DATE DUE

FE 18 95			
MR 25 05			

DEMCO 38-296

HUMAN DEVELOPMENT REPORT 1999

Published
for the United Nations
Development Programme
(UNDP)

New York   Oxford
Oxford University Press
1999

Oxford University Press
Oxford   New York
Athens   Auckland   Bangkok   Bombay
Calcutta   Cape Town   Dar es Salaam   Delhi
Florence   Hong Kong   Istanbul   Karachi
Kuala Lumpur   Madras   Madrid   Melbourne
Mexico City   Nairobi   Paris   Singapore
Taipei   Tokyo   Toronto

and associated companies in
Berlin   Ibadan

Copyright ©1999
by the United Nations Development Programme
1 UN Plaza, New York, New York, 10017, USA

Published by Oxford University Press, Inc.
198 Madison Avenue, New York, New York, 10016

Oxford is a registered trademark of Oxford University Press

ISBN 0-19-521561-3 (cloth)
ISBN 0-19-521562-1 (paper)

9 8 7 6 5 4 3 2 1
Printed in the United States of America on acid-free, recycled paper, using soy-based ink.

Cover and design: Gerald Quinn, Quinn Information Design, Cabin John, Maryland

Editing, desktop composition and production management: Communications Development Incorporated, Washington, DC, New York,
San Francisco and London

DEDICATED TO THE MEMORY OF

MAHBUB UL HAQ (1934–98)

CREATOR OF THE HUMAN DEVELOPMENT REPORT

Foreword

This is the first *Human Development Report* that bears my signature as Administrator. For a new Administrator, the *Human Development Report* is a crown jewel of UNDP. Its robust editorial independence and its unapologetic scholarship have led its authors to say the unthinkable, and they then have the pleasure of watching conventional opinion catch up. I believe that Mahbub ul Haq, to whom this tenth Report is dedicated, would be proud that the tradition is being so vigorously maintained.

This year's Report comes down clearly in favour of the power of globalization to bring economic and social benefits to societies: the free flow of money and trade is matched by the liberating power of the flow of ideas and information driven by new technologies.

However, as it has so effectively in the past, the Report champions the agenda of the world's weak, those marginalized by globalization, and calls for a much bolder agenda of global and national reforms to achieve globalization with a human face. It cautions that globalization is too important to be left as unmanaged as it is at present, because it has the capacity to do extraordinary harm as well as good. I fully endorse this view.

Let me comment on only two aspects of the Report's wide-ranging recommendations for change in how global society is organized.

First, governance. My own view is that we are seeing the emergence of a new, much less formal structure of global governance, where governments and partners in civil society, the private sector and others are forming functional coalitions across geographic borders and traditional political lines to move public policy in ways that meet the aspirations of a global citizenry. Some issue campaigns have led to shifts in global policy, such as the antilandmine campaign and the

campaign for millennium debt relief. These coalitions use the convening power and the consensus-building, standard-setting and implementing roles of the United Nations, the Bretton Woods institutions and international organizations, but their key strength is that they are bigger than any of us and give new expression to the UN Charter's "We, the peoples." We must not suffocate this new diplomacy with new institutions, but first try to adapt and strengthen those we have—not least by reaching out to these new global coalitions of stakeholders.

Second, markets. In listing the negative impacts of markets on people, it is important not to appear to be rejecting markets as the central organizing principle of global economic life. Markets need institutions and rules—and too frequently in the global setting they are not yet adequately subjected to the control of either. But the unleashing of competition within countries and between countries has ushered in for many an era of prosperity and liberty.

Where I fully agree with the authors is that this empowerment has been uneven—leaving countries, regions, ethnic and religious groups, classes and economic sectors the victims of increased inequality. Sixty countries have been getting steadily poorer since 1980. The losers from globalization are both a huge human and political waste and the source of disappointment and often tragedy for themselves and the families that depend on them. Markets have brought dislocation and heartache as well as remarkable advances. As the authors argue, these failures, unaddressed, will compound and encroach on the security of today's market winners.

Public health problems, immigration and refugees, environmental degradation and broader social and political breakdown are the new security challenges that breed in a context of unattended global inequality. For all our sakes we need to work together to build the frameworks of a new global society and economy that respect differences, protect the weak and regulate the strong. We must do so, however, in ways that are innovative and reflective of the new forces in our societies—and that keep markets free but fair.

Mark Malloch Brown

The analysis and policy recommendations of the Report do not necessarily reflect the views of the United Nations Development Programme, its Executive Board or its Member States. The Report is the fruit of a collaborative effort by a team of eminent consultants and advisers and the Human Development Report team. Richard Jolly, Special Adviser to the Administrator, together with Sakiko Fukuda-Parr, Director of the Human Development Report Office, led the effort.

Team for the preparation of
Human Development Report 1999

Principal Coordinator
Richard Jolly

UNDP team
Director: Sakiko Fukuda-Parr
Deputy Director: Selim Jahan
Members: Håkan Björkman, Sarah Burd-Sharps, Haishan Fu, Laura Mourino-Casas, Andreas Pfeil, Kate Raworth and Pablo Rodas, in collaboration with Özer Babakol, Marixie Mercado, Irina Nemirovsky, Guy Ranaivomanana, Nadia Rasheed and Tamahi Yamauchi

Editor: Bruce Ross-Larson
Designer: Gerald Quinn

Panel of consultants
Adebayo Adedeji, Philip Alston, Galal Amin, Lourdes Arizpe, Isabella Bakker, Yusuf Bangura, David Bigman, Bob Deacon, Meghnad Desai, Nancy Folbre, Stephany Griffith-Jones, Gerry Helleiner, K.S. Jomo, Azizur Rahman Khan, Martin Khor Kok Peng, Jong-Wha Lee, Michael Lipton, Nguyuru Lipumba, Raisul Awal Mahmood, Ranjini Mazumdar, Süle Özler, Theodore Panayotou, Alejandro Ramirez, Mohan Rao, Changyong Rhee, Ewa Ruminska-Zimny, Arjun Sengupta, Victor Tokman, Albert Tuijnman and John Whalley
Human development index revision: Sudhir Anand and Amartya Sen

Acknowledgements

The preparation of the Report would not have been possible without the support and valuable contributions of a large number of individuals and organizations.

Many organizations generously shared their experience, research materials and data: the Food and Agriculture Organization, International Data Corporation, International Fund for Agricultural Development, International Labour Organisation, International Monetary Fund, International Organization for Migration, International Telecommunication Union, Inter-Parliamentary Union, Joint United Nations Programme on HIV/AIDS, Office of the United Nations High Commissioner for Refugees, Organisation for Economic Co-operation and Development, Rural Advancement Foundation International, Stockholm University, United Nations Centre for Social Development and Humanitarian Affairs, United Nations Children's Fund, United Nations Conference on Trade and Development, United Nations Department of Economic and Social Affairs, United Nations Division for the Advancement of Women, United Nations Economic and Social Commission for Asia and the Pacific, United Nations Economic and Social Commission for Western Asia, United Nations Economic Commission for Africa, United Nations Economic Commission for Europe, United Nations Economic Commission for Latin America and the Caribbean, United Nations Educational, Scientific and Cultural Organization, United Nations International Drug Control Programme, United Nations Office at Vienna/Crime Prevention and Criminal Justice Division, United Nations Population Division, United Nations Research Institute for Social Development, United Nations Statistical Division, World Bank, World Health Organization, World Resources Institute and World Times.

The Report benefited greatly from intellectual advice and guidance provided by the external Advisory Panel of eminent experts, which included Lourdes Beneria, Nancy Birdsall, Kwesi Botchwey, Manuel Castells, Ha-Joon Chang, Robert Douglas, Muni Figueres, Carlos Fortin, Ellen Johnson-Sirleaf, Louka T. Katseli, John Langmore, Nora Lustig, Maureen O'Neil, Yung Chul Park, Juan F. Rada, Gert Rosenthal and Paul Streeten.

The team expresses its special thanks to Gordon Conway and Lincoln Chen of the Rockefeller Foundation for their support for the Bellagio Conference and to those who facilitated and chaired consultations in Geneva, London, Paris, Seoul and Tokyo: Carlos Fortin, Ryokichi Hirono, Jacques Loup and Clare Short. The Report benefited greatly from these and other discussions with Raja Zaharaton Raja Zainal Abdin, Montek Singh Ahluwalia, Sultan Ahmad, Halis Akder, Yilmaz Akyuz, Qazi Shamsul Alam, Azita Amjadi, Aya Aoki, Arjun Appadurai, Lourdes Arizpe, Maria Baquero, Hazel Bennett, Jean-Claude Berthelemy, Yves Berthelot, Ram Binod Bhattari, Yonas Biru, David E. Bloom, Tom Boden, Carlos Hernando Gomez Buendia, Bernadette Burke, Shashua Chen, Kim Woo Choong, S. K. Chu, Patrick Cornu, Elizabeth Crayford, Jacqueline Damon, Liang Dan, Isabelle Decarroux, V. V. Desai, John Dixon, Le Dang Doah, Susan Douglas, Jean-Christophe Dumont, Heba El-Laithy, Doris Ma Fat, Julio Frenk, Susan Gearhart, Dorota Gierycz, Thomas Gladwin, Erlinda Go, Greta Greathouse, Joseph Grinblat, Odd Gulbrandsen, the late Mahbub ul Haq, Hazel Henderson, Ricardo Henriques, Mark Hereward,

Evelyne Herfkens, Barry Herman, Alan Heston, Kenneth Hill, Karl Hoghesand, Michael Hopkins, Shinsuke Horiuchi, Bela Hovy, Morimitsu Inaba, Hilde Frafjord Johnson, Gareth Jones, Bela Kadar, Kazuko Kano, Devash Kapur, Mats Karlsson, Robert King, Jon Lickerman, Patrick Low, Nyein-Nyein Lwin, Robert Lynn, Christian Morrisson, Srdan Mrkic, Scott Murray, Daw Yi Yi Myint, Takeshi Nakano, Geraldo Nascimiento, Peter Newell, David Nitkin, Farhad Noorbakhsh, Michimasa Numata, Naoki Ono, Elsie Onubogu, Saeed Ordoubadi, Manuel Otero, G. L. Peiris, Bernard Perrollaz, Antonella Picchio, Christine Pintat, Jason Potts, Thomson Prentice, Will Prince, Madanmohan Rao, Martin Ravallion, Wolfgang Rhomberg, E. Riordan, Jerzey Rozanski, Jagdish Saighal, Orlando Sakay, Claude Sauvageot, Karl Sauvant, Enid Schoettle, Simon Scott, John Sewell, Ali Mojtahed Shabestari, Donald Shih, A. K. Shivakumar, S. Simeant, Ajit Singh, Timothy Smeeding, Babar Sobhan, Budhy T. Socdijoko, Shiv Someshwar, Frances Stewart, Namgoong Suk, Robert Summers, Eric Swanson, Françoise Tandart, Simon Tay, Shigeki Tejima, Raj Thamotheram, Harald Trabold Nubler, Lourdes Urdaneta-Ferran, Mark Uzan, Joann Vanek, Maria Vaquero, Michael Ward, Tessa Wardlow, Robin White, Saskia E. Wieringa, Erna Witoelar, Jinishiro Yanabuta, Long Yongtu, Tsuneaki Yoshida, Akiko Yuge, Anne Zammitt, Frederique Zegel and He Zengke.

Colleagues in UNDP provided extremely useful comments, suggestions and inputs during the drafting of the Report. In particular, the authors would like to express their gratitude to Thelma Awori, Nilufer Cagatay, Georges Chapelier, Shabbir Cheema, Djibril Diallo, Abdoulaye Mar Dieye, Moez Doraid, Hans d'Orville, Ligia Elizondo, Fawaz Fokeladeh, Anne Forrester, Ariel Français, Enrique Ganuza, Isabelle Grunberg-Filatov, Michael Heyn, Noeleen Heyzer, Nay Htun, Henry Jackelen, Mbaya Kankwenda, Inge Kaul, Anton Kruiderink, Kerstin Leitner, Thierry Lemaresquier, Khalid Malik, Andrei Marcu, Elena Martinez, Brenda McSweeney, Saraswathi Menon, Luong Nguyen, Omar Noman, John Ohiorhenuan, Minh Pham, Ravi Rajan, Jordan Ryan, Nessim Shallon, Sarah L.

Timpson, Antonio Vigilante, Mourad Wahba, Eimi Watanabe, Phillips Young, Raul Zambrano and Fernando Zumbado.

A number of offices in UNDP and national human development report teams provided support and information. They include many UNDP country offices, including special contributions from UNDP Indonesia and Malaysia, UNDP's Regional Bureaux and the Bureau for Development Policy. The United Nations Office for Project Services provided the team with critical administrative support. Particular thanks go to Martha Barrientos, Maria Hemsy, Oscar Hernandez, Liliana Izquierdo, Serene Ong and Ingolf Schuetz-Mueller.

The Report also benefited from the dedicated work of interns. Thanks are due to Myriam Benlamlih, Fe Conway, Michael E. Davidian, Petter Meirik, Joachim Reiter, Jessica Rothenberg-Aalami, Kerstin Schuetz-Mueller, Sahba Sobhani and Hye Yoen Kim.

Secretarial and administrative support for the Report's preparation were provided by Luz Asuncion, Sonia Barolette, Oscar Bernal, Renuka Corea-Lloyd, Rekha Kalekar, Chato Ledonio-O'Buckley and Marjorie Victor. And as in previous years, the Report benefited from the editing and pre-press production of Communications Development Incorporated's Bruce Ross-Larson, Garrett Cruce, Terrence Fischer, Wendy Guyette, Paul Holtz, Damon Iacovelli, Megan Klose, Daphne Levitas, Terra Lynch, Donna McGreevy, Laurel Morais, Alison Smith and Alison Strong.

The team expresses sincere appreciation to the Administrator's peer reviewers, Kwesi Botchwey and Diane Elson.

The authors are deeply indebted to the late Mahbub ul Haq, the originator of the *Human Development Report*s. His vision and commitment will continue to inspire the Reports.

The authors are especially grateful to James Gustave Speth, who, as UNDP Administrator, guided and inspired the preparation of *Human Development Report*s 1994, 1995, 1996, 1997, 1998 and 1999. His strong intellectual leadership and unqualified commitment to this series made these publications possible.

Thankful for all the support that they have received, the authors assume full responsibility for the opinions expressed in the Report.

Contents

CHAPTER FIVE

Reinventing global governance—for humanity and equity   97

References   115

SPECIAL CONTRIBUTIONS

BOXES

FIGURES

HUMAN DEVELOPMENT INDICATORS

What do the human development indices reveal?   127

Monitoring human development: enlarging people's choices . . .

AIDS	Acquired immunodeficiency syndrome
CGIAR	Consultative Group on International Agricultural Research
CIS	Commonwealth of Independent States
ECOSOC	Economic and Social Council (of the United Nations)
EU	European Union
FDI	Foreign direct investment
GATT	General Agreement on Tariffs and Trade
GDI	Gender-related development index
GDP	Gross domestic product
GEM	Gender empowerment measure
GNP	Gross national product
HIPCs	Heavily indebted poor countries
HDI	Human development index
HIV	Human immunodeficiency virus
HPI	Human poverty index
IMF	International Monetary Fund
NGO	Non-governmental organization
ODA	Official development assistance
OECD	Organisation for Economic Co-operation and Development
PPP	Purchasing power parity
TRIPS	Trade-Related Aspects of Intellectual Property Rights
UNCTAD	United Nations Conference on Trade and Development
UNDP	United Nations Development Programme
UNESCO	United Nations Educational, Scientific and Cultural Organization
UNICEF	United Nations Children's Fund
WHO	World Health Organization
WTO	World Trade Organization

Globalization with a human face

"The real wealth of a nation is its people. And the purpose of development is to create an enabling environment for people to enjoy long, healthy and creative lives. This simple but powerful truth is too often forgotten in the pursuit of material and financial wealth." Those are the opening lines of the first *Human Development Report,* published in 1990. This tenth *Human Development Report*—like the first and all the others—is about people. It is about the growing interdependence of people in today's globalizing world.

Globalization is not new, but the present era has distinctive features. Shrinking space, shrinking time and disappearing borders are linking people's lives more deeply, more intensely, more immediately than ever before.

More than $1.5 trillion is now exchanged in the world's currency markets each day, and nearly a fifth of the goods and services produced each year are traded. But globalization is more than the flow of money and commodities—it is the growing interdependence of the world's people. And globalization is a process integrating not just the economy but culture, technology and governance. People everywhere are becoming connected—affected by events in far corners of the world. The collapse of the Thai baht not only threw millions into unemployment in South-East Asia—the ensuing decline in global demand meant slowdowns in social investment in Latin America and a sudden rise in the cost of imported medicines in Africa.

Globalization is not new. Recall the early sixteenth century and the late nineteenth. But this era is different:

- *New markets*—foreign exchange and capital markets linked globally, operating 24 hours a day, with dealings at a distance in real time.
- *New tools*—Internet links, cellular phones, media networks.
- *New actors*—the World Trade Organization (WTO) with authority over national governments, the multinational corporations with more economic power than many states, the global networks of non-governmental organizations (NGOs) and other groups that transcend national boundaries.
- *New rules*—multilateral agreements on trade, services and intellectual property, backed by strong enforcement mechanisms and more binding for national governments, reducing the scope for national policy.

Globalization offers great opportunities for human advance—but only with stronger governance.

This era of globalization is opening many opportunities for millions of people around the world. Increased trade, new technologies, foreign investments, expanding media and Internet connections are fuelling economic growth and human advance. All this offers enormous potential to eradicate poverty in the 21st century—to continue the unprecedented progress in the 20th century. We have more wealth and technology—and more commitment to a global community—than ever before.

Global markets, global technology, global ideas and global solidarity can enrich the lives of people everywhere, greatly expanding their choices. The growing interdependence of people's lives calls for shared values and a shared commitment to the human development of all people.

People everywhere are becoming connected— affected by events in far corners of the world

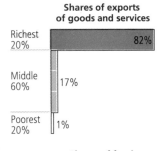

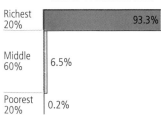
The post–cold war world of the 1990s has sped progress in defining such values—in adopting human rights and in setting development goals in the United Nations conferences on environment, population, social development, women and human settlements.

But today's globalization is being driven by market expansion—opening national borders to trade, capital, information—outpacing governance of these markets and their repercussions for people. More progress has been made in norms, standards, policies and institutions for open global markets than for people and their rights. And a new commitment is needed to the ethics of universalism set out in the Universal Declaration of Human Rights.

Competitive markets may be the best guarantee of efficiency, but not necessarily of equity. Liberalization and privatization can be a step to competitive markets—but not a guarantee of them. And markets are neither the first nor the last word in human development. Many activities and goods that are critical to human development are provided outside the market—but these are being squeezed by the pressures of global competition. There is a fiscal squeeze on public goods, a time squeeze on care activities and an incentive squeeze on the environment.

When the market goes too far in dominating social and political outcomes, the opportunities and rewards of globalization spread unequally and inequitably—concentrating power and wealth in a select group of people, nations and corporations, marginalizing the others. When the market gets out of hand, the instabilities show up in boom and bust economies, as in the financial crisis in East Asia and its worldwide repercussions, cutting global output by an estimated $2 trillion in 1998-2000. When the profit motives of market players get out of hand, they challenge people's ethics—and sacrifice respect for justice and human rights.

The challenge of globalization in the new century is not to stop the expansion of global markets. The challenge is to find the rules and institutions for stronger governance—local, national, regional and global—to preserve the advantages of global markets and competition, but also to provide enough space for human, community and environmental resources to ensure that globalization works

for people—not just for profits. Globalization with:

- *Ethics*—less violation of human rights, not more.
- *Equity*—less disparity within and between nations, not more.
- *Inclusion*—less marginalization of people and countries, not more.
- *Human security*—less instability of societies and less vulnerability of people, not more.
- *Sustainability*—less environmental destruction, not more.
- *Development*—less poverty and deprivation, not more.

The opportunities and benefits of globalization need to be shared much more widely.

Since the 1980s many countries have seized the opportunities of economic and technological globalization. Beyond the industrial countries, the newly industrializing East Asian tigers are joined by Chile, the Dominican Republic, India, Mauritius, Poland, Turkey and many others linking into global markets, attracting foreign investment and taking advantage of technological advance. Their export growth has averaged more than 5% a year, diversifying into manufactures.

At the other extreme are the many countries benefiting little from expanding markets and advancing technology—Madagascar, Niger, the Russian Federation, Tajikistan and Venezuela among them.

These countries are becoming even more marginal—ironic, since many of them are highly "integrated", with exports nearly 30% of GDP for Sub-Saharan Africa and only 19% for the OECD. But these countries hang on the vagaries of global markets, with the prices of primary commodities having fallen to their lowest in a century and a half. They have shown little growth in exports and attracted virtually no foreign investment. In sum, today, global opportunities are unevenly distributed—between countries and people (see figure).

If global opportunities are not shared better, the failed growth of the last decades will continue. More than 80 countries still have per capita incomes lower than they were a decade or more ago. While 40 countries have sustained average per capita income growth of more than 3% a year since 1990, 55 countries, mostly in Sub-Saharan Africa and Eastern Europe and the Commonwealth of Independent States (CIS), have had declining per capita incomes.

Many people are also missing out on employment opportunities. The global labour market is increasingly integrated for the highly skilled—corporate executives, scientists, entertainers and the many others who form the global professional elite—with high mobility and wages. But the market for unskilled labour is highly restricted by national barriers.

Inequality has been rising in many countries since the early 1980s. In China disparities are widening between the export-oriented regions of the coast and the interior: the human poverty index is just under 20% in coastal provinces, but more than 50% in inland Guizhou. The countries of Eastern Europe and the CIS have registered some of the largest increases ever in the Gini coefficient, a measure of income inequality. OECD countries also registered big increases in inequality after the 1980s—especially Sweden, the United Kingdom and the United States.

Inequality between countries has also increased. The income gap between the fifth of the world's people living in the richest countries and the fifth in the poorest was 74 to 1 in 1997, up from 60 to 1 in 1990 and 30 to 1 in 1960. In the nineteenth century, too, inequality grew rapidly during the last three decades, in an era of rapid global integration: the income gap between the top and bottom countries increased from 3 to 1 in 1820 to 7 to 1 in 1870 and 11 to 1 in 1913.

By the late 1990s the fifth of the world's people living in the highest-income countries had:
- 86% of world GDP—the bottom fifth just 1%.
- 82% of world export markets—the bottom fifth just 1%.
- 68% of foreign direct investment—the bottom fifth just 1%.
- 74% of world telephone lines, today's basic means of communication—the bottom fifth just 1.5%.

Some have predicted convergence. Yet the past decade has shown increasing concentration of income, resources and wealth among people, corporations and countries:

- OECD countries, with 19% of the global population, have 71% of global trade in goods and services, 58% of foreign direct investment and 91% of all Internet users.
- The world's 200 richest people more than doubled their net worth in the four years to 1998, to more than $1 trillion. The assets of the top three billionaires are more than the combined GNP of all least developed countries and their 600 million people.
- The recent wave of mergers and acquisitions is concentrating industrial power in megacorporations—at the risk of eroding competition. By 1998 the top 10 companies in pesticides controlled 85% of a $31 billion global market—and the top 10 in telecommunications, 86% of a $262 billion market.
- In 1993 just 10 countries accounted for 84% of global research and development expenditures and controlled 95% of the US patents of the past two decades. Moreover, more than 80% of patents granted in developing countries belong to residents of industrial countries.

All these trends are not the inevitable consequences of global economic integration—but they have run ahead of global governance to share the benefits.

The past decade has shown increasing concentration of income, resources and wealth among people, corporations and countries

---

Globalization is creating new threats to human security—in rich countries and poor.

One achievement of recent decades has been greater security for people in many countries—more political freedom and stability in Chile, peace in Central America, safer streets in the United States. But in the globalizing world of shrinking time, shrinking space and disappearing borders, people are confronting new threats to human security—sudden and hurtful disruptions in the pattern of daily life.

Financial volatility and economic insecurity. The financial turmoil in East Asia in 1997–99 demonstrates the risks of global financial markets. Net capital flows to Indonesia, the Republic of Korea, Malaysia, the Philippines and Thailand rocketed in the 1990s, reaching $93 billion in 1996. As turmoil hit market after market, these flows reversed overnight—with an outflow of

$12 billion in 1997. The swing amounted to 11% of the precrisis GDPs of these countries. Two important lessons come out of this experience.

First, the human impacts are severe and are likely to persist long after economic recovery.

Bankruptcies spread. Education and health budgets came under pressure. More than 13 million people lost their jobs. As prices of essentials rose sharply, real wages fell sharply, down some 40–60% in Indonesia. The consequences go deeper—all countries report erosion of their social fabric, with social unrest, more crime, more violence in the home.

Recovery seems to be on the way, most evidently in Korea and least in Indonesia. But while output growth, payment balances, interest rates and inflation may be returning to normal, human lives take longer to recover. A review of financial crises in 80 countries over the past few decades shows that real wages take an average of three years to pick up again, and that employment growth does not regain precrisis levels for several years after that.

Second, far from being isolated incidents, financial crises have become increasingly common with the spread and growth of global capital flows. They result from rapid buildups and reversals of short-term capital flows and are likely to recur. More likely when national institutions regulating financial markets are not well developed, they are now recognized as systemic features of global capital markets. No single country can withstand their whims, and global action is needed to prevent and manage them.

Job and income insecurity. In both poor and rich countries dislocations from economic and corporate restructuring, and from dismantling the institutions of social protection, have meant greater insecurity in jobs and incomes. The pressures of global competition have led countries and employers to adopt more flexible labour policies with more precarious work arrangements. Workers without contracts or with new, less secure contracts make up 30% of the total in Chile, 39% in Colombia.

France, Germany, the United Kingdom and other countries have weakened worker dismissal laws. Mergers and acquisitions have come with corporate restructuring and massive layoffs. Sustained economic growth has not reduced unemployment in Europe—leaving it at 11% for a decade, affecting 35 million. In Latin America growth has created jobs, but 85% of them are in the informal sector.

Health insecurity. Growing travel and migration have helped spread HIV/AIDS. More than 33 million people were living with HIV/AIDS in 1998, with almost 6 million new infections in that year. And the epidemic is now spreading rapidly to new locations, such as rural India and Eastern Europe and the CIS. With 95% of the 16,000 infected each day living in developing countries, AIDS has become a poor person's disease, taking a heavy toll on life expectancy, reversing the gains of recent decades. For nine countries in Africa, a loss of 17 years in life expectancy is projected by 2010, back to the levels of the 1960s.

Cultural insecurity. Globalization opens people's lives to culture and all its creativity—and to the flow of ideas and knowledge. But the new culture carried by expanding global markets is disquieting. As Mahatma Gandhi expressed so eloquently earlier in the century, "I do not want my house to be walled in on all sides and my windows to be stuffed. I want the cultures of all the lands to be blown about my house as freely as possible. But I refuse to be blown off my feet by any." Today's flow of culture is unbalanced, heavily weighted in one direction, from rich countries to poor.

Weightless goods—with high knowledge content rather than material content—now make for some of the most dynamic sectors in today's most advanced economies. The single largest export industry for the United States is not aircraft or automobiles, it is entertainment—Hollywood films grossed more than $30 billion worldwide in 1997.

The expansion of global media networks and satellite communications technologies gives rise to a powerful new medium with a global reach. These networks bring Hollywood to remote villages—the number of television sets per 1,000 people almost doubled between 1980 and 1995, from 121 to 235. And the spread of global brands—Nike, Sony—is setting new social standards from Delhi to Warsaw to Rio de Janeiro. Such onslaughts of

Globalization opens people's lives to culture and all its creativity—and to the flow of ideas and knowledge

foreign culture can put cultural diversity at risk, and make people fear losing their cultural identity. What is needed is support to indigenous and national cultures—to let them flourish alongside foreign cultures.

Personal insecurity. Criminals are reaping the benefits of globalization. Deregulated capital markets, advances in information and communications technology and cheaper transport make flows easier, faster and less restricted not just for medical knowledge but for heroin—not just for books and seeds but for dirty money and weapons.

Illicit trade—in drugs, women, weapons and laundered money—is contributing to the violence and crime that threaten neighbourhoods around the world. Drug-related crimes increased from 4 per 100,000 people in Belarus in 1990 to 28 in 1997, and from 1 per 100,000 to 8 in Estonia. The weapons trade feeds street crime as well as civil strife. In South Africa machine guns are pouring in from Angola and Mozambique. The traffic in women and girls for sexual exploitation—500,000 a year to Western Europe alone—is one of the most heinous violations of human rights, estimated to be a $7 billion business.

The Internet is an easy vehicle for trafficking in drugs, arms and women through nearly untraceable networks. In 1995 the illegal drug trade was estimated at 8% of world trade, more than the trade in motor vehicles or in iron and steel. Money laundering—which the International Monetary Fund (IMF) estimates at equivalent to 2–5% of global GDP—hides the traces of crime in split seconds, with the click of a mouse.

At the root of all this is the growing influence of organized crime, estimated to gross $1.5 trillion a year, rivalling multinational corporations as an economic power. Global crime groups have the power to criminalize politics, business and the police, developing efficient networks, extending their reach deep and wide.

Environmental insecurity. Chronic environmental degradation—today's silent emergency—threatens people worldwide and undercuts the livelihoods of at least half a billion people. Poor people themselves, having little choice, put pressure on the environment, but so does the consumption of the rich. The growing export markets for fish, shrimp, paper and many other products mean depleted stocks, less biodiversity and fewer forests. Most of the costs are borne by the poor—though it is the world's rich who benefit most. The fifth of the world's people living in the richest countries consume 84% of the world's paper.

Political and community insecurity. Closely related to many other forms of insecurity is the rise of social tensions that threaten political stability and community cohesion. Of the 61 major armed conflicts fought between 1989 and 1998, only three were between states—the rest were civil.

Globalization has given new characteristics to conflicts. Feeding these conflicts is the global traffic in weapons, involving new actors and blurring political and business interests. In the power vacuum of the post–cold war era, military companies and mercenary armies began offering training to governments—and corporations. Accountable only to those who pay them, these hired military services pose a severe threat to human security.

New information and communications technologies are driving globalization—but polarizing the world into the connected and the isolated.

With the costs of communications plummeting and innovative tools easier to use, people around the world have burst into conversation using the Internet, mobile phones and fax machines. The fastest-growing communications tool ever, the Internet had more than 140 million users in mid-1998, a number expected to pass 700 million by 2001.

Communications networks can foster great advances in health and education. They can also empower small players. The previously unheard voices of NGOs helped halt the secretive OECD negotiations for the Multilateral Agreement on Investment, called for corporate accountability and created support for marginal communities. Barriers of size, time and distance are coming down for small businesses,

With the costs of communications plummeting and innovative tools easier to use, people around the world have burst into conversation

for governments of poor countries, for remote academics and specialists.

Information and communications technology can also open a fast track to knowledge-based growth—a track followed by India's software exports, Ireland's computing services and the Eastern Caribbean's data processing.

Despite the potential for development, the Internet poses severe problems of access and exclusion. Who was in the loop in 1998?

- *Geography divides.* Thailand has more cellular phones than Africa. South Asia, home to 23% of the world's people, has less than 1% of Internet users.
- *Education is a ticket to the network high society.* Globally, 30% of users had at least one university degree.
- *Income buys access.* To purchase a computer would cost the average Bangladeshi more than eight years' income, the average American, just one month's wage.
- *Men and youth dominate.* Women make up just 17% of the Internet users in Japan, only 7% in China. Most users in China and the United Kingdom are under 30.
- *English talks.* English prevails in almost 80% of all Websites, yet less than one in 10 people worldwide speaks it.

This exclusivity is creating parallel worlds. Those with income, education and—literally—connections have cheap and instantaneous access to information. The rest are left with uncertain, slow and costly access. When people in these two worlds live and compete side by side, the advantage of being connected will overpower the marginal and impoverished, cutting off their voices and concerns from the global conversation.

This risk of marginalization does not have to be a reason for despair. It should be a call to action for:

- *More connectivity:* setting up telecommunications and computer hardware.
- *More community:* focusing on group access, not just individual ownership.
- *More capacity:* building human skills for the knowledge society.
- *More content:* putting local views, news, culture and commerce on the Web.
- *More creativity:* adapting technology to local needs and opportunities.

- *More collaboration:* developing Internet governance to accommodate diverse national needs.
- *More cash:* finding innovative ways to fund the knowledge society everywhere.

Global technological breakthroughs offer great potential for human advance and for eradicating poverty—but not with today's agendas.

Liberalization, privatization and tighter intellectual property rights are shaping the path for the new technologies, determining how they are used. But the privatization and concentration of technology are going too far. Corporations define research agendas and tightly control their findings with patents, racing to lay claim to intellectual property under the rules set out in the agreement on Trade-Related Aspects of Intellectual Property Rights (TRIPS).

Poor people and poor countries risk being pushed to the margin in this proprietary regime controlling the world's knowledge:

- In defining research agendas, money talks, not need—cosmetic drugs and slow-ripening tomatoes come higher on the priority list than drought-resistant crops or a vaccine against malaria.
- From new drugs to better seeds, the best of the new technologies are priced for those who can pay. For poor people, they remain far out of reach.
- Tighter property rights raise the price of technology transfer, blocking developing countries from the dynamic knowledge sectors. The TRIPS agreement will enable multinationals to dominate the global market even more easily.
- New patent laws pay scant attention to the knowledge of indigenous people. These laws ignore cultural diversity in the way innovations are created and shared—and diversity in views on what can and should be owned, from plant varieties to human life. The result: a silent theft of centuries of knowledge from some of the poorest communities in developing countries.
- Despite the risks of genetic engineering, the rush and push of commercial interests are putting profits before people.

A broader perspective is needed. Intellectual property rights were first raised as a multilateral trade issue in 1986 to crack down on counterfeit goods. The reach of those rights now goes far beyond that—into the ownership of life. As trade, patents and copyright determine the paths of technology—and of nations—questioning today's arrangements is not just about economic flows. It is about preserving biodiversity. Addressing the ethics of patents on life. Ensuring access to health care. Respecting other cultures' forms of ownership. Preventing a growing technological gap between the knowledge-driven global economy and the rest trapped in its shadows.

The relentless pressures of global competition are squeezing out care, the invisible heart of human development.

Caring labour—providing for children, the sick and the elderly, as well as all the rest of us, exhausted from the demands of daily life—is an important input for the development of human capabilities. It is also a capability in itself. And it is special—nurturing human relationships with love, altruism, reciprocity and trust. Without enough care, individuals do not flourish. Without attention and stimulus, babies languish, failing to reach their full potential. And without nurturing from their families, children underperform in school.

Human support to others is essential for social cohesion and a strong community. It is also essential for economic growth. But the market gives few incentives and few rewards for it. Societies everywhere have allocated women much of the responsibility and the burden for care—women spend two-thirds of their work time in unpaid activities, men only a quarter. Women predominate in caring professions and domestic service. Families, nations and corporations have been free-riding on caring labour provided mostly by women, unpaid or underpaid.

But today's competitive global market is putting pressures on the time, resources and incentives for the supply of caring labour. Women's participation in the formal labour market is rising, yet they continue to carry the burden of care—women's hours spent in unpaid work remain high. In Bangladesh women in the garment industry spend 56 hours a week in paid employment on top of 31 hours in unpaid work—a total of 87 hours, compared with 67 by men. Men's share of unpaid care work is increasing slowly in Europe and other OECD countries but not in most developing countries and in Eastern Europe.

Meanwhile, fiscal pressures are cutting back on the supply of state-provided care services. Tax revenue declined in poor countries from 18% of GDP in the early 1980s to 16% in the 1990s. Public services deteriorated markedly—the result of economic stagnation, structural adjustment programmes or the dismantling of state services, especially in the transition economies of Eastern Europe and the CIS.

And global economic competition has put pressure on the wages for caring labour, as the wage gap increases between tradable and non-tradable sectors, and between the skilled and unskilled.

How can societies design new arrangements for care in the global economy? The traditional model of a patriarchal household is no solution—a new approach must build gender equity into sharing the burdens and responsibility for care. New institutional mechanisms, better public policy and a social consensus are needed to provide incentives for rewarding care and increasing its supply and quality:
- Public support for care services—such as care for the elderly, day care for children and protection of social services during crises.
- Labour market policies and employer action to support the care needs of employees.
- More gender balance and equity in carrying the burden of household care services.

Each society needs to find its own arrangements based on its history and conditions. But all societies need to devise a better solution. And all need to make a strong commitment to preserving time and resources for care—and the human bonds that nourish human development.

National and global governance have to be reinvented—with human development and equity at their core.

None of these pernicious trends—growing marginalization, growing human insecurity,

All need to make a strong commitment to preserving time and resources for care—and the human bonds that nourish human development

growing inequality—is inevitable. With political will and commitment in the global community, they can all be reversed. With stronger governance—local, national, regional and global—the benefits of competitive markets can be preserved with clear rules and boundaries, and stronger action can be taken to meet the needs of human development.

Governance does not mean mere government. It means the framework of rules, institutions and established practices that set limits and give incentives for the behaviour of individuals, organizations and firms. Without strong governance, the dangers of global conflicts could be a reality of the 21st century—trade wars promoting national and corporate interests, uncontrolled financial volatility setting off civil conflicts, untamed global crime infecting safe neighbourhoods and criminalizing politics, business and the police.

With the market collapse in East Asia, with the contagion to Brazil, Russia and elsewhere and with the threat of a global recession still looming, global governance is being re-examined. But the current debate is:

• Too narrow, limited to the concerns of economic growth and financial stability and neglecting broader human concerns such as persistent global poverty, growing inequality between and within countries, exclusion of poor people and countries and persisting human rights abuses.

• Too geographically unbalanced, dominated by the largest economies—usually the G-7, sometimes just the G-1, and only occasionally bringing in the large newly industrializing countries. Most small and poor developing countries are excluded, as are people's organizations.

Nor does the debate address the current weaknesses, imbalances and inequities in global governance—which, having developed in an ad hoc way, leaves many gaps.

• Multilateral agreements have helped establish global markets without considering their impacts on human development and poverty.

• The structures and processes for global policy-making are not representative. The key economic structures—the IMF, World Bank, G-7, G-10, G-22, OECD, WTO—are dominated by the large and rich countries, leaving poor countries and poor people with little influence and little voice, either for lack of membership or for lack of capacity for effective representation and participation. There is little transparency in decisions, and there is no structured forum for civil society institutions to express their views.

• There are no mechanisms for making ethical standards and human rights binding for corporations and individuals, not just governments.

In short, stronger national and global governance are needed for human well-being, not for the market.

Reinventing governance for the 21st century must start with strong commitments:

• *TO GLOBAL ETHICS, JUSTICE AND RESPECT FOR THE HUMAN RIGHTS OF ALL PEOPLE.* Global governance requires a common core of values, standards and attitudes, a widely felt sense of responsibility and obligations—not just by individuals, but by governments, corporations and civil society organizations. The core values of respect for life, liberty, justice, equality, tolerance, mutual respect and integrity underlie the Charter of the United Nations and the Universal Declaration of Human Rights. They now need to be the guiding objectives of globalization with a human face.

• *TO HUMAN WELL-BEING AS THE END, WITH OPEN MARKETS AND ECONOMIC GROWTH AS MEANS.* Human development and social protection have to be incorporated in the principles and practices of global governance. Recent advances in global governance have been built on concepts and principles of economic efficiency and competitive markets. These are important but not enough, just as they would be in national governance.

• *TO RESPECT FOR THE DIVERSE CONDITIONS AND NEEDS OF EACH COUNTRY.* Economic policy-making should be guided by pragmatism rather than ideology—and a recognition that what works in Chile does not necessarily work in Argentina, what is right for Mauritius may not work for Madagascar. Open markets require institutions to function, and policies to ensure equitable distribution of benefits and opportunities. And with the great diversity of institutions and traditions, countries around the world need flexibility in adapting economic policies and timing their implementation.

• *To the accountability of all actors.* Multilateral agreements and international human rights regimes hold only national governments accountable. National governance holds all actors accountable within national borders, but it is being overtaken by the rising importance of supranational global actors (multinational corporations) and international institutions (IMF, World Bank, WTO, Bank for International Settlements). Needed are standards and norms that set limits and define responsibilities for all actors.

The agenda for action to secure human development in this era of globalization should focus on seven key challenges, each requiring national and international action.

1. Strengthen policies and actions for human development, and adapt them to the new realities of the global economy.

Social policies—and national governance—are even more relevant today to make globalization work for human development and to protect people against its new threats. New policies are needed to tackle:

• Changing labour markets—not by going back to the old rigidities of labour market policies that protect elite labour, but by promoting job-creating growth, investing in workers' skills, promoting labour rights and making informal work more productive and remunerative. This is the new road to flexibility in the labour market.

• Shrinking fiscal resources of states, the results of liberalizing trade and financial markets, of the global tax competition and of the growth of the underground economy—by generating more revenue from new sources, such as taxes on income and land, abysmally low in many developing countries, or on value added; by improving efficiency in tax administration, cutting costs and increasing collections; by reducing military spending globally, still as high as a third of education and health spending.

• Increasing pressures on people's ability to provide caring labour in the family and community and on the state's ability to support it—by restoring strong commitments to preserving time, resources and rewards for care and restoring gender balance in the distribution of costs and burdens.

• Declining cultural diversity—by supporting national cultures, not by shutting out imports but by supporting local culture, arts and artists.

All countries need to rethink their social policies—for redistribution, for safety nets, for the universal provision of social services. The current debate focuses on the choice between a targeted, minimum cost approach, as in such countries as the United Kingdom and the United States, and a more universalist approach, as in the Nordic countries and several continental European countries. What is appropriate for developing countries? An approach that combines human development and poverty eradication with social protection.

2. Reduce the threats of financial volatility—of the boom and bust economy—and all their human costs.

Last year's financial crisis in East Asia spotlighted the inadequacies of national and global governance in managing economic and financial integration. Dominating the financial markets are the big players—from the United States to Brazil to China. But all countries are affected by the swings of the world economy—from South Africa to the Lao People's Democratic Republic—particularly if they have opened their economies. While countries need to manage their vulnerabilities to these swings, international action is needed to manage and prevent financial instability. Policy should focus on:

• Liberalizing the capital account more carefully, with less international pressure and greater flexibility for countries to decide on the pace and phasing based on their institutional capacities.

• Subjecting financial institutions to greater transparency and accountability. Developing countries need to strengthen the legal and regulatory institutions in their financial sectors.

• Integrating macroeconomic management and social policies to reduce the impact of financial turmoil on the economy and to minimize the social costs.

• Strengthening international action to regulate and supervise banking systems—building on the provisions of the Basle Committee and

Social policies—and national governance—are even more relevant today to make globalization work for human development and to protect people against its new threats

Stronger global cooperation and action are needed to address the growing problems beyond the scope of national governments to manage

the G-10 in requiring greater transparency and disclosure of information both nationally and internationally. The UN Economic and Social Council (ECOSOC), the World Bank and the IMF should conduct an international study of regulatory gaps, especially for short-term bank loans, for reversible portfolio flows and for the activities of hedge funds.

• Instituting standstill provisions on debt service to the IMF, the World Bank and the regional development banks, as proposed by the recent UN task force on the architecture of the international financial system.

• Developing better institutions of early warning and crisis management. The international community mobilized more than $170 billion in the 1997–99 financial crisis for Thailand, Indonesia, Korea, Russia and Brazil. But what ultimately is needed is a true lender of last resort, with more resources than the IMF is now equipped to provide. A world central bank to perform the functions of a lender of last resort should be seriously considered.

• Establishing an international lender of last resort for people—to complement financial packages. The real losses and risks from financial crises are felt by people, and a parallel funding mechanism should be established to protect them—and their rights to development.

3. Take stronger global action to tackle global threats to human security.

Stronger global cooperation and action are needed to address the growing problems beyond the scope of national governments to manage.

• The fight against global crime requires national police to take cooperative action as rapidly as the crime syndicates do. Dismantling bank secrecy and providing witness protection for foreign investigations would dramatically improve the effectiveness of the global fight against global crime. The proposed United Nations Convention against Transnational Organized Crime is an important first step deserving support.

• The "loud emergencies" of environmental degradation (acid rain, global warming and ozone depletion) have transboundary consequences, particularly for poor people and nations. Such emergencies demand global action, with initiatives building on the progress at the global conferences in Kyoto and Buenos Aires and on proposals for tradable permits and clean development mechanisms.

• Violations of human rights are often observed in export processing zones and in the factories of multinational corporations. The international community should formulate codes of conduct for multinationals to safeguard workers' rights.

• More global action is essential to address HIV/AIDS, which is penetrating borders everywhere. Efforts should be directed at disseminating the benefits of research from developed to developing countries, providing medicines and preventive measures at reasonable cost in developing countries and strengthening public health systems in the developing world.

4. Enhance public action to develop technologies for human development and the eradication of poverty.

The potential of the new technologies for human development and poverty eradication must be tapped.

• Intellectual property rights under the TRIPS agreement need comprehensive review to redress their perverse effects undermining food security, indigenous knowledge, biosafety and access to health care.

• The governance of global communications—especially the Internet—must be broadened to embrace the interests of developing countries in decisions on Internet protocols, taxation, domain name allocation and telephony costs.

• Public investments are needed in technologies for the needs of poor people and poor countries—in everything from seeds to computers. An international programme should be launched to support this, based on the model of the Consultative Group on International Agricultural Research (CGIAR).

• New funds must be raised to ensure that the information revolution leads to human development. A "bit" tax and a patent tax could raise funds from those who already have access to technology, with the proceeds used to extend the benefits to all.

5. Reverse the marginalization of poor, small countries.

Nearly 30 years ago the Pearson Commission began its report with the recognition that "the widening gap between the developed and the developing countries has become the central problem of our times." But over the past three decades the income gap between the world's richest fifth and its poorest fifth has more than doubled, to 74 to 1. And with that gap comes migration, environmental pressure, conflict, instability and other problems rooted in poverty and inequality.

Narrowing the gaps between rich and poor and the extremes between countries should become explicit global goals—to be rigorously monitored by ECOSOC and the Bretton Woods institutions. These would complement the goals for poverty reduction and social advance agreed to in the global conferences of the 1990s.

Action can start at the national level. All countries need strong and coherent policies for managing their integration into the rapidly changing global economy:

• To capture the opportunities of markets in trade and investment, each country should adopt a coordinated policy package. As the better-performing countries in each region have shown— the Dominican Republic, Ireland, Poland, Tunisia—the fundamentals do not stop with sound macroeconomic management. They must build on widely spread human capabilities, better incentive structures and sound governance.

• To negotiate more favourable provisions in multilateral agreements, poor and small countries should pursue active participation in the global dialogues on multilateral agreements— from their development to negotiations to implementation. In trade, for example, to negotiate for more rapid implementation of the agreement on textiles and clothing, for a reduction of agricultural tariffs and subsidies and for a slower pace in implementing the TRIPS agreement.

Poor and small countries can gain from collective action to link negotiations on intellectual property rights with rights to emit carbon into the atmosphere—and to link environmental assets, like rain forests, to negotiations on trade, debt and investment. They can also gain in negotiations by pooling resources for policy analysis and developing common negotiating positions. Regional collective action is a first step in this direction.

Stronger international action is needed to support growth and accelerate human development in marginalized countries. This requires reversing the decline in flows of official development assistance (ODA), down by almost a fifth in real terms since 1992. Even without increasing resources, ODA can be much better targeted to the countries in greatest need, and to achieving key human development goals. Another priority is debt relief for the 41 heavily indebted poor countries (HIPCs), whose debt service amounted to $11.1 billion in 1996 and whose debt payments have been squeezing spending on education and health. The HIPC initiative is welcome—but it delivers too little too late. Why not reduce the ceiling for a country's debt burden from 200–250% of exports to 100% or less? And why not reduce from six years to three (or even one) the performance requirement for eligibility?

6. Remedy the imbalances in the structures of global governance with new efforts to create a more inclusive system.

Poor countries and poor people have little influence and little voice in today's global policymaking forums. The most important and influential is the G-7, whose members control the Bretton Woods institutions through voting rights, and the UN Security Council by occupying three of the five permanent seats. There is no developing country equivalent to the G-7 or OECD—with similar levels of resources, consultation and policy coordination—though there have been many efforts to develop collective third world positions through such bodies as the G-15, the G-24 and the G-77.

Four actions could be rapidly set in motion to strengthen the bargaining position of the poor and small countries:

• *Provide legal aid.* WTO dispute settlement mechanisms can be fair only when the parties to a dispute have access to expert services of equal calibre to argue their case. An independent legal aid centre is needed to support poor countries.

• *Appoint an ombudsman* to respond to grievances and investigate injustices.

Narrowing the gaps between rich and poor and the extremes between countries should become explicit global goals

• *Support policy research.* OECD countries arrive at multilateral forums with a battery of policy research to formulate and defend their positions. The UNDP South Centre set up to support developing countries is still grossly underfunded.

• *Rely more on regional solidarity and regional institutions* to develop common positions for negotiations. Regional support would help in crises, as with the regional fund for financial stability proposed in 1997. By using peer pressure, it would also help to maintain policies and practices consistent with economic and financial stability.

At the other extreme is the concentration of influence in rich countries, institutions and corporations—influence not yet used to ensure that globalization works for human development. The voting patterns of the Bretton Woods organizations need to be reviewed. Greater public accountability and more transparency would make their operations more democratic and increase their credibility. Multinational corporations influence the lives and welfare of billions of people, yet their accountability is limited to their shareholders, with their influence on national and international policy-making kept behind the scenes. If they were brought into the structures of global governance, their positions would become more transparent, and their social responsibilities subject to greater public accountability.

• A multilateral code of conduct needs to be developed for multinational corporations. Today, they are held to codes of conduct only for what national legislation requires on the social and environmental impact of their operations. True, they have in recent years taken up voluntary codes of ethical conduct. But multinationals are too important for their conduct to be left to voluntary and self-generated standards.

• National policies ensure free competition in national markets, but there is no parallel in global markets. *Human Development Report 1994* proposed a world antimonopoly authority to monitor and implement competition rules for the global market. That authority could be included in the mandate of the WTO.

• A task force should be established on global economic governance—with perhaps 10 industrial and 10 developing countries, but also with representatives of civil society and private financial and corporate actors. That task force would report to the key institutions of global governance: to ECOSOC, the IMF, the World Bank, as well as to the WTO.

• A joint World Bank–UN task force should be set up to investigate global inequalities and suggest policies and actions on how they can be narrowed over the next two or three decades. The task force should report to ECOSOC and to the World Bank Development Committee.

7. Build a more coherent and more democratic architecture for global governance in the 21st century.

Just as the nineteenth-century mechanisms of national government were inadequate for the challenges of the postwar era, so today's institutions of international governance are inadequate for the challenges of the 21st century. Many of the basic elements of national governance will be needed in a more robust structure of global governance. An essential aspect of global governance, as of national governance, is responsibility to people—to equity, to justice, to enlarging the choices of all.

Some of the key institutions of global governance needed for the 21st century include:

• A stronger and more coherent United Nations to provide a forum for global leadership with equity and human concerns.

• A global central bank and lender of last resort.

• A World Trade Organization that ensures both free and fair international trade, with a mandate extending to global competition policy with antitrust provisions and a code of conduct for multinational corporations.

• A world environment agency.

• A world investment trust with redistributive functions.

• An international criminal court with a broader mandate for human rights.

• A broader UN system, including a two-chamber General Assembly to allow for civil society representation.

Even before these long-term changes are initiated or achieved, many actions could be taken in the next one to three years:

- Developing countries could take collective—especially regional—initiatives to strengthen their positions in global negotiations in trade, intellectual property rights and other areas.
- Individual countries could set up a high-level group to coordinate policy on globalization and manage their integration for a more positive impact on human development.
- Donor countries could accelerate action on debt relief and redirect aid in favour of poorer countries and human development priorities.
- An independent legal aid facility and ombudsman could be created to support the poor and weak countries in the WTO.
- All countries could cooperate more to fight global crime, relaxing restrictive bank secrecy laws.
- New sources of financing for the global technology revolution could be investigated, to ensure that it is truly global and that its potential for poverty eradication is mobilized. Two proposals: a bit tax to generate resources, and a public programme for development technology similar to CGIAR's programme for food.
- A representative task force could be set up to review global economic governance, including some 20 or so countries—large and small, rich and poor—but also the private sector and the civil society. It could report jointly to ECOSOC, the IMF Interim Committee and the World Bank Development Committee.

●　　　●　　　●

The surge of globalization over the past decade or two is only a beginning. The globally integrated world will require stronger governance if it is to preserve the advantages of global market competition, and to turn the forces of globalization to support human advance.

On the eve of the millenium, people are unusually expectant of a more fundamental diagnosis, more ready to receive it, more eager to act on it. Millenium fever is already stimulating many groups to sketch out their visions of the future—for their community, their country and their planet. The future of global governance—objectives, institutions, responsibilities and actions—needs to be part of this exploration by people everywhere. And the Millenium Assembly of the United Nations is a global forum that could provide powerful momentum for moving the agenda forward.

Stronger governance is needed to preserve the advantages of global market competition, and to turn the forces of globalization to support human advance

TEN YEARS OF HUMAN DEVELOPMENT

When I was arguing that helping a one-meal family

to become a two-meal family, enabling a woman without a change of clothing

to afford to buy a second piece of clothing, is a development miracle,

I was ridiculed. That is no development, I was reminded sternly.

Development is growth of the economy, they said; growth will bring everything.

We carried out our work as if we were engaged in some very undesirable activities.

When UNDP's Human Development Report came out we felt vindicated.

We were no longer back-street operators, we felt we were in the mainstream.

Thanks, Human Development Report.

PROFESSOR MUHAMMAD YUNUS, FOUNDER, GRAMEEN BANK, BANGLADESH

Ten years of human development

SPECIAL CONTRIBUTION

In 1990 the time had come for a broad approach to improving human well-being that would cover all aspects of human life, for all people, in both high-income and developing countries, both now and in the future. It went far beyond narrowly defined economic development to cover the full flourishing of all human choices. It emphasized the need to put people—their needs, their aspirations and their capabilities—at the center of the development effort. And the need to assert the unacceptability of any biases or discrimination, whether by class, gender, race, nationality, religion, community or generation. Human development had arrived.

The first *Human Development Report* of UNDP, published in 1990 under the inspiration and leadership of its architect, Mahbub ul Haq, came after a period of crisis and retrenchment, in which concern for people had given way to concern for balancing budgets and payments. It met a felt need and was widely welcomed. Since then it has caused considerable academic discussion in journals and seminars. It has caught the world's imagination, stimulating criticisms and debate, ingenious elaborations, improvements and additions.

Human development is the process of enlarging people's choices—not just choices among different detergents, television channels or car models but the choices that are created by expanding human capabilities and functionings—what people do and can do in their lives. At all levels of development a few capabilities are essential for human development, without which many choices in life would not be available. These capabilities are to lead long and healthy lives, to be knowledgeable and to have access to the resources needed for a decent standard of living—and these are reflected in the human development index. But many additional choices are valued by people. These include political, social, economic and cultural freedom, a sense of community, opportunities for being creative and productive, and self-respect and human rights. Yet human development is more than just achieving these capabilities; it is also the process of pursuing them in a way that is equitable, participatory, productive and sustainable.

Choices will change over time and can, in principle, be infinite. Yet infinite choices without limits and constraints can become pointless and mindless. Choices have to be combined with allegiances, rights with duties, options with bonds, liberties with ligatures. Today we see a reaction against the extreme individualism of the free market approach towards what has come to be called communitarianism. The exact combination of individual and public action, of personal agency and social institutions, will vary from time to time and from problem to problem. Institutional arrangements will be more important for achieving environmental sustainability, personal agency more important when it comes to the choice of household articles or marriage partners. But some complementarity will always be necessary.

Getting income is one of the options people would like to have. It is important but not an all-important option. Human development includes the expansion of income and wealth, but it includes many other valued and valuable things as well.

For example, in investigating the priorities of poor people, one discovers that what matters most to them often differs from what outsiders assume. More income is only one of the things poor people desire. Adequate nutrition, safe water at hand, better medical services, more and better schooling for their children, cheap transport, adequate shelter, continuing employment and secure livelihoods and productive, remunerating, satisfying jobs do not show up in higher income per head, at least not for some time.

There are other non-material benefits that are often more highly valued by poor people than material improvements. Some of these partake in the characteristics of rights, others in those of states of mind. Among these are good and safe working conditions, freedom to choose jobs and livelihoods, freedom of movement and speech, liberation from oppression, violence and exploitation, security from persecution and arbitrary arrest, a satisfying family life, the assertion of cultural and religious values, adequate leisure time and satisfying forms of its use, a sense of purpose in life and work, the opportunity to join and actively participate in the activities of civil society and a sense of belonging to a community. These are often more highly valued than income, both in their own right and as a means to satisfying and productive work. They do not show up in higher income figures. No policy-maker can guarantee the achievement of all, or even the majority, of these aspirations, but policies can create the opportunities for their fulfilment.

P. P. Streeten

PAUL STREETEN

Human Development Reports have had a significant impact worldwide.
Up until the publication of these Reports, discussions on development centred on economic growth, using variables
such as per capita income growth. Of course these economic variables also generate some social benefits. But this view
of development had been quite limited. While a country could perfectly well be considered highly developed, income
might be concentrated in the hands of a few, and poverty worsening.... Speaking as President of Brazil,
until today the country is plagued by a lot of problems—income concentration, poverty, and so on.
If we do not adopt a development model that responds to the needs of the majority,
this development will not be long-lasting.

FERNANDO HENRIQUE CARDOSO, PRESIDENT, BRAZIL

This year's Report marks the tenth anniversary of the *Human Development Report*. Each year since being launched in 1990, the Report has focused on different themes and introduced new concepts and approaches. But the central concern has always been people as the purpose of development, and their empowerment as participants in the development process. The Report puts economic growth into perspective: it is a means—a very important one—to serve human ends, but it is not an end in itself.

ACCOUNTING FOR THE FIRST 10 YEARS

How has human development changed since the Report was first published in 1990? A balance sheet of human development in 1990–97 shows tremendous progress—but also enduring deprivations and new setbacks.

POLICY PROPOSALS OVER THE YEARS

Each year the *Human Development Report* has made strong policy recommendations, for both national and international action. The proposals, some emphasizing suggestions by others, some putting forward new approaches, have drawn both criticism and praise. But most important, they have helped to open policy debates to wider possibilities.

GLOBAL PROPOSALS

Global proposals have been aimed at contributing to a new paradigm of sustainable human development—based on a new concept of human security, a new partnership of developed and developing countries, new forms of international cooperation and a new global compact.

THE 20:20 INITIATIVE (1992). With the aim of turning both domestic and external priorities to basic human concerns, this initiative proposed that every developing country allocate 20% of its domestic budget, and every donor 20% of its official development assistance (ODA), to ensuring basic health care, basic education, access to safe water and basic sanitation, and basic family planning packages for all couples.

GLOBAL HUMAN SECURITY FUND (1994). This fund would tackle drug trafficking, international terrorism, communicable diseases, nuclear proliferation, natural disasters, ethnic conflicts, excessive international migration and global environmental pollution and degradation. The fund of $250 billion a year would be financed with $14 billion from a proportion of the peace dividend (20% of the amount saved by industrial countries and 10% of that saved by developing countries through a 3% reduction in global military spending); $150 billion from a 0.05% tax on speculative international capital movements; $66 billion from a global energy tax ($1 per barrel of oil or its equivalent in coal consumption) and $20 billion from a one-third share of ODA.

A NEW GLOBAL ARCHITECTURE (1994). A globalizing world needs new institutions to deal with problems that nations alone cannot solve:
• An economic security council—to review the threats to human security.
• A world central bank—to take on global macroeconomic management and supervision of international banking.
• An international investment trust—to recycle international surpluses to developing countries.
• A world antimonopoly authority—to monitor the

The issues raised by this Report [Human Development Report 1995] are of central importance to all of us....
In country after country women have demonstrated that when given the tools of opportunity—education, health
care, access to credit, political participation and legal rights—they can lift themselves out of poverty, and as
women realize their potential, they lift their families, communities and nations as well.... This Report not only
provides a graphic portrait of the problems facing today's women, but also opens up the opportunity for a serious
dialogue about possible solutions. It challenges governments, communities and individuals to enter
into this conversation in a common effort to overcome shared problems.

HILLARY RODHAM CLINTON, FIRST LADY, THE UNITED STATES

activities of multinational corporations and ensure that markets are competitive.

A TIMETABLE TO ELIMINATE LEGAL GENDER DISCRIMINATION
(1995). As of December 1998, 163 countries had ratified the 1979 Convention on the Elimination of All Forms of Discrimination Against Women (CEDAW), but others—including the United States—had not. Women's rights are human rights. There should be a timetable for recognizing legal equality between women and men everywhere, say by 2005, using CEDAW as the framework.

NATIONAL PROPOSALS

National proposals have focused on the centrality of people in development, on the need for a new partnership between the state and the market and on new forms of alliance between governments, institutions of civil society, communities and people.

RESTRUCTURING SOCIAL EXPENDITURES (1991). Resources
should be reallocated to basic human priority concerns through in analysis of a country's total expenditure, social expenditure and human priority spending ratios. The key is to move away from military spending towards social spending—and to shift the focus to primary human concerns: better education, health services and safe water accessible to poor people.

A CRITICAL THRESHOLD OF 30% FOR WOMEN'S REPRESENTA-
TION (1995). Women must have a critical 30% representation in all decision-making processes—economic, political and social—nationally and locally. Reaching this threshold is essential to enable women to influence decisions that affect their lives. And to achieve gender equal-

ity, social norms and practices must be changed, and women's access to social services, productive resources and all other opportunities made equal to men's.

PRO-POOR GROWTH (1996). The quality of economic growth
is as important as its quantity. For human development, growth should be job-creating rather than *jobless*, poverty-reducing rather than *ruthless*, participatory rather than *voiceless*, culturally entrenched rather than *rootless* and environment-friendly rather than *futureless*. A growth strategy that aims for a more equitable distribution of assets, that is job-creating and labour-intensive, and that is decentralized can achieve such growth.

AGENDA FOR POVERTY ERADICATION (1997). People's
empowerment is the key to poverty elimination and at the centre of a six-point agenda:
• Empower individuals, households and communities to gain greater control over their lives and resources.
• Strengthen gender equality to empower women.
• Accelerate pro-poor growth in low-income countries.
• Improve the management of globalization.
• Ensure an active state committed to eradicating poverty.
• Take special actions for special situations to support progress in the poorest and weakest countries.

HUMAN DEVELOPMENT AS A NATIONAL TOOL

The human development approach has tremendous potential for analysing situations and policies at the national level. Two Human Development Centres have been established—the first in Islamabad, Pakistan, and the second in Guanajuanto, Mexico. More than 260 national and subnational human development reports

TEN YEARS OF HUMAN DEVELOPMENT

*The Human Development Report has become an important instrument of policy
and the concept of the human development index a fundamental tool in formulation of policy by government....
Growth and advancement must be measured by the extent to which it impacts positively on people,
but the starting point must be human development. We need to focus particularly
on the sectors of society that are the most disadvantaged—
women, youth, children, the elderly and the disabled.*

THABO MBEKI, DEPUTY PRESIDENT, SOUTH AFRICA

have been produced over the years by 120 countries, in addition to nine regional reports. In each country these serve to bring together the facts, influence national policy and mobilize action. They have introduced the human development concept into national policy dialogue—not only through human development indicators and policy recommendations, but also through the country-led process of consultation, data collection and report writing.

SOUTH AFRICA—UNDERSTANDING THE FULL COSTS OF HIV/AIDS

South Africa has one of the fastest-spreading HIV epidemics in the world. The country's 1998 human development report provided startling information on how this will affect human development. Many of the advances achieved during the short life of the new democracy will be reversed if the epidemic goes unchecked. Developing and drafting the report brought critical gaps in information to light. The economic costs alone, in lost labour and sick days, are far greater than initially realized. The report has prompted plans for further study of the full costs—direct and indirect—of the epidemic to the government, to communities and to households.

INDIA—STATE REPORTS INFLUENCING POLICY

Many of India's 25 states rival medium-size countries in size, population and diversity. National-level aggregation would hide these important regional disparities. UNDP India has therefore supported the preparation of human development reports by state governments.

The government of Madhya Pradesh was the first to prepare a state report, in 1995, which helped bring human development into political discourse and planning. Its second report, in 1998, reflects the influence the first report had on planning. Social services now account for more than 42% of plan investment, compared with 19% in the previous plan budget. This success bodes well for other states, such as Gujarat, Karnataka and Rajasthan, preparing their first human development reports in 1999.

KUWAIT—INTRODUCING THE HUMAN DEVELOPMENT PERSPECTIVE

Kuwait's first human development report, in 1997, raised awareness of the human development concept and its relevance to the country's struggle to shift from dependence on oil towards a knowledge-based economy. The report's production and promotion helped advance new thinking in academia, research institutions and the government. The Ministry of Planning has started to incorporate the human development approach in its indicators for strategic planning and to monitor human development. The Arab Planning Institute has revised its curriculum to reflect the human development concept. And after the success of the first report, the Ministry of Planning is following up with a second, fully funded by the government.

GUATEMALA—ALERTING THE COUNTRY TO THE NEED FOR DATA

Guatemala's first human development report, in 1998, overcame data limitations to spotlight socio-economic disparities across regions, with a strong emphasis on statistics. Seen as the most complete document on Guatemalan society after the civil war, the report has

We, the people of the Earth, are one large family. The new epoch offers new challenges and new global problems, such as environmental catastrophes, exhaustion of resources, bloody conflicts and poverty. Every time I see children begging in the street, my heart is broken—it is our challenge and our shame that we are still unable to help those who are vulnerable—children in the first place. Whatever are the problems or perspectives for the future— the human dimension is what should be applied as the measure of all events, towards the implications of every political decision to be made. That is why the idea of human development promoted by UNDP is so important for us. I would like to thank UNDP for bringing to life both the important concept of human development, and these Reports.

EDUARD SHEVARDNADZE, PRESIDENT, GEORGIA

become a crucial source of information for NGOs, universities and the international community. And it has led Guatemala's government and civil society to recognize that the national system of statistics urgently needs strengthening—not only to support technical studies, but also to inform citizens as a requirement for democracy.

LATVIA AND LITHUANIA—NETWORKING ON HUMAN DEVELOPMENT

Latvia and Lithuania have published national human development reports every year since 1995. The reports have covered the social effects of transition, human settlements, social cohesion and poverty. Starting out by encouraging national debate on development challenges, the reports have now inspired a cross-border academic network. Scholars from three universities in each country are jointly developing a course curriculum to provide a multidisciplinary overview of human development and its relevance to Latvia and Lithuania. The reports will be part of the course curriculum.

CAMBODIA—HIGHLIGHTING GENDER DISCRIMINATION

Published annually since 1997, Cambodia's human development reports have provided a unique overview of human development in a country where scarcity of reliable statistical data has been a major obstacle in developing sustainable social and economic policies. The 1998 report drew public attention to the persistent discrimination against women in access to education and health care. This message was reinforced by a television documentary and four short spots on women in different occupations, broadcast by all five national television stations. The reports have received an enthusiastic response, and several NGOs and provincial government units are using them to train field staff and community workers. Encouraged by this reception, UNDP and the Cambodian government recently began transferring ownership of the report fully into Cambodian hands. The initiative, with the participation of many NGOs, seeks to strengthen local capacity in compiling and analysing data on human development.

A balance sheet of human development, 1990-97

GLOBAL PROGRESS | GLOBAL DEPRIVATION

HEALTH

In 1997, 84 countries enjoyed a life expectancy at birth of more than 70 years, up from 55 countries in 1990. The number of developing countries in the group has more than doubled, from 22 to 49. Between 1990 and 1997 the share of the population with access to safe water nearly doubled, from 40% to 72%.

During 1990-97 the number of people infected with HIV/AIDS more than doubled, from less than 15 million to more than 33 million. Around 1.5 billion people are not expected to survive to age 60. More than 880 million people lack access to health services, and 2.6 billion access to basic sanitation.

EDUCATION

Between 1990 and 1997 the adult literacy rate rose from 64% to 76%.
During 1990-97 the gross primary and secondary enrolment ratio increased from 74% to 81%.

In 1997 more than 850 million adults were illiterate. In industrial countries more than 100 million people were functionally illiterate. More than 260 million children are out of school at the primary and secondary levels.

FOOD AND NUTRITION

Despite rapid population growth, food production per capita increased by nearly 25% during 1990-97.
The per capita daily supply of calories rose from less than 2,500 to 2,750, and that of protein from 71 grams to 76.

About 840 million people are malnourished.
The overall consumption of the richest fifth of the world's people is 16 times that of the poorest fifth.

INCOME AND POVERTY

During 1990-97 real per capita GDP increased at an average annual rate of more than 1%.
Real per capita consumption increased at an average annual rate of 2.4% during the same period.

Nearly 1.3 billion people live on less than a dollar a day, and close to 1 billion cannot meet their basic consumption requirements.
The share in global income of the richest fifth of the world's people is 74 times that of the poorest fifth.

WOMEN

During 1990-97 the net secondary enrolment ratio for girls increased from 36% to 61%.
Between 1990 and 1997 women's economic activity rate rose from 34% to nearly 40%.

Nearly 340 million women are not expected to survive to age 40.
A quarter to a half of all women have suffered physical abuse by an intimate partner.

CHILDREN

Between 1990 and 1997 the infant mortality rate was reduced from 76 per 1,000 live births to 58.
The proportion of one-year-olds immunized increased from 70% to 89% during 1990-97.

Nearly 160 million children are malnourished.
More than 250 million children are working as child labourers.

ENVIRONMENT

Between 1990 and 1997 the share of heavily polluting traditional fuels in the energy used was reduced by more than two-fifths.

Every year nearly 3 million people die from air pollution—more than 80% of them from indoor air pollution—and more than 5 million die from diarrhoeal diseases caused by water contamination.

HUMAN SECURITY

Between two-thirds and three-quarters of the people in developing countries live under relatively pluralist and democratic regimes.

At the end of 1997 there were nearly 12 million refugees.

ASSESSING HUMAN DEVELOPMENT

SPECIAL CONTRIBUTION

The human development index (HDI), which the *Human Development Report* has made into something of a flagship, has been rather successful in serving as an alternative measure of development, supplementing GNP. Based as it is on three distinct components—indicators of longevity, education and income per head—it is not exclusively focused on economic opulence (as GNP is). Within the limits of these three components, the HDI has served to broaden substantially the empirical attention that the assessment of development processes receives.

However, the HDI, which is inescapably a crude index, must not be seen as anything other than an introductory move in getting people interested in the rich collection of information that is present in the *Human Development Report*. Indeed, I must admit I did not initially see much merit in the HDI itself, which, as it happens, I was privileged to help devise. At first I had expressed to Mahbub ul Haq, the originator of the *Human Development Report,* considerable scepticism about trying to focus on a crude index of this kind, attempting to catch in one simple number a complex reality about human development and deprivation. In contrast to the coarse index of the HDI, the rest of the *Human Development Report* contains an extensive collection of tables, a wealth of information on a variety of social, economic and political features that influence the nature and quality of human life. Why give prominence, it was natural to ask, to a crude summary index that could not begin to capture much of the rich information that makes the *Human Development Report* so engaging and important?

This crudeness had not escaped Mahbub at all. He did not resist the argument that the HDI could not be but a very limited indicator of development. But after some initial hesitation, Mahbub persuaded himself that the dominance of GNP (an overused and oversold index that he wanted to supplant) would not be broken by any set of tables. People would look at them respectfully, he argued, but when it came to using a summary measure of development, they would still go back to the unadorned GNP, because it was crude but convenient. As I listened to Mahbub, I heard an echo of T. S. Eliot's poem "Burnt Norton": "Human kind/Cannot bear very much reality".

"We need a measure", Mahbub demanded, "of the same level of vulgarity as GNP—just one number—but a measure that is not as blind to social aspects of human lives as GNP is." Mahbub hoped that not only would the HDI be something of an improvement on—or at least a helpful supplement to—GNP, but also that it would serve to broaden public interest in the other variables that are plentifully analysed in the *Human Development Report.*

Mahbub got this exactly right, I have to admit, and I am very glad that we did not manage to deflect him from seeking a crude measure. By skilful use of the attracting power of the HDI, Mahbub got readers to take an involved interest in the large class of systematic tables and detailed critical analyses presented in the *Human Development Report.* The crude index spoke loud and clear and received intelligent attention and through that vehicle the complex reality contained in the rest of the Report also found an interested audience.

AMARTYA SEN, 1998 NOBEL LAUREATE IN ECONOMICS

Countries and regions that have produced human development reports

ARAB STATES

Algeria, *1999*
Bahrain, *1997*
Egypt, *1994, 1995, 1996, 1997/98*
Iraq, *1995*
Jordan, *1998*
Kuwait, *1997, 1998*
Lebanon, *1997, 1999*
Libyan Arab Jamahiriya, *1998*
Morocco, *1997, 1999*
Occupied Palestinian territory, *1997*
Somalia, *1998*
Sudan, *1998*
Syrian Arab Republic, *1999*
Tunisia, *1999*
United Arab Emirates, *1998*
Yemen, *1998*

ASIA AND THE PACIFIC

Bangladesh, *1992, 1993, 1994, 1995, 1996, 1997*
Cambodia, *1997, 1998, 1999*
China, *1997, 1999*
India, Gujarat,[a] *1999*
India, Karnataka,[a] *1999*
India, Madhya Pradesh,[a] *1995, 1998*
India, Rajasthan,[a] *1999*
Iran, Islamic Rep. of, *1999*
Korea, Rep. of, *1998*
Lao People's Dem. Rep., *1998*
Maldives, *1999*
Mongolia, *1997, 1999*
Myanmar, *1998*
Nepal, *1998*
Pakistan, *1992*
Palau, *1999*
Papua New Guinea, *1999*
Philippines, *1994, 1997, 1999*
Samoa (Western), *1998*
Sri Lanka, *1998*
Thailand, *1999*
Vanuatu, *1996*
Viet Nam, *1998*

EASTERN EUROPE AND THE CIS

Albania, *1995, 1996, 1997, 1998*
Armenia, *1995, 1996, 1997, 1998*
Azerbaijan, *1995, 1996, 1997, 1998, 1999*
Belarus, *1995, 1996, 1997, 1998*
Bosnia and Herzegovina, *1999*
Bulgaria, *1995, 1996, 1997, 1998, 1999*

Bulgaria, Sofia,[a] *1997*
Croatia, *1997, 1998*
Czech Republic, *1996, 1997, 1998*
Estonia, *1995, 1996, 1997, 1998*
Georgia, *1995, 1996, 1997, 1998*
Hungary, *1995, 1996, 1998*
Kazakhstan, *1995, 1996, 1997, 1998, 1999*
Kyrgyzstan, *1995, 1996, 1997, 1998, 1999*
Latvia, *1995, 1996, 1997, 1998, 1999*
Lithuania, *1995, 1996, 1997, 1998, 1999*
Macedonia, *1997, 1998*
Malta, *1996*
Moldova, Rep. of, *1995, 1996, 1997, 1998*
Poland, *1995, 1996, 1997, 1998, 1999*
Romania, *1995, 1996, 1997, 1998*
Russian Federation, *1995, 1996, 1997, 1998*
Slovakia, *1995, 1997, 1998*
Tajikistan, *1995, 1996, 1997, 1998*
Turkey, *1995, 1996, 1997, 1998*
Turkmenistan, *1995, 1996, 1997, 1998*
Ukraine, *1995, 1996, 1997, 1998*
Uzbekistan, *1995, 1996, 1997, 1998*
Yugoslavia, *1996, 1997*

LATIN AMERICA AND THE CARIBBEAN

Argentina, *1995, 1996, 1997, 1998, 1999*
Argentina, Buenos Aires,[a] *1996, 1997, 1998, 1999*
Belize, *1997*
Bolivia, *1998*
Bolivia, Cochabamba,[a] *1995*
Bolivia, La Paz,[a] *1995*
Bolivia, Santa Cruz,[a] *1995*
Brazil, *1996*
Chile, *1996, 1998*
Colombia, *1998*
Costa Rica, *1995, 1996, 1997, 1998*
Cuba, *1996, 1999*
Dominican Republic, *1997, 1999*
Ecuador, *1999*
El Salvador, *1997, 1999*
Guatemala, *1998, 1999*
Guyana, *1996*
Honduras, *1998, 1999*
Nicaragua, *1997*

Paraguay, *1995, 1996*
Peru, *1997*
Trinidad and Tobago, *1999*
Uruguay, *1999*
Venezuela, *1995, 1996, 1997, 1998*

SUB-SAHARAN AFRICA

Angola, *1997, 1998, 1999*
Benin, *1997, 1998*
Botswana, *1997*
Burkina Faso, *1997*
Burundi, *1997*
Cameroon, *1991, 1993, 1996, 1998*
Cape Verde, *1998*
Central African Republic, *1996*
Chad, *1997*
Comoros, *1997, 1998*
Côte d'Ivoire, *1997*
Equatorial Guinea, *1996*
Ethiopia, *1997, 1998*
Gambia, *1997*
Ghana, *1997*
Guinea, *1997*
Guinea-Bissau, *1997*
Kenya, *1999*
Lesotho, *1998*
Liberia, *1997*
Madagascar, *1996*
Malawi, *1997, 1998*
Mali, *1995, 1997, 1998*
Mauritania, *1996, 1997, 1998*
Mozambique, *1998*
Namibia, *1996, 1997*
Niger, *1997, 1998*
Nigeria, *1996, 1997*
Sierra Leone, *1996*
South Africa, *1998*
Swaziland, *1997*
Tanzania, U. Rep. of, *1997*
Togo, *1995, 1997*
Uganda, *1996, 1997*
Zambia, *1997*
Zimbabwe, *1998*

REGIONAL REPORTS

Africa, *1995*
Southern African Development Community, *1998*
Europe and the CIS, *1995, 1996*
Pacific Islands, *1994, 1998*
South Asia, *1997, 1998, 1999*

a. Subnational report.
Source: Human Development Report Office.

CHAPTER 1

Human development in this age of globalization

Globalization, a dominant force in the 20th century's last decade, is shaping a new era of interaction among nations, economies and people. It is increasing the contacts between people across national boundaries—in economy, in technology, in culture and in governance. But it is also fragmenting production processes, labour markets, political entities and societies. So, while globalization has positive, innovative, dynamic aspects—it also has negative, disruptive, marginalizing aspects.

Today's interactions between nations and people are deeper than ever (figure 1.1).

• World exports, now $7 trillion, averaged 21% of GDP in the 1990s, compared with 17% of a much smaller GDP in the 1970s.

• Foreign direct investment topped $400 billion in 1997, seven times the level in real terms in the 1970s. Portfolio and other short-term capital flows grew substantially, and now total more than $2 trillion in gross terms, almost three times those in the 1980s.

• The daily turnover in foreign exchange markets increased from around $10–20 billion in the 1970s to $1.5 trillion in 1998.

• Between 1983 and 1993 cross-border sales and purchases of US Treasury bonds increased from $30 billion a year to $500 billion.

• International bank lending grew from $265 billion in 1975 to $4.2 trillion in 1994.

• People travel more—with tourism more than doubling between 1980 and 1996, from 260 million to 590 million travellers a year.

• Despite the tight restrictions, international migration continues to grow. So have workers' remittances, reaching $58 billion in 1996.

• Time spent on international telephone calls rocketed from 33 billion minutes in 1990 to 70 billion minutes in 1996 (figure 1.2).

• Travel, the Internet and the media have stimulated exponential growth in the exchange of ideas and information, and people today engage more than ever in associations that span national borders—from informal networks to formal organizations.

Driving this global integration are policy shifts to promote economic efficiency through the liberalization and deregulation of national markets and the retreat of the state from many economic activities, including a restructuring of the welfare state. Driving integration even faster are the recent innovations in information and communications technology. But global integration is still very partial—for one thing, the flow of labour is restricted, with borders closed to the unskilled.

The world today has more opportunities for people than 20, 50 or 100 years ago. Child death rates have fallen by half since 1965, and a child born today can expect to live a decade longer than a child born then. In developing countries the combined primary and secondary enrolment ratio has more than doubled—and the proportion of children in primary school has risen from less than half to more than three-quarters. Adult literacy rates have also risen, from 48% in 1970 to 72% in 1997. Most states are now independent, and more than 70% of the world's people live under fairly pluralist democratic regimes.

The world is more prosperous, with average per capita incomes having more than tripled as global GDP increased ninefold, from $3 trillion to $30 trillion, in the past 50 years. The share of people enjoying medium human development rose from 55% in 1975 to 66% in 1997, and the share in low human development fell from 20% to 10%.

But these trends mask great unevenness—in the advances and in the new setbacks.

While globalization has positive, innovative, dynamic aspects—it also has negative, disruptive, marginalizing aspects

FIGURE 1.1

Global integration has progressed rapidly but unevenly . . .

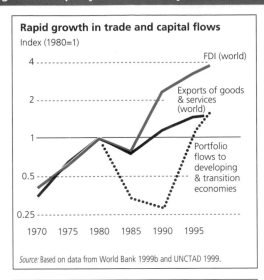

Rapid growth in trade and capital flows
Index (1980=1)

FDI (world)

Exports of goods & services (world)

Portfolio flows to developing & transition economies

Source: Based on data from World Bank 1999b and UNCTAD 1999.

Cross-border mergers and acquisitions

The growth in cross-border mergers and acquisitions (M&As) has become a striking trend and a major driver of FDI. In 1997 there were 58 transactions that exceeded $1 billion each. Large M&As have been concentrated in financial services, insurance, life sciences, telecommunications and the media.

US$ billions

Annual cross-border mergers and acquisitions

42% of total FDI

59% of total FDI

Source: UNCTAD 1998c.

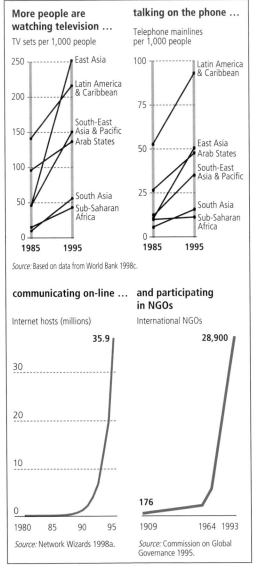

More people are watching television ...
TV sets per 1,000 people

East Asia
Latin America & Caribbean
South-East Asia & Pacific
Arab States
South Asia
Sub-Saharan Africa

talking on the phone ...
Telephone mainlines per 1,000 people

Latin America & Caribbean
East Asia
Arab States
South-East Asia & Pacific
South Asia
Sub-Saharan Africa

Source: Based on data from World Bank 1998c.

communicating on-line ...
Internet hosts (millions)

35.9

Source: Network Wizards 1998a.

and participating in NGOs
International NGOs

28,900

176

Source: Commission on Global Governance 1995.

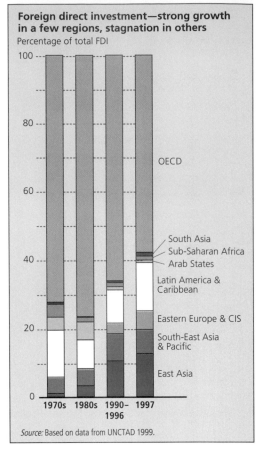

Foreign direct investment—strong growth in a few regions, stagnation in others
Percentage of total FDI

OECD
South Asia
Sub-Saharan Africa
Arab States
Latin America & Caribbean
Eastern Europe & CIS
South-East Asia & Pacific
East Asia

Source: Based on data from UNCTAD 1999.

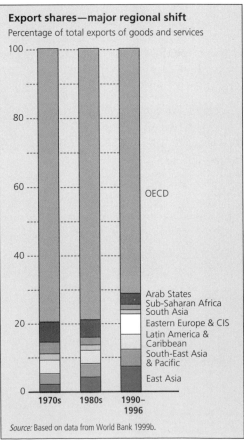

Export shares—major regional shift
Percentage of total exports of goods and services

OECD
Arab States
Sub-Saharan Africa
South Asia
Eastern Europe & CIS
Latin America & Caribbean
South-East Asia & Pacific
East Asia

Source: Based on data from World Bank 1999b.

Country performance varies widely within regions

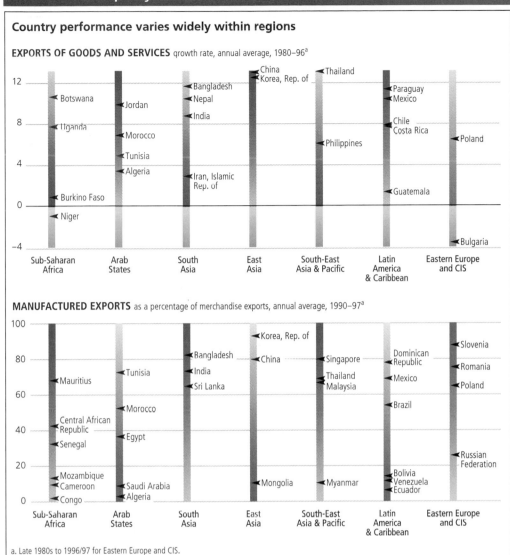

EXPORTS OF GOODS AND SERVICES growth rate, annual average, 1980–96[a]

(Regions: Sub-Saharan Africa; Arab States; South Asia; East Asia; South-East Asia & Pacific; Latin America & Caribbean; Eastern Europe and CIS)

Labeled points include: Botswana, Uganda, Burkino Faso, Niger; Jordan, Morocco, Tunisia, Algeria; Bangladesh, Nepal, India, Iran, Islamic Rep. of; China, Korea, Rep. of; Thailand, Philippines; Paraguay, Mexico, Chile, Costa Rica, Guatemala; Poland, Bulgaria.

MANUFACTURED EXPORTS as a percentage of merchandise exports, annual average, 1990–97[a]

(Regions: Sub-Saharan Africa; Arab States; South Asia; East Asia; South-East Asia & Pacific; Latin America & Caribbean; Eastern Europe and CIS)

Labeled points include: Mauritius, Central African Republic, Senegal, Mozambique, Cameroon, Congo; Tunisia, Morocco, Egypt, Saudi Arabia, Algeria; Bangladesh, India, Sri Lanka; Korea, Rep. of, China, Mongolia; Singapore, Thailand, Malaysia, Myanmar; Dominican Republic, Mexico, Brazil, Bolivia, Venezuela, Ecuador; Slovenia, Romania, Poland, Russian Federation.

a. Late 1980s to 1996/97 for Eastern Europe and CIS.

Top 20 recipients
Among developing and transition countries

Workers' remittances 1996, millions of current US$		Foreign direct investment 1997, millions of current US$		Portfolio and other flows 1997, millions of current US$	
India	9,326	China	45,300	Brazil	18,495
Mexico	4,224	Brazil	16,330	Mexico	16,028
Turkey	3,542	Mexico	12,101	Thailand	11,181
Egypt	2,798	Singapore	10,000	Argentina	10,132
Lebanon	2,503	Argentina	6,327	Indonesia	10,070
Morocco	2,165	Russian Federation	6,241	China	9,920
China	1,672	Chile	5,417	Malaysia	7,596
Jordan	1,544	Indonesia	5,350	Russian Federation	4,975
Pakistan	1,461	Poland	5,000	Turkey	4,913
Bangladesh	1,217	Venezuela	4,893	Colombia	4,417
Brazil	1,213	Malaysia	3,754	India	3,817
Yemen	1,123	Thailand	3,600	Czech Republic	3,459
El Salvador	1,086	India	3,264	Philippines	3,192
Algeria	1,045	Hong Kong, China (SAR)	2,600	Chile	2,712
Croatia	985	Colombia	2,447	Venezuela	2,411
Nigeria	947	Korea, Rep. of	2,341	Peru	2,273
Dominican Republic	847	Taiwan, province of China	2,248	Romania	1,551
Sri Lanka	832	Hungary	2,085	South Africa	1,281
Indonesia	796	Peru	2,000	Pakistan	1,246
Tunisia	736	Kazakhstan	1,320	Slovenia	1,033
Totalling 88% of remittances		**Totalling 85% of FDI**		**Totalling 94% of flows**	

How the benefits of integration are distributed
Annual averages

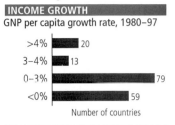

INCOME GROWTH
GNP per capita growth rate, 1980–97

	Number of countries
>4%	20
3–4%	13
0–3%	79
<0%	59

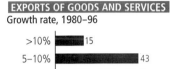

EXPORTS OF GOODS AND SERVICES
Growth rate, 1980–96

	Number of countries
>10%	15
5–10%	43
1–5%	46
<1%	9

As a percentage of GDP, 1990–97

	Number of countries
>50%	43
25–50%	66
10–25%	53
<10%	10

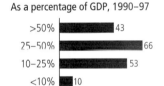

MANUFACTURED EXPORTS
As a percentage of merchandise exports, 1990–97

	Number of countries
>50%	58
25–50%	29
10–25%	26
<10%	28

TAXES ON INTERNATIONAL TRADE
As a percentage of current revenue, 1990–96

	Number of countries
>50%	2
25–50%	19
10–25%	36
<10%	51

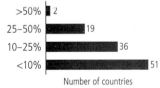

WORKERS' REMITTANCES
US$ millions, 1990–96

	Number of countries
>1,000	14
500–1,000	10
100–500	19
<100	113

Note: The number of countries varies from 108 to 172 depending on the database used.

Source: All figures based on data from World Bank 1999b and UNCTAD 1999.

FIGURE 1.2
International telephone calls
Minutes per person per year, 1995

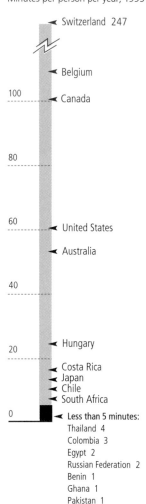

Switzerland 247

Belgium

100 Canada

80

60 United States

Australia

40

20 Hungary

Costa Rica
Japan
Chile
South Africa

0 Less than 5 minutes:
Thailand 4
Colombia 3
Egypt 2
Russian Federation 2
Benin 1
Ghana 1
Pakistan 1

Source: UNESCO 1998b.

Despite the tremendous progress in the 20th century, the world today faces huge backlogs of deprivation and inequality that leave huge disparities within countries and regions.

Poverty is everywhere. Measured by the human poverty index (HPI-1), more than a quarter of the 4.5 billion people in developing countries still do not have some of life's most basic choices—survival beyond age 40, access to knowledge and minimum private and public services.

• Nearly 1.3 billion people do not have access to clean water.

• One in seven children of primary school age is out of school.

• About 840 million are malnourished.

• An estimated 1.3 billion people live on incomes of less than $1 (1987 PPP$) a day.

In industrial countries, too, human poverty and exclusion are hidden among statistics of success, revealing enormous disparities within countries. Measured by the human poverty index (HPI-2), one person in eight in the richest countries of the world is affected by some aspect of human poverty: long-term unemployment, a life shorter than 60 years, an income below the national poverty line or a lack of the literacy needed to cope in society.

The HPI disaggregated for a country's regions also shows wide disparities. In India, for example, the level of human poverty in the state of Bihar (54%) is more than twice that in Kerala.

Gender disparities remain large, too. In developing countries there are still 60% more illiterate women than illiterate men, and female enrolment at the primary level is still 6% lower than male enrolment. Disparities are starkest in the political and economic arena, with women nearly closed out of political life. In only five countries do they occupy more than 30% of parliamentary seats, and in 31 they occupy fewer than 5%. The gender empowerment measure and the gender development index show inequalities in every country (see indicator tables 2 and 3).

THE WORLD HAS CHANGED

Over the past decade dramatic events have changed the global political order, brought technological progress and shifted economic policies—events defining the character of globalization and greatly accelerating it. The end of the cold war unleashed a wave of global political integration. Information and communications technology has launched millions of global conversations. And the Marrakesh Agreement of 1994 changed the rules of global trade. All this in the wake of a global ideological shift.

POLITICAL ORDER

The fall of the Berlin Wall in 1989 and the end of the cold war removed political and economic barriers—bringing more than 400 million people in Eastern Europe and the Commonwealth of Independent States (CIS) and almost 1.3 billion people in China and Viet Nam into the world of global contacts and communications. Ideas and information began to flow freely as countries lifted censorship, travel restrictions and prohibitions on political parties and civil society organizations. And foreign investment poured into China, Viet Nam, Poland and the Russian Federation—as did McDonald's, Hollywood movies and CNN real-time global news.

TECHNOLOGICAL PROGRESS

The launching of the Internet's World Wide Web in 1990 followed by the free distribution of Netscape in 1994 turned an established but little-known technology for the scientific community into a user-friendly web for people. This not only brought far wider access at lower cost. It also brought a whole new structure of communication, allowing simultaneous transfers of information in words, numbers and images to points around the world. And it shrank the world of communications, making interaction possible at a distance in real time.

The average cost of processing information fell from $75 per million operations to less than a hundredth of a cent in 1960–90. Airline operating costs per mile came down by half in 1960–90. The cost of a three-minute telephone call from New York to London fell from $245 in 1930 (in 1990 prices) to under $50 in 1960 to $3 in 1990 to about 35 cents in 1999. These innovations in communications technology transform the possibilities for building social solidarity and for mobilizing people across the globe in network societies.

ECONOMIC GOVERNANCE

The Marrakesh Agreement—signed in April 1994, ending the Uruguay Round of the General Agreement on Tariffs and Trade (GATT)—reduced virtually all tariffs and other barriers. It also introduced a "rules based" system of global regulation in trade. And it broke ground in establishing the World Trade Organization (WTO) to enforce the agreement, with far-reaching authority to review country policies and settle disputes.

Multilateral agreements extend to new areas—services such as banking and insurance, and intellectual property rights. Unprecedented in scope and commitment, these multilateral agreements bind national governments in their domestic policy choices, driving a convergence of policy in a world of enormously diverse conditions.

A GLOBAL IDEOLOGICAL SHIFT

National and international economic policies shifted sharply in the 1970s and 1980s towards more reliance on the market—diminishing the role of the state. Ever-growing numbers of developing countries adopted an open trade approach, shifting away from import substitution policies. By 1997 India had reduced its tariffs from an average of 82% in 1990 to 30%, Brazil from 25% in 1991 to 12%, and China from 43% in 1992 to 18%. Driven by technocrats, the changes were strongly supported by International Monetary Fund (IMF) and World Bank financing as part of comprehensive economic reform and liberalization packages. Conditions of membership in the WTO and the Organisation for Economic Co-operation and Development (OECD) were important incentives.

Country after country undertook deep unilateral liberalization, not just in trade but in foreign direct investment. In 1991, for example, 35 countries introduced changes in 82 regulatory regimes, in 80 of them moving to liberalize or promote foreign direct investment. In 1995 the pace accelerated, with even more countries—65—changing regimes, most continuing the trend of liberalization.

After the breakdown of the Bretton Woods system of fixed exchange rates in 1971, OECD countries abolished most restrictions on capital flows, and today capital of all kinds moves among them virtually without restriction. The deregulation of financial markets has been slower in developing countries but is progressing nonetheless, with encouragement from the IMF and OECD. Argentina, Mexico and Thailand opened their capital markets. India liberalized trade radically but not its capital markets. China discouraged short-term capital flows. And Chile followed the unique route of reducing excessive short-term volatility of flows by introducing a deposit tax.

Countries of Eastern Europe and the CIS began the dramatic transition from centrally planned economic systems to market democracies. China, Mongolia and Viet Nam also began to liberalize their economies and dramatically reshape their trading relationships, opening their economies to trade and foreign direct investment.

These changes sped the pace of globalization and deepened the interactions among people. They have also defined the character of global integration, giving rise to new markets, new actors, new rules and new tools (box 1.1). And they have created an era of globalization that is intensifying contacts—not just between countries but between people.

The landscape is changing in three distinct ways:
- *Shrinking space.* People's lives—their jobs, incomes and health—are affected by events on the other side of the globe, often by events they do not know about.
- *Shrinking time.* Markets and technologies now change with unprecedented speed, with action at a distance in real time, with impacts on people's lives far away. An example is the rapid reversal of capital flows to the East Asian markets and its contagion from Thailand to Indonesia to Korea—and also to faraway South Africa.
- *Disappearing borders.* National borders are breaking down, not only for trade, capital and information but also for ideas, norms, cultures and values. Borders are also breaking down in economic policy—as multilateral

Unprecedented in scope and commitment, these multilateral agreements bind national governments in their domestic policy choices, driving a convergence of policy in a world of enormously diverse conditions

BOX 1.1

Globalization—what's really new?

Some argue that globalization is not new, and that the world was more integrated a century ago. Trade and investment as a proportion of GDP were comparable, and with borders open, many people were migrating abroad. What's new this time?

New markets
• Growing global markets in services—banking, insurance, transport.
• New financial markets—deregulated, globally linked, working around the clock, with action at a distance in real time, with new instruments such as derivatives.
• Deregulation of antitrust laws and proliferation of mergers and acquisitions.
• Global consumer markets with global brands.

New actors
• Multinational corporations integrating their production and marketing, dominating world production.
• The World Trade Organization—the first multilateral organization with authority to enforce national governments' compliance with rules.
• An international criminal court system in the making.
• A booming international network of NGOs.
• Regional blocs proliferating and gaining importance—European Union, Association of South-East Asian Nations, Mercosur, North American Free Trade Association, Southern African Development Community, among many others.

• More policy coordination groups—G-7, G-10, G-22, G-77, OECD.

New rules and norms
• Market economic policies spreading around the world, with greater privatization and liberalization than in earlier decades.
• Widespread adoption of democracy as the choice of political regime.
• Human rights conventions and instruments building up in both coverage and number of signatories—and growing awareness among people around the world.
• Consensus goals and action agenda for development.
• Conventions and agreements on the global environment—biodiversity, ozone layer, disposal of hazardous wastes, desertification, climate change.
• Multilateral agreements in trade, taking on such new agendas as environmental and social conditions.
• New multilateral agreements—for services, intellectual property, communications—more binding on national governments than any previous agreements.
• The Multilateral Agreement on Investment under debate.

New (faster and cheaper) tools of communication
• Internet and electronic communications linking many people simultaneously.
• Cellular phones.
• Fax machines.
• Faster and cheaper transport by air, rail and road (box table 1.1).
• Computer-aided design.

BOX TABLE 1.1
Declining cost of transport and communications
(1990 US$)

Year	Sea freight (average ocean freight and port charges per ton)	Air transport (average revenue per passenger mile)	Telephone call (3 minutes, NY/London)	Computers (index, 1990 = 100)
1920	95	—	—	—
1930	60	0.68	245	—
1940	63	0.46	189	—
1950	34	0.30	53	—
1960	27	0.24	46	12,500
1970	27	0.16	32	1,947
1980	24	0.10	5	362
1990	29	0.11	3	100

Source: IMF 1997a.

agreements and the pressures of staying competitive in global markets constrain the options for national policy, and as multinational corporations and global crime syndicates integrate their operations globally.

What does all this mean for human development? People's lives around the globe are linked more deeply, more intensely, more immediately than ever before. This opens many opportunities, giving new power to good and bad, to global women's movements as well as to global crime syndicates. But it also exposes people to risks from changes far away. National governments cannot cope with these vulnerabilities and risks on their own—because their autonomy is weakening, and because "global bads" such as drugs and illegal arms travel the world with ease.

GLOBAL INTEGRATION—
RAPID BUT UNBALANCED

Global integration is proceeding at breakneck speed and with amazing reach. But the process is uneven and unbalanced, with uneven participation of countries and people in the expanding opportunities of globalization—in the global economy, in global technology, in the global spread of cultures and in global governance. The new rules of globalization—and the players writing them—focus on integrating global markets, neglecting the needs of people that markets cannot meet. The process is concentrating power and marginalizing the poor, both countries and people (box 1.2).

GLOBAL ECONOMY

The steady expansion of exports and the phenomenal growth of capital flows mask enormous disparities in experience across countries and regions.
• World exports of goods and services almost tripled between the 1970s and 1997 in real terms. Botswana, China, the Dominican Republic and the Republic of Korea enjoyed 10–13% average annual growth in their exports. But many countries did not share in the benefits, with exports declining in Bulgaria, Niger, Togo and Zambia.
• Since the 1970s the share of manufactures in merchandise exports has grown considerably

for some countries—from 13% to 71% in Mauritius, 32% to 81% in Mexico, 25% to 78% in Tunisia. But for 28 countries manufactures still make up less than 10% of merchandise exports.

• In 1997 foreign direct investment zoomed to $400 billion, seven times the level of the 1970s, but 58% of it went to industrial countries, 37% to developing countries and just 5% to the transition economies of Eastern Europe and the CIS (see figure 1.1).

• More than 80% of the foreign direct investment in developing and transition economies in the 1990s has gone to just 20 countries, mainly China. For 100 countries foreign direct investment has averaged less than $100 million a year since 1990, and for nine countries net flows have been negative.

• Some 94% of the portfolio and other short-term capital flows to developing and transition economies went to just 20 of them in 1996, the year before the East Asian crisis (see figure 1.1). Today only 25 developing countries have access to private markets for bonds, commercial bank loans and portfolio equity. The rest are shut out by their lack of credit rating.

To sum up: the top fifth of the world's people in the richest countries enjoy 82% of the expanding export trade and 68% of foreign direct investment—the bottom fifth, barely more than 1%.

These trends reinforce economic stagnation and low human development. And they have further marginalized many developing countries from the most dynamic areas of global economic growth. The 1980s and 1990s have seen strong growth in the trade of manufactures, services and "knowledge goods". While some developing countries have made major advances, others have missed out entirely. Manufacturing exports should have been a step towards transforming their economies and creating more jobs. But only 33 countries managed to sustain 3% annual growth in GNP per capita during 1980–96. For 59 countries—mainly in Sub-Saharan Africa and Eastern Europe and the CIS—GNP per capita declined.

Economic integration is thus dividing developing and transition economies into those that are benefiting from global opportunities and those that are not. The uneven divide cuts across levels of income and human development—and across regions. Contrast China, Chile, Costa Rica, Mauritius and Poland with Cameroon, Niger, Venezuela and Russia.

Ironically, those left behind are deeply integrated in world trade. Sub-Saharan Africa has a higher export-to-GDP ratio (29% in the 1990s) than Latin America (15%). But Africa's exports are still mainly in primary commodities, and foreign direct investment is concentrated in mineral extraction—so the region's apparent integration is actually a vulnerability to the whims of the primary commodity markets.

Countries are not the only major actors—more and more it is multinational corporations that dominate global markets. Their foreign affiliates accounted for an estimated $9.5 trillion in sales in 1997. Their value added was 7% of world GDP in 1997, up from 5% in the mid-1980s. Their share of world exports increased as well, from a quarter in the late 1980s to a third in 1995. US-based multinationals account for more than a quarter of US GDP—$2 trillion

---

BOX 1.2

Shrinking time, shrinking space, disappearing borders—but for whom?

Have time, space and borders collapsed into a global village? It depends on who you are.

Financial dealers are at the pinnacle of connections. Instant communications, free flows of capital and constant updates from around the world enable money markets from London to Jakarta, from Tokyo to New York, to act as a unit in real time.

Multinational corporations, too, are roaming global markets and integrating production. Cross-border mergers and acquisitions (majority foreign-owned) accounted for 59% of total foreign direct investment in 1997.

Tourists travel more outside their countries—but more than half are travelling from high-income countries.

NGOs on-line can campaign around the world, with their messages travelling across borders in seconds. Through email and media networks, people are giving their support to associations across borders—from informal networks to formal organizations.

High-skilled labour also travels the global village. With Internet access in nearly every country, the highly educated are increasingly on-line and in touch around the world. In 1998 more than 250,000 African professionals were working in the United States and Europe. Immigrants with skills in computing technologies are in high demand—in the European Union alone, 500,000 information technology jobs go unfilled because of lack of national skills. The United States offers a special visa to professional immigrants to keep high-tech industries staffed.

Unskilled labour, by contrast, runs up against hurdles. Many families are divided across international borders as a result of the increasingly tight restrictions in the rich countries on immigration of unskilled labour. Millions of people do not even have passports—difficult to get in some countries—let alone the visas required to travel abroad.

The collapse of space, time and borders may be creating a global village, but not everyone can be a citizen. The global, professional elite faces low borders, but billions of others find borders as high as ever.

Source: Human Development Report Office.

TABLE 1.1

Top corporations had sales totalling more than the GDP of many countries in 1997

Country or corporation	GDP or total sales (US$ billions)
General Motors	**164**
Thailand	154
Norway	153
Ford Motor	**147**
Mitsui & Co.	**145**
Saudi Arabia	140
Mitsubishi	**140**
Poland	136
Itochu	**136**
South Africa	129
Royal Dutch/Shell Group	**128**
Marubeni	**124**
Greece	123
Sumitomo	**119**
Exxon	**117**
Toyota Motor	**109**
Wal Mart Stores	**105**
Malaysia	98
Israel	98
Colombia	96
Venezuela	87
Philippines	82

Source: Forbes Magazine 1998.

TABLE 1.2

Unemployment rate in selected OECD countries
(percentage of the labour force)

Country or group	Average 1985–95	1997	1999 a
Iceland	2.3	3.9	2.7
Japan	2.5	3.4	4.6
Norway	4.3	4.1	3.7
United States	6.3	4.9	5.0
Belgium	11.1	12.7	11.5
Spain	19.5	20.8	17.8
European Union	9.9	11.2	10.3
OECD	7.1	7.2	7.3

a. Projections.
Source: OECD 1998a and 1998b.

of $7.3 trillion. And the large multinationals are becoming even larger as takeovers and mergers proliferate.

Capital is becoming even more concentrated globally as megacorporations merge, often across borders—Chrysler and Daimler, Hoechst and Rhone-Poulenc, Exxon and Mobil. From 1990 to 1997 the annual number of mergers and acquisitions more than doubled, from 11,300 to 24,600. Cross-border mergers and acquisitions accounted for $236 billion in 1997. Multinational corporations now dwarf some governments in economic power (table 1.1).

Generating employment? Conventional economic theory predicts that trade liberalization will increase productivity and wages, especially for tradable goods, thus expanding jobs and opportunities for poor people. Sometimes the theory has been right. In the 1980s and 1990s great progress in reducing global poverty and advancing human development was propelled by many countries seizing global opportunities.
- China, Indonesia, the Republic of Korea, Malaysia and many others achieved rapid economic growth, and linked that growth to advancing human development and reducing poverty.
- Many countries generated good employment opportunities by tapping into global markets—take software programming in Bangalore, India, computer assembly in Costa Rica, high-tech services in Ireland.
- Others used foreign direct investment to improve the quality of employment. Foreign-owned companies in Hungary accounted for more than 80% of manufacturing investment in 1996, a third of employment and three-quarters of export earnings.

But expansion of trade does not always mean more employment and better wages. In the OECD countries employment creation has lagged behind GDP growth and the expansion of trade and investment. Despite 2–3% growth in per capita GDP over the past two decades, unemployment did not decline, staying at around 7%, with a higher rate in the European Union (10–11%) and lower rates in Japan, Norway and the United States (table 1.2). More than 35 million people are unemployed, and another

10 million have given up looking for a job. Among the youth, one in five is unemployed.

People are facing job losses alongside job creation in many countries—from corporate restructuring, mergers and acquisitions, the spread of globally integrated production by multinational corporations and, in the OECD countries, shifts to knowledge-based sectors.

A common perception in the OECD countries is that jobs are being exported to the South. OECD imports of manufactures from developing countries have certainly increased since 1970, but such imports were just 2% of the combined GDP of the OECD countries in 1996. So, it is not surprising that trade and immigration contributed only about a tenth of the increase in wage dispersion in the United States in the early 1980s. Moreover, North-South trade has mainly raised wages for skilled labour in OECD countries through exports, not depressed wages for unskilled labour. So, "dislocation" of jobs to the South does not appear to be the main source of job stress in the North.

Expanding opportunities—migration. Migration in today's globalizing world is also marked by uneven human opportunities and uneven human impacts. An estimated 130–145 million people live outside their countries, up from 104 million in 1985 and 84 million in 1975. These estimates include only legally registered immigrants, so the real number is much higher. For many countries workers' remittances are a major source of foreign exchange, sometimes the primary source (see figure 1.1).

Three points about migration. First, global employment opportunities may be opening for some, but they are closing for most others. The global market for high-skilled labour is now more integrated, with high mobility and standardized wages. But the market for unskilled labour is highly restricted by national barriers, even though it accounts for a larger share of international migration. Australia, Canada and the United States have programmes to attract skilled migrants, so the brain drain from developing countries continues. As many as 30,000 African PhDs live abroad, while the continent is left with only one scientist and engineer per 10,000 people.

Second, undocumented migration continues unabated. The United States alone has an estimated 4 million undocumented immigrants. European countries estimate that half their immigrants are undocumented, up from a quarter in the mid-1980s. Developing countries also host large numbers of undocumented immigrants—3 million in Côte d'Ivoire in 1988, 1 million in Thailand and 700,000 in Malaysia in 1997, 1 million in Gabon in 1993, 1 million in Argentina in 1996. Lacking papers, illegal immigrants face not only discrimination but also denial of human rights. They often have to accept wages and conditions that do not meet minimum labour standards. And they often have to pay traffickers—as much as $35,000 from China to the United States. Trafficking is a booming business, moving 4 million people a year, generating $7 billion.

Third, there is a gender face to much migration. At least 50 million migrants are women, 30 million in developing countries. A large share of migrants from the Philippines, Sri Lanka and elsewhere are women. Many end up in activities that are dirty, dangerous and demeaning.

GLOBAL CULTURE

Contacts between people and their cultures—their ideas, their values, their ways of life—have been growing and deepening in unprecedented ways. Television now reaches families everywhere. For many, the exposure to new cultures is exciting, even empowering. For others, it is disquieting, as they try to cope with a rapidly changing world.

As Mahatma Gandhi expressed so eloquently earlier in the century, "I do not want my house to be walled in on all sides and my windows to be stuffed. I want the cultures of all the lands to be blown about my house as freely as possible. But I refuse to be blown off my feet by any." Today's flow of culture and cultural products is heavily weighted in one direction—from rich countries to poor.

The rise of culture as an economic good has added to the identification of culture with commodities that can be sold and traded—crafts, tourism, music, books, films. Although the spread of ideas and images enriches the world, there is a risk of reducing cultural concerns to protecting what can be bought and sold, neglecting community, custom and tradition.

Culture has become important economically. A UNESCO study shows that world trade in goods with cultural content—printed matter, literature, music, visual arts, cinema and photographic, radio and television equipment—almost tripled between 1980 and 1991, from $67 billion to $200 billion. It continues to grow. For the United States the largest single export industry is not aircraft, computers or automobiles—it is entertainment, in films and television programmes. Hollywood films grossed more than $30 billion worldwide in 1997, and in 1998 a single movie, *Titanic,* grossed more than $1.8 billion.

The vehicles for this trade in cultural goods are the new technologies. Satellite communications technology from the mid-1980s gave rise to a powerful new medium with a global reach and to such global media networks as CNN. The number of television sets per 1,000 people worldwide almost doubled between 1980 and 1995, from 121 to 235. The 1990s have seen a boom in multimedia industries, with sales of the world's largest 50 multimedia companies reaching $110 billion in 1993. The development of the Internet is also spreading culture around the world, over an expanded telecommunications infrastructure of fiber optics and parabolic antennas.

But the global market for cultural products is becoming concentrated, driving out small and local industries. At the core of the entertainment industry—film, music and television—there is a growing dominance of US products, and many countries are seeing their local industries wither (figures 1.3 and 1.4). Although India makes the most films each year, Hollywood reaches every market, getting more than 50% of its revenues from overseas, up from just 30% in 1980. It claimed 70% of the film market in Europe in 1996, up from 56% in 1987—and 83% in Latin America and 50% in Japan. By contrast, foreign films rarely make it big in the United States, taking less than 3% of the market there.

Once-thriving film industries around the world declined in the 1970s and 1980s, a result of the rise of television. Mexico once produced more than 100 films a year, but despite a resurgence of cinema attendance, local production

For the United States the largest single export industry is not aircraft, computers or automobiles—it is entertainment, in films and television programmes

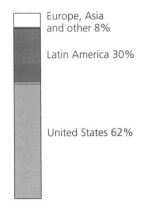

FIGURE 1.3

Less than a third of television programming in Latin America originates in the region

Percentage of total programming by origin

Europe, Asia and other 8%

Latin America 30%

United States 62%

Source: UNESCO 1998b.

FIGURE 1.4

Domestic film industries struggle to hold market share

Domestic share of film distribution, 1990–93 (percent)

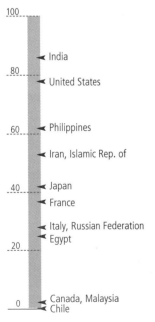

Source: UNESCO 1998b.

had dropped to less than 40 films by 1995, and to less than 10 by 1998. Hollywood has captured the resurgence of attendance since the mid-1990s, leaving domestic industries to struggle.

Faced with such threats, many countries argue that cultural goods should be exempt from free trade agreements. The Uruguay Round acknowledged the special nature of cultural goods, granting some exemptions. The North American Free Trade Agreement (NAFTA) required substantial negotiations before limited exemptions or exclusions of cultural industries were adopted. The issue was reopened in the negotiations for the Multilateral Agreement on Investments, polarizing countries that see cultural goods as an economic good or service like any other (Germany, Japan, the United Kingdom, the United States) and countries that see cultural goods as having intrinsic value to be protected for artistic diversity and national identity (Canada, France).

People are concerned about the spread of "global consumer culture" and cultural homogenization. Global producers market global products—brands like Nike and Sony that symbolize the life styles that people aspire to. But there are countervailing trends. Culture does not always flow in one direction. Salsa music from the Caribbean, the cuisines of Ethiopia and Thailand and many other traditions are spreading globally, and more nations are becoming multiethnic. Local cultures have also taken on renewed vigour and significance as political movements promote local culture and local identity. In the post–cold war world local culture has often replaced ideology in politics, as the rise of fundamentalist movements reflects.

The debate among anthropologists on whether there is cultural homogenization remains open. There are no surveys showing that people are becoming alike. And while some argue that globalization is an ideological process imposing a global culture, others argue that while cultural products flow around the world, people receive and use them differently.

GLOBAL GOVERNANCE

Governance is not government—it is the framework of rules, institutions and practices

that set limits on the behaviour of individuals, organizations and companies. In today's integrating world there is clear need for global governance for the good of society, economy and environment. And a form of global governance is indeed emerging—but the imbalances in the process are cause for concern.

Intergovernmental policy-making in today's global economy is in the hands of the major industrial powers and the international institutions they control—the World Bank, the International Monetary Fund, the Bank for International Settlements. Their rule-making may create a secure environment for open markets, but there are no countervailing rules to protect human rights and promote human development. And developing countries, with about 80% of the world's people but less than a fifth of global GDP, have little influence.

Ad hoc and self-selected policy groups have emerged in the past decade to make de facto global economic policy, outside the United Nations or any other formal system with democratic processes and participation. The finance ministers of the major industrial countries are in daily telephone contact—and their staff in email contact—shaping the annual G-7 meetings to discuss global economic and political issues. The United States took the initiative in 1998 to form the G-22—from the G-7 and 15 others, including the largest emerging economies—to review the global financial system in the wake of the East Asian crisis. The G-10 central bankers still guide the supervision of banking systems. All these groups play a key part in international economic policy-making, yet only the G-22 has any consultation with developing countries, and then only with a select few.

Poor countries participate little in the formulation and implementation of the new rules that govern global markets. The 1994 Uruguay Round of GATT shows the difficulties facing small and poor countries. Of the 29 least developed countries in the WTO, only 12 had missions in Geneva, most staffed with a handful of people to cover the gamut of UN work. Few African countries had delegations supported by staff or in-depth analysis to defend their national interests, weaknesses that carry through all negotiating and dispute settlement procedures. Many small and poor countries had difficulty even ensuring representation at meetings. And although the WTO is representative in its voting structure, its procedures, which rely on consensus for decision-making and on committees with selected membership, leave much scope for the delegations with more resources to influence outcomes. Indeed, the 1996 ministerial meeting in Singapore agreed on the need to review these procedures.

Compounding these weaknesses in negotiating capacity is the breakup of the common "South" position on global trade issues in the 1990s—and the pursuit of diverging interests. The different situations of developing countries—from the newly industrializing to the least developed—only deepen the schisms.

The rapidly increasing multilateral agreements—the new rules—are highly binding on national governments and constrain domestic policy choices, including those critical for human development. They drive a convergence of policies in a world of enormous diversity in conditions—economic, social, ecological. For example, most developing countries previously exempted agriculture, medicines and other products from national patent laws, but with the passage of the agreement on Trade-Related Aspects of Intellectual Property Rights (TRIPS), almost all knowledge-based production is now subject to tight intellectual property protection, unified internationally. Further, the TRIPS agreement is unbalanced: it provides an enabling environment for multinationals, tightening their dominant ownership of technology, impeding and increasing the cost of transfer to developing countries.

These new rules and institutions advance global markets. But there has been much less progress in strengthening rules and institutions to promote universal ethics and norms—especially human rights to promote human development and to empower poor people and poor countries. Fortunately, two important forces of social governance are gaining strength.

Institutions of human rights. Helped by the end of the cold war and the global communications network, awareness is growing of the violations of human rights and the possibilities for democratic governance. The international

legal framework for human rights is a great achievement, starting with the Universal Declaration of Human Rights in 1948. And since the 1980s the system has been gaining ground. A high commissioner for human rights was appointed, and it was agreed to establish an international criminal court. And the Convention on the Rights of the Child has achieved nearly universal ratification in just a decade, while earlier conventions have yet to be universally ratified after three decades (figure 1.5).

But the lack of mechanisms for enforcement is glaring. The human rights regime holds only national governments accountable—not individuals, corporations or institutions. The 1998 agreement to create an international criminal court, with 120 countries in favour and only 7 against, was a landmark, bringing a forum for enforcement of international justice. But it applies only to war crimes, crimes against humanity and genocide.

Ironically, more attention has gone to enforcing labour and environmental standards in expanding free trade, using strong trade sanctions to punish countries that violate them. The Multilateral Agreement on Investment was being developed in the OECD to provide a predictable market for multinationals, protecting their rights. But no consideration went to their responsibilities to people—their responsibilities to limit their behaviour, to bind their obligation to respect human rights and to promote the development interests of the communities they touch.

Global NGO networks. One big development in opening opportunities for people to participate in global governance has been the growing strength and influence of NGOs—in both the North and the South. NGOs have been effective advocates for human development, maintaining pressure on national governments, international agencies and corporations to live up to commitments and to protect human rights and environmental standards. Their campaigns have reversed policy—as with their opposition to the Multilateral Agreement on Investment. When developing country governments have found it difficult to stay unified in negotiations, the NGOs have often come forward with alternative approaches. Some NGOs

NGOs have been effective advocates for human development, maintaining pressure on national governments, international agencies and corporations to live up to commitments and to protect human rights and environmental standards

FIGURE 1.5
Uneven ratification of human rights conventions
Total countries ratifying

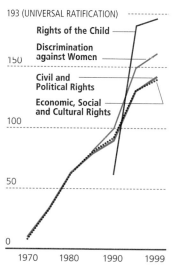

Source: UN 1999c.

now have more members than some countries have citizens. A recent study estimates that the non-profit organizations in just 22 countries are a $1.1 trillion sector, employing 19 million people (see figure 1.1).

SOCIAL FRAGMENTATION—REVERSALS IN PROGRESS AND THREATS TO HUMAN SECURITY

Uneven globalization is bringing not only integration but also fragmentation—dividing communities, nations and regions into those that are integrated and those that are excluded.

Social tensions and conflicts are ignited when there are extremes of inequality between the marginal and the powerful. Indonesia shows what can happen when an economic crisis sets off latent social tensions between ethnic groups—or between the rich and poor.

Recent research on complex humanitarian emergencies concluded that "horizontal inequalities" between groups—whether ethnic, religious or social—are the major cause of the current wave of civil conflicts. Inequalities—and insecurities—matter not only in incomes but in political participation (in parliaments, cabinets, armies and local governments), in economic assets (in land, human capital and communal resources) and in social conditions (in education, housing and employment).

The shrinking of time and space is creating new threats to human security. The fast-changing world presents many risks of sudden disruptions in the patterns of daily life—in jobs and livelihoods, in health and personal safety, in the social and cultural cohesion of communities (box 1.3). Threats to human security can now speed their way around the world—the collapse of financial markets, HIV/AIDS, global warming, global crime. Global threats are increasing, outgrowing national abilities to tackle them, and outpacing international responses.

WIDENING DISPARITIES IN INCOME

Gaps in income between the poorest and richest people and countries have continued to widen. In 1960 the 20% of the world's people in the richest countries had 30 times the income of the poorest 20%—in 1997, 74 times as much. This continues the trend of nearly two centuries (figure 1.6).

Gaps are widening both between and within countries. In East Asia per capita incomes today are more than seven times what they were in 1960, three times what they were in 1980. But in Sub-Saharan African and other least developed countries, per capita incomes today are lower than they were in 1970. The transition economies of Eastern Europe and the CIS have experienced the fastest rise in inequality ever. Russia now has the greatest inequality—the income share of the richest 20% is 11 times that of the poorest 20%. Income inequalities also grew markedly in China, Indonesia, Thailand and other East and South-East Asian countries that had achieved high growth while improving income distribution and reducing poverty in earlier decades.

BOX 1.3

The concept of human security

Human Development Report 1994 presented the concept of human security. Human development is a broader concept—a process of widening the range of people's choices. Human security means that people can exercise these choices safely and freely—and that they can be fairly confident that the opportunities they have today will not be lost tomorrow. With advancing globalization, new issues of global security have since emerged, but the conceptual framework from 1994 is still relevant for analysing today's global issues.

Human security has two main aspects:
• Safety from such chronic threats as hunger, disease and repression.
• Protection from sudden and hurtful disruptions in the patterns of daily life—whether in homes, in jobs or in communities. Such threats exist at all levels of national income and development.

Threats to human security
The loss of human security can be a slow, silent process—or an abrupt, loud emergency. Humans can be at fault—with bad policy choices. So can the forces of nature. Or it can be a combination of the two—when environmental degradation leads to a natural disaster, followed by human tragedy.

The many threats to human security, differing for individuals at different times, fall into seven main categories:
• Economic insecurity.
• Food insecurity.
• Health insecurity.
• Personal insecurity.
• Environmental insecurity.
• Community and cultural insecurity.
• Political insecurity.

Threats to global security
When human security is under threat anywhere, it can affect people everywhere. Famines, ethnic conflicts, social disintegration, terrorism, pollution and drug trafficking can no longer be confined within national borders. Some global challenges to human security arise because threats within countries rapidly spill beyond national frontiers, such as greenhouse gases and trade in drugs. Other threats take on a global character because of the disparities between countries—disparities that encourage millions of people to leave their homes in search of a better life, whether the receiving country wants them or not. And frustrations over inequality—in incomes and in political power—often build up into serious civil conflicts between groups, whether ethnic, religious or social.

Source: UNDP 1994.

Recent studies show inequality rising in most OECD countries during the 1980s and into the early 1990s. Of 19 countries, only one showed a slight improvement. The deterioration was worst in Sweden, the United Kingdom and the United States. In the United Kingdom the number of families below the poverty line rose by 60% in the 1980s, in the Netherlands, by nearly 40%. And in Australia, Canada, the United Kingdom and the United States at least half the single-parent households with children have incomes below the poverty line. Contrast that with the staggering concentration of wealth among the ultra-rich. The net worth of the world's 200 richest people increased from $440 billion to more than $1 trillion in just the four years from 1994 to 1998. The assets of the three richest people were more than the combined GNP of the 48 least developed countries.

JOB AND INCOME INSECURITY

In both poor countries and rich, dislocations from economic and corporate restructuring and dismantled social protection have meant heavy job losses and worsening employment conditions. Jobs and incomes have become more precarious. The pressures of global competition have led countries and employers to adopt more flexible labour policies, and work arrangements with no long-term commitment between employer and employee are on the rise.

In Latin America, for example, reforms in labour laws increased labour market flexibility, and more flexible contracts were introduced. By 1996 the share of workers without contracts or with new kinds of contracts increased to 30% in Chile, 36% in Argentina, 39% in Colombia and 41% in Peru. In Egypt an increasingly common practice is to require new recruits to sign a resignation letter before taking the job. Belgium, France, Germany and the United Kingdom all weakened their worker dismissal laws. And the Netherlands, Spain and the United Kingdom decentralized wage bargaining.

With ever-changing technology, people need ever-changing skills—yet even in the richest countries many lack the basics. Despite universal primary and secondary education in OECD countries, one person in six is functionally illiterate—unable to fill out a job application, excluded from the rapidly changing world that demands new skills in processing information. With unemployment a luxury few can afford, people who cannot get formal employment end up in the informal sector. In Latin America in the 1990s, informal employment has expanded from 52% to 58%, and 85 of every 100 jobs created are informal.

As multinationals merge, corporate restructuring means job losses (box 1.4). Though the loss of corporate jobs may be compensated by employment creation elsewhere, it adds to the insecurity of people in their jobs and lives.

BUST AND BOOM ECONOMIES— FINANCIAL VOLATILITY

The financial crisis in East Asia destabilized the lives of millions and reduced the prospects for growth in that region and in the world. In Indonesia, the Republic of Korea, Malaysia, the Philippines and Thailand human costs were

---

BOX 1.4

Merry Christmas—and have a Happy New Year elsewhere

With mergers and acquisitions come corporate restructuring, downsizing and layoffs. It is impossible to say whether the downsizing following a merger would have been avoided if the two corporations had not merged, but it is clear that the layoffs disrupt the lives of many. Reports in the *New York Times* and the *Financial Times* in one month, from 7 December 1998 to 4 January 1999, tell part of the relentless story of corporate layoffs.
• *NYT*, 7 December 1998. "Deutsche Telekom plans to eliminate 20,000 jobs by the year 2000 and will seek partners for possible mergers. . . . The job reductions are part of Deutsche Telekom's effort to cut costs to help offset lower prices, as the company, a former monopoly, winds up its first year in a more competitive market."
• *FT*, 8 December 1998. "Last week's announcements that Exxon was to buy Mobil (with job losses projected at 9,000) and that Deutsche Bank planned to acquire Bankers Trust (5,500 jobs to go) both came in industries that are becoming accustomed to consolidation through merger. . . . In Exxon's case, the announced job losses represent only those that will be lost in the immediate aftermath of the merger: many thousands more are likely to be cut later as the merged company sheds unprofitable refineries, oil wells and service stations."
• *NYT*, 16 December 1998. "Citigroup, one of the country's largest financial services companies, said yesterday that it planned to eliminate about 10,400 jobs, or about 6 percent of its workforce. . . . Citigroup said 65 percent, or about 6,760, of the cuts would be overseas. The rest, about 3,640 positions, will be in the US."
• *NYT*, 4 January 1999. "The largest private oil company, the Royal Dutch/Shell Group, said last month that it would . . . cut some of its 105,000 employees. . . . In addition, thousands of jobs will be cut by Texaco, Conoco, Shell and Chevron. British Petroleum and Amoco, whose merger was approved on Wednesday by the FTC, plan to shed 6,000 jobs."

Source: New York Times 1998a, 1998b and 1999b; Financial Times 1998b.

FIGURE 1.6

Widening gaps between rich and poor since the early 19th century

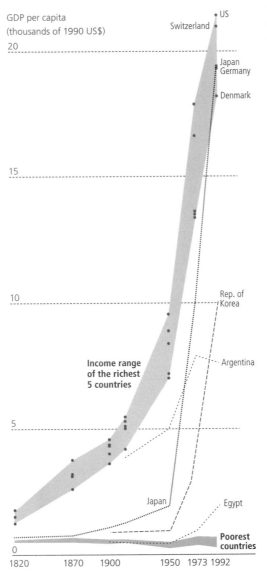

GDP per capita
(thousands of 1990 US$)

World inequalities have been rising steadily for nearly two centuries. An analysis of long-term trends in world income distribution (between countries) shows that the distance between the richest and poorest country was about 3 to 1 in 1820, 11 to 1 in 1913, 35 to 1 in 1950, 44 to 1 in 1973 and 72 to 1 in 1992. More amazing is that the British in 1820 had an income about six times that of the Ethiopians in 1992!

These trends mask the fact that many countries have caught up with the most advanced. Japan, for example, had scarcely 20% of US income in 1950, 90% in 1992. Southern Europe has seen a similar trend—with 26% of US income in 1950 and 53% in 1992. Some Arab states have also seen big increases in income.

Richest and poorest countries, 1820–1992
GDP per capita (1990 US$)

Richest

1820	1900	1992
UK 1,756	UK 4,593	US 21,558
Netherlands 1,561	New Zealand 4,320	Switzerland 21,036
Australia 1,528	Australia 4,299	Japan 19,425
Austria 1,295	US 4,096	Germany 19,351
Belgium 1,291	Belgium 3,652	Denmark 18,293

Poorest

Indonesia 614	Myanmar 647	Myanmar 748
India 531	India 625	Bangladesh 720
Bangladesh 531	Bangladesh 581	Tanzania,
Pakistan 531	Egypt 509	U. Rep. of 601
China 523	Ghana 462	Congo, Dem. Rep.
		of the 353
		Ethiopia 300

Source: Maddison 1995.

The world's 200 richest people are getting richer—fast

Net worth of the 200 richest people

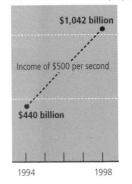

They are global, citizens of both rich and poor countries:

North America	65
Europe	55
Other industrial countries	13
Eastern Europe & CIS	3
Asia & the Pacific	30
Arab States	16
Latin America & Caribbean	17
Sub-Saharan Africa	1

They could do a lot for world poverty:

The assets of the 3 richest people are more than the combined GNP of all least developed countries.

The assets of the 200 richest people are more than the combined income of 41% of the world's people.

A yearly contribution of 1% of the wealth of the 200 richest people could provide universal access to primary education for all ($7–8 billion).

Source: Based on data from *Forbes Magazine* 1998.

Worsening inequality in OECD countries during the 1980s

Earnings inequality

- Almost all countries had an increase in wage inequality during the 1980s except Germany and Italy.
- Earnings inequality increased most in the UK and the US, and least in the Nordic countries.
- The increasing demand for skilled workers coupled with differences across countries in the growth of supply of skilled workers explain a large part of differences in earnings inequality.
- At any given time there are large earnings inequalities between men and women.

Disposable income inequality

- Increases in household income inequality were lower than those in earnings inequality in most nations, since disposable income (after taxes and transfers) is better distributed than market income.
- Still, income inequality increased in most OECD countries in the 1980s and early 1990s.
- Trends in inequality were not closely associated with levels. Some nations with low inequality experienced some of the largest increases.
- Reductions in social welfare spending and regressive changes in income taxes account for only a small part of the increase in disposable income inequality in most nations.

Country	Inequality in:	
	Market income	Disposable income
UK 1981–91	▲	▲
US 1980–93	▲	▲
Sweden 1980–93	▲	▲
Australia 1980–81 to 89–90	△	△
Denmark 1981–90	△	△
New Zealand 1981–89	△	△
Japan 1981–90	△	△
Netherlands 1981–89	△	△
Norway 1982–89	△	△
Belgium 1985–92	△	△
Canada 1980–92	△	○
Israel 1979–92	△	○
Finland 1981–92	▲	○
France 1979–89	○	○
Portugal 1980–90	○	○
Spain 1980–90		○
Ireland 1980–87	△	○
Germany 1983–90 [a]	△	○
Italy 1977–91	▽	▽

Interpretation		Change in Gini
▲	Extremely large increase	30% or more
▲	Large increase	16 to 29%
△	Small increase	5 to 10%
○	Zero	–4% to +4%
▽	Small decline	–5% or more

a. Data refer to the Federal Republic of Germany before reunification.
Source: Gottschalk and Smeeding 1997.

Recovery, but no improvement in distribution: the experience of Latin America

The period of rapid growth in the region, beginning in the 1960s and lasting until the outbreak of the debt crisis in 1982, led to an improvement in income distribution. Between 1970 and 1982 the income gap between the richest 20% of the population and the poorest 20% fell from 23 to 1 to 18 to 1. But these improvements were short-lived. In the 1980s the 10% of the population with the highest incomes increased its share by more than 10 percent—at the cost of all other groups. The poorest 10% suffered a 15% drop in their share of income, wiping out the improvements in distribution before the crisis.

The economies of the region have undergone great changes in the 1990s. High inflation has been halted, deep economic reforms have been adopted to support market operations, and productivity and economic growth have been restored. But the concentration of income has remained nearly unchanged, with the region's Gini coefficient staying at around 0.58.

But trends have varied across countries. In Brazil, Chile and Mexico income inequality worsened in the 1980s, but this trend was halted in the 1990s. In Colombia and Costa Rica distribution patterns have remained quite stable. In Honduras and Jamaica income distribution worsened in the early 1990s.

One of the most striking features of income distribution in Latin America is the huge gap between the top and bottom 20%.

Income distribution in selected Latin American countries

Share of household income (percent)

Country	Poorest 20%	Richest 20%	Gini coefficient[a]
Uruguay	5.0	48.7	0.43
Costa Rica	4.3	50.6	0.46
Peru	4.4	51.3	0.46
Ecuador	2.3	59.6	0.57
Brazil	2.5	63.4	0.59
Paraguay	2.3	62.3	0.59

a. A Gini coefficient of zero represents perfect equality, a coefficient of one perfect inequality.
Source: IADB 1998.

Worsening inequality in Eastern Europe and the CIS

The transition from centrally planned to market economies was accompanied by large changes in the distribution of national wealth and income. Data on income inequality indicate that these changes were the fastest ever recorded. In less than a decade income inequality as measured by the Gini coefficient increased from an average of 0.25–0.28 to 0.35–0.38, surpassing OECD levels. Inequality increased most in the Russian Federation and other CIS countries, least in Eastern Europe. In Ukraine and the Russian Federation the annual increase in the Gini coefficient was three to four times as high as in the United States and United Kingdom.

Gini coefficient

	1987/88	1993/95	Increase
Ukraine	0.23	0.47	0.24
Russia	0.24	0.48	0.24
Lithuania	0.23	0.37	0.14
Hungary	0.21	0.23	0.02
Poland	0.26	0.28	0.02

Source: Milanovic 1998; Ruminska-Zimny 1999.

The collapse of the East Asian financial markets— economies recovering, but human recovery will take longer

The exchange rate and inflation seem to have stabilized in the Republic of Korea, Malaysia and Thailand. Malaysia's stock index has begun to recover, and liquidity is returning to the financial system. Consumer spending is increasing—motor vehicle sales rose from 19,000 in November 1998 to nearly 23,000 in December. These developments are welcome. But they mask the continuing human costs of the crisis.

Past crises show that while economies regain output growth and macroeconomic balances—inflation, exchange rates, balance of payments—fairly quickly, it takes longer for employment and wages to recover. An analysis of more than 300 economic crises in more than 80 countries since 1973 shows that output growth recovered to precrisis levels in one year on average. But real wage growth took about four years to recover, and employment growth five years. Income distribution worsened on average for three years, improving over precrisis levels by the fifth year.

The human costs of the East Asian crisis have been wide-ranging and widespread.
• *Bankruptcies.* Among small businesses especially, bankruptcies soared with currency and stock market plunges and rocketing interest rates. A total of 435 Malaysian firms were declared bankrupt in the nine months from July 1997 to March 1998. Such bankruptcies are a loss of livelihood for owners and employees of small firms, which unlike large businesses and banks did not receive rescue packages.
• *Rising poverty.* In Indonesia, the poorest country affected, an additional 40 million people (or 20% of the population) are estimated to have fallen into poverty. In Korea and Thailand poverty is expected to rise, with 12% of the population affected in each country—5.5 million in Korea and 6.7 million in Thailand.
• *Surging unemployment.* Virtually unknown for many years in Korea and Malaysia, unemployment rose in all countries—by 0.3 million in Malaysia, 0.5 million in Thailand, 1 million in Indonesia and 1.5 million in Korea. Real wages declined: average real wages in Korea fell by nearly

10% in the 12 months following April 1997.

Job losses hit women, the youth and unskilled workers hardest in Korea. Employment declined by 7.1% among women between April 1997 and April 1998, compared with 3.8% for men. The number of unemployed among those aged 15–29 doubled in 1997–98, from 300,000 to 600,000, and it tripled for the unskilled, rising from 1.7% to 5.4%. Migrant workers were also hit hard. Lacking valid papers, many were sent back to their home countries.
• *Reduced schooling.* Families under stress are taking children out of school. In Thailand one study estimates that nearly 100,000 students are not pursuing either primary or secondary education because of the crisis. In Korea enrolment registered small declines at primary and middle school levels. But drop-outs at the higher level increased by 36% in 1998.
• *Reduced public services.* When family incomes are under stress, people need to rely more on public services to finance education and health. In most countries efforts were made to protect public expenditures, but strains are evident in many activities. In Thailand the budget of the Ministry of Public Health was reduced by 10%, and the community and social services budget by 7.6%. In the Philippines health expenditures declined by about 10%, and the budget shows reductions in family health and nutrition (6%) and communicable disease control (10%). Malaysia initially cut all expenditures by 18–20%, but then introduced a stimulus package.
• *Increased social stress and fragmentation.* Felt in many communities, though difficult to document, increasing domestic violence, street crime and suicides are reported in all countries. In Korea the Hotline for Women received escalating numbers of calls from women suffering domestic violence—seven times as many as in the previous year. The incidence of suicides also went up, from 620 a month in 1996 to more than 900 a month in mid-1998. Unemployment was often reported as the cause of intolerable human pain and social tension.

Source: Lee and Rhee 1999; World Bank 1998a; Kakwani 1998; Korea Institute for Social Information and Research 1999; UNFPA 1998; UNDP Country Office, Malaysia 1999.

---

severe. Escalating prices of essentials such as food and medicines were accompanied by increases in bankruptcies, unemployment, suicides, domestic violence and other consequences. Signs of economic recovery are beginning to emerge in 1999. But studies of past economic crises show that unemployment persists long after inflation subsides and exchange rates recover. People take longer to recover than economies (box 1.5).

An analysis of this crisis spotlights two important lessons about global capital markets. The first is that financial volatility is a permanent feature of today's globally integrated financial markets (figure 1.7). The East Asian crisis is not an isolated accident—it is a symptom of general weakness in global capital markets. Recent UNCTAD studies show a rising frequency of financial crises with the growth in international capital flows of the 1990s. Flows can be volatile, fed by herd behaviour and inadequate information for investors around the world, with investor confidence and risk ratings tumbling overnight. Technological innovations link global financial markets in real time, allowing instantaneous decisions around the world. Markets have also become increasingly sophisticated, with financial innovations that have made available countless financial instruments—from derivatives to hedge funds. In theory, these instruments were intended to transfer and spread risk. In practice, they have become part of the volatility of today's capital markets.

A central feature of the financial crisis in East Asia was the massive new inflows of short-term capital, followed by sudden reversals (box 1.6). A rapid buildup in the early 1990s followed the deregulation of capital controls and the restructuring of financial policies. Net financial inflows to Indonesia, Korea, Malaysia, the Philippines and Thailand totalled $93 billion in 1996. In 1997, as turmoil hit financial markets, these flows reversed in just weeks to a net outflow of $12 billion, a swing of $105 billion, or 11% of the precrisis GDPs of the five countries.

The second lesson is that extreme caution is required in opening up to foreign short-term (often speculative) capital, especially when financial market institutions are not well developed. There are increasing doubts among economists about the benefits of short-term flows. They do not have the same potential as long-term investments to contribute to development. They can even be disastrous, creating macroeconomic imbalances, overvaluing the currency, reducing international competitiveness and seriously destabilizing domestic banking systems.

CONTAGION AND THREAT OF A WORLDWIDE RECESSION

The reversals in human development are spreading—with the contagion to financial markets in Brazil, Russia and elsewhere, but also through slowdowns in global economic growth. IMF, World Bank and UN projections of growth in 1998 show a slowdown of 1–2 percentage points to around 2%, the lowest in five years. Many poor countries are suffering lower export prices due to shrinking world demand. Petroleum exporters have been hit particularly hard, and Angola and Kuwait could lose about a quarter of their export earnings and have their GDPs decline by 14–18%. The impact has also been severe for African countries dependent on primary commodity exports. Because of the collapse in the copper market, Zambia can expect a 26% decline in its copper exports—and a 9% decline in its GDP (table 1.3). World Bank projections of GDP growth in Sub-Saharan Africa for 1999 were revised downward from 4.5% to 3.2%.

GLOBAL CRIME

Globalization opens many opportunities for crime, and crime is rapidly becoming global, outpacing international cooperation to fight it. There are now 200 million drug users, threatening neighbourhoods around the world. In the past decade the production of opium more than tripled and that of coca leaf more than doubled. In Belarus drug-related crimes increased from 4 per 100,000 people to 28 in 1990–97, in Estonia from 1.4 per 100,000 to almost 8. The illegal drug trade in 1995 was estimated at $400 billion, about 8% of world trade, more than the share of iron and steel or of motor vehicles, and roughly the same as textiles (7.5%) and gas and oil (8.6%).

Illegal trafficking in weapons is a growing business—destabilizing societies and governments, arming conflicts in Africa and Eastern Europe. Light weapons have the most immediate impact on people's lives. Used in every conflict around the world, they have caused 90% of war casualties since 1945. In El Salvador the homicide rate increased 36% after the end of the civil war. In South Africa machine guns pouring in from Angola and Mozambique are being used in more and more crimes. In Alba-

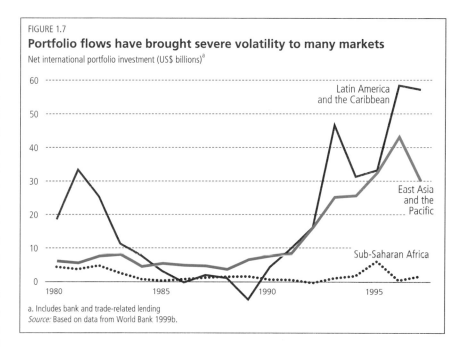

FIGURE 1.7
Portfolio flows have brought severe volatility to many markets
Net international portfolio investment (US$ billions)[a]

a. Includes bank and trade-related lending
Source: Based on data from World Bank 1999b.

BOX 1.6
Buildup and reversal of short-term capital flows—lessons of East Asia

Capital to East Asia and Latin America increased dramatically in the 1990s. Between 1990 and 1996 financial capital flows to the East Asian countries averaged more than 5% of GDP. The most extreme cases: Thailand and Malaysia. Capital inflows to these two countries averaged more than 10% of GDP during the 1990s, reaching 13% and 17% of GDP in one year. Capital flows then abruptly reversed in 1997. For Thailand capital outflows between 1996 and 1998 amounted to about 20% of GDP. The other countries faced a similar fate.

The large inflows before the reversal had had negative effects, contributing to the appreciation of real exchange rates and delayed devaluation in a time of increasing current account deficits, and reducing international competitiveness. They also expanded domestic bank lending and increased the financial system's vulnerability to reversals of capital flows. An UNCTAD study found no case in any country, developed or developing, where a large increase in liquidity in the banking sector did not lead to overextended lending, a worsening in the quality of assets and laxer risk management.

Not just the amount but the structure of capital inflows determines a country's vulnerability. External borrowings were concentrated in short-term debt. Thailand and Korea had short- to long-term debt ratios of nearly 50% before the crisis. The ratio of short-term debt to GDP was also high in Indonesia, Korea and Thailand, in sharp contrast to China, Malaysia and the Philippines. It is no wonder that the crisis erupted in Thailand and then spread to Indonesia and Korea, leaving the other countries less affected.

Source: Lee and Rhee 1999; UNCTAD 1998b.

nia there were five times as many murders in 1997 as in 1996, a rise attributed to the illegal arming of civilians.

Another thriving industry is the illegal trafficking in women and girls for sexual exploitation, a form of slavery and an inconceivable violation of human rights. In Western Europe alone, about 500,000 women and girls from developing and transition economies are entrapped in this slave trade each year. Women lose not only their freedom, but their dignity and often their health. If they return to their homes, they are often rejected by their families and communities.

At the heart of all this is the growing power and influence of organized crime syndicates, estimated to gross $1.5 trillion a year—a major economic power rivalling multinational corporations. The sheer concentration of their power and money criminalizes business, politics and government. Look at the Six Triads in China, the Medellín and Cali cartels in Colombia, the Mafia in Italy, the Yakuza in Japan, the Juarez, Tijuana and Gulf cartels in Mexico, the Cosa Nostra in the United States and the organizations in Nigeria, Russia and South Africa. All have operations extending beyond national borders, and they are now developing strategic alliances linked in a global network, reaping the benefits of globalization (box 1.7).

THE SPREAD OF HIV/AIDS

Global travel spreads more than ideas. The latest estimates by UNAIDS and the World Health Organization show that more than 33 million people were living with HIV/AIDS at the end of 1998. The spread of the virus continues unabated, with 11 men, women and children becoming infected each minute—about 6 million in 1998. AIDS causes 2.5 million deaths a year, more than twice as many as the 1 million deaths from malaria. Yet some experts say that we are only a tenth of the way into the epidemic.

AIDS is now a poor people's epidemic, with 95% of all HIV-infected people in developing countries. HIV/AIDS has taken a heavy toll on the life expectancy built up over the past three decades. A loss of 17 years in life expectancy is projected for the nine countries in Africa with an HIV prevalence of 10% or more—Botswana, Kenya, Malawi, Mozambique, Namibia, Rwanda, South Africa, Zambia and Zimbabwe—down to 47 years by 2010, back to the life expectancy of the 1960s.

HIV is also spreading fast in areas thought to be relatively free of the virus—in China and even in the vast rural areas of India, where some studies show higher prevalence rates than in urban areas. Eastern Europe and the CIS had appeared to be spared the worst in the early 1990s, but new surveys show stupendous increases in Belarus, Moldova, Russia and Ukraine. There, too, HIV/AIDS is often associated with poverty, spreading among marginalized people, especially through drug use.

CIVIL CONFLICT, GLOBAL UNREST

Civil conflicts have been flaring for decades. What's new today is the complex interaction of interests, the blurred line between conflict and business. Defence is becoming privatized, and international private military firms are proliferating. In some countries mercenaries often sell their services for mining and energy concessions and set up affiliates in air transport, road building and trading. And more and more, the clients of mercenaries are multinational corporations seeking to protect their mining interests in conflict-prone countries.

Executive Outcomes, Sandline International and Military Professional Resources Incorporated offer military services and training to governments and large corporations

At the heart of all this is the growing power and influence of organized crime syndicates, estimated to gross $1.5 trillion a year

TABLE 1.3
The Asian crisis hurts distant economies and people
(percent)

Commodity price decline	Country	Fall in export earnings [a] 1998	Fall in GDP [a] 1998
Petroleum—25%	Angola	25	18
	Gabon	21	13
	Kuwait	25	14
	Nigeria	24	4
	Venezuela	20	6
Copper—31%	Zambia	26	9
	Mongolia	10	6
	Chile	10	3

a. Estimated.
Source: UNCTAD 1998b.

and have been particularly active in Africa. The Mobutu government in its final days spent some $50 million in a desperate attempt to stay in power in the Democratic Republic of the Congo. The rise of military companies is linked to the post–cold war power vacuum. Major powers are less inclined to intervene militarily, especially in low-level conflicts.

Accountable only to those who pay, such businesses are hard to regulate. So far, domestic and international laws seeking to limit mercenaries' operations have been ineffective. The annual reports of the UN Human Rights Special Rapporteur on Mercenaries have regularly urged governments to develop legislation that bans the use of mercenaries in their territories.

*ENVIRONMENTAL DEGRADATION—
A SILENT EMERGENCY*

Environmental degradation is a global problem that surpasses the scope of national governments. Globalization can improve prospects for environmental management—through the spread of environment-friendly technologies, standards and pressures by consumers and activists. It can also add pressures for environmental exploitation—export-led demand for paper leading to deforestation, and demand for fish leading to overfishing.

Environmental degradation is a chronic and "silent emergency" that threatens the livelihoods of some of the poorest people of the world. Scientists predict a steady rise in global temperatures and sea levels, inundating as much as 17% of the land area in Bangladesh, 12% in Egypt and almost all of the Maldives. Renewable resources are being depleted rapidly and unsustainably: fish stocks are three-quarters of what they once were. Water availability today is 60% of 1970 levels, as is forest coverage. All this threatens the economic security, food security and health security of the world's poorest people.

People are also vulnerable to the "loud emergencies" of the environment. In 1997 and 1998 El Niño and La Niña brought wild swings in temperature and rainfall. El Niño is estimated to have displaced nearly 5 million people, injured 118 million and caused almost

22,000 deaths. The worldwide costs of the El Niño disaster were judged to be as high as $33 billion. Many scientists believe that the ferocity of the El Niño storms was due to global warming. The storms ruined harvests and fuelled forest fires from Indonesia to Brazil. La Niña hurricanes and floods killed 9,000 people and left more than a million homeless in Nicaragua and Honduras.

WHAT'S TO BE DONE?

Globalization expands the opportunities for unprecedented human advance for some but shrinks those opportunities for others and erodes human security. It is integrating economy, culture and governance but fragmenting societies. Driven by commercial market forces, globalization in

---

BOX 1.7

Why crime syndicates like globalization

Globalization creates new and exciting opportunities, and among the most enterprising and imaginative opportunists are the world's criminals.

Free movement of capital, say private sector investors, is a precondition of increased foreign investment. But the precipitous removal of currency controls, before a proper regulatory environment has been established, is the perfect condition for money laundering. And sure enough, Eastern European banks became a regular transfer point in the flow of dirty money.

Lowering the barriers to international trade and the transit of goods across borders is generally seen as a good thing. But it also helps the luxury car hijacked on a Johannesburg street to reappear for sale in Moscow.

Think of the organization required to effect such a transfer, or to ship illegal Bangladeshi immigrants to England or Ukrainian girls to a life of prostitution in the Netherlands. As the multinational corporations have led the drive to globalize the world's economy, so the "crime multinationals"—the organized crime syndicates—have been quick to exploit it. The Chinese triads are in the restaurant trade in London. The Sicilian Mafia is selling heroin in New York. And the Japanese Yakuza are financing pornography in the Netherlands.

The breakdown of the old order in emerging markets—whether through industrialization, automation and the rise of skill-based economies or through the dislocation of war or economic collapse—creates a burgeoning underclass ripe for exploitation by the crime multinationals. The unemployed in the South African townships make easy recruits for criminal gangs, which have fostered South Africa's rise as a major transshipment point for the worldwide drug trade.

Technological advances create new vulnerabilities. A computer hacker in Russia came close to stealing millions of dollars from Citibank in New York. Nigerian con men take advantage of the semblance of legitimacy that the fax machine gives a forged document. New technology also creates new crimes, such as the piracy of intellectual property—music, films and software.

Paradoxically, the rise of such criminal activities undermines the initiatives that create the opportunity. Who wants to invest in a country where a business partner may turn out to be a gangster who settles arguments with a gun? Who in the international community will want to be seen supporting a government mired in the corruption to which unchecked criminal activity so often leads? The control of organized crime must be ranked high on the international agenda as well as national ones.

Source: Helsby 1999.

---

this era seeks to promote economic efficiency, generate growth and yield profits. But it misses out on the goals of equity, poverty eradication and enhanced human security.

• First, not just new but stronger policies to protect and promote human development are needed, including policies often called "social protection".

• Second, many problems of human development go beyond what nations can tackle on their own and require more international cooperation.

• Third, action to protect and promote human development must come not only from nations but from communities, NGOs and corporations.

Economic growth, an important input for human development, can translate into human development only if the expansion of private income is equitable and only if growth generates public provisioning that is invested in human development—in schools and health centres, not arms. Human development also depends on unpaid work by men and women in the household or community, providing the "care" so essential to human survival. And it depends on the natural environment, another essential resource for all, particularly for poor people who derive their livelihood from natural resources (figure 1.8).

The rapid expansion of global markets—the conditions for people, corporations and nations to compete globally, the urge to privatize and downsize public action in search of economic efficiency—creates an environment in which the needs of human development can be easily neglected, with spending subject to a fiscal squeeze. Reduced public spending weakens institutions of redistribution, leading to inequalities. And as individuals compete in the global economy, they spend time in honing their skills and working at a paid job—putting a time squeeze on caring activities. Care is also squeezed by reductions in public spending. And free market prices do not capture the full environmental costs of production and consumption, putting a squeeze on the natural environment.

Stronger policies for human development —more investment to equip people for the globally competitive economy, and to participate in the global network society—are needed to promote human development. But they are also needed to make globalization work. Ultimately, people and nations will reject global integration and global interdependence if they do not gain from it and if it increases their vulnerability. Pressures will mount to retreat to isolationism in economic policy, culture and political priorities.

To pursue human development, globalization has to mean:

• *Ethics*—less, not more violation of human rights and disregard of human values.

• *Development*—less, not more poverty of countries and people.

• *Equity*—less, not more disparity between and within nations and generations.

• *Inclusion*—less, not more marginalization and exclusion of countries and people.

• *Human security*—less, not more vulnerability of countries and people.

• *Sustainability*—less, not more depletion and degradation of the environment.

FIGURE 1.8
Provisioning for human development

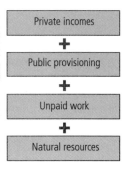

Source: Human Development Report Office.

HDI rank	Exports of goods and services Total (US$ millions) 1997	As % of GDP 1997	Index (1985=100) 1997	Imports of goods and services Total (US$ millions) 1997	As % of GDP 1997	Index (1985=100) 1997	Manufactures as % of merchandise exports 1997	Index (1985=100) 1997
High human development	4,993,093 T	20	156	4,866,827 T	20	154	80	113
1 Canada	234,297 [a]	40 [a]	162 [a]	211,487 [a]	36 [a]	165 [a]	63	107
2 Norway	64,230 [a]	41 [a]	138 [a]	50,620 [a]	32 [a]	98 [a]	24	81
3 United States	856,000 [a]	12 [a]	200 [a]	965,700 [a]	13 [a]	151 [a]	81	116
4 Japan	456,889 [a]	10 [a]	106 [a]	432,269 [a]	9 [a]	164 [a]	95	98
5 Belgium	183,718 [a]	68 [a]	135 [a]	171,012 [a]	64 [a]	140 [a]	..	..
6 Sweden	100,672 [a]	40 [a]	147 [a]	83,713 [a]	33 [a]	134 [a]	80	100
7 Australia	81,856 [a]	20 [a]	164 [a]	79,579 [a]	20 [a]	154 [a]	29	183
8 Netherlands	212,504 [a]	54 [a]	127 [a]	187,182 [a]	47 [a]	121 [a]	71	139
9 Iceland	2,649 [a]	36 [a]	100 [a]	2,612 [a]	36 [a]	95 [a]	12	129
10 United Kingdom	340,685 [a]	30 [a]	128 [a]	349,600 [a]	30 [a]	136 [a]	83	127
11 France	368,605 [a]	24 [a]	130 [a]	328,652 [a]	21 [a]	132 [a]	78	106
12 Switzerland	106,413 [a]	36 [a]	113 [a]	94,088 [a]	32 [a]	126 [a]	93	101
13 Finland	47,347 [a]	38 [a]	142 [a]	37,251 [a]	30 [a]	129 [a]	83	108
14 Germany	569,614 [a]	24 [a]	..	541,018 [a]	23 [a]	..	83	97
15 Denmark	64,916 [a]	35 [a]	129 [a]	56,229 [a]	31 [a]	123 [a]	63	110
16 Austria	93,400 [a]	41 [a]	133 [a]	94,628 [a]	41 [a]	136 [a]	88 [a]	103 [a]
17 Luxembourg	15,467 [a]	91 [a]	94 [a]	13,729 [a]	81 [a]	85 [a]	..	..
18 New Zealand	18,921 [a]	29 [a]	134 [a]	18,337 [a]	28 [a]	149 [a]	29 [a]	131 [a]
19 Italy	324,046 [a]	27 [a]	149 [a]	260,606 [a]	21 [a]	140 [a]	89	105
20 Ireland	53,981 [a]	76 [a]	166 [a]	43,237 [a]	61 [a]	128 [a]	81	125
21 Spain	148,125 [a]	26 [a]	157 [a]	143,065 [a]	25 [a]	212 [a]	78 [a]	110 [a]
22 Singapore	..	..	..	..	..	..	84	164
23 Israel	31,065	32	113	43,873	45	131	92	111
24 Hong Kong, China (SAR)	225,481	132	218	232,082	135	246	89	103
25 Brunei Darussalam	..	..	..	..	..	..	..	..
26 Cyprus	..	..	..	..	..	..	56	101
27 Greece	18,841 [a]	15 [a]	148 [a]	29,295 [a]	24 [a]	166 [a]	52	106
28 Portugal	33,658 [a]	31 [a]	147 [a]	41,672 [a]	38 [a]	202 [a]	86	113
29 Barbados	..	..	..	..	..	..	54	64
30 Korea, Rep. of	168,683	38	185	171,885	39	192	92 [a]	101 [a]
31 Bahamas	..	..	..	..	..	..	..	..
32 Malta	2,795	84	..	3,117	94	..	97 [a]	106 [a]
33 Slovenia	10,458	57	..	10,635	58	..	89	..
34 Chile	20,716	27	136	22,540	29	206	16	227
35 Kuwait	15,974	53	..	12,407	41	..	14	..
36 Czech Republic	29,950	58	..	32,808	63	..	85	..
37 Bahrain	6,357	104	..	4,370	72	..	12 [a]	257 [a]
38 Antigua and Barbuda	..	..	..	..	..	..	..	..
39 Argentina	29,318	9	148	34,899	11	367	34	160
40 Uruguay	4,511	23	150	4,563	23	251	37	105
41 Qatar	..	..	..	..	..	..	..	..
42 Slovakia	10,976	56	..	12,366	64	..	79	..
43 United Arab Emirates	..	..	..	..	..	..	..	..
44 Poland	35,616	26	220	41,170	30	272	73	116
45 Costa Rica	4,360	46	188	4,529	48	192	25 [a]	113 [a]
Medium human development	1,255,577 T	26	159	1,270,896 T	26	159	58	..
46 Trinidad and Tobago	2,912	49	103	3,316	56	94	44	241
47 Hungary	20,801	45	150	21,013	46	174	77	115
48 Venezuela	25,735	29	152	17,692	20	112	12	120
49 Panama	7,759 [a]	94 [a]	88 [a]	7,520 [a]	91 [a]	99 [a]	17	136
50 Mexico	121,772	30	249	121,896	30	302	81	298

A1.1 Trade flows

HDI rank	Exports of goods and services Total (US$ millions) 1997	As % of GDP 1997	Index (1985 = 100) 1997	Imports of goods and services Total (US$ millions) 1997	As % of GDP 1997	Index (1985=100) 1997	Manufactures as % of merchandise exports 1997	Index (1985=100) 1997
51 Saint Kitts and Nevis	120 [a]	48 [a]	..	184 [a]	74 [a]	..	34	..
52 Grenada	132 [a]	45 [a]	104 [a]	193 [a]	65 [a]	95 [a]	13 [a]	284 [a]
53 Dominica	125	51	141	155	64	107	49 [a]	140 [a]
54 Estonia	3,614	77	..	4,148	89	..	66	..
55 Croatia	8,014 [a]	42 [a]	..	10,200 [a]	53 [a]	..	69	..
56 Malaysia	92,877	94	193	91,360	93	215	76 [a]	279 [a]
57 Colombia	14,553	15	164	17,422	18	226	31	182
58 Cuba	..	..	..	..	..	..	..	..
59 Mauritius	2,725	62	137	2,879	65	151	71	156
60 Belarus	13,469	60	..	14,386	64	..	..	..
61 Fiji	1,204	57	..	1,240	59	..	..	..
62 Lithuania	5,224	55	..	6,237	65	..	70	..
63 Bulgaria	6,178	61	27	5,619	56	15	..	..
64 Suriname	..	..	..	..	..	..	..	..
65 Libyan Arab Jamahiriya	..	..	..	..	..	..	..	..
66 Seychelles	365	68	185	438	81	238	(.) [a]	5 [a]
67 Thailand	72,382	47	194	71,340	46	182	71	188
68 Romania	10,359	30	..	12,802	37	..	79	..
69 Lebanon	1,558	10	..	8,056	54	..	..	..
70 Samoa (Western)	75 [a]	43 [a]	..	127 [a]	73 [a]	..	..	..
71 Russian Federation	102,196	23	..	90,065	20	..	23	..
72 Ecuador	5,930	30	144	5,734	29	107	9	1,128
73 Macedonia, TFYR	880	40	..	1,232	56	..	..	..
74 Latvia	2,791	50	..	3,352	61	..	58	..
75 Saint Vincent and the Grenadines	144 [a]	52 [a]	72 [a]	176 [a]	64 [a]	81 [a]	13	..
76 Kazakhstan	7,810	35	..	8,280	37	..	..	..
77 Philippines	40,284	49	218	48,777	59	293	45	166
78 Saudi Arabia	62,991	45	..	43,017	31	..	9 [a]	294 [a]
79 Brazil	61,982	8	131	83,556	10	266	54	123
80 Peru	8,182	13	107	10,617	17	179	17	138
81 Saint Lucia	406 [a]	68 [a]	..	417 [a]	70 [a]	..	25 [a]	99 [a]
82 Jamaica	2,109	51	101	2,645	64	144	69 [a]	130 [a]
83 Belize	320	49	83	334	51	86	13	51
84 Paraguay	2,226	22	285	2,477	24	439	15	277
85 Georgia	623	12	..	1,192	23	..	..	..
86 Turkey	46,675	25	..	57,698	30	..	75	123
87 Armenia	330	20	..	952	58	..	..	..
88 Dominican Republic	7,221	48	273	7,595	51	237	..	..
89 Oman	..	..	..	..	..	..	17	26
90 Sri Lanka	5,507	36	155	6,569	44	112	..	..
91 Ukraine	20,126	41	..	22,009	44	..	..	..
92 Uzbekistan	..	..	..	..	..	..	..	..
93 Maldives	..	..	..	..	..	..	..	..
94 Jordan	3,572	51	163	5,186	74	138	..	..
95 Iran, Islamic Rep. of	..	..	..	..	..	..	..	..
96 Turkmenistan	..	..	..	..	..	..	..	..
97 Kyrgyzstan	675	38	..	815	46	..	38 [a]	..
98 China	207,303	23	163	166,759	18	81	85	..
99 Guyana	783	100	..	854	109	..	..	..
100 Albania	292	12	..	915	37	..	65	..

A1.1 Trade flows

HDI rank	Exports of goods and services Total (US$ millions) 1997	Exports As % of GDP 1997	Exports As % of GDP Index (1985 = 100) 1997	Imports of goods and services Total (US$ millions) 1997	Imports As % of GDP 1997	Imports As % of GDP Index (1985=100) 1997	Manufactures as % of merchandise exports 1997	Manufactures as % of merchandise exports Index (1985=100) 1997
101 South Africa	35,848	28	130	34,365	27	174	55 [a]	..
102 Tunisia	8,251	44	140	8,719	46	107	78	175
103 Azerbaijan	833	19	..	1,649	37	..	..	..
104 Moldova, Rep. of	984	53	..	1,432	76	..	..	..
105 Indonesia	60,106	28	125	60,700	28	119	42	325
106 Cape Verde	108	25	..	272	64	..	..	..
107 El Salvador	2,741	24	135	3,930	35	194	39	151
108 Tajikistan	..	..	..	..	..	..	..	..
109 Algeria	14,681	31	134	10,534	22	45	3	187
110 Viet Nam	11,480	46	..	13,443	54	..	..	..
111 Syrian Arab Republic	5,343	30	161	7,189	40	61	..	..
112 Bolivia	1,644	21	183	2,334	29	194	16	4,219
113 Swaziland	1,075	82	118	1,265	96	76	..	..
114 Honduras	1,673	37	91	2,131	47	116	27	739
115 Namibia	1,726	53	95	1,908	58	78	..	..
116 Vanuatu	..	..	..	..	..	..	..	..
117 Guatemala	3,186	18	120	4,193	24	173	30	147
118 Solomon Islands	..	..	..	..	..	..	..	..
119 Mongolia	471	55	..	513	60	..	10 [a]	..
120 Egypt	15,251	20	124	18,820	25	58	40	400
121 Nicaragua	803 [a]	41 [a]	197 [a]	1,294 [a]	66 [a]	170 [a]	25	389
122 Botswana	2,857 [a]	56 [a]	87	1,901	38	68 [a]	..	..
123 São Tomé and Principe	12	28	..	41	94	..	..	..
124 Gabon	3,296	64	138	2,165	42	61	2 [a]	..
125 Iraq	..	..	..	..	..	..	..	..
126 Morocco	9,342	28	164	10,622	32	144	49	122
127 Lesotho	309	33	151	1,215	128	62	..	..
128 Myanmar	..	..	..	..	..	..	..	..
129 Papua New Guinea	2,605	56	142	2,782	60	96	..	..
130 Zimbabwe	3,227	36	163	3,829	43	196	32	109
131 Equatorial Guinea	489	101	544	630	129	531	..	..
132 India	44,107	12	171	59,230	16	119	72 [a]	125 [a]
133 Ghana	1,657	24	170	2,640	38	155	..	..
134 Cameroon	2,443	27	89	2,041	22	116	8 [a]	..
135 Congo	1,767	77	146	1,565	68	71	..	..
136 Kenya	2,994	29	110	3,787	37	199	25	222
137 Cambodia	920	30	..	1,281	42	..	..	..
138 Pakistan	10,009	16	137	12,955	21	83	86	139
139 Comoros	30	16	219	76	39	77	..	..
Low human development	49,958 T	28	147	56,692 T	31	105	..	..
140 Lao People's Dem. Rep.	418	24	..	721	41	..	..	..
141 Congo, Dem. Rep. of the	1,463	24	75	1,350	22	57	..	..
142 Sudan	..	..	..	..	..	..	3 [a]	161 [a]
143 Togo	464	31	78	550	37	66	..	..
144 Nepal	1,296	26	228	1,856	38	188	95	161
145 Bhutan	120	31	..	160	42	..	..	..
146 Nigeria	16,286	41	106	13,677	34	57	..	..
147 Madagascar	773	22	125	1,064	30	86	28	271
148 Yemen	2,489	44	..	2,966	52	..	..	..
149 Mauritania	435	40	53	533	49	51	..	..
150 Bangladesh	5,075	12	286	7,656	18	164	87 [a]	133 [a]

A1.1 Trade flows

	Exports of goods and services			Imports of goods and services			Manufactures as % of merchandise exports	
	Total (US$ millions)	As % of GDP		Total (US$ millions)	As % of GDP			
			Index (1985 = 100)			Index (1985=100)		Index (1985=100)
HDI rank	1997	**1997**	1997	1997	**1997**	1997	**1997**	1997
151 Zambia	1,276	33	99	1,474	38	93	..	..
152 Haiti	236	8	131	650	23	225	..	..
153 Senegal	1,481	33	106	1,730	38	79	..	..
154 Côte d'Ivoire	4,777	47	131	4,055	40	107	..	..
155 Benin	531	25	58	696	33	62	..	..
156 Tanzania, U. Rep. of	1,259 [a]	22 [a]	..	2,118 [a]	36 [a]	..	..	..
157 Djibouti	207	41	..	285	57	..	..	..
158 Uganda	826	13	163	1,335	20	114	..	..
159 Malawi	613	24	100	870	35	99	..	..
160 Angola	5,196	68	174	5,003	65	183	..	..
161 Guinea	694	18	..	811	21	..	..	..
162 Chad	271	17	102	562	35	60	..	..
163 Gambia	191	47	82	248	61	93	..	..
164 Rwanda	110	6	63	451	24	185	..	..
165 Central African Republic	213	21	119	236	23	82	43 [a]	..
166 Mali	644	25	163	889	35	70	..	..
167 Eritrea	201	31	..	583	89	..	..	..
168 Guinea-Bissau	56	21	384	106	40	44	..	..
169 Mozambique	500	18	216	937	34	59	17 [a]	..
170 Burundi	96	10	97	136	14	63	..	..
171 Burkina Faso	331	14	83	721	30	85	..	..
172 Ethiopia	1,017	16	100	1,682	26	88	..	..
173 Niger	300	16	71	440	24	48	..	..
174 Sierra Leone	116	14	273	140	17	296	..	..

a. Data refer to 1996.

Source: Columns 1–8: World Bank 1999b.

HDI rank	Net foreign direct Investment flows (US$ millions) 1985	1997	Net portfolio Investment flows a (US$ millions) 1985	1997	Net bank and trade-related lending b (US$ millions) 1985	1997	Net official development assistance (ODA) disbursed or received c (net disbursements) Total (US$ millions) 1997	As % of GNP 1997	Per capita (US$) 1997	External debt Total (US$ millions) 1997	As % of GNP 1997	Debt service ratio d (%) 1997	Sovereign long-term debt rating e 1998
High human development	44,388 T	266,225 T	..	..	..	..	48,324 T	0.2	66 [f]	..	..	..	..
1 Canada	1,357	8,246	..	..	..	..	2,045	0.3	64 [f]	..	..	..	AA+
2 Norway	−426	3,181	..	..	..	..	1,306	0.9	308 [f]	..	..	..	AAA
3 United States	20,010	90,748	..	..	..	..	6,878	0.1	30 [f]	..	..	..	AAA
4 Japan	642	3,224	..	..	..	..	9,358	0.2	79 [f]	..	..	..	AAA
5 Belgium	1,051 [g]	12,550 [g]	..	..	..	..	764	0.3	88 [f]	..	..	..	AA+
6 Sweden	393	9,659	..	..	..	..	1,731	0.8	222 [f]	..	..	..	AA+
7 Australia	2,063	9,584	..	..	..	..	1,061	0.3	59 [f]	..	..	..	AA
8 Netherlands	1,505	8,725	..	..	..	..	2,947	0.8	212 [f]	..	..	..	AAA
9 Iceland	24	3	..	..	..	..	..	..	..	..	..	..	A+
10 United Kingdom	5,480	36,897	..	..	..	..	3,433	0.3	55 [f]	..	..	..	AAA
11 France	2,595	18,280	..	..	..	..	6,307	0.5	125 [f]	..	..	..	AAA
12 Switzerland	1,267	3,500	..	..	..	..	911	0.3	148 [f]	..	..	..	AAA
13 Finland	110	1,543	..	..	..	..	379	0.3	81 [f]	..	..	..	AA
14 Germany	490	−195	..	..	..	..	5,857	0.3	87 [f]	..	..	..	AAA
15 Denmark	111	2,570	..	..	..	..	1,637	1.0	342 [f]	..	..	..	AA+
16 Austria	173	1,700	..	..	..	..	527	0.3	72 [f]	..	..	..	AAA
17 Luxembourg	..	..	..	..	..	..	95	0.6	226 [f]	..	..	..	AAA
18 New Zealand	1,266	1,343	..	..	..	..	154	0.3	38 [f]	..	..	..	AA+
19 Italy	1,072	3,523	..	..	..	..	1,266	0.1	33 [f]	..	..	..	AA
20 Ireland	164	4,152	..	..	..	..	187	0.3	51 [f]	..	..	..	AA+
21 Spain	1,968	5,556	..	..	..	..	1,234	0.2	34 [f]	..	..	..	AA
22 Singapore	1,047	10,000	..	..	..	..	1 [h]	(.)	0	..	..	..	AAA
23 Israel	99	3,407	..	..	..	..	1,192 [h]	1.2	241	..	..	..	A−
24 Hong Kong, China (SAR)	−142	2,600	..	..	..	..	8 [h]	(.)	1	..	..	..	A
25 Brunei Darussalam	4	5	..	..	..	..	(.) [h]	..	1	..	..	..	..
26 Cyprus	58	175	..	..	..	..	49 [h]	0.6	71	..	..	..	A+
27 Greece	447	1,500	..	..	..	..	..	..	..	..	..	..	BBB
28 Portugal	274	1,713	..	..	..	..	250	0.3	25 [f]	..	..	..	AA
29 Barbados	5	18	21	84	17	−20	3	..	12	644.3	..	7.5 [i]	..
30 Korea, Rep. of	234	2,341	1,271	2,704	1,388	6,264	−160 [i]	(.)	−4	143,372.5	32.8	8.6	BB+
31 Bahamas	30	89	..	..	..	..	3 [h]	..	12	..	..	..	..
32 Malta	19	110	..	..	(.)	93	22	0.7	62	1,033.9	30.6	2.1	A
33 Slovenia	..	321	..	−37	..	−69	97	0.5	49	4,762.1	26.0	3.9	A
34 Chile	144	5,417	..	1,525	684	2,695	136	0.2	10	31,440.1	42.4	20.4	A−
35 Kuwait	7	45	..	..	..	..	2 [h]	(.)	2	..	..	..	A
36 Czech Republic	..	1,301	..	221	−118	311	107 [h]	0.2	10	21,456.3	41.8	14.1	A−
37 Bahrain	101	15	205	..	28	..	84	1.6	165	7,084.0 [i]	138.4 [i]	..	..
38 Antigua and Barbuda	16	28	..	..	..	..	4	0.8	62	280.0 [i]	59.7 [i]	..	..
39 Argentina	919	6,327	−151	11,250	2,501	1,939	222	0.1	7	123,221.4	38.7	58.7	BB
40 Uruguay	1	200	89	451	−72	22	57	0.3	18	6,652.0	33.6	15.4	BBB−
41 Qatar	8	55	..	..	..	..	1 [h]	..	2	..	..	..	BBB
42 Slovakia	..	170	..	37	−171	872	67 [h]	0.3	13	9,989.0	51.7	12.2	BB+
43 United Arab Emirates	−221	100	..	..	..	..	4 [h]	..	2	..	..	..	..
44 Poland	15	5,000	−15	1,748	−178	131	641 [h]	0.5	17	39,889.5	29.5	6.1	BBB−
45 Costa Rica	70	500	..	41	45	7	..	..	..	3,548.4	38.1	11.8	BB
Medium human development	10,311 T	126,766 T	3,916 T	53,433 T	11,076 T	51,478 T	24,130 T	0.6	6	1,720,856.1 T	32.9	18.0	..
46 Trinidad and Tobago	1	340	56	−150	96	−94	33	0.6	27	2,161.5	38.8	19.6	BB+
47 Hungary	..	2,085	495	598	1,212	−72	152 [h]	0.3	15	24,373.4	55.0	29.7	BBB
48 Venezuela	68	4,893	−65	256	−517	938	28	(.)	1	35,541.5	41.6	31.3	B+
49 Panama	67	340	−20	461	26	−48	124	1.5	51	6,338.0	75.4	16.4	BB+
50 Mexico	1,984	12,101	−477	2,526	−341	5,530	108	(.)	1	149,689.9	38.4	32.4	BB

A1.2 Resource flows

HDI rank	Net foreign direct investment flows (US$ millions)		Net portfolio investment flows [a] (US$ millions)		Net bank and trade-related lending [b] (US$ millions)		Net official development assistance (ODA) disbursed or received [c] (net disbursements)			External debt		Debt service ratio [d] (%)	Sovereign long-term debt rating [e]
							Total (US$ millions)	As % of GNP	Per capita (US$)	Total (US$ millions)	As % of GNP		
	1985	1997	1985	1997	1985	1997	1997	1997	1997	1997	1997	1997	1998
51 Saint Kitts and Nevis	8	25	..	..	..	-1	7	2.7	168	62.0	24.3	3.9	..
52 Grenada	4	22	..	..	-1	-1	8	2.7	86	105.3	34.9	5.7 i	..
53 Dominica	3	20	..	..	..	..	14	6.2	194	161.4	43.5	8.2	..
54 Estonia	..	262	..	82	..	-2	65 h	1.4	42	658.4	14.5	1.4	BBB+
55 Croatia	..	348	..	485	..	1,524	44	0.2	9	6,841.5	35.2	11.9	BBB-
56 Malaysia	695	3,754	2,253	2,014	-2,162	2,192	-241 j	-0.3	-13	47,228.2	50.5	7.5	BBB-
57 Colombia	1,023	2,447	-1	1,184	392	2,984	274	0.3	8	31,777.4	34.4	26.6	BBB-
58 Cuba	(.)	13	..	..	212	..	67	..	6	35,344.0 i	..	..	..
59 Mauritius	8	38	..	624	-19	94	42	1.0	39	2,471.6	56.7	10.9	..
60 Belarus	..	163	..	..	..	-31	43 h	0.2	4	1,161.5	5.2	1.8	..
61 Fiji	22	12	..	..	11	-12	44	2.2	59	213.4	10.5	3.0	..
62 Lithuania	..	355	..	90	..	193	102 h	1.1	27	1,540.5	16.4	6.0	BBB-
63 Bulgaria	..	497	..	69	887	3	206 h	2.1	24	9,858.3	101.3	14.4	B
64 Suriname	21	12	..	..	9	..	77	11.4	191	118.0 i	17.5 i	..	..
65 Libyan Arab Jamahiriya	119	110	..	..	271	..	9	..	2	3,363.0 i	..	..	..
66 Seychelles	12	49	..	..	5	-3	15	2.8	212	149.1	28.2	4.0	..
67 Thailand	163	3,600	179	1,418	794	-1,719	626	0.4	11	93,415.7	62.6	15.4	BBB-
68 Romania	..	1,224	..	422	-645	637	197 h	0.6	9	10,442.1	30.2	15.7	B-
69 Lebanon	7	150	..	808	-30	112	239	1.6	65	5,036.2	32.8	14.4	BB-
70 Samoa (Western)	(.)	1	-1	..	(.)	..	28	14.4	173	156.3	80.1	3.8	..
71 Russian Federation	..	6,241	..	6,666	1,564	-454	718 h	0.2	5	125,645.2	28.7	6.5	CCC-
72 Ecuador	62	577	-2	-135	203	387	172	0.9	16	14,918.4	79.4	31.0	..
73 Macedonia, TFYR	..	16	..	..	..	-7	149	6.8	78	1,542.5	70.8	8.8	..
74 Latvia	..	418	..	23	..	15	81 h	1.5	30	503.3	9.0	4.4	BBB
75 Saint Vincent and the Grenadines	2	42	..	..	(.)	-2	6	2.2	56	257.8	94.8	8.3 i	..
76 Kazakhstan	..	1,320	..	400	..	436	131	0.6	8	4,278.0	19.5	6.5	B+
77 Philippines	12	1,253	-71	2,704	868	238	689	0.8	11	45,433.3	53.0	9.2	BB+
78 Saudi Arabia	491	400	150	..	564	..	15	(.)	1	19,222.0 i	13.5 i	..	..
79 Brazil	1,441	16,330	-215	5,056	365	18,669	487	0.1	3	193,662.8	24.1	57.4	BB-
80 Peru	1	2,000	..	-110	81	1,175	488	0.8	22	30,495.7	48.8	30.9	BB
81 Saint Lucia	17	45	..	..	..	..	24	4.1	160	151.7	25.7	3.3 i	..
82 Jamaica	-9	180	..	200	41	40	71	1.8	29	3,912.9	97.7	16.2	..
83 Belize	4	23	..	..	-3	-7	14	2.3	72	383.4	62.2	9.2	..
84 Paraguay	1	200	..	..	-5	23	116	1.2	27	2,052.5	20.8	5.0	BB-
85 Georgia	..	100	..	..	..	(.)	246	4.7	45	1,445.5	27.4	6.4	..
86 Turkey	99	606	-6	2,552	6	8,864	-1 j	(.)	(.)	91,205.4	47.1	18.4	B
87 Armenia	..	43	..	..	..	..	168	9.6	47	665.5	38.0	5.8	..
88 Dominican Republic	36	250	..	-2	20	-2	76	0.5	11	4,238.7	29.0	6.2	B+
89 Oman	161	90	..	263	501	-234	20	..	11	3,601.7	..	5.9	BBB-
90 Sri Lanka	26	140	..	148	44	-4	345	2.3	20	7,638.1	51.2	6.4	..
91 Ukraine	..	623	..	..	..	796	176 h	0.4	3	10,901.3	22.2	6.6	..
92 Uzbekistan	..	85	..	..	..	150	130	0.5	6	2,760.5	11.2	12.9	..
93 Maldives	1	10	..	..	-3	5	26	8.4	119	160.3	51.8	6.7	..
94 Jordan	25	70	..	160	190	-122	462	6.8	130	8,234.1	121.0	11.1	BB-
95 Iran, Islamic Rep. of	-38	50	..	..	-200	-353	196	0.2	4	11,816.4	9.6	32.2	..
96 Turkmenistan	..	121	..	..	..	762	11	0.4	3	1,771.2	62.5	34.7	..
97 Kyrgyzstan	..	83	..	..	..	..	240	14.1	54	928.2	54.4	6.3	..
98 China	1,659	45,300	971	11,787	1,895	4,805	2,040	0.2	2	146,697.0	16.6	8.6	BBB+
99 Guyana	2	90	..	..	-5	-5	272	39.9	340	1,610.6	236.0	17.6	..
100 Albania	..	48	..	..	..	-1	155	6.2	48	706.0	28.1	7.1	..

HDI rank	Net foreign direct investment flows (US$ millions) 1985	1997	Net portfolio investment flows [a] (US$ millions) 1985	1997	Net bank and trade-related lending [b] (US$ millions) 1985	1997	Net official development assistance (ODA) disbursed or received [c] (net disbursements) Total (US$ millions) 1997	As % of GNP 1997	Per capita (US$) 1997	External debt Total (US$ millions) 1997	As % of GNP 1997	Debt service ratio [d] (%) 1997	Sovereign long-term debt rating [e] 1998
101 South Africa	−449	1,705	..	2,016	..	−131	497	0.4	14	25,221.6	20.0	12.8	BB+
102 Tunisia	108	360	..	586	109	1	194	1.1	23	11,322.7	62.8	16.0	BBB−
103 Azerbaijan	..	872	..	..	..	8	182	4.2	25	503.7	11.7	6.8	..
104 Moldova, Rep. of	..	43	..	75	..	121	63	3.5	15	1,039.8	57.4	10.9	..
105 Indonesia	310	5,350	−40	3,417	195	2,769	832	0.4	5	136,173.5	65.3	30.0	CCC+
106 Cape Verde	..	13	..	..	1	1	110	26.2	317	220.0	52.5	5.5	..
107 El Salvador	12	41	−9	..	−42	50	294	2.6	57	3,281.8	29.4	7.0	BB
108 Tajikistan	..	4	..	..	..	(.)	101	5.0	19	901.1	44.6	4.6	..
109 Algeria	(.)	7	429	8	111	−557	248	0.6	10	30,920.6	69.0	27.2	..
110 Viet Nam	(.)	1,200	..	−94	..	287	997	4.1	15	21,629.3	89.4	7.8	..
111 Syrian Arab Republic	37	80	..	..	85	−11	199	1.2	16	20,864.7	126.4	9.3	..
112 Bolivia	10	500	−1	−3	−35	213	717	9.2	107	5,247.5	67.6	32.5	BB−
113 Swaziland	12	75	..	..	9	..	27	1.9	34	368.2	25.4	2.5	..
114 Honduras	28	80	..	−30	36	33	308	6.7	61	4,697.8	102.8	20.9	..
115 Namibia	16	131	..	..	..	..	166	5.0	120	85.0 [i]	2.6 [i]	..	..
116 Vanuatu	5	30	..	..	(.)	(.)	27	11.6	178	47.9	20.5	1.5	..
117 Guatemala	62	130	−10	106	19	−30	302	1.7	34	4,085.7	23.2	9.9	..
118 Solomon Islands	1	22	..	..	6	−4	42	11.4	126	135.4	36.9	2.4	..
119 Mongolia	..	7	..	..	..	9	248	25.2	110	717.9	72.9	11.7	..
120 Egypt	1,178	834	10	1,813	550	−109	1,947	2.5	36	29,849.1	39.0	9.0	BBB−
121 Nicaragua	..	92	..	..	13	−16	421	..	..	5,677.4	305.6	31.7	..
122 Botswana	54	100	..	..	−12	−5	125	2.6	95	562.0	11.5	5.2 [i]	..
123 São Tomé and Principe	..	..	..	..	(.)	..	34	87.5	287	260.7	671.2	52.0	..
124 Gabon	15	−100	(.)	..	96	−5	40	0.9	40	4,284.5	95.7	13.1	..
125 Iraq	(.)	..	..	..	1,627	..	281	..	15	21,912.0 [i]	..	..	..
126 Morocco	20	500	−21	243	237	−140	462	1.4	19	19,320.8	59.5	26.6	BB
127 Lesotho	5	29	..	..	−6	13	93	7.3	53	659.8	51.9	6.4	..
128 Myanmar	..	80	..	−2	−56	102	45	..	1	5,074.1	..	8.0	..
129 Papua New Guinea	83	300	19	..	167	−57	349	8.6	89	2,272.5	56.3	15.0	..
130 Zimbabwe	4	70	−29	−20	−40	−18	327	3.9	33	4,961.3	58.5	22.0	..
131 Equatorial Guinea	2	40	..	..	1	..	24	4.9	67	283.2	57.8	1.4	..
132 India	106	3,264	320	4,035	1,954	920	1,678	0.4	2	94,404.2	24.9	19.6	BB
133 Ghana	6	200	..	46	35	27	493	7.3	32	5,982.0	88.6	29.5	..
134 Cameroon	316	45	..	..	−241	−29	501	5.9	43	9,292.9	109.2	20.4	..
135 Congo	13	9	..	..	97	..	268	14.7	117	5,070.8	278.4	6.2	..
136 Kenya	29	40	..	12	8	−119	457	4.6	19	6,485.8	64.7	21.5	..
137 Cambodia	..	200	..	..	..	−3	372	12.2	42	2,128.7	69.9	1.1	..
138 Pakistan	131	800	..	627	−170	757	597	1.0	5	29,664.5	47.5	35.2	CC
139 Comoros	..	2	..	..	(.)	..	28	14.5	63	197.4	101.9	3.9	..
Low human development	980 T	2,449 T	..	..	178 T	−1,125 T	13,285 T	10.5	28	173,123.7 T	93.4	13.1	..
140 Lao People's Dem. Rep.	..	90	..	..	..	..	341	19.5	82	2,319.9	132.4	6.5	..
141 Congo, Dem. Rep. of the	69	1	(.)	..	−35	..	168	3.2	4	12,329.6	232.3	0.9	..
142 Sudan	−3	(.)	..	..	..	..	187	2.1	8	16,326.1	182.4	9.2	..
143 Togo	16	1	..	..	−14	−6	124	8.6	34	1,339.0	92.6	8.1	..
144 Nepal	1	20	..	..	5	−11	414	8.4	22	2,397.7	48.6	6.9	..
145 Bhutan	..	..	..	..	..	−2	70	21.3	113	89.3	27.2	5.1	..
146 Nigeria	486	1,000	..	4	−955	−258	202	11.0	25	28,455.1	75.6	7.8	..
147 Madagascar	(.)	17	..	..	5	−1	838	24.3	71	4,104.7	119.2	27.0	..
148 Yemen	3	50	..	..	6	..	366	7.3	27	3,856.3	76.7	2.6	..
149 Mauritania	7	3	..	..	2	−2	250	23.9	120	2,453.2	234.7	24.2	..
150 Bangladesh	1	145	..	11	−3	−28	1,009	2.3	9	15,125.3	35.1	10.6	..

HDI rank	Net foreign direct investment flows (US$ millions)		Net portfolio investment flows [a] (US$ millions)		Net bank and trade-related lending [b] (US$ millions)		Net official development assistance (ODA) disbursed or received [c] (net disbursements)			External debt		Debt service ratio [d] (%)	Sovereign long-term debt rating [e]
							Total (US$ millions)	As % of GNP	Per capita (US$)	Total (US$ millions)	As % of GNP		
	1985	1997	1985	1997	1985	1997	1997	1997	1997	1997	1997	1997	1998
151 Zambia	52	70	..	..	12	9	618	16.9	77	6,757.8	184.6	19.9	..
152 Haiti	5	3	..	..	−4	..	332	11.8	50	1,057.2	37.7	15.9	..
153 Senegal	−16	30	..	..	−5	14	427	9.6	57	3,670.6	82.9	15.3	..
154 Côte d'Ivoire	29	50	(.)	18	(.)	−436	444	4.7	37	15,608.6	165.3	27.4	..
155 Benin	(.)	3	..	..	−18	..	225	10.7	46	1,624.3	76.9	9.1	..
156 Tanzania, U. Rep. of	15	250	..	..	46	−15	963	13.0	37	7,177.1	97.2	12.9	..
157 Djibouti	(.)	5	..	..	(.)	..	87	17.5	163	283.6	57.1	3.1	..
158 Uganda	−4	250	..	..	6	−1	840	12.8	50	3,707.9	56.5	22.1	..
159 Malawi	6	2	..	..	−29	−1	350	14.1	40	2,206.0	89.0	12.4	..
160 Angola	278	350	..	..	1,042	−374	436	9.9	46	10,159.8	231.8	15.9	..
161 Guinea	1	1	..	..	18	−24	382	10.3	65	3,520.4	95.3	21.5	..
162 Chad	54	15	..	..	−6	..	225	14.3	38	1,026.5	65.2	12.5	..
163 Gambia	−1	13	..	..	(.)	..	40	10.0	42	430.1	107.6	11.6	..
164 Rwanda	15	1	..	..	−3	..	592	32.0	83	1,110.9	60.0	13.3	..
165 Central African Republic	3	6	..	..	−1	..	92	9.2	31	885.3	88.2	6.2	..
166 Mali	3	15	..	..	−2	..	455	18.4	52	2,945.1	119.2	10.5	..
167 Eritrea	..	..	..	..	..	..	123	14.8	38	75.5	9.1	0.1	..
168 Guinea-Bissau	1	2	..	..	20	..	125	49.7	126	921.3	366.5	17.3	..
169 Mozambique	(.)	35	..	..	54	2	963	37.4	67	5,990.6	232.9	18.6	..
170 Burundi	1	1	..	..	−3	..	119	12.6	21	1,065.5	112.6	29.0	..
171 Burkina Faso	−1	1	..	..	−9	..	370	15.5	41	1,297.1	54.3	11.8	..
172 Ethiopia	(.)	15	..	..	59	23	637	10.1	12	10,078.5	159.0	9.5	..
173 Niger	−9	1	..	..	−7	−14	341	18.4	87	1,579.1	86.3	19.5	..
174 Sierra Leone	−31	4	..	..	−4	..	130	16.0	32	1,148.7	141.4	21.2	..

a. Portfolio investment flows (net) include non-debt-creating portfolio equity flows (the sum of country funds, depository receipts and direct purchases of shares by foreign investors) and portfolio debt flows (bond issues purchased by foreign investors).

b. Bank and trade-related lending covers commercial bank lending and other private credits.

c. Data in italics refer to net ODA disbursed by Development Assistance Committee member countries.

d. Total debt service as a percentage of exports of goods and services.

e. Ratings cover foreign currency debt and refer to the fourth quarter of the year specified.

f. Data refer to an average for 1996 and 1997, per capita of the donor country.

g. Data refer to Belgium and Luxembourg.

h. Data refer to net official aid.

i. Data refer to 1996.

j. Data refer to net ODA receipts.

Source: Columns 1 and 2: calculated on the basis of data from UNCTAD 1999; *columns 3–6:* World Bank 1999b; *column 7:* OECD 1999a and 1999b; *columns 8 and 9:* calculated on the basis of data from OECD 1999a and 1999b, UN 1998h and World Bank 1999b; *columns 10-12:* World Bank 1999b; *column 13:* Standard & Poor's 1999.

HDI rank	International tourism departures		Main telephone lines		Televisions		Fax machines		Personal computers		Internet hosts
	Thousands 1996	Index (1985 = 100) 1996	Per 1,000 people 1996	Index (1990 = 100)[a] 1996	Per 1,000 people 1996	Index (1990 = 100)[a] 1996	Per 1,000 people 1996	Index (1990 = 100)[a] 1996	Per 1,000 people 1996	Index (1990 = 100)[a] 1996	per 1,000 people 1998
High human development	433,035 T	284	502	132	595	123	44.6	395	204.5	254	34.50
1 Canada	18,973	144	602	118	709 [b]	124 [b]	26.7	267	243.6	270	53.50
2 Norway	3,085	517	555	114	569	140	..	..	284.5	..	71.80
3 United States	50,763 [b]	146 [b]	640	125	806 [b]	110 [b]	64.6 [b]	334 [b]	362.4	178	88.90
4 Japan	16,695	337	489	113	700	117	113.7	210	128.0	221	11.00
5 Belgium	5,645	85	465	121	464 [b]	106 [b]	18.7	271	167.3	194	16.00
6 Sweden	6,582	120	682	103	476 [b]	105 [b]	50.9	265	214.9	193	35.10
7 Australia	2,732	181	519	122	666	137	26.3 [b]	170 [b]	311.3	223	42.70
8 Netherlands	10,261 [b]	153 [b]	543	121	495 [b]	106 [b]	32.3 [b]	200 [b]	232.0	257	34.60
9 Iceland	190	198	576	119	447 [b]	148 [b]	..	..	205.4 [b]	550 [b]	78.70
10 United Kingdom	41,873 [b]	194 [b]	528	121	612 [b]	144 [b]	30.8 [b]	240 [b]	192.6	238	23.30
11 France	18,151	206	564	117	598 [b]	114 [b]	32.7 [b]	328 [b]	150.7	220	7.87
12 Switzerland	10,860	128	640	115	493	128	29.2	249	408.5	..	27.90
13 Finland	4,918	1,002	549	105	605	126	34.9	239	195.2	200	108.00
14 Germany	76,100	169	538	138	493	106	22.0	259	233.2	292	14.90
15 Denmark	4,955 [b]	155 [b]	618	112	533 [b]	102 [b]	47.6 [b]	250 [b]	304.1	271	17.90
16 Austria	12,683 [b]	255 [b]	469	117	496	110	35.4 [b]	335 [b]	148.9	251	18.40
17 Luxembourg	..	..	592	133	628	196	36.3	429	..	..	16.60
18 New Zealand	920 [b]	243 [b]	499	121	517	123	18.1 [b]	232 [b]	266.1	..	49.70
19 Italy	15,991 [b]	173 [b]	440	113	436 [b]	103 [b]	31.4 [b]	1,056 [b]	92.3	252	5.75
20 Ireland	2,000 [h]	..	395	141	469	161	..	..	170.4	161	12.80
21 Spain	12,644 [b]	222 [b]	392	122	509	129	17.8	485	94.2	336	6.26
22 Singapore	3,305	628	513	148	361	107	29.6	271	216.8	..	15.10
23 Israel	2,259 [b]	408 [b]	441	156	300 [b]	139 [b]	24.7 [b]	400 [b]	116.3	..	14.20
24 Hong Kong, China (SAR)	3,445	304	547	139	388	158	49.8	283	150.5	..	20.50
25 Brunei Darussalam	300	333	263	225	417	202	7.0 [b]	175 [b]	..	..	2.41
26 Cyprus	360 [b]	243 [b]	485	149	146	105	..	..	40.9 [b]	600 [b]	5.89
27 Greece	1,620 [b]	147 [b]	509	135	442 [b]	235 [b]	3.8	435	35.3	211	3.89
28 Portugal	2,358	1,275	375	157	367	201	5.0 [b]	476 [b]	67.4	261	4.74
29 Barbados	..	..	370	134	287 [b]	110 [b]	6.8 [b]	137 [b]	57.5 [b]	..	5.44
30 Korea, Rep. of	4,649	961	430	148	326	165	8.9 [b]	174 [b]	131.7	376	4.27
31 Bahamas	..	..	315	128	233 [b]	114 [b]	..	..	..	..	1.96
32 Malta	180	170	483	141	497	71	16.0	412	80.6 [b]	600 [b]	3.00
33 Slovenia	..	..	333	157	375 [b]	..	8.9	452	47.8 [b]	..	9.85
34 Chile	1,070 [b]	193 [b]	156	261	277	148	1.8 [b]	439 [b]	45.1	433	2.07
35 Kuwait	..	..	232	118	373 [b]	109 [b]	23.7	..	74.1	1,389	3.98
36 Czech Republic	48,614	..	273	174	406 [b]	..	7.7	1,746	67.9	..	6.73
37 Bahrain	..	..	241	154	429	124	10.6	226	66.8	..	0.62
38 Antigua and Barbuda	..	..	423	175	412 [b]	117 [b]	12.9	243	..	..	3.69
39 Argentina	3,550 [b]	203 [b]	174	198	345 [b]	148 [b]	1.7	400	34.1	..	1.75
40 Uruguay	..	..	209	161	305 [b]	81 [b]	3.5 [b]	..	22.0 [b]	..	5.02
41 Qatar	..	..	239	145	538	158	18.6	1,095	62.7	..	0.09
42 Slovakia	318	..	232	175	384	..	10.3	2,203	186.1	..	2.65
43 United Arab Emirates	..	..	308	186	282	386	18.8	289	66.7	..	6.07
44 Poland	44,713	1,070	169	198	418	144	1.4 [b]	944 [b]	36.2	560	2.57
45 Costa Rica	273 [b]	165 [b]	155	187	221	121	..	..	..	..	0.85
Medium human development	120,037 T	..	54	432	182	200	0.7	1,167	7.2	..	0.24
46 Trinidad and Tobago	261 [b]	97 [b]	168	133	318 [b]	107 [b]	1.6	116	19.2 [b]	..	3.13
47 Hungary	12,064	218	261	267	442 [b]	105 [b]	4.4 [b]	464 [b]	44.1	..	8.20
48 Venezuela	534 [b]	154 [b]	117	179	180 [b]	125 [b]	1.1 [b]	..	21.1	..	0.63
49 Panama	188	186	122	151	229 [b]	153 [b]	..	..	..	..	0.86
50 Mexico	9,001	330	95	165	193 [b]	143 [b]	2.4 [b]	367 [b]	29.0	..	0.92

A1.3 Information flows

HDI rank	International tourism departures		Main telephone lines		Televisions		Fax machines		Personal computers		Internet hosts per 1,000 people
	Thousands 1996	Index (1985 = 100) 1996	Per 1,000 people 1996	Index (1990 = 100)[a] 1996	Per 1,000 people 1996	Index (1990 = 100)[a] 1996	Per 1,000 people 1996	Index (1990 = 100)[a] 1996	Per 1,000 people 1996	Index (1990 = 100)[a] 1996	1998
51 Saint Kitts and Nevis	..	..	382	161	244 [b]	111 [b]	11.0	..	..	..	0.17
52 Grenada	..	..	243	159	..	..	2.7	180	..	..	0.14
53 Dominica	..	..	264	161	183	260	5.6	180	..	..	1.23
54 Estonia	217	..	299	137	449	122	8.8 [b]	..	6.7 [b]	..	13.20
55 Croatia	..	..	309	169	267	117	10.1	1,363	20.9	..	1.34
56 Malaysia	20,642 [b]	1,124 [b]	183	238	228	178	5.0 [b]	250 [b]	42.8	..	2.09
57 Colombia	1,073	164	118	192	185	192	3.6	402	23.3	..	0.52
58 Cuba	55	550	32	106	199	100	..	..	..	..	0.01
59 Mauritius	120	..	162	331	219 [b]	138 [b]	22.0	..	31.9 [b]	900 [b]	0.34
60 Belarus	703	..	208	135	292 [b]	109 [b]	0.9 [b]	..	..	..	0.07
61 Fiji	67	558	88	165	94	682	3.8 [b]	198 [b]	..	..	0.17
62 Lithuania	2,864	..	268	127	376	107	1.5	..	6.5 [b]	..	2.87
63 Bulgaria	3,006	564	313	122	361	136	1.8 [b]	..	29.8 [b]	..	0.81
64 Suriname	90 [b]	170 [b]	132	155	208	164	1.9	400	..	..	0.34
65 Libyan Arab Jamahiriya	185 [b]	..	68	173	143	178	..	..	..	..	(.)
66 Seychelles	31 [b]	344 [b]	196	171	191	290	8.5	235	..	..	0.60
67 Thailand	1,845	339	70	317	167	169	2.1	1,977	16.7	..	0.03
68 Romania	5,737 [b]	499 [b]	140	134	226	113	0.9 [b]	519 [b]	5.3 [b]	1,200 [b]	0.62
69 Lebanon	..	..	149	154	355	123	..	..	24.3	..	0.46
70 Samoa (Western)	..	..	50	201	45	121	..	..	..	..	..
71 Russian Federation	21,331 [b]	..	175	125	386	106	0.4	..	23.7	..	1.05
72 Ecuador	279	208	73	175	148 [b]	193 [b]	..	..	3.9 [b]	..	0.21
73 Macedonia, TFYR	..	..	170	129	170 [b]	..	1.2	..	..	..	0.21
74 Latvia	1,798	..	298	119	598	151	0.3 [b]	..	7.9 [b]	..	3.40
75 Saint Vincent and the Grenadines	..	..	171	148	234 [b]	173 [b]	13.3	..	..	..	0.03
76 Kazakhstan	..	..	116	144	275 [b]	97 [b]	0.2	..	..	..	0.14
77 Philippines	1,400 [b]	185 [b]	25	293	125	300	0.7 [b]	500 [b]	9.3	670	0.21
78 Saudi Arabia	..	..	106	162	263 [b]	118 [b]	8.4 [b]	556 [b]	37.2	184	0.01
79 Brazil	2,943	308	96	161	289	148	2.2	389	18.4	..	1.04
80 Peru	508 [b]	360 [b]	60	254	142	163	0.6 [b]	827 [b]	5.9 [b]	..	0.15
81 Saint Lucia	..	..	235	199	301 [b]	200 [b]	..	..	..	..	0.25
82 Jamaica	..	..	142	335	326	254	..	..	4.6	..	0.67
83 Belize	..	..	133	171	180	129	..	..	27.8 [b]	..	2.26
84 Paraguay	418	..	36	157	144 [b]	323 [b]	..	..	..	..	0.15
85 Georgia	..	..	105	105	474 [b]	232 [b]	..	..	..	..	0.26
86 Turkey	4,261	236	224	208	309	152	1.6	311	13.8	440	0.54
87 Armenia	..	..	154	103	217 [b]	109 [b]	..	..	..	..	0.16
88 Dominican Republic	175	..	83	195	84	113	0.3	..	..	..	0.63
89 Oman	..	..	86	189	591	118	2.5	419	10.9	833	0.30
90 Sri Lanka	494	207	14	210	82	250	..	..	3.3	2,000	0.04
91 Ukraine	..	..	181	131	341	103	(.)	..	5.6 [b]	..	0.43
92 Uzbekistan	..	..	67	109	190 [b]	118 [b]	..	..	..	..	0.01
93 Maldives	32	457	63	265	39	197	14.3 [b]	1,489 [b]	12.3 [b]	..	0.34
94 Jordan	1,141	141	60	136	..	..	7.3 [b]	..	7.2	..	0.10
95 Iran, Islamic Rep. of	1,000	102	95	265	164	276	..	..	32.7	..	(.)
96 Turkmenistan	..	..	74	154	163 [b]	105 [b]	..	..	..	..	0.07
97 Kyrgyzstan	42 [b]	..	75	109	..	..	..	..	..	..	0.04
98 China	5,061	..	45	802	252	172	0.2 [b]	688 [b]	3.0	..	0.02
99 Guyana	..	..	60	386	42 [b]	117 [b]	..	..	..	..	0.09
100 Albania	16	..	17	160	161	211	..	..	..	..	0.03

HDI rank	International tourism departures		Main telephone lines		Televisions		Fax machines		Personal computers		Internet hosts per 1,000 people
	Thousands 1996	Index (1985=100) 1996	Per 1,000 people 1996	Index (1990=100)[a] 1996	Per 1,000 people 1996	Index (1990=100)[a] 1996	Per 1,000 people 1996	Index (1990=100)[a] 1996	Per 1,000 people 1996	Index (1990=100)[a] 1996	1998
101 South Africa	2,775	544	100	128	123	141	2.4 [b]	..	37.7	..	3.82
102 Tunisia	1,778 [b]	247 [b]	64	193	156 [b]	215 [b]	3.1	1,120	6.7 [b]	286 [b]	0.01
103 Azerbaijan	..	..	85	104	212	114	..	..	..	..	0.04
104 Moldova, Rep. of	71 [b]	..	140	128	307	100	0.1	1,620	2.6	..	0.15
105 Indonesia	1,782 [b]	470 [b]	21	393	232	435	0.4 [b]	567 [b]	4.8	..	0.10
106 Cape Verde	..	..	64	306	45	1,800	2.5	..	..	..	(.)
107 El Salvador	348 [b]	93 [b]	56	260	250	305	..	..	..	..	0.02
108 Tajikistan	..	..	42	103	279	165	0.3	..	..	..	0.01
109 Algeria	1,810 [b]	63 [b]	44	161	68	115	0.2	388	3.4	400	(.)
110 Viet Nam	..	..	16	1,204	180	519	0.3	3,960	3.3	..	(.)
111 Syrian Arab Republic	2,485 [b]	390 [b]	82	242	91 [b]	176 [b]	1.4	..	1.4	..	(.)
112 Bolivia	258 [b]	..	43	178	202 [b]	200 [b]	..	..	..	..	0.09
113 Swaziland	..	..	22	151	96 [b]	600 [b]	1.3	352	..	..	0.47
114 Honduras	150 [b]	115 [b]	31	216	80 [b]	122 [b]	..	..	..	..	0.04
115 Namibia	..	..	54	161	29 [b]	150 [b]	..	..	12.7	..	0.39
116 Vanuatu	10 [b]	333 [b]	26	172	13	169	3.3 [b]	..	..	..	0.27
117 Guatemala	333	218	31	180	122 [b]	274 [b]	..	..	2.8 [b]	..	0.92
118 Solomon Islands	..	..	18	165	7 [b]	..	2.1 [b]	626 [b]	..	..	0.06
119 Mongolia	..	..	39	139	63	108	2.3	..	..	..	0.01
120 Egypt	2,812	167	50	189	126 [b]	130 [b]	..	..	5.8	..	0.05
121 Nicaragua	282	..	26	240	170 [b]	292 [b]	..	..	..	..	0.17
122 Botswana	460	767	48	274	27	201	2.3	416	6.7	..	0.41
123 São Tomé and Principe	..	..	20 [b]	114 [b]	165 [b]	..	1.3 [b]	..	..	..	..
124 Gabon	..	..	32	169	76 [b]	233 [b]	0.5	263	6.3	..	0.02
125 Iraq	200 [b]	125 [b]	33	100	78 [b]	123 [b]	..	..	..	..	..
126 Morocco	1,212	221	46	310	..	..	..	..	1.7 [b]	..	0.02
127 Lesotho	..	..	9 [b]	144 [b]	13 [b]	250 [b]	0.3 [b]	228 [b]	..	..	0.01
128 Myanmar	..	..	4	255	7	270	(.)	1,006	..	..	..
129 Papua New Guinea	51 [b]	..	11	156	4	183	..	..	..	..	0.01
130 Zimbabwe	256 [b]	111 [b]	15	141	29 [b]	107 [b]	0.4 [b]	276 [b]	6.7	4,000	0.07
131 Equatorial Guinea	..	..	9	282	98	1,333	0.2 [b]	..	..	..	..
132 India	3,056 [b]	154 [b]	15	287	64	222	0.1 [b]	1,400 [b]	1.5	..	0.01
133 Ghana	..	..	4	176	41 [b]	311 [b]	0.3 [b]	260 [b]	1.2 [b]	2,747 [b]	0.02
134 Cameroon	..	..	5	175	..	..	..	..	1.5 [b]	..	(.)
135 Congo	..	..	8	135	7	154	..	..	..	..	(.)
136 Kenya	295 [b]	..	8	149	19 [b]	141 [b]	0.1 [b]	190 [b]	1.6	625	0.04
137 Cambodia	31	..	1	161	9	132	0.0	..	..	..	0.01
138 Pakistan	..	..	18	282	24	156	1.2 [b]	6,913 [b]	1.2 [b]	1,033 [b]	0.02
139 Comoros	..	..	8	153	4	231	..	..	..	..	0.02
Low human development	..	..	4	144	36	538	0.2	..	..	..	(.)
140 Lao People's Dem. Rep.	..	..	6	380	10	162	..	..	1.1	..	(.)
141 Congo, Dem. Rep. of the	..	..	1	106	41 [b]	4,500 [b]	0.1 [b]	..	..	..	..
142 Sudan	..	..	4	160	80 [b]	124 [b]	0.3	..	0.7	..	(.)
143 Togo	..	..	6	229	14	273	3.8	4,776	..	..	0.02
144 Nepal	70 [b]	103 [b]	5	197	4	226	..	..	..	..	0.01
145 Bhutan	..	..	10	325	19	..	1.7	..	..	..	(.)
146 Nigeria	50 [b]	59 [b]	4 [b]	140 [b]	55 [b]	174 [b]	..	..	..	..	(.)
147 Madagascar	38	158	3	125	..	..	..	..	..	..	(.)
148 Yemen	..	..	13	164	278 [b]	135 [b]	0.2 [b]	358 [b]	..	..	(.)
149 Mauritania	..	..	4	174	82	664	1.7	1,343	5.3	..	0.01
150 Bangladesh	935	537	3	131	7	160	(.) [b]	..	..	..	(.)

HDI rank	International tourism departures		Main telephone lines		Televisions		Fax machines		Personal computers		Internet hosts
	Thousands	Index (1985 = 100)	Per 1,000 people	Index (1990 = 100)[a]	Per 1,000 people	Index (1990 = 100)[a]	Per 1,000 people	Index (1990 = 100)[a]	Per 1,000 people	Index (1990 = 100)[a]	per 1,000 people
	1996	1996	1996	1996	1996	1996	1996	1996	1996	1996	1998
151 Zambia	..	..	9	120	80	264	0.1	141	..	..	0.03
152 Haiti	..	..	8 [b]	133 [b]	5 [b]	117 [b]	..	..	..	..	0.02
153 Senegal	..	..	11	214	38 [b]	121 [b]	..	..	7.2 [b]	333 [b]	0.04
154 Côte d'Ivoire	5	..	9	178	58	117	..	..	1.4	..	0.02
155 Benin	415 [b]	..	6	221	73 [b]	533 [b]	0.2	739	..	..	(.)
156 Tanzania, U. Rep. of	148	463	3	127	..	..	..	..	..	..	0.02
157 Djibouti	..	..	13	143	73	196	0.1	69	6.9 [b]	..	..
158 Uganda	..	..	2	172	26	292	0.1	430	0.5	..	0.01
159 Malawi	..	..	4	133	..	..	0.1	349	..	..	..
160 Angola	..	..	5	75	51 [b]	965 [b]	..	..	..	..	(.)
161 Guinea	..	..	2	143	8 [b]	133 [b]	0.1	125	0.3	..	(.)
162 Chad	11	42	1	149	2	150	0.0	243	..	..	..
163 Gambia	..	..	19	346	..	..	1.0	577	..	..	(.)
164 Rwanda	..	..	..	..	..	..	..	..	..	..	..
165 Central African Republic	..	..	3	194	5	131	0.1	..	..	..	..
166 Mali	..	..	2	191	11	150	..	..	0.3 [b]	..	(.)
167 Eritrea	..	..	5	..	7	..	0.3	..	..	..	..
168 Guinea-Bissau	..	..	7	133	..	..	0.5 [b]	..	..	..	(.)
169 Mozambique	..	..	3	126	3 [b]	150 [b]	..	..	0.8	..	(.)
170 Burundi	35	..	2	191	2	240	0.7	667	..	..	..
171 Burkina Faso	..	..	3	210	6	138	..	..	..	..	0.01
172 Ethiopia	133	..	3	119	4 [b]	217 [b]	(.)	663	..	..	(.)
173 Niger	10 [b]	29 [b]	2	166	..	..	(.) [b]	218 [b]	..	..	(.)
174 Sierra Leone	..	..	4	129	17	177	0.4	..	..	..	(.)

a. Data refer to change in total value.
b. Data refer to 1995.
Source: Columns 1 and 2: World Bank 1998c; *columns 3–10:* ITU 1997; *column 11:* Network Wizards 1998a.

CHAPTER 2

New technologies and the global race for knowledge

The recent great strides in technology present tremendous opportunities for human development—but achieving that potential depends on how technology is used. What is technology's impact on globalization—and globalization's impact on technology?

THE RACE FOR KNOWLEDGE

With the knowledge economy at the forefront of global interaction, much attention has become focused on new technologies: on information and communications technologies and on biotechnology. Why do these stand out?

For both, there have been fundamental leaps in innovation—not just better ways of doing old things but radically new ways of doing previously unimagined things. The fusion of computing and communications—especially through the Internet—has broken the bounds of cost, time and distance, launching an era of global information networking. In biotechnology the ability to identify and move genetic materials across species types has broken the bounds of nature, creating totally new organisms with enormous but unknown implications.

Both technologies are fuelling globalization, opening new markets and giving rise to new actors. Communications change economic competition, empowerment and culture, inspiring global conversation. Genetic engineering leads to complex links between farmers and indigenous people in biorich countries and the multinational pharmaceutical and agricultural industries.

And both technologies are being shaped by globalization. Writing computer programmes and revealing genetic codes have replaced the search for gold, the conquest of land and the command of machinery as the path to economic

power. Knowledge is the new asset: more than half of the GDP in the major OECD countries is now knowledge-based. With such importance placed on these technologies, the new rules of globalization—liberalization, privatization and tighter intellectual property rights—are shaping their control and use, with many consequences for human development.

Globalization's rules have set off a race to lay claim to knowledge. A global map for the new technologies is being drawn up faster than most people are able to understand the implications—let alone respond to them—and faster than anyone's certainty of the ethical and developmental impacts. The global gap between haves and have-nots, between know and know-nots, is widening:

- In private research agendas money talks louder than need.
- Tightened intellectual property rights keep developing countries out of the knowledge sector.
- Patent laws do not recognize traditional knowledge and systems of ownership.
- The rush and push of commercial interests protect profits, not people, despite the risks in the new technologies.

THE NEW TECHNOLOGIES—DRIVERS OF GLOBALIZATION

Communications technology sets this era of globalization apart from any other. The Internet, mobile phones and satellite networks have shrunk space and time. Bringing together computers and communications unleashed an unprecedented explosion of ways to communicate at the start of the 1990s. Since then tremendous productivity gains, ever-falling costs and rapidly growing networks of computers have

The global gap between haves and have-nots, between know and know-nots, is widening

transformed the computing and communications sector. If the automobile industry had the same productivity growth, a car today would cost $3.

In the early 1990s the Internet shifted from a specialized tool of the scientific community to a more user-friendly network transforming social interaction (box 2.1). The number of Internet hosts—computers with a direct connection—rose from less than 100,000 in 1988 to more than 36 million in 1998. More than 143 million people were estimated to be Internet users in mid-1998—and by 2001 that number is expected to be more than 700 million. The Internet is the fastest-growing tool of communication ever (figure 2.1).

Its speed and cost advantages are clear. A 40-page document can be sent from Madagascar to Côte d'Ivoire, for example, by five-day courier for $75, by 30-minute fax for $45 or by two-minute email for less than 20 cents—and the email can go to hundreds of people at no extra cost. The choice is easy, if the choice is there.

As the communications revolution turns digital, it promises far-reaching change, globally, nationally and locally. Network communications connect everything to everything else, creating a network society that forces complex and contradictory shifts:

• *Decentralization versus recentralization.* Old economic boundaries around nations have given way to new centres of power in the private sector. Multinational corporations have spread their activities around the world thanks to fast and cheap communications, computer-aided design and the standardization of tasks—yet they can still coordinate and control their worldwide operations as a unit. They operate in an arena beyond the jurisdiction and accountability of any one country, in a global context that does not yet have an adequate framework for regulating them. At the same time network communications have been a tremendous levelling force for small businesses, enabling them to compete—and succeed—in lucrative niches of the global market.

• *Fragmentation versus integration.* Cutting across the tradition of national communities is the rise of on-line communities, drawn together by politics, ethnicity, interests, gender, work or social cause. Using the network, they fire up debates and rally instant responses, bringing a new lobbying power to previously silent voices on the global stage. At the same time network communications can forge closer local communities, providing community information and making local government more transparent.

• *Homogenization versus diversity.* The global entertainment and media industry—spreading opinion, culture and politics—is dominated by a handful of major companies. They control both distribution networks and the programming, including news and films, sent by cable and satellite television into households across the world. At the same time the declining costs of technology have allowed a diversity of voices and cultures to be aired. Multilingual Internet sites and radio programming in local languages reach out to minority groups. Programmes on satellite television bring news and culture from home to many diasporas around the world, including Chinese, Indian and Korean communities.

These changes are still in flux. But information and communications technology can be a tremendous force for human development for all those connected—by providing information, enabling empowerment and raising productivity.

PROVIDING INFORMATION

Developing countries suffer many of the world's most virulent and infectious diseases, yet often have the least access to information

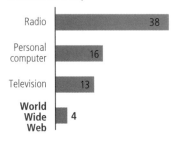

FIGURE 2.1
How long before new technologies gain widespread acceptance?
(years from inception to 50 million users)

Radio 38
Personal computer 16
Television 13
World Wide Web 4

Source: Economist 1998b.

BOX 2.1

What is the Internet?

The Internet—a centreless web of computer networks—was funded by the US Department of Defence in the late 1960s as a strategy for communicating during a nuclear attack. Soon it was used to link technically skilled science and university communities. In the early 1990s user-friendly innovations—the creation of the World Wide Web, the distribution of free browsers—turned the arcana of computer language into the simple point and click of a mouse, making the Internet more widely accessible.

At the same time computers became much cheaper, and the network took off.

Even people in the industry did not foresee the revolution. In 1977 a computer industry executive said "there is no reason why anyone would want a computer in their home". Today more than 50 million households in the United States and almost 50 million in Europe have at least one computer at home—and many have two.

The Web began as a free-for-all, an unregulated domain, with a spirit of exploration and spontaneity. Now that it is of commercial interest, laws and regulations are needed in areas of privacy, liability, censorship, taxation and intellectual property.

Source: Security Distributing and Marketing 1998; CNBC 1998; Human Development Report Office.

---

for combating them. A US medical library subscribes to around 5,000 journals, but the Nairobi University Medical School Library, long regarded as a flagship centre in East Africa, now receives just 20 journals, compared with 300 a decade ago. In Brazzaville, Congo, the university has only 40 medical books and a dozen journals, all from before 1993. Worse, the library in a large district hospital consists of a single bookshelf filled mostly with novels.

Distance learning, through teleconferencing and, increasingly, the Internet, can bring critical knowledge to information-poor hospitals and schools in developing countries (box 2.2). The potential is great—but technology alone is not a solution. Three cautions:

• Information-poor schools and hospitals are often poorly connected. In South Africa, the best-connected African country, many hospitals and about 75% of schools have no telephone line. Even at the university level, where there is connection, up to 1,000 people can depend on just one terminal. A single computer is not enough: an entire telecommunications infrastructure is needed.

• Equipment is a necessity, but to be part of a solution distance learning requires institutions, skills and good management. Distance learning technology is of little use without relevant course content and strong staff support. Zambia saw an exodus of 7,000 teachers between 1986 and 1990, largely due to a shrinking education budget. Technology cannot work where there are no support staff to help pupils get the best from the network.

• Information is only one of many needs. Email is no substitute for vaccines, and satellites cannot provide clean water. High-profile technology projects risk overshadowing basic priorities. As one health worker in Kathmandu said, "Our priorities are hygiene, sanitation, safe drinking water . . . how is access to the Internet going to change that?" The main constraint is inadequate resources for health and education systems as a whole.

ENABLING EMPOWERMENT

Communications technology opens new opportunities for small players to enter the global marketplace and political arena.

Giving voice to NGOs. The heat of the moment will not wait for a letter to travel halfway around the world: people's movements must respond fast to have an impact. Instant network communications have brought this power to NGOs, creating a tremendously important countervailing force out of previously silent voices in the global arena.

The rise of these new actors is felt across the board (box 2.3). Socially excluded and minority groups have created cybercommunities to find strength in on-line unity and fight the silence on abuses of their rights. In India DATPERS, the Dalit and Tribal People Electronic Resource Site, exposes the exclusion of 250 million low-caste people, coordinating international human rights campaigns and keeping the community in touch. During the Indonesian riots of 1998 the ethnic Chinese minority used the Web to draw the attention of the world to their plight.

Women have been innovative in using global communications for their needs. In Mexico City an NGO called Mujer a Mujer—Woman to Woman—emailed contacts in California for assistance when plans for a new textile factory were announced in their community. The women went to meet the management with a bulky portfolio detailing the company's practices, profits and ownership—

BOX 2.2

HealthNet for better patient care

HealthNet is a networked information service supporting health care workers in more than 30 developing countries, including 22 in Africa. It uses radio- and telephone-based computer networks and a low-earth-orbit satellite. Slower than the Internet, it is also cheaper, and accessible in areas with no telecommunications infrastructure.

The network provides summaries of the latest medical research, email connectivity and access to medical libraries. Doctors in Central Africa used it to share information on the 1995 outbreak of the Ebola virus. Burn surgeons in Mozambique, Tanzania and Uganda use it to consult one another on reconstructive surgery techniques. Malaria researchers at a remote site in northern Ghana use the system to communicate daily with the London School of Hygiene and Tropical Medicine.

HealthNet's communications system also supports ProMED mail, created by the Program for Monitoring Emerging Diseases. A moderated, free email list started in 1994, it now has more than 11,000 direct subscribers in more than 135 countries—and thousands more over the Web—who report, discuss and request assistance for outbreaks of emerging infectious diseases. The aim of ProMED is fast reporting—of cholera in the Philippines, E. coli in Japan, Delta hepatitis in the upper Amazon, dengue fever in Malaysia, yellow fever in Switzerland and Ebola in Gabon. The speed of communication—often faster than official channels, yet just as reliable—translates into faster assistance, earlier warnings to neighbouring countries and greater awareness among health workers.

Source: SatelLife 1998.

information impossible to find in Mexico City, and even on the Web, but available in the United States for a small database access fee. And one inspired group used the Internet to build community across the lines in war-torn former Yugoslavia in 1994, creating the Electronic Witches to link women from different ethnic groups. Gathering at Internet-linked computers around the country, often in universities, groups of women sent messages to one another, sharing their concerns, their grief over the bombing of the city of Tuzla and their survival strategies. One message advised that burning just one running shoe would be enough to bake a loaf of bread.

Creating commerce for small businesses. Telephone, email and the Internet give small businesses access to markets and bring much-needed savings in cost and time. A study in Ghana found that workers in small-scale industries without telecommunications can waste up to half their work time travelling from place to place.

Starting from a small base, electronic commerce is booming. The market was valued at $2.6 billion in 1996, and by 2002 it is expected to be more than $300 billion, promising to transform the way business is done around the world. The potential is not limited to companies with sophisticated Websites, or to customers with credit cards and electronic banking. There are many ways of using the Internet to do business—from making contacts and checking prices to displaying goods and entering into contracts. Small businesses everywhere are exploiting the opportunities.

PEOPLink is a fair trade organization selling crafts over the Internet, linking the work of more than 130,000 artisans across 14 countries of Africa, Asia and Latin America. By recording their work with a digital camera, the trading partners can display their products on the Internet and receive orders from around the world.

Tropical Whole Foods, a UK company selling fairly traded dried fruit from cooperatives and small businesses in Burkina Faso, South Africa, Uganda and Zambia, has transformed communications with email. Daily messages are exchanged to pass on business advice and share accounts and production figures, preventing stockpiles and shortages and keeping all partners informed of the current state of trade. In the past such tight coordination would have been possible only for multinational corporations with integrated data networks. Now innovative small businesses can find their niche and compete alongside giants.

Empowering governments of poor countries. In 1990 more than 90% of data on Africa were stored and managed in the United States and Europe, inaccessible to African policy-makers and academics. The Internet is bringing the data back home. Policy-makers can also gain access to international expertise and ongoing debates, strengthening their negotiating positions for a much-needed greater presence in international forums. The Small Islands Developing States Network, SIDSNet, is a forum for its 42 member nations—from Malta and Mauritius to Cuba and Comoros—to share data and experience on common concerns: energy options, sustainable tourism, coastal and marine resources and biodiversity.

BOX 2.3

Defending Gorbachev, defeating the Multilateral Agreement on Investment—how the Internet made a difference

Leaflets and banners are out. Email and Websites are in—as the new tool of protest movements in this global era. Click, connect and the campaign begins.

• In August 1991 an attempted coup against President Mikhail Gorbachev of the Soviet Union was defeated—a part in this was played by a small but determined network society. Coup leaders seized control of television and radio stations, the traditional communications, to block the sounds of dissent, but they did not think to shut down the telephone network. Russia's fledgling and little-known computer network set to work, supplying information to computer nodes and fax machines across the Soviet Union, broadcasting Boris Yeltsin's declaration of defiance and providing a link between Moscow and the rest of the world. The supply of information galvanized people's resistance and helped prevent the coup from gaining momentum.

• In 1997 the leading countries of the OECD began negotiating an agreement behind closed doors to set up a global framework of rules on investment. The Multilateral Agreement on Investment aimed to prevent governments from favouring domestic investors and to remove restrictions on multinational corporations investing in developing countries—highly sensitive issues. When the proposal was posted on the Internet, a coalition of NGOs—environmental organizations, consumer groups, trade unions and church groups—united forces to question the direction of the debate, gain the attention of the press and expose the agreement's shortcomings. By the end of 1998 there were campaigns against the agreement in more than half the OECD countries participating in the discussions and many more in developing countries. With public pressure putting negotiators in an uncomfortable position, and with disagreement among the players, the negotiations broke down.

Source: Rohozinski 1998; Kobrin 1998.

Informing remote specialists. Isolated academics and scientists can take part in Internet conferences, keeping up to date on discussions and developments in their fields. Contacts made can become technical support groups, which are of tremendous value to remote specialists. By allowing participants to share and discuss papers on-line, Internet conferences can easily involve more than 1,000 people worldwide, without any of the costs of travel.

RAISING PRODUCTIVITY

With the knowledge sector at the forefront of global economic opportunity, getting into knowledge production can be a fast track to growth. By creating a basic capacity to operate imported technology, countries can progress, climbing the rungs of the ladder, by learning to duplicate, to adapt to their own needs and, finally, to innovate. The Eastern Caribbean has seized the opportunity to step onto the first rung, using its low-cost, semi-skilled labour to export data processing services (box 2.4). In Sweden, too, remote communities have specialized in data processing, airline ticketing and hotel reservations, creating productive employment to keep young people from heading for the cities. India has forged ahead, specializing in software programming for export (figure 2.2). Japan and the first tier of newly industrializing countries have climbed the furthest—they focused their industrial strategies on creating knowledge-intensive industries and have built up strong national capacities in research and development. Indeed, Japan is perhaps the ultimate proof that comparative advantage is not a fixed given, but can be created in the information economy.

ADDRESSING CENSORSHIP

Many governments recognize the tremendous potential of the Internet and use it to provide public information: from the Indian Ministry of Finance to the Malaysian Ministry of Agriculture, government agencies are using Websites to increase the transparency of their operations. Several countries, however, have attempted to censor and control this popular empowerment. Some monitor Web searches and have blocked access to sites providing foreign news or airing

political criticism. Others have even made use of the Internet a punishable crime.

But censoring the Internet is difficult, ultimately impossible, since it was designed by the US Department of Defence to operate even if under nuclear attack and to hunt for ways around obstacles when access is blocked. Web discussion groups write the equivalent of thousands of broadsheet newspapers every day—an impossible volume to oversee. The Global Internet Liberty Campaign brings together civil liberties groups, journalists and NGOs to persuade national governments not to restrict access to the Internet because of its tremendous potential for human development. Compared with most traditional tools for development, information and communications technologies can reach many more people, go geographically deeper, work faster and at lower cost.

ACCESS TO THE NETWORK SOCIETY—WHO IS IN THE LOOP AND ON THE MAP?

The power and importance of communications technology are clear. But is it leading to globalization or polarization in communications?

The information revolution has only just begun on a worldwide scale, and its networks are spreading wider every day. But they are heavily concentrated in a very few countries.

In Cambodia in 1996, there was less than 1 telephone for every 100 people. In Monaco, by

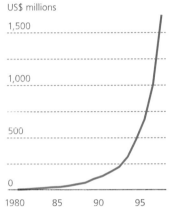

FIGURE 2.2
Software exports from India
US$ millions

Source: Heeks 1998.

BOX 2.4

Trading places—the rise of data processing

As early as 1980 electronic data entry services were being exported: bulky paper slips were sent by air freight to countries with good computing skills and low wages. The industry was hampered, however, by the unreliability of freight delivery and the costs of volume, time and distance. Electronic commerce has removed those constraints. Claims processing, electronic publishing, secretarial work, airline ticketing and customer support have migrated overseas through the Internet.

The Eastern Caribbean seized this opportunity. Combining excellent telecommunications with low wages for semi-skilled computer work, the islands have attracted many US companies. In 1994 hourly wages for data entry in the United States were $7–8. Compare that with less than $1.50 in Dominica, Grenada, Saint Kitts and Nevis, Saint Lucia and Saint Vincent.

The appeal is heating up the competition among offshore teleports, and the cost of overseas calls is often a determining factor—compare Jamaica's 22 cents a minute with Saint Lucia's $1.85 in 1994. That is why developing countries need to move into high-tech, low-cost digital communications technology to be competitive in the global knowledge sector.

Source: Schware and Hume 1994.

FIGURE 2.3
Teledensity
Telephone mainlines per 100 people

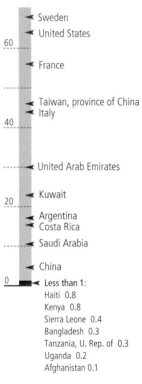

Source: ITU 1998.

contrast, there were 99 telephones for every 100 people. A widely accepted measure of basic access to telecommunications is having 1 telephone for every 100 people—a teledensity of 1. Yet as we enter the next century, a quarter of countries still have not achieved even this basic level. Many of those countries are in Sub-Saharan Africa and among the least developed countries (figure 2.3). At the present average speed of telecommunications spread, Côte d'Ivoire and Bhutan would take until 2050 to achieve the teledensity that Germany and Singapore have today.

Beyond basic landline connections, the disparities are even more stark. In mid-1998 industrial countries—home to less than 15% of people—had 88% of Internet users. North America alone—with less than 5% of all people—had more than 50% of Internet users. By contrast, South Asia is home to over 20% of all people but had less than 1% of the world's Internet users (figure 2.4).

Thailand has more cellular phones than the whole of Africa. There are more Internet hosts in Bulgaria than in Sub-Saharan Africa (excluding South Africa). The United States has more computers than the rest of the world combined, and more computers per capita than any other country. Just 55 countries account for 99% of global spending on information technology. Most telephones in developing countries are in the capital city, although most people live in rural areas. Connections are often poor in the rainy season, and the costs of calls are very high. In several African countries average monthly Internet connection and use costs run as high as $100—compared with $10 in the United States.

Yet even if telecommunications systems are installed and accessible, without literacy and basic computer skills people will have little access to the network society. In 1995 adult literacy was less than 40% in 16 countries, and primary school enrolments less than 80% in 24 countries. In Benin, for example, more than 60% of the population is illiterate, so the possibilities of expanding access beyond today's 2,000 Internet users are heavily constrained. Even for the newest and most advanced technologies, the most basic and long-standing policy lies at the heart of the solution: investment in education.

WELCOME TO THE NETWORK HIGH SOCIETY

Within each region it is only the tip of each society that has stepped into the global loop—worldwide, just 2% of all people. What sets these people apart from the rest? Current access to the Internet runs along the fault lines of national societies, dividing educated from illiterate, men from women, rich from poor, young from old, urban from rural. National Internet surveys in 1998 and 1999 revealed that:

• *Income buys access.* The average South African user had an income seven times the national average, and 90% of users in Latin America came from upper-income groups. More than 30% of users in the United Kingdom had salaries above $60,000. Buying a computer would cost the average Bangladeshi more than eight years' income, compared with just one month's wage for the average American.

• *Education is a ticket to the network high society.* Globally, 30% of users have at least one university degree—in the United Kingdom it is 50%, in China almost 60%, in Mexico 67% and in Ireland almost 70%.

• *Men dominate.* Women accounted for 38% of users in the United States, 25% in Brazil, 17% in Japan and South Africa, 16% in Russia, only 7% in China and a mere 4% in the Arab States. The trend starts early: in the United States five times as many boys as girls use computers at home, and parents spend twice as much on technology products for their sons as they do for their daughters.

• *Youth dominate too.* The average age of users in the United States was 36; in China and the United Kingdom, under 30.

• *Ethnicity counts.* In the United States the difference in use by ethnic groups widened between 1995 and 1998. Disparity exists even among US university students. More than 80% attending elite private colleges used the Internet regularly, compared with just over 40% attending public institutions, where African-American students are more likely to enrol.

• *English talks.* English is used in almost 80% of Websites and in the common user interfaces—the graphics and instructions. Yet less than 1 in 10 people worldwide speaks the language.

Geographic barriers may have fallen for communications, but a new barrier has emerged, an invisible barrier that, true to its name, is like a world wide web, embracing the connected and silently—almost imperceptibly—excluding the rest. The typical Internet user worldwide is male, under 35 years old, with a college education and high income, urban-based and English-speaking—a member of a very elite minority worldwide. The consequence? The network society is creating parallel communications systems: one for those with income, education and—literally—connections, giving plentiful information at low cost and high speed; the other for those without connections, blocked by high barriers of time, cost and uncertainty and dependent on outdated information. With people in these two systems living and competing side by side, the advantages of connection are overpowering. The voices and concerns of people already living in human poverty—lacking incomes, education and access to public institutions—are being increasingly marginalized. Determined efforts are needed to bring developing countries—and poor people everywhere—into the global conversation.

MAKING GLOBAL COMMUNICATIONS TRULY GLOBAL

The past decade has proven the tremendous potential of global communications to provide information, enable empowerment and raise productivity. But it has also exposed the risks of dividing and polarizing societies, threatening greater marginalization of those left out and left behind.

What lies in between is proactive policy. The greatest danger is the complacent belief that a profitable and growing industry will solve the problem by itself. But the market alone will make global citizens only of those who can afford it. Fulfilling the potential of global communications for development demands relentless effort in reaching out to extend and enhance the loop. Seven goals on the road to an information society:

- *Connectivity*—setting up telecommunications and computer networks.
- *Community*—focusing on group access, not individual ownership.

- *Capacity*—building human skills for the knowledge society.
- *Content*—putting local views, news, culture and commerce on the Web.
- *Creativity*—adapting technology to local needs and constraints.
- *Collaboration*—devising Internet governance for diverse needs around the world.
- *Cash*—finding innovative ways to fund the knowledge society.

Connectivity. A telecommunications infrastructure is needed, but the infrastructure costs are immense, and many governments are turning to the private sector. Opening telecommunications and Internet provider services to the market can massively increase connectivity. But schemes are needed to ensure that the market does not focus only on lucrative urban customers. When Senegal privatized telephone services, operators were required under licence to install public telephones in 50% of the rural villages containing

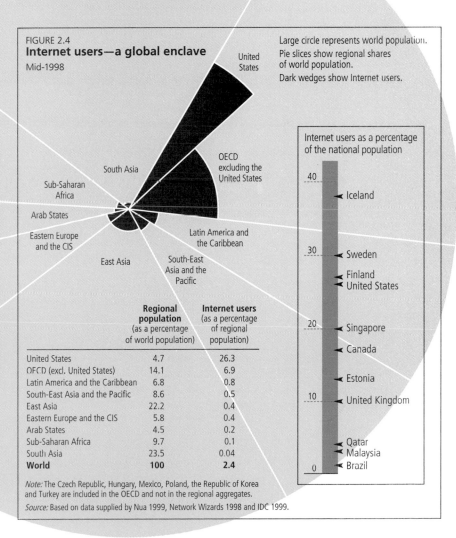

FIGURE 2.4
Internet users—a global enclave
Mid-1998

Large circle represents world population.
Pie slices show regional shares of world population.
Dark wedges show Internet users.

United States
OECD excluding the United States
South Asia
Sub-Saharan Africa
Arab States
Eastern Europe and the CIS
East Asia
South-East Asia and the Pacific
Latin America and the Caribbean

Internet users as a percentage of the national population

40 — Iceland
30 — Sweden
Finland
United States
20 — Singapore
Canada
Estonia
10 — United Kingdom
Qatar
Malaysia
0 — Brazil

	Regional population (as a percentage of world population)	Internet users (as a percentage of regional population)
United States	4.7	26.3
OECD (excl. United States)	14.1	6.9
Latin America and the Caribbean	6.8	0.8
South-East Asia and the Pacific	8.6	0.5
East Asia	22.2	0.4
Eastern Europe and the CIS	5.8	0.4
Arab States	4.5	0.2
Sub-Saharan Africa	9.7	0.1
South Asia	23.5	0.04
World	**100**	**2.4**

Note: The Czech Republic, Hungary, Mexico, Poland, the Republic of Korea and Turkey are included in the OECD and not in the regional aggregates.

Source: Based on data supplied by Nua 1999, Network Wizards 1998 and IDC 1999.

more than 3,000 people by 2000. In the Philippines new mobile phone operators—usually serving an elite market—are also required to install 400,000 landlines—serving poor communities—within five years. Computing hardware and software are needed to transform telephone lines into Internet connections, and policies are needed to promote this. To encourage computer ownership, the governments of Bangladesh and Mauritius, for example, eliminated tariffs and taxes on personal computers.

The satellite revolution promises greater connectivity, since every point on the globe can be reached instantly without a need for expensive land-based infrastructure. User costs are still very high, but with several major satellite networks due to be launched before 2001, com-petition could bring rapidly falling prices in the future.

Competition is hard to ensure in the telecommunications industry—especially for local calls, as even the most developed countries have seen. Strong regulation and antitrust laws, well implemented, are needed to ensure that private markets are competitive markets and that public needs are met. This will be a challenge for all countries.

Community access. To bring connectivity to people, community access is key, not individual ownership. The concept of one household, one phone is unrealistic in many developing countries, especially in rural areas and among poor communities everywhere. A

BOX 2.5

Innovating with the Internet

The Internet is an evolving tool and can be creatively used in many ways. Some countries are at the forefront of innovating to make this technology work for their needs.

Egypt—enriching telecentres
At the end of 1998 there was less than one Internet user for every 1,600 people in Egypt. Connections are increasing daily, but mainly among the wealthy and well educated in urban areas. To reach out to people in poor and remote areas, UNDP has launched three pilot Technology Access Community Centres (TACCs) in the governorate of Sharkeya.

Each TACC telecentre, equipped with Internet connection and many computers, is located in a public building or a local chamber of commerce to ensure that it is accessible to all—individuals, civil society groups, small businesses, low-income communities. But the centres provide far more than walk-in access. They offer training in computer literacy, email and Web searches, Webpage creation, desktop publishing, computer maintenance and technical support. These skills can be used for distance learning, telemedicine, networking and electronic commerce. Future plans include integrating women's health centres into the TACCs. Internet access is initially free to encourage people to explore the potential. Later, low fees will be supplemented by charges on other services: fax, photocopies and training programmes. This is the way forward for telecentres.

Estonia—raising the roof
Estonia, among the first of Eastern Europe's transition economies expected to enter the European Union, is wasting no time catching up. Along with economic reform, the country has made great efforts to promote access to the Internet for its 1.4 million citizens. Small countries, often disadvantaged by their size in other areas, can be among the first to create an information society. As President Lennart Meri of Estonia has said, "The Internet is the roof of the world for a small nation."

Public Internet access points are provided throughout the country, even on remote islands in the Baltic Sea. In schools the Tiger Leap Programme, launched in 1996, provides information-based learning systems for all pupils, rapidly modernizing education and creating strong conditions for an open learning environment. Its scope has widened, aiming to create an open and democratic society by providing access to modern communications for all, not just school pupils, city dwellers and the well-off. With few natural resources, Estonia has realized that its wealth is its people and is investing in them for the 21st century.

The country has indeed tiger-leaped ahead of other transition economies in integrating into the information society. More than one in 10 Estonians are now on-line—using the Internet—and Estonia ranks among the top 15 countries in Europe in computers per capita, ahead of France and Italy. Surveys of users show that they use the World Wide Web mainly to find information for work, for school and for leisure—spending little time playing games or watching videos. Clearly, in Estonia the Internet is becoming a learning tool, not an entertainment centre.

India—reaching the villages
Some of the remotest villages in the world have modern communication. Ironically, it usually brings only satellite television full of images of distant lives, irrelevant to local issues.

The M.S. Swaminathan Research Foundation in South India is trying to change this—to tackle local problems. The Village Information Project in Pondicherry began with an in-depth study of village needs—and only when this was complete did it turn to technology. Reconditioned second-hand computers were donated by Byte by Byte, a Tokyo-based organization that collects discarded equipment from companies such as Reuters and Ford Motors and sends them off for second lives around the world.

Even in villages without telephones, the Village Information Project brings people the knowledge they need. Free-standing, solar-powered computers are updated daily with information relayed through radio handsets and cell phones from a regional centre with direct Internet access. The village computer acts as a bulletin board for the availability of medicine in health centres and credit in microfinance schemes, for market prices, transport services and input costs, for warnings of pest, weather and water risks and for educational materials for schoolchildren.

Source: M.S. Swaminathan Research Foundation 1998; Mehta 1999; UNDP 1998b; BMF Gallup Media 1999.

more appropriate approach is to create multi-media community centres—or "telecentres"—in places accessible to those often blocked out of institutions: poor people and communities, women and youth. From Peru to Kazakhstan, basic telecentres have been set up in post offices, community centres, libraries, video shops, police stations and health clinics, providing local community access to telephone and fax services, email and the World Wide Web. But providing access takes more than providing computers. Telecentres need to become hubs for skills training and capacity building. Egypt is leading the way in this approach (box 2.5).

Capacity. Building people's capacity to use the Internet starts in schools. The Costa Rican government has installed computers in rural schools across the country to give all pupils a chance to learn the new skills. In Hungary the ambitious Sulinet (Schoolnet) has enabled students in more than two-thirds of secondary schools to browse the Net from their classrooms. The annual NetDay initiative in the United States has used volunteers to connect more than 140,000 schools at a fraction of the commercial cost. Beyond classroom connections, support staff are essential for on-line learning, and teachers need training. In Finland teachers receive more than a month of training in how to use information technology in the classroom. In Lesotho the Technical Enhanced Learning Institutes in Southern Africa (TELISA) were launched in 1998 to renew regional education with professional development for teachers.

Content. The information highway cannot be a one-way street. Websites need to be created locally, adding new voices to the global conversation and making content relevant to communities. The first step is language and culture. The government of Tamil Nadu, India, is promoting keyboard standardization, software interfaces and Websites in Tamil, spoken by 75 million people worldwide. In Estonia the highly effective Tiger Leap Programme is developing educational software to teach the Estonian language and the history of the country (see box 2.5). The Vietnamese community

in California's Silicon Valley uses email to keep culture strong for the worldwide diaspora. As one user said of the discussion group, "Vietnet brought everybody closer. Many ideas, feelings, poems and opinions were exchanged. . . . Many people from faraway states and different continents came to visit."

Local content can enhance community participation and institutional transparency. In India the state government of Andhra Pradesh is setting up a network to connect telecentre access points with government services and offices. The Infoville Project in Villena, Spain, has created a "virtual" town hall by subsidizing access to a community intranet with local information, government services, banking, retail, schools and health services on-line.

Creativity. The context for communications varies greatly around the world, yet solutions have focused on industrial countries. Creativity is needed to adapt the possibilities of technology to the needs of poor countries and poor people. In rural Bolivia most farmers have never seen a computer, but they already have access to the Internet. How? Farmers with crop concerns can give questions to a community leader, who relays the inquiry to the radio station, where it is sent to UNDP's communications centre. The question is then posted on the Internet and answers received are emailed back to the radio station and broadcast. In South India, too, creativity has tailored computer technology to local community needs (see box 2.5).

Collaboration. The Internet has rapidly become not only a global communications tool but a great source of economic potential. Its evolution, at first ad hoc, is being shaped into a system of governance—with rules on domain names, taxation, privacy and protection of intellectual property rights. But governance should not be framed by the United States, the European Union or the OECD alone. Commercial interests may be at stake—but so is the right of access to communications for all people. Internet and telecommunications need global governance framed by global interests.

To bring connectivity to people, community access is key, not individual ownership

BOX 2.6

Preparing for the information age—set the wheels in motion

The importance of building an information society is clear. The question for governments faced with scarce resources is not whether to invest—but how much and where. What are the areas that strengthen a nation's capacity to make the most of information and communications technology? The Information Society Index, prepared by the World Times and the International Data Corporation, gives one way of measuring a country's preparedness, across four types of infrastructure:

• *Information*—creating the capacity to send and receive information by telephone, television, radio and fax.
• *Computer*—extending access to computers in schools, workplaces and homes, building networks and using software.
• *Internet*—expanding the use of the Internet in schools, workplaces and homes and enabling electronic commerce.
• *Social*—building people's capacity to use information through education, freedom of the press and civil liberty.

For each indicator, the closer a country is to the outside of the wheel, the closer it is to the best performance yet achieved. A complete wheel would mean the smoothest ride in the information age.

The index has been calculated for the 55 countries, which account for 99% of global information technology spending. This puts the focus on indicators most relevant to industrial countries. An interesting future challenge would be to adapt the index to include indicators more relevant to progress in developing countries. Even in this group of 55 there is great disparity, shown in the range of wheels below.

The United States is the most prepared information economy, but small countries can be early adopters and leaders of the information revolution. Finland, the Netherlands and Singapore have all surpassed many of the traditional industrial economies in coverage and preparedness. The wheels show that there are many dimensions to being prepared for the information age, and each country must tackle its weaknesses.

Circle shows best country's achievement

INTERNET	COMPUTERS	INFORMATION	SOCIAL
1 Business Internet use	5 Personal computers for education use	11 Fax ownership	19 Newspaper readership
2 Education Internet use	6 PCs for government and commercial use	12 Radio ownership	20 Tertiary enrolment
3 Home Internet use	7 PCs for home use	13 Cable TV subscription	21 Secondary enrolment
4 E-commerce spending	8 PCs installed	14 TV ownership	
	9 Networked PCs	15 Cost of phone call	
	10 Software spending	16 Cellular phone ownership	
		17 Telephone line error rate	
		18 Telephone lines installed	

Source: World Times and IDC 1999.

Cash. There is an urgent need to find the resources to fund the global communications revolution—to ensure that it is truly global. One proposal is a "bit tax"—a very small tax on the amount of data sent through the Internet. The costs for users would be negligible: sending 100 emails a day, each containing a 10-kilobyte document (a very long one), would raise a tax of just 1 cent. Yet with email booming worldwide, the total would be substantial. In Belgium in 1998, such a tax would have yielded $10 billion. Globally in 1996, it would have yielded $70 billion—more than total official development assistance that year.

How quickly are different countries preparing for global communications? Many factors are involved, and the race to join the information society has set off at a fast pace. It will determine many of the winners and losers in the globalized world (box 2.6).

THE NEW RULES OF GLOBALIZATION— SHAPING THE PATH OF TECHNOLOGY

New technologies promise many advances for human development. Gene therapy could tackle diseases such as cystic fibrosis and cancer. Genetically altered crops could reduce the need to use polluting herbicides and pesticides. The information and communications industry could provide entry points for developing countries into producing for the knowledge-intensive economy. Yet the path of technology is not predetermined—many avenues of research could be pursued, but only a few are followed.

Technology may be globalizing communications, but globalization—and its new rules—is also shaping the path of new technologies. Over the past 20 years increasing privatization of research and development, ever-growing liberalization of markets and the tightening of intellectual property rights have set off a race to lay claim to knowledge, and this has changed technology's path. The risk is that poor people's and poor countries' interests are being left on the sidelines.

PRIVATIZATION OF RESEARCH

The knowledge sector is a fast-growing area of the global economy: between 1980 and 1994 the share of high-technology products in international trade doubled, from 12% to 24%. Yet in the 1990s, with many governments facing a squeeze on budgets, the proportion of public funding for research and development in science and technology has fallen around the world, to be replaced by private industry. Research and development has also shifted away from developing countries. Their share in the global total dropped from 6% in the mid-1980s to 4% in the mid-1990s.

The trend has been particularly strong in agriculture and biotechnology. In the early 1980s most crop and seed development in the United States was under public research. Patents were rarely sought and rarely enforced; saving and trading of seed was commonplace. This changed when new legislation encouraged closer cooperation with the private sector, enabling companies to profit from products developed largely with public funds. The intellectual property of public and university research was increasingly passed over to private industry: the portion of public sector patents in biotechnology sold under exclusive licence to the private sector rose from just 6% in 1981 to more than 40% by 1990.

With increasing privatization of research and rising costs for risky innovations, the 1990s have seen a boom in the number and value of mergers and acquisitions. The biggest year ever was 1998, especially for biotechnology, telecommunications and computing industries (figure 2.5). As a result economic power has consolidated among a very few players. By 1995 the world's top 20 information and communications corporations had combined revenue of more than $1 trillion—equivalent to the GDP of the United Kingdom.

In biotechnology genetic engineering underlies the new direction of pharmaceuticals, food, chemicals, cosmetics, energy and seeds. This is blurring the boundaries between the sectors, creating mega "life sciences" corporations. Indeed, across all knowledge-intensive industries, a select group of corporations controls ever-growing shares of the global market. In 1998, how much of the global market did the top 10 corporations in each industry control? In commercial seed, 32% of a $23 billion industry; in pharmaceuticals, 35% of

$297 billion; in veterinary medicine, 60% of $17 billion; in computers, almost 70% of $334 billion; in pesticides, 85% of $31 billion; and in telecommunications, more than 86% of $262 billion. The lesson is clear: privatization does not automatically lead to competition.

TIGHTER INTELLECTUAL PROPERTY RIGHTS

At the creation of the World Trade Organization in 1994, the most far-reaching multilateral agreement on intellectual property was drawn up: Trade-Related Aspects of Intellectual Property Rights, or TRIPS (box 2.7).

The past two decades have seen a huge rise in patent claims. The World Intellectual Property Organization's Patent Cooperation Treaty accepts a single international application valid in many countries. The number of applications made annually soared from less than 3,000 in 1979 to more than 54,000 in 1997—and those applications in 1997 were equivalent to nearly 3.5 million individual national applications (figure 2.6). According to the director of research and development at one of the largest biotechnology corporations, "the most important publications for our researchers are not chemistry journals but patent office journals around the world."

Yet the claims to intellectual property are concentrated among very few countries.

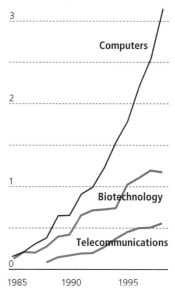

FIGURE 2.5
Worldwide mergers and acquisitions
Deals annually (thousands)

Total value of mergers and acquisitions
US$ billions

Sector	1988	1998
Computers	21.4	246.7
Biotechnology	9.3	172.4
Telecommunications	6.8	265.8

Source: Securities Data Company 1999.

BOX 2.7

What is TRIPS?

Intellectual property issues were first raised under the General Agreement on Tariffs and Trade in 1986 to clamp down on trade in counterfeit goods. With many industrial countries interested in tying negotiations on trade liberalization to tighter control over technology, this narrow focus was soon extended to include many other areas. The agreement on Trade-Related Aspects of Intellectual Property Rights, or TRIPS, came into effect in 1995 under the World Trade Organization (WTO). It affects such diverse areas as computer programming and circuit design, pharmaceuticals and transgenic crops.

Although each country implements intellectual property rights law at the national level, the TRIPS agreement

imposes minimum standards on patents, copyright, trademarks and trade secrets. These standards are derived from the legislation of industrial countries, applying the form and level of protection of the industrial world to all WTO members. This is far tighter than existing legislation in most developing countries and often conflicts with their national interests and needs. Developing countries have been given until 2000 to adjust their laws, least developed countries until 2005.

The WTO's TRIPS agreement can be enforced through the integrated dispute settlement system. This effectively means that if a country does not fulfil its intellectual property rights obligations, trade sanctions can be applied against it—a serious threat.

Source: South Centre 1997.

FIGURE 2.6
The race for patents
Annual applications under World Intellectual Property Organization's Patent Cooperation Treaty (thousands)

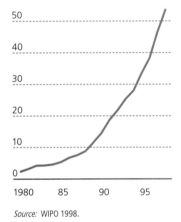

Source: WIPO 1998.

Industrial countries hold 97% of all patents worldwide. In 1995 more than half of global royalties and licensing fees were paid to the United States, mostly from Japan, the United Kingdom, France, Germany and the Netherlands. Indeed, in 1993 just 10 countries accounted for 84% of global research and development, controlled 95% of the US patents of the past two decades and captured more than 90% of cross-border royalties and licensing fees—and 70% of global royalty and licensing fee payments were between parent and affiliate in multinational corporations. By contrast, the use of intellectual property rights is alien to many developing countries. More than 80% of the patents that have been granted in developing countries belong to residents of industrial countries.

IMPACTS ON PEOPLE

These new rules of globalization—privatization, liberalization and tighter intellectual property rights—are shaping the path of technology, creating new risks of marginalization and vulnerability:

• In defining research agendas, money talks louder than need—cosmetic drugs and slow-ripening tomatoes come higher on the list than a vaccine against malaria or drought-resistant crops for marginal lands. Tighter control of innovation in the hands of multinational corporations ignores the needs of millions. From new drugs to better seeds for food crops, the best of the new technologies are designed and priced for those who can pay. For poor people, the technological progress remains far out of reach.

• Tighter intellectual property rights raise the price of technology transfer, and risk blocking developing countries out of the dynamic knowledge sector in areas such as computer software and generic drugs.

• New patent laws pay scant attention to the knowledge of indigenous people, leaving it vulnerable to claim by others. These laws ignore cultural diversity in creating and sharing innovations—and diversity in views on what can and should be owned, from plant varieties to human life. The result is a silent theft of centuries of knowledge from developing to developed countries.

• Despite the risks of genetic engineering, the rush and push of commercial interests are putting profits before people.

PRIVATE RESEARCH AGENDAS—MONEY TALKS LOUDER THAN NEED

Genetic engineering is largely the product of private commercial research in industrial countries. The top five biotechnology firms, based in the United States and Europe, control more than 95% of gene transfer patents. It can take 10 years and $300 million to create a new commercial product—so, not surprisingly, companies want to protect their innovations and ensure that they reap profits. But this approach focuses research on high-income markets. In 1998, of the 27 million hectares of land under transgenic—genetically altered—crops, more than 95% was in North America and Europe. Research has focused on the wants of rich farmers and consumers: tomatoes with longer shelf lives or herbicide-resistant soyabeans and yellow maize to be used mainly for poultry feed. Seed varieties are engineered to be suitable for mechanized mass production with labour-saving techniques, designed for industrial and intensive farming conditions.

Far less time and money have been given to the needs of farmers in developing countries: increasing nutritional value, disease resistance and robustness. Similarly, research is lacking on water-saving plant varieties for smallholders. Instead, many major corporations are seeking patents for the innovation of linking genetic characteristics to chemical triggers. What for? One likely use is to create seeds that will germinate and bear fruit only when used with the company's brand of fertilizers or herbicides—increasing sales through dependency on inputs. With agrochemical, plant breeding and seed distribution companies merging into megacorporations, farming communities risk becoming caught in a chain of biological and licensing controls.

Local plant breeding is essential for adapting seeds to the ecosystem and maintaining biodiversity. The 1.4 billion rural people relying on farm-saved seed could see their interests marginalized. With increasing control and homogenization of the market by major agribusinesses, the competitiveness of alternative varieties and the scope for producing alternative crops will most likely decline, depleting local genetic diversity.

In the pharmaceutical industry private interests cannot be expected to meet all public needs. Almost all research on diseases in developing countries has been done by international organizations or the military in industrial countries. Of the annual health-related research and development worldwide, only 0.2% goes for pneumonia, diarrhoeal diseases and tuberculosis—yet these account for 18% of the global disease burden. In the United States between 1981 and 1991, less than 5% of drugs introduced by the top 25 companies were therapeutic advances. Some 70% of drugs with therapeutic gain were produced with government involvement. Vaccines are the most cost-effective technologies known in health care, preventing illness in a one-time dose. But they generate smaller profits and have higher potential liabilities than treatments used repeatedly. As a result a consortium of US pharmaceutical companies has united to develop antiviral agents against HIV, but not to produce a vaccine against AIDS.

TIGHTER INTELLECTUAL PROPERTY RIGHTS ARE BLOCKING DEVELOPING COUNTRIES FROM THE KNOWLEDGE SECTOR

The costs of industrial catch-up for Japan and the first-tier newly industrializing economies in East Asia were greatly reduced by the weak enforcement of intellectual property rights in the region before the mid-1980s. Tighter control under the TRIPS agreement has closed off old opportunities and increased the costs of access to new technologies.

In the pharmaceutical industry, prior to the TRIPS agreement, countries such as China, Egypt and India allowed patents on pharmaceutical processes but not final products. This approach supported the development of domestic industries using different methods to produce mainly generic drugs, similar to but far cheaper than the original brand names. The difference is highlighted by contrasting drug prices in Pakistan, where there are patents, to India, where there are none (figure 2.7).

When Glaxo Wellcome launched AZT as an inhibitor of AIDS, it cost $10,000 per patient each year. As sales increased, the price fell to $3,000—still far out of reach for most people in developing countries. An Indian company then produced a generic—Zidovir 100—and exported it to Belgium, Tanzania and Uganda at less than half the price. The TRIPS agreement requires 20-year patents on both processes and products, so India and others must change national patent laws, making such opportunities impossible in the future. As gene therapy comes to dominate the pharmaceutical industry, this will significantly limit the industry's potential in developing countries.

Countries can choose to require patent holders to give licences to competitors—but the process is long and the fees may be prohibitive. Imposing price controls on industry, calculated as a mark-up on costs, is another option, but multinationals often avoid low prices by using loopholes in transfer pricing—artificially inflating the cost of inputs transferred from country to country within the multinational's domain. In India multinational companies have sometimes charged 2, 4 or even 10 times the prices they would charge for inputs in Europe and the United States in order to avoid controlled low prices. They have little interest in pricing drugs for the market in developing countries because they are maximizing global, not national, profits and do not want to set a low-price precedent.

In the computer industry, software is one of the fastest-growing areas and can be a way for new countries to get into producing for the knowledge sector. In 1994 the global market for final, packaged software was $79 billion, of which OECD countries accounted for 94%. With a small but growing number of developing countries entering the competition, it is not surprising that the battle over intellectual property rights for software is a fierce one. Protection is certainly needed: programmes are expensive to develop, while pirating them is cheap and easy. Even before Microsoft launched Windows 95 at $100, it was on sale on the streets of Beijing for $9. Many firms have lost billions of dollars of trade in this way. At the same time excessively tight intellectual property rights would eliminate competition and innovation in this industry

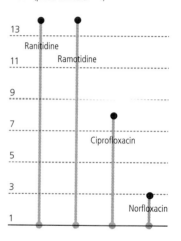

FIGURE 2.7
Drug prices and patent costs

Price in Pakistan
Index (price in India = 1)

Source: Lanjouw 1997.

underlying global communications. A careful balance needs to be struck.

The TRIPS agreement followed the United States in placing software, like music and novels, under copyright law, with strong and universal protection. The United States has started to grant patents on software in addition to copyright, creating stronger control over programme interfaces and tightening control over the industry. But there is leeway. The TRIPS agreement does not prohibit making copies for reverse engineering—a process of unravelling computer programmes to see how they work, generating ideas and innovation. With programmes such as Word and Excel becoming computing standards, reverse engineering is essential for smaller producers to create software that is compatible and competitive, and it must be protected in future reviews of the agreement. If it were forbidden, the development of competitive products would be drastically limited. And different computers around the world would not be able to interact with one another—defeating the aim of connecting the network society.

PATENT LAWS DO NOT RECOGNIZE TRADITIONAL KNOWLEDGE AND SYSTEMS OF OWNERSHIP

Biodiversity is of great importance to drug development, and developing countries are the source of an estimated 90% of the world's store of biological resources. More than half of the world's most frequently prescribed drugs are derived from plants or synthetic copies of plant chemicals—and this trend is growing. Plant-based drugs are part of standard medical treatment for heart conditions, childhood leukaemia, lymphatic cancer and glaucoma, with a global value over the counter of more than $40 billion a year.

In the same way that many Arab states benefited from industrialization's thirst for the petroleum that lay beneath their land, so now biorich countries could have the chance to benefit from biotechnology's demand for the rare germ plasm found on their land. Many indigenous communities have a further claim to biotechnology's bounty because they have been the cultivators, researchers and protectors of their plants—indeed, it is their long-acquired knowledge of nature's potential that is valuable to pharmaceutical companies today. Bioprospectors have for many years taken samples of plant material and documented their traditional medicinal uses. Without the consent of local people, this knowledge has been used to develop highly profitable drugs. In any other situation this would be called industrial espionage—theft of both the genetic materials and the long-acquired knowledge of using them to develop medicines.

The rosy periwinkle found in Madagascar, for example, contains anticancer properties, and drugs developed from it give $100 million in annual sales to a US-based multinational pharmaceutical company, Eli Lilly—but virtually nothing for Madagascar.

Plant material was once treated as common property, but a landmark US legal case in 1980 awarded a patent on a genetically altered organism, launching the first step in the race to patent life. Yet patent laws were drawn up in 19th-century Europe during the industrial revolution; their legal frameworks have been extended to cover global markets during the information revolution. Three fundamental concerns:

• The inventions born of genetic engineering bring radically new characteristics. Can a framework of property rights first designed to protect industrial machinery really cope fairly and effectively with the complexities of genetically manipulated organisms?

• Scientific research now takes place under a regime based on ownership and control. It rewards research according to short-term profitability, not according to the needs to protect biodiversity, ensure sustainable and ethical use of genetic resources or meet the essential needs of people.

• The attempt to create a global market in property rights imposes one conception of ownership and innovation on a culturally diverse reality, benefiting private industrial research but not public institutes or farming communities (table 2.1).

In 1995 two researchers at the University of Mississippi Medical Center were granted the US patent for using turmeric to heal wounds. But in India this was a long-standing art, common knowledge and practice for thousands of

Developing countries are the source of an estimated 90% of the world's store of biological resources

years. To get the patent repealed, the claim had to be backed by written evidence—an ancient Sanskrit text was eventually presented as proof and the patent removed—but this only highlighted the absurd imposition of one culture's systems on another culture's traditions.

As a result of these problems, there has been increasing recognition of the need to protect the knowledge of indigenous people. The Convention on Biological Diversity of 1992 recognizes the need to protect property rights but also the need for companies to gain prior informed consent before conducting research—but this convention is not legally binding until countries translate it into national law, and indigenous communities have often received little attention or protection under national law.

In the absence of legislation, more and more strategic alliances are being struck between pharmaceutical firms and governments or indigenous groups in resource-rich countries. Merck Pharmaceuticals has an agreement with the non-profit National Institute of Biodiversity, INBio, in Costa Rica to pay $1.1 million for access to 10,000 plant and insect samples. If any leads to a successful drug, Costa Rica would receive a 2–3% royalty share, yielding a possible $20–30 million each year.

From Australia and Ecuador to Thailand and Uganda, bioprospectors have made agreements with local communities, taking out patents based on local knowledge in exchange for a share of profits. Royalties promised are commonly 1–2%, though sometimes as low as 0.1% and as high as 3–4%. Even if just a 2% royalty were charged on genetic resources that had been developed by local innovators in the South, it is estimated that the North would owe more than $300 million in unpaid royalties for farmers' crop seeds and more than $5 billion in unpaid royalties for medicinal plants. But this rate is low because negotiations are on an uneven footing. When one company wanted to bioprospect in Yellowstone National Park, the United States Park Service secured a 10% royalty share. Negotiating power is everything.

THE RUSH AND PUSH OF COMMERCIAL INTERESTS PROTECT PROFITS, NOT PEOPLE— DESPITE THE RISKS IN THE NEW TECHNOLOGIES

Genetically modified foods come from plants to which extra genes have been introduced to add qualities such as resistance to pests or frost. The genes are taken from other plants, animals or micro-organisms and are often introduced by attaching them to a virus. There are several risks in this process. Genes introduced to make plants tolerant to herbicides and insecticides could escape in pollen and create highly resilient weeds that displace other wild plants and change the balance of the ecosystem. Similarly, over time powerful new strains of insects

More strategic alliances are being struck between pharmaceutical firms and the governments or indigenous groups in resource-rich countries

TABLE 2.1
Who has real access to intellectual property claims?

Issue	Multinational corporations	Public research institutes	Farming communities
Under intellectual property law the inventor must be named.	Employee contracts ensure that inventors surrender most or all rights to the company.	Employee contracts can ensure that inventors surrender most or all rights to the institute.	The concept of an individual inventor is alien to many communities and can cause conflict.
The criteria for patents include novelty and an inventive step.	Companies' focus on micro-improvements usually manages to meet the criteria.	Focused more on research, institutes often cannot meet the strict criteria.	Since these criteria have little to do with the process of community invention, they are hard to meet.
Legal advice from highly specialized patent lawyers is expensive.	Companies have in-house legal departments and ready access to expert consultants.	Institutes have little in-house capacity and limited access to expensive expertise.	Communities usually cannot afford or obtain either basic or expert advice.
Patent holders must defend their patents under civil law.	Companies employ aggressive tactics, using patent claims to stake out their market turf.	Institutes often lack strong patent defence and give in to political pressure not to challenge the private sector.	Communities find it almost impossible to monitor—let alone confront—patent infringements around the world.

Source: RAFI 1998.

and weeds resistant to herbicides and insecticides could develop. New toxins could have damaging effects in the food chain, and viruses could escape from virus-containing crops. The impacts could be particularly serious in developing countries where biodiversity is high and essential for sustainable agriculture. Yet it can take 10–15 years before environmental damage becomes evident. Despite the promised commercial gains, many developing countries are extremely concerned about the potential impact (box 2.8).

The growing use of transgenic crops raises important issues—about the safety of transferring organisms into new environments, questions of liability for damage that are not covered under international law and the need for far more transparency in information. Responses to these issues have varied dramatically.

The United States, exporting $50 billion of agricultural products a year and planting transgenic varieties for 25–45% of its major crops, claims that strict safety rules will impede billions of dollars of global exports annually in seed, grains and even products like breakfast cereals and cotton clothing. But consumer movements and farmers have often reacted strongly to transgenic crops, pulling them out of fields and rejecting them in shops. Ten years ago the risk of humans being infected by bovine spongiform encephalopathy (BSE, or mad cow disease) was said to be negligible—but it happened. Once

bitten, twice shy, European consumers especially are now questioning altered foods. Science is moving so fast and so little information has been shared, it is not surprising that people fear that technology is out of control.

With new technologies, profits should not come first—but nor should panic. Precaution is needed, and this was the motivation for the Biosafety Protocol under the Convention on Biological Diversity. The protocol would require exports of genetically manipulated organisms to be approved in advance by the importing country. The negotiations collapsed in February 1999 after the main exporting countries—the United States, Canada, Australia, Argentina, Uruguay and Chile—fell into open disagreement with the European Union and many developing countries. Biosafety is still critical—all the more so as transgenic crops become more widespread.

THE NEED TO RESHAPE TECHNOLOGY'S PATH

Policies are urgently needed to turn the advances in the new technologies into advances for all of humankind—and to prevent the rules of globalization from blocking poor people and poor countries out of the knowledge economy.

THE NEED TO BROADEN GOVERNANCE

Intellectual property rights were first raised in GATT in 1986 to crack down on counterfeit goods. Their reach has gone far beyond that into the ownership of life itself. As trade and intellectual property law increasingly come to determine the path of nations—and the path of technology—questioning present arrangements is not just about economic flows. It is about preserving biodiversity, carefully considering the ethics of patents on life, ensuring access to health care, respecting other cultures' forms of ownership and preventing a widening of the technological gap between the knowledge-driven global economy and the rest trapped in its shadows.

At a time of such dramatic breakthroughs in new technologies, it is indefensible that human poverty should persist as it does. What is more startling is that the current path could be leading to greater marginalization and vulnerability

Policies are urgently needed to turn the advances in the new technologies into advances for all of humankind

---

BOX 2.8

Ethics and technology—a luxury concern?

The ability to manipulate genetic resources is running far ahead of the understanding of where to place the ethical limits. Sheep, mice and human cells have already been cloned—all considered impossible only 10 years ago. The new technologies have sparked many debates about the limits of science and the ethics of tampering with the essence of life.

Some argue that ethical questions are a luxury for the wealthy and should not hinder technological change in the developing world, especially when the race is on to establish a competitive edge. But this is surely wrong. The pursuit of human development is the first priority, and all concerns—social, financial, ethical, environmental—need to be

taken into account. This is especially true of the new technologies whose social and environmental implications are still unknown. To ask who gains and who loses, and what are the benefits and what are the costs, is precisely to ask the ethical questions.

Far from being able to ignore these issues, developing countries often find themselves at the centre. They are home to much of the world's biodiversity. And neglecting the ethical issues surrounding genetic engineering will lead to their continued neglect in economic forums. For developing countries the ethics of technology are far from a luxury—they are a basic.

Source: Shiva 1997.

of poor people. The relentless march of intellectual property rights needs to be stopped and questioned. Developments in the new technologies are running far ahead of the ethical, legal, regulatory and policy frameworks needed to govern their use. More understanding is needed—in every country—of the economic and social consequences of the TRIPS agreement. Many people have started to question the relationship between knowledge ownership and innovation. Alternative approaches to innovation, based on sharing, open access and communal innovation, are flourishing, disproving the claim that innovation necessarily requires patents (box 2.9).

Broader governance is also needed in the communications industry. Governance of the Internet has until recently been ad hoc and largely biased towards the needs of high-tech countries. Debates over taxing electronic commerce, allocating domain names and creating privacy laws need to be opened up to include the needs and concerns of developing countries, which have an equal interest in the evolution of this tremendous tool.

Participation in the governance of technology must also be widened. Race car drivers would not be the best advisers on public transport, and scientists at the cutting edge of the technological revolution cannot alone decide its path. This calls for collaboration—in national and global forums—between industry, independent scientists and technicians, governments, regulators, civil society organizations and the mass media.

PUBLIC INVESTMENT IN TECHNOLOGIES FOR DEVELOPMENT

The path of technology must be reshaped if developing countries are to see an advance in sustainable agriculture, wide access to global communications and improvements in the health of their populations. The new structure of science requires new initiatives. New technologies promise many advances for human

At a time of such dramatic breakthroughs in new technologies, it is indefensible that human poverty should persist

---

BOX 2.9

Questioning the ownership of knowledge

Innovation is one of the most important processes for human development. It pushes human capability forward and keeps cultures thriving. It is also at the heart of the human quest to expand knowledge. But are patents always the best way to promote innovation in new technologies? There are good reasons to question this common claim.

Experts question current trends
Some scientists are appalled by the scramble for patents for commercial gain, believing that it damages research openness about discoveries that should be shared for the common good. With the "stacking"—tactical purchase—of patents by corporations, the terrain of medical and agricultural research is quickly being carved up and fenced off. Ideas are no longer shared across the boundaries of different research groups.

History tells another story
Many of today's developed countries—ironically now the strongest advocates of tighter intellectual property rights—themselves had loose rules when they were setting up their national industries, changing their tune only after they became technology exporters.

Canada and Italy had no trouble attracting foreign investors even when they lacked patent protection. In Switzerland in 1883, a leading textile manufacturer defended loose laws, saying "Swiss industrial development was fostered by the absence of patent protection. If [it] had been in effect, neither the textile industry nor the machine-building industry . . . would have flourished as they did."

Empirical evidence shows no clear link
Despite the fierce defence of the need for intellectual property rights in new technologies, there is no conclusive evidence to back it up. Do tighter intellectual property rights increase trade in knowledge-intensive goods? Unclear. A 1999 World Bank study examining the experience of more than 80 countries found that the effect of intellectual property rights on trade flows in high-tech goods was insignificant. Do tighter intellectual property rights increase foreign direct investment in high-tech goods? Studies say yes for pharmaceuticals—along with higher prices—but for other knowledge goods foreign direct investment usually depends on market size, technological infrastructure and macroeconomic policy. Do tighter intellectual property

rights spur multinational corporations to carry out in-country research and development? Apparently not: studies have found that competitive markets are the biggest influence on research and development, not patents. All this evidence is inconclusive—but while the jury is still out, how can the judge decide?

There is living proof of successful alternatives
Alternative ways of innovating are alive—and doing very well. The Internet is testament to the power of cooperative, decentralized approaches to solving problems. Rejecting the tight control over software given by copyright, a reverse movement has been launched "copyleft", turning standard practice on its head. Rather than guarding the source codes to programmes, software developers allow users to view, modify and innovate with them—as long as they keep the new codes open too. The result? Arguably the best software around. Apache, a Web server developed communally by programmers in their spare time, is one of the most reliable and up-to-date products available—and is installed on 50% of publicly accessible Web servers. Its no-secrets policy makes it an ideal tool for teaching and experimenting in programming.

Source: Gerster 1998; Fink and Braga 1999; Leonard 1997; GRAIN 1998; UNCTAD 1997.

---

development, but public institutions cannot afford them alone and private industry will not develop them alone. Jointly they can. Innovative policy is needed to ensure that much-needed solutions for human development are pursued. Incentives are needed to turn research towards the pressing needs of the world, not just of those who pay. One proposal is for the Consultative Group on International Agricultural Research (CGIAR) to reroute genetic research to wider needs (box 2.10).

A representative group of independent scientists is needed to identify the critically important technological challenges—those that, if solved, would substantially improve the human development of the world's poorest people and address the global challenges to human security faced by all. Every five years the group could offer financial incentives and public recognition to researchers, public and private alike, for innovations that would be used for global public interests. What would be high on the list? In agriculture, sustainable, robust and biosafe crops. In medical research, vaccines for malaria and HIV. In communications technology, personal computers powered by solar strips and wind-up or dynamo drives, resistant to sand and humidity; software for touch screens; and prepaid chip card software for electronic commerce without credit cards. In environmental science, diverse sources of renewable energy. What would fund such initiatives? A levy on patents registered under the World Intellectual Property Organization is one possibility. A levy

Incentives are needed to turn research towards the pressing needs of the world, not just of those who pay

of just $100 on each patent would have raised $350 million in 1998 alone, equivalent to the annual budget of the world's largest international research organization in agriculture, the CGIAR. Alternatively, funding could be reallocated from the research subsidies, grants and tax breaks now given to industry.

PUSHING FOR CHANGE IN MULTILATERAL AGREEMENTS

The WTO is planning a review of the TRIPS agreement. But these discussions must not simply push into new issues. Intellectual property rights agreements were signed before most governments and people understood the social and economic implications of patents on life. They were also negotiated with far too little participation from many developing countries now feeling the impact of their conditions. There is a clear need for a full and broad review of existing legislation, not an additional, unsustainable burden of new conditions.

The choice is not between patents on everything or on nothing. Rather, the question is, how much should be patentable? How can the system be structured to take into account diverse interests and diverse needs?

The review needs to ensure that the room for manoeuvre granted in the TRIPS agreement is respected in practice. Interpretation of the agreement is obviously not a unilateral matter, and proposals by developing countries have often been rejected by G-7 countries keen to maintain their industrial interests. In the event of disagreement, dispute resolution mechanisms involve intense negotiating among lawyers—expensive and complex. The advantage in costs and expertise clearly does not lie with developing countries.

To strengthen their bargaining positions in pushing for change, countries need to present frameworks that provide alternatives to the provisions of the TRIPS agreement. Work is already well under way. Many countries are exploring possible sui generis legislation for plant varieties to protect farmers' rights. The difficulty is the need for legislation to meet many diverse interests within each country. One strong and coordinated international proposal is the Convention of Farmers and Breed-

---

BOX 2.10

Rerouting the genetic revolution—the CGIAR proposal

The Consultative Group on International Agricultural Research (CGIAR) proposes to redirect the path of modern biotechnology by providing public research to meet the needs of all humanity. Responsible for a major collection of crop species—numbering 600,000 accessions—it has called for an end to patenting genes drawn from gene banks. It has also banned the use of genetically sterile seeds—"terminator technology"—in its own research. The CGIAR's current budget for crop biotechnology is just $12 million a year—compare that with US private sector spending on biotechnology research: $9 billion in 1997 alone.

The CGIAR plans to rejuvenate a strong public research system to ensure that breakthroughs in science are translated into breakthroughs for people—reducing malnutrition, poverty and environmental degradation, keeping the findings as public property. Also needed are "rules of engagement" for the public and private sectors, based on the premise that access to the means of food production is as much a human right as access to food. The CGIAR could also lead the way in combining the search for solutions with precautions against risk—following the equity and biosafety protocols of the Convention on Biological Diversity.

Source: CGIAR 1998.

ers (CoFaB). It offers developing countries an alternative to following European legislation by focusing legislation on needs to protect farmers' rights to save and reuse seed and to fulfil the food and nutritional security goals of their people.

For indigenous people's interests, too, open debate is needed across countries to bring together the most up-to-date thinking for use by negotiators and policy-makers. The framework needs to consider collective rights to knowledge and resources, the need for prior informed consent for use of materials and knowledge—not just the consent of the government but also of the indigenous groups concerned—and the need for transparency in the findings of research. Some initiatives have already been taken. Indigenous people's organizations around the world such as the Indigenous Peoples Biodiversity Network are seeking guidelines for legal recognition of their intellectual property. Thailand, the Philippines and Australian aboriginal groups have all taken steps to protect indigenous knowledge.

Developing countries facing similar challenges can benefit from consultation and co-operation to create model laws, collaborate in training public officials and devise strategies to help industries adversely affected by the new regime. Spreading awareness of the issues at stake is important in building coalitions among national interest groups, regional organizations and international civil society campaigns. Presenting counter-proposals as a united negotiating bloc would greatly strengthen the possibility for change. In March 1999 the International South Group Network drew together representatives from 17 southern and East African countries to discuss a joint position on the upcoming World Trade Organization round and the review of the TRIPS agreement, greatly strengthening the clarity and force of the message to be delivered from countries in the region.

The TRIPS agreement was drawn up with remarkably little analysis of its expected economic impacts. The costs of implementation—revising laws, training officers, testing and enforcing patents—are high, yet the benefits are unclear. If the agreement is to be reviewed, then let it be a review in everyone's interests. A transparent cost review mechanism should be established within the World Trade Organization, to track the costs of implementing the TRIPS agreement, the effects on consumer prices, the cost of anti-competitive effects and the impact on technology flows. And most important, it should examine the impact on biodiversity, on farming communities and on access to medical resources and scientific information.

PUTTING PRECAUTION BEFORE PROFITS

The potentially great benefits of the new biotechnology come with risks attached: national and international guidelines are urgently needed as transgenic crop production grows. Each country needs to draw up biosafety measures, to monitor changes in biodiversity, demand transparency and labelling of products, consider the social, economic and ethical impacts and promote research into areas of national need. Regional coordination is needed for sharing data and experience, for sharing in the costs of training officials and for developing rules of trading.

Much greater attention must be given to understanding the potential environmental and health hazards of genetically altered crops—an especially important task in countries where the science base and media coverage are narrow and there is extensive fragmentation of the food chain into many smallholders, processors and traders.

Participation in the process must be widened. Knowledge is needed not only of the latest technologies but also of local ecosystems and food chains, local culture and systems of exchange, socio-economic conditions and political and market stability. This calls for broad collaboration. Some countries are already on this path with established and representative biotechnology advisory groups. France's government has adopted the precautionary principle, promising to survey the development of the genetic revolution and increase public transparency on findings. The European Parliament favours creating a registry of tested and accepted transgenic products, making a database available to the public.

To strengthen their bargaining positions in pushing for change, countries need to present frameworks that provide alternatives to the provisions of the TRIPS agreement

* * *

Information and communications technologies and biotechnology hold great potential for human development. But strong policy action is needed nationally and internationally to ensure that the new rules of globalization are framed to turn the new technologies towards people's needs. Thus questions need to be asked on how it is used. Does the control, direction and use of technology:

- Promote innovation and sharing of knowledge?
- Restore social balance or concentrate power in the hands of a few?
- Favour profits or precaution?
- Bring benefits for the many or profits for the few?
- Respect diverse systems of property ownership?
- Empower or disempower people?
- Make technology accessible to those who need it?

Global governance of technology must respect and encompass diverse needs and cultures. Public investment—through new funding—is essential to develop products and systems for poor people and countries. Precaution is needed in exploring new applications, no matter how great their commercial promise. Only then will the rules of globalization allow technological breakthroughs to be steered to the needs of people, not just profits.

CHAPTER 3

The invisible heart—
care and the global economy

Studies of globalization and its impact on people focus on incomes, employment, education and other opportunities. Less visible, and often neglected, is the impact on care and caring labour—the task of providing for dependants, for children, the sick, the elderly and (do not forget) all the rest of us, exhausted from the demands of daily life. Human development is nourished not only by expanding incomes, schooling, health, empowerment and a clean environment but also by care. And the essence of care is in the human bonds that it creates and supplies. Care, sometimes referred to as social reproduction, is also essential for economic sustainability.

Globalization is putting a squeeze on care and caring labour. Changes in the way that men and women use their time put a squeeze on the time available for care. The fiscal pressures on the state put a resource squeeze on public spending on care services. And the wage gap between the tradable and non-tradable sectors puts an incentive squeeze on the supply of care services in the market. Gender is a major factor in all these impacts, because women the world over carry the main responsibility for these activities, and most of the burden.

In a globally competitive labour market, how can we preserve time to care for ourselves and our families, neighbours and friends? In a globally competitive economy, how do we find the resources to provide for those unable to provide for themselves? And how can societies distribute the costs and burdens of this work equitably—between men and women, and between the state and the family or community, including the private sector (box 3.1)?

To answer these questions requires an understanding of what care is, how it is provided, who bears the costs and the burdens and

what the critical paths are to negotiating an equitable solution. These are little-explored issues, but an exciting new body of work is probing them.

HUMAN DEVELOPMENT, CAPABILITIES AND CARE

The role of care in the formation of human capabilities and in human development is fundamental. Without genuine care and nurturing, children cannot develop capabilities, and adults have a hard time maintaining or expanding theirs. But the supply of care is not merely an input into human development. It is also an output, an intangible yet essential capability—a factor of human well-being.

Most adults need care in the emotional sense, even if not in the economic sense of relying on one another. A clear manifestation of this is the positive effect of social support and social relationships on life expectancy—at least as significant as the negative effects of cigarette smoking, hypertension and lack of physical exercise. Married adults enjoy lower risks of mortality than those who are unmarried.

The difference that care makes for child health and survival is also well documented. A UNICEF analysis identifies caring as the third underlying factor in preventing child malnutrition, after household food security and access to water, health care and sanitation facilities. It is what translates available food and health resources into healthy growth and development. For example, risks of malnutrition and illness depend significantly on whether a child is breast-fed and how long, at what age it is given complementary foods and whether it receives immunizations on schedule. Many studies show that malnourished children grow

Globalization is putting a squeeze on care and caring labour

faster when they receive verbal and cognitive stimulation—special attention can encourage a child in pain to eat.

Another link between human development and care relates to equity for the providers of caring labour. These activities are often identified with women's unpaid work in the domestic sector. This is an important source, but there are others. Not just the family but the community plays an important role. So do men, though their contribution is smaller than women's in most countries. The private sector provides domestic service,

teaching, nursing and similar services. The public sector also provides many services in these areas (figure 3.1).

But in almost all societies the gender division of labour hands the responsibility for caring labour to women, much of it without remuneration—in the family or as voluntary activity in the community. *Human Development Report 1995* estimated that women spend two-thirds of their working hours on unpaid work (men spend just a fourth), and most of those hours are for caring work. The hours are long and the work physically hard—fetching water and fuel, for example—especially in rural areas of developing countries. In Nepal women work 21 more hours each week than men, and in India, 12 more hours. In Kenya 8- to 14-year-old girls spend 5 hours more on household chores than boys. These inequalities in burden are an important part of the obstacles women face in their life choices and opportunities.

Women also make up a disproportionate share of workers in domestic service and in professions such as child care, teaching, therapy and nursing. These occupations offer low pay relative to their requirements for education, skills and other qualifications—another source of gender biases in opportunities.

CARE—OR "TENDER LOVING CARE"

Care can mean a feeling of care, an emotional involvement or a state of mind. Personal identity and personal contact—especially face-to-face contact—are key elements of care services, involving a sense of connection between the givers and receivers. The care-giver may be motivated by affection, altruism or social norms of obligation. The care-receiver has a sense of being cared for. These elements are frequently there even when the care-giver is a paid employee. Individuals often choose caring jobs because they are a way to express caring motives and earn a living at the same time.

The commitment to care for others is usually thought to be altruistic—involving love and emotional reciprocity. But it is also a social obligation, socially constructed and enforced by social norms and rewards. A compelling example: when a mother gets up for the fifth

BOX 3.1

If we are going to compete, let it be in a game of our choosing

Once upon a time the goddesses decided to hold a competition, a kind of Olympics, among the nations of the world. This was not an ordinary race in which the distance was determined and the winner would be the runner who took the shortest time, but a contest to see which society, acting as a team, could move all its members forward.

When the gun went off, one nation assumed that the race would not last long. It urged all its citizens to start running as quickly as possible. It was every person for himself. Very soon the young children and the elderly were left behind, but none of the fast runners bothered to help them out because it would have slowed them down.

At first those who were in front were exhilarated by their success. But as the race continued some became tired or hurt and fell by the wayside. Gradually all the runners grew exhausted and sick, and there was no one to replace them. It became clear that this nation would not win the race.

Everyone's attention turned to a second nation, which adopted a slightly different strategy. It sent all its young men out ahead to compete, but required all the women to come along behind, carrying the children, the sick and the elderly and caring for the runners who needed help. The nation's leaders explained to the women that this was a natural and efficient arrangement from which everyone could benefit. They provided great incentives for the men to run fast, and gave them authority over the women.

At first this seemed to work, but the women found that they could run just as fast as the men if they were not burdened with caring for the weak. They began to

argue that the work they were doing—caring for the runners—was just as important as the running and deserved equal reward. The men refused to make any changes. The nation began to waste a great deal of energy in bargaining and negotiation. Gradually it became clear that this nation, too, was losing the race.

So attention turned to a third nation, which had started out moving quite slowly, though making steady progress. In this nation everyone was required both to run and to take care of those who could not run. Both men and women were given incentives to compete, to run as fast as possible, but the rules required them all to share in carrying the burden of care.

Having agreed to rules that rewarded both kinds of contribution to the collective effort, people were free to choose their own speed, to find a balance between individual effort and collective responsibility. This freedom and equality contributed to their solidarity. Of course, it was this nation that won the race.

Perhaps this is a utopian fairy tale. But the global economic system tells us that we are all in a race. It tells us to hurry up. It tells us all to worry about our speed. But it does not tell us how long the race will last—or what the best long-term strategy is. And it does not tell us how victory will be defined. If we are going to compete, let it be a game of our own choosing. That is, in a nutshell, the challenge of the new global order: how to define a world economy that preserves the advantages of market competition, but establishes strict limits and rules that prevent competition from taking a destructive turn.

Source: Folbre 1999.

time in the night to soothe her crying child, it is not necessarily because she gets pleasure from doing so. She may feel quite irritated. But she accepts a social obligation to care for her child, even at some cost to her health or happiness.

The word *care* often refers to looking after people who cannot take care of themselves: children, the sick, the needy, the elderly. But this misses the fact that even the healthiest and happiest of adults require a certain amount of care. Their need for that care may ebb and flow, but it sometimes comes in tidal waves.

GLOBALIZATION AND CARE

Economic analysis of care offers three insights into the impact of globalization on human development:

• Women's increased participation in the labour force and shifts in economic structures are transforming the ways care services are provided. Needs once provided almost exclusively by unpaid family labour are now being purchased from the market or provided by the state.

• Increases in the scope and speed of transactions are increasing the size of markets, which are becoming disconnected from local communities. As market relationships become less personal, reliance on families as a source of emotional support tends to increase—just as they are becoming less stable economically and demographically.

• Perhaps most important, the expansion of markets tends to penalize altruism and care. Both individuals and institutions have been free-riding on the caring labour that mainly women provide. Whether women will continue to provide such labour without fair remuneration is another matter.

Globalization is dominated by the expansion of markets and rewards profitability and efficiency. While economic growth reflects increasing private and public incomes, human development needs people to provide goods and services that fall outside the market—such as care and other unpaid services. A country can speed the growth of GDP by encouraging a shift in production from unpaid services such as care to market commodities. Care thus has clear analogies to environmental resources,

with the characteristics of a resource outside the market. But a deficit of care services not only destroys human development—it also undermines economic growth.

This may be just what is happening in many OECD countries today, where there is a shortage of reliable, skilled labour in the midst of widespread unemployment. And despite universal schooling, there are widespread gaps in skills. Data from the International Adult Literacy Surveys in OECD countries show that nearly half the population in almost all these countries score below the level needed to be trained for a skilled occupation.

The traditional restrictions on women's activities once guaranteed that women would specialize in providing care. Globalization's shifts in employment patterns have promoted and to some extent enforced the participation of women in wage employment. The supply of unpaid care services may be reduced, and daughters, cousins or nieces may have to take on more of the work. Nonetheless, women in most countries continue to carry the "double burden" of care services—ending up exhausted.

A challenge for human development is to find the incentives and rewards that ensure the supply of services—from the family, the community, the state and the market—all recognizing the need for gender equality and distributing the burdens and costs of care fairly (boxes 3.2 and 3.3).

Noble. But trends are moving in the opposite direction. In OECD countries the problem is that globalization has pulled back on state services and pushed more to private services. Many social commentators protest the ensuing deterioration in quality.

In the transition economies of Eastern Europe and the CIS these trends have been dramatic, contributing to the huge human costs of the transition. The dismantling and weakening of the welfare state have meant cuts and deterioration in services in health and education—across the board—contributing to the deteriorating human outcomes. Life expectancy was lower in 1995 than in 1989 in 7 of 18 countries—falling as much as five years since 1987. Enrolment in kindergarten declined dramatically—falling from 64% to 36% of 3- to 6-year-olds in Lithuania between

FIGURE 3.1
Four sources of caring labour

Source: Human Development Report Office.

1989 and 1995, and from 69% to 54% in Russia. Responsibility for pre-primary education was transferred from the state to parents, with enormous consequences for mothers of children this age.

CARE AND MARKET REWARDS

The market gives almost no rewards for care. Much of it is unpaid—most of it provided by women, some by men. The market also penalizes individuals who spend time in these activities, which take time away from investing in skills for paid work or from doing paid work.

Care services are also provided in the market, usually underremunerated. What explains the financial penalty for doing caring work? Gender bias is one factor. A second is the intrinsic reward people get from helping others, allowing employers to fill jobs at lower pay. A third is that people feel queasy about putting a price on something as sacred as care.

And global economic competition has tended to reinforce these trends, as the wage gap increases between the tradable and non-tradable sectors. Wages for teaching, domestic service and other caring work have stagnated—or even fallen—in the industrial countries.

Care produces goods with widespread benefits for those who do not pay for them

Care produces goods with social externalities—widespread benefits for those who do not pay for them. It creates human and social capital—the next generation, workers with human and social skills who can be relied on, who are good citizens. But mothers cannot demand a fee from employers who hire their children. This care will be underproduced and overexploited unless non-market institutions ensure that everyone shares the burden of providing it. The traditional patriarchal family, and gender biases in society that limit opportunities for women outside the role of wife and mother, have been the traditional way to solve this problem. But this is obviously inequitable, and no solution at all.

REDISTRIBUTING THE COSTS AND RESPONSIBILITIES OF CARE— TO FAMILY, STATE AND CORPORATION

Where do the effects of globalization fit in the larger conflicts over the distribution of the costs of care? Consider a mother who devotes much time and energy to enhancing her children's capabilities and a country that devotes much of its national budget to family welfare. In the short run both are at a competitive disadvantage: they devote fewer resources to directly productive activities. But in the long run their position depends on their ability to claim some share of the economic benefits produced by the next generation.

The family today is a small welfare state. Women invest time and energy in children—essentially a "family public good". They pay most of the costs—while other family members claim a greater share of the benefits. What they do is far less transferable outside the family than investments in a career. The resulting loss of bargaining power can mean less consumption or leisure time for women, even if they remain married and enjoy some of their husband's market income.

Public spending on children is modest compared with that by parents. Take public spending in the United States, about 38 percent of all spending. Over the past 30 years the elderly in the United States have received far more than the young for a simple reason—the elderly have more votes than parents with chil-

---

BOX 3.2

Globalization leads to the feminization of labour— but the outcome is mixed

Many empirical studies now allow analysis of how shifts in trade patterns affect employment. A study covering 165 countries from 1985 to 1990 concludes that greater trade openness increases women's share of paid employment. Further analysis of plant-level data from Colombia and from Turkey—both with rapid export growth—shows that firms producing for export employ more female workers, often in skilled functions.

But increasing participation has not always meant less discrimination. Women constitute a large share of workers in informal subcontracting, often in the garment industry—at low wages and under poor conditions. Highly competitive international markets in garments also mean that

the work is volatile—with contracts moving with small changes in costs or trade regulations.

Globalization has also been associated with home work, tele-work and part-time work. In the United Kingdom the share of workers with unconventional work arrangements rose from 17% in 1965 to 40% in 1991. In 1985 the shares of such work arrangements were up to 15% in Japan, 33% in the Republic of Korea and 50% in Mexico, Peru and Sri Lanka. And in Greece and Portugal women constitute 90% of the home workers. This is a mixed blessing. Informal work arrangements can accommodate women's care obligations in the family. But such jobs are often precarious and poorly paid.

Source: Özler 1999.

---

dren. Studies in Western and Eastern European countries show similar biases against children. Parents who invest in the next generation of workers are not explicitly rewarded for their efforts. Their efforts are socially important but economically unproductive.

For much of the past 200 years nations have exercised a lot of control over the production of care services such as education, health and provision for dependants. The analogy of the family to the state is clear. Both institutions demand commitment to the welfare of the collective rather than the individual. But on the negative side, both institutions can generate oppressive hierarchies that interfere with the development of human capabilities.

Take a multinational corporation, tired of the frustrations of negotiating taxation and regulation with host governments, that buys a small island, writes a constitution and announces a new country—Corporation Nation. A citizen automatically receives a highly paid job. Sounds good, but some restrictions apply. Individuals must have advanced educational credentials, be physically and emotionally healthy, have no children and be under the age of 60. They do not have to emigrate but can work from their country over the Internet. And they immediately lose their new citizenship if they require retraining, become seriously ill, acquire children or reach the age of 60.

Corporation Nation can free-ride on the human capabilities of its citizen workers without paying for their production or their maintenance when ill or old. It can offer high wages to attract the best workers from around the world without threatening its profitability. Footloose capital of the globalized economy weakens the connections between corporations and communities, and the obligations to citizens. Why then would multinational firms remain in countries that tax them to support the production of human capabilities when they can go elsewhere and free-ride? They will remain for a while, out of habit and loyalty. But the ones that jump first to take advantage of new opportunities will win the race if the finish line is defined by maximizing the short-term value of market output.

THE CHALLENGE OF CARE IN THE GLOBAL ECONOMY

How can societies design new arrangements for care in the global economy—to make sure that it is not squeezed out?

Many fear that there is no alternative to the traditional model of the patriarchal household in which women shoulder much of the responsibility through unpaid work. The resurgence of religious fundamentalism around the world testifies to the anxieties about changing traditional patriarchal relationships that have ensured a supply of caring labour. Many social conservatives fear that globalization fuels market-based individualism at the expense of

---

BOX 3.3

More paid work doesn't reduce unpaid work

Women are responsible for most unpaid care work—a social norm slow to change. A review of time-use surveys in *Human Development Report 1995* showed a general trend to greater gender equality in unpaid work in the OECD countries, but no equalization in developing countries and a deterioration in the transition economies of Eastern Europe and the CIS.

Bangladesh had one of the largest increases in the share of women participating in the labour force—from 5% in 1965 to 42% in 1995. This has been important for export growth, with women as the main workers in the garment industry. But women still spend many hours in unpaid work. A survey of men and women working in formal urban manufacturing activities shows that women put in on average 31 hours a week in unpaid work—cooking, looking after children, collecting fuel, food and water (box table 3.3). Men put in 14 hours in activities such as house repair. Workers in the informal sector show similar patterns.

Women in Eastern Europe and the CIS spend more hours in paid employment than those in most other countries. But the gender disparity in sharing the burden of unpaid work remains stark, and it is worsening under the economic dislocations of the transition. In Bulgaria men's total work burden was 15% less than women's in 1977 but 17% less in 1988. Women increased their share of both paid and unpaid work—in 1977 men did 52% as much household work as women, but in 1988 only 48% as much. In Moldova women work 73.5 hours each week.

In OECD countries men's contribution to unpaid work has been increasing. But a woman who works full time still does a lot of unpaid work. Once she has a child, she can expect to devote 3.3 more hours a day to unpaid household work. Married women who are employed and have children under 15 carry the heaviest work burden—almost 11 hours a day.

BOX TABLE 3.3
Time spent in paid and unpaid work in Bangladesh, 1995
(hours per week)

	Formal sector workers		Informal sector workers	
	Men	Women	Men	Women
Unpaid work	14	31	14	24
Paid employment	53	56	23	21
Total	67	87	37	45

Source: Zohir 1998; UNDP 1995.

---

social commitments to family and community. A consistent theme of religious fundamentalism worldwide: re-establish rules that restrict women's rights for fear that women will abandon caring responsibilities.

At the other end of the spectrum is market provision of care—but often the people who need care cannot afford to pay for it. And finally there is state provision. But the search for efficiency in today's global economy imposes a "market discipline" that is at variance with quality. Cost-minimizing standards drive down quality in schools, hospitals and child-care centres. So public services alone are not a total answer, though state support must be a big part of it.

In all this, the challenge is to strike a balance between individual rights and social obligations of care. Competitive market societies emphasize values that encourage individualism—and say little about obligations and commitment to the family and community. The extreme responses of the patriarchal backlash and the marketization of care require far less effort and negotiation than the democratic response, which requires serious thinking about how to enforce responsibilities for care in the community.

So the first step must be to challenge social norms—to build commitment of both men and women to their responsibilities for caring labour. Societies—through public and corporate policy—then need to acknowledge care as a priority human need that they have a social obligation to foster.

A clear policy path is to support incentives and rewards for caring work, both paid and unpaid, to increase its supply and quality. This does not mean sending women back to the traditional role of housewife and mother, closing off other opportunities. It means sharing unpaid care services between men and women, reducing men's paid work time and increasing their time on family care. And it means increasing the supply of state-supported care services. Nordic countries have a long tradition of such approaches, which give public recognition and payment for care, rewarding family commitment but without reinforcing traditional gender roles (box 3.4).

BOX 3.4

Support for men's child-care responsibilities in Western Europe

Although several countries in Western Europe have encouraged gender-neutral family-oriented work policies, in 1995 only 5% of the male workforce in the European Union (EU) worked part time, and only 5% of fathers took paternity leave. Men often cite their work environment as a constraint when explaining their reluctance to make full use of parental and paternal leave rights or to work part-time to care for a child. Private sector employers in particular are seen as unsupportive of such arrangements. Traditionally it has been women who have had to move into part-time labour or take a career break after the birth of a child. EU Commissioner for Employment and Social Affairs Padraig Flynn has stated that "even where there are policy instruments aimed at breaking down the gender imbalance in caring . . . the assumption that caring is the responsibility of women persists."

Time use

Austria. Men spend an average of 70% of their time in paid labour, 30% in unpaid; women spend an average of 30% of their time in paid labour, 70% in unpaid. Women make up 98% of part-time employees.

Denmark. About 65% of men in the labour force work 30–39 hours a week, 30% work more and 5% less; 69% of women work 30–39 hours, 11% work more and 20% work less. In 1987 men spent 10 hours a week in unpaid work, women 21 hours; in 1997 men spent 13 hours in unpaid work, and women 18.

Germany. A third of women work less than 35 hours a week; only 2–3% of men do so.

Italy. Married women with children spend 7.5 hours each day in care work, men 1.5 hours.

Netherlands. Women spend twice as much time in unpaid work at home as men (women 32 hours, men 16). But women who work more than 30 hours a week spend only 18 hours in unpaid housework, compared with 19 hours for their husbands.

Spain. Women spend seven times as many hours doing domestic work as men.

Paternal and parental leave

Denmark. Fathers are allowed a 2-week paternal leave for the birth or adoption of a child. They can also use the last 10 weeks of maternity leave (10% of fathers do this). And there is a 4-week extension for fathers only.

Finland. Fathers may take 6–18 days of paternal leave, and 158 days of parental leave can be shared after maternity leave ends (parental leave is used by only 3% of fathers). One parent can take unpaid leave until the child is three. And parents are allowed 2–4 days a year to care for a sick child.

Italy. During the child's first year a 6-month parental leave can be taken after maternity leave ends (at 30% pay).

Norway. Employees may take parental leave for 42 weeks (at 100% pay) or 52 weeks (at 80% pay). Fathers must use at least 4 weeks of the parental leave; otherwise that period is lost. Parents may also combine their leave with part-time work. Employees are allowed 10–15 days each year to care for a sick child, single parents 20–30 days.

Sweden. Employees are allowed 10 days' paternal leave for the birth or adoption of a child, 450 days' parental leave (at 80% pay). One parent, usually the father, has an absolute right to one month (at 85% pay). Parents have the right to a 25% reduction in their work hours until a child is eight; child care is a legal right.

Source: Flynn 1998; EU Network 1998.

Citizens could be given tax credits for contributing care services that develop long-term relationships between individuals. And this model could be extended further. For example, many young adults benefit from public support for higher education. They could repay the costs through mandatory national service that takes some responsibility for children and other dependants in their community. The care services they could provide would be at least as valuable as military service, and they could develop important skills as well as reinforce the value of care.

Policies to foster more caring labour appear unproductive or costly only to those who define them as narrowly contributing to GDP or short-term profit. The erosion of family and community solidarity imposes enormous costs reflected in inefficient and unsuccessful education efforts, high crime rates and a social atmosphere of anxiety and resentment. The nurturing of human capabilities has always been difficult and expensive. In the past it was assured by a gender division of labour based on the subordination of women. Today, however, the cost of providing caring labour should be confronted explicitly and distributed fairly—between men and women, and among the state, the family or community and the employer.

CHAPTER 4

National responses to make globalization work for human development

Globalization has swung open the door to opportunities in the world's markets. But markets can go too far and squeeze the non-market activities so critical for human development. Because of a *fiscal squeeze,* the public provision of social services is being constrained. Because of a *time squeeze,* the personal provision of (unpaid) caring services is being reduced. And because of a perverse *incentive squeeze,* the environmental resources so essential for human development are being degraded.

The markets in today's global system are creating wonderful opportunities, but distributing them unevenly—and the volatility of markets is creating new vulnerabilities. What's worse, the success of the global markets has marginalized many non-market activities for human development, making human well-being even more vulnerable.

What can countries do to make globalization work for human development?

• Capture global opportunities in trade, capital flows and migration.

• Protect people against the vulnerabilities that globalization creates.

• Overcome the resource squeeze from the shrinking fiscal autonomy of the state.

For national action to succeed in these areas, countries have to generate pro-poor growth that reduces inequalities and enhances human capabilities. They also have to create effective alliances of all actors. And they have to formulate strategies for better managing their needs and interests in today's globalizing world. None of these tasks is easy. With deeper integration of economies in the global system, the demand for convergence of policies is high. But without strong national governance, neither the opportunities nor the threats of global-

ization can be effectively managed for human development.

CAPTURING GLOBAL OPPORTUNITIES

Comparative disadvantage in markets and resources need not be a constraint. With appropriate policies, countries can capture global opportunities in trade, finance and employment and translate them into more human development.

ENHANCING TRADE

The standard policy prescription for the developing world has been to liberalize trade and provide incentives to produce for export. Many developing countries have reduced their tariffs, removed distortions in exchange rates and trimmed fiscal deficits. The CFA countries have devalued the CFA franc. Eritrea, Ethiopia and Mozambique have achieved current account convertibility for their currencies. Several South Asian countries have removed import restrictions. Transition economies in Eastern Europe and the CIS have made tax incentives a key part of their strategies. And several Arab states are liberalizing financial services.

Has this helped growth? Yes, in many countries. Botswana, Chile, China, India, the Republic of Korea and Mauritius had a burst of exports—and a boost in per capita income. The lessons are clear: countries can accelerate growth through trade liberalization if they have sound macroeconomic management, good infrastructure and social services, and strong governance with an appropriate institutional framework. Critical in all this is human development. Just look at Botswana and Mali. Both opened their economies. But Botswana's per capita income grew at nearly 6% a year in 1980–96, while Mali's shrank 0.8% a year. In the mid-1980s Botswana was far ahead of Mali in human development (figure 4.1).

Translating trade and growth into human development. Even though there is a strong link between trade and growth, there is no automatic link with human development (table 4.1). Egypt and Pakistan achieved annual export growth of more than 5% and per capita income growth of more than 3% in 1985–97, yet both still have far to go in human development. At the other extreme, countries can open their economies, but generate neither growth nor human development. Russia generated trade and attracted private capital flows by opening in the 1990s, yet economic stagnation and human deprivation are serious (box 4.1).

By contrast, the Republic of Korea managed trade and growth to improve its human development. Since 1960 life expectancy has risen from 54 years to 74. Infant mortality has come down from 85 per 1,000 live births to 6. More than 96% of its people are expected to survive beyond age 40, and 98% of adults are literate.

The main elements of the Republic of Korea's success:
• A pro-growth strategy, with a commitment to poverty reduction.
• Bold economic reforms, with sound macro-economic policies and a focus on price reforms.
• Institutions oriented to the market, with a restructuring of banking and financial institutions.
• An emphasis on rural areas and agriculture, with widespread land reform.
• Extensive public provision of social services.
• Redistributive income policies, creating more labour-intensive employment and instituting measures for social protection.

Similar policies in Botswana, Chile, Malaysia and Thailand have also translated good performance in trade into economic growth—and into the well-being of their people.

A major lesson is that capturing global opportunities in trade requires a comprehensive package, evident when contrasting Russia with Poland. From the beginning of its transition to the market, Poland opened its economy,

FIGURE 4.1
Differences in human development—Botswana and Mali, mid-1980s

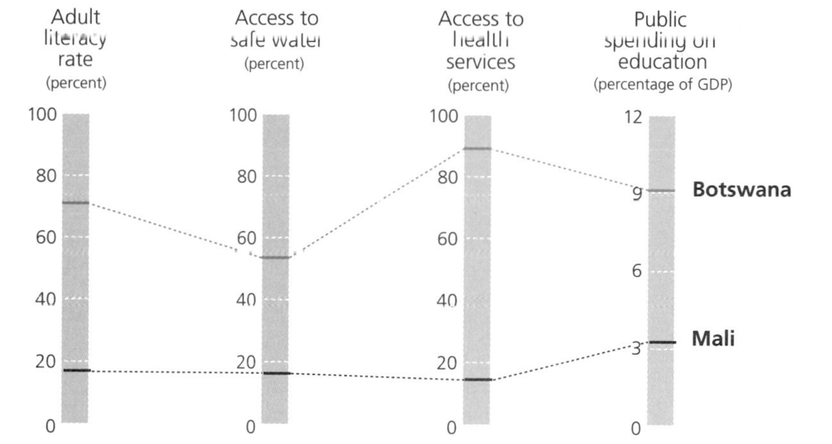

Source: UNDP 1990.

TABLE 4.1
Trade, economic growth and human development—no automatic link
(percent)

Country	Annual growth of exports 1985–97	Per capita income growth 1985–97	Reduction in human development index (HDI) shortfall 1985–97
Stronger links			
Singapore	12.9	6.2	45
Mauritius	7.9	3.7	38
Hong Kong, China (SAR)	13.0	4.8	33
Weaker links			
Pakistan	9.0	3.0	17
Uganda	8.0	2.4	5

Source: Human Development Report Office.

BOX 4.1
More trade, more capital, more human deprivation—Russia

In 1997 Russia's exports to the rest of the world were $56 billion—and its inflows of foreign direct investment $6 billion, 30% of the total to the region. But its economic growth was a meagre 0.4%. In 1989–96 its Gini coefficient deteriorated from 0.24 to 0.48, a doubling of inequality. Wages fell 48%, with the share of wage income down from 74% to 55% and that of rent and other income up almost fourfold, from 5% to 23%.

There are also serious human deprivations. Between 1989 and 1996 male life expectancy declined by more than four years to 60, two years less than the average

for developing countries. The under-five mortality rate is 25 per 1,000 live births, compared with 14 in Poland. Homicides and illegal drug trafficking have increased.

What went wrong? Sometimes Russia's problems are seen as only a financial crisis—partly due to the East Asian crisis, unfavourable external conditions and a lack of progress in building market institutions. A broader view sees deeper causes: bad governance, no rule of law, a criminal society, concentrated power, an imperfect market economy.

Source: Ruminska-Zimny 1999.

built up institutions, put in place democratic and participatory processes and ensured transparency and accountability (box 4.2).

Maintaining labour and environmental standards. Capturing trade opportunities is complicated by labour and environmental standards, for violating them hurts human development.

When wages less than the minimum are imposed on female garment workers in Bangladesh, that is a violation of the minimum wage law. When the workplace is put under lock and key with workers inside, that is a violation of human rights. When hundreds of these women die in a fire because they cannot get out, that is a human tragedy. When 27 million workers in the world's 845 export processing zones are not allowed to organize in unions, that is a violation of workers' rights as well as human rights. And continuing degradation of the environment for economic gain increases the vulnerability of current generations—and deprives future generations of the opportunities that are their due.

Does lowering labour and environmental standards give developing countries a competitive edge in capturing trade opportunities? No. Are developed countries using these standards as grounds for unfairly restricting trade? Possibly. And do developing countries lose if they improve their labour and environmental standards? Again, no.

Empirical evidence suggests that lowering labour standards does not make a country more competitive, especially if the country does nothing to improve productivity. It is not so much cheap labour as low per-unit labour cost that attracts investment. The irony is that developed countries themselves take advantage of lower labour standards by outsourcing production, $585 billion worth (in 1994 prices) and more than two-fifths of the exports from developing countries. Enhancing labour standards will not harm developing countries if they can improve productivity.

In labour standards there is a strong movement among trade unions and NGOs to ensure workers' welfare in the developing world. But there is no substitute for government action on legal and regulatory frameworks, on codes of conduct for business and on monitoring and punishing violations of labour standards.

On the whole, developing countries will be better served, in trade and in human development, if they maintain appropriate environmental standards. Repeated tests of the pollution haven hypothesis—that investment and production migrate from countries with high environmental standards to those with low standards—have failed to find systematic evidence in its favour. Moreover, trade liberalization affects the environment through many routes—some positive, some negative. The net result can be anything, and thus does not justify lowering environmental standards a priori. Consumers in developed countries can help if they are willing to pay for such standards through social labelling and eco-labelling. And developing countries, through regional collective action, can set regional environmental standards that provide them with better bargaining tools in trade negotiations.

In environmental standards country experience offers specific policy recommendations:
- Abolish policies that distort trade and have negative environmental impacts. In the 1990s,

---

BOX 4.2

Opening the Polish economy with institutional reforms

In the late 1980s, when Poland embarked on opening its economy, it took a "shock therapy" approach to macroeconomic management. In the first few years of transition income and consumption dropped by some 20% and unemployment and poverty increased. But in 1994 human development trends started improving and economic growth took off. Consumption increased, and unemployment fell from more than 16% in 1993 to less than 10% in 1997.

What made the difference? Poland shifted in the mid-1990s from a piecemeal to a comprehensive approach. The building blocks of the programme were institutional reforms, policy consistency and popular participation.

At the beginning of the transition Poland established a democratic system with market institutions, including property rights and a transparent financial sector. There was strong political will to advance reforms and a consensus on the transition strategy. Policies aimed at building the market system with a comprehen-

sive approach towards privatization and the modernization of the industrial base. This differed from the rushed and uncontrolled privatization in Russia, from the market option in Hungary and from the equity option in the Czech Republic. By negotiating with banks and other partners, and in some cases undertaking debt swaps, Poland solved the debt problems of state enterprises.

Openness policies remained consistent despite changes in government, and there was a consensus on opening to the world economy, joining the OECD, European Union and North Atlantic Treaty Organization (NATO) and adopting internal policies related to privatization, economic restructuring and decentralization. All policies balanced market and equity considerations.

And all policies were the subject of public debate—in parliament and the media. This gave a sense of transparency and ownership, facilitating consensus. Compare that with Russia, where a narrow group of people made decisions whenever policies were subject to internal conflict.

Source: Ruminska-Zimny 1999.

a decade in which Indonesia cut pesticide subsidies from $128 million to zero, the country's exports grew 7% a year.

• Correct market failures with good incentive systems. In Norway energy taxes have helped cut carbon dioxide emissions in some sectors by more than a fifth since 1991.

• Provide more incentives for transferring "clean" technologies to help developing countries follow environment-friendly growth paths. In Lithuania 35% of companies started cleaner production in the 1990s.

• Create the legal and institutional framework to comply with environmental standards. In 1997 Brazil passed an environmental law to protect natural resources, imposing fines of up to $44 million or prison terms of up to four years for illegal logging or killing wild animals.

• Improve the effectiveness of environmental policies through an alliance of communities, NGOs and other institutions of civil society.

One last point. Developed countries should realize that using trade restrictions in the name of environmental standards is protectionist and, for domestic environmental problems, inefficient. For transboundary problems, it is both inefficient and inequitable.

ATTRACTING CAPITAL— CONTROLLING ITS VOLATILITY

Private capital flows, particularly foreign direct investment, have helped developing countries to grow and to enhance human development. But again, the link between foreign direct investment, growth and human development is not automatic (table 4.2). And empirical evidence suggests that short-term speculative capital makes for financial volatility and little long-term contribution to an economy.

Attracting long-term capital flows. To attract foreign direct investment, the traditional macroeconomic package calls for liberalizing capital, providing incentives, formulating a conducive industrial policy and implementing pragmatic technology and labour policies.

• Countries thus need a comprehensive policy package, not ad hoc measures. Consider India, which liberalized its investment rules,

offered investment incentives and promoted foreign investment opportunities (box 4.3).

• National governance conditions the domestic policy and economic framework, affecting attitudes towards foreign direct investment and operational efficiency and profits. Important in all this is political openness—ensuring a democratic system, promoting transparency and accountability, unleashing the press and civil society and maintaining political stability through the work of democratic political institutions. That is perhaps why Poland, with a GDP a fifth of Russia's, received $18 billion of foreign direct investment in 1991–97, while Russia received only $13 billion. In Latin America, too,

TABLE 4.2
Foreign direct investment, economic growth and human development— no automatic link

Country	Foreign direct investment flows (US$ billions)		Per capita income growth rate (%)	Reduction in human development index (HDI) shortfall (%)
	1985	1997	1985–97	1985–97
Stronger links				
Chile	0.2	5.2	3.7	47
China	2.3	43.5	8.3	45
Korea, Rep. of	0.3	2.2	6.5	35
Weaker links				
India	0.1	3.1	3.7	13
Romania	0.0	1.1	-0.6	-2

Source: Human Development Report Office.

BOX 4.3
Liberalizing foreign investment in India

Foreign direct investment flows to India in the 1980s were insignificant, not much more than $1 billion. But in the early 1990s India removed restrictions on ownership, loosened regulations on currency transactions, expedited the review and approval process for foreign investment through "one-stop" coordination and encouraged imports of new technology.

The outcome: new opportunities for foreign investment. In 1988 the stock of foreign direct investment in India was $1.2 billion—in 1994, $2.5 billion. Inflows rose from $91 million in 1988 to $300 million in 1994 to $3 billion in 1997.

India developed seven export processing zones, where foreign investors

receive tax incentives and can bring in duty-free imports. India also promoted private foreign investment in the country and identified enterprises for joint ventures. The government advertised broadly in newspapers and other media in foreign countries. It arranged international fairs. It sent trade delegations to countries. It cranked up its missions abroad.

What helped in this? Good human capital, enhanced technological power, market size, democratic traditions and stable politics. But they are not new. What made the breakthrough possible was the liberalization of foreign investment and a new set of strong incentives.

Source: Lim and Siddall 1997.

the democratization of politics explains higher inflows of foreign direct investment in the 1990s. Increasingly, there are demands for government insurance against political risks for foreign direct investment. In many cases foreign investors are willing to undertake commercial risks, but require protection against political risks.

• Educating people and moving their skills up the ladder are essential for raising productivity—and for attracting foreign direct

investment. The quality of labour and its skill level are an important element in capturing global opportunities. For the workers, skill ensures better pay. Education and training are essential to build the necessary human capital.

• Countries need to complement liberalization policies with technology policies, as Brazil, China, India and Malaysia have done. Look at the results in India, which has been providing incentives for research and development and working with foreign multinationals in high-tech areas.

That's what is needed to have foreign direct investment. But what does it take for foreign direct investment and growth to contribute to human development? First, investments in infrastructure and services should have a direct impact on human development. Second, foreign direct investment must be tailored to national priorities, in activities that have spillovers—in creating more employment, bringing in high technology, building future human capital (box 4.4). Third, countries need to minimize the adverse impacts of foreign direct investment (such as creating inequalities), provide domestic enterprises with necessary incentives and protect their interests.

National action on multinational corporations should focus on:

• *Providing appropriate incentives.* Countries might give economic incentives to multinational corporations, but these should not come at a cost to domestic enterprises (box 4.5).

• *Bringing the operations of multinationals under national rules.* While keeping the incentive structures for multinationals intact, their operations should be subject to all national rules and regulations—ranging from general laws to economic regulations.

• *Ensuring social responsibility.* In the absence of an enforceable international framework governing the operations of multinational corporations, pressing companies to adopt voluntary codes of conduct guaranteeing minimum labour standards for all their international operations has become a key strategy for enforcing labour standards—an issue discussed in chapter 5.

Managing the volatility of short-term capital. The recent financial crisis in East Asia has renewed the debate on the effectiveness of

---

BOX 4.4

Foreign direct investment for human development in Malaysia

In 1993 foreign direct investment accounted for nearly 25% of gross fixed capital formation in Malaysia, which has used it to generate growth and enhance human well-being. With per capita income growth of more than 4% a year in 1980–95, Malaysia reduced income poverty from 29% to 13% and lowered its Gini coefficient from 0.49 in 1980 to 0.45 in 1993. The income of the poorest 20% has increased from $431 in 1970 to $1,030 (1985 PPP$). Wage employment grew at more than 8% a year in 1970–92, and unemployment has fallen from 8% to 4%.

Look at what that has done for human development. Life expectancy is 72 years. Adult literacy is 85%. Primary enrolments are 91%. Infant mortality has come down in the past 20 years from 30 per 1,000 live births to 11. And more than 88% of Malaysians have access to safe water and health services.

Foreign direct investment played a big part in these achievements. The Malaysian approach has been to use foreign direct investment for economic growth and human development, with

economic measures backed by social and structural measures. An active affirmative action policy for Malays reduced social and economic disparities. Technocratic governance ensured efficiency, and institutional reforms supported the policy measures.

The recent financial crisis spotlights four principles:

• A high priority on policies friendly to human development and good governance helps a country take advantage of globalization's opportunities.

• Human and physical capital cannot insulate a country from the harm of globalization—and can indeed attract much more short-term capital than a country can cope with.

• Rapid access to larger amounts of capital, labour and natural resources can distort the development process, leaving it unsustainable.

• A slower, more sustainable pace of growth—with a strong emphasis on human development—may be a better way to take advantage of the opportunities and minimize the vulnerabilities.

Source: Jomo 1999.

BOX 4.5

Incentives to multinationals—and nationals—in Mauritius

Mauritius gave incentives to multinational corporations in export processing zones, simultaneously protecting domestic industries. Enterprises in the zones had tariff-free access to imports of machinery and inputs, free repatriation of profits, a 10-year tax holiday and implicit assurance that wage increases would be moderate. But domestic firms also got tax holidays and protection from imports. In the mid-1980s the average effective tariff

for manufactured imports was 89%.

The combination fuelled an export boom in garments to European markets, generating new opportunities for women. And because incentives went to all industries, the boom didn't drive up wages in the rest of the economy. New profit opportunities were created at the margin, leaving old opportunities undisturbed. There were no identifiable losers, only winners.

Source: Rodrik 1999.

capital controls to inhibit volatile, short-term flows. Earlier the focus was on capital controls to limit capital flight. Now it's on controls to alter the volume and composition of capital flows (box 4.6).

To avoid the speculative movement of hot money, the Republic of Korea favoured a gradual opening of its financial markets, even though there were pressures to fully liberalize its capital markets to become an OECD member. Rather than opening capital markets directly to foreign investors, the government chose to do it indirectly, allowing domestic financial institutions to borrow from abroad and distribute the borrowed funds in domestic markets.

Malaysia approached crisis management and recovery with a multipronged strategy of fiscal austerity, caps on bank lending, bank recapitalization and capital controls. Its ban on foreigners taking money out of the stock market for a year has attracted much attention. Although new foreign direct investment commitments fell by 12% in 1998, that is not bad given the regional slump. And in recent months Malaysia has eased capital controls, allowing investors to repatriate capital by paying an exit tax equal to 30% of the principal. The impact is not yet clear, but the experience shows that tight fiscal policy alone cannot calm panic and restore the capital flows essential for fast recovery. In addition to relaxing capital controls, Malaysia has recently increased public spending to spur demand and avoid a recession.

GETTING THE MOST FROM MIGRATION— BOTH WAYS

To aid the migration of unskilled workers, labour-sending countries such as Jordan, Pakistan and the Philippines have set up overseas employment units to capture opportunities for employment and protect workers' well-being. Policies for opening accounts with banks and financial institutions also helped migrant workers—and were good for remittances back home. Egypt managed to get $4.7 billion in remittances in 1995—close to the $6 billion it earned from Suez Canal receipts, oil exports and tourism combined. The Philippines received $7 billion in remittances in 1996, and Mexico $4 billion. Albania received three times as much from the 600,000 Albanians working abroad in 1993 as it did from foreign investment.

Countries also need stronger legal frameworks and tougher laws to punish those involved in human trafficking. NGOs and other institutions of civil society can play an important part in uncovering the story of human trafficking (box 4.7).

When developing countries open their economies and develop a strong private sector, they can reverse their brain drains. In Taiwan (province of China) this is called *rencai huiliu*—the "return flow of human talent". A survey of US multinational corporations in Taiwan

---

BOX 4.6

Short-term capital controls in Chile

In the early 1990s Chile experienced a surge in capital inflows that created a conflict between maintaining a tight monetary policy and spurring export competitiveness. In 1991 the Central Bank attempted to resolve this by imposing a one-year unremunerated reserve requirement on foreign loans, primarily designed to discourage short-term borrowing without affecting foreign direct investment. Between 1991 and 1997 the rate of reserve requirement was increased and its coverage extended in several steps to cover most forms of foreign financing except foreign direct investment.

The empirical evidence on the effectiveness of the Chilean controls in reducing short-term capital flows is ambiguous. It is difficult to be conclusive in the absence of a counterfactual, but national data for Chile's external debt suggest that the controls affected the maturity composition of net capital inflows only after 1995, when they were strengthened. Data from the Bank for International Settlements present a somewhat different picture. The figures for short-term external borrowing substantially exceed those reported in Chilean sources, and the maturity structure of foreign bank borrowing appears quite different from what the national data imply.

Analysts, too, are divided on the effectiveness of the Chilean approach. Some suggest that the controls were effective, but only for a short while. Others suggest that they were not effective before 1995. And still others argue that they were always ineffective.

Source: IMF 1998b.

BOX 4.7

Revealing the human trafficking in Eastern Europe and the CIS

An estimated 500,000 women are trafficked each year from Eastern Europe and the CIS to Western Europe. An estimated 15,000 Russians and Eastern Europeans work in Germany's red-light districts. In the Netherlands 57% of the trafficked women are under 21.

The Global Survival Network played a big part in exposing this slave trade, after studying it between 1995 and 1997. The researchers interviewed police and government officials, NGOs, and women trafficked overseas. It also went undercover to get information from companies dealing with trafficking and traffickers.

The outcome: *Crime and Servitude: An Exposé of the Traffic in Women for Prostitution from the Newly Independent States.* This very useful report showed the size and depth of the problem, heightened awareness of the trafficking in people and made concrete recommendations for actions to rein in the traffickers and assist the victims.

Source: Global Survival Network 1997.

(province of China) found that no fewer than 35% of expatriate staff were of Chinese extraction. In both Hong Kong (China, SAR) and mainland China there is a high demand for ABCs (American-born Chinese). The brain drain may also have reversed in India and the Republic of Korea. Would that it could in Africa.

There is also a need to protect unskilled workers who return home. Return migration can occur for several reasons. There could be a slowdown of the economy in receiving countries (oil-producing countries in the 1980s). Countries might want to speed the climb up the skills ladder by importing cheap foreign labour (the Republic of Korea and Singapore). Or there could be political or social problems (some 2.7 million people returned to Russia after having emigrated to other republics, finding it infeasible to stay if they could not speak the national language).

Return migration can cause political, social and cultural disruption in the home countries, as it did for many Asian and Arab countries after the Gulf War in 1991 and as it is doing today in many countries in Eastern Europe and the CIS. Bangladesh, the Philippines and Thailand have long had in place measures to integrate returnees in the economy and society with little disruption.

PROTECTING PEOPLE AGAINST VULNERABILITIES

People everywhere are more vulnerable. Changing labour markets are making people insecure in their jobs and livelihoods. The erosion of the welfare state removes safety nets. And the financial crisis is now a social crisis. All

Evidence does not show that flexible labour markets contribute to competitiveness, and the trade-off between worker protection and competitiveness may be illusory

this is happening as globalization erodes the fiscal base of countries, particularly developing countries, shrinking the public resources and institutions to protect people (box 4.8).

COPING WITH CHANGING LABOUR MARKETS

The structure and composition of labour markets in both developing and developed countries are changing rapidly. Some are moving towards jobs that are highly skilled and highly productive. But there are also pressures to be more flexible, as emphasized in chapter 1—and that can mean throwing out the protection of workers' incomes, rights and working conditions. Yet evidence does not show that flexible labour markets contribute to competitiveness, and the trade-off between worker protection and competitiveness may be illusory. Belgium, France, Germany and the United Kingdom weakened labour laws, but with little effect on unemployment. Spain and the Netherlands decentralized wage bargaining and Italy eliminated automatic wage indexation, but also failed to reduce unemployment.

Developing countries have responded to the changing labour markets in different ways—sometimes successfully, sometimes not. Malaysia and the Republic of Korea used price policies to ensure an affordable food supply for workers. By fixing the domestic price of rice above the export price, they maintained the domestic supply. And through subsidies, they ensured that workers could afford it. That allowed them to devalue their currencies to capture trade opportunities while protecting workers.

Countries in Latin America attempted to deal with changing labour markets through wage flexibility, allowing a widening gap between formal and informal sector wages. But that did not increase trade or foreign direct investment. So, they are now trying to make their informal sectors more productive, more vibrant and more sensitive to workers' rights. The lesson: making labour markets flexible by abandoning conditions that protect labour does not help in dealing with changing labour markets and capturing global opportunities.

The new vulnerabilities in labour markets in developing countries call for:

BOX 4.8

Social protection for Tunisia's poor

Under the pressure of globalization Tunisia cut public spending, but without hurting the poor. Food subsidies fell less in Tunisia than in some other Arab countries, going from 3% to 2% of GDP in recent years, compared with a fall in Morocco from 5.5% of GDP to 0.5% between 1981 and 1993. Also important:

Tunisia has reduced its ratio of military to social spending in the past 30 years from 45% to 31%, one of the smallest in the Arab States.

Tunisian labour unions, though not large, were instrumental in setting a minimum wage and in maintaining food subsidies for the poor.

Source: Amin 1999.

- Expanding employment, with a focus on creating reasonably productive jobs.
- Constantly upgrading the skills of workers, particularly the unskilled, through training, on-the-job dissemination of technical know-how and building the flexibility in skills needed to move around.
- Maintaining reasonable compensation, the minimum wage and accepted labour standards and rights.
- Increasing the productivity of the informal sector—through tax holidays, duty exemptions, lower interest rates and access to credit.

The transition economies of Eastern Europe and the CIS swiftly transformed labour policies. Wage setting by the state was replaced by income policies, now being abandoned. The region has the old tripartite commissions bringing together unions, employers and governments. But in many countries economic and social conditions have deteriorated so much that unemployment is high and real wages are low. Many enterprises, particularly those in the public sector, cannot pay workers. Workers can be protected only if an adequate legal system, sound institutions and good governance are put in place. Only if macroeconomic policies are undertaken to reverse economic stagnation and enhance human development. Only if social policies are pursued for the protection of people.

In the developed world deindustrialization and declines in manufacturing employment are due mainly to slow growth, outmoded patterns of growth and the expansion of high-skilled, high-productivity jobs. Finance, insurance, real estate, health care and business services have become the most dynamic sectors in job creation, with a doubling in their share of employment. But there are large disparities in skills and wages between service sectors. And part-time and precarious, low-productivity, low-wage jobs are the norm for low-skilled workers in the formal sector. The labour market is also changing because of growing links with developing countries—more imports, outsourcing of investments and immigration. But no more than a tenth of the unemployment in industrial countries can be attributed to these links.

How to overcome the vulnerabilities in labour markets? With political commitment and strong will, as in Ireland (box 4.9). What specific actions are needed? More growth, particularly pro-labour growth. How can this be achieved through expansionary monetary policy as well as other measures? That is explained later on. Addressing the vulnerabilities of workers in labour markets calls for:

- *Providing education and training.* Unskilled workers need training to upgrade skills and be flexible in adapting to different situations. Training by governments, direct or indirect, could be supported by an employers' training tax. Employers should also provide training to their employees, encouraged by tax refunds. Just look at the way Sweden has taken

---

BOX 4.9

Ireland's social partnership agreements

Since 1988 Ireland has used social partnership agreements to help the Irish act together to pursue strategic goals and recognize the actions of each part of the community. The idea is to have a national strategy against poverty and inequality.

One essential agreement is for moderate wage increases—to ensure work for everybody. It has kept society together through continuous increases in real take-home pay and employment growth without neglecting competitiveness.

The results are impressive. Since 1994 Ireland's GDP growth has been more than 7% a year, twice the developed world average. Since 1992 Ireland has created nearly 220,000 jobs, more than the rest of the European Union could manage. It cut unemployment in half between 1986 and 1998, and has raised real wages for the average industrial worker about 10% a year since 1990. Inflation remains at 2%, and the national debt is down from 122% of GDP in 1986 to 55% in 1998.

The challenge in all this progress is to reduce poverty and inequality. About 10% of the Irish are not expected to survive age 60, 23% are functionally illiterate, and nearly a fifth are income-poor.

Source: National Economic and Social Forum 1997; Ireland 1998.

BOX 4.10

Upgrading skills and achieving worker flexibility in Sweden

Globalization has brought changes in Swedish firms' organization, increased capital-intensive production and raised the requirements for knowledge. The results for workers: greater demand for vocational education, skills, broad competence and flexibility.

Sweden has helped workers meet these challenges through programmes to build their skills and increase their flexibility. Its active labour market policy absorbs 7% of the government's budget, $5 billion for a workforce of 4.4 million. More than 70% goes to training and placement programmes. In contrast to the Netherlands, the Swedish government does not support job creation at the low-wage, low-productivity end of the market. Its labour market policy has always been part of a policy of full employment that emphasizes equitable wage policies and promoting labour mobility.

Unemployment is lower in Sweden than in Australia, Belgium, Canada, Denmark, Finland, France, Germany, Italy and Spain. Although problems of structural unemployment remain, skills formation and training have contributed to equity and helped prevent long-term unemployment.

Source: Bakker 1999.

TABLE 4.3
Adjustment and greater income inequality, 1987–88 to 1993–95

Country by type of adjustment	Increase in income inequality [a]
Non-compensatory	
Russian Federation	0.24
Ukraine	0.24
Estonia	0.12
Compensatory	
Bulgaria	0.11
Latvia	0.08
Belarus	0.05
Populist	
Slovenia	0.03
Poland	0.02
Hungary	0.02

a. The increase in income inequality refers to the increase in the Gini coefficient. A Gini coefficient of zero means perfect equality, a coefficient of one perfect inequality.
Source: Rodas-Martini 1999.

TABLE 4.4
Major and minor collectors of trade taxes, 1990–96

Country	Taxes on international trade as % of total government revenue
Major collectors	
Lesotho	54.8
Madagascar	47.2
Mauritius	40.6
Dominican Republic	40.4
Lebanon	40.2
Minor collectors	
Lithuania	3.6
South Africa	2.6
Brazil	1.6
Singapore	1.3
Estonia	1.2

Source: Human Development Report Office.

workers' training seriously in dealing with changing labour markets (box 4.10).
• *Supporting the unemployed in finding jobs.* Job search assistance complements training for the unemployed. And public employment may be a real possibility for targeting such disadvantaged workers as the long-term unemployed or workers with disabilities.
• *Maintaining workers' benefits and rights.* Setting minimum wages at moderate levels does not hurt employment, and it can reduce wage gaps between men and women. Health insurance, maternity benefits, parental leave and unemployment insurance are all important for workers' welfare. And prior notice of dismissal and rights of association and collective bargaining are workers' rights.
• *Managing transitional labour markets.* Policies should support change in the gender roles in households—to value caring activities differently—and encourage the use of information technology.

MANAGING THE SOCIAL COSTS OF FINANCIAL CRISIS

Financial volatility brings huge social costs, as evidenced by the debt debacle in Latin America in the 1980s, the financial collapse in Eastern Europe and the CIS in the early 1990s and the recent East Asian crisis. The costs go beyond job losses, food insecurity and reduced social services. Weak social insurance systems and sudden unemployment also cause serious psychological and social stress, pushing up circulatory disease and suicide. Some households may even turn to prostitution and crime, leading to the spread of disease, family breakdown, increased violence and ethnic hatred. So, with restoring economic stability, one of the big issues national governments face in a crisis is minimizing the social costs and protecting people.

The financial crises of the 1980s and 1990s show that countries need to:
• Target poor people through public works programmes and food subsidies.
• Protect public spending for basic social services for poor people.
• Put in place such formal protections as unemployment insurance.
• Avoid excessive fiscal restraint.

• Align macroeconomic policies to ensure their compatibility with poverty reduction.

Besides public works programmes, countries can rely on private job placement services to ensure job and income security for poor people, as Thailand did. Income transfers for the needy are also important. To maintain food security, countries have targeted low-cost food supply to poor people. Allowing poor people to cultivate unused land can help to alleviate hunger and absorb some of the urban unemployed.

Social services for poor people are crucial. Indonesia has kept children in school by reducing or waiving school fees and providing more scholarships to poor students. And it has targeted 18 million families in a program to protect basic health services in 1998–2000, ensuring basic health services in health centres, nutritional improvements, midwife services and a health guarantee scheme at the district level. In any kind of transition—whether a financial crisis or trade volatility or economic transition—how people fare depends largely on the kind of social protection. When countries cushion people's living standards against economic declines through social transfers, they minimize the rise in inequality (table 4.3).

OVERCOMING THE RESOURCE SQUEEZE

The fiscal resource base of developing countries is being squeezed in four ways:
• *Trade liberalization.* Efficiency objectives, as well as multilateral commitments, have led many developing countries to reduce trade taxes, particularly import taxes. Trade taxes have always been a revenue-raising device for developing countries, where they account for an average of a third of tax revenue (table 4.4). Losing that base has hurt revenue generation in these countries (figure 4.2).
• *Globalization of the tax base.* With most tax systems designed when economies were primarily domestic, it is difficult to tax operations that are transnational. A typical US company may earn up to 50% of its profit outside the country. Through transfer pricing, multinational corporations can make it even more difficult for national governments to tax them. And the rise in electronic com-

merce is posing a fresh challenge to revenue collection.

- *Tax competition.* With capital tending to prefer low-tax situations, countries compete in lowering their corporate and capital gains taxes, reducing tax receipts. Of 35 Commonwealth countries that had an individual income tax before 1990, 29 reduced their rates by 1990, and none increased them. And tax-exempt export processing zones compete with one another and with the domestic economy. Tax competition led all OECD countries except Switzerland and Turkey to reduce the rate in their top tax bracket in 1985–90, from an average of 52% to 42%.

- *Growth of the underground economy.* The growth of the "black", or "underground", economy has also reduced tax revenue in many countries. India's underground economy is estimated at 20% of GDP, comparable in size to Chile, Colombia, Kenya and Nigeria. In the European Union the untaxed economy is estimated to be 25% of GDP. Russia estimates that its tax revenue is less than half of what it would be if tax laws were implemented, and that organized crime generates $900 million a year. The global drug business generates $400 billion a year—8% of all international trade.

As the resource base in developing countries shrinks, the demand for public resources grows—a double jeopardy. All the structural changes of globalization increase the demand for public resources—but in the face of reduced revenues, governments are pulling back. Public spending on health and education in countries with low human development declined from 2.0% of GDP in 1986–90 to 1.8% in 1991–96. Capital spending fell in the same period from 6.5% of public expenditure to 6.1%.

Economic and industrial change increases calls on public authorities to offset the effects of stronger competition by subsidizing ailing firms—or helping exporting firms in their struggle for global competitiveness. And seeking to boost growth, public authorities are luring investment capital with various incentives, all with a price.

Governments also have to put up public funds to stabilize their exchange rates. Where capital inflows are sterilized to avoid currency appreciation, open market operations usually lead to losses for the central bank—up to 1% of GDP in some Latin America countries. In Jamaica central bank losses from exchange rate guarantees exceeded 5% of GDP in the early 1990s. Thailand spent $23.4 billion, or three-fourths of its foreign exchange holdings, in the first half of 1997 to resist devaluation and shore up financial institutions.

Governments differ in their wishes and capacities to provide social protection. In industrial countries government expenditure increased from just under 30% of GDP in 1960 to nearly 50% in 1995. More than half this increase was due to higher social transfers, up from 9% of GDP to 20%. A recent OECD report recorded an increase in member countries' national costs of subsidies from $39 billion in 1989 to $49 billion in 1993. Meanwhile, many countries have cut social spending to balance their books. Confronted by the challenges to welfare states posed by globalization, new thinking has emerged in the discourse within and among supranational organizations about the future of welfare (box 4.11).

Two conflicting models are emerging. One is a modified version of liberalism—liberalism with a safety net, the US model of welfare but more

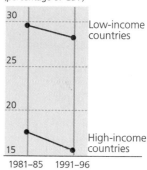

FIGURE 4.2
Reduced revenue generation— loss of fiscal strength

Trade taxes
(percentage of trade)

Low-income countries

High-income countries

1981–85   1991–96

Tax revenue
(percentage of GDP)

Low-income countries

High-income countries

1981–85   1991–96

Source: Mohan J. Rao 1999a.

BOX 4.11
Responses to the eroding welfare state

With the erosion of the welfare state, people in the developed world are even less secure and even more vulnerable—smashed or marginalized by market forces, their survival endangered, with much of the burden falling on women.

- *The neoliberal response.* Britain, New Zealand, the United States and to less degree Australia and Canada believe that the market should supplement a very basic social safety net. But market decay—typified by wage deregulation and low pay—is accompanying welfare decay, eroding both public and private coverage in health and pensions among young and low-wage workers. Welfare gaps will therefore widen, and costs will shift to families and individuals. A double jeopardy: the low-wage labour market requires higher income maintenance transfers and creates a disincentive to work.

- *The Scandinavian response.* With declining fiscal resources in recent years, there is now more emphasis on workfare,

and benefits are tied more closely to contributions. High unemployment means more reliance on private sector jobs and services, putting pressure on a "social investment" approach.

- *The continental European response.* Continental Europe is subsidizing unskilled workers' exit from the labour market, mainly through early retirement. This creates a dual problem of mass retirement and mass unemployment, pushing up financial requirements and social contributions. The strong incentive to participate in the informal sector or to pursue self-employment further undermines the welfare state's tax base.

Built-in labour market rigidities stem from most families' dependence on the male earner's pay and social rights. So, it is argued, welfare states need to be scaled down. Dutch social policy suggests the possibility of updating policies without abandoning job growth and social solidarity.

Source: Deacon 1999.

---

committed to targeting benefits to poor people. The second, based more on the European welfare system, is more universalist. It argues that the middle class should be brought into the welfare system—to ensure political support, and thus a sustainable tax base, for the system. This approach maintains that without support from the middle class, services for poor people become poor services. This point is borne out in the evidence showing that more targeted programmes result in more inequality (table 4.5).

To cope with the shrinking fiscal autonomy of the state, particularly in developing countries, national governments might focus on:

• *Generating more revenue from direct taxes,* such as income and property taxes. Direct taxes are often extremely low. In many South Asian countries agriculture accounts for more than 33% of GDP, but contributes less than 6% to total tax revenue. Imposing property taxes on big landholdings would generate significant resources in the region.

• *Introducing a value added tax.* A broad-based value added tax can be more effective in generating resources than an income tax. But it may be more regressive, requiring a choice between efficiency and equity, a choice that can be tackled only through a full analysis of the impact of both taxes in a country.

• *Making tax laws simple,* easy and transparent and making tax administration efficient. Countries may need to formulate new institutional arrangements and mechanisms for tax administration.

• *Restructuring expenditures* by taking resources away from the military and redirecting them to health and education. Countries in Eastern Europe and the CIS have recently done this.

GENERATING PRO-POOR GROWTH— REDUCING INEQUALITIES AND ENHANCING HUMAN CAPABILITIES

To generate growth the main policy components are ensuring sound macroeconomic management and macroeconomic stability, boosting domestic demand by appropriately adjusting real interest rates, adopting fiscal discipline, accelerating industrial production, reforming financial sector institutions and promoting good governance. But economic growth alone is not enough. It must be pro-poor growth—expanding the capabilities, opportunities and life choices of poor people (figure 4.3). To ensure the generation of pro-poor growth, national action should:

• Restore full employment and expansion of opportunities as a high priority of economic policy.

• Remove antipoor biases in the macroeconomic framework.

• Invest in the capabilities of poor people by restructuring public expenditure and taxation.

• Ensure access of poor people to productive resources, including credit.

• Increase the productivity of small-scale agriculture.

• Promote microenterprises and the informal sector.

• Emphasize labour-intensive industrialization to expand employment opportunities.

Reducing inequality in the developing world requires the following additional actions, through alliances of governments, firms and NGOs:

• Build human capabilities through education and ensure access of poor people to education. Education has been found to be the most important asset in explaining income disparities, and wage dispersion among skill levels has become significant.

TABLE 4.5
Social welfare systems and income inequality, 1998

Country by type of social welfare system	Income inequality (Gini coefficient) [a]
Non-targeted	
Encompassing—based on contribution	
Norway	0.23
Finland	0.23
Sweden	0.22
Corporatist—compulsory membership, but separate social programme	
France	0.29
Germany	0.24
Basic security and targeted	
United States	0.33
Australia	0.31
United Kingdom	0.29

a. A Gini coefficient of zero means perfect equality, a coefficient of one perfect inequality.
Source: Rodas-Martini 1999.

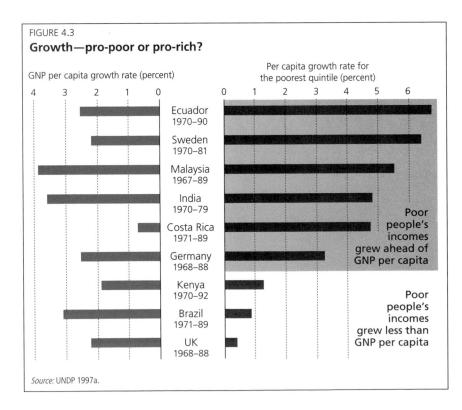

FIGURE 4.3
Growth—pro-poor or pro-rich?

Source: UNDP 1997a.

- Make public provision of safe water, health services and housing accessible to poor people.
- Make more financial assets and productive resources available to poor people and create productive and remunerative jobs for them.
- Reduce inequality through progressive income taxation and other redistributive policies.
- Provide income transfers and other social protection during adjustment and crisis—and pursue antipoverty programmes for the poorest.

Both redistributive policies and social protection are important means for reducing inequality. But in many developing countries redistributive tools, such as subsidies, favour the rich (figure 4.4). This is particularly true in urban health facilities and universities. Of course, national action to generate pro-poor growth and reduce inequality may be constrained by measures at the international level—a point discussed in chapter 5.

CREATING EFFECTIVE ALLIANCES OF NATIONAL ACTORS

An alliance among the government, NGOs, local firms and multinational corporations can go far to foster cooperation towards common goals. An alliance does not mean submission by any one actor to the others. The work of each actor can complement that of others, under such universal guidelines as respecting the rule of law, not violating human rights, and being fair, transparent and accountable. A strong, democratically elected government is especially important, allowing representatives of the people to express their aspirations and be accountable to them. All this is easier said than done, for elite groups and other interest groups benefit from the present nature and structure of globalization. They also share power with global elites.

NGOs have emerged as major actors—both in size and in impact. In the United States employment in the NGO sector is nearly 9 million, in the European Union nearly 6 million and in Japan more than 2 million—and in Brazil 1 million, in Argentina 350,000 and in Colombia 270,000. The share of resources accruing to NGOs has steadily increased, even though official aid transfers have been steadily declining. NGO revenues in the United States total $566

billion, in Japan $264 billion and in the United Kingdom $78 billion. In the developing world NGO budgets are nearly $1.2 billion, more than $200 million in Mexico alone. And among the transition economies their budgets are more than $1.4 billion in Hungary and nearly $900 million in the Czech Republic. The point: NGOs are a strong force—both as advocates and as providers of services.

NGOs can often do more than developing country governments in meeting the basic needs of citizens—using fewer resources. NGOs also create opportunities for people and protect them against the new vulnerabilities of globalization. And they have become important pressure groups, protecting people's rights and watching over other actors. The 1998 Birmingham Declaration for Debt Relief to the poorest countries is an important achievement. During the 1998 election in Germany more than 80 NGOs came together to get a commitment from national political parties to increase aid funding to 0.7% of the country's GDP.

For a long time governments and NGOs were adversarial, each suspicious of the other, but that is changing. NGOs' relationships with local firms and with multinational corporations are also improving steadily. And the donor community is coming to recognize NGOs as development partners (box 4.12).

How can the private sector be pulled in? By allowing it to work creatively, and by encouraging its innovativeness. This requires complemen-

An alliance among the government, NGOs, local firms and multinational corporations can go far to foster cooperation towards common goals

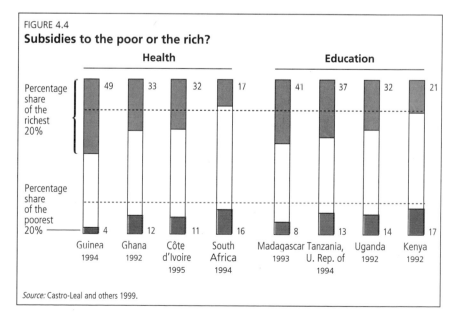

FIGURE 4.4

Subsidies to the poor or the rich?

	Health				Education			
Percentage share of the richest 20%	49	33	32	17	41	37	32	21
Percentage share of the poorest 20%	4	12	11	16	8	13	14	17
	Guinea 1994	Ghana 1992	Côte d'Ivoire 1995	South Africa 1994	Madagascar 1993	Tanzania, U. Rep. of 1994	Uganda 1992	Kenya 1992

Source: Castro-Leal and others 1999.

NGOs as a powerhouse in national alliances

In the outcry against child labour—with threats of boycotts and other trade restrictions—NGOs in South Asia have often joined with local manufacturers and the government to lobby against the arbitrary imposition of social clauses within the World Trade Organization. In 1998 a group of NGOs lobbied the World Bank and other international donors to fund detailed research on the human impact of structural adjustment policies.

NGOs everywhere are making bigger contributions to national development efforts. In Uganda NGOs are collaborating with the government, private sector and communities in a project on nutrition and early childhood development funded by a $34 million credit from the International Development Association, using their expertise to give primary care providers better access to infrastructure. Proshika MUK, an NGO in Bangladesh, does participatory rural appraisals of the national budget to encourage the government to examine how spending decisions affect the poor and to adopt a pro-poor budget.

Source: Human Development Report Office.

Meeting the challenges of globalization—Fundación Chile

Fundación Chile, a joint initiative by the Chilean government and the private sector, combines research and development with a creative vision for market opportunities and a commitment to sustainable development.

The first step is to identify a product that Chile may not yet produce but for which there could be a significant market. Next, Fundación Chile masters the technology through long experimentation. If the product can be adapted to local conditions, a company is created for commercial production. When production is exported, the process is complete and Fundación Chile sells the company—30 so far—to Chilean interests.

Take salmon, which did not exist in Chile. Given the high price of salmon in the world market and the demand in Japan, Fundación Chile introduced salmon in Chile's rivers in the early 1990s. By 1995 salmon exports amounted to almost $500 million, creating thousands of jobs.

Source: Human Development Report Office.

Using national human development reports to outline impacts and priorities

National and local human development reports—expected to number 260 by the end of 1999—provide a great opportunity to outline how a country or community is affected by globalization. Some possible elements:

• An analysis of how people have been affected by globalization in the past 5-10 years, with a balance sheet of gains and losses, quantified as much as possible. It should cover which groups of people gained or lost, what enabled the gains and what caused the losses.

• An analysis of gains and losses in the different elements of human security.

• Priorities for action by local communities, by urban and rural groups and by the national government.

• Indicators for monitoring the impact of globalization and the effectiveness of national policy to manage it.

• A common position on globalization for the different sectors of government—covering finance, planning, trade, agriculture, health and so on.

Globalization should be the topic of one chapter or the theme for an entire national human development report. The chapter or report might set out key priorities in national policy for managing globalization to enhance human development.

Source: Human Development Report Office.

tary domestic and trade policies to guarantee a competitive market environment, regulating any monopoly or oligopoly, particularly if it provides essential services. In many cases the private sector has demanded subsidies, protection and infrastructure from government to benefit from global markets. But in other cases local firms have accepted the challenge of tackling globalization for the good of the country (box 4.13).

Bringing multinational corporations into these alliances is the most difficult. Not only outsiders, they are empires—with money, power, affiliates, subsidiaries and the support of the international system. They are often seen as creating enclaves in national economies, and it is extremely difficult to bring them under national rules and regulations. To make them partners in the development process, they require support, but they also need to respect national rules and be accountable, transparent and sensitive to social responsibilities.

FORMULATING STRATEGIES FOR EMERGING NEW ISSUES IN THE GLOBAL SYSTEM

National action is essential to capture global opportunities in trade, capital flows and migration—and to protect people against the uncertainties and vulnerabilities of globalization (box 4.14). But the success of national action hinges on how effectively countries can negotiate at the global level.

Globalization's many facets require a focus, but efforts today are divided among different ministries and departments. Some are led by the ministry of trade, some by the ministry of finance and some by the ministry of planning. This fragmentation not only weakens the capacity of developing country governments to develop a powerful and consolidated strategy at global forums. It also limits their ability to capture global opportunities. That is why each developing country should set up a coordinated mechanism for dealing with globalization. And whatever the mechanism chosen—presidential task force, global planning commission, special interministerial unit—it must be given the visibility, power and flexibility as well as the technical expertise and political clout to handle the complexities of globalization.

CHAPTER 5

 # Reinventing global governance— for humanity and equity

What area of policy is most important for managing globalization? Harmonizing global competition and free market approaches with steady and expanding support for human development and human rights in all countries, developed and developing. This is at the heart of a new perspective, a new global ethic, a new approach to globalization. And it requires a range of actions, from the broad to the specific.

Reinventing global governance is not an option—it is an imperative for the 21st century. The preceding chapters have spelled out possibilities for human development—and the pitfalls. They have also spelled out the failures of governance in getting the most from the opportunities—and in avoiding the pitfalls.

The costs of these failures are much larger than generally realized. Consider the output losses from the East Asian crisis and its global repercussions. Over the three years from 1998 to 2000 these are estimated at nearly $2 trillion. These losses are:
- About 2% of global economic production in these years—and more than the combined annual income of Sub-Saharan Africa, the Arab States and South Asia.
- Enough to double the incomes of the poorest fifth of the world's people.
- About twice the additional finance required over the next decade to achieve the goals of basic education, primary health care, family planning, nutrition, water and sanitation for all.
- Well over 10 times the $170 billion mobilized internationally to prevent the economic slowdown.

And as chapter 1 made so painfully clear, the cold statistics of economic loss convey few of the human costs—interrupted treatment for hospital patients, rioting and looting in the streets, rising unemployment and declining school attendance. This has become the worst setback to the global economy since the 1930s.

For developing countries there have long been losses from the inadequacies and inequalities in global governance. Some result from weaknesses in global markets for capital —and some from restricted access to developed country markets for exports and technology. Restrictions on migration are still a major contradiction with the principles of the open global economy and one with a high cost to developing countries. *Human Development Report 1992* estimated the total cost of denying market opportunities to developing countries as roughly $500 billion a year, almost 10 times the amount they receive each year in aid.

With the Asian crisis in 1998, the need for fresh thinking about global governance has again been recognized. Initially, the crisis was attributed to weaknesses of domestic policy and action within the countries affected, even though only months before the same countries had been hailed as Asian "miracles of development". But the need for changes in international governance is now widely accepted, and the international community has begun to seek solutions with renewed vigour.

Even so, the debate on international reform is:
- Too narrow in scope—usually excluding human development as an objective, underplaying the importance of employment and environmental sustainability and largely neglecting economic and social rights.
- Too geographically unbalanced—dominated by the concerns of the industrial countries, with secondary attention to the emerging and large

Reinventing global governance is not an option—it is an imperative for the 21st century

economies. The poorest and least developed countries are largely neglected.

• Too driven by the economic and financial interests of the rich countries—often those of the G-7, sometimes just the G-1.

Is it too ambitious to think and plan more boldly? Recall the remarkable vision and human concerns of the 1940s, when the United Nations and Bretton Woods institutions were created. At that time full employment was a key objective, along with:

• Fulfilment of economic and social rights.

• Measures for economic stability, including stability of commodity prices.

• An integral view of the United Nations and Bretton Woods institutions.

The entire structure rested on the Charter of the United Nations, one of the most remarkable and pioneering documents of the 20th century. The far-seeing principles of the UN Charter were reinforced three years later in the 30 articles of the Universal Declaration of Human Rights (boxes 5.1 and 5.2).

Fundamental rethinking of policy and governance is again required. It must be broad and fair, and it must restore an integrated approach covering social as well as economic issues. Key priorities:

• Putting human concerns and human rights at the centre of international policy and action.

• Protecting human security and reducing vulnerability on a worldwide scale.

• Narrowing the extremes of inequality between and within countries.

• Increasing equity in negotiation and structures of international governance.

• Building a new global architecture for the 21st century.

In short, reform driven by concern for people, not for capital.

PUTTING HUMAN CONCERNS AND RIGHTS AT THE CENTRE OF GLOBAL GOVERNANCE

Changes in international governance are needed so that the international system does much more to support, and much less to hinder, international, national and local actions for human development. Five specifics:

STRENGTHEN GLOBAL ETHICS AND RESPONSIBILITY

Global governance with a human face requires shared values, standards and attitudes—a wide acceptance of human responsibilities and obligations. Those values include respect—for life, liberty, justice and equality. And they include tolerance and mutual caring.

Such values underlie the UN Charter and the Universal Declaration of Human Rights. They now need to be translated into the principles and practices of global governance. How? With a strong political commitment propelled by public awareness and support (see the special contribution by Ted Turner).

BOX 5.1

Keynes's vision for global governance

The architecture of international governance set up after the Second World War was in several respects more advanced than that of today.

• There was an integral view of the United Nations and Bretton Woods institutions, working together as part of the whole UN system.

• Economic and social rights were key objectives. The UN Charter emphasized that "conditions of stability and well-being are necessary for peaceful and friendly relations among nations" and "all members pledge themselves to take joint and separate action in cooperation with the organization for 'promoting' higher standards of living, full employment, and conditions of economic and social progress and development."

• The International Monetary Fund and the World Bank were to be complemented by a third body, an international trade organization.

• Full employment was a basic goal, to be supported in all international economic operations.

Keynes went much further than the governments of the time were prepared to accept. He proposed a fund with access to resources equal to half of world imports. The IMF today controls liquidity equal to less than 3% of world imports. He envisaged the IMF as a world central bank, issuing its own reserve currency (Bancor). In the 1970s the IMF was permitted to create a limited amount of special drawing rights

(SDRs), but these constitute less than 3% of global liquidity today.

Keynes placed the burden of adjustment on both surplus and deficit countries, even envisaging a penalty interest rate of 1% a month on outstanding trade surpluses. In practice, deficit nations (mostly developing countries) have had to bear the main burden of adjustment—except for the United States, which can avoid adjustment because its deficit serves to supply dollars needed for liquidity by the global system. The IMF now exercises some monetary discipline only on developing countries, which are responsible for less than 10% of global liquidity.

The international trade organization, as envisaged by Keynes, had functions far beyond the present World Trade Organization. Keynes's international trade organization was not only to maintain free trade but also to help stabilize world commodity prices, essentially through buffer stock arrangements.

Keynes went even further. He recognized that the long-term international prices for commodities must be fixed in relation to both the economic conditions for efficient production and the human conditions for proper nutritional and other requirements to ensure a decent standard of living among primary producers (a principle that Keynes recognized would also apply to producers of manufactured goods).

Direct concern for nutrition and decent living standards has yet to be incorporated into the principles of international trade.

Source: Keynes 1980.

BRING PRINCIPLES OF HUMAN DEVELOPMENT
AND SOCIAL PROTECTION INTO THE
CONCEPTS AND PRACTICES OF GLOBAL
ECONOMIC GOVERNANCE

Global competition and market efficiency are the big objectives of current efforts to restructure global economic governance. Important, but they are too narrow internationally, just as they would be nationally. Global governance needs to incorporate human development priorities for people in all parts of the world—for poverty reduction, equity, sustainability and human development.

Until recently social and welfare policy were matters for national action. With globalization, this has been changing. In the industrial countries global economic competition is putting welfare states under pressure, as chapter 4 showed. In many developing countries education, health and the more limited range of welfare provisions have come under even greater pressure. Structural adjustment policies have often cut back primary health care and basic education, with reduced subsidies and increased charges restricting access to these services for poor people.

At the same time the institutions of global governance have leaned hard on national governments to adopt their preferred systems of social protection—marginal for the International Monetary Fund, social safety nets for the World Bank and a broader and more pragmatic range of social policy options and mechanisms for other UN agencies. Human development policy, as promoted in the *Human Development Reports*, is an example.

But a broader, more coherent set of international principles is required—as some governments are beginning to recognize. Such principles should be built on:
- Economic, social and cultural rights as well as political and civil ones.
- The goals and commitments of the global conferences of the 1990s.
- Democratic and equitable governance, globally and nationally.

The World Bank Group and the IMF need to explore how these principles are brought into their policies and operations.

ADOPT REGIONAL AND GLOBAL AGREEMENTS
TO PREVENT RACES TO THE BOTTOM

International bargaining can be tough—and in the heat of the moment minor or major concessions may be made in wages, labour standards

---

BOX 5.2

The successes and failures of global governance since 1945

Although political negotiations never permitted full realization of the international economic and political architecture as originally proposed, its practical impact was remarkable. From the late 1940s to the early 1970s world economic growth was faster, economic stability greater and unemployment lower than in any comparable period in history. Moreover, more than 70 countries moved from colonial status to political independence, most achieving economic growth rates during the 1960s higher than ever before and often higher than ever since.

Of course, the structures of global governance were far from perfect. The cold war polarized many operations. Inflation was often high. The terms of trade of many primary producing countries fell. The poorest and least developed countries became more marginalized. Various international efforts introduced changes in global governance to tackle these problems.
- The International Development Association was established in 1960 to expand the flows of concessional finance to poor countries.
- UNCTAD was established in 1964 to improve the analysis and negotiation of trade and development issues.

Nonetheless, global governance was recognized to be inadequate, especially for the developing countries. A high-level international group, the Pearson Commission, was established to propose ways to improve aid and development policy. It reported its recommendations in 1969 in *Partners in Development.*

In 1971 the United States abandoned the Bretton Woods system of fixed exchange rates. In the mid and late 1970s, after two decades of declining oil prices, the price of petroleum almost quadrupled, shifting global income distribution in favour of the oil-producing countries. The suddenness of the adjustment set back the global economy. Output in the OECD economies fell. There was a surge in flows of petro-dollars to non-oil developing countries, from commercial banks lending with little overall control or supervision. Welcomed at the time, it was later seen to have laid the foundation for the major debt crises and adjustment problems of the 1980s.

A second major international commission was established, the Brandt Commission. Its report in 1980, *North-South: A Programme for Survival,* showed how industrial and developing countries could share in actions and transfers to stimulate growth in developing countries as a way to achieve a more dynamic global economy. But little of the message was implemented. Instead, the global emphasis shifted to what countries must do on their own, especially in implementing liberalization and adjustment. The need for complementary action by the international community was muted. Debt in the poorest developing countries rose rapidly, commodity prices fell, and aid remained far below commitments, especially for the least developed countries.

There followed a lost decade for development in most of Latin America and Sub-Saharan Africa. Per capita income fell in more than 40 countries in the two regions, often with serious human setbacks for large parts of the population. School enrolment ratios fell in 20 countries.

None of these results can be blamed entirely on the inadequacies of global governance. But the fact remains that since 1980 the majority of countries in Sub-Saharan Africa, many in Latin America and most of those in transition have experienced disastrous failures in growth, often with serious increases in poverty and setbacks in human security. Although there have been some improvements over the 1990s, per capita income in some 40 developing countries is still less than it was 20 or more years ago. The economic decline in many of these countries has already been much worse than anything felt by the industrial countries during the Great Depression.

Source: Haq and others 1995; Rodrik 1999.

and environmental regulations. One way to avoid these pressures is to establish regional frameworks of minimum standards and to strengthen regional agreements to work within them. Labour standards need to support the abilities of people to provide care for their families and communities—not to have global competition undermine them. Mercosur and the European Union have taken steps in this direction.

Such agreements, carefully defined, can raise living standards and protect the environment, without setting back employment or discouraging foreign investment. Collective regional action can ensure that the decisions are based on the needs of people in the countries concerned.

DEVELOP A GLOBAL CODE OF CONDUCT FOR MULTINATIONAL CORPORATIONS—AND A GLOBAL FORUM FOR THEIR MONITORING

Multinational corporations are already a dominant part of the global economy—yet many of their actions go unrecorded and unaccounted. They must, however, go far beyond reporting just to their shareholders. They need to be brought within the frame of global governance, not just the patchwork of national laws, rules and regulations.

Because of the activism of NGOs and other institutions of civil society, many multinational corporations are taking their social responsibili-

ties more seriously. Mattel, the toy-producing enterprise, and Disney World, the entertainment giant, have codes of conduct for their plants in Asia. Mattel is the only multinational corporation in China that has won the Social Accountability 8000—a certificate of workplace standards that Asia Monitor, a watchdog NGO, calls for. Disney has done more than 10,000 inspections to ensure proper working conditions for its workers in Asia.

Codes of conduct have moved from vague promises to detailed rules, with the best codes now monitored by outside auditors (box 5.3). But multinationals should be socially responsible from the beginning, not only after having been caught neglecting responsibilities. Codes of conduct should also be developed for banks and financial institutions, covering secrecy and risk assessment.

Incentives and publicity can help. The Council for Economic Priorities, a US-based NGO, gives annual awards and public recognition to Fortune 500 companies demonstrating exceptional performance in community partnership, employee empowerment and gender equity, environmental stewardship, social mission and human rights.

But multinational corporations are too important and too dominant a part of the global economy for voluntary codes to be enough. Globally agreed principles of performance are needed for:

Multinational corporations need to be brought within the frame of global governance, not just the patchwork of national laws, rules and regulations

Partnership with the United Nations

Even as communications, transportation and technology are driving global economic expansion, headway on poverty is not keeping pace. It is as if globalization is in fast-forward, and the world's ability to understand and react to it is in slow motion.

But there are promising signs.

First is the ascendance of new means for global progress—the emergence of a more vibrant and engaged civil society. The private sector is another growing force for progress. Private investment in developing countries now dwarfs foreign assistance as a source of resources for progress.

On the other hand, governments are financially and politically challenged as never before. And increasingly, the expertise of

new global challenges resides outside government.

All of these trends point us towards the need and potential for public-private partnerships. These kinds of partnership are urgently needed as government assistance is cut even as the demands and needs for international cooperation grow.

While the private sector, trade and investment hold promise for broad progress in the future, too few countries and sectors are benefiting from globalization. Worldwide economic progress must address sustainable human development.

That is why the UNDP and its UN colleagues are ever-more important. All those who care about the world around them must care about and support the United Nations. The United Nations is the place where nations work together

to address global issues, protect the environment, eliminate poverty, empower women and promote children's health. And the United Nations needs the support of all sectors—business, government, NGOs and the philanthropic world.

Secretary-General Kofi Annan is doing all that he can to make the United Nations a better, more responsive and more open institution. It is up to the rest of us to join him in rededicating our support for the United Nations and its efforts to create a more peaceful, prosperous and poverty-free world.

Ted Turner
Founder, CNN

- Human concerns—to ensure compliance with labour standards and human rights.
- Economic efficiency—to ensure fair trade and competitive markets.
- Environmental sustainability—to avoid degradation and pollution.

Also needed is a global forum to bring multinational corporations into open debate with other parts of the global community—unions, NGOs and government. The results could be practical and positive. The first major conference hosted by the UK-based Ethical Trading Initiative, in London at the end of 1998, brought together hundreds of people from a range of companies, trade unions and NGOs to discuss fair trade issues and company codes of conduct. Six of the nine UK companies among the top 100 multinationals now have codes in draft. In the space of a few years, the fair trade movement and the promotion of fairly traded products have gone from the margin to the mainstream in promoting labour rights, and retail sales of fairly traded goods are worth more than $250 million in Europe alone. This could be replicated at the global level in many ways.

STRENGTHEN THE GLOBAL COMMITMENT TO HUMANE GOVERNANCE

People's expanding awareness of their connections with the wider world is part of globalization. Securing political support for more humane global governance will depend on increasing that awareness even more—and on making people conscious of their being citizens of the world, not just their countries.

Many things already contribute to a sense of global responsibility:
- Education, especially the opportunity for young people to learn about the lives and situations of people in other parts of the world.
- The media's treatment of international news and events, explaining them from the viewpoints of other countries.
- Networks of NGOs, such as the Third World Network and the UN-NGO Forum.
- Trade union activities focusing on global issues.
- Opportunities to study abroad and to travel and work with people from other countries.

- Interactions in professional groups.
- Parliamentary, religious and other groups committed to strengthening international understanding and exchange.

And these are just a start (box 5.4).

PROTECTING HUMAN SECURITY IN ECONOMIC CRISIS

The biggest human setbacks of the past two years emanate from the Asian economic crisis. The crisis has already stimulated strong support from the World Bank and the UN system in response to human needs in the countries

---

BOX 5.3

Social auditing of multinational corporations

The demand for social auditing—a thorough check as to whether multinationals are living up to their social responsibilities—is on the rise. In addition to emerging social auditors, accounting firms such as Deloitte & Touche, PricewaterhouseCoopers and Ernst & Young are also carrying out social auditing.

Last year 1,500 inspections were done in the Guangdong province of China, where there is a large concentration of multinationals. Nike has said that it would arrange for inspections of all its plants worldwide. At the same time Nike has raised the salaries of workers hurt by currency devaluation, increased its minimum working age to 18 and switched to less toxic glues. Mattel has also worked hard. Independent auditors have paid visits to its factories and those of its suppliers, and local activists play a role in its social auditing.

Source: OECD 1999a.

BOX 5.4

Globalization without Poverty—a European initiative

The Council of Europe, with 40 member states, recently launched Globalization without Poverty. This initiative brings together national governments, intergovernmental organizations, NGOs, parliamentarians, local authorities, the media and communications agencies in joint efforts to renew the commitment in Europe to global poverty eradication. The permanent North-South Centre of the Council of Europe, based in Lisbon, is the secretariat for these efforts.

The campaign aims to promote the idea of social inclusiveness in Europe and new concepts of global citizenship that focus on the rights and responsibilities of citizens living in a global society. Some initiatives, such as the Action Week against Poverty, will be Europe-wide; many others are national or local. The project aims to remind people, in line with the overall policy of the Council of Europe, that extreme poverty and social exclusion are a denial of human rights.

One initiative, the Global Forum on Poverty Eradication, has been inspired by the work of the Forum of the Poor in Thailand. It aims to listen to—and learn from—the experiences of the poor, both in Europe and in the South. Its goal is to develop an agenda for action that will contain recommendations and proposals on how extreme poverty can be eradicated and especially on how societies can be mobilized to achieve this goal.

By emphasizing poverty eradication on a global scale, the forum attempts to offset ideas of personal insecurity and "Fortress" Europe as a response to European inwardness in thought and action. The campaign message: "Europe is not a planet, but part of One World, and that creates both opportunities and responsibilities."

Source: Human Development Report Office.

directly affected. More important for the long run, it has stirred a major rethinking of the improvements needed in global governance to avoid recurrence and further contagion.

REDUCING FINANCIAL INSECURITY

Extremes of vulnerability are a systemic problem of financial liberalization on a global scale and call for new global measures of prevention and preparedness. Already the economic costs and human consequences of these setbacks add up to an important agenda of priorities.

Developing and adopting new international codes of conduct for banks and financial institutions, improving information and transparency and enhancing international financial supervision and regulation are all part of the new consensus. So is recognition of the IMF's need for increased financial resources to enable it to act more quickly and preemptively as lender of last resort. Such resources could be obtained by increasing government financial commitments to the IMF, enhancing the use of IMF special drawing rights (SDRs) or selling some of its gold holdings.

Those who balk at the political difficulties of getting agreement to such measures should recall the risks and costs of not doing so. The willingness of the United States to act as lender of last resort to Mexico in 1994-95, and the speed of its support, did much to limit the depth and contagion of the Mexican financial crisis and to achieve rapid recovery. Money alone is not enough, however. Financial support must be accompanied by economic reform and restructuring—taking account of human goals, not just economic and financial ones.

PREVENTING FUTURE FINANCIAL CRISES

The financial crises of the 1990s have been systemic—with finance surging in and out of countries at a speed and volume beyond the capacity of any country on its own to control.

In addition to the measures to reduce financial insecurity, poor countries need special support. A recent UN task force on financial architecture proposed various measures to help prevent further crisis and contagion, including:

- *Removing the requirement that countries liberalize capital accounts as a condition for borrowing.* The extent and phasing of capital account liberalization should be a matter for each developing or transition economy to decide on the basis of its needs and capacities. International pressures for abrupt or premature liberalization have often proved counterproductive.
- *Incorporating standstill provisions into the rules for borrowing from the international financial institutions.* These would give countries under financial pressure the right to delay debt servicing.
- *Developing regional and subregional initiatives to support monetary and financial management.* Stronger regional collective action could be stabilizing—pooling reserve funds, strengthening financial monitoring, maintaining open trade even under pressure. The experience of Western Europe, from the Payments Union in the early postwar years to the euro today, underscores the value of such arrangements.
- *Increasing technical support.* The cost of processing all the information required for financial negotiation and decision-making is very high for small and poor countries. The international institutions have a special responsibility to help countries gain rapid and easy access to such information and analysis.

PROTECTING PEOPLE DURING PERIODS OF CRISIS AND ADJUSTMENT

Time and time again when under economic pressure, countries find themselves sacrificing the needs of their children on the altar of economic orthodoxy—cutting schools, clinics and hospitals to balance their budgets and pay their debts. The challenge is greatest in poor countries, where the coverage of schools and health services is already limited. By cutting the investment budget, countries ease the pressures on both capital and recurrent accounts—but at the cost of postponing the vital goals of health and education for all.

This spotlights the importance of adopting long-run human goals—and maintaining progress towards them, with international support to make this possible. Countries should be

Stronger regional collective action could be stabilizing—pooling reserve funds, strengthening financial monitoring, maintaining open trade even under pressure

encouraged to set goals and dates for achieving universal access to education and health—as set out in the World Summit for Social Development, in other global conferences of the 1990s and in the Development Assistance Committee goals for the 21st century. At a minimum, all countries should be encouraged to make some progress towards these goals each year—no matter how severe the economic pressures.

Stronger international support is needed for protecting people in crisis. The way industrial countries respond to a flood or earthquake within their borders is instructive here. It would be unthinkable and politically unacceptable in an industrial country today to allow a natural disaster to leave citizens without health services or children without schooling for years on end. Yet this happens often in developing countries. A lender of last resort for social protection would thus be useful—perhaps as a special window of the World Bank.

REDUCING OTHER CAUSES OF HUMAN INSECURITY

Threats to human security are being exacerbated by globalization in other ways. Three threats show the range of actions required.

CONTROLLING GLOBAL CRIME

The virulent synergy between globalization and organized crime calls for new global instruments to back national actions and control the international links. An international convention against transnational organized crime is under preparation. Among the key measures:
• Encouraging cooperation in law enforcement and surveillance, with support for advanced investigative techniques.
• Enhancing international judicial cooperation, including the transfer of cases from one jurisdiction to another and the use of video-conferencing for cross-examination.
• Obliging states to develop effective programmes for protecting witnesses and legal professionals.
• Criminalizing money laundering and developing cooperative actions to track and prevent it.

Special actions are needed to deal with trafficking in women and children and smuggling migrants and firearms.

The media, NGOs and other institutions of civil society have played an important role in uncovering the untold story of human trafficking and forcing action. Needed now are more formal international processes of reporting and reviewing actions. Also needed are international negotiations between labour-sending and labour-receiving countries and with international organizations. Such negotiations should lead to codes of conduct both for labour-sending and for labour-receiving countries, laws for eliminating exploitation of migrant workers and violations of their human rights, and severe penalties for traffickers (box 5.5). The UN Convention for the Suppression of Traffic in Persons and the Exploitation of the Prostitution of Others, approved by the General Assembly in 1949, focuses on trafficking as a criminal commercial enterprise. Only 70 countries have adopted this convention.

PROTECTING CULTURAL DIVERSITY

Culture, community and human security are intertwined—but too often undermined by the invasions of globalization. The World Commission on Culture and Development recognized the broad principle of protecting cultural diversity while encouraging cultural exchange. Balancing the two is difficult and controversial—but countries wishing to protect their cultural heritage need to be permitted to do so.

Four examples of actions:
• Regional and private efforts could encourage much more two-way cultural communication—so that films, music, literature and television programming flow between and within developing regions, not just to them from industrial countries.
• Policy-makers have to rethink state, community and international institutions and policies to permit local populations to choose their languages and way of life. At the same time institutions should be created that encourage a dialogue between leaders of different cultural groups to negotiate exchanges and promote better mutual understanding.
• An international forum could be held on international violence and pornography—

Culture, community and human security are intertwined—but too often undermined by the invasions of globalization whether in videos, television programming or interactive games and services—and on national efforts to moderate and control these activities and safeguard children from their influence.

• New partnerships between governments, corporations, private voluntary associations and other stakeholders should be developed. The effects of global markets on local cultural indus-

tries, both good and bad, should be more clearly recognized, so that policy can protect and enhance their cultural and economic flowering.

PRESERVING THE ENVIRONMENT

Despite widespread public support for environmental action, the driving forces of globalization still put profit before environmental protection, preservation and sustainability. The international body charged with building a bridge between environmental and trade policy, the World Trade Organization's committee on trade and environment, has focused mostly on fitting environmental concerns into existing trade regimes, not on seeking a true synergy between environment and trade as equal policy objectives. The committee sees its role as limiting unilateral state actions in the name of environmental protection to protect the trading system—not as creating a paradigm shift from a negative trade-environment relationship to a positive one, a relationship that promotes sustainable trade, investment and growth.

The committee has focused on some important questions: Should WTO members agree on general exemptions for trade-restricting measures in multilateral environmental agreements? And how can eco-labelling schemes be protected and not classed as non-tariff trade barriers? But other issues demand attention: How can trade measures encourage countries to remove the perverse subsidies for energy, chemicals and water that distort trade and damage the environment? And how can they lead countries to internalize the environmental costs of production? Why not establish a "green round" on international trade to coordinate joint actions on eliminating environmentally damaging subsidies and internalizing environmental costs?

NARROWING GLOBAL GAPS

Nearly 30 years ago the Pearson Commission report began with the recognition that "the widening gap between the developed and the developing countries has become the central problem of our times." Today, global inequalities in income and living standards have reached grotesque proportions. The gap in per capita income (GNP) between the countries with the

---

BOX 5.5

Global crime—the international response

The risk to the positive aspects of globalization posed by the growth of global organized crime has been recognized at the highest levels: it was on the agenda for the G-7 meeting in Birmingham a couple of years ago. Such recognition is critical, because the response to global crime must be global, not national.

Con men operating out of Amsterdam sell bogus US securities by telephone to Germans; the operation is controlled by an Englishman resident in Monaco, with his profits in Panama. Which police force should investigate? In which jurisdiction should a prosecution be mounted? There may even be a question about whether a crime has been committed, although if all the actions had taken place in a single country there would be little doubt.

The first principle of a global response to crime is cooperation. Law enforcement agencies, police, prosecutors and intelligence services need to work with their opposite numbers across borders, breaking down what is often generations of suspicion and even enmity. This is not easy, but there are precedents at the national level. A crime in the United States may be investigated by city, state or federal police; among the federal agencies may be the Federal Bureau of Investigation, the Drug Enforcement Administration, the Secret Service, US Customs and the Internal Revenue Service. These groups do not always get on with each other, but they have learned to cooperate to attack crime that cuts across their jurisdictions and competencies.

Part of the suspicion that law enforcement agencies in the developed world have of their counterparts elsewhere is based on corruption. The traffic policeman in Mexico, the customs officer in Nigeria, the prosecutor in Russia may all face a choice between operating honestly or feeding their family. When compared with the needs of education and health care, support for the

law enforcement budget may not seem a high priority, but short-term savings may result in heavy long-term costs.

The second principle is effective and appropriate regulation. When a political system changes from a centrally planned economy or a police state to a liberal, free market, democratic society, there are huge pressures, from within and from the international community, to remove oppressive regulations; but there is less push to replace them with the sort of legal framework and institutions that have grown up over centuries in societies that have long had such political systems. This is a dangerous mistake.

For example, encouraging an indigenous banking system is an important development goal, and bank secrecy legislation may seem a good short cut. But without a strong bank regulatory framework, and an institution with the muscle to impose it, the result will be a flood of dirty money followed by bank failures. The end result is bailout costs for the central bank and loss of international market credibility for the future.

Similarly, privatization without a strong system of corporate law, and a judicial system that is an effective administrator and guarantor of its application, becomes a lottery. Sometimes a sound enterprise, a good local partner and management team, and consistent government regulation align to produce a spectacular investment success. But more often cronyism in the privatization process and abuse of minority shareholder interests lead to failure, and the local courts offer little hope of redress.

Comparing the goal of increasing economic freedom with imposing new bureaucratic contraints is an unequal battle. But the liberalization of the economic and political system must march in lock-step with the growth of laws and the institutions that administer them. New freedoms bring new responsibilities.

Source: Helsby 1999.

richest fifth of the world's people and those with the poorest fifth widened from 30 to 1 in 1960, to 60 to 1 in 1990, to 74 to 1 in 1995. The marginalization of the least developed countries continues, accelerating as a result of the Asian crisis.

Narrowing such gaps is the unlisted item on the global agenda. Extremes of inequality permeate and poison globalization and polarize many reasonable and desirable attempts to manage it better. The issues of global inequality are too fundamental to be swept under the carpet. On the eve of the 21st century, with the newfound awareness of globalization's possibilities, new approaches are needed:

• Taking consistent international actions to support faster growth, and adopting stronger measures to support pro-poor growth in poorer countries.

• Removing constraints on poor countries in trade, investment and technology.

• Refocusing aid to support poverty reduction, especially in the poorest and least developed countries.

• Accelerating debt relief for the highly indebted poor countries.

These proposals are not new, but they are rarely pursued with the energy and resolve required, nor with the clear recognition that the extremes between the richest and poorest countries are counter-productive for the very process of globalization. One of the main reasons globalization stalled in the early 20th century was rising global inequalities.

Pro-poor growth is needed—both for reducing poverty and for making growth a stronger and more indigenous process. Particularly important is accelerating growth in the poorest and least developed countries, with growth rates of at least 3% per capita maintained for three decades. An important step would be to establish an international transfer mechanism to encourage resource flows to poor countries—through private investment and through purposeful allocation of global revenues derived from taxing pollution or charging for use of the global commons (see below). Another would be to create an international task force to focus on possible actions to address the widening gaps between rich and poor countries, including setting time-bound goals for narrowing the gaps between the industrial countries and the poorest and least developed countries.

As Professor Jan Tinbergen, the first Nobel Prize winner in economics, wrote a few years ago, "there should also be redistribution at the international level through development cooperation. . . . As the world economy becomes increasingly integrated, so the redistribution of world income should become similar to that within well-governed nations" (*Human Development Report 1994*, p. 88).

PROMOTING FAIRER TRADE,
ESPECIALLY FOR THE POOREST COUNTRIES

Both developing and developed countries need to do more to ensure greater benefits for

Extremes of inequality permeate and poison globalization and polarize many reasonable and desirable attempts to manage it better

---

BOX 5.6

Renegotiating Lomé—one size doesn't fit all

For almost 25 years this pioneering treaty of development cooperation guaranteed the African, Caribbean and Pacific (ACP) states financial aid and preferential market access to Europe. The current Lomé convention will expire in February 2000. The European Union and 71 ACP states are engaged in negotiations to renew it.

The first of four treaties under this framework was signed in Lomé, the capital of Togo, in 1975. It started out with high ideals. Its fundamental principles called for equality between the partners, respect for their sovereignty, mutual interest and interdependence and the right of each partner to determine its own political, social, cultural and economic policy options.

The European Union is suggesting substantial changes to the Lomé convention. European policy-makers argue that Lomé did not work. They say that the convention did little to pull the ACP states out of poverty. Moreover, European policy priorities have shifted. Donor fatigue, new partners in Eastern Europe and budgetary constraints due to the strict Maastricht criteria contributed to a change in European attitude towards the ACP states. In addition, the European Union claims that Lomé is not in accord with the rules of the World Trade Organization.

If the European Union's plans are implemented, a large group of ACP states may experience a massive deterioration in market access to Europe, reversing transfer of payments from some ACP countries to the European Union.

Under these plans, free trade areas, private investment and conditionality may replace preferential market access and unconditional financial aid. The European Union intends to maintain Lomé preferences for the 41 least developed ACP countries. But the 30 other developing countries may be given the choice of forming a free trade area with the European Union or joining the General System of Preferences.

What can be done?

• Europeans must not abandon their commitments to the ACP states. They should realize that Lomé applied one set of policies to 71 different countries. This one-size-fits-all approach eventually did not work. A renewal of the Lomé treaty must therefore recognize the political, economic and cultural diversity of the ACP states.

• Previously, financial support was given as a lump sum to ACP governments. A future Lomé treaty should direct resources to promote specific sectors or to build institutions. This can be achieved only when donor and recipient countries cooperate closely.

• The European Union should pursue a mix of policies. Free trade areas can benefit sectors that can compete. More vulnerable sectors, such as agriculture, should either receive financial aid or be temporarily exempted from trade liberalization.

Source: Kennan and Stevens 1997.

---

developing countries in trade, improving market access and the terms of trade, especially for the poorest and least developed countries (box 5.6). Trade liberalization can benefit developing countries, and they should in principle be willing to engage in new multilateral negotiations. But before new global trade talks start, developing countries must be assured that previous agreements and promises will be kept. The Multi-Fibre Arrangement must be eliminated, as promised by developed countries. And the use of antidumping measures against the poorest countries must be curbed.

Speeding the elimination of domestic agricultural support and export subsidies in the industrial countries would help ensure access to markets for agricultural products. And regulations governing food safety, animal and plant health and the safety of farm workers need to be implemented in ways that minimize the risk that they will be used as protectionist measures—say, by:
- Devising multilateral standards and encouraging the spread of mutual recognition and equivalency agreements.
- Requiring product labels that include the origin and attributes of each product.
- Ensuring credible regulatory agencies that are separate from those responsible for farm support programmes.

International support to help poor countries expand agricultural exports would offer triple benefits. It would encourage production in areas of the world with many comparative advantages and much lower use of fertilizers and pesticides than is typical in industrial countries. It would help maintain crop and seed diversity. And it would encourage exports and production as a step towards economic development in poor countries.

A new round of trade negotiations—the millenium round—is in the works (box 5.7). Much is at stake, and developing countries need to be ahead of the issues, not behind them.

REDUCING THE DEBT OF THE POOREST COUNTRIES

Slow progress in tackling the accumulated debt of the 41 heavily indebted poor countries (HIPCs) is one of the clearest examples of how globalization has been failing the poorest and least developed countries (box 5.8). For several years most commentators have agreed that the debt of these countries is excessive and unpayable. Yet the actions have so far been minute in relation to the needs.

The debt burden has undermined growth, health and education. Only 2 HIPCs have achieved growth rates of more than 2% per capita since 1980, while 9 did so between 1965 and 1980. Debt service payments exceed annual expenditure on health and education in 9 HIPCs, and they exceed health spending in 29, including 23 in Sub-Saharan Africa (table 5.1). Tanzania's debt service payments are nine times what it spends on primary health care and four times what it spends on primary education.

BOX 5.7

Developing countries and trade— active participation in the millennium round

Five years after the end of the Uruguay Round, preparations for a new round of multilateral trade negotiations are under way. Negotiations might deal not only with the reduction of tariff and non-tariff barriers in such critical areas as textiles and agriculture. They could focus also on non-trade issues such as environmental and labour standards and competition rules.

Developing countries need to understand these developments, be ahead and not behind them, identify areas of key interest and help shape more forcefully the global trade structure. Trade liberalization can, after all, be a win-win situation.

Developing countries could consider these policy and strategy options for the next round of multilateral trade negotiations:
- *Review and implement existing agreements before new agreements.* Before negotiators talk about such issues as environmental or labour standards, they need to make sure that all parties keep the commitments made in the Uruguay Round. For example, OECD countries need to implement the Agreement on Textiles and Clothing to free developing countries from the regime of the Multi-Fibre Arrangement.
- *Talk about all property rights.* Property rights include intellectual property rights as well as rights to emit carbon into the atmosphere. Many rich countries seem to have overused their right to pollute. If they want to continue to do so, developing countries could link these property rights in trade negotiations and demand compensation. An aggressive pursuit of property rights could yield the developing countries both potential economic benefits and negotiating leverage.
- *Win-win: environmental concessions and trade liberalization.* Broadening the negotiating agenda to include issues such as the environment does not have to be disadvantageous to developing countries. It can also open opportunities. Countries with significant environmental assets (rain forests in Brazil, Cameroon, the Democratic Republic of the Congo, Costa Rica, Indonesia, Malaysia, Thailand) could make concessions to achieve benefits in other areas. In exchange for protecting or even rebuilding rain forests, developing countries could ask OECD countries to level the playing field in trade, investment or antidumping measures.
- *Together, if you can.* Developing countries need to get better organized and negotiate in groups. Their political leverage increased during the Uruguay Round. Today, developing countries account for 30% of world trade. Regional or sectoral alliances may help developing countries increase their standing in trade negotiations.

Source: Whalley 1999.

Under the HIPC initiative, it takes six years for a country to become eligible for debt relief. This period should be sharply reduced, by half or more. The debt sustainability ratio—the amount of debt that is deemed manageable by an indebted country—must also be lowered, from 200–250% of a country's annual exports to 100% or less (table 5.2). Debt payments are deemed bearable at 20–25% of a country's annual exports. This should be reduced to 10% or less. In short, the poorest countries need more support and more breathing space to restore growth and accelerate human development.

The sum required to fund the HIPC initiative has been officially estimated at $7 billion—less than 5% of the $170 billion mobilized for East Asia and Brazil (though it is needed on grant not loan terms). One argument against faster debt relief is that the resources for it would have to come from other concessional funds, "robbing Peter to pay Paul". This need not be. Debt relief for the poorest countries could and should be financed from new and additional resources. These could come from sales of IMF gold or new allocations of SDRs—even from special contributions, just as for the bailout of the Long-Term Capital Management fund. By the test of human development, Sub-Saharan countries and the other HIPCs deserve more support.

MORE AID, BETTER ALLOCATED, MORE USEFUL

Although official development assistance (ODA) has fallen since 1994 (table 5.3), there are some signs of recovery. Six donor countries of 21 increased their ODA in 1997, Canada and the United Kingdom by the most. And four continue to exceed the 0.7% of GNP target by an easy margin—Denmark, the Netherlands, Norway and Sweden. The increases will help offset the much faster decline in aid budgets in relation to other public expenditures.

Implementing the commitments to the least developed countries remains one of the highest priorities, especially the commitment that each donor allocate a minimum of 0.15% of its GNP to these countries. Few of the poorest countries have much chance of receiving substantial foreign direct investment, so they depend on aid, especially for expanding basic health and education and raising growth rates.

A MULTILATERAL AGREEMENT ON INVESTMENT—FOR PEOPLE

Negotiations on the Multilateral Agreement on Investment collapsed—a casualty of unreconciled differences of philosophy among developed countries. More serious was the secrecy surrounding the negotiations and the failure to bring in all the countries involved. Negotiations on a new agreement must start with a more equitable process and clearer acceptance of the need to achieve equitable results not just for capital—but for people.

The process of negotiating the agreement will determine its success. Talks need to be open. Participation of developing countries and of civil society is crucial. National treatment of capital must be tied to the concept of sustainable development. Most-favored-nation principles for investment do not preclude

---

BOX 5.8

Debt—a need for accelerated action

External debt continues to be a heavy burden for developing countries. In 1997 the total debt of developing countries reached almost $2.2 trillion. Hardest hit have been the 41 heavily indebted poor countries (HIPCs), 33 of them in Africa. Their debt burden, $245 billion in 1996, drains public budgets, absorbs resources needed for human development and inhibits economic growth.

Since 1980 the debt of the HIPCs has more than tripled, two-thirds the result of arrears unpaid or earlier debt. Moreover, the nature of debt has changed. In 1980 more than half of all debt was owed to private creditors—in 1997 barely a fifth. Today's debt crisis is about official debt—increasingly debt owed to multilateral institutions such as the International Monetary Fund and the World Bank. The shift from private debt to official and multilateral debt opens the door for policy-makers to find solutions to the debt crisis.
• An acceleration of debt forgiveness under the HIPC initiative is essential. Too few of the poorest countries are eligible under the initiative, which may leave some countries in a very tight spot. The envisaged

period of six years of good performance before eligibility should be reduced to three years or even less, provided debtor countries work closely with the World Bank and the IMF and follow agreed principles.
• In some cases partial or total debt forgiveness by the Paris Club is also needed. Denmark's cancellation of developing country debt worth $635 million and Germany's debt initiative are leading examples for OECD countries. Other industrial countries have forgiven debt arising from earlier aid support—but not all.
• Showing how debt payments squeeze a country's capacity to provide education and health to all its children would help to bring home to the general public the wider significance of the debt problem—and the urgent need for action.
• Cancellation of all debt of the most impoverished developing countries is the objective pursued by the Jubilee 2000 initiative. Sponsored by many churches and NGOs, the initiative links the year 2000 with the biblical concept of debt forgiveness.

Source: UNCTAD 1998b; UN 1998b.

---

codes of conduct for big corporations. Governments must retain full discretion to set environmental and labour standards.

NARROWING TECHNOLOGY GAPS

In an era of sweeping technological advance, it is inexcusable that human poverty should persist—and that the technological gaps are widening. Poor people and countries need a better

deal from technology's breakthroughs.

• Global governance of intellectual property rights under the agreement on Trade-Related Aspects of Intellectual Property Rights, or TRIPS, must be broadly and fully reviewed to create a system that does not block developing countries from knowledge or threaten food security, indigenous knowledge, biosafety and access to health care.

• The TRIPS agreement must recognize the rights of local communities to their traditional and indigenous knowledge—and encourage fair and just compensation for the use of this knowledge.

• Consumers and producers in developing countries must be protected. Price controls should be permitted or encouraged on certain patented products for production by poor farmers and for basic health and education. Price controls are especially important for pharmaceutical products, with treatments for HIV/AIDS an obvious example.

• Governance of global communications—especially the Internet—must be broadened to include the very strong interests of developing countries in decisions on Internet protocols, taxation, domain name allocation and telephony costs.

• Public investment is needed in technologies to meet the needs of poor people and countries, from drought-resistant, robust seeds to humidity-resistant, solar-powered computers.

• New funding mechanisms should be created to ensure that the information revolution leads to human development, not human polarization. Two proposals—a bit tax and a patent tax—would raise funds from those who already have access to technology and use them to help extend the benefits more widely.

SPECIFIC ACTIONS TO STRENGTHEN THE BARGAINING POSITION OF POOR COUNTRIES IN GLOBAL GOVERNANCE

Large inequalities of economic power and influence are embedded in most international institutions. Often this is justified on the grounds that those with the largest stake in the outcomes have most to lose—and that they must have greater influence to ensure "respon-

TABLE 5.1
Eight heavily indebted poor countries, 1995

Country	External debt US$ billions	As % of GNP	Debt service as % of GNP	Public expenditure On education (% of GNP) [a]	On health (% of GDP) [a]	On military (% of GDP)
Nicaragua	10	670	19	4	4	2
Angola	12	501	20	..	4	3
Guyana	2	394	20	5	..	1
Guinea-Bissau	1	380	7	..	1	3
Congo	6	350	11	6	2	3
Mozambique	6	327	9	6	5	5
Congo, Dem. Rep. of the	13	242	0.5	..	0.2	0.3
Mauritania	2	231	12	5	2	3

a. Data are for most recent year available during 1990–95.
Source: World Bank 1998c.

TABLE 5.2
External debt of the 41 heavily indebted poor countries, 1992–96

	1992	1993	1994	1995	1996
Total debt (US$ billions)	229	235	247	254	245
Debt service (US$ billions)	10	8	9	12	11
Debt service/exports (%)	21	17	19	20	16
Debt stocks/exports (%)	461	495	493	431	344

Source: UN 1998b.

TABLE 5.3
Who gets aid?
(official development assistance in current US$ billions, except where otherwise specified)

	1988	1993	1994	1995	1996	1997
Net ODA	48	56	60	60	58	50
Bilateral	37	39	41	41	39	32
Multilateral	11	17	19	19	19	18
Net ODA (1995 US$ billions)	61	59	62	60	57	48
Share of ODA to least developed countries (%)	28	27	27	28	24	27
ODA to least developed countries	13	15	16	17	14	14
ODA to five largest recipients						
China	2.5	3.3	3.3	3.5	2.6	2.0
Egypt	1.9	2.4	2.7	2.0	2.2	2.0
India	2.4	1.5	2.3	1.7	1.9	1.7
Israel	1.5	1.3	1.3	0.3	2.2	..
Bangladesh	2.2	1.4	1.8	1.3	1.3	1.0

Source: OECD 1996a and 1999a.

sible" decisions. If stake means financial outcome, this may be true. But if stake refers to the number of people affected, often hurt, this justification looks very thin (table 5.4).

Voting arrangements need to be revised—for fairness, efficiency and political viability. If they are not, those shut out may change their minds about the virtues of participating in the system. There must also be some agreement on the need to give much more attention to the interests of the poor countries and, over time, to narrow the gaps between them and the better-off countries.

Improving institutional accountability is a priority in the reform of international gover-

nance. Decision-making in international trade and finance needs to be more transparent, and independent evaluations of international public policies can be a first step towards increased accountability. The World Bank's Operations Evaluation Department and the IMF's independent external evaluation of its Enhanced Structural Adjustment Facility programmes are first steps in the right direction. Other priorities:

• Establishing an ombudsman mechanism within the WTO, World Bank and IMF to investigate cases of alleged bias and injustice in their operations.

TABLE 5.4
Global institutions and their membership

Institution		Membership	Share of world GDP (%) 1997	Share of world population (%) 1997
P-5	Security Council	China, France, Russian Federation, United Kingdom, United States	40.9	30.6
G-7	Western economic powers	Canada, France, Germany, Italy, Japan, United Kingdom, United States	64.0	11.8
G-10	Western economic powers	Belgium, Canada, France, Germany, Italy, Japan, Netherlands, Sweden, Switzerland, United Kingdom, United States	67.8	12.5
G-22	Western economic powers and emerging markets	Argentina, Australia, Brazil, Canada, China, France, Germany, Hong Kong (China, SAR), India, Indonesia, Italy, Japan, Republic of Korea, Malaysia, Mexico, Poland, Russian Federation, Singapore, South Africa, Thailand, United Kingdom, United States	81.7	64.8
G-24	Major developing countries	Algeria, Argentina, Brazil, Colombia, Democratic Republic of the Congo, Côte d'Ivoire, Egypt, Ethiopia, Gabon, Ghana, Guatemala, India, Islamic Republic of Iran, Lebanon, Mexico, Nigeria, Pakistan, Peru, Philippines, Sri Lanka, Syrian Arab Republic, Trinidad and Tobago, Venezuela, Yugoslavia	8.9	34.6
G-77	Developing and transition countries	Afghanistan, Algeria, Angola, Antigua and Barbuda, Argentina, Bahamas, Bahrain, Bangladesh, Barbados, Belize, Benin, Bhutan, Bolivia, Bosnia and Herzegovina, Botswana, Brazil, Brunei Darussalam, Burkina Faso, Burundi, Cambodia, Cameroon, Cape Verde, Central African Republic, Chad, Chile, China, Colombia, Comoros, Congo, Democratic Republic of the Congo, Costa Rica, Côte d'Ivoire, Cuba, Cyprus, Djibouti, Dominica, Dominican Republic, Ecuador, Egypt, El Salvador, Equatorial Guinea, Eritrea, Ethiopia, Fiji, Gabon, Gambia, Ghana, Grenada, Guatemala, Guinea, Guinea-Bissau, Guyana, Haiti, Honduras, India, Indonesia, Islamic Republic of Iran, Iraq, Jamaica, Jordan, Kenya, Democratic People's Republic of Korea, Kuwait, Lao People's Democratic Republic, Lebanon, Lesotho, Liberia, Libyan Arab Jamahiriya, Madagascar, Malawi, Malaysia, Maldives, Mali, Malta, Marshall Islands, Mauritania, Mauritius, Federated States of Micronesia, Mongolia, Morocco, Mozambique, Myanmar, Namibia, Nepal, Nicaragua, Niger, Nigeria, Oman, Pakistan, Occupied Palestinian territory, Panama, Papua New Guinea, Paraguay, Peru, Philippines, Qatar, Romania, Rwanda, Saint Kitts and Nevis, Saint Lucia, Saint Vincent and the Grenadines, Samoa (Western), São Tomé and Principe, Saudi Arabia, Senegal, Seychelles, Sierra Leone, Singapore, Solomon Islands, Somalia, South Africa, Sri Lanka, Sudan, Suriname, Swaziland, Syrian Arab Republic, United Republic of Tanzania, Thailand, Togo, Tonga, Trinidad and Tobago, Tunisia, Turkmenistan, Uganda, United Arab Emirates, Uruguay, Vanuatu, Venezuela, Viet Nam, Yemen, Yugoslavia,[a] Zambia, Zimbabwe	16.9	76.0

a. Cannot participate in the activities of the G-77.
Source: Human Development Report Office.

- Encouraging the involvement, formal or informal, of NGOs and non-official professional groups in the discussion and review of proposals and policies, especially those affecting groups underrepresented in the formal structures (box 5.9).
- Adapting legal aid to provide support to and strengthen the bargaining position of weak countries. Legal aid and capacity-building programmes for the poorest countries could increase the participation of poor countries in international trade and financial organizations, allowing them to establish missions and hire experienced staff. Some Latin American countries, backed by two or three members of the European Union, floated the idea of funding a legal centre to help developing countries prepare or defend cases under the WTO's dispute settlement system.
- Setting some long-term goals and broad guidelines for narrowing global income gaps and securing larger shares of the benefits from trade and financial agreements for poor countries and people.

Developing countries can do much more to strengthen their own bargaining capacity and positions. Priorities here include:
- *Building and strengthening third world and regional collective organizations.* There is no developing country group equivalent to the G-7 or to the OECD, even though at times there have been efforts to strengthen such bodies as the G-15, the G-24 or even the G-77.
- *Using regional economic arrangements to develop and coordinate common positions in negotiations on economic issues.* In Latin America Mercosur and the Andean Community have already proved useful in establishing negotiating positions during trade talks with the United States, Canada and the European Union. In the 1990s the number of regional trade agreements increased significantly. Greater efforts are needed, especially in Sub-Saharan Africa, to transform regional or subregional economic integration schemes into strong platforms of common interest.
- *Developing regional initiatives on financial and monetary matters.* Such initiatives could focus on providing early warning of financial crises, supplementing international resources and formulating structural adjustment programmes while encouraging a move to peer review of national programmes and ensuring that the programmes relate more closely to recipient countries' economic and financial systems.
- *Ensuring stronger professional support to the poorest and least developed countries in negotiations,* especially those relating to trade, investment and growth prospects and to long-term institutional restructuring. The G-24 research programme offers some support to developing country representatives and decision-makers in trade and finance, but it is still primarily donor-funded and has no full-time or on-site staff. It merits fuller support from developing countries themselves.

START NOW
TO BUILD THE GLOBAL ARCHITECTURE REQUIRED FOR THE 21ST CENTURY

With the new challenges of globalization, and the need to ensure stronger action on old problems and new, the time has come to rethink the

---

BOX 5.9

NGOs and global advocacy

During the 1970s activists were urged to "think globally and act locally". Over the past 10–15 years a vibrant NGO community has emerged in the South with a profound impact on development practice and thinking. Alternative NGO-sponsored conferences took place alongside all the global UN conferences of the 1990s. Activists from both South and North joined to lobby governments and international agencies to give greater priority to the world's poor and marginalized.

In response to lobbying against some of its policies, the World Bank reached out to its NGO critics, which now play a much bigger role in Bank-funded projects. Other changes include the appointment of NGO-liaison officers in most Bank country offices and a greater recognition of the importance and input of NGOs to the Bank's work. NGOs have also held the Bank accountable to its own procedures and policies. NGO submissions to the World Bank Inspection Panels on the Arun III Hydroelectric Project in Nepal weighed heavily in the Bank's decision not to finance the project.

NGOs have put pressure on all the UN agencies as well as governments to follow up on the goals and commitments of the global conferences.

For the Kyoto protocol, NGOs have been pushing for an agreement that will have a significant impact on global greenhouse gas emissions rather than one that settles for cosmetic changes. At the Kyoto meeting NGOs pressured national governments and multilateral agencies to release a 10-point call for action. The declaration forms the basis for ongoing NGO advocacy and lobbying on climate change. Similar declarations have been submitted by a group of NGOs from Eastern and Central Europe. Friends of the Earth and the World Wildlife Fund for Nature have been active in raising awareness about how private sector concerns appear to be dominating the discussions on how the protocol is to be implemented. They have also raised concerns that the final outcome will have no meaningful impact on greenhouse gas emissions.

Source: Human Development Report Office.

global architecture. Some of the key elements of an improved international architecture:

• A stronger and more coherent UN system, with greater commitment from all countries.
• A global central bank.
• A world investment trust with redistributive functions and transfer mechanism.
• A world environment agency.
• A revised World Trade Organization, fairer and with an expanded mandate.
• An international criminal court with a broader mandate for human rights.
• A broader United Nations, including a two-chamber General Assembly to allow for civil society representation.

Earlier *Human Development Report*s recognized the need for major changes in global governance if human development was to be achieved on a global scale. The recent crises underscored this need and made people and governments more aware of the case for fundamental changes—and more ready to consider them.

New and stronger international institutions of global governance can be seen as global public goods. At the national level, public goods have been recognized as vital when the market has neither the incentive nor the mechanisms to meet a public need. With growing globalization, international public goods are now needed for similar reasons (box 5.10).

This new perspective is much more than a change of terminology. To recognize the need for global goods is to accept the importance of actions of global governance beyond the capacity of individual countries to provide, to establish a rationale for new forms of financial support that countries need to ensure but to recognize also that without special efforts such support may not be forthcoming. These issues become matters for political advocacy and education on globalization, in which all countries have a role and a stake. Five basic elements are needed in a new international architecture of global economic governance.

STRENGTHEN THE UNITED NATIONS SYSTEM, GIVING IT GREATER COHERENCE TO RESPOND TO BROADER NEEDS OF HUMAN SECURITY

More actions have been taken in the past few years to strengthen the UN system than in any

previous decade: high-level global conferences to establish goals and commitments, internal reforms to increase focus and efficiency, the creation of a UN Development Group bringing together the development agencies to strengthen field-level action and initiatives to encourage closer working relationships with the World Bank and the IMF.

In parallel with these, the Economic and Social Council (ECOSOC) has adopted several

---

BOX 5.10

Global public goods—the missing element

Earlier we thought the ozone layer was out there. But now it is in here, a key issue on the national policy agendas of most countries. The reason is that to avoid further depletion of the ozone shield, the use of chlorofluorocarbons has to be reduced in every country. The same point can be made for the atmosphere: energy use has to change *everywhere* to reduce the risk of global warming.

Conversely, health, employment and equity, previously thought to be quintessential domestic concerns, now figure on international policy agendas. Take the 1995 World Summit on Social Development, which focused on issues of poverty, employment and social cohesion.

Why this intermingling of concerns and agendas?

• *Open borders*. While borders continue to be important, they have become porous as a result of falling tariffs, loosening capital controls and spreading information technology. Openness allows global goods and bads to travel with ever-greater ease. So, good health, reduced greenhouse gas emissions and peace and security in all countries matter even more.
• *Systemic risks*. International financial markets produce boom and bust cycles and present inherent risks. If global warming is allowed to proceed, we may face climatic changes with as yet difficult to predict consequences. And if global inequity continues unchecked, the global social fabric could come under severe strain. Because of the growing number of systemic risks, the international community faces the challenge of staying within limits (sustainable pollution levels), achieving specific targets (for poverty reduction) or providing risk insurance (for countries affected by financial contagion).

• *Transnational actors*. In business and civil society the number of transnational actors has been growing. And these actors are placing more pressure on governments to harmonize policy—such as standardizing market rules for banking supervision or recognizing universal human rights.

These trends turn many national public goods and bads into global public goods and bads—and place global concerns, notably those about the natural global commons, on national policy agendas. So, the number of global public goods—*non-rival* and *non-excludable*—is growing. Non-rivalry means that one person's consumption of a good does not detract from another's enjoyment of it. Non-excludability means that it is difficult and costly, if not impossible, to prevent a person from enjoying a public good once it exists. Peace is one such non-rival, non-excludable public good.

Today's policy-making is ill equipped to handle today's global public good issues. Three major policy deficits exist:
• *A jurisdictional gap*—While the policy issues are global in nature, policy-making is still primarily national in focus and scope.
• *A participation gap*—While we are living in a multi-actor world, international cooperation is still primarily intergovernmental.
• *An incentive gap*—While cooperation works only if it offers a clear and fair deal to all parties, today's international cooperation is often stalled by concerns about equity and fairness.

Sustainable, broad-based development depends on closing these three gaps—on restocking the toolkit of policy-makers to equip them for cooperating in the provision of global public goods.

Source: Kaul, Grunberg and Stern 1999.

---

new ways of working, including holding joint meetings with the IMF–World Bank Development Committee and inviting distinguished specialists to address the council. These have been important for enlivening debate and improving relevance in ECOSOC—but the council still has not been given the status of senior decision-making body on economic and social matters as envisaged by its founders. Collective decision-making on economic and social matters remains with a variety of other bodies—the G-7, the World Bank, the IMF, the WTO. As a result, global decision-making still lacks coherence and geographic balance, with key decisions made in different bodies and no clear mechanism to bring the elements together.

Various suggestions have been made to remedy this. Earlier *Human Development Reports*—and the Commission on Global Governance in 1995—proposed an economic security council, with equal numbers of developed and developing countries and veto powers in each group to build confidence. Some have suggested that the existing ECOSOC should set up an executive committee with delegated powers for decision-making on certain matters or split into two bodies, one for decision-making on economic matters and the other for social matters.

Other mechanisms would be possible, depending mostly on what could command a political consensus. Three critical needs:

• For a broad consensus among industrial and developing countries, rich and poor, and for a stronger and more open decision-making process on next steps in economic and social issues of global governance.

• For national governments to work out arrangements to harmonize their national positions and representation in the institutions of global government. Today, global management suffers because many countries lack coherence between positions taken by their finance ministries (which generally represent them in the Bretton Woods institutions), their foreign ministries (which generally represent them in the United Nations in New York) and other ministries (which represent them in the World Health Organization, Food and Agriculture Organization, UNESCO, International Labour Organisation and other bodies of the United Nations).

• For clear agreement on a division of labour among the United Nations, the World Bank and the IMF.

The issues in reforming global governance are a good starting point. Because the issues are so wide-ranging, a joint committee could be set up at the highest level to steer discussions and negotiations, recognizing that governments will probably choose to pursue most matters in existing institutions. But to get legitimacy and balanced representation in the final result, the United Nations will have to be involved in the overall process and the final decision-making.

MOVE TO A GLOBAL CENTRAL BANK

Just as countries need central banks, so the world needs a central bank in the 21st century. The recent establishment of the European Central Bank demonstrates the perceived need among some of the richest industrial countries.

A world central bank would help stabilize global economic activity by performing several vital functions:
• Acting as lender of last resort.
• Regulating financial institutions and flows.
• Calming financial markets when they become jittery or disorderly.
• Creating and regulating new international liquidity.

Enlarging the mandate of the IMF would be one approach, though this would need to be accompanied by measures to ensure greater sensitivity to human concerns and broader perspectives on economic and social policy. Another would be to establish a world financial authority.

The Asian crisis has demonstrated the need for a global monetary authority to have access to much greater financial resources. Keynes's original proposal was that the global monetary authority should have access to resources equivalent to 50% of world imports. The US counter-proposal was for 15%. Even with the special efforts during the recent crisis, IMF resources remain less than 3% of world imports.

Several mechanisms are available to expand global financial resources, including a renewed issue of special drawing rights and agreements with the main central banks to permit enlarged swap arrangements. Quick access to funding

Keynes's original proposal was that the global monetary authority should have access to resources equivalent to 50% of world imports

may be as important as the size of the resources available. Procedures to achieve this need to be explored, such as advance agreements on provisional lines of credit.

CREATE A GLOBAL INVESTMENT TRUST AND TRANSFER MECHANISM

There is an urgent need for new mechanisms to generate additional flows of resources to poor developing countries as well as new funding for global public goods. Private investment flows are important, but experience shows two major problems. First is their volatility, especially portfolio flows. Second is the tendency for foreign direct investment to be concentrated in a small number of developing countries. In 1997 almost 70% of all foreign direct investment to developing and transition economies went to just 10 countries.

There are several possible ways to generate such additional revenues:
• Mobilize resources as a by-product of revenues raised from polluter-pays charges on global pollution.
• Charge rents or royalties on the use of such "global commons" as under-seabed mineral resources or radio waves.
• Introduce taxes on such items as international air tickets.
• Implement the Tobin tax proposal—to levy a charge on short-term financial movements and restrain volatile flows of short-term finance. Some of the proceeds could be invested in poor countries.
• Blend concessional finance with private lending and make the proceeds available as a third window for middle-income countries.
Separately or together, these proposals could improve the operation of the global economy and generate billions of dollars a year.

CREATE A WORLD ENVIRONMENT AGENCY

The Earth Summit in Rio de Janeiro in 1992 estimated the cost for developing countries to adopt sustainable development practices at $600 billion a year, of which $475 billion would need to come out of their own resources and $125 billion from new and additional international resources.

The Global Environment Facility (GEF), established in 1991, is a poor cousin to these ambitious plans. Jointly implemented by the World Bank, UNDP and the United Nations Environment Programme (UNEP), the GEF provides funding aimed at achieving environmental benefits in four areas: climate change, loss of biodiversity, pollution of international waters and depletion of the ozone layer. At Rio the scope of the GEF's funding was broadened to include land degradation, primarily desertification and deforestation, where this is linked to the four focal areas. Since 1992 some $2 billion has been pledged for activities supported by the GEF.

Relative to today's global economy—and the global challenge of sustainability—present structures and levels of global support are minuscule. Needed is a world environment agency, possibly developed from UNEP, with much larger resources and broader functions:
• To oversee the global environment, presenting reports and posing issues for review and policy-making.
• To broker deals.
• To serve as a clearing bank.

One important focus of that agency would be to encourage the removal of perverse subsidies and shift the resources released to direct support of environmental protection and other measures (including employment creation). An Earth Council study estimated that developing and transition economies spend $220–270 billion a year on such perverse subsidies, mostly for energy and water. Some estimates suggest an even higher figure. Massive resources are clearly being wasted, and there is a strong case for beneficial reallocation.

For its clearinghouse functions, the agency would oversee trade in permits for greenhouse gas emissions, along the lines explored in the Clean Development Mechanism proposed in the Kyoto and Buenos Aires climate conferences. Emission rights could be borrowed or lent, but not sold—thus keeping the market competitive and avoiding any risk that developing countries might lose long-term control over their rights. In addition to promoting environmental sustainability, the clearinghouse would be a new mechanism for mobilizing additional financial resources for developing countries, especially the poorest.

These proposals could improve the operation of the global economy and generate billions of dollars a year

Environmental governance should also be improved—by reviving the proposal that the Trusteeship Council of the United Nations be given a new mandate to preside over issues relating to the use and protection of the global commons, guided by concern for the security of the planet.

MAKE THE WORLD TRADE ORGANIZATION FAIRER AND GIVE IT A MANDATE OVER MULTINATIONAL CORPORATIONS

The World Trade Organization, still on an upward trajectory following its creation in 1995, marks a major step forward from its predecessor, GATT. It has established a rule-based system for monitoring international trade and for settling disputes. More than 130 countries now belong to it. And its voting system offers fairer representation than that of the Bretton Woods institutions.

But it is far from adequate, given the long-term priorities for improving the situation of developing countries. And although its playing field is apparently more level, the very unequal size of the players often pits Gulliver against a single Lilliputian.

Other functions for the WTO need to be explored in the long run. Multinational corporations are involved in more than 60% of world trade and dominate the production, distribution and sale of many goods from developing countries, especially in the cereal, mining and tobacco markets. About a third of world trade is conducted as intrafirm trade within multinational corporations, bypassing altogether the free play of genuine market competition. The mandate of the WTO needs to be expanded to give it anti-monopoly functions over the activities of multinational corporations, including production, working in close collaboration with national competition and antitrust agencies.

Achieving a comprehensive global competition policy might not be feasible, but progress could be made on several fronts.
• Agreements could provide for international oversight of the implementation of domestic competition policy rather than for international rules.
• An international agreement could be limited to the issue of price discrimination and predation, which would allow the elimination of antidumping rules.
• There may be opportunities for increased cooperation through bilateral and regional agreements where differences in antitrust laws are smaller. A multilateral agreement could be negotiated to lay out a set of minimum standards for national policies in areas of international consensus.

One strong reason for adopting an international agreement on competition policies is to eliminate antidumping actions, initiated when countries are deemed to be dumping or selling below cost.

ALL THESE ACTIONS BEGIN WITH PEOPLE

The world is rushing headlong into greater integration—driven mostly by economic forces and guided mostly by a philosophy of market profitability and economic efficiency.

Much debate is under way—but it is too narrowly focused, too geographically unbalanced and driven too much by economic and financial interests. People in all parts of the world need to join in the debate and to make clear their interests and concerns. The process of reinventing global governance must be broader, and human development can provide a framework for this exploration. It is time to change.

People in all parts of the world need to join in the debate and to make clear their interests and concerns

References

Background papers, country and regional studies and background notes for Human Development Report 1999

Background papers

Adedeji, Adebayo. 1999. "Globalisation and Marginalisation in Sub-Saharan Africa."

Al-Samarrai, Samer, and Patrick Belser. 1999. "Education, Globalization and the 'Low-Skill Trap'."

Alston, Philip. 1999. "Governance, Human Rights, and the Normative Areas."

Anderson, Edward. 1999. "Globalisation and Inequality in Historical Perspective."

Arizpe, Lourdes. 1999. "Culture, Globalisation, and International Trade."

Bangura, Yusuf. 1999. "Globalization, Technocratic Policy-Making and Democratisation."

Belser, Patrick. 1999. "Globalisation, International Labour Standards, and Multilateral Institutions."

Bigman, David. 1999. "Global Income Distribution."

Desai, Meghnad. 1999a. "Global Governance."

Folbre, Nancy. 1999. "Care and the Global Economy."

Griffith-Jones, Stephany, and J. Kimmis. 1999. "Capital Flows: How to Curb Their Volatility."

Helleiner, Gerry, and Ademola Oyejide. 1999. "Global Economic Governance, Global Negotiations, and the Developing Countries."

Hopkins, Michael. 1999a. "Corporate Social Responsibility of Business and Human Development."

———. 1999b. "Towards an Index to Measure the Social Responsibility of Business and Human Development."

Khor Kok Peng, Martin. 1999. "Foreign Investment Policy, the Multilateral Agreement on Investment and Development Issues."

Lee, Jong-Wha, and Changyong Rhee. 1999. "Social Impacts of the Asian Crisis: Policy Challenges and Lessons."

Mahmood, Raisul Awal. 1999. "Globalisation, International Migration and Human Development: Linkages and Implications."

Mazumdar, Ranjini. 1999. "Globalisation and the Media: Currents and Counter Currents."

Özler, Süle. 1999. "Globalisation, Employment, and Gender."

Panayotou, Theodore. 1999. "Globalisation and Environment."

Ramirez, Alejandro Magana. 1999. "Impact of Globalisation on National Film Industries."

Rao, Mohan J. 1999a. "Globalization and the Fiscal Autonomy of the State."

———. 1999b. "Openness, Poverty and Inequality."

Rodas-Martini, Pablo. 1999. "Income Inequality within and between Countries: The Main Issues in the Literature."

Sengupta, Arjun. 1999. "Financial Management of Globalization of Developing Countries."

Tokman, Viktor E., and Emilio Klein. 1999. "Social Stratification under Tension in a Globalized Era."

Tuijnman, Albert. 1999. "International Indicators of Educational Attainment."

UNDP (United Nations Development Programme) Country Office, Thailand. 1999. "Responding to the Thai Economic Crisis."

Whalley, John. 1999. "Developing Countries in the Global Economy: A Forward-Looking View."

Country and regional studies

Amin, Galal. 1999. "Globalisation and Human Development in the Arab World."

Bakker, Isabella. 1999. "Globalisation and Human Development in the Rich Countries: Lessons from Labour Markets and Welfare States."

Jomo, Kwame Sundaram. 1999. "Globalisation and Human Development in East Asia."

Khan, Azizur Rahman. 1999. "Globalisation and Human Development in South Asia."

Lipumba, Nguyuru I. 1999. "Opportunities and Challenges of Globalisation: Can Sub-Saharan Africa Avoid Marginalisation?"

Ruminska-Zimny, Ewa. 1999. "Globalisation and Human Development in Transition Economies."

Background notes

Deacon, Bob. 1999. "The Social Impact of Globalization on Developed Economics."

Desai, Meghnad. 1999b. "Equity Issues in Global Governance."

Goldstone, Leo. 1998. "Statistical Note on Human Development Report Indicators and Tables."

Korea Institute for Social Information and Research. 1999. "The Economic Crisis in Korea: Its Effects and Prospects for Recovery—A Random Assessment."

Lipton, Michael. 1999a. "Globalization, Liberalization, and Competition."

———. 1999b. "Globalized Agricultural Technology and Human Development."

———. 1999c. "Impact of Globalization on the Poor."

RAFI (Rural Advancement Foundation International). 1999a. "Background Note on Biotechnology Patenting."

UNDP (United Nations Development Programme) Country Office, Indonesia. 1999. "Mitigating the Social Impact of the Economic Crisis: Approaches to Social Safety Net Programmes in Indonesia."

UNDP (United Nations Development Programme) Country Office, Malaysia. 1999. "Globalization and Human Development: The Case of Malaysia."

Bibliographic note

Chapter 1 draws on the following: Adedeji 1999, Amin 1999, Anderson 1999, Arizpe 1999, Bakker 1999, Belser 1999, Castells 1996, Deacon 1999, Desai 1999a and 1999b, Eatwell and Taylor 1998a and 1998b, Giddens 1990, Griffith-Jones and Kimmis 1999, Helleiner and Oyejide 1999, IMF 1999, Jomo 1999, Khor Kok Peng 1998 and 1999, Lee and Rhee 1999, Lipton 1999a, 1999b and 1999c, Lipumba 1999, Mahmood 1999, Mazumdar 1999, OECD 1997d and 1998b, Özler 1999, Panayotou 1999, Ramirez 1999, Rodas-Martini 1999, Ruminska-Zimny 1999, Tokman and Klein 1999, UN 1998f and 1998g, UNAIDS and WHO 1998b, UNCTAD 1998b and 1998c, UNDCP 1997, UNDP 1994, 1995 and 1998c, UNDP Country Office, Indonesia 1999, UNDP Country Office, Malaysia 1999, UNDP Country Office, Thailand 1999, Whalley 1999 and World Bank 1998a.

Chapter 2 draws on the following: *Biotechnology and Development Monitor* 1998, Bond 1997, Brown and Flavin 1999, *Budapest Sun* 1998, Castells 1998, CNN Interactive 1999, Corner House 1998, d'Orville 1999, Drahos 1997, *Ecologist* 1998, *Financial Times* 1998, Fink and Braga 1999, Foo 1999, *Fortune Magazine* 1999, GetIt 1998, GRAIN 1998, Hakansta 1998, Hamelink 1997, Headcount 1998, *Irish Times* 1998, ITU 1998, Jensen 1998, Lanfranco 1998, Lipton 1999b, Mansell and When 1998, Mehta 1999, Mooney 1998, My Vuong 1999, National Research Council and the World Bank 1995, National Science Foundation 1998, NetDay 1999, *New York Times* 1999a, ODI 1999, OECD 1996b and 1996c, Oxfam 1998, Panos 1998, PEOPLink 1999, Poster 1997, Pradesh 1998, RAFI 1998, 1999a, 1999b, 1999c and 1999d, Madanmohan Rao 1999, Richardson 1998, Schoettle and Grant 1998, SIDSnet 1998, South Centre 1997, UNCTAD 1996b and 1998c, UNDP 1998b, UNESCO 1998d, von Weizsacker 1998, *Weekly Mail and Guardian* 1998, White 1999, WIPO 1997 and 1998 and World Bank 1999a.

Chapter 3 draws mainly on Folbre 1999. It also draws on the following: Elson 1998, England and Folbre 1998, Özler 1999, Ruminska-Zimny 1997, UNDP 1995, UNICEF 1998b and Zohir 1998.

Chapter 4 draws on the following: Adedeji 1999, Agosin 1995, Al-Samarrai and Belser 1999, Amin 1999, Bakker 1999, Bangura 1999, Belser 1999, Castro-Leal and others 1999, Dasgupta 1998, Deacon 1999, Edwards and Edwards 1991, Ghai and de Alcantara 1994, Global Survival Network 1997, Griffith-Jones and Kimmis 1999, Grunberg 1998, Gupta, Davoodi and Alonso-Terme 1998, Hausman and Rojas-Suarez 1996, Helleiner and Oyejide 1999, IADB 1998, IMF 1998b and 1999b, International Confederation of Free Trade Unions 1998, Jomo 1999, Khan 1999, Khan and Muqtada 1997, Khor Kok Peng 1999, Kobrin 1998, Lawrence, Rodrik and Whalley 1996, Lee 1998, Lee and Rhee 1999, Lim and Siddall 1997, Lipton 1999a, Lipumba 1999, Mahmood 1999, OECD 1998c, Panayotou 1999, Ranis and Stewart 1998, Mohan J. Rao 1999a and 1999b, Robson 1997, Rodas-Martini 1999, Rodrik 1997 and 1999, Ruminska-Zimny 1999, Spinanger 1998, Stalker 1997, Tokman and Klein 1999, UN 1998h, UNCTAD 1998a and 1998b, UNDP 1997b, UNDP Country Office, Indonesia 1999, UNESCO 1998b, Visser and Hemerijck 1997, Wahba and Mohieldin 1998, Whalley 1999, Woods 1998, World Bank 1995, 1998a and 1998b and Yoon and Rhee 1998.

Chapter 5 draws on the following: Agosin, Crespi and Tussie 1998, Arizpe 1999, Bergsten 1998, Brandt Commission 1980, Castells 1996–99, Commission on Global Governance 1995, Desai 1999a and 1999b, Dubey 1996, Eatwell 1996, *Economist* 1998a, Eichengreen 1999, Frankel 1997, Griffith-Jones and Kimmis 1999, Group of 22 1998, Haq 1995, Haq, Grunberg and Kaul 1996, Helleiner and Oyejide 1999, Jomo 1999, Kay 1997, Kenen 1994, Keynes 1980, Kobrin 1998, Küng 1996, Lee 1998, Lee and Rhee 1999, Lipumba 1999, Lister 1997, Michaelopoulos 1998, Panayotou 1999, Pearson Commission 1969, Randel and German 1997, Rodrik 1999, Sachs 1998, Schott 1994, South Centre 1998, Stewart and Daws 1996, UN 1998a and 1998b, UNCTAD 1996a and 1998b, USAID 1999, Whalley 1999, Whalley and Hamilton 1996, World Bank 1998a and 1999a and World Commission on Culture and Development 1995.

References

Agosin, Manuel R. 1995. "Foreign Direct Investment in Latin America." In Manuel R. Agosin, ed., *Foreign Direct Investment in Latin America*. Washington, DC: Inter-American Development Bank.

Agosin, Manuel R., Gustavo Crespi and Diana Tussie. 1995. "Developing Countries and the Uruguay Round: An Evaluation and Issues for the Future." *International Monetary and Financial Issues for the 1990s*. New York: United Nations Conference on Trade and Development.

Alesina, Alberto. 1998. "The Political Economy of Macroeconomic Stabilizations and Income Inequality: Myth and Reality." In Vito Tanzi and Ke-young Chu, eds., *Income Distribution and High-Quality Growth*. Cambridge, Mass.: MIT Press.

Alston, Julian, Philip Pardey and Johannes Roseboom. 1998. "Financing Agricultural Research: International Investment Patterns and Policy Perspectives." IFPRI Reprint 388. Reprinted from *World Development* 26 (6). International Food Policy Research Institute, Washington, DC.

Anand, Sudhir, and Amartya Sen. 1999. "The Income Component in the HDI—Alternative Formulations." Occasional Paper. United Nations Development Programme, Human Development Report Office, New York.

Bergsten, C. Fred. 1998. "Reviving the Asian Monetary Fund." International Economics Policy Brief 98-8. Washington, DC.

Biotechnology and Development Monitor. 1998. "Pharmaceuticals: The Role of Biotechnology and Patents." 34(June): 13–15.

BIS (Bank for International Settlements). 1998. *68th Annual Report*. Basle.

BMF Gallup Media. 1999. "Internet Users among Population in Estonia." [http://www.bmf.ee]. 27 March 1999.

Bond, James. 1997. "The Drivers of the Information Revolution—Cost, Computing Power and Convergence." Viewpoint 118. World Bank, Finance, Private Sector and Infrastructure Network, Washington, DC.

Brandt Commission (Independent Commission on International Development Issues). 1980. *North-South: A Programme for Survival*. Cambridge, Mass.: MIT Press.

Brown, Lester, and Christopher Flavin. 1999. *State of the World 1999*. London: Earthscan.

Budapest Sun. 1998. "Teachers Buckling under Strain of National Internet Program." 23 April. [http://www.proquest.com]. 9 March 1999.

Cambodia, Ministry of Planning. 1998. *Cambodia Human Development Report 1998*. Phnom Penh.

Camdessus, Michel. 1998. "Money Laundering: The Importance of International Countermeasures." Address delivered at the Plenary Meeting of the Financial Action Task Force on Money Laundering, 10 February, Paris. [http://www.imf.org/external/np/speeches/1998/021098.htm]. February 1999.

Castells, Manuel. 1996. *The Rise of the Network Society*. Cambridge: Blackwell.

——. 1996–99. *The Information Age*. Vols. 1–3. Oxford: Blackwell.

——. 1998. "Information Technology, Globalisation and Social Development." Paper presented at United Nations Research Institute for Social Development (UNRISD) conference on Information Technology and Social Development, 22–24 June, Geneva.

Castro-Leal, Florencia, Julia Dayton, Lionel Demery and Kalpana Mehra. 1999. "Public Social Spending in Africa: Do the Poor Benefit?" *World Bank Research Observer* 14(1): 49–72.

CDIAC (Carbon Dioxide Information Analysis Center). 1999a. "CO_2 Emissions." [http://www.cdiac.esd.ornl.gov/ftp/ndp030/global96.ems]. February 1999.

——. 1999b. "CO_2 Emissions." [http://www.cdiac.esd.ornl.gov/ftp/ndp030/nation96.ems]. February 1999.

CGIAR (Consultative Group on International Agricultural Research). 1998. "'The Bio-Technology Revolution'—New Opportunities and Risks for the Poor and the Environment." [http://www.cgiar.org]. 29 January 1999.

Chilliah, Raja J., and R. Sudarshan. 1999. *Income Poverty and Beyond: Human Development in India*. New Delhi: Social Science Press.

CNBC. 1998. "Future File." [http://www.cnbc.com]. 10 November 1998.

CNN Interactive. 1999. "China Shuts Down Popular Internet Forum." [http://www.cnn.com]. 5 February 1999.

Commission on Global Governance. 1995. *Our Global Neighborhood: The Report of the Commission on Global Governance*. New York: Oxford University Press.

Corner House. 1998. "Food? Health? Hope? Genetic Engineering and World Hunger." Briefing 10. Dorset, England.

Dasgupta, Biplab. 1998. *Structural Adjustment, Global Trade and the New Political Economy of Development*. London: Zed Books.

d'Orville, Hans. 1999. Email correspondence on proposals for a bit tax. 11 March.

Drahos, Peter. 1997. "States and Intellectual Property: The Past, the Present and the Future." [http://138.77.20.51/impart/drahos.htm]. 8 December 1997.

Dubey, Muchkund. 1996. *An Unequal Treaty: World Trading Order after GATT*. New Delhi: New Age International.

Eatwell, John. 1996. "International Financial Liberalization: The Impact on World Development." Office of Development Studies Discussion Paper 12. United Nations Development Programme, New York.

Eatwell, John, and Lance Taylor. 1998a. "The Case for a World Financial Authority." Paper presented at the workshop on the United Nations' Position in International Financial Architecture, 26–27 November, Santiago.

——. 1998b. "International Capital Markets and the Future of Economic Policy." Center for Economic Policy Analysis Working Paper Series 3. New School for Social Research, New York.

Ecologist. 1998. "The Monsanto Files: Can We Survive Genetic Engineering?" (special edition) 28(5).

Economist. 1998a. "The Resources Lie Within." 7 November, pp. 19–21.

——. 1998b. "The World in Figures: Industries." *The World in 1999*, p. 82.

Edwards, Sebastian, and Alejandra Cox Edwards. 1991. *Monetarism and Liberalization: The Chilean Experience*. Chicago: University of Chicago Press.

Eichengreen, Barry. 1999. *Toward a New International Financial Architecture: A Practical Post-Asia Agenda*. Washington, DC: Institute for International Economics.

Elson, Diane. 1998. "The Economic, the Political and the Domestic: Businesses, States and Households in the

Organisation of Production." *New Political Economy* 3(2): 189–208.

England, Paula, and Nancy Folbre. 1998. "The Cost of Caring." In Ronnie J. Steinberg and Deborah Figart, eds., *The Annals of the American Academy of Political and Social Science on Emotional Labour*. London: Sage.

EU Network. 1998. *New Ways Information Bulletin 2*. Brussels.

FAO (Food and Agriculture Organization of the United Nations). 1997. Correspondence on daily per capita calorie supply. July. Rome.

——. 1998. "Daily Per Capita Supply of Calories." [http://www.fao.org/NEWS/1998/981204-e.htm]. February 1999.

——. 1999. "Food Balance Sheets." [http://www.apps.fao.org/lim500/nphwrap.pl?FoodBalanceSheet&Domain=FoodBalanceSheet]. February 1999.

Financial Times. 1998a. "Spain's Pace-Setting Project for Europe." 5 November.

——. 1998b. "U.S. Corporate Axe Casts Shadow over Europe." 8 December.

Fink, Carsten, and Carlos A. Primo Braga. 1999. "How Stronger Protection of Intellectual Property Rights Affects International Trade Flows." World Bank, Science and Technology Thematic Group and the Energy, Mining and Telecommunications Department, Washington, DC.

Fischer, Stanley. 1999. "On the Need for an International Lender of Last Resort." International Monetary Fund, Washington, DC. [http://www.imf.org]. 17 February 1999.

Flynn, Padraig. 1998. Speech presented at the Conference of EU Ministers for Women, 5–6 May, Belfast.

Foo, Jacky. 1999. Email correspondence on the organization and impact of Internet conferences. 19 January.

Forbes Magazine. 1997a. "Forbes 500 Annual Directory." [http://www.forbes.com]. April 1999.

——. 1997b. "The International 800." [http://www.forbes.com]. April 1999.

——. 1998. "The World's Richest People." 6 July.

Frankel, Jeffrey A. 1997. *Regional Trading Blocs in the World Economic System*. Washington, DC: Institute for International Economics.

Gerster, Richard. 1998. "Patents and Development: A Non-Governmental Organization View Prior to Revision of the TRIPS Agreement." *Journal of World Intellectual Property* 1(4): 608.

GetIt. 1998. *The Internet for Policymakers*. CD-ROM. Singapore.

Ghai, Dharam, and Cynthia Hewitt de Alcantara. 1994. *Globalization and Social Integration: Patterns and Processes*. Geneva: United Nations Research Institute for Social Development.

Ghosh, Bimal. 1997. "Migration and Development: Some Selected Issues." Panama City.

Giddens, Anthony. 1990. *The Consequences of Modernity*. Cambridge, England: Polity Press.

Global Survival Network. 1997a. *Bought & Sold*. Documentary. Washington, DC.

——. 1997b. *Crime and Servitude: An Exposé of the Traffic of Women for Prostitution from the Newly Independent States*. New York.

Gottschalk, Peter, and Timothy M. Smeeding. 1997. "Cross-National Comparisons of Earnings and Income Inequality." *Journal of Economic Literature* 35(2): 633–87.

GRAIN (Genetic Resources Action International). 1998. "Intellectual Property Rights and Biodiversity: The Economic Myths." [http://www.grain.org]. 28 February 1999.

Group of 22. 1998. *Summary of Reports on the International Financial Architecture*. Washington, DC.

Grunberg, Isabelle. 1998. "Double Jeopardy: Globalization, Liberalization and the Fiscal Squeeze." *World Development* 26(4): 591–606.

Gupta, Sanjeev, Hamid Davoodi and Rosa Alonso-Terme. 1998. "Does Corruption Affect Income Inequality and Poverty?" International Monetary Fund, Fiscal Affairs Department, Washington, DC.

Hakansta, Carin. 1998. "The Battle on Patents and AIDS Treatment." *Biotechnology and Development Monitor* 34(March): 17–19.

Hamelink, Cees. 1997. "New Information and Communication Technologies, Social Development and Cultural Change." UNRISD Discussion Paper 86. United Nations Research Institute for Social Development, Geneva.

Haq, Mahbub ul. 1995. *Reflections on Human Development*. New York: Oxford University Press.

Haq, Mahbub ul, Isabelle Grunberg and Inge Kaul, eds. 1996. *The Tobin Tax: Coping with Financial Volatility*. New York: Oxford University Press.

Haq, Mahbub ul, Richard Jolly, Paul Streeten and Khadija Haq. 1995. *The UN and the Bretton Woods Institutions: New Challenges for the Twenty-First Century*. Houndmills: Macmillan.

Hausman, Ricardo, and Liliana Rojas-Suarez. 1996. *Volatile Capital Flows: Taming Their Impact on Latin America*. Baltimore, Md.: Johns Hopkins University Press.

Headcount. 1998. "Global E-Commerce." [http://www.headcount.com]. 12 November 1998.

Heeks, Richard. 1998. "The Uneven Profile of Indian Software Exports." Development Infomatics Working Paper Series WP 3. Institute for Development Policy, Manchester.

Helsby, Thomas. 1999. Correspondence on globalization and crime. Kroll Associates. March.

Heston, Alan, and Robert Summers. 1999. Data on real GDP per capita (PPP$). March. University of Pennsylvania, Department of Economics, Philadelphia.

IADB (Inter-American Development Bank). 1998. *Facing Up to Inequality in Latin America: Economic and Social Progress in Latin America, 1998–99 Report*. Baltimore, Md.: Johns Hopkins University Press.

IDC (International Data Corporation). 1999. Email correspondence on Internet user data for 1998 for Latin America, South-East Asia and Eastern Europe. 18 and 30 March. Mountain View, Calif., Prague and Singapore.

IDEA (Institute for Democracy and Electoral Assistance). 1997. *Voter Turnout from 1945 to 1997: A Global Report*. Stockholm.

IISS (International Institute for Strategic Studies). 1998. *The Military Balance 1998–99*. London: Oxford University Press.

ILO (International Labour Office). 1995. *World Labour Report 1995*. Geneva.

——. 1996. *Estimates and Projections of the Economically Active Population, 1950–2010*. 4th ed. Diskette. Geneva.

——. 1998. *Labour Statistics Database*. Geneva.

———. Various years. *Yearbook of Labour Statistics.* Geneva.

IMF (International Monetary Fund). 1997a. *World Economic Outlook.* May. Washington, DC.

———. 1997b. *World Economic Outlook.* October. Washington, DC.

———. 1998a. "Debt Relief for Low-Income Countries: The HIPC Initiative." [http://www.imf.org]. 23 December 1998.

———. 1998b. *World Economic Outlook.* October. Washington, DC.

———. 1998c. *World Economic Outlook and International Capital Markets: Interim Assessment, December 1998.* Washington, DC.

———. 1999a. *Balance of Payments Statistics.* CD-ROM. Washington, DC.

———. 1999b. "Opportunities for Africa." *Finance and Development* (special issue) 36(1).

International Confederation of Free Trade Unions. 1998. *Fighting for Workers' Human Rights in a Global Economy.* Brussels.

International Federation of Red Cross and Red Crescent Societies. 1995. *World Disasters Report 1995.* Geneva.

International Organization for Migration. 1994. "Trafficking in Migrants: Characteristics and Trends in Different Regions of the World." Discussion paper. Geneva.

———. 1996a. *CIS Migration Report.* Geneva.

———. 1996b. *Irregular Migration and Migrant Trafficking: An Overview.* Geneva.

———. 1996c. "Trafficking in Migrants: Some Global and Regional Perspectives." Paper submitted by the International Organization for Migration for the Regional Conference on Migration, 13 and 14 March, Puebla, Mexico.

———. 1996d. "Trafficking of Women to the European Union: Characteristics, Trends and Policy Issues." Paper for the Conference on Trafficking in Women for Sexual Exploitation, June, Vienna.

———. 1997a. *Trafficking in Migrants: The Baltic Route.* Geneva.

———. 1997b. *Trafficking in Migrants: IOM Policy and Activities.* Geneva.

———. 1997c. *Trafficking in Women to Japan for Sexual Exploitation: A Survey of the Case of Filipino Women.* Geneva.

———. 1998a. *Information Campaign against Trafficking in Women from Ukraine.* Geneva.

———. 1998b. "Statement by International Organization for Migration to Third Regional Seminar on Irregular Migration and Migrant Trafficking in East and Southeast Asia." Bangkok.

IPU (Inter-Parliamentary Union). 1999a. "Women in Parliaments." [http://www.ipu.org/wmn-e/classif.htm]. February 1999.

———. 1999b. Correspondence on date of latest elections, political parties represented and women's rights to vote and to stand for election. February. Geneva.

Ireland, Department of Taoiseach. 1998. "Overview of Irish Economic Performance." Social Policy Unit. Dublin.

Irish Times. 1998. "Girls Just Want to Have Equal Access." 28 September, p. 18.

ITU (International Telecommunication Union). 1997. *World Telecommunication Indicators.* Database. Geneva.

———. 1998. *World Telecommunication Development Report 1998.* Geneva.

Jensen, Mike. 1998. "African Internet Connectivity." [http://www3.sn.apc.org/africa/afstat.htm]. 19 November 1998.

Kakwani, Nanak. 1998. "Impact of Economic Crisis on Employment, Unemployment and Real Income." National Economic and Social Development Board, Development Evaluation Division, and Asian Development Bank, Bangkok.

Kaul, Inge, Isabelle Grunberg and Marc Stern, eds. 1999. *Global Public Goods: International Cooperation in the 21st Century.* New York: Oxford University Press.

Kay, Cristobal, ed. 1997. *Globalisation, Competitiveness, and Human Security.* London: International Specialized Book Services.

Kenen, Peter B. 1994. *Managing the World Economy: Fifty Years after Bretton Woods.* Washington, DC: Institute for International Economics.

Kennan, Jane, and Christopher Stevens. 1997. "From Lomé to the GSP: Implications for the ACP of Losing Lomé Trade Preferences." Institute of Development Studies, Sussex, England.

Keynes, John Maynard. 1980. *The Collected Writings of John Maynard Keynes.* Vols. 25–27. London: Macmillan.

Khan, Azizur Rahman, and M. Muqtada. 1997. *Employment Expansion and Macroeconomic Stability under Increasing Globalization.* ILO Studies Series. Geneva: International Labour Office.

Khor Kok Peng, Martin. 1998. "Why Capital Controls and International Debt Restructuring Mechanisms Are Necessary to Prevent and Manage Financial Crises." Penang.

Klugman, Jeni. 1999. "Social and Economic Policies to Prevent Complex Humanitarian Emergencies: Lessons from Experience." Policy Brief 2. United Nations University/World Institute for Development Economics Research, Helsinki.

Kobrin, Stephen J. 1998. "The MAI and the Clash of Globalizations." *Foreign Policy* 112(fall): 97–109.

Küng, Hans. 1996. *Global Responsibility: In Search of a New World Ethic.* New York: Continuum.

Kuwait, Ministry of Planning, and UNDP (United Nations Development Programme). 1997. *Human Development Report: The State of Kuwait 1997.* Kuwait City.

Lal Das, Bhagirath. 1998. *The WTO Agreement: Deficiencies, Imbalances and Required Changes.* Penang: Third World Network.

Lanfranco, Sam. 1998. "To What Extent Has the 'Wiring of Asia' Been Used for Job Training and Skills Development among the Poor?" [http://www.oneworld.org]. 2 November 1998.

Lanjouw, Jean. 1997. "The Introduction of Pharmaceutical Product Patents in India: 'Heartless Exploitation of the Poor and Suffering?'" Economic Growth Center Discussion Paper 775. Yale University, Economic Growth Center, New Haven, Conn.

Lawrence, Robert Z., Dani Rodrik and John Whalley. 1996. *Emerging Agenda for Global Trade: High Stakes for Developing Countries.* Policy Essay 20. Washington, DC: Overseas Development Council.

Lee, Eddy. 1998. *The Asian Financial Crisis.* Geneva: International Labour Office.

Leonard, Andrew. 1997. "Apache's Free-Software Warriors." [http://www.salonmagazine.com]. 11 March 1999.

Lim, Lin Lean, ed. 1998. *The Sex Sector: The Economic and Social Bases of Prostitution in Southeast Asia.* Geneva: International Labour Office.

Lim, Linda Y.C., and Nathaniel S. Siddall. 1997. "Investment Dynamism in Asian Developing Countries." In John H. Dunning and Khalil A. Hamdani, eds., *The New Globalism and Developing Countries*. Tokyo: United Nations Press.

Lipton, Michael. 1996. "Poverty-Basic and Annex Tables: Notes on Method." Background paper for *Human Development Report 1997*. United Nations Development Programme, Human Development Report Office, New York.

Lister, Marjorie. 1997. *The European Union and the South: Relations with Developing Countries*. New York: Routledge.

Maddison, Angus. 1995. *Monitoring the World Economy, 1820–1992*. Paris: Organisation for Economic Co-operation and Development, Development Centre.

Madhya Pradesh, Government of. 1998. *The Madhya Pradesh Human Development Report*. Bhopal.

Mansell, Robin, and Uta Wehn, eds. 1998. *Knowledge Societies: Information Technology for Sustainable Development*. Oxford: Oxford University Press.

McGrew, Anthony. 1997. "Globalization: Conceptualizing a Moving Target." Paper presented at the seminar on International Solidarity and Globalization: In Search of New Strategies, October, Stockholm.

Mehta, Geeta. 1999. Correspondence by fax on byte by byte and the M.S. Swaminathan Research Foundation. 15 February.

Michaelopoulos, Constantine. 1998. "Developing Countries' Participation in the World Trade Organization." Policy Research Working Paper 1906. World Bank, Washington, DC, and World Trade Organization, Geneva.

Milanovic, Branko. 1998. *Income, Inequality and Poverty during the Transition from Planned to Market Economy*. Washington, DC: World Bank.

Mooney, Pat Roy. 1996. "Private Parts: Privatization and the Life Industry." *Development Dialogue* (special issue) no. 1–2: 13–181.

M.S. Swaminathan Research Foundation. 1998. "Communication Technology: Bridging the Urban-Rural Divide." [http://www.mssrf.org]. 18 March 1999.

My Vuong, Theresa. 1999. "Vietnamese Forge Worldwide Online Community." [http://www.mercurycenter.com]. 24 February 1999.

National Defense University. 1997. "Strategic Assessment: Flashpoints and Force Structures: Chapter 16." [http://www.ndu.edu/ndu/inss/sa97/sa97ch16.html]. December 1999.

National Economic and Social Forum. 1997. *A Framework for Partnership: Enriching Strategic Consensus through Participation*. Forum Report 16. Dublin.

National Research Council and World Bank. 1995. *Marshaling Technology for Development: Proceedings of a Symposium*. Washington, DC: National Academy Press.

National Science Foundation. 1998. "US and International Research and Development." [http://www.nsf.gov]. 27 February 1999.

Nepal South Asia Centre. 1998. *Nepal Human Development Report 1998*. Kathmandu.

NetDay. 1999. "NetDay FAQs." [http://www.netday96.com]. 9 February 1999.

Network Wizards. 1998a. "Internet Domain Survey July 1998." [http://www.nw.com]. March 1999.

———. 1998b. "Number of Internet Hosts." [http://www.nw.com]. 22 October 1998.

New York Times. 1998a. "Citigroup Says It Will Cut 10,400 Jobs." 16 December.

———. 1998b. "20,000 More Jobs Cut for Deutsche Telekom." 7 December.

———. 1999a. "College Freshmen's Internet Use a Way of Life, but Disparities Emerge." 25 January, p. A11.

———. 1999b. "Unthinkable Happened throughout Oil Industry." 4 January.

Nua. 1999. "How Many Online." [http://www.nua.ie]. 1 March 1999.

ODI (Overseas Development Institute). 1999. "The Debate on Genetically Modified Organisms: Relevance to the South." Briefing Paper. 1 January. London.

OECD (Organisation for Economic Co-operation and Development). 1996a. *Development Co-operation 1995 Report*. Development Assistance Committee Report. Paris.

———. 1996b. *The Knowledge-Based Economy*. Paris.

———. 1996c. *Science, Technology and Industry Outlook*. Paris.

———.1997a. *Education Policy Analysis*. Paris.

———.1997b. *Employment Outlook*. Paris.

———. 1997c. *Environmental Data: Compendium 1997*. Paris.

———. 1997d. *Implementing the OECD Jobs Strategy: Lessons from Member Countries' Experience*. Paris.

———.1998a. *Economic Outlook*. Paris.

———.1998b. *Employment Outlook*. Paris.

———.1998c. *Open Markets Matter: The Benefits of Trade and Investment Liberalization*. Paris.

———. 1999a. *Development Co-operation 1998 Report*. Development Assistance Committee Report. Paris.

———. 1999b. *Geographical Distribution of Financial Flows to Aid Recipients*. Paris.

———. Forthcoming. *Environmental Data: Compendium 1999*. Paris.

Oxfam. 1998. "Biotechnology in Crops: Issues for the Developing World." [http://www.oxfam.org]. 26 February 1999.

Panos. 1998. "The Internet and Poverty." Panos Briefing 28. [http://www.oneworld.org]. 7 November 1998.

Pearson Commission (Commission on International Development). 1969. *Partners in Development*. New York: Praeger.

PEOPLink. 1999. [http://www.peoplink.org]. 24 February 1999.

Poster, Mark. 1997. "Nations, Identities and Global Technologies." Paper presented to the Media and Culture Group of the University of British Columbia, January, Vancouver.

Pradesh, Siddartha. 1998. "Country Study: India—Local Species (Turmeric, Neem, Basmati)." [http://www.itd.org/issues/india6.htm]. 17 December 1998.

Pritchett, Lant. 1997. "Divergence, Big Time." *Journal of Economic Perspectives* 11(3): 3–17.

Psacharopoulos, George, and Zafiris Tzannatos, eds. 1992. *Case Studies on Women's Employment and Pay in Latin America*. Washington, DC: World Bank.

RAFI (Rural Advancement Foundation International). 1998. *Seed Industry Consolidation: Who Owns Whom?* [http://www.rafi.org]. 7 January 1999.

———.1999b. "The Gene Giants: Masters of the Universe?" [http://www.rafi.org]. 18 March 1999.

———.1999c. "RAFI: Traitor Tech: 'Damaged Goods' from the GeneGiants." [post-0-matic@rafi.org]. 29 March.

———. 1999d. "Traitor Technology: The Terminator's Wider Implications." [http://www.rafi.org]. 26 February 1999.

Randel, Judith, and Tony German. 1997. *The Reality of Aid 1997/8: An Independent Review of Development Cooperation.* London: Earthscan.

Ranis, Gustav, and Frances Stewart. 1998. *A Pro-Human Development Adjustment Framework for the Countries of East and South-East Asia.* A United Nations Development Programme Policy Document. New York: United Nations Development Programme.

Rao, Madanmohan. 1999. "The Internet for All: From Access to Agenda." [http://www.cpsr.org]. 22 January 1999.

Richardson, Barry. 1998. "Intellectual Property Rights of Indigenous Knowledge." [http://www.mp.wa.gov.au/jscott/isssmoke.html]. 9 December 1998.

Robson, Peter. 1997. *The Economics of International Integration.* 3d ed. London: Unwin Hyman.

Rodrik, Dani. 1997. *Has Globalization Gone Too Far?* Washington, DC: Institute for International Economics.

———. 1999. *Making Openness Work: The New Global Economy and the Developing Countries.* Baltimore, Md.: Johns Hopkins University Press.

Rohozinski, Rafal. 1998. "Mapping Russian Cyberspace: Perspective on Democracy and the Net." Paper presented at the United Nations Research Institute for Social Development (UNRISD) conference on Information Technology and Social Development, 22–24 June, Geneva.

Ruminska-Zimny, Ewa. 1997. "Human Poverty in Transition Economies: Regional Overview for the *Human Development Report 1997.*" Occasional Paper Series. United Nations Development Programme, Human Development Report Office, New York.

Sachs, Jeffrey. 1998. "Proposals for Reform of the Global Financial Infrastructure." Harvard Institute for International Development, Cambridge, Mass.

Sahai, Suman. 1999. Email correspondence on the Proposal for the Convention of Farmers and Breeders. 18 March.

SatelLife. 1998. "HealthNet." [http://www.healthnet.org]. 9 November 1998.

Schoettle, Enid C.B., and Kate Grant. 1998. *Globalisation: A Discussion Paper.* New York: The Rockefeller Foundation.

Schott, Jeffrey J. 1994. *The Uruguay Round. An Assessment.* Washington, DC: Institute for International Economics.

Schware, Robert, and Susan Hume. 1994. "The Global Information Industry and the Eastern Caribbean." Viewpoint 17. World Bank, Finance, Private Sector and Infrastructure Network, Washington, DC.

Securities Data Company. 1998. Correspondence by fax on unpublished data on announced worldwide mergers and acquisitions. Media Relations Division. 14 December. Newark, N.J.

———. 1999. Correspondence by fax on mergers of biotechnology, telecommunications and computer companies. 2 March.

Security Distributing and Marketing. 1998. "Home Networks Imminent." [http://www.umi.com]. 5 March 1999.

Shiva, Vandana. 1997. "Bioethics: A Third World Issue." [http://www.gene.free.de:80/gentech/1997/Jul-Aug/msg00498.html] 7 January 1999.

SIDSnet (Small Island Developing States Network). 1998. "Small Island Developing States Network." [http://www.sidsnet.org.] 1 December 1998.

SIPRI (Stockholm International Peace Research Institute). 1998. *SIPRI Yearbook 1998.* New York: Oxford University Press.

Skrobanek, Siriporn, Nataya Boonpakdi and Chutima Janthakeero. 1997. *The Traffic in Women: Human Realities of the International Sex Trade.* London: Zed Books.

Smeeding, Timothy. 1997. "Financial Poverty in Developed Countries: The Evidence from the Luxembourg Income Study." *Human Development Papers 1997: Poverty and Human Development.* New York: United Nations Development Programme.

South Centre. 1997. *The TRIPS Agreement: A Guide for the South.* Geneva.

———. 1998. *The WTO Multilateral Trade Agenda and the South.* Geneva.

Spinanger, Dean. 1998. "Background Statistics on Anti-Dumping Measures." Paper presented to a meeting of the Ad Hoc Expert Group of the Secretary General of the United Nations Conference on Trade and Development (UNCTAD), Kiel Institute of World Economics, September, Kiel, Germany.

Stalker, Peter. 1997. *Global Nations: The Impact of Globalization on International Migration.* Geneva: International Labour Office, Employment and Training Department.

Standard & Poor's. 1999. Email correspondence on sovereign ratings history. 9 March.

Stewart, Frances, and Sam Daws. 1996. "An Economic Social Security Council at the United Nations." Prepared for a conference in honour of the 85th birthday of Professor Sir Hans Singer, May, Innsbruck, New York.

UN (United Nations). 1993. "Statistical Chart on World Families." Statistics Division and the Secretariat for the International Year of the Family. New York.

———. 1994. *Women's Indicators and Statistics Database.* Version 3. CD-ROM. Statistics Division. New York.

———. 1995. *The World's Women 1970–95: Trends and Statistics.* New York.

———. 1996a. "Factsheet on Women in Government as at January 1996." Division for the Advancement of Women. New York.

———. 1996b. *World Urbanization Prospects: The 1996 Revision.* Database. Population Division. New York.

———. 1997a. *Energy Statistics Yearbook 1995.* New York.

———. 1997b. *World Investment Report.* New York and Geneva.

———. 1998a. *Basic Facts about the United Nations.* New York.

———. 1998b. *Debt Situation of the Developing Countries as of Mid-1998.* Report of the secretary-general. New York.

———. 1998c. *Energy Statistics Yearbook 1996.* New York.

———. 1998d. *Guatemala: Los Contrastes del Desarrollo Humano-Edicion 1998.* Auspiciado por el Sistema de las Naciones Unidas. Guatemala City.

———. 1998e. "Statement by International Organization for Migration to 53rd Session of the General Assembly." New York.

———. 1998f. *Towards a New International Financial Architecture.* Executive Committee of Economic and Social Affairs, Task Force. New York.

———. 1998g. *World Economic and Social Survey 1998.* New York.

———. 1998h. *World Population Prospects 1950–2050: The 1998 Revision.* Database. Population Division. New York.

———. 1999a. *Demographic Yearbook 1997*. New York.

———. 1999b. *Fifth United Nations Survey of Crime Trends and Operations of Criminal Justice Systems*. United Nations Office at Vienna, Crime Prevention and Criminal Justice Division. Vienna. [http://www.ifs.univie.ac.at/~uncjin/wcs]. March 1999.

———. 1999c. "Multilateral Treaties Deposited with the Secretary-General." New York. [http://www.un.org/Depts/Treaty]. March 1999.

UNAIDS (Joint United Nations Programme on HIV/AIDS) and WHO (World Health Organization). 1998a. *Aids Epidemic Update: December 1998*. Geneva. [http://www.who.org/emc_hiv/global_report/data/globalrep_e.pdf]. March 1999.

———. 1998b. *Report on the Global HIV/AIDS Epidemic*. Geneva. [http://www.who.org/emc_hiv/global_report/data/globrep_e.pdf].

UNCTAD (United Nations Conference on Trade and Development). 1996a. *Globalisation and Liberalisation: Effects of International Economic Relations on Poverty*. Geneva.

———. 1996b. *The TRIPS Agreement and Developing Countries*. New York and Geneva.

———. 1997. *World Investment Report*. New York and Geneva.

———. 1998a. *The Least Developed Countries 1998 Report*. New York and Geneva.

———. 1998b. *Trade and Development Report 1998*. New York and Geneva.

———. 1998c. *World Investment Report*. New York and Geneva.

———. 1999. Email correspondence on unpublished data on foreign direct investment. Division on Transnational Corporations and Investment. 20 January. New York and Geneva.

UNDCP (United Nations International Drug Control Programme). 1997. *World Drug Report*. Vienna.

UNDP (United Nations Development Programme). 1990. *Human Development Report 1990*. New York: Oxford University Press.

———. 1994. *Human Development Report 1994*. New York: Oxford University Press.

———. 1995. *Human Development Report 1995*. New York: Oxford University Press.

———. 1997a. *Human Development Report 1997*. New York: Oxford University Press.

———. 1997b. *The Shrinking State: Governance and Sustainable Human Development*. Regional Bureau for Europe and the CIS. New York.

———. 1998a. *Albanian Human Development Report 1998*. Tirana.

———. 1998b. *Estonian Human Development Report 1998*. Tallinn.

———. 1998c. *Human Development Report 1998*. New York: Oxford University Press.

———. 1998d. *Human Development Report: Kazakhstan 1998—Social Integration and the Role of the State in the Transition Period*. Almaty.

———. 1998e. *National Human Development Report: Belarus—State, Governance, People*. Minsk.

———. 1998f. *Social Implications of the Asian Financial Crisis*. United Nations Development Programme–Economic Management and Development for Asian and the Pacific. Joint Policy Studies 9. Seoul: Korea Development Institute.

UNDP (United Nations Development Programme) and Botswana, Government of. 1997. *Botswana Human Development Report 1997*. Gaborone.

UNDP (United Nations Development Programme) and UNAIDS (Joint United Nations Programme on HIV/AIDS). 1998. *HIV/AIDS and Human Development—South Africa*. Pretoria.

UNECE (United Nations Economic Commission for Europe). 1999a. *Trends in Europe and North America 1998–99*. New York and Geneva.

———. 1999b. Correspondence on injuries and deaths from road accidents. March. New York and Geneva.

UNESCO (United Nations Educational, Scientific and Cultural Organization). 1996. Correspondence on gross enrolment ratios. December. Paris.

———. 1997. Correspondence on gross enrolment ratios. November. Paris.

———. 1998a. *Statistical Yearbook 1998*. Paris.

———. 1998b. *World Cultural Report*. Paris.

———. 1998c. *World Education Report 1998*. Paris.

———. 1998d. *World Science Report 1998*. Paris.

———. 1999a. Correspondence on adult literacy rates. January. Paris.

———. 1999b. Correspondence on gross enrolment ratios. April. Paris.

———. 1999c. Correspondence on gross enrolment ratios. February. Paris.

———. 1999d. Correspondence on net enrolment ratios. February. Paris.

———. 1999e. Correspondence on rate of survival to grade 5 of primary education. February. Paris.

UNFPA (United Nations Population Fund) in collaboration with the Australian National University. 1998. *Southeast Asian Population in Crisis: Challenges to the Implementation of the ICPD Programme of Action*. New York.

UNHCHR (United Nations High Commissioner for Human Rights). 1998. *The Right of Peoples to Self-Determination and Its Application to Peoples under Colonial or Alien Domination or Foreign Occupation*. Report submitted by the special rapporteur on mercenaries. Geneva.

UNHCR (United Nations High Commissioner for Refugees). 1998. *Refugees and Others of Concern to UNHCR: 1997, Statistical Overview*. Geneva.

UNICEF (United Nations Children's Fund). 1998a. *Progress of Nations 1998*. New York: Oxford University Press.

———. 1998b. *The State of the World's Children 1998*. New York: Oxford University Press.

———. 1999a. *The State of the World's Children 1999*. New York: Oxford University Press.

———. 1999b. Correspondence on infant mortality and under-five mortality rates. February. New York.

Uppsala Conflict Data Project. 1999. Correspondence on major armed conflict. Uppsala University, Department of Peace and Conflict Research. March. Uppsala, Sweden.

USAID (United States Agency for International Development). 1999. "Women as Chattel: The Emerging Global Market in Trafficking." *Gender Matters Quarterly*, no. 1. Office of Women in Development, Gender Research Project. Washington, DC.

Visser, Jelle, and Anton Hemerijck. 1997. *A Dutch Miracle: Job Growth, Welfare Reform and Corporatism in the Netherlands*. Amsterdam: Amsterdam University Press.

von Weizsacker, Christine. 1998. "Promises of Paradise: Diverse, Multi-Layered and Conflicting Global Perspectives." Policy paper presented at the symposium on Amending Directive 90/220/EEC: Safety and Control of GMOs, convened by the Austrian Federal Chancellery, 23 September, Vienna.

Wahba, Jackline, and Mahmoud Mohieldin. 1998. "Liberalizing Trade in Financial Services: The Uruguay Round and the Arab Countries." *World Development* 26(7): 1331–48.

Weekly Mail and Guardian. 1998. "Indigenous Knowledge at Risk." Johannesburg. 18 December.

Whalley, John, and Colleen Hamilton. 1996. *The Trading System after the Uruguay Round.* Washington, DC: Institute for International Economics.

White, Kathryn. 1999. Email correspondence on the electronic witches of Bosnia. 25 March.

WHO (World Health Organization). 1997. *Tobacco or Health: A Global Status Report.* Geneva.

———.1998a. *The World Health Report 1998.* Geneva.

———. 1998b. *World Health Statistics Annual 1996.* Geneva.

WIPO (World Intellectual Property Organization). 1997. *Implications of the TRIPS Agreement on Treaties Administered by WIPO.* Geneva.

———.1998. *General Information.* Geneva.

WMO (World Meteorological Organisation). 1998. "The First Intergovernmental Meeting of Experts Reviews the 1997–98 El Niño Event." 17 November. Geneva.

Woods, Ngaire. 1998. "Editorial Introduction: Globalization: Definitions, Debates and Implications." *Oxford Development Studies* 26(1): 5–13.

World Bank. 1993. *World Development Report 1993: Investing in Health.* New York: Oxford University Press.

———.1995. *World Development Report 1995: Workers in an Integrating World.* New York: Oxford University Press.

———.1996. *World Bank Atlas 1996.* Washington, DC.

———. 1997a. *World Development Indicators 1997.* Washington, DC.

———. 1997b. *World Development Indicators 1997.* CD-ROM. Washington, DC.

———. 1998a. *East Asia: The Road to Recovery.* Washington, DC.

———. 1998b. *Global Development Finance 1998.* Washington, DC.

———. 1998c. *World Development Indicators 1998.* CD-ROM. Washington, DC.

———. 1999a. *Global Economic Prospects and the Developing Countries 1998/99.* Washington, DC.

———. 1999b. *World Development Indicators 1999.* CD-ROM. Washington, DC.

———. 1999c. *World Development Report 1998/99: Knowledge for Development.* New York: Oxford University Press.

———. 1999d. "The World Bank Responds to Hurricane Mitch." [http://www.worldbank.org/html/extdr/offrep/lac/mitch.htm]. March 1999.

———.1999e. Correspondence on the percentage of population with access to health services. Development Economics Data Group. March. Washington, DC.

———.1999f. Correspondence on unpublished World Bank data on GDP per capita (PPP$) for 1997. Development Economics Data Group. February. Washington, DC.

World Commission on Culture and Development. 1995. *Our Creative Diversity.* Paris: United Nations Educational, Scientific and Cultural Organization.

World Times and IDC (International Data Corporation). 1999. *The 1999 World Times/IDC Information Society Index: Measuring Progress towards a Digital Future.* Boston.

WRI (World Resources Institute). 1998. *World Resources 1998–99.* New York: Oxford University Press.

Yoon, Je Cho, and Changyong Rhee. 1998. "The East Asian Crisis and Macroeconomic Adjustment." Presented at the World Bank Conference on Asian Corporate Recovery, Corporate Governance and Role of Governments, 31 March–12 April, Bangkok.

Zohir, Salma Chaudhuri. 1998. "Gender Implications of Industrial Reforms and Adjustment in the Manufacturing Sector of Bangladesh." PhD diss. University of Manchester.

HUMAN DEVELOPMENT INDICATORS

What do the human development indices reveal?

Since first being published in 1990, the *Human Development Report* has developed and constructed several composite indices to measure different aspects of human development.

The human development index (HDI) has been constructed every year since 1990 to measure average achievements in basic human development in one simple composite index and to produce a ranking of countries. The gender-related development index (GDI) and the gender empowerment measure (GEM), introduced in *Human Development Report 1995*, are composite measures reflecting gender inequalities in human development. While the GDI captures achievements in basic human development adjusted for gender inequality, the GEM measures gender inequality in economic and political opportunities. *Human Development Report 1997* introduced the concept of human poverty and formulated a composite measure of it—the human poverty index (HPI). While the HDI measures average

achievements in basic dimensions of human development, the HPI measures deprivations in those dimensions. Table 1 presents the basic dimensions of human development reflected in the human development indices, and the indicators used to measure them, and table 2 shows the top and bottom five countries in the rankings for each of the indices.

THE NEW HDI—
BETTER DATA, BETTER METHOD

The concept of human development is much deeper and richer than what can be captured in any composite index or even by a detailed set of statistical indicators. Yet to monitor progress in human development, a simple tool is needed. Thus the HDI reflects achievements in the most basic human capabilities—leading a long life, being knowledgeable and enjoying a decent standard of living. Three variables have been chosen to represent those dimensions

---

TABLE 1
HDI, GDI, HPI-1, HPI-2—same dimensions, different measurements

Index	Longevity	Knowledge	Decent standard of living	Participation or exclusion
HDI	Life expectancy at birth	1. Adult literacy rate 2. Combined enrolment ratio	Adjusted per capita income in PPP$	—
GDI	Female and male life expectancy at birth	1. Female and male adult literacy rate 2. Female and male combined enrolment ratio	Adjusted per capita income in PPP$, based on female and male earned income shares	—
HPI-1 For developing countries	Percentage of people not expected to survive to age 40	Adult illiteracy rate	1. Percentage of people without access to safe water 2. Percentage of people without access to health services 3. Percentage of underweight children under five	—
HPI-2 For industrialized countries	Percentage of people not expected to survive to age 60	Adult functional illiteracy rate	Percentage of people living below the income poverty line (50% of median personal disposable income)	Long-term unemployment rate (12 months or more)

Source: Human Development Report Office.

—life expectancy, educational attainment and income.

The HDI is a more comprehensive measure than per capita income. Income is only a means to human development, not an end. Nor is it the sum total of human lives. Thus by focusing on areas beyond income and treating income as a proxy for a decent standard of living, the HDI provides a more comprehensive picture of human life than income does.

With normalization of the values of the variables that make up the HDI, its value ranges from 0 to 1. (The method for constructing the HDI is explained in detail in the technical note.) The HDI value for a country shows the distance that it has already travelled towards the maximum possible value of 1 and also allows comparisons with other countries. The difference between the value achieved by a country and the maximum possible value shows the country's shortfall—how far the country has to go. A challenge for every country is to find ways to reduce its shortfall.

The HDI has been evolving, and this year its methodology has been significantly refined on the basis of a thorough review of its concept and formulation. The changes are summarized in the technical note and discussed in detail in Anand and Sen (1999). This year's HDI also reflects new and improved data for 1997 for the indicators included in the HDI. And the availability of time series on various indicators has made it possible to construct a trend HDI for every five years for 1975–97.

• *Methodological changes.* Until now, in calculating the HDI, income above the cut-off point of world average per capita income has been discounted using a drastic discounting formula. In the new methodology this discounting has been made more gradual by taking the logarithm of income throughout. The rationale for the new treatment of income is given in the technical note.

• *New and improved data series.* This year's HDI is based on improved life expectancy data from the United Nations Population Division and revised data on adult literacy and combined gross primary, secondary and tertiary enrolment ratios from UNESCO. Data on purchasing power parities (PPP) have been

TABLE 2
Top and bottom five countries in the human development indices

Index	Top five	Bottom five
HDI	Canada Norway United States Japan Belgium	Burundi Burkina Faso Ethiopia Niger Sierra Leone
GDI	Canada Norway United States Australia Sweden	Guinea-Bissau Burundi Burkina Faso Ethiopia Niger
GEM	Norway Sweden Denmark Canada Germany	Jordan Mauritania Togo Pakistan Niger
HPI-1	Barbados Trinidad and Tobago Uruguay Costa Rica Cuba	Central African Republic Ethiopia Sierra Leone Burkina Faso Niger
HPI-2	Sweden Netherlands Germany Norway Italy	New Zealand Spain United Kingdom Ireland United States

Source: Human Development Report Office.

TABLE 3
Changes in HDI ranks due to revisions of data and methodology

Country	HDI 1998 Report Rank [a]	HDI 1998 Report Value	HDI 1999 Report Rank	HDI 1999 Report Value	Rank changes due to revised data — Life expectancy	Rank changes due to revised data — Adult literacy	Rank changes due to revised data — Gross enrolment	Rank changes due to revised data — Income (PPP$)	Rank changes due to refined methodology	Total rank changes
Brazil	62	0.809	79	0.739	−1	−1	+1	+3	−19	−17
Estonia	76	0.758	54	0.773	−1	0	+1	+17	+5	+22
Botswana	96	0.678	122	0.609	−8	+2	0	+9	−29	−26

a. Ranks have been recalculated to reflect the exclusion of the Democratic People's Republic of Korea from the HDI ranking in this year's Report.
Source: Human Development Report Office.

WHAT DO THE HUMAN DEVELOPMENT INDICES REVEAL?

updated by the World Bank following the more comprehensive 1997–98 surveys by the International Comparison Programme (ICP).

Because of these changes, this year's HDI is not comparable with last year's. The improvements in methodology and data affect the HDI ranks of almost all countries. Thus if a country ranks lower or higher on the HDI this year compared with last year, that does not necessarily mean that its state of human development has deteriorated or improved. A drop or rise in rank could be attributed to the change in methodology or data. Moreover, the HDI rank of a country also depends on the performance of other countries. The examples of Brazil, Estonia and Botswana show how the improvements in methodology and data can affect countries' rankings (table 3).

What does the 1999 HDI reveal?

The HDI reveals the following state of human development:

- Of the 174 countries for which the HDI has been constructed this year, 45 are in the high human development category (with an HDI value equal to or more than 0.800), 94 in the medium human development category (0.500–0.799) and 35 in the low human development category (less than 0.500). Sixteen countries have experienced reversals in human development since 1990 due to the HIV/AIDS pandemic (mostly in Sub Saharan Africa) or economic stagnation (in Sub-Saharan Africa and Eastern Europe and the CIS).

- Canada, Norway and the United States are at the top of the HDI ranking, and Sierra Leone, Niger and Ethiopia at the bottom. Wide disparities in global human development persist. Canada's HDI value of 0.932 is more than three times Sierra Leone's 0.254. Thus Canada has a shortfall in human development of only about 7%, Sierra Leone one of 75%.

- Disparities between regions can be significant, with some regions having more ground to cover in making up shortfalls than others (figure 1). Sub-Saharan Africa has more than twice as far to go as Latin America and the Caribbean, South Asia three times as far as East Asia (excluding China). Disparities within regions can also be substantial. In South-East

Asia and the Pacific HDI values range from 0.491 in the Lao People's Democratic Republic to 0.888 in Singapore. Among the Arab States they range from 0.412 in Djibouti to 0.833 in Kuwait.

- The link between economic prosperity and human development is neither automatic nor obvious. Two countries with similar income per capita can have very different HDI values; countries with similar HDI values can have very different income levels (figure 2 and table 4). Of the 174 countries, 92 rank higher on the HDI than on GDP per capita (PPP$), suggesting that these countries have been effective in converting income into human development. But for 77 countries the HDI rank is lower than the GDP per capita (PPP$) rank. These countries have been less successful in translating economic prosperity into better lives for people.

- New data series from the United Nations Population Division show that people in many countries live a much longer and healthier life than just two decades ago. In 31 of the 174

TABLE 4		
Similar HDI, different income, 1997		
Country	HDI value	Real GDP per capita (PPP$)
Spain	0.894	15,930
Singapore	0.888	28,460
Georgia	0.729	1,960
Turkey	0.728	6,350
Morocco	0.582	3,310
Lesotho	0.582	1,860

Source: Human Development Report Office.

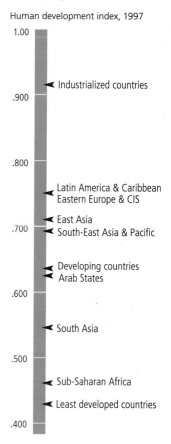

FIGURE 1
Human development varies among regions

Human development index, 1997

Source: Human Development Report Office

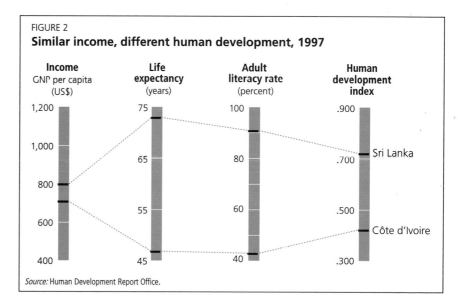

FIGURE 2
Similar income, different human development, 1997

Source: Human Development Report Office.

countries included in the HDI, life expectancy has increased by more than a fifth since 1975.

But the data also tell a tragic story. Between 1975 and 1997 life expectancy fell in 18 countries—10 in Africa, 8 in Eastern Europe and the CIS. In 4 countries, all in Sub-Saharan Africa, life expectancy declined by more than 10%: Zambia (17%), Zimbabwe (17%), Uganda (15%) and Botswana (14%) (figure 3). These large declines in such a relatively short time reveal the devastating effects of HIV/AIDS. For these countries, the HDI rank also dropped.

TRENDS IN HUMAN DEVELOPMENT, 1975–97

Between 1975 and 1997 most countries made substantial progress in human development, reducing their shortfall from the maximum possible value of the HDI. Of the 79 countries for which HDI trends between 1975 and 1997 are available, 54 made up more than 20% of their shortfall, 31 more than 30% and 19 more than 40%. And 6 countries managed a shortfall reduction of more than 50% (table 5). Zambia is the only country among those with data that had a lower HDI in 1997 than in 1975, largely as a result of the effects of HIV/AIDS on life expectancy.

The HDI trends also show that the speed of human progress is uneven. Countries can start at similar levels of human development, but advance at different speeds (figure 4). And countries can start at different levels of human development, yet end up in similar places. Whatever the initial situation, progress is often determined by the policy measures countries take to enhance their people's well-being.

HUMAN POVERTY AND DEPRIVATION

The human poverty index is a multidimensional measure of poverty. It brings together in one composite index the deprivation in four basic dimensions of human life—a long and healthy life, knowledge, economic provisioning and social inclusion. These dimensions of deprivation are the same for both developing and industrialized countries. Only the indicators to measure them differ, to reflect the different realities in these countries and because of data limitations.

For developing countries the deprivation in a long and healthy life is measured by the percentage of people not expected to survive to age 40, deprivation in knowledge by illiteracy and deprivation in economic provisioning by the percentage of people lacking access to health services and safe water and the percentage of children under five who are moderately or severely underweight . Two observations. First, for economic provisioning in developing countries, public provisioning is more important than private income. At the same time more than four-fifths of private income is spent on food. Thus in developing countries lack of access to health services and safe water and the level of malnutrition capture deprivation in economic provisioning more practically than other indicators. Second, the absence of a suitable indicator and lack of data prevent the human poverty index from reflecting deprivation in social inclusion in developing countries.

For industrialized countries deprivation in a long and healthy life is measured by the percentage of people not expected to survive to age 60, deprivation in knowledge by functional illiteracy, deprivation in economic provisioning by income poverty (as private income is the most important source of economic provisioning in

FIGURE 3
Setbacks in Africa
Life expectancy (years)

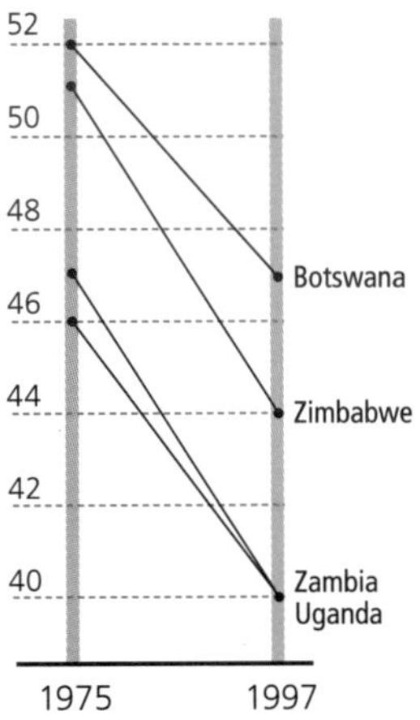

Source: UN 1998h.

TABLE 5
Fastest and slowest progress in human development, 1975–97
For 79 countries with available data

	Country	1975 HDI	1997 HDI	Shortfall reduction 1975–97 (%)
Starting from high human development (0.800–1.000)				
Fastest progress	Australia	0.838	0.922	52.0
	Norway	0.850	0.927	51.5
	Canada	0.862	0.932	50.5
Slowest progress	Austria	0.836	0.904	42.0
	New Zealand	0.843	0.901	37.0
	Denmark	0.861	0.905	31.5
Starting from medium human development (0.500–0.799)				
Fastest progress	Singapore	0.737	0.888	57.5
	Korea, Rep. of	0.680	0.852	54.0
	Hong Kong, China (SAR)	0.757	0.880	51.0
Slowest progress	South Africa	0.637	0.695	16.0
	Romania	0.722	0.752	11.0
	Zimbabwe	0.539	0.560	4.5
Starting from low human development (0–0.499)				
Fastest progress	Indonesia	0.471	0.681	40.0
	Egypt	0.432	0.616	32.5
	Swaziland	0.497	0.644	29.0
Slowest progress	Burundi	0.282	0.324	6.0
	Central African Republic	0.342	0.378	5.5
	Zambia	0.453	0.431	–4.0

Source: Human Development Report Office.

WHAT DO THE HUMAN DEVELOPMENT INDICES REVEAL?

industrialized countries) and deprivation in social inclusion by long-term unemployment.

The components and the results of the HPI-1 (for developing countries) and HPI-2 (for industrialized countries) are presented in indicator tables 4 and 5. The technical note presents a detailed discussion of the methodology for constructing the HPI-1 and HPI-2.

WHAT DOES THE HPI-1 REVEAL?

Calculated for 92 developing countries, the HPI-1 reveals the following:
• Human poverty ranges from a low 2.6% in Barbados to a high 65.5% in Niger. Several countries have an HPI-1 of less than 10%: Bahrain, Barbados, Chile, Costa Rica, Cuba, Fiji, Jordan, Panama, Trinidad and Tobago and Uruguay. These developing countries have overcome severe levels of poverty.
• The HPI-1 exceeds 33% in 37 of the 92 countries, implying that human poverty affects at least a third of the people in these countries. Others have still further to go in reducing human poverty. The HPI-1 exceeds 50% in Benin, Burkina Faso, the Central African Republic, Chad, Ethiopia, Guinea, Guinea-Bissau, Mali, Nepal, Niger and Sierra Leone, suggesting that poverty affects at least half the population.
• A comparison of HDI and HPI-1 values shows the distribution of achievements in human progress. Countries can have similar HDI values but different HPI values (figure 5).

WHAT DOES THE HPI-2 REVEAL?

The HPI-2 shows that human poverty is not confined to developing countries.
• Among the 17 industrialized countries included in the HPI-2, Sweden has the lowest human poverty, with 7%, followed by the Netherlands and Germany, with 8.3% and 10.4%. The industrialized countries with the highest poverty according to the HPI-2 are the United States (16.5%), Ireland (15.3%) and the United Kingdom (15.1%).
• A high HDI value does not automatically imply low levels of human deprivation. All 17 countries included in the HPI-2 have an HDI of at least 0.894, suggesting that they have achieved high levels of human development.

Yet their levels of human poverty vary. Sweden and the United Kingdom have almost the same HDI values, 0.923 and 0.918. But Sweden has an HPI-2 value of only 7%, while the United Kingdom's is 15.1%.

DISPARITIES WITHIN COUNTRIES

Differences in human development exist not only between countries and between North and South. National human development data, disaggregated by region, gender, ethnic group or rural and urban areas, reveal significant disparities within countries. And disparities of all kinds are interrelated and overlapping.

. . . BETWEEN RURAL AND URBAN AREAS . . .

When the HDI and the HPI are disaggregated along the rural-urban divide, they document higher progress in human development and less deprivation for people in urban areas than for those in rural areas. The rural-urban divide in Botswana provides a good example.

According to Botswana's national human development report, the country's HPI-1 dropped from 32.2% to 22% between 1991 and 1996. Yet poverty persists even today, though at very different levels in urban and rural areas (figure 6). People in Botswana's urban areas are better off, with an HPI-1 of 11.7%. In rural areas the HPI is more than twice as high—27%.

. . . BETWEEN REGIONS OR DISTRICTS . . .

• In India the disaggregated HPI-1 shows strong disparities in poverty between states. Human deprivation is highest in the state of Bihar, in northeastern India, where the HPI-1 is 54%. The state of Kerala, in South India, has an HPI-1 of only 23%.
• The Mangistau and Zhambyl oblasts in Kazakhstan have very similar life expectancy and school enrolments. But they have very different HDI values, reflecting very different income levels. Mangistau has an HDI of 0.835 and a GDP per capita (PPP$) of $8,285— Zhambyl an HDI of 0.594 and a GDP per capita (PPP$) of only $1,650.
• In Cuba the provinces with big cities— Havana and Cienfuegos—on the southern

FIGURE 4

Different human progress

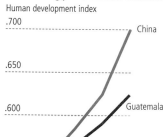

Same starting point, different outcomes
Human development index

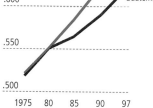

Same outcome, different paths
Human development index

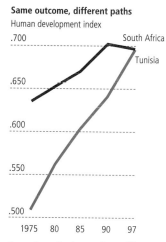

Source: Human Development Report Office.

coast have the highest HDI values, 0.728 and 0.720. The lowest HDI values can be found in the provinces of Granma and Las Tunas, 0.372 and 0.435.

. . . BETWEEN ETHNIC GROUPS . . .

• In Nepal Brahmins have a life expectancy of 61 years, Muslims a life expectancy of only 49. Adult literacy among the Brahmins is 58%, among the Muslims only 22%.

. . . AND BETWEEN MEN AND WOMEN . . .

The HDI is a measure of average achievements and thus masks the differences in human development for men and women. So, other measures are needed to capture gender inequalities.

The gender-related development index attempts to capture achievement in the same dimensions as the HDI—life expectancy, educational attainment and income—but adjusts the results for gender inequality. The technical note presents a detailed discussion of the methodology of the GDI and of its components. Just as in the HDI, income in the GDI has been treated according to the refined methodology, so the GDI ranks of countries have been affected just as their HDI ranks have been.

This year the GDI has been calculated for 143 countries. The GDI values and ranks reveal the following:

• The closer a country's GDI is to its HDI, the less gender disparity there is in the country. But the GDI for every country is lower than its HDI, implying that there is gender inequality in every society.

• For 43 of the 143 countries for which the GDI has been calculated this year, the GDI rank is lower than the HDI rank, revealing the unequal progress in building women's capabilities compared with men's. In these countries—including Ecuador, Luxembourg and the United Arab Emirates—the average achievements in human development have not been equally distributed between men and women.

• For 60 countries the GDI rank is higher than the HDI rank, suggesting a more equitable distribution of human development between men and women. These countries are diverse: they include industrialized countries such as Australia and Sweden, transition economies in Eastern Europe and the CIS such as the Czech Republic and Slovenia and developing countries such as Thailand and Uruguay. These results show that greater gender equality in human development does not depend on income level or stage of development. And they show that it can be achieved across a range of cultures.

. . . INCLUDING IN POLITICAL AND PROFESSIONAL LIFE

The gender empowerment measure captures gender inequality in key areas of economic and political participation and decision-making. It thus focuses on women's opportunities rather than their capabilities as measured in the GDI. The methodology and the components of the GEM are discussed in detail in the technical note.

The GEM has been calculated this year for 102 countries, revealing the following:

• The top three countries are Nordic—Norway, Sweden and Denmark. These countries are not only good at strengthening the basic capabilities of women, they have also opened many opportunities for them to partic-

FIGURE 5
Same HDI, different HPI-1, 1997

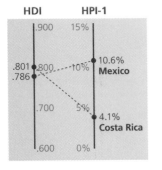

Source: Human Development Report Office.

FIGURE 6
Disparity in human poverty within Botswana

Urban-rural HPI-1, 1996

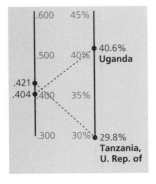

a. Used as a proxy for the percentage of people not expected to survive to age 40.
Source: UNDP and the Government of Botswana 1997.

WHAT DO THE HUMAN DEVELOPMENT INDICES REVEAL?

ipate in economic and political life. The GEM values are lowest in Niger (0.120), Pakistan (0.176) and Togo (0.185), implying that in these societies opportunities for women are much constrained.

• Only one country of the 102 has achieved a value of more than 0.800, and only 33 countries a GEM of more than 0.500. Seventy countries have GEM values less than 0.500. Thus many countries have much further to go in extending broad economic and political opportunities to women.

• Some developing countries outperform much richer industrialized countries in gender equality in political and professional activities. Costa Rica and Trinidad and Tobago are ahead of France and Italy, Israel outperforms Japan, and the Bahamas outranks Portugal. Greece's GEM value, at 0.404, is less than three-fourths that of Costa Rica, at 0.550. The crucial message of the GEM: high income is not a prerequisite for creating opportunities for women.

• Different regions of the same country allow women different roles in public life. The disaggregated GEM for Nepal shows large disparities between two districts, Lalitpur and Jumla (figure 7).

• • • •

The composite indices of human development do not by themselves provide a comprehensive profile of human development in a country. To gain a complete picture, these indices must be supplemented with other indicators of human development (see indicator tables 8–30).

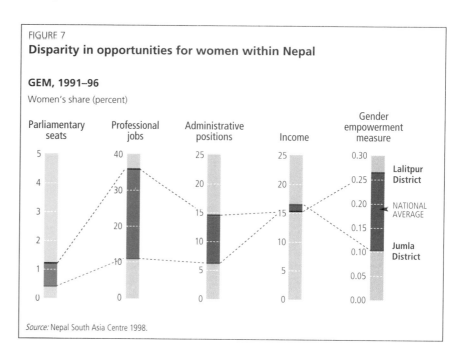

FIGURE 7

Disparity in opportunities for women within Nepal

GEM, 1991–96

Women's share (percent)

Source: Nepal South Asia Centre 1998.

HDI rank	Life expectancy at birth (years) 1997	Adult literacy rate (%) 1997	Combined first-, second- and third-level gross enrolment ratio (%) 1997	Real GDP per capita (PPP$) 1997	Life expectancy index	Education index	GDP index	Human development index (HDI) value 1997	Real GDP per capita (PPP$) rank minus HDI rank[a]
High human development	77.0	98.3	89	21,647	0.87	0.95	0.90	0.904	–
1 Canada	79.0	99.0 [b]	99	22,480	0.90	0.99	0.90	0.932	12
2 Norway	78.1	99.0 [b]	95	24,450	0.89	0.98	0.92	0.927	5
3 United States	76.7	99.0 [b]	94	29,010	0.86	0.97	0.95	0.927	0
4 Japan	80.0	99.0 [b]	85	24,070	0.92	0.94	0.92	0.924	5
5 Belgium	77.2	99.0 [b]	100 [c]	22,750	0.87	0.99	0.91	0.923	6
6 Sweden	78.5	99.0 [b]	100 [c]	19,790	0.89	0.99	0.88	0.923	18
7 Australia	78.2	99.0 [b]	100 [c]	20,210	0.89	0.99	0.89	0.922	15
8 Netherlands	77.9	99.0 [b]	98	21,110	0.88	0.99	0.89	0.921	9
9 Iceland	79.0	99.0 [b]	87	22,497 [d]	0.90	0.95	0.90	0.919	3
10 United Kingdom	77.2	99.0 [b]	100 [c]	20,730	0.87	0.99	0.89	0.918	9
11 France	78.1	99.0 [b]	92	22,030	0.89	0.97	0.90	0.918	4
12 Switzerland	78.6	99.0 [b]	79	25,240	0.89	0.92	0.92	0.914	-6
13 Finland	76.8	99.0 [b]	99	20,150	0.86	0.99	0.89	0.913	10
14 Germany	77.2	99.0 [b]	88	21,260	0.87	0.95	0.89	0.906	2
15 Denmark	75.7	99.0 [b]	89	23,690	0.84	0.96	0.91	0.905	-5
16 Austria	77.0	99.0 [b]	86	22,070	0.87	0.95	0.90	0.904	-2
17 Luxembourg	76.7	99.0 [b]	69	30,863 [d]	0.86	0.89	0.96	0.902	-16
18 New Zealand	76.9	99.0 [b]	95	17,410	0.87	0.98	0.86	0.901	9
19 Italy	78.2	98.3	82	20,290	0.89	0.93	0.89	0.900	2
20 Ireland	76.3	99.0 [b]	88	20,710	0.86	0.95	0.89	0.900	0
21 Spain	78.0	97.2	92	15,930	0.88	0.95	0.85	0.894	9
22 Singapore	77.1	91.4	73	28,460	0.87	0.85	0.94	0.888	-18
23 Israel	77.8	95.4	80	18,150	0.88	0.90	0.87	0.883	3
24 Hong Kong, China (SAR)	78.5	92.4	65	24,350	0.89	0.83	0.92	0.880	-16
25 Brunei Darussalam	75.5	90.1	72	29,773 [d]	0.84	0.84	0.95	0.878	-23
26 Cyprus	77.8	95.9	79 [e]	14,201 [d]	0.88	0.90	0.83	0.870	6
27 Greece	78.1	96.6	79	12,769 [d]	0.89	0.91	0.81	0.867	8
28 Portugal	75.3	90.8	91	14,270	0.84	0.91	0.83	0.858	3
29 Barbados	76.4	97.6	80	12,001 [d]	0.86	0.92	0.80	0.857	8
30 Korea, Rep. of	72.4	97.2	90	13,590	0.79	0.95	0.82	0.852	3
31 Bahamas	73.8	95.8	74	16,705 [d]	0.81	0.88	0.85	0.851	-3
32 Malta	77.2	91.1	78	13,180	0.87	0.87	0.81	0.850	2
33 Slovenia	74.4	99.0 [f]	76	11,800	0.82	0.91	0.80	0.845	5
34 Chile	74.9	95.2	77	12,730	0.83	0.89	0.81	0.844	2
35 Kuwait	75.9	80.4	57	25,314 [d]	0.85	0.73	0.92	0.833	-30
36 Czech Republic	73.9	99.0 [b]	74	10,510	0.81	0.91	0.78	0.833	3
37 Bahrain	72.9	86.2	81	16,527 [d]	0.80	0.85	0.85	0.832	-8
38 Antigua and Barbuda	75.0 [g]	95.0 [g, h]	76 [b]	9,692 [d]	0.83	0.89	0.76	0.828	5
39 Argentina	72.9	96.5	79	10,300	0.80	0.91	0.77	0.827	1
40 Uruguay	73.9	97.5	77	9,200	0.82	0.91	0.75	0.826	5
41 Qatar	71.7	80.0	71	20,987 [d]	0.78	0.77	0.89	0.814	-23
42 Slovakia	73.0	99.0 [b]	75	7,910	0.80	0.91	0.73	0.813	9
43 United Arab Emirates	74.8	74.8	69	19,115 [d]	0.83	0.73	0.88	0.812	-18
44 Poland	72.5	99.0 [f]	77	6,520	0.79	0.92	0.70	0.802	18
45 Costa Rica	76.0	95.1	66	6,650	0.85	0.85	0.70	0.801	16
Medium human development	66.6	75.9	64	3,327	0.69	0.72	0.58	0.662	–
46 Trinidad and Tobago	73.8	97.8	66	6,840	0.81	0.87	0.71	0.797	11
47 Hungary	70.9	99.0 [f]	74	7,200	0.76	0.91	0.71	0.795	8
48 Venezuela	72.4	92.0	67	8,860	0.79	0.84	0.75	0.792	-2
49 Panama	73.6	91.1	73	7,168 [d]	0.81	0.85	0.71	0.791	7
50 Mexico	72.2	90.1	70	8,370	0.79	0.83	0.74	0.786	-3

MONITORING HUMAN DEVELOPMENT: ENLARGING PEOPLE'S CHOICES . . .

HDI rank	Life expectancy at birth (years) 1997	Adult literacy rate (%) 1997	Combined first-, second- and third-level gross enrolment ratio (%) 1997	Real GDP per capita (PPP$) 1997	Life expectancy index	Education index	GDP index	Human development index (HDI) value 1997	Real GDP per capita (PPP$) rank minus HDI rank[a]
51 Saint Kitts and Nevis	70.0 [g]	90.0 [g, h]	78 [b]	8,017 [d]	0.75	0.86	0.73	0.781	-1
52 Grenada	72.0 [i]	96.0 [g, h]	78 [b]	4,864 [d]	0.78	0.90	0.65	0.777	22
53 Dominica	74.0 [g]	94.0 [i]	77 [b]	4,320	0.82	0.88	0.63	0.776	27
54 Estonia	68.7	99.0 [b]	81	5,240	0.73	0.93	0.66	0.773	15
55 Croatia	72.6	97.7	67	4,895 [d]	0.79	0.88	0.65	0.773	18
56 Malaysia	72.0	85.7	65	8,140	0.78	0.79	0.73	0.768	-7
57 Colombia	70.4	90.9	71	6,810	0.76	0.84	0.70	0.768	1
58 Cuba	75.7	95.9	72	3,100 [b]	0.84	0.88	0.57	0.765	47
59 Mauritius	71.4	83.0	63	9,310	0.77	0.76	0.76	0.764	-15
60 Belarus	68.0	99.0 [f]	80	4,850	0.72	0.93	0.65	0.763	15
61 Fiji	72.7	91.8	80	3,990	0.79	0.88	0.62	0.763	26
62 Lithuania	69.9	99.0 [f]	75	4,220	0.75	0.91	0.62	0.761	22
63 Bulgaria	71.1	98.2	70	4,010	0.77	0.89	0.62	0.758	23
64 Suriname	70.1	93.5	71 [b]	5,161 [d]	0.75	0.86	0.66	0.757	6
65 Libyan Arab Jamahiriya	70.0	76.5	92	6,697 [d]	0.75	0.82	0.70	0.756	-6
66 Seychelles	71.0 [g]	84.0 [g, h]	61 [b]	8,171 [d]	0.77	0.76	0.73	0.755	-18
67 Thailand	68.8	94.7	59	6,690	0.73	0.83	0.70	0.753	-7
68 Romania	69.9	97.8	68	4,310	0.75	0.88	0.63	0.752	13
69 Lebanon	69.9	84.4	76	5,940	0.75	0.82	0.68	0.749	-4
70 Samoa (Western)	71.3	98.0 [g, h]	66	3,550	0.77	0.87	0.60	0.747	22
71 Russian Federation	66.6	99.0 [f]	77	4,370	0.69	0.92	0.63	0.747	8
72 Ecuador	69.5	90.7	73	4,940	0.74	0.85	0.65	0.747	0
73 Macedonia, TFYR	73.1	94.0 [b]	70	3,210	0.80	0.86	0.58	0.746	28
74 Latvia	68.4	99.0 [f]	71	3,940	0.72	0.90	0.61	0.744	15
75 Saint Vincent and the Grenadines	73.0 [g]	82.0 [g, h]	78 [b]	4,250 [d]	0.80	0.81	0.63	0.744	8
76 Kazakhstan	67.6	99.0 [b]	76	3,560	0.71	0.91	0.60	0.740	15
77 Philippines	68.3	94.6	82	3,520	0.72	0.90	0.59	0.740	16
78 Saudi Arabia	71.4	73.4	56	10,120	0.77	0.67	0.77	0.740	-37
79 Brazil	66.8	84.0	80	6,480	0.70	0.83	0.70	0.739	-16
80 Peru	68.3	88.7	78	4,680	0.72	0.85	0.64	0.739	-3
81 Saint Lucia	70.0 [g]	82.0 [h, i]	74 [b]	5,437 [d]	0.75	0.79	0.67	0.737	14
82 Jamaica	74.8	85.5	63	3,440	0.83	0.78	0.59	0.734	15
83 Belize	74.7	75.0 [h, j]	72	4,300	0.83	0.74	0.63	0.732	-1
84 Paraguay	69.6	92.4	64	3,980	0.74	0.83	0.61	0.730	4
85 Georgia	72.7	99.0 [g, h]	71	1,960	0.80	0.90	0.50	0.729	37
86 Turkey	69.0	83.2	61	6,350	0.73	0.76	0.69	0.728	-22
87 Armenia	70.5	98.8 [b]	72	2,360	0.76	0.90	0.53	0.728	26
88 Dominican Republic	70.6	82.6	66	4,820	0.76	0.77	0.65	0.726	-12
89 Oman	70.9	67.1	58	9,960 [d]	0.76	0.64	0.77	0.725	-47
90 Sri Lanka	73.1	90.7	66	2,490	0.80	0.82	0.54	0.721	22
91 Ukraine	68.8	99.0 [h, j]	77	2,190	0.73	0.92	0.52	0.721	27
92 Uzbekistan	67.5	99.0 [i]	76	2,529 [d]	0.71	0.91	0.54	0.720	19
93 Maldives	64.5	95.7	74	3,690	0.66	0.89	0.60	0.716	-3
94 Jordan	70.1	87.2	66 [b]	3,450	0.75	0.80	0.59	0.715	2
95 Iran, Islamic Rep. of	69.2	73.3	72	5,817 [d]	0.74	0.73	0.68	0.715	-29
96 Turkmenistan	65.4	98.0 [g, h]	90 [k]	2,109 [d]	0.67	0.95	0.51	0.712	24
97 Kyrgyzstan	67.6	97.0 [g, h]	69	2,250	0.71	0.88	0.52	0.702	19
98 China	69.8	82.9	69	3,130	0.75	0.78	0.57	0.701	6
99 Guyana	64.4	98.1	64	3,210	0.66	0.87	0.58	0.701	2
100 Albania	72.8	85.0 [b]	68	2,120	0.80	0.79	0.51	0.699	19

HDI rank	Life expectancy at birth (years) 1997	Adult literacy rate (%) 1997	Combined first-, second- and third-level gross enrolment ratio (%) 1997	Real GDP per capita (PPP$) 1997	Life expectancy index	Education index	GDP index	Human development index (HDI) value 1997	Real GDP per capita (PPP$) rank minus HDI rank[a]
101 South Africa	54.7	84.0	93	7,380	0.50	0.87	0.72	0.695	-47
102 Tunisia	69.5	67.0	70	5,300	0.74	0.68	0.66	0.695	-34
103 Azerbaijan	69.9	96.3 [b]	71	1,550	0.75	0.88	0.46	0.695	34
104 Moldova, Rep. of	67.5	98.3	70	1,500	0.71	0.89	0.45	0.683	35
105 Indonesia	65.1	85.0	64	3,490	0.67	0.78	0.59	0.681	-11
106 Cape Verde	68.9	71.0	77	2,990	0.73	0.73	0.57	0.677	1
107 El Salvador	69.1	77.0	64	2,880	0.74	0.73	0.56	0.674	1
108 Tajikistan	67.2	98.9	69	1,126 [d]	0.70	0.89	0.40	0.665	46
109 Algeria	68.9	60.3	68	4,460	0.73	0.63	0.63	0.665	-31
110 Viet Nam	67.4	91.9	62	1,630	0.71	0.82	0.47	0.664	23
111 Syrian Arab Republic	68.9	71.6	60	3,250	0.73	0.68	0.58	0.663	-11
112 Bolivia	61.4	83.6	70	2,880	0.61	0.79	0.56	0.652	-4
113 Swaziland	60.2	77.5	73	3,350	0.59	0.76	0.59	0.644	-15
114 Honduras	69.4	70.7	58	2,220	0.74	0.66	0.52	0.641	3
115 Namibia	52.4	79.8	82	5,010	0.46	0.81	0.65	0.638	-44
116 Vanuatu	67.4	64.0 [g, h]	47	3,480	0.71	0.58	0.59	0.627	-21
117 Guatemala	64.0	66.6	47	4,100	0.65	0.60	0.62	0.624	-32
118 Solomon Islands	71.7	62.0 [g, h]	46	2,310	0.78	0.57	0.52	0.623	-3
119 Mongolia	65.8	84.0	55	1,310	0.68	0.74	0.43	0.618	26
120 Egypt	66.3	52.7	72	3,050	0.69	0.59	0.57	0.616	-14
121 Nicaragua	67.9	63.4	63	1,997 [d]	0.71	0.63	0.50	0.616	0
122 Botswana	47.4	74.4	70	7,690	0.37	0.73	0.72	0.609	-70
123 São Tomé and Principe	64.0 [g]	75.0 [l]	57 [b]	1,851 [d]	0.65	0.69	0.49	0.609	3
124 Gabon	52.4	66.2	60 [k]	7,550	0.46	0.64	0.72	0.607	-71
125 Iraq	62.4	58.0 [g, h]	51	3,197 [d]	0.62	0.56	0.58	0.586	-22
126 Morocco	66.6	45.9	49	3,310	0.69	0.47	0.58	0.582	-27
127 Lesotho	56.0	82.3	58	1,860	0.52	0.74	0.49	0.582	-2
128 Myanmar	60.1	83.6	55	1,199 [d]	0.59	0.74	0.41	0.580	23
129 Papua New Guinea	57.9	73.7	37	2,654 [d]	0.55	0.61	0.55	0.570	-19
130 Zimbabwe	44.1	90.9	68	2,350	0.32	0.83	0.53	0.560	-16
131 Equatorial Guinea	50.0	79.9	64 [e]	1,817 [d]	0.42	0.75	0.48	0.549	-3
132 India	62.6	53.5	55	1,670	0.63	0.54	0.47	0.545	-1
133 Ghana	60.0	66.4	42	1,640	0.58	0.58	0.47	0.544	-1
134 Cameroon	54.7	71.7	43	1,890	0.50	0.62	0.49	0.536	-11
135 Congo	48.6	76.9	68	1,620	0.39	0.74	0.46	0.533	-1
136 Kenya	52.0	79.3	50	1,190	0.45	0.69	0.41	0.519	16
137 Cambodia	53.4	66.0 [j]	61	1,290	0.47	0.64	0.43	0.514	10
138 Pakistan	64.0	40.9	43	1,560	0.65	0.41	0.46	0.508	-3
139 Comoros	58.8	55.4	39	1,530	0.56	0.50	0.46	0.506	-1
Low human development	50.6	48.5	39	982	0.43	0.45	0.38	0.416	–
140 Lao People's Dem. Rep.	53.2	58.6	55	1,300	0.47	0.57	0.43	0.491	6
141 Congo, Dem. Rep. of the	50.8	77.0 [h, i]	39	880	0.43	0.64	0.36	0.479	21
142 Sudan	55.0	53.3	34	1,560	0.50	0.47	0.46	0.475	-7
143 Togo	48.8	53.2	61	1,490	0.40	0.56	0.45	0.469	-3
144 Nepal	57.3	38.1	59	1,090	0.54	0.45	0.40	0.463	11
145 Bhutan	60.7	44.2	12	1,467 [d]	0.60	0.33	0.45	0.459	-3
146 Nigeria	50.1	59.5	54	920	0.42	0.58	0.37	0.456	15
147 Madagascar	57.5	47.0 [h, j]	39	930	0.54	0.44	0.37	0.453	13
148 Yemen	58.0	42.5	49	810	0.55	0.45	0.35	0.449	18
149 Mauritania	53.5	38.4	41	1,730	0.47	0.39	0.48	0.447	-20
150 Bangladesh	58.1	38.9	35	1,050	0.55	0.38	0.39	0.440	6

HDI rank	Life expectancy at birth (years) 1997	Adult literacy rate (%) 1997	Combined first-, second- and third-level gross enrolment ratio (%) 1997	Real GDP per capita (PPP$) 1997	Life expectancy index	Education index	GDP index	Human development index (HDI) value 1997	Real GDP per capita (PPP$) rank minus HDI rank[a]
151 Zambia	40.1	75.1	49	960	0.25	0.67	0.38	0.431	8
152 Haiti	53.7	45.8	24	1,270	0.48	0.39	0.42	0.430	-4
153 Senegal	52.3	34.6	35	1,730	0.46	0.35	0.48	0.426	-24
154 Côte d'Ivoire	46.7	42.6	40	1,840	0.36	0.42	0.49	0.422	-27
155 Benin	53.4	33.9	42	1,270	0.47	0.37	0.42	0.421	-7
156 Tanzania, U. Rep. of	47.9	71.6	33	580	0.38	0.59	0.29	0.421	16
157 Djibouti	50.4	48.3	21	1,266 d	0.42	0.39	0.42	0.412	-7
158 Uganda	39.6	64.0	40	1,160	0.24	0.56	0.41	0.404	-5
159 Malawi	39.3	57.7	75	710	0.24	0.63	0.33	0.399	10
160 Angola	46.5	45.0 h, j	27	1,430	0.36	0.39	0.44	0.398	-17
161 Guinea	46.5	37.9	28	1,880	0.36	0.34	0.49	0.398	-37
162 Chad	47.2	50.3	29	970	0.37	0.43	0.38	0.393	-4
163 Gambia	47.0	33.1	41	1,470	0.37	0.36	0.45	0.391	-22
164 Rwanda	40.5	63.0	43	660	0.26	0.56	0.31	0.379	6
165 Central African Republic	44.9	42.4	26	1,330	0.33	0.37	0.43	0.378	-21
166 Mali	53.3	35.5	25	740	0.47	0.32	0.33	0.375	1
167 Eritrea	50.8	25.0 j	27	820	0.43	0.26	0.35	0.346	-2
168 Guinea-Bissau	45.0	33.6	34	861 d	0.33	0.34	0.36	0.343	-5
169 Mozambique	45.2	40.5	25	740	0.34	0.35	0.33	0.341	-2
170 Burundi	42.4	44.6	23	630	0.29	0.37	0.31	0.324	1
171 Burkina Faso	44.4	20.7	20	1,010	0.32	0.20	0.39	0.304	-14
172 Ethiopia	43.3	35.4	24	510	0.31	0.32	0.27	0.298	1
173 Niger	48.5	14.3	15	850	0.39	0.14	0.36	0.298	-9
174 Sierra Leone	37.2	33.3	30 e	410	0.20	0.32	0.24	0.254	0
All developing countries	64.4	71.4	59	3,240	0.66	0.67	0.58	0.637	–
Least developed countries	51.7	50.7	37	992	0.44	0.46	0.38	0.430	–
Sub-Saharan Africa	48.9	58.5	44	1,534	0.40	0.54	0.46	0.463	–
Arab States	65.1	58.6	59	4,094	0.67	0.59	0.62	0.626	–
East Asia	70.0	83.4	69	3,601	0.75	0.79	0.60	0.712	–
East Asia (excluding China)	72.8	96.1	85	14,300	0.80	0.92	0.83	0.849	–
South-East Asia and the Pacific	65.9	87.9	65	3,697	0.68	0.80	0.60	0.695	–
South Asia	62.7	52.2	52	1,803	0.63	0.52	0.48	0.544	–
South Asia (excluding India)	63.0	48.4	47	2,147	0.63	0.48	0.51	0.542	–
Latin America and the Caribbean	69.5	87.2	72	6,868	0.74	0.82	0.71	0.756	–
Eastern Europe and the CIS	68.6	98.7	76	4,243	0.73	0.91	0.63	0.754	–
Industrialized countries	77.7	98.7	92	23,741	0.88	0.96	0.91	0.919	–
World	66.7	78.0	63	6,332	0.69	0.73	0.69	0.706	–

a. A positive figure indicates that the HDI rank is better than the real GDP per capita (PPP$) rank, a negative the opposite.

b. Human Development Report Office estimate.

c. Capped at 100%.

d. Heston and Summers 1999.

e. UNESCO 1997.

f. Capped at 99.0%.

g. UNICEF 1999a.

h. Data refer to a year or period other than that specified in the column heading, differ from the standard definition or refer to only part of the country.

i. UNICEF 1998b.

j. Human Development Report Office estimate based on national sources.

k. UNESCO 1996.

l. World Bank 1997b.

Source: Column 1: unless otherwise noted, calculated on the basis of data from UN 1998h; *column 2:* unless otherwise noted, calculated on the basis of data from UNESCO 1999a; *column 3:* unless otherwise noted, UNESCO 1999b; *column 4:* unless otherwise noted, calculated on the basis of data from World Bank 1999f; *columns 5-9:* Human Development Report Office calculations.

HDI rank	Gender-related development index (GDI) 1997		Life expectancy at birth (years) 1997		Adult literacy rate (%) 1997		Combined first-, second- and third-level gross enrolment ratio (%) 1997		Real GDP per capita (PPP$) 1997 [a]		HDI rank minus GDI rank [b]
	Rank	Value	Female	Male	Female	Male	Female	Male	Female	Male	
High human development	–	0.902	80.2	73.7	98.1	98.6	90	88	15,827	27,656	–
1 Canada	1	0.928	81.8	76.1	99.0 [c]	99.0 [c]	100 [d]	96	17,254 [e]	27,806 [e]	0
2 Norway	2	0.927	81.1	75.2	99.0 [c]	99.0 [c]	98	93	20,872 [f]	28,095 [f]	0
3 United States	3	0.926	80.1	73.4	99.0 [c]	99.0 [c]	97	91	23,540	34,639	0
4 Japan	8	0.917	82.9	76.8	99.0 [c]	99.0 [c]	83	86	14,625	33,893	-4
5 Belgium	6	0.918	80.6	73.8	99.0 [c]	99.0 [c]	100 [d]	100 [d]	15,249	30,565	-1
6 Sweden	5	0.919	80.8	76.3	99.0 [c]	99.0 [c]	100 [d]	95	17,829	21,789	1
7 Australia	4	0.921	81.1	75.5	99.0 [c]	99.0 [c]	100 [d]	100 [d]	16,526	23,944	3
8 Netherlands	9	0.916	80.7	75.0	99.0 [c]	99.0 [c]	97	100	14,483	27,877	-1
9 Iceland	7	0.918	81.3	76.8	99.0 [c]	99.0 [c]	89	86	19,183 [g]	25,777 [g]	2
10 United Kingdom	11	0.915	79.8	74.5	99.0 [c]	99.0 [c]	100 [d]	99	15,736	25,917	-1
11 France	10	0.916	82.0	74.2	99.0 [c]	99.0 [c]	94	91	17,176	27,134	1
12 Switzerland	12	0.909	81.8	75.4	99.0 [c]	99.0 [c]	76	83	16,802	33,878	0
13 Finland	13	0.908	80.6	73.0	99.0 [c]	99.0 [c]	100 [d]	94	15,045	25,522	0
14 Germany	15	0.904	80.2	73.9	99.0 [c]	99.0 [c]	87	89	16,780	25,962	-1
15 Denmark	14	0.904	78.3	73.0	99.0 [c]	99.0 [c]	91	87	19,733	27,741	1
16 Austria	17	0.898	80.2	73.7	99.0 [c]	99.0 [c]	85	86	14,099	30,337	-1
17 Luxembourg	19	0.894	79.9	73.3	99.0 [c]	99.0 [c]	69	69	17,326 [g]	44,955 [g]	-2
18 New Zealand	16	0.900	79.7	74.1	99.0 [c]	99.0 [c]	99	92	13,757	21,177	2
19 Italy	18	0.894	81.2	75.0	97.8	98.8	83	80	12,634 [e]	28,405 [e]	1
20 Ireland	20	0.892	79.2	73.6	99.0 [c]	99.0 [c]	90	86	11,585 [f]	29,973 [f]	0
21 Spain	21	0.888	81.5	74.5	96.2	98.4	94	89	9,568 [e]	22,569 [e]	0
22 Singapore	22	0.883	79.3	74.9	87.0	95.9	71	74	18,947	37,833	0
23 Israel	23	0.879	79.7	75.7	93.4	97.5	81	79	12,387 [e]	24,007 [e]	0
24 Hong Kong, China (SAR)	24	0.875	81.4	75.8	88.4	96.1	67	64	15,180	32,688	0
25 Brunei Darussalam	25	0.872	78.1	73.4	86.0	93.7	73	71	17,637 [e, g]	40,781 [e, g]	0
26 Cyprus	..	..	80.0	75.5	93.5	98.4	..	..	8,095 [g]	20,329 [g]	..
27 Greece	26	0.861	80.7	75.6	94.9	98.3	79	79	8,248 [f, g]	17,429 [f, g]	0
28 Portugal	28	0.853	78.8	71.8	88.3	93.7	93	88	9,445	19,469	-1
29 Barbados	27	0.854	78.7	73.7	97.0	98.2	80	80	9,252 [e, g]	14,946 [e, g]	1
30 Korea, Rep. of	30	0.845	76.0	68.8	95.5	98.9	84	94	8,388	18,708	-1
31 Bahamas	29	0.849	77.1	70.5	96.4	95.1	77	71	13,296 [e, g]	20,232 [e, g]	1
32 Malta	32	0.834	79.3	74.9	91.7	90.5	77	78	5,733 [e]	20,772 [e]	-1
33 Slovenia	31	0.842	78.2	70.6	99.0 [h]	99.0 [h]	78	74	9,137 [e]	14,619 [e]	1
34 Chile	33	0.832	78.3	72.3	94.9	95.4	76	78	5,853 [i]	19,749 [i]	0
35 Kuwait	35	0.825	78.2	74.1	77.5	83.1	59	56	13,481 [e, g]	36,544 [e, g]	-1
36 Czech Republic	34	0.830	77.4	70.3	99.0 [c]	99.0 [c]	74	74	7,952 [f]	13,205 [f]	1
37 Bahrain	38	0.813	75.3	71.1	80.7	89.9	84	79	5,512 [e, g]	24,772 [e, g]	-2
38 Antigua and Barbuda	..	..	..	..	..	..	..	..	..	..	..
39 Argentina	37	0.814	76.8	69.7	96.5	96.6	82	77	4,835 [i]	15,976 [i]	0
40 Uruguay	36	0.823	78.0	70.5	97.8	97.0	81	74	6,305 [i]	12,275 [i]	2
41 Qatar	41	0.796	75.4	70.0	81.2	79.6	74	69	5,193 [e, g]	29,165 [e, g]	-2
42 Slovakia	39	0.811	76.7	69.2	99.0 [c]	99.0 [c]	76	74	6,366 [e]	9,532 [e]	1
43 United Arab Emirates	45	0.790	76.5	73.9	76.8	73.9	72	66	4,544 [e, g]	27,373 [e, g]	-4
44 Poland	40	0.800	76.9	68.2	99.0 [h]	99.0 [h]	78	77	5,061 [e]	8,060 [e]	2
45 Costa Rica	42	0.795	78.9	74.3	95.1	95.0	65	66	3,643	9,575	1
Medium human development	–	0.658	68.7	64.8	67.3	83.3	60	68	2,220	4,414	–
46 Trinidad and Tobago	44	0.790	76.2	71.5	97.0	98.7	66	67	4,101 [e]	9,600 [e]	0
47 Hungary	43	0.792	74.9	66.8	99.0 [h]	99.0 [h]	75	73	5,372	9,194	2
48 Venezuela	46	0.786	75.7	70.0	91.6	92.5	68	66	5,006 [e]	12,661 [e]	0
49 Panama	47	0.786	76.4	71.8	90.4	91.7	74	72	4,140 [e, g]	10,135 [e, g]	0
50 Mexico	48	0.778	75.5	69.5	87.9	92.3	69	71	4,594	12,216	0

2 Gender-related development index

HDI rank	Gender-related development index (GDI) 1997 Rank	Value	Life expectancy at birth (years) 1997 Female	Male	Adult literacy rate (%) 1997 Female	Male	Combined first-, second- and third-level gross enrolment ratio (%) 1997 Female	Male	Real GDP per capita (PPP$) 1997 [a] Female	Male	HDI rank minus GDI rank [b]
51 Saint Kitts and Nevis	..	..	..	..	..	..	..	..	..	..	..
52 Grenada	..	..	..	..	..	..	..	..	..	..	..
53 Dominica	..	..	..	..	..	..	..	..	..	..	..
54 Estonia	49	0.772	74.5	63.0	99.0 [c]	99.0 [c]	83	80	4,236 [g]	6,372 [g]	0
55 Croatia	50	0.769	76.5	68.8	96.4	99.0 [h]	68	67	3,557 [e, g]	6,325 [e, g]	0
56 Malaysia	52	0.763	74.3	69.9	81.0	90.2	66	64	5,115 [e]	11,081 [e]	-1
57 Colombia	51	0.765	74.3	67.3	90.8	91.0	71	70	4,725 [i]	8,945 [i]	1
58 Cuba	53	0.762	78.0	74.2	95.9	95.9	73	70	2,013 [e, j]	4,181 [e, j]	0
59 Mauritius	57	0.754	75.1	67.9	79.2	86.9	63	62	4,893 [e]	13,745 [e]	-3
60 Belarus	54	0.761	73.9	62.2	98.5	99.0 [h]	82	78	3,909 [e]	5,912 [e]	1
61 Fiji	60	0.749	74.9	70.6	89.4	94.1	79	81	1,897 [e]	6,014 [e]	-4
62 Lithuania	55	0.759	75.6	64.3	99.0 [h]	99.0 [h]	77	73	3,323	5,221	2
63 Bulgaria	56	0.757	74.7	67.6	97.6	98.8	73	68	3,256 [e]	4,801 [e]	2
64 Suriname	..	..	72.7	67.5	91.6	95.4	..	..	2,794 [e, g]	7,569 [e, g]	..
65 Libyan Arab Jamahiriya	68	0.732	72.2	68.3	62.9	88.7	92	92	2,373 [e, g]	10,699 [e, g]	-9
66 Seychelles	..	..	..	..	..	..	..	..	..	..	..
67 Thailand	58	0.751	72.0	65.8	92.8	96.7	59	58	5,000	8,382	2
68 Romania	59	0.750	73.9	66.2	96.7	98.9	68	68	3,221 [e]	5,435 [e]	2
69 Lebanon	66	0.734	71.7	68.1	78.3	91.2	77	76	2,793 [e]	9,239 [e]	-4
70 Samoa (Western)	..	..	73.6	69.3	..	..	67	65	1,560 [e]	5,379 [e]	..
71 Russian Federation	61	0.745	72.8	60.6	98.8	99.0 [h]	80	74	3,503 [e]	5,356 [e]	2
72 Ecuador	70	0.728	72.5	67.3	88.8	92.7	67	78	1,925 [i]	7,927 [i]	-6
73 Macedonia, TFYR	63	0.742	75.3	70.9	94.0 [c]	94.0 [c]	70	70	2,257 [e]	4,163 [e]	2
74 Latvia	62	0.743	74.4	62.5	99.0 [h]	99.0 [h]	72	69	3,330	4,664	4
75 Saint Vincent and the Grenadines	..	..	..	..	..	..	..	..	..	..	..
76 Kazakhstan	64	0.738	72.5	62.8	99.0 [c]	99.0 [c]	79	74	2,804 [e]	4,358 [e]	3
77 Philippines	65	0.736	70.2	66.5	94.3	94.8	85	80	2,510	4,513	3
78 Saudi Arabia	78	0.703	73.4	69.9	62.5	81.0	53	58	2,284 [e]	16,385 [e]	-9
79 Brazil	67	0.733	71.0	63.1	83.9	84.1	77	82	3,813	9,205	3
80 Peru	71	0.726	70.9	65.9	83.7	93.9	77	80	2,335 [e]	7,061 [e]	0
81 Saint Lucia	..	..	..	..	..	..	..	..	..	..	..
82 Jamaica	69	0.731	76.8	72.9	89.6	81.2	63	62	2,756 [e]	4,138 [e]	3
83 Belize	..	..	76.1	73.4	..	..	72	72	1,617 [e]	6,928 [e]	..
84 Paraguay	74	0.717	72.0	67.5	91.1	93.8	64	65	1,918	6,009	-1
85 Georgia	..	..	76.8	68.5	..	..	71	70	1,521 [e]	2,440 [e]	..
86 Turkey	73	0.722	71.7	66.5	73.9	92.4	54	67	4,681	7,982	1
87 Armenia	72	0.726	73.6	67.2	98.8 [c]	98.8 [c]	68	75	1,928 [e]	2,816 [e]	3
88 Dominican Republic	75	0.716	73.1	69.0	82.3	82.8	69	63	2,374 [e]	7,186 [e]	1
89 Oman	85	0.686	73.3	68.9	55.0	76.9	57	60	2,339 [e, g]	16,654 [e, g]	-8
90 Sri Lanka	76	0.712	75.4	70.9	87.6	94.0	67	65	1,452	3,545	2
91 Ukraine	..	..	73.7	63.8	..	..	80	74	1,691	2,763	..
92 Uzbekistan	..	..	70.7	64.3	..	..	74	78	2,019 [c, g]	3,047 [c, g]	..
93 Maldives	77	0.711	63.3	65.7	95.6	95.7	75	74	2,698 [e]	4,630 [e]	2
94 Jordan	..	..	71.5	68.9	81.8	92.2	..	..	1,429	5,336	..
95 Iran, Islamic Rep. of	81	0.696	70.0	68.5	65.8	80.7	68	76	2,453 [e, g]	9,084 [e, g]	-1
96 Turkmenistan	..	..	68.9	61.9	..	..	..	..	1,642 [e, g]	2,586 [e, g]	..
97 Kyrgyzstan	..	..	71.9	63.3	..	..	71	68	1,798 [e]	2,720 [e]	..
98 China	79	0.699	72.0	67.9	74.5	90.8	67	71	2,485 [e]	3,738 [e]	2
99 Guyana	83	0.691	67.9	61.1	97.5	98.7	64	64	1,760 [e]	4,696 [e]	-1
100 Albania	80	0.696	75.9	69.9	85.0 [c]	85.0 [c]	68	67	1,501 [e]	2,711 [e]	3

HDI rank	Gender-related development index (GDI) 1997		Life expectancy at birth (years) 1997		Adult literacy rate (%) 1997		Combined first-, second- and third-level gross enrolment ratio (%) 1997		Real GDP per capita (PPP$) 1997[a]		HDI rank minus GDI rank[b]
	Rank	Value	Female	Male	Female	Male	Female	Male	Female	Male	
101 South Africa	84	0.689	58.1	51.5	83.2	84.7	94	93	4,637 [e]	10,216 [e]	0
102 Tunisia	87	0.681	70.7	68.4	55.8	78.1	68	72	2,742 [e]	7,806 [e]	-2
103 Azerbaijan	82	0.691	74.1	65.5	96.3 [c]	96.3 [c]	73	69	1,164 [e]	1,952 [e]	4
104 Moldova, Rep. of	86	0.681	71.5	63.5	97.4	99.0 [h]	71	69	1,221 [e]	1,805 [e]	1
105 Indonesia	88	0.675	67.0	63.3	79.5	90.6	61	68	2,359 [e]	4,626 [e]	0
106 Cape Verde	90	0.667	71.3	65.5	62.5	82.1	76	79	1,985 [e]	4,152 [e]	-1
107 El Salvador	89	0.667	72.5	66.5	74.2	80.1	63	64	1,688 [e]	4,120 [e]	1
108 Tajikistan	92	0.662	70.2	64.2	98.3	99.0 [h]	65	73	850 [e, g]	1,404 [e, g]	-1
109 Algeria	93	0.642	70.3	67.5	47.7	72.7	64	71	1,896 [e]	6,962 [e]	-1
110 Viet Nam	91	0.662	69.6	64.9	89.0	95.1	59	64	1,385 [e]	1,882 [e]	2
111 Syrian Arab Republic	95	0.640	71.2	66.7	56.5	86.5	56	63	1,397 [e]	5,064 [e]	-1
112 Bolivia	94	0.641	63.2	59.8	76.8	90.7	64	75	1,589 [i]	4,187 [i]	1
113 Swaziland	96	0.636	62.5	57.9	76.3	78.9	71	74	2,082 [e]	4,720 [e]	0
114 Honduras	98	0.631	72.3	67.5	70.2	71.1	59	57	1,130 [e]	3,293 [e]	-1
115 Namibia	97	0.633	53.0	51.8	78.5	81.2	84	80	3,439 [e]	6,594 [e]	1
116 Vanuatu	..	..	69.5	65.5	..	..	44	49	..	..	..
117 Guatemala	101	0.608	67.2	61.4	58.9	74.2	43	51	1,861 [e]	6,298 [e]	-2
118 Solomon Islands	..	..	73.9	69.7	..	..	44	48	1,886 [e]	2,710 [e]	..
119 Mongolia	99	0.616	67.3	64.4	78.6	89.3	61	49	1,057 [e]	1,562 [e]	1
120 Egypt	103	0.603	67.9	64.7	40.5	64.7	66	77	1,800	4,264	-2
121 Nicaragua	100	0.609	70.6	65.8	63.4	63.3	65	61	1,169 [e, g]	2,835 [e, g]	2
122 Botswana	102	0.606	48.4	46.2	76.9	71.7	72	69	5,990 [e]	9,460 [e]	1
123 São Tomé and Principe	..	..	..	..	..	..	..	..	..	..	..
124 Gabon	..	..	53.8	51.1	56.8	76.1	..	..	5,678 [e]	9,468 [e]	..
125 Iraq	..	..	63.9	60.9	..	..	44	57	970 [e, g]	5,347 [e, g]	..
126 Morocco	106	0.565	68.5	64.8	32.7	59.3	42	55	1,909 [e]	4,709 [e]	-2
127 Lesotho	105	0.570	57.3	54.7	92.5	71.5	62	53	1,145 [e]	2,598 [e]	0
128 Myanmar	104	0.576	61.8	58.5	78.8	88.5	54	55	882 [e, g]	1,519 [e, g]	2
129 Papua New Guinea	107	0.564	58.7	57.2	64.7	82.0	33	40	1,915 [e, g]	3,348 [e, g]	0
130 Zimbabwe	108	0.555	44.7	43.6	87.6	94.3	66	71	1,764 [e]	2,945 [e]	0
131 Equatorial Guinea	..	..	51.6	48.4	70.1	90.5	..	..	1,066 [e, g]	2,589 [e, g]	..
132 India	112	0.525	62.9	62.3	39.4	66.7	47	62	902 [e]	2,389 [e]	-3
133 Ghana	109	0.540	61.8	58.3	56.5	76.5	37	47	1,428 [e]	1,854 [e]	1
134 Cameroon	110	0.527	56.0	53.4	64.6	79.0	39	48	1,191 [e]	2,598 [e]	1
135 Congo	111	0.527	50.8	46.3	69.8	84.6	62	76	1,179 [e]	2,082 [e]	1
136 Kenya	113	0.517	53.0	51.1	71.8	86.9	49	50	1,013	1,366	0
137 Cambodia	..	..	55.0	51.5	..	..	54	68	1,163 [e]	1,426 [e]	..
138 Pakistan	116	0.472	65.1	62.9	25.4	55.2	28	56	701 [e]	2,363 [e]	-2
139 Comoros	114	0.500	60.2	57.4	48.2	62.9	35	42	1,124 [e]	1,936 [e]	1
Low human development	–	0.404	51.5	49.7	35.8	57.2	33	44	691	1,277	–
140 Lao People's Dem. Rep.	115	0.483	54.5	52.0	46.8	71.1	48	62	1,033 [e]	1,563 [e]	1
141 Congo, Dem. Rep. of the	..	..	52.3	49.2	..	..	31	47	648 [e]	1,117 [e]	..
142 Sudan	117	0.453	56.4	53.6	41.3	65.4	31	37	741 [e]	2,375 [e]	0
143 Togo	118	0.450	50.1	47.6	38.3	68.7	47	75	998 [e]	1,991 [e]	0
144 Nepal	121	0.441	57.1	57.6	20.7	55.7	49	69	763 [e]	1,409 [e]	-2
145 Bhutan	119	0.444	62.0	59.5	30.3	58.1	10	14	985 [e, g]	1,940 [e, g]	1
146 Nigeria	120	0.442	51.5	48.7	50.8	68.5	48	61	553 [e]	1,293 [e]	1
147 Madagascar	..	..	59.0	56.0	..	..	39	39	712 [e]	1,151 [e]	..
148 Yemen	128	0.408	58.4	57.4	21.0	64.2	27	70	579 [e]	1,038 [e]	-6
149 Mauritania	122	0.438	55.1	51.9	27.8	49.4	36	45	1,283 [e]	2,185 [e]	1
150 Bangladesh	123	0.428	58.2	58.1	27.4	49.9	30	40	767 [e]	1,320 [e]	1

MONITORING HUMAN DEVELOPMENT: ENLARGING PEOPLE'S CHOICES . . .

HDI rank	Gender-related development index (GDI) 1997 Rank	Value	Life expectancy at birth (years) 1997 Female	Male	Adult literacy rate (%) 1997 Female	Male	Combined first-, second- and third-level gross enrolment ratio (%) 1997 Female	Male	Real GDP per capita (PPP$) 1997[a] Female	Male	HDI rank minus GDI rank[b]
151 Zambia	125	0.425	40.6	39.5	67.5	83.3	46	53	753	1,172	0
152 Haiti	124	0.426	56.2	51.4	43.4	48.3	24	25	928[e]	1,624[e]	2
153 Senegal	127	0.417	54.2	50.5	24.8	44.5	31	40	1,253[e]	2,209[e]	0
154 Côte d'Ivoire	130	0.404	47.3	46.2	33.7	51.0	32	48	991[e]	2,656[e]	-2
155 Benin	129	0.405	55.2	51.7	20.9	47.8	30	54	1,048[e]	1,499[e]	0
156 Tanzania, U. Rep. of	126	0.418	49.1	46.8	62.0	81.7	32	33	549	612	4
157 Djibouti	..	..	52.0	48.7	35.0	62.2	17	24	..	..	..
158 Uganda	131	0.397	40.4	38.9	53.0	75.2	36	44	944[e]	1,378[e]	0
159 Malawi	132	0.390	39.6	38.9	43.4	72.8	70	79	600[e]	823[e]	0
160 Angola	..	..	48.1	44.9	..	..	25	29	1,127[e]	1,741[e]	..
161 Guinea	134	0.381	47.0	46.0	23.9	52.0	19	36	1,530[e]	2,226[e]	-1
162 Chad	135	0.378	48.7	45.7	37.1	64.0	19	38	730[e]	1,216[e]	-1
163 Gambia	133	0.384	48.6	45.4	26.4	40.1	35	48	1,115[e]	1,834[e]	2
164 Rwanda	..	..	41.7	39.4	55.6	70.7	42	44	..	..	..
165 Central African Republic	137	0.365	46.9	42.9	30.1	56.0	20	33	1,032	1,645	-1
166 Mali	136	0.367	54.6	52.0	28.3	43.1	20	31	583[e]	902[e]	1
167 Eritrea	..	..	52.4	49.3	..	..	24	30	568	1,076	..
168 Guinea-Bissau	139	0.318	46.5	43.5	18.3	49.7	24	43	580[e, g]	1,151[e, g]	-1
169 Mozambique	138	0.326	46.6	43.9	25.0	56.7	20	29	612[e]	872[e]	1
170 Burundi	140	0.317	43.8	41.0	36.1	53.8	20	25	527[e]	738[e]	0
171 Burkina Faso	141	0.291	45.2	43.6	11.2	30.4	15	24	807[e]	1,214[e]	0
172 Ethiopia	142	0.287	44.3	42.4	29.2	41.5	18	31	349[e]	670[e]	0
173 Niger	143	0.286	50.1	46.9	7.2	21.7	11	19	636[e]	1,069[e]	0
174 Sierra Leone	..	..	38.7	35.8	20.0	47.5	..	..	246[e]	581[e]	..
All developing countries	–	0.630	66.1	63.0	62.9	80.0	55	64	2,088	4,374	–
Least developed countries	–	0.415	52.6	50.8	38.1	58.8	32	43	731	1,258	–
Sub-Saharan Africa	–	0.454	50.3	47.5	49.6	65.9	39	49	1,063	2,004	–
Arab States	–	0.609	67.1	64.2	46.4	70.6	54	64	1,730	6,449	–
East Asia	–	0.709	72.2	68.0	75.4	91.2	67	72	2,757	4,398	–
East Asia (excluding China)	–	0.843	76.2	69.5	94.0	98.2	81	88	8,824	19,641	–
South-East Asia and the Pacific		0.692	67.0	63.9	84.4	92.2	63	66	2,605	4,794	–
South Asia	–	0.525	63.1	62.3	38.6	65.0	44	60	950	2,606	–
South Asia (excluding India)	–	0.524	63.7	62.3	36.2	60.0	39	55	1,073	3,171	–
Latin America and the Caribbean	–	0.749	73.0	66.5	86.2	88.3	71	73	3,837	9,951	–
Eastern Europe and the CIS	–	0.752	73.7	63.8	98.4	98.8	77	74	3,314	5,226	–
Industrialized countries	–	0.915	80.9	74.5	98.6	98.9	93	90	17,660	30,050	–
World	–	0.700	68.9	64.7	71.1	84.3	60	67	4,523	8,103	–

a. Data refer to the latest available year.

b. The HDI ranks used in this column are those recalculated for the universe of 143 countries. A positive figure indicates that the GDI rank is better than the HDI rank, a negative the opposite.

c. Human Development Report Office estimate.

d. Capped at 100%.

e. No wage data available. An estimate of 75%, the mean for all countries with wage data, was used for the ratio of the female non-agricultural wage to the male non-agricultural wage.

f. The manufacturing wage was used for the Czech Republic, Greece, Ireland and Norway.

g. Real GDP per capita (PPP$) data from Heston and Summers 1999.

h. Capped at 99.0%.

i. Wage data based on Psacharopoulos and Tzannatos 1992.

j. Real GDP per capita (PPP$) based on Human Development Report Office estimate.

Source: Columns 1 and 2: Human Development Report Office calculations; *columns 3 and 4:* calculated on the basis of data from UN 1998h; *columns 5 and 6:* unless otherwise noted, calculated on the basis of data from UNESCO 1999a; *columns 7 and 8:* UNESCO 1999b; *columns 9 and 10:* unless otherwise noted, calculated based on estimates from the following: for real GDP per capita (PPP$), World Bank 1999f; for share of economically active population and for female non-agricultural wages as a percentage of male non-agricultural wages, ILO, *Yearbook of Labour Statistics 1996* and *Yearbook of Labour Statistics 1998;* for female and male populations, UN 1998h; *column 11:* Human Development Report Office calculations.

HDI rank	Gender empowerment measure (GEM)		Seats in parliament held by women (as % of total) [a]	Female administrators and managers (as % of total) [b]	Female professional and technical workers (as % of total) [b]	Women's real GDP per capita (PPP$) [b]
	Rank	Value				
High human development	–	..	17.3	..	..	15,827
1 Canada	4	0.742	23.3	42.2	51.1	17,254 [c]
2 Norway	1	0.810	36.4	30.6	58.5	20,872 [d]
3 United States	8	0.708	12.5	44.3	53.1	23,540
4 Japan	38	0.494	8.9	9.3	44.1	14,625
5 Belgium	17	0.610	15.8	18.8	50.5	15,249
6 Sweden	2	0.777	42.7	27.9	63.7	17,829
7 Australia	9	0.707	25.9	43.3	25.5	16,526
8 Netherlands	10	0.702	31.6	16.8	44.8	14,483
9 Iceland	7	0.721	25.4	23.1	53.2	19,183 [e]
10 United Kingdom	16	0.614	12.3	33.0	43.7	15,736
11 France	36	0.499	9.1	9.4 [f]	41.4 [f]	17,176
12 Switzerland	14	0.655	20.3	29.1	23.0	16,802
13 Finland	6	0.737	33.5	26.6	62.5	15,045
14 Germany	5	0.740	29.8	26.6	49.0	16,780
15 Denmark	3	0.765	37.4	20.0	62.8	19,733
16 Austria	12	0.684	24.7	21.8	50.4	14,099
17 Luxembourg	15	0.624	20.0	8.6 [f]	37.7 [f]	17,326 [e]
18 New Zealand	11	0.700	29.2	24.2	49.6	13,757
19 Italy	26	0.523	10.0	53.8	17.8	12,634 [c]
20 Ireland	20	0.556	13.7	17.3	48.0	11,585 [d]
21 Spain	22	0.555	19.9	12.0	48.1	9,568 [c]
22 Singapore	32	0.512	4.8	34.3	16.1	18,947
23 Israel	37	0.496	7.5	19.2	53.8	12,387 [c]
24 Hong Kong, China (SAR)	..	..	..	..	..	15,180
25 Brunei Darussalam	..	..	..	..	..	17,637 [c, e]
26 Cyprus	68	0.385	5.4	10.2 [f]	40.8 [f]	8,095 [e]
27 Greece	66	0.404	6.3	12.1	44.2	8,248 [d, e]
28 Portugal	19	0.571	13.0	36.6	52.4	9,445
29 Barbados	..	..	..	..	..	9,252 [c, e]
30 Korea, Rep. of	78	0.336	3.7	4.2	45.0	8,388
31 Bahamas	13	0.658	19.6	34.8	51.4	13,296 [c, e]
32 Malta	..	..	9.2	..	..	5,733 [c]
33 Slovenia	42	0.486	7.8	28.3	53.1	9,137 [c]
34 Chile	54	0.449	9.0	18.5	51.6	5,853 [g]
35 Kuwait	72	0.355	0.0	5.2 [f]	36.8 [f]	13,481 [c, e]
36 Czech Republic	27	0.521	13.9	23.2	54.1	7,952 [d]
37 Bahrain	..	..	..	..	..	5,512 [c, e]
38 Antigua and Barbuda	..	..	11.1	..	..	..
39 Argentina	..	..	22.8	..	..	4,835 [g]
40 Uruguay	56	0.441	6.9	28.2	63.7	6,305 [g]
41 Qatar	..	..	..	..	..	5,193 [c, e]
42 Slovakia	34	0.509	12.7	30.7	59.7	6,366 [c]
43 United Arab Emirates	96	0.239	0.0	1.6 [f]	25.1 [f]	4,544 [c, e]
44 Poland	35	0.504	12.9	33.5	61.2	5,061 [c]
45 Costa Rica	23	0.550	19.3	26.6	47.8	3,643
Medium human development	–	..	10.0	..	..	2,220
46 Trinidad and Tobago	24	0.540	19.4	23.3	53.3	4,101 [c]
47 Hungary	48	0.458	8.3	32.8	60.9	5,372
48 Venezuela	43	0.484	12.2	22.9	57.1	5,006 [c]
49 Panama	47	0.467	9.7	27.6 [h]	49.2 [h]	4,140 [c, e]
50 Mexico	33	0.511	16.9	19.8	45.2	4,594

HDI rank	Gender empowerment measure (GEM)		Seats in parliament held by women (as % of total) [a]	Female administrators and managers (as % of total) [b]	Female professional and technical workers (as % of total) [b]	Women's real GDP per capita (PPP$) [b]
	Rank	Value				
51 Saint Kitts and Nevis	..	..	13.3	..	..	..
52 Grenada	..	..	..	..	..	..
53 Dominica	..	..	9.4	..	..	..
54 Estonia	46	0.468	10.9	36.5	66.8	4,236 [c]
55 Croatia	..	..	7.2	..	..	3,557 [c,e]
56 Malaysia	52	0.451	10.3	19.2	43.2	5,115 [c]
57 Colombia	31	0.515	12.2	38.8	45.6	4,725 [g]
58 Cuba	21	0.556	27.6	18.5 [f]	47.8 [f]	2,013 [c,i]
59 Mauritius	61	0.427	7.6	22.6	38.4	4,893 [c]
60 Belarus	..	..	..	..	..	3,909 [c]
61 Fiji	79	0.327	5.8	48.3	10.5	1,897 [c]
62 Lithuania	28	0.517	17.5	35.2	67.5	3,323
63 Bulgaria	49	0.457	10.8	28.9 [f]	57.0 [f]	3,256 [c]
64 Suriname	60	0.428	15.7	13.3	69.0	2,794 [c,e]
65 Libyan Arab Jamahiriya	..	..	..	..	..	2,373 [c,e]
66 Seychelles	..	..	23.5	..	..	..
67 Thailand	64	0.407	6.6	20.4	54.5	5,000
68 Romania	67	0.400	5.6	28.1	56.4	3,221 [c]
69 Lebanon	..	..	2.3	..	..	2,793 [c]
70 Samoa (Western)	..	..	4.1	..	..	1,560 [c]
71 Russian Federation	..	..	7.5	..	..	3,503 [c]
72 Ecuador	29	0.516	17.4	27.5	46.6	1,925 [g]
73 Macedonia, TFYR	..	..	7.5	..	..	2,257 [c]
74 Latvia	30	0.515	17.0	37.5	66.4	3,330
75 Saint Vincent and the Grenadines	..	..	4.8	..	..	..
76 Kazakhstan	..	..	11.4	..	..	2,804 [c]
77 Philippines	45	0.480	12.9	34.8	65.1	2,510
78 Saudi Arabia	..	..	..	..	..	2,284 [c]
79 Brazil	70	0.367	5.9	17.3 [f]	63.3	3,813
80 Peru	63	0.421	10.8	20.0	39.4	2,335 [c]
81 Saint Lucia	..	..	14.3	..	..	..
82 Jamaica	..	..	16.3	..	..	2,756 [c]
83 Belize	39	0.492	13.5	36.6	38.8	1,617 [c]
84 Paraguay	65	0.405	8.0	22.6	54.1	1,918
85 Georgia	73	0.355	6.9	18.3 [j]	41.8 [j]	1,521 [c]
86 Turkey	85	0.280	2.4	8.6	33.0	4,681
87 Armenia	..	..	6.3	..	..	1,928 [c]
88 Dominican Republic	25	0.528	14.5	44.8	49.9	2,374 [c]
89 Oman	..	..	..	..	..	2,339 [c,e]
90 Sri Lanka	80	0.321	5.3	17.6	30.7	1,452
91 Ukraine	..	..	7.9	..	..	1,691
92 Uzbekistan	..	..	6.0	..	..	2,019 [c,e]
93 Maldives	76	0.342	6.3	14.0 [f]	34.6 [f]	2,698 [c]
94 Jordan	98	0.220	2.5	4.6 [j]	28.7 [j]	1,429
95 Iran, Islamic Rep. of	88	0.264	4.9	3.5 [f]	32.6 [f]	2,453 [c,e]
96 Turkmenistan	..	..	18.0	..	..	1,642 [c,e]
97 Kyrgyzstan	..	..	4.8	..	..	1,798 [c]
98 China	40	0.491	21.8	11.6 [f]	45.1 [f]	2,485 [c]
99 Guyana	57	0.434	15.6	12.8 [f]	47.5 [f]	1,760 [c]
100 Albania	..	..	..	..	..	1,501 [c]

HDI rank	Gender empowerment measure (GEM)		Seats in parliament held by women (as % of total) [a]	Female administrators and managers (as % of total) [b]	Female professional and technical workers (as % of total) [b]	Women's real GDP per capita (PPP$) [b]
	Rank	Value				
101 South Africa	18	0.582	28.4	17.4 [h]	46.7 [h]	4,637 [c]
102 Tunisia	75	0.353	7.4	12.7 [j]	35.6 [j]	2,742 [c]
103 Azerbaijan	..	..	12.0	..	..	1,164 [c]
104 Moldova, Rep. of	..	..	8.9	..	..	1,221 [c]
105 Indonesia	71	0.362	11.4	6.6 [f]	40.8 [f]	2,359 [c]
106 Cape Verde	62	0.426	11.1	23.3 [f]	48.4 [f]	1,985 [c]
107 El Salvador	41	0.491	16.7	25.3	44.5	1,688 [c]
108 Tajikistan	..	..	2.8	..	..	850 [c, e]
109 Algeria	92	0.245	3.8	5.9 [f]	27.6 [f]	1,896 [c]
110 Viet Nam	..	..	26.2	..	..	1,385 [c]
111 Syrian Arab Republic	81	0.317	10.4	2.9	37.0	1,397 [c]
112 Bolivia	..	..	..	..	..	1,589 [g]
113 Swaziland	69	0.378	6.3	24.1	61.2	2,082 [c]
114 Honduras	53	0.450	9.4	39.2	56.3	1,130 [c]
115 Namibia	..	..	17.3	..	..	3,439 [c]
116 Vanuatu	..	..	0.0	..	..	..
117 Guatemala	44	0.482	12.5	32.4 [f]	45.2 [f]	1,861 [c]
118 Solomon Islands	..	..	2.0	..	..	1,886 [c]
119 Mongolia	..	..	7.9	..	..	1,057 [c]
120 Egypt	86	0.275	2.0	16.4	28.4	1,800
121 Nicaragua	..	..	10.8	..	..	1,169 [c, e]
122 Botswana	51	0.454	8.5	25.7	52.8	5,990 [c]
123 São Tomé and Principe	..	..	9.1	..	..	..
124 Gabon	..	..	9.6	..	..	5,678 [c]
125 Iraq	..	..	6.4	..	..	970 [c, e]
126 Morocco	84	0.301	0.7	25.6 [f]	31.3 [h]	1,909 [c]
127 Lesotho	55	0.449	10.6	33.4 [f]	56.6 [f]	1,145 [c]
128 Myanmar	..	..	..	..	..	882 [c, e]
129 Papua New Guinea	91	0.255	1.8	11.6 [f]	29.5 [f]	1,915 [c, e]
130 Zimbabwe	58	0.430	14.7	15.4 [f]	40.0 [f]	1,764 [c]
131 Equatorial Guinea	89	0.257	8.8	1.6 [f]	26.8 [f]	1,066 [c, e]
132 India	95	0.240	8.3	2.3 [f]	20.5 [f]	902 [c]
133 Ghana	..	..	9.0	..	..	1,428 [c]
134 Cameroon	87	0.265	5.6	10.1 [f]	24.4 [f]	1,191 [c]
135 Congo	..	..	12.0	..	..	1,179 [c]
136 Kenya	..	..	3.6	..	..	1,013
137 Cambodia	..	..	8.2	..	..	1,163 [c]
138 Pakistan	101	0.176	2.0	4.3	21.0	701 [c]
139 Comoros	..	..	0.0	..	..	1,124 [c]
Low human development	–	..	8.9	..	..	691
140 Lao People's Dem. Rep.	..	..	21.2	..	..	1,033 [c]
141 Congo, Dem. Rep. of the	..	..	..	..	..	648 [c]
142 Sudan	97	0.227	5.3	2.4 [f]	28.8 [f]	741 [c]
143 Togo	100	0.185	1.2	7.9 [f]	21.2 [f]	998 [c]
144 Nepal	..	..	4.5	..	..	763 [c]
145 Bhutan	..	..	2.0	..	..	985 [c, e]
146 Nigeria	..	..	..	..	..	553 [c]
147 Madagascar	..	..	8.0	..	..	712 [c]
148 Yemen	..	..	0.7	..	..	579 [c]
149 Mauritania	99	0.197	2.2	7.7 [f]	20.7 [f]	1,283 [c]
150 Bangladesh	83	0.304	9.1	4.9	34.7	767 [c]

HDI rank	Gender empowerment measure (GEM) Rank	Value	Seats in parliament held by women (as % of total) [a]	Female administrators and managers (as % of total) [b]	Female professional and technical workers (as % of total) [b]	Women's real GDP per capita (PPP$) [b]
151 Zambia	82	0.310	10.3	6.1 [f]	31.9 [f]	753
152 Haiti	..	..	..	..	..	928 [c]
153 Senegal	..	..	..	..	..	1,253 [c]
154 Côte d'Ivoire	..	..	8.0	..	..	991 [c]
155 Benin	..	..	7.2	..	..	1,048 [c]
156 Tanzania, U. Rep. of	..	..	17.5	..	..	549
157 Djibouti	..	..	0.0	..	..	..
158 Uganda	..	..	18.1	..	..	944 [c]
159 Malawi	90	0.256	5.7	4.8 [f]	34.7 [f]	600 [c]
160 Angola	..	..	15.5	..	..	1,127 [c]
161 Guinea	..	..	8.8	..	..	1,530 [c]
162 Chad	..	..	2.4	..	..	730 [c]
163 Gambia	93	0.243	2.0	15.5 [h]	23.7 [h]	1,115 [c]
164 Rwanda	..	..	17.1	..	..	..
165 Central African Republic	94	0.242	6.4	9.0 [f]	18.9 [f]	1,032
166 Mali	74	0.353	12.2	19.7 [f]	19.0 [f]	583 [c]
167 Eritrea	50	0.456	21.0	16.8	29.5	568
168 Guinea-Bissau	..	..	10.0	..	..	580 [c, e]
169 Mozambique	59	0.428	25.2	11.3 [f]	20.4 [f]	612 [c]
170 Burundi	..	..	6.0	..	..	527 [c]
171 Burkina Faso	77	0.337	10.5	13.5 [f]	25.8 [f]	807 [c]
172 Ethiopia	..	..	2.0	..	..	349 [c]
173 Niger	102	0.120	1.2	8.3	8.0	636 [c]
174 Sierra Leone	..	..	..	..	..	246 [c]
All developing countries	–	..	10.0	..	..	2,088
Least developed countries	–	..	8.7	..	..	731
Sub-Saharan Africa	–	..	11.2	..	..	1,063
Arab States	–	..	3.7	..	..	1,730
East Asia	–	..	4.6	..	..	2,757
East Asia (excluding China)	–	..	4.5	..	..	8,824
South-East Asia and the Pacific	–	..	12.3	..	..	2,605
South Asia	–	..	6.0	..	..	950
South Asia (excluding India)	–	..	5.2	..	..	1,073
Latin America and the Caribbean	–	..	15.3	..	..	3,837
Eastern Europe and the CIS	–	..	9.1	..	..	3,314
Industrialized countries	–	..	19.0	..	..	17,660
World	–	..	12.0	..	..	4,523

a. Data are as of 5 February 1999.

b. Data refer to latest available year.

c. No wage data available. An estimate of 75%, the mean for all countries with wage data available, was used for the ratio of the female non-agricultural wage to the male non-agricultural wage.

d. The manufacturing wage was used for the Czech Republic, Greece, Ireland and Norway.

e. Real GDP per capita (PPP$) from Heston and Summers 1999.

f. Calculated on the basis of data from UN 1994 and ILO, *Yearbook of Labour Statistics 1993* and *Yearbook of Labour Statistics 1994*.

g. Wage data based on Psacharopoulos and Tzannatos 1992.

h. Calculated on the basis of data from UN 1994 and ILO, *Yearbook of Labour Statistics 1994* and *Yearbook of Labour Statistics 1995*.

i. Real GDP per capita (PPP$) based on Human Development Report Office estimate.

j. Calculated on the basis of data from UN 1995 and ILO, *Yearbook of Labour Statistics 1997*.

Source: Columns 1 and 2: Human Development Report Office calculations; *column 3:* IPU 1999a; *columns 4 and 5:* unless otherwise noted, ILO, *Yearbook of Labour Statistics 1998;* column 6: unless otherwise noted, calculated based on estimates from the following: for real GDP per capita (PPP$), World Bank 1999f; for share of economically active population, ILO, *Yearbook of Labour Statistics 1998;* for female non-agricultural wages as a percentage of male non-agricultural wages, ILO, *Yearbook of Labour Statistics 1998;* for female and male populations, UN 1998h.

HDI rank	Human poverty index (HPI-1) 1997 Rank	Value (%)	People not expected to survive to age 40 (as % of total population) 1997	Adult illiteracy rate (%) 1997	Population without access — To safe water (%) 1990-1997[a]	To health services (%) 1981-1992[a]	To sanitation (%) 1990-1997[a]	Under-weight children under age five (%) 1990-1997[a]	Real GDP per capita (PPP$) Poorest 20% 1980-1994[a]	Richest 20% 1980-1994[a]	Richest 20% to poorest 20% 1980-1994[a]	Population below income poverty line (%) $1 a day (1985 PPP$) 1989-1994[a]	National poverty line 1989-1994[a]
High human development	–	..	4.7	4.7	14	..	14	3	..	..	..	..	..
22 Singapore	..	..	2.3	8.6	0 [b]	0	..	..	4,934	47,311	9.6	..	..
24 Hong Kong, China (SAR)	..	..	2.2	7.6	..	..	..	..	5,821	50,666	8.7	..	..
25 Brunei Darussalam	..	..	3.2	9.9	..	4	..	..	..	..	..	..	..
26 Cyprus	..	..	3.2	4.1	0	0	3	..	..	..	..	..	..
29 Barbados	1	2.6	3.2	2.4	0	0	0	5 [b]	..	..	..	..	..
30 Korea, Rep. of	..	..	4.7	2.8	7	0	0	..	..	..	..	..	..
31 Bahamas	..	..	5.8	4.2	6	0	18	..	..	..	..	..	..
34 Chile	6	4.8	4.5	4.8	9	5	..	1	1,558	27,145	17.4	15.0	..
35 Kuwait	..	..	2.9	19.6	..	0	..	6 [b]	..	..	..	..	..
37 Bahrain	10	9.8	4.7	13.8	6	0	3	9	..	..	..	..	..
38 Antigua and Barbuda	..	..	..	..	..	0	4	10 [b]	..	..	..	..	12.0
39 Argentina	..	..	5.6	3.5	29	..	32	..	..	..	..	..	26.0
40 Uruguay	3	4.0	5.1	2.5	5 [b]	0 [b,c]	..	5	..	..	..	..	..
41 Qatar	..	..	4.9	20.0	..	0	3	6	..	..	..	..	..
43 United Arab Emirates	27	17.7	3.1	25.2	3	10	8	14	..	..	..	..	..
45 Costa Rica	4	4.1	4.0	4.9	4	3	16	2	1,136	14,399	12.7	18.9	11.0
Medium human development	–	25.3	11.9	26.2	26	..	57	30	..	..	..	..	..
46 Trinidad and Tobago	2	3.5	4.1	2.2	3	1	21	7 [b]	..	..	..	..	21.0
48 Venezuela	16	12.4	6.5	8.0	21	_ [d]	42	5	1,505	24,411	16.2	11.8	31.0
49 Panama	8	9.0	6.4	8.9	7	18	17	7	589	17,611	29.9	25.6	..
50 Mexico	13	10.6	8.3	9.9	15	9	28	14 [b]	1,437	19,383	13.5	14.9	34.0
51 Saint Kitts and Nevis	..	..	..	..	0	0	0	..	..	..	..	..	15.0
52 Grenada	..	..	..	..	..	..	..	..	..	..	..	..	20.0
53 Dominica	..	..	..	..	4	0	20	5 [b]	..	..	..	..	33.0
56 Malaysia	18	14.2	4.9	14.3	22	12	6	19	1,923	22,447	11.7	5.6	16.0
57 Colombia	12	10.5	10.1	9.1	15	13	15	8	1,042	16,154	15.5	7.4	19.0
58 Cuba	5	4.7	4.5	4.1	7	0	34	9	..	..	..	..	..
59 Mauritius	15	12.1	4.9	17.0	2	1	0	16	..	..	..	..	11.0
61 Fiji	7	8.6	5.0	8.2	23	1	8	8	..	..	..	..	..
64 Suriname	..	..	7.4	6.5	..	9	..	..	..	..	..	..	..
65 Libyan Arab Jamahiriya	22	16.4	6.4	23.5	3	0	2	5	..	..	..	..	..
66 Seychelles	..	..	..	..	..	1	..	6 [b]	..	..	..	..	..
67 Thailand	29	18.7	10.5	5.3	19	41	4	19	1,778	16,732	9.4	0.1	13.0
69 Lebanon	14	11.3	7.5	15.6	6	5	37	3	..	..	..	..	..
70 Samoa (Western)	..	..	5.5	..	32	0	..	..	..	..	..	..	..
72 Ecuador	25	16.8	11.1	9.3	32	20	24	17 [b]	1,188	11,572	9.7	30.4	35.0
75 Saint Vincent and the Grenadines	..	..	..	..	11	20	2	..	..	..	..	..	17.0
77 Philippines	20	16.3	9.2	5.4	16	_ [d]	25	28	842	6,190	7.4	27.5 [b]	41.0
78 Saudi Arabia	..	..	5.9	26.6	5 [b]	2	14	..	..	..	..	..	..
79 Brazil	19	15.8	11.5	16.0	24	_ [d]	30	6	578	18,563	32.1	28.7	17.0
80 Peru	23	16.6	11.6	11.3	33	_ [d]	28	8	813	8,366	10.3	49.4	32.0
81 Saint Lucia	..	..	..	..	15	0	..	..	..	..	..	..	25.0
82 Jamaica	17	13.6	5.1	14.5	14	_ [d]	11	10	922	7,553	8.2	4.7	32.0
83 Belize	..	..	6.1	..	17	5	43	6	..	..	..	..	35.0
84 Paraguay	21	16.4	8.7	7.6	40	_ [d]	59	4	..	..	..	..	22.0
86 Turkey	24	16.7	9.6	16.8	51	0	20	10	..	..	..	..	..
88 Dominican Republic	26	17.7	9.0	17.4	35	_ [d]	22	6	775	10,277	13.3	19.9	21.0
89 Oman	39	23.7	6.4	32.9	15	11	22	23	..	..	..	..	..
90 Sri Lanka	33	20.4	5.3	9.3	43	10	37	34	1,348	5,954	4.4	4.0	22.0
93 Maldives	43	25.4	13.5	4.3	40	25	56	43	..	..	..	..	..
94 Jordan	9	9.8	7.1	12.8	2	10	23	9	1,292	10,972	8.5	2.5	15.0
95 Iran, Islamic Rep. of	34	20.4	9.7	26.7	10	27	19	16	..	..	..	..	..

HDI rank	Human poverty index (HPI-1) 1997 Rank	Value (%)	People not expected to survive to age 40 (as % of total population) 1997	Adult illiteracy rate (%) 1997	Population without access — To safe water (%) 1990-1997[a]	To health services (%) 1981-1992[a]	To sani-tation (%) 1990-1997[a]	Under-weight children under age five (%) 1990-1997[a]	Real GDP per capita (PPP$) — Poorest 20% 1980-1994[a]	Richest 20% 1980-1994[a]	Richest 20% to poorest 20% 1980-1994[a]	Population below income poverty line (%) — $1 a day (1985 PPP$) 1989-1994[a]	National poverty line 1989-1994[a]
98 China	30	19.0	7.9	17.1	33	_ [d]	76	16	722	5,114	7.1	29.4	11.0
99 Guyana	11	10.2	13.8	1.9	9	4	12	12	..	..	..	..	43.0
101 South Africa	31	19.1	23.4	16.0	13	_ [d]	13	9	516	9,897	19.2	23.7	..
102 Tunisia	38	23.1	7.8	33.0	2	10	20	9	1,460	11,459	7.8	3.9	14.0
105 Indonesia	46	27.7	12.8	15.0	25	57	41	34	1,422	6,654	4.7	14.5	8.0
106 Cape Verde	40	24.7	10.4	29.0	49	18	76	14	..	..	..	..	44.0
107 El Salvador	35	20.6	10.9	23.0	34	_ [d]	10	11	..	..	..	..	38.0
109 Algeria	52	28.8	9.1	39.7	22	_ [d]	9	13	1,922	12,839	6.7	1.6 [b]	..
110 Viet Nam	51	28.7	11.6	8.1	57	_ [d]	79	41	406	2,288	5.6	..	51.0
111 Syrian Arab Republic	32	20.1	8.5	28.4	14	1	33	13	..	..	..	..	..
112 Bolivia	36	21.1	18.4	16.4	37	_ [d]	42	16	703	6,049	8.6	7.1	..
113 Swaziland	45	27.6	20.8	22.5	50	45	41	10 [b]	..	..	..	..	..
114 Honduras	41	24.8	11.5	29.3	24	38	26	18	399	6,027	15.1	46.5	53.0
115 Namibia	42	25.0	30.0	20.2	17	_ [d]	38	26	..	..	..	..	..
116 Vanuatu	..	..	10.0	..	23	20	72	20 [b]	..	..	..	..	..
117 Guatemala	50	28.3	15.6	33.4	23	40	17	27	357	10,710	30.0	53.3	58.0
118 Solomon Islands	..	..	5.8	..	39 [b]	20	..	21 [b]	..	..	..	..	..
119 Mongolia	28	18.2	11.2	16.0	60	0	14	10	..	..	..	..	36.0
120 Egypt	57	33.0	10.3	47.3	13	1	12	15	1,653	7,809	4.7	7.6	..
121 Nicaragua	48	28.1	12.4	36.6	38	_ [d]	65	12	479	6,293	13.1	43.8	50.0
122 Botswana	44	27.5	35.0	25.6	10	14	45	17	..	..	..	34.7 [b]	..
123 São Tomé and Principe	..	..	..	..	18	12	65	16	..	..	..	..	46.0
124 Gabon	..	..	30.6	33.8	33	13	..	..	..	..	..	..	..
125 Iraq	..	..	17.4	..	19	2	25	23	..	..	..	..	..
126 Morocco	67	39.2	11.8	54.1	35	38	42	9	1,079	7,570	7.0	1.1	13.0
127 Lesotho	37	23.0	25.1	17.7	38	20	62	16	137	2,945	21.5	50.4 [b]	26.0
128 Myanmar	55	32.3	18.1	16.4	40	52	57	43	..	..	..	..	..
129 Papua New Guinea	47	27.8	18.8	26.3	68	4	17	30 [b]	..	..	..	..	..
130 Zimbabwe	53	29.2	39.8	9.1	21	29	48	16	420	6,542	15.6	41.0	26.0
131 Equatorial Guinea	..	..	33.7	20.1	5	..	46	..	..	..	..	..	..
132 India	59	35.9	16.1	46.5	19	25	71	53	527	2,641	5.0	52.5	..
133 Ghana	60	36.2	21.1	33.6	35	75	45	27	790	4,220	5.3	..	31.0
134 Cameroon	62	38.1	27.2	28.3	50	85	50	14	..	..	..	..	..
135 Congo	56	32.3	34.9	23.1	66	_ [d]	31	17 [b]	..	..	..	..	..
136 Kenya	49	28.2	29.8	20.7	47	_ [d]	23	23	238	4,347	18.3	50.2	37.0
137 Cambodia	..	..	28.0	..	70	_ [d]	81	52	..	..	..	..	..
138 Pakistan	71	42.1	14.7	59.1	21	15	44	38	907	4,288	4.7	11.6	34.0
139 Comoros	58	34.6	20.6	44.6	47	18	77	26	..	..	..	..	..
Low human development	–	44.9	32.3	53.5	43	..	63	38	..	..	..	..	..
140 Lao People's Dem. Rep.	66	38.9	29.5	41.4	56	33	82	40	700	2,931	4.2	..	46.0
141 Congo, Dem. Rep. of the	..	..	32.2	..	58	41	82	34	..	..	..	..	..
142 Sudan	61	36.8	27.1	46.7	27	30	49	34	..	..	..	..	..
143 Togo	65	38.4	34.5	46.8	45	_ [d]	59	19	..	..	..	..	17.3
144 Nepal	85	51.9	22.5	61.9	29	90	84	47	455	1,975	4.3	53.1 [b]	..
145 Bhutan	70	41.8	20.2	55.8	42	20	30	38 [b]	..	..	..	..	..
146 Nigeria	63	38.2	33.4	40.5	51	33	59	36	308	3,796	12.3	28.9	21.0
147 Madagascar	..	..	22.3	..	74	35	60	40	203	1,750	8.6	72.3	59.0
148 Yemen	78	49.2	21.8	57.5	39	84	76	39	..	..	..	..	..
149 Mauritania	77	47.5	29.2	61.6	26	70	68	23	290	3,743	12.9	31.4 [b]	57.0

HDI rank	Human poverty index (HPI-1) 1997 Rank	Human poverty index (HPI-1) 1997 Value (%)	People not expected to survive to age 40 (as % of total population) 1997	Adult illiteracy rate (%) 1997	Population without access To safe water (%) 1990-1997[a]	Population without access To health services (%) 1981-1992[a]	Population without access To sani-tation (%) 1990-1997[a]	Under-weight children under age five (%) 1990-1997[a]	Real GDP per capita (PPP$) Poorest 20% 1980-1994[a]	Real GDP per capita (PPP$) Richest 20% 1980-1994[a]	Real GDP per capita (PPP$) Richest 20% to poorest 20% 1980-1994[a]	Population below income poverty line (%) $1 a day (1985 PPP$) 1989-1994[a]	Population below income poverty line (%) National poverty line 1989-1994[a]
150 Bangladesh	73	44.4	21.5	61.1	5	26	57	56	606	2,445	4.0	28.5	48.0
151 Zambia	64	38.4	46.9	24.9	62	25	29	24	216	2,797	12.9	84.6	86.0
152 Haiti	74	46.1	26.7	54.2	63	55	75	28	..	..	..	54.0	..
153 Senegal	80	49.6	28.5	65.4	37	60	61	22	299	5,010	16.8	54.0	..
154 Côte d'Ivoire	76	46.8	37.3	57.4	58	40	61	24	551	3,572	6.5	17.7[b]	..
155 Benin	83	50.9	29.0	66.1	44	58	73	29	..	..	..	..	33.0
156 Tanzania, U. Rep. of	54	29.8	35.5	28.4	34	7	14	27	217	1,430	6.6	16.4	50.0
157 Djibouti	69	40.8	33.3	51.7	10	63	45	18	..	..	..	..	..
158 Uganda	68	40.6	47.4	36.0	54	29	43	26	309	2,189	7.1	50.0	55.0
159 Malawi	72	42.2	47.8	42.3	53	20	97	30	..	..	..	42.1	..
160 Angola	..	..	38.4	..	69	76	60	42	..	..	..	..	..
161 Guinea	82	50.5	38.3	62.1	54	55	69	26 [b, e]	270	4,518	16.7	26.3	..
162 Chad	86	52.1	37.4	49.7	76	74	79	39	..	..	..	..	..
163 Gambia	81	49.9	37.7	66.9	31	_ [d]	63	26	..	..	..	..	64.0
164 Rwanda	..	..	46.1	37.0	..	..	..	27	359	1,447	4.0	45.7[b]	53.0
165 Central African Republic	88	53.6	40.4	57.6	62	88	73	27	..	..	..	..	..
166 Mali	87	52.8	33.6	64.5	34	80	94	40	..	..	..	..	..
167 Eritrea	..	..	31.8	..	78	_ [d]	87	44	..	..	..	..	..
168 Guinea-Bissau	84	51.8	40.6	66.4	57	36	54	23 [b]	90	2,533	28.1	87.0	49.0
169 Mozambique	79	49.5	39.8	59.5	37	70	46	27	..	..	..	..	..
170 Burundi	75	46.1	43.2	55.4	48	20	49	37	..	..	..	..	..
171 Burkina Faso	91	59.3	40.5	79.3	58	30	63	30	..	..	..	..	..
172 Ethiopia	89	55.8	42.3	64.6	75	45	81	48	..	..	..	33.8[b]	..
173 Niger	92	65.5	35.7	85.7	52	70	83	43	296	1,742	5.9	61.5	..
174 Sierra Leone	90	57.7	51.0	66.7	66	64	89	29	..	..	..	..	75.0
All developing countries	–	27.7	14.6	28.4	28	..	57	31	..	..	..	..	..
Least developed countries		44.9	30.8	51.6	41	..	63	40	..	..	..	..	..
Sub-Saharan Africa		40.6	34.6	42.4	50	..	56	32	..	..	..	..	..
Arab States		32.4	13.1	41.3	18	..	29	19	..	..	..	..	..
East Asia		19.0	7.8	16.6	32	..	73	16	..	..	..	..	..
East Asia (excluding China)		..	4.7	3.9	10	..	1	..	..	..	..	..	..
South-East Asia and the Pacific		25.0	12.4	11.8	31	..	41	34	..	..	..	..	..
South Asia		36.6	16.1	47.8	18	..	64	48	..	..	..	..	..
South Asia (excluding India)		38.6	16.1	51.6	15	..	46	39	..	..	..	..	..
Latin America and the Caribbean		14.5	9.9	12.8	22	..	29	10	..	..	..	..	..
Eastern Europe and the CIS	–	..	8.3	..	..	..	..	..	..	..	..	..	..
Industrialized countries	–	..	3.1	..	..	..	..	..	..	..	..	..	..
World	–	..	12.5	..	..	..	..	29 [f]	..	..	..	..	..

a. Data refer to the most recent year available during the period specified in the column heading.

b. Data refer to a year or period other than that specified in the column heading, differ from the standard definition or refer to only part of the country.

c. Human Development Report Office estimate based on national sources.

d. For the purpose of calculating the HPI-1, an estimate of 25%, the unweighted average for the 97 countries with data, was applied.

e. UNICEF 1998b.

f. UNICEF 1999a.

Source: Columns 1 and 2: Human Development Report Office calculations; column 3: UN 1998h; column 4: calculated on the basis of data from UNESCO 1999a; columns 5 and 7: calculated on the basis of data from UNICEF 1999a; column 6: unless otherwise noted, calculated on the basis of data from World Bank 1999e; column 8: UNICEF 1999a; columns 9 -11: calculated on the basis of data from World Bank 1995; column 12: World Bank 1997a; column 13: World Bank 1997a and Lipton 1996.

HDI rank	Human poverty index (HPI-2) 1997		People not expected to survive to age 60 (as % of total population) 1997	People who are functionally illiterate (% age 16-65) 1995 [a]	Long-term unemploy-ment (as % of labour force) 1997 [b]	Real GDP per capita (PPP$)			Population below income poverty line (%)	
	Rank	Value (%)				Poorest 20% 1980-94 [c]	Richest 20% 1980-94 [c]	Richest 20% to poorest 20% 1980-94 [c]	50% of median income 1989-94 [c, d]	$14.40 a day (1985 PPP$) 1989-95 [c, e]
High human development	–	13.5	11.0	19.2	4.2	..	..	..	..	..
1 Canada	9	12.0	9.3	16.6	1.3	5,971	42,110	7.1	11.7	5.9
2 Norway	4	11.3	9.1	16.8 [f]	0.8	6,315	37,379	5.9	6.6	2.6
3 United States	17	16.5	12.6	20.7	0.5	5,800	51,705	8.9	19.1	14.1
4 Japan	8	12.0	8.2	16.8 [f]	0.7	8,987	38,738	4.3	11.8	3.7
5 Belgium	11	12.4	10.1	18.4 [g]	5.8	7,718	35,172	4.6	5.5	12.0
6 Sweden	1	7.0	8.7	7.5	1.4	7,160	33,026	4.6	6.7	4.6
7 Australia	12	12.5	8.9	17.0	2.4	4,077	39,098	9.6	12.9	7.8
8 Netherlands	2	8.3	9.3	10.5	3.3	7,109	31,992	4.5	6.7	14.4
9 Iceland	..	..	8.4	..	0.7	..	..	..	..	..
10 United Kingdom	15	15.1	9.8	21.8	3.3	3,963	38,164	9.6	13.5	13.1
11 France	7	11.9	11.3	16.8 [f]	4.8	5,359	40,098	7.5	7.5	12.0 [h]
12 Switzerland	..	..	9.8	18.9	1.0	5,907	50,666	8.6	..	..
13 Finland	6	11.9	11.3	16.8 [f]	6.4	5,141	30,682	6.0	6.2	3.8
14 Germany	3	10.4	10.7	14.4	4.3	6,594	37,963	5.8	5.9	11.5
15 Denmark	10	12.2	12.8	16.8 [f]	1.8	5,454	38,986	7.1	7.5 [h]	7.6
16 Austria	..	..	10.9	..	1.4	..	..	..	..	8.0
17 Luxembourg	..	..	10.6	..	0.9	..	..	..	5.4 [h]	4.3 [h]
18 New Zealand	13	12.8	11.1	18.4	1.3	4,264	37,369	8.8	9.2	..
19 Italy	5	11.6	9.0	16.8 [f]	8.1	6,174	37,228	6.0	6.5	2.0
20 Ireland	16	15.3	10.0	22.6	7.1	..	..	..	11.1 [h]	36.5 [h]
21 Spain	14	13.0	10.1	16.8 [f]	12.5	5,669	24,998	4.4	10.4	21.1
23 Israel	..	..	9.3	..	..	4,539	29,957	6.6	..	..
27 Greece	..	..	8.9	..	5.6	..	..	..	..	..
28 Portugal	..	..	12.6	..	4.1	..	..	..	..	..
32 Malta	..	..	8.4	..	..	..	..	..	..	..
33 Slovenia	..	..	14.6	..	..	..	..	..	..	<1.0 [i]
36 Czech Republic	..	..	14.2	..	1.2	4,426	15,764	3.6	..	<1.0 [i]
42 Slovakia	..	..	16.4	..	..	3,344	8,823	2.6	..	<1.0 [i]
44 Poland	..	..	17.3	42.6	5.0	2,186	8,605	3.9	11.6	20.0 [i]
Medium human development	–	..	26.1	..	..	..	..	..	..	..
47 Hungary	..	..	21.6	..	5.3	2,878	11,088	3.9	10.0	4.0 [i]
54 Estonia	..	..	23.8	..	..	1,191	8,357	7.0	..	37.0 [i]
55 Croatia	..	..	16.4	..	..	..	..	..	.. ..	
60 Belarus	..	..	26.1	..	..	2,355	6,981	3.0	..	22.0 [i]
62 Lithuania	..	..	23.3	..	..	1,260	6,547	5.2	..	30.0 [i]
63 Bulgaria	..	..	18.3	..	..	1,793	8,489	4.7	..	15.0 [i]
68 Romania	..	..	20.7	..	..	1,714	6,485	3.8	..	59.0 [i]
71 Russian Federation	..	..	29.7	..	..	881	12,804	14.5	22.1	50.0 [i]
73 Macedonia, TFYR	..	..	14.0	..	..	..	..	..	..	..
74 Latvia	..	..	25.0	..	..	2,405	9,193	3.8	..	22.0 [i]
76 Kazakhstan	..	..	25.8	..	..	1,391	7,494	5.4	..	65.0 [i]
85 Georgia	..	..	17.5	..	..	..	..	..	..	..
87 Armenia	..	..	19.8	..	..	..	..	..	..	..
91 Ukraine	..	..	24.1	..	..	1,544	5,753	3.7	..	63.0 [i]
92 Uzbekistan	..	..	25.1	..	..	..	..	..	..	63.0 [i]
96 Turkmenistan	..	..	27.6	..	..	1,048	6,694	6.4	..	61.0 [i]
97 Kyrgyzstan	..	..	25.4	..	..	..	..	..	..	88.0 [i]
100 Albania	..	..	13.9	..	..	..	..	..	..	..
103 Azerbaijan	..	..	22.1	..	..	..	..	..	..	..
104 Moldova, Rep. of	..	..	25.7	..	..	818	4,918	6.0	..	66.0 [i]
108 Tajikistan	..	..	25.3	..	..	..	..	..	..	..

HDI rank	Human poverty index (HPI-2) 1997		People not expected to survive to age 60 (as % of total population) 1997	People who are functionally illiterate (% age 16-65) 1995 [a]	Long-term unemploy-ment (as % of labour force) 1997 [b]	Real GDP per capita (PPP$)			Population below income poverty line (%)	
	Rank	Value (%)				Poorest 20% 1980-94 [c]	Richest 20% 1980-94 [c]	Richest 20% to poorest 20% 1980-94 [c]	50% of median income 1989-94 [c, d]	$14.40 a day (1985 PPP$) 1989-95 [c, e]
All developing countries	–	..	28.1	..	..	..	..	..	..	..
Eastern Europe and the CIS	–	..	24.7	..	..	..	..	..	..	..
Industrialized countries	–	13.5	10.6	18.0	4.2	..	..	..	..	..
World	–	..	25.3	..	..	..	..	..	..	..

a. Based on level 1 prose. Data refer to 1995 or a year around 1995.

b. Data refer to unemployment lasting at least 12 months or more.

c. Data refer to the most recent year available during the period specified in the column heading.

d. Poverty is measured at 50% of the median adjusted disposable personal income.

e. Based on US poverty line.

f. For the purpose of calculating the HPI-2, an estimate of 16.8%, the unweighted average for level 1 prose (excluding Poland) was applied.

g. Data refer to Flanders.

h. Data refer to a year or period other than that specified in the column heading.

i. Income poverty line is $4 (1990 PPP$) a day per person.

Source: Columns 1 and 2: Human Development Report Office calculations; *column 3:* UN 1998h; *column 4:* OECD 1997a; *column 5:* OECD 1998b; *columns 6-8:* calculated on the basis of data from World Bank 1995; *columns 9 and 10:* Smeeding 1997 and Milanovic 1998.

MONITORING HUMAN DEVELOPMENT: ENLARGING PEOPLE'S CHOICES . . .

HDI rank	Human development index (HDI) value					GDP per capita (1987 US$)				
	1975	1980	1985	1990	1997	1975	1980	1985	1990	1997
High human development	..	..	..	..	0.904	11,459	12,409	13,220	15,052	16,576
1 Canada	0.862	0.879	0.901	0.924	0.932	11,832	13,509	14,783	15,895	16,525
2 Norway	0.850	0.869	0.000	0.091	0.927	14,517	17,991	20,634	21,975	27,620
3 United States	0.865	0.885	p0.897	0.911	0.927	15,264	16,756	18,000	19,652	21,541
4 Japan	0.851	0.875	0.890	0.906	0.924	13,825	16,384	18,691	22,928	25,084
5 Belgium	..	..	..	..	0.923	11,527	13,354	13,760	15,897	16,809 [a]
6 Sweden	0.859	0.869	0.880	0.888	0.923	16,049	16,903	18,346	20,018	20,309
7 Australia	0.838	0.855	0.867	0.880	0.922	10,439	11,388	12,328	13,070	15,186
8 Netherlands	0.856	0.868	0.883	0.896	0.921	12,599	13,855	14,406	16,283	18,369
9 Iceland	0.853	0.874	0.884	0.902	0.919	13,903	18,002	19,441	21,474	23,112
10 United Kingdom	0.840	0.848	0.856	0.876	0.918	9,310	10,161	11,121	12,899	14,096
11 France	0.848	0.864	0.875	0.896	0.918	12,763	14,564	15,342	17,485	18,554
12 Switzerland	..	..	..	..	0.914	22,043	24,291	25,417	28,114	26,441 [a]
13 Finland	0.834	0.855	0.871	0.893	0.913	13,374	15,140	16,888	19,576	19,816
14 Germany	..	..	..	..	0.906	..	..	..	..	..
15 Denmark	0.861	0.869	0.878	0.885	0.905	15,080	16,858	19,190	20,511	23,303
16 Austria	0.836	0.849	0.863	0.886	0.904	11,901	14,006	15,028	17,201	18,594
17 Luxembourg	..	..	..	..	0.902	13,782	15,231	17,133	22,501	28,010 [a]
18 New Zealand	0.843	0.852	0.862	0.872	0.901	9,801	9,824	10,820	10,782	11,565
19 Italy	0.824	0.842	0.852	0.875	0.900	9,629	11,763	12,637	14,595	15,548
20 Ireland	0.811	0.824	0.839	0.863	0.900	6,675	7,791	8,489	10,804	15,779
21 Spain	0.814	0.834	0.851	0.871	0.894	6,415	6,657	6,992	8,618	9,591
22 Singapore	0.737	0.767	0.796	0.834	0.888	4,557	6,016	7,451	10,200	15,467
23 Israel	..	..	..	..	0.883	7,121	7,653	8,109	9,097	..
24 Hong Kong, China (SAR)	0.757	0.796	0.823	0.859	0.880	3,895	5,939	7,201	9,897	12,439
25 Brunei Darussalam	..	..	..	..	0.878	12,842	17,052	12,255	11,193	..
26 Cyprus	..	..	..	..	0.870	2,390	4,165	5,146	6,828	..
27 Greece	0.792	0.814	0.835	0.846	0.867	4,552	5,338	5,557	6,044	6,583
28 Portugal	0.735	0.758	0.786	0.815	0.858	3,117	3,721	3,794	4,897	5,564
29 Barbados	..	..	..	..	0.857	4,427	5,456	5,139	6,008	..
30 Korea, Rep. of	0.680	0.716	0.761	0.804	0.852	1,461	1,929	2,677	4,132	6,251
31 Bahamas	..	..	..	..	0.851	6,477	10,265	11,159	11,227	..
32 Malta	..	..	..	..	0.850	2,391	3,718	4,279	5,601	..
33 Slovenia	..	..	..	..	0.845	..	..	..	..	..
34 Chile	..	..	..	..	0.844	1,199	1,579	1,526	1,923	2,677 [a]
35 Kuwait	..	..	..	..	0.833	24,353	18,431	11,440	..	..
36 Czech Republic	..	..	..	..	0.833	..	..	3,411	3,680	3,329 [a]
37 Bahrain	..	..	..	..	0.832	..	10,037	7,344	7,240	7,997 [a]
38 Antigua and Barbuda	..	..	..	..	0.828	..	2,982	3,797	5,250	..
39 Argentina	0.776	0.790	0.798	0.803	0.827	3,779	3,999	3,333	3,150	4,021
40 Uruguay	0.759	0.779	0.783	0.803	0.826	2,144	2,590	2,079	2,407	2,992
41 Qatar	..	..	..	..	0.814	..	..	..	..	..
42 Slovakia	..	..	0.798	0.803	0.813	..	..	3,436	3,622	3,432
43 United Arab Emirates	0.735	0.767	0.780	0.803	0.812	29,249	29,887	19,971	16,858	15,300
44 Poland	..	0.774	0.778	0.780	0.802	..	1,687	1,622	1,559	1,926
45 Costa Rica	0.741	0.766	0.767	0.783	0.801	1,589	1,766	1,552	1,684	1,865
Medium human development	..	..	..	..	0.662	651	779	790	902	935
46 Trinidad and Tobago	0.746	0.776	0.784	0.787	0.797	3,794	5,218	4,414	3,759	3,990
47 Hungary	..	..	..	..	0.795	1,756	2,059	2,312	2,456	2,372 [a]
48 Venezuela	0.740	0.753	0.761	0.780	0.792	3,175	3,022	2,540	2,537	2,685
49 Panama	..	..	..	..	0.791	2,277	2,399	2,558	2,235	2,688 [a]
50 Mexico	..	..	..	..	0.786	1,591	1,923	1,893	1,873	1,910 [a]

HDI rank	Human development index (HDI) value					GDP per capita (1987 US$)				
	1975	1980	1985	1990	1997	1975	1980	1985	1990	1997
51 Saint Kitts and Nevis	..	..	..	..	0.781	..	1,767	2,156	3,083	..
52 Grenada	..	..	..	..	0.777	..	1,223	1,498	1,884	..
53 Dominica	..	..	..	..	0.776	1,087	1,140	1,492	1,989	2,196 [a]
54 Estonia	..	0.788	0.798	0.790	0.773	..	3,354	3,712	3,683	2,984
55 Croatia	..	..	..	..	0.773	..	..	..	..	..
56 Malaysia	0.614	0.654	0.691	0.718	0.768	1,253	1,688	1,902	2,262	3,387
57 Colombia	..	..	..	..	0.768	880	1,020	1,027	1,163	1,321 [a]
58 Cuba	..	..	..	..	0.765	..	..	..	..	..
59 Mauritius	0.635	0.661	0.692	0.728	0.764	1,098	1,297	1,550	2,129	2,752
60 Belarus	..	..	..	0.793	0.763	..	..	..	2,738	2,013
61 Fiji	0.674	0.696	0.708	0.735	0.763	1,641	1,817	1,688	1,880	1,986
62 Lithuania	..	..	..	0.780	0.761	..	..	..	2,684	2,013
63 Bulgaria	..	0.752	0.776	0.777	0.758	..	2,344	2,870	3,176	2,332
64 Suriname	..	..	..	..	0.757	1,159	1,214	1,539	1,953	..
65 Libyan Arab Jamahiriya	..	..	..	..	0.756	10,459	13,219	6,926	..	..
66 Seychelles	..	..	..	..	0.755	2,551	3,459	3,513	4,400	4,632
67 Thailand	0.604	0.647	0.678	0.717	0.753	557	718	854	1,291	1,870
68 Romania	0.722	0.756	0.762	0.745	0.752	1,105	1,511	1,722	1,452	1,457
69 Lebanon	..	..	..	..	0.749	..	..	..	..	..
70 Samoa (Western)	..	..	..	..	0.747	..	655	615	626	633 [a]
71 Russian Federation	..	0.753	0.769	0.786	0.747	2,250	3,219	3,050	4,507	2,742
72 Ecuador	0.645	0.693	0.715	0.726	0.747	1,027	1,226	1,199	1,170	1,257
73 Macedonia, TFYR	..	..	..	..	0.746	..	..	..	..	..
74 Latvia	..	0.765	0.780	0.778	0.744	2,290	2,689	3,060	3,530	2,153
75 Saint Vincent and the Grenadines	..	..	..	..	0.744	725	940	1,222	1,627	..
76 Kazakhstan	..	..	..	..	0.740	..	..	..	1,782	1,015 [a]
77 Philippines	0.646	0.680	0.683	0.711	0.740	568	679	562	619	652
78 Saudi Arabia	0.595	0.651	0.671	0.707	0.740	8,970	10,225	5,744	5,434	5,057
79 Brazil	0.639	0.672	0.687	0.708	0.739	1,662	2,045	1,942	1,948	2,107
80 Peru	0.641	0.669	0.691	0.703	0.739	1,197	1,170	1,035	849	1,112
81 Saint Lucia	..	..	..	..	0.737	..	..	1,737	2,472	..
82 Jamaica	..	..	..	..	0.734	1,585	1,286	1,195	1,459	1,433 [a]
83 Belize	..	..	..	..	0.732	1,279	1,598	1,430	1,991	2,111
84 Paraguay	0.655	0.688	0.695	0.706	0.730	741	1,055	992	1,028	1,047
85 Georgia	..	..	..	..	0.729	..	..	..	..	..
86 Turkey	..	..	..	..	0.728	1,284	1,323	1,478	1,735	1,940 [a]
87 Armenia	..	..	..	..	0.728	550	715	890	848	..
88 Dominican Republic	0.617	0.654	0.685	0.693	0.726	726	815	819	837	1,032
89 Oman	..	..	..	..	0.725	3,789	3,587	5,733	5,653	..
90 Sri Lanka	0.605	0.641	0.671	0.694	0.721	278	328	401	439	551
91 Ukraine	..	..	..	..	0.721	..	..	..	1,165	496
92 Uzbekistan	..	..	..	..	0.720	..	..	..	..	..
93 Maldives	..	..	..	..	0.716	..	..	421	594	749 [a]
94 Jordan	..	..	..	..	0.715	1,209	2,098	2,238	1,771	2,006
95 Iran, Islamic Rep. of	..	..	..	..	0.715	4,386	2,980	3,275	2,734	..
96 Turkmenistan	..	..	..	..	0.712	..	..	..	..	..
97 Kyrgyzstan	..	..	..	..	0.702	..	..	..	210	111
98 China	0.521	0.554	0.588	0.624	0.701	109	138	210	285	564
99 Guyana	..	..	..	..	0.701	624	584	447	394	..
100 Albania	..	0.699	0.706	0.702	0.699	..	696	696	640	562

HDI rank	Human development index (HDI) value					GDP per capita (1987 US$)				
	1975	1980	1985	1990	1997	1975	1980	1985	1990	1997
101 South Africa	0.637	0.652	0.671	0.700	0.695	2,656	2,745	2,543	2,468	2,336
102 Tunisia	0.510	0.566	0.608	0.640	0.695	980	1,177	1,272	1,310	1,670
103 Azerbaijan	..	..	..	0.755	0.695	..	..	..	1,130	402
104 Moldova, Rep. of	..	..	..	..	0.683	..	..	..	..	..
105 Indonesia	0.471	0.533	0.586	0.630	0.681	265	349	417	537	785
106 Cape Verde	..	..	0.573	0.610	0.677	..	..	718	790	856
107 El Salvador	..	..	..	..	0.674	1,082	976	813	837	1,011 [a]
108 Tajikistan	..	..	..	..	0.665	..	..	..	718	240 [a]
109 Algeria	0.511	0.556	0.605	0.637	0.665	2,315	2,683	2,966	2,624	2,352
110 Viet Nam	..	..	..	..	0.664	..	..	..	..	..
111 Syrian Arab Republic	..	..	..	..	0.663	998	1,168	1,132	1,040	1,288 [a]
112 Bolivia	0.524	0.558	0.584	0.611	0.652	250	252	208	220	244
113 Swaziland	0.497	0.528	0.556	0.605	0.644	717	699	693	961	947
114 Honduras	0.515	0.563	0.595	0.616	0.641	834	999	928	927	969
115 Namibia	..	0.604	0.620	0.644	0.638	..	1,880	1,571	1,515	1,670
116 Vanuatu	..	..	..	..	0.627	..	820	962	914	836
117 Guatemala	0.517	0.552	0.563	0.588	0.624	910	1,060	883	902	990
118 Solomon Islands	..	..	..	..	0.623	312	434	496	583	606 [a]
119 Mongolia	..	..	..	..	0.618	..	..	..	..	..
120 Egypt	0.432	0.479	0.531	0.573	0.616	467	678	827	900	1,015
121 Nicaragua	..	..	..	..	0.616	1,904	1,338	1,198	845	1,022 [d]
122 Botswana	0.501	0.565	0.624	0.670	0.609	621	959	1,301	1,781	2,101
123 São Tomé and Principe	..	..	..	..	0.609	..	..	..	496	454
124 Gabon	..	..	..	..	0.607	6,562	5,225	4,883	4,422	4,575
125 Iraq	..	..	..	..	0.586	5,178	6,600	3,586	1,621	..
126 Morocco	0.426	0.473	0.508	0.540	0.582	641	782	822	916	927
127 Lesotho	0.471	0.512	0.537	0.569	0.582	171	242	229	286	391
128 Myanmar	..	..	..	..	0.580	..	..	..	..	..
129 Papua New Guinea	..	..	..	..	0.570	947	881	848	802	1,060 [a]
130 Zimbabwe	0.539	0.562	0.619	0.609	0.560	828	783	782	842	830
131 Equatorial Guinea	..	..	..	..	0.549	..	..	376	357	944
132 India	..	..	..	..	0.545	251	262	305	374	465 [a]
133 Ghana	0.431	0.461	0.475	0.506	0.544	456	438	365	391	437
134 Cameroon	0.422	0.467	0.519	0.534	0.536	735	871	1,183	911	756
135 Congo	0.450	0.499	0.545	0.531	0.533	829	907	1,281	1,092	946
136 Kenya	0.453	0.498	0.521	0.544	0.519	332	370	354	392	372
137 Cambodia	..	..	..	..	0.514	..	..	..	111	139
138 Pakistan	0.347	0.377	0.414	0.455	0.508	222	258	313	364	417
139 Comoros	..	0.470	0.495	0.500	0.506	..	458	500	475	380
Low human development	..	..	..	..	0.416	332	331	297	305	282
140 Lao People's Dem. Rep.	..	..	0.405	0.434	0.491	..	..	293	322	415
141 Congo, Dem. Rep. of the	..	..	..	..	0.479	307	241	225	190	97
142 Sudan	..	..	..	..	0.475	1,065	1,026	943	891	..
143 Togo	0.395	0.441	0.438	0.456	0.469	430	474	404	394	363
144 Nepal	0.289	0.327	0.368	0.411	0.463	153	151	169	185	219
145 Bhutan	..	..	..	..	0.459	..	312	393	517	..
146 Nigeria	0.322	0.379	0.395	0.419	0.456	349	373	277	311	315
147 Madagascar	..	..	..	..	0.453	324	305	246	245	209
148 Yemen	..	..	..	..	0.449	..	..	..	..	..
149 Mauritania	0.343	0.366	0.386	0.402	0.447	512	523	477	466	513
150 Bangladesh	0.318	0.336	0.369	0.400	0.440	134	145	165	179	218

HDI rank	Human development index (HDI) value					GDP per capita (1987 US$)				
	1975	1980	1985	1990	1997	1975	1980	1985	1990	1997
151 Zambia	0.453	0.467	0.483	0.460	0.431	438	380	329	302	300
152 Haiti	..	..	..	0.432	0.430	353	428	372	340	258
153 Senegal	0.326	0.344	0.369	0.393	0.426	716	661	664	676	674
154 Côte d'Ivoire	0.374	0.407	0.415	0.416	0.422	1,169	1,181	992	893	899
155 Benin	0.306	0.342	0.370	0.377	0.421	316	337	381	332	371
156 Tanzania, U. Rep. of	..	..	..	..	0.421	..	..	..	..	..
157 Djibouti	..	..	..	..	0.412	..	..	..	..	..
158 Uganda	..	..	0.373	0.364	0.404	..	..	426	470	602
159 Malawi	0.328	0.352	0.366	0.367	0.399	155	167	159	154	166
160 Angola	..	..	..	..	0.398	..	..	832	847	662
161 Guinea	..	..	..	0.352	0.398	..	..	..	409	447
162 Chad	0.286	0.310	0.341	0.366	0.393	196	208	226	215	211
163 Gambia	0.270	0.303	0.332	0.354	0.391	259	278	278	275	256
164 Rwanda	0.323	0.368	0.411	0.321	0.379	247	340	341	316	222
165 Central African Republic	0.342	0.361	0.383	0.384	0.378	523	480	472	418	387
166 Mali	0.246	0.274	0.289	0.319	0.375	239	268	242	260	271
167 Eritrea	..	..	..	..	0.346	..	..	..	..	..
168 Guinea-Bissau	0.249	0.248	0.279	0.302	0.343	217	157	194	209	234
169 Mozambique	..	0.302	0.294	0.334	0.341	..	165	123	173	199
170 Burundi	0.282	0.308	0.340	0.343	0.324	179	195	219	229	162
171 Burkina Faso	0.237	0.257	0.280	0.290	0.304	223	237	255	257	290
172 Ethiopia	..	..	0.258	0.281	0.298	..	..	139	153	171
173 Niger	0.247	0.269	0.267	0.283	0.298	391	430	318	308	269
174 Sierra Leone	..	..	..	..	0.254	256	260	227	227	159 [a]
All developing countries	..	..	..	..	0.637	600	686	693	745	908
Least developed countries	..	..	..	..	0.430	287	282	276	277	245
Sub-Saharan Africa	..	..	..	..	0.463	671	661	550	542	518
Arab States	..	..	..	..	0.626	2,327	2,914	2,252	1,842	..
East Asia	..	..	..	..	0.712	176	233	336	470	828
East Asia (excluding China)	..	..	..	..	0.849	1,729	2,397	3,210	4,809	7,018
South-East Asia and the Pacific	..	..	..	..	0.695	481	616	673	849	1,183
South Asia	..	..	..	..	0.544	404	365	427	463	432
South Asia (excluding India)	..	..	..	..	0.542	857	662	768	709	327
Latin America and the Caribbean	..	..	..	..	0.756	1,694	1,941	1,795	1,788	2,049
Eastern Europe and the CIS	..	..	..	..	0.754	..	..	..	2,913	1,989
Industrialized countries	..	..	..	..	0.919	12,589	14,206	15,464	17,618	19,283
World	..	..	..	..	0.706	2,888	3,136	3,174	3,407	3,610

a. Data refer to 1996.

Source: Columns 1-5: Human Development Report Office calculations; *columns 6-10:* calculated on the basis of data from World Bank 1999b.

7 Trends in human development and economic growth

HDI rank	Reduction in shortfall (1 - HDI) in human development index (HDI) value (%)				GDP per capita (1987 US$)						
	1975-80	1980-85	1985-90	1990-97	1975[a]	Lowest value during 1975-97[a]	Year	Highest value during 1975-97[a]	Year	1997[a]	Average annual rate of change (%) 1975-97[a]
High human development	..	..	..	..	..	..	..	..	..	..	..
1 Canada	12.1	18.2	22.8	10.4	11,832	11,832	1975	16,525	1997	16,525	1.5
2 Norway	12.9	8.0	9.7	33.1	14,517	14,517	1975	27,620	1997	27,620	3.0
3 United States	14.7	10.4	13.5	17.9	15,264	15,264	1975	21,541	1997	21,541	1.6
4 Japan	16.2	11.5	14.8	19.5	13,825	13,825	1975	25,084	1997	25,084	2.8
5 Belgium	..	..	..	..	11,527	11,527	1975	16,809	1996	16,809 [b]	1.8
6 Sweden	7.0	8.2	7.1	30.8	16,049	15,845	1977	20,309	1997	20,309	1.1
7 Australia	10.6	8.0	10.4	35.0	10,439	10,439	1975	15,186	1997	15,186	1.7
8 Netherlands	8.4	10.8	11.7	23.7	12,599	12,599	1975	18,369	1997	18,369	1.7
9 Iceland	14.6	7.9	15.5	16.9	13,903	13,903	1975	23,112	1997	23,112	2.3
10 United Kingdom	4.9	5.8	13.9	33.5	9,310	9,310	1975	14,096	1997	14,096	1.9
11 France	10.2	8.6	16.9	20.5	12,763	12,763	1975	18,554	1997	18,554	1.7
12 Switzerland	..	..	..	..	22,043	21,936	1976	28,114	1990	26,441 [b]	0.9
13 Finland	12.1	11.1	17.6	18.1	13,374	13,238	1977	19,816	1997	19,816	1.8
14 Germany	..	..	..	..	..	..	..	..	..	..	..
15 Denmark	5.9	6.8	5.7	17.0	15,080	15,080	1975	23,303	1997	23,303	2.0
16 Austria	8.4	9.1	16.5	16.5	11,901	11,901	1975	18,594	1997	18,594	2.1
17 Luxembourg	..	..	..	..	13,782	13,782	1975	28,010	1996	28,010 [b]	3.4
18 New Zealand	5.5	7.0	7.6	22.7	9,801	9,446	1978	11,639	1995	11,565	0.8
19 Italy	10.0	6.7	15.5	20.0	9,629	9,629	1975	15,548	1997	15,548	2.2
20 Ireland	6.9	8.7	14.9	27.0	6,675	6,661	1976	15,779	1997	15,779	4.0
21 Spain	10.6	10.3	13.2	18.5	6,415	6,415	1975	9,591	1997	9,591	1.8
22 Singapore	11.2	12.4	18.8	32.5	4,557	4,557	1975	15,467	1997	15,467	5.7
23 Israel	..	..	..	..	7,121	6,899	1977	10,505	1995	10,505 [c]	2.0
24 Hong Kong, China (SAR)	16.3	13.0	20.2	15.2	3,895	3,895	1975	12,439	1997	12,439	5.4
25 Brunei Darussalam	..	..	..	..	12,842	10,574	1995	19,148	1979	10,574 [c]	-1.0
26 Cyprus	..	..	..	..	2,390	2,390	1975	7,543	1994	7,543 [d]	6.2
27 Greece	10.6	11.3	6.7	13.6	4,552	4,552	1975	6,583	1997	6,583	1.7
28 Portugal	8.8	11.4	13.4	23.3	3,117	3,117	1975	5,564	1997	5,564	2.7
29 Barbados	..	..	..	..	4,427	4,419	1976	6,376	1989	5,779 [c]	1.3
30 Korea, Rep. of	11.2	15.9	17.9	24.6	1,461	1,461	1975	6,251	1997	6,251	6.8
31 Bahamas	..	..	..	..	6,477	6,477	1975	11,362	1989	10,037 [c]	2.2
32 Malta	..	..	..	..	2,391	2,391	1975	6,986	1995	6,986 [c]	5.5
33 Slovenia	..	..	..	..	..	..	..	..	..	..	..
34 Chile	..	..	..	..	1,199	1,199	1975	2,677	1996	2,677 [h]	3.9
35 Kuwait	..	..	..	..	24,353	10,578	1988	25,125	1979	17,971 [c]	-1.5
36 Czech Republic	..	..	..	..	3,395 [e]	2,937	1993	3,726	1989	3,329 [b]	-0.2
37 Bahrain	..	..	..	..	10,03 [f]	6,921	1987	10,037	1980	7,997 [b]	-1.4
38 Antigua and Barbuda	..	..	..	..	2,982 [f]	2,982	1980	5,878	1994	5,878 [d]	5.0
39 Argentina	6.0	3.7	2.4	12.1	3,779	3,150	1990	4,021	1997	4,021	0.3
40 Uruguay	8.3	2.1	9.2	11.7	2,144	2,061	1984	2,992	1997	2,992	1.5
41 Qatar	..	..	..	..	..	..	..	..	..	..	..
42 Slovakia	..	..	2.6	4.8	3,340 [e]	2,741	1993	3,715	1989	3,432	0.2
43 United Arab Emirates	12.1	5.5	10.6	4.6	29,249	14,124	1994	29,887	1980	15,300	-2.9
44 Poland	..	1.8	0.8	10.0	1,687 [f]	1,421	1992	1,926	1997	1,926	0.8
45 Costa Rica	9.6	0.1	7.2	8.2	1,589	1,513	1983	1,908	1995	1,865	0.7
Medium human development	..	..	..	..	..	..	..	..	..	..	..
46 Trinidad and Tobago	12.1	3.5	1.6	4.6	3,794	3,646	1993	5,356	1981	3,990	0.2
47 Hungary	..	..	..	..	1,756	1,756	1975	2,511	1989	2,372 [b]	1.4
48 Venezuela	5.2	3.0	8.2	5.2	3,175	2,455	1989	3,384	1977	2,685	-0.8
49 Panama	..	..	..	..	2,277	2,108	1989	2,688	1996	2,688 [b]	0.8
50 Mexico	..	..	..	..	1,591	1,591	1975	2,043	1981	1,910 [b]	0.9

	Reduction in shortfall (1 - HDI) in human development index (HDI) value (%)				GDP per capita (1987 US$)						Average annual rate of change (%)
						Lowest value during		Highest value during			
HDI rank	1975-80	1980-85	1985-90	1990-97	1975 [a]	1975-97 [a]	Year	1975-97 [a]	Year	1997 [a]	1975-97 [a]
51 Saint Kitts and Nevis	..	..	..	..	1,427 [g]	1,427	1977	3,895	1995	3,895 [c]	5.7
52 Grenada	..	..	..	..	1,223 [f]	1,223	1980	2,023	1995	2,023 [c]	3.4
53 Dominica	..	..	..	..	1,087	967	1979	2,196	1996	2,196 [b]	3.4
54 Estonia	..	4.7	-3.8	-7.9	3,354 [f]	2,443	1994	4,015	1989	2,984	-0.7
55 Croatia	..	..	..	..	..	..	..	..	..	..	..
56 Malaysia	10.3	10.8	8.8	17.7	1,253	1,253	1975	3,387	1997	3,387	4.6
57 Colombia	..	..	..	..	880	880	1975	1,321	1996	1,321 [b]	2.0
58 Cuba	..	..	..	..	..	..	..	..	..	..	..
59 Mauritius	7.1	9.1	11.6	13.4	1,098	1,098	1975	2,752	1997	2,752	4.3
60 Belarus	..	..	..	-14.2	2,460 [h]	1,739	1995	2,778	1989	2,013	-2.0
61 Fiji	6.8	4.0	9.1	10.5	1,641	1,641	1975	1,995	1996	1,986	0.9
62 Lithuania	..	..	..	-8.5	2,482 [h]	1,808	1993	2,799	1989	2,013	-2.1
63 Bulgaria	..	9.5	0.3	-8.5	2,344 [f]	2,332	1997	3,510	1988	2,332	0.0
64 Suriname	..	..	..	..	1,159	1,113	1983	2,765	1987	2,089 [c]	3.0
65 Libyan Arab Jamahiriya	..	..	..	..	10,459	5,466	1989	13,731	1979	5,466 [i]	-4.5
66 Seychelles	..	..	..	..	2,551	2,551	1975	4,920	1993	4,632	2.8
67 Thailand	10.8	8.8	12.0	12.9	557	557	1975	1,896	1996	1,870	5.7
68 Romania	12.2	2.2	-7.1	2.8	1,105	1,105	1975	1,756	1986	1,457	1.3
69 Lebanon	..	..	..	..	..	..	..	..	..	..	..
70 Samoa (Western)	..	..	..	..	638 [j]	560	1994	703	1979	633 [b]	0.0
71 Russian Federation	..	6.5	7.5	-18.5	2,250	2,250	1975	4,665	1989	2,742	0.9
72 Ecuador	13.3	7.2	3.9	7.6	1,027	1,027	1975	1,257	1997	1,257	0.9
73 Macedonia, TFYR	..	..	..	..	..	..	..	..	..	..	..
74 Latvia	..	6.2	-0.9	-14.9	2,290	1,884	1993	3,558	1989	2,153	-0.3
75 Saint Vincent and the Grenadines	..	..	..	..	725	725	1975	1,813	1995	1,813 [c]	4.7
76 Kazakhstan	..	..	..	..	1,880 [h]	1,001	1995	1,922	1988	1,015 [b]	-6.6
77 Philippines	9.6	1.1	8.7	10.1	568	562	1985	695	1982	652	0.6
78 Saudi Arabia	13.8	5.9	11.0	11.1	8,970	5,057	1997	10,225	1980	5,057	-2.6
79 Brazil	9.1	4.5	6.7	10.7	1,662	1,662	1975	2,107	1997	2,107	1.1
80 Peru	7.8	6.7	3.8	12.2	1,197	849	1990	1,225	1981	1,112	-0.3
81 Saint Lucia	..	..	..	..	1,737 [k]	1,737	1985	2,721	1994	2,721 [d]	5.1
82 Jamaica	..	..	..	..	1,585	1,195	1985	1,585	1975	1,433 [b]	-0.5
83 Belize	..	..	..	..	1,279	1,252	1976	2,153	1993	2,111	2.3
84 Paraguay	9.8	2.1	3.8	8.0	741	741	1975	1,112	1981	1,047	1.6
85 Georgia	..	..	..	..	..	..	..	..	..	..	..
86 Turkey	..	..	..	..	1,284	1,284	1975	1,940	1996	1,940 [b]	2.0
87 Armenia	..	..	..	..	550	251	1993	946	1989	283 [c]	-3.3
88 Dominican Republic	9.8	9.0	2.6	10.7	726	726	1975	1,032	1997	1,032	1.6
89 Oman	..	..	..	..	3,789	3,587	1980	5,763	1995	5,763 [c]	2.1
90 Sri Lanka	9.1	8.5	6.8	8.9	278	278	1975	551	1997	551	3.2
91 Ukraine	..	..	..	..	1,181 [h]	496	1997	1,247	1989	496	-8.3
92 Uzbekistan	..	..	..	..	..	..	..	..	..	..	..
93 Maldives	..	..	..	..	421 [k]	421	1985	749	1996	749 [b]	5.4
94 Jordan	..	..	..	..	1,209	1,209	1975	2,308	1986	2,006	2.3
95 Iran, Islamic Rep. of	..	..	..	..	4,386	2,503	1988	4,977	1976	3,156 [c]	-1.6
96 Turkmenistan	..	..	..	..	..	..	..	..	..	..	..
97 Kyrgyzstan	..	..	..	..	45 [h]	45	1987	210	1990	111	9.4
98 China	6.8	7.7	8.6	20.7	109	101	1976	564	1997	564	7.8
99 Guyana	..	..	..	..	624	394	1990	630	1976	542 [c]	-0.7
100 Albania	..	2.2	-1.2	-0.9	696 [f]	442	1992	728	1982	562	-1.3

HDI rank	Reduction in shortfall (1 - HDI) in human development index (HDI) value (%)				GDP per capita (1987 US$)						
	1975-80	1980-85	1985-90	1990-97	1975 [a]	Lowest value during 1975-97 [a]	Year	Highest value during 1975-97 [a]	Year	1997 [a]	Average annual rate of change (%) 1975-97 [a]
101 South Africa	4.0	5.5	9.0	-1.8	2,656	2,270	1993	2,848	1981	2,336	-0.6
102 Tunisia	11.4	9.7	8.2	15.2	980	980	1975	1,670	1997	1,670	2.5
103 Azerbaijan	..	..	..	-24.6	1,415 [h]	389	1995	1,415	1987	402	-11.8
104 Moldova, Rep. of	..	..	..	..	..	..	..	..	..	..	..
105 Indonesia	11.6	11.3	10.7	13.8	265	265	1975	785	1997	785	5.1
106 Cape Verde	..	..	8.6	17.2	547 [l]	547	1981	856	1997	856	2.8
107 El Salvador	..	..	..	..	1,082	800	1986	1,165	1978	1,011 [b]	-0.3
108 Tajikistan	..	..	..	..	789 [m]	240	1996	813	1988	240 [b]	-11.2
109 Algeria	9.2	11.2	8.0	7.5	2,315	2,315	1975	2,966	1985	2,352	0.1
110 Viet Nam	..	..	..	..	..	..	..	..	..	..	..
111 Syrian Arab Republic	..	..	..	..	998	991	1989	1,288	1996	1,288 [b]	1.2
112 Bolivia	7.3	5.9	6.5	10.6	250	207	1987	266	1978	244	-0.1
113 Swaziland	6.2	6.0	10.9	9.9	717	652	1979	961	1990	947	1.3
114 Honduras	10.0	7.3	5.2	6.4	834	834	1975	1,027	1979	969	0.7
115 Namibia	..	4.0	6.4	-1.7	1,880 [f]	1,515	1990	1,880	1980	1,670	-0.7
116 Vanuatu	..	..	..	..	947 [n]	793	1992	968	1984	836	-0.7
117 Guatemala	7.4	2.4	5.7	8.8	910	862	1986	1,060	1980	990	0.4
118 Solomon Islands	..	..	..	..	312	312	1975	651	1995	606 [b]	3.2
119 Mongolia	..	..	..	..	..	..	..	..	..	..	..
120 Egypt	8.3	10.1	8.9	10.2	467	467	1975	1,015	1997	1,015	3.6
121 Nicaragua	..	..	..	..	1,904	772	1993	2,069	1977	1,022 [b]	-2.9
122 Botswana	12.8	13.5	12.4	-18.5	621	621	1975	2,101	1997	2,101	5.7
123 São Tomé and Principe	..	..	..	..	525 [h]	454	1997	525	1987	454	-1.4
124 Gabon	..	..	..	..	6,562	3,766	1987	8,617	1976	4,575	-1.6
125 Iraq	..	..	..	..	5,178	776	1991	8,313	1979	776 [o]	-11.2
126 Morocco	8.0	6.7	6.5	9.2	641	641	1975	968	1996	927	1.7
127 Lesotho	7.6	5.1	7.1	2.9	171	171	1975	391	1997	391	3.8
128 Myanmar	..	..	..	..	..	..	..	..	..	..	..
129 Papua New Guinea	..	..	..	..	947	802	1990	1,120	1994	1,060 [b]	0.5
130 Zimbabwe	5.0	13.0	-2.6	-12.6	828	695	1979	869	1991	830	0.0
131 Equatorial Guinea	..	..	..	..	376 [k]	345	1991	944	1997	944	8.0
132 India	..	..	..	..	251	250	1976	465	1996	465 [b]	3.0
133 Ghana	5.2	2.6	5.8	7.9	456	343	1983	465	1978	437	-0.2
134 Cameroon	7.8	9.8	3.0	0.6	735	676	1976	1,229	1986	756	0.1
135 Congo	9.0	9.2	-3.1	0.3	829	719	1977	1,334	1984	946	0.6
136 Kenya	8.2	4.7	4.7	-5.4	332	327	1976	392	1990	372	0.5
137 Cambodia	..	..	..	..	105 [h]	105	1987	139	1997	139	2.9
138 Pakistan	4.6	5.9	7.1	9.6	222	222	1975	417	1997	417	2.9
139 Comoros	..	4.7	1.0	1.2	458 [f]	380	1997	502	1984	380	-1.1
Low human development	..	..	..	..	..	..	..	..	..	..	..
140 Lao People's Dem. Rep.	..	..	4.8	10.1	287 [e]	276	1988	415	1997	415	2.9
141 Congo, Dem. Rep. of the	..	..	..	..	307	97	1997	307	1975	97	-5.1
142 Sudan	..	..	..	..	1,065	891	1990	1,240	1977	924 [o]	-0.9
143 Togo	7.6	-0.5	3.2	2.4	430	287	1993	474	1980	363	-0.8
144 Nepal	5.3	6.1	6.9	8.8	153	151	1980	219	1997	219	1.7
145 Bhutan	..	..	..	..	312 [f]	312	1980	571	1995	571 [c]	4.1
146 Nigeria	8.5	2.4	4.0	6.3	349	260	1984	386	1977	315	-0.5
147 Madagascar	..	..	..	..	324	208	1996	324	1975	209	-2.0
148 Yemen	..	..	..	..	..	..	..	..	..	..	..
149 Mauritania	3.5	3.2	2.5	7.6	512	462	1992	540	1976	513	0.0
150 Bangladesh	2.7	5.0	4.8	6.8	134	134	1975	218	1997	218	2.2

7 Trends in human development and economic growth

	Reduction in shortfall (1 - HDI) in human development index (HDI) value (%)				GDP per capita (1987 US$)						Average annual rate of change (%)
HDI rank	1975-80	1980-85	985-90	1990-97	1975[a]	Lowest value during 1975-97[a]	Year	Highest value during 1975-97[a]	Year	1997[a]	1975-97[a]
151 Zambia	2.5	3.0	-4.4	-5.4	438	281	1995	451	1976	300	-1.7
152 Haiti	..	..	..	..	353	254	1994	428	1980	258	-1.4
153 Senegal	2.7	3.9	3.7	5.6	716	624	1993	756	1976	674	-0.3
154 Côte d'Ivoire	5.3	1.5	0.1	1.0	1,169	804	1994	1,399	1978	899	-1.2
155 Benin	5.2	4.3	1.0	7.2	316	311	1976	382	1986	371	0.7
156 Tanzania, U. Rep. of	..	..	..	..	..	..	..	..	..	..	..
157 Djibouti	..	..	..	..	..	..	..	..	..	..	..
158 Uganda	..	..	-1.5	6.4	460 [p]	419	1986	602	1997	602	1.9
159 Malawi	3.6	2.0	0.3	5.1	155	134	1994	172	1979	166	0.3
160 Angola	..	..	..	..	832 [k]	543	1994	899	1988	662	-1.9
161 Guinea	..	..	..	7.0	386 [m]	386	1986	447	1997	447	1.4
162 Chad	3.4	4.5	3.7	4.4	196	178	1976	284	1977	211	0.3
163 Gambia	4.5	4.2	3.2	5.8	259	250	1996	293	1981	256	-0.1
164 Rwanda	6.5	6.8	-15.3	8.5	247	168	1994	354	1983	222	-0.5
165 Central African Republic	2.9	3.4	0.3	-1.0	523	364	1993	547	1977	387	-1.4
166 Mali	3.7	2.2	4.2	8.3	239	234	1982	287	1979	271	0.6
167 Eritrea	..	..	..	..	..	..	..	..	..	..	..
168 Guinea-Bissau	-0.1	4.2	3.2	5.9	217	157	1980	234	1997	234	0.3
169 Mozambique	..	-1.2	5.6	1.1	165 [f]	115	1984	199	1997	199	1.1
170 Burundi	3.7	4.6	0.5	-3.0	179	160	1996	234	1991	162	-0.5
171 Burkina Faso	2.6	3.1	1.4	2.1	223	223	1975	290	1997	290	1.2
172 Ethiopia	..	..	3.2	2.4	179 [p]	131	1992	179	1983	171	-0.4
173 Niger	3.0	-0.2	2.1	2.1	391	269	1996	455	1979	269	-1.7
174 Sierra Leone	..	..	..	..	256	156	1995	260	1980	159 [b]	-2.2
All developing countries	..	..	..	..	..	..	..	..	..	..	..
Least developed countries	..	..	..	..	..	..	..	..	..	..	..
Sub-Saharan Africa	..	..	..	..	..	..	..	..	..	..	..
Arab States	..	..	..	..	..	..	..	..	..	..	..
East Asia	..	..	..	..	..	..	..	..	..	..	..
East Asia (excluding China)	..	..	..	..	..	..	..	..	..	..	..
South-East Asia and the Pacific	..	..	..	..	..	..	..	..	..	..	..
South Asia	..	..	..	..	..	..	..	..	..	..	..
South Asia (excluding India)	..	..	..	..	..	..	..	..	..	..	..
Latin America and the Caribbean	..	..	..	..	..	..	..	..	..	..	..
Eastern Europe and the CIS	..	..	..	..	..	..	..	..	..	..	..
Industrialized countries	..	..	..	..	..	..	..	..	..	..	..
World	..	..	..	..	..	..	..	..	..	..	..

a. The earliest year for which data are given is 1975, and the latest year 1997, unless otherwise specified.
b. 1996.
c. 1995.
d. 1994.
e. 1984.
f. 1980.
g. 1977.
h. 1987.
i. 1989.
j. 1978.
k. 1985.
l. 1981.
m. 1986.
n. 1979.
o. 1991.
p. 1983.

Source: Columns 1-4: Human Development Report Office calculations; *columns 5-10:* World Bank 1999b; *column 11:* calculated on the basis of data from World Bank 1999b.

MONITORING HUMAN DEVELOPMENT: ENLARGING PEOPLE'S CHOICES . . .

Technical note. Computing the indices

The human development index

The HDI is based on three indicators: longevity, as measured by life expectancy at birth; educational attainment, as measured by a combination of adult literacy (two-thirds weight) and the combined gross primary, secondary and tertiary enrolment ratio (one-third weight); and standard of living, as measured by real GDP per capita (PPP$).

Fixed minimum and maximum values
To construct the index, fixed minimum and maximum values have been established for each of these indicators:
- Life expectancy at birth: 25 years and 85 years.
- Adult literacy rate: 0% and 100%.
- Combined gross enrolment ratio: 0% and 100%.
- Real GDP per capita (PPP$): $100 and $40,000 (PPP$).

For any component of the HDI individual indices can be computed according to the general formula:

$$\text{Index} = \frac{\text{Actual } x_i \text{ value} - \text{minimum } x_i \text{ value}}{\text{Maximum } x_i \text{ value} - \text{minimum } x_i \text{ value}}$$

If, for example, the life expectancy at birth in a country is 65 years, the index of life expectancy for this country would be:

$$\text{Life expectancy index} = \frac{65 - 25}{85 - 25} = \frac{40}{60} = 0.667$$

Treatment of income
Constructing the income index is a little more complex. Over the years the *Human Development Report* has used a particular formula to do this, explained below. This year a thorough review of the treatment of income in the HDI was done, based on the work of Anand and Sen (1999).

Income enters into the HDI as a surrogate for all the dimensions of human development not reflected in a long and healthy life and in knowledge—in a nutshell, it is a proxy for a decent standard of living. The basic approach in the treatment of income has been driven by the fact that achieving a respectable level of human development does not require unlimited income. To reflect this, income has always been discounted in calculating the HDI. The issue is, how should it be discounted, and at what level?

In previous years the practice was to discount income above the threshold level of the world average income, using the following formula:

$$W(y) = y^* \text{ for } 0 < y < y^*$$
$$= y^* + 2[(y - y^*)^{1/2}] \text{ for } y^* < y < 2y^*$$
$$= y^* + 2(y^{*1/2}) + 3[(y - 2y^*)^{1/3}] \text{ for } 2y^* < y < 3y^*$$

where y is the actual per capita income in PPP$ and y^* is the threshold per capita income (PPP$) at the world average income in the year for which the HDI is constructed. The world average income was taken as the threshold income on the premise that each person should have the income that the world on average enjoys.

To calculate the discounted value of the maximum income of $40,000 (PPP$), the following formula was used:

$$W(y) = y^* + 2(y^{*1/2}) + 3(y^{*1/3}) + 4(y^{*1/4}) + 5(y^{*1/5}) + 6(y^{*1/6}) + 7[(40,000 - 6y^*)^{1/7}]$$

This is because $40,000 (PPP$) is between $6y^*$ and $7y^*$. With the above formula, the discounted value of the maximum income of $40,000 (PPP$) is $6,311 (PPP$).

The main problem with this formula is that it discounts the income above the threshold level very heavily, penalizing the countries in which income exceeds the threshold level. It reduces the $34,000 (PPP$) between the threshold and maximum

level of income to a mere $321 (PPP$). In many cases income loses its relevance as a proxy for all dimensions of human development other than a long and healthy life and knowledge.

This year's refinement in the treatment of income attempts to rectify this problem by putting the methodology on a more solid analytical foundation. The rationale and the formula adopted in the refinement are discussed in detail in Anand and Sen (1999). To summarize, in the construction of this year's HDI, income is treated using the following formula:

$$W(y) = \frac{\log y - \log y_{\min}}{\log y_{\max} - \log y_{\min}}$$

There are several advantages to this formula. First, it does not discount income as severely as the formula used earlier (technical note figure 1). Second, it discounts all income, not just the income above a certain level. Third, as the figure shows, the asymptote starts quite late, so middle-income countries are not penalized unduly; moreover, as income rises further in these countries, they will continue to receive recognition for their increasing income as a potential means for further human development.

Illustration of the HDI methodology
The construction of the HDI is illustrated with two examples—Germany and China, an industrialized and a developing country.

Country	Life expectancy (years)	Adult literacy rate (%)	Combined gross enrolment ratio (%)	Real GDP per capita (PPP$)
Germany	77.2	99.0	88.1	21,260
China	69.8	82.9	68.9	3,130

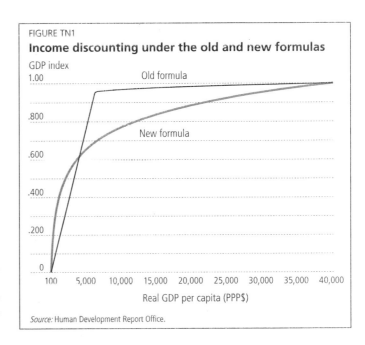

FIGURE TN1
Income discounting under the old and new formulas

Source: Human Development Report Office.

Life expectancy index

$$\text{Germany} = \frac{77.2 - 25}{85 - 25} = \frac{52.2}{60} = 0.870$$

$$\text{China} = \frac{69.8 - 25}{85 - 25} = \frac{44.8}{60} = 0.747$$

Adult literacy index

$$\text{Germany} = \frac{99.0 - 0}{100 - 0} = \frac{99.0}{100} = 0.990$$

$$\text{China} = \frac{82.9 - 0}{100 - 0} = \frac{82.9}{100} = 0.829$$

Combined gross enrolment index

$$\text{Germany} = \frac{88.1 - 0}{100 - 0} = 0.881$$

$$\text{China} = \frac{68.9 - 0}{100 - 0} = 0.689$$

Educational attainment index

Germany $= [2(0.990) + 1(0.881)]/3 = 0.954$

China $= [2(0.829) + 1(0.689)]/3 = 0.782$

Adjusted real GDP per capita (PPP$) index

$$\text{Germany} = \frac{\log (21{,}260) - \log (100)}{\log (40{,}000) - \log (100)} = 0.895$$

$$\text{China} = \frac{\log (3{,}130) - \log (100)}{\log (40{,}000) - \log (100)} = 0.575$$

Human development index

The HDI is a simple average of the life expectancy index, educational attainment index and adjusted real GDP per capita (PPP$) index, and so is derived by dividing the sum of these three indices by 3.

Country	Life expectancy index	Educational attainment index	Adjusted real GDP (PPP$) index	Sum of the three indices	HDI
Germany	0.870	0.954	0.895	2.719	0.906
China	0.747	0.782	0.575	2.104	0.701

Comparing HDI values across years

The HDI values in this year's Report are not strictly comparable with those in last year's because of the change in the treatment of income in the HDI. Comparability is also affected by significant revision in the data series for some indicators, particularly the income data (PPP$) from the World Bank. As a result of these changes, both HDI values and rankings for many countries this year differ considerably from those in last year's Report. Technical note table 1 shows the changes in countries' HDI rankings and the source of those changes—whether refinement of the treatment of income or revision of data.

The table makes two clear points. First, most of the changes in HDI rankings can be attributed to the changes in the treatment of income. Second, although a simple comparison of the HDI values in last year's Report with those in this year's shows an apparent deterioration, a comparison using the new treatment of income in both cases shows an improvement in the HDI value for every country.

The gender-related development index and the gender empowerment measure

For comparisons among countries the GDI and the GEM are limited to data widely available in international data sets. For this year's Report we have endeavoured to use the most recent, reliable and internally consistent data. Collecting more extensive and more reliable gender-disaggregated data is a challenge that the international community should squarely face. We continue to publish results on the GDI and the GEM—based on the best available estimates—in the expectation that it will help increase the demand for such data.

The gender-related development index

The GDI uses the same variables as the HDI. The difference is that the GDI adjusts the average achievement of each country in life expectancy, educational attainment and income in accordance with the disparity in achievement between women and men. (For a detailed explanation of the GDI methodology see technical note 1 in *Human Development Report 1995.*) For this gender-sensitive adjustment we use a weighting formula that expresses a moderate aversion to inequality, setting the weighting parameter, ϵ, equal to 2. This is the harmonic mean of the male and female values.

The GDI also adjusts the maximum and minimum values for life expectancy, to account for the fact that women tend to live longer than men. For women the maximum value is 87.5 years and the minimum value 27.5 years; for men the corresponding values are 82.5 and 22.5 years.

Calculating the index for income is fairly complex. Values of real per capita GDP (PPP$) for women and men are calculated from the female share (s_f) and male share (s_m) of earned income. These shares, in turn, are estimated from the ratio of the female wage (w_f) to the male wage (w_m) and the percentage shares of women (ea_f) and men (ea_m) in the economically active population. When data on the wage ratio are not available, a value of 75%, the weighted mean of the wage ratios for all countries with wage data, is used. The estimates of female and male per capita income (PPP$) are treated in the same way as income is treated in the HDI and then used to compute the equally distributed income index.

$$\text{Female share of the wage bill} = \frac{(w_f/w_m) \times ea_f}{[(w_f/w_m) \times ea_f] + ea_m}$$

Assuming that the female share of earned income is exactly equal to the female share of the wage bill,

$$s_f = \frac{(w_f/w_m) \times ea_f}{[(w_f/w_m) \times ea_f] + ea_m}$$

If it is now assumed that the total GDP (PPP$) of a country ($Y$) is also divided between women and men according to s_f, the total GDP (PPP$) going to women is given by ($s_f \times Y$) and the total GDP (PPP$) to men by $[Y - (s_f \times Y)]$.

Per capita GDP (PPP$) of women is $y_f = s_f \times Y/N_f$, where N_f is the total female population.

Per capita GDP (PPP$) of men is $y_m = [Y - (s_f \times Y)]/N_m$, where N_m is the total male population.

Treating income the same way as in the construction of the HDI, the adjusted income for women, $W(y_f)$, is given by:

$$W(y_f) = \frac{\log y_f - \log y_{\min}}{\log y_{\max} - \log y_{\min}}$$

The adjusted income for men, $W(y_m)$, is given by:

$$W(y_m) = \frac{\log y_m - \log y_{\min}}{\log y_{\max} - \log y_{\min}}$$

The equally distributed income index is given by:

{[female population share × (adjusted female per capita PPP$ GDP)$^{-1}$]
+ [male population share × (adjusted male per capita PPP$ GDP)$^{-1}$]}$^{-1}$

The indices for life expectancy, educational attainment and income are added together with equal weight to derive the final GDI value.

Illustration of the GDI methodology
We choose Cameroon to illustrate the steps for calculating the gender-related development index. The parameter of inequality aversion, ϵ, equals 2. (Any discrepancies in results are due to numbers' being rounded up.)

Population (millions)
Total   13.924
Females   7.009
Males   6.915

Percentage share of population
Females   50.3
Males   49.7

Step one
Computing the equally distributed life expectancy index

Life expectancy at birth (years)
Females   56.0
Males   53.4

Life expectancy index
Females $(56.0 - 27.5)/60 = 0.476$
Males $(53.4 - 22.5)/60 = 0.516$

Equally distributed life expectancy index
{[female population share × (female life expectancy index)$^{-1}$] + [male population share × (male life expectancy index)$^{-1}$]}$^{-1}$
$[0.503(0.476)^{-1} + 0.497(0.516)^{-1}]^{-1} = 0.495$

Step two
Computing the equally distributed educational attainment index

Adult literacy rate (percent)
Females   64.6
Males   79.0

Adult literacy index
Females $(64.6 - 0)/100 = 0.646$
Males $(79.0 - 0)/100 = 0.790$

Combined gross enrolment ratio (percent)
Females   39.2
Males   47.6

Combined gross enrolment index
Females $(39.2 - 0)/100 = 0.392$
Males $(47.6 - 0)/100 = 0.476$

Educational attainment index
2/3(adult literacy index) + 1/3(combined gross enrolment index)
Females   2/3(0.646) + 1/3(0.392) = 0.561
Males   2/3(0.790) + 1/3(0.476) = 0.685

Equally distributed educational attainment index
{[female population share × (educational attainment index)$^{-1}$] + [male population share × (educational attainment index)$^{-1}$]}$^{-1}$
$[0.503(0.561)^{-1} + 0.497(0.685)^{-1}]^{-1} = 0.616$

Step three
Computing the equally distributed income index

Percentage share of the economically active population
Females (ea_f)   38.3
Males (ea_m)   61.7

*Ratio of female non-agricultural wage
to male non-agricultural wage (w_f/w_m): 0.750*

GDP per capita: $1,890 (PPP$)

Total GDP (PPP$): $1,890 × 13.924 million = $26,316 million (PPP$)

$$s_f = \frac{0.750 \times 0.383}{(0.750 \times 0.383) + 0.617}$$

$$= \frac{0.287}{0.287 + 0.617}$$

$$= 0.318$$

Female total GDP (PPP$) = 0.318 × $26,316 million (PPP$) = $8,368 million (PPP$)
Male total GDP (PPP$) = $26,316 million (PPP$) − $8,368 million (PPP$)
= $17,948 million (PPP$)

Per capita female GDP (PPP$) = $8,368 million/7.009 million = $1,194 (PPP$)
Per capita male GDP (PPP$) = $17,948 million/6.915 million = $2,596 (PPP$)

$W(y_f)$ = [log (1,194) − log (100)]/[log (40,000) − log (100)]
= (3.076 − 2.000)/(4.602 − 2.000)
= 1.076/2.602
= 0.414

$W(y_m)$ = [log (2,596) − log (100)]/[log (40,000) − log (100)]
= (3.415 − 2.000)/(4.602 − 2.000)
= 1.415/2.602
= 0.544

Equally distributed income index
({female population share × $[W(y_f)]^{-1}$} + {male population share × $[W(y_m)]^{-1}$})$^{-1}$
$[0.503 \times (0.414)^{-1} + 0.497 \times (0.544)^{-1}]^{-1}$
$= [0.503 \times 2.415 + 0.497 \times 1.838]^{-1}$
$= [2.128]^{-1}$
$= 0.469$

Step four
Computing the GDI
1/3(0.495 + 0.616 + 0.469) = 0.527

The gender empowerment measure
The GEM uses variables constructed explicitly to measure the relative empowerment of women and men in political and economic spheres of activity.

The first two variables are chosen to reflect economic participation and decision-making power: women's and men's percentage shares of administrative and managerial positions and their percentage shares of professional and technical jobs. These are broad, loosely defined occupational categories. Because the relevant population for each is different, we calculate a separate index for each and then add the two together.

The third variable, women's and men's percentage shares of parliamentary seats, is chosen to reflect political participation and decision-making power.

For all three of these variables we use the methodology of population-weighted $(1 - \epsilon)$ averaging to derive an "equally distributed equivalent percentage" (EDEP) for both sexes taken together. Each variable is indexed by dividing the EDEP by 50%.

An income variable is used to reflect power over economic resources. It is calculated in the same way as for the GDI except that unadjusted rather than adjusted real GDP per capita is used.

The three indices—for economic participation and decision-making, political participation and decision-making, and power over economic resources—are added together to derive the final GEM value.

Illustration of the GEM methodology

We choose Algeria to illustrate the steps in calculating the GEM. The parameter of inequality aversion, ϵ, equals 2. (Any discrepancies in results are due to numbers' being rounded up.)

Population (millions)
Total   29.394
Females   14.518
Males   14.876

Percentage share of population
Females   49.39
Males   50.61

STEP ONE
Calculating indices for parliamentary representation and administrative and managerial, and professional and technical, positions

Percentage share of parliamentary representation
Females   3.82
Males   96.18

Percentage share of administrative and managerial positions
Females   5.9
Males   94.1

Percentage share of professional and technical positions
Females   27.6
Males   72.4

Calculating the EDEP for parliamentary representation
$[0.494(3.82)^{-1} + 0.506(96.18)^{-1}]^{-1} = 7.4$
Calculating the EDEP for administrative and managerial positions
$[0.494(5.9)^{-1} + 0.506(94.1)^{-1}]^{-1} = 11.2$
Calculating the EDEP for professional and technical positions
$[0.494(27.6)^{-1} + 0.506(72.4)^{-1}]^{-1} = 40.2$
Indexing parliamentary representation
$7.4/50 = 0.149$
Indexing administrative and managerial positions
$11.2/50 = 0.224$
Indexing professional and technical positions
$40.2/50 = 0.804$
Combining the indices for administrative and managerial, and professional and technical, positions
$(0.224 + 0.804)/2 = 0.514$

STEP TWO
Calculating the index for female and male income

Percentage share of the economically active population
Females (ea_f) 26.2
Males (ea_m) 73.8

Ratio of female non-agricultural wage to male non-agricultural wage (w_f/w_m): 0.750

Per capita GDP (PPP$): $4,460 (PPP$)

Total GDP (PPP$): $4,460 \times 29.394$ million = $131,097 million (PPP$)

$$s_f = \frac{0.750 \times 0.262}{(0.750 \times 0.262) + 0.738}$$

$$= \frac{0.197}{0.197 + 0.738}$$

$$= 0.210$$

Female total GDP (PPP$) = $0.210 \times \$131,097$ million (PPP$) = $27,530 million (PPP$)
Male total GDP (PPP$) = $131,097 million (PPP$) − $27,530 million (PPP$)
      = $103,567 million (PPP$)
Per capita female GDP (PPP$) = $27,530 million/14.518 million = $1,896 (PPP$)
Per capita male GDP (PPP$) = $103,567 million/14.876 million = $6,962 (PPP$)

$$\text{Index of female per capita GDP} = \frac{1,896 - 100}{40,000 - 100}$$

$$= \frac{1,796}{39,900}$$

$$= 0.045$$

$$\text{Index of male per capita GDP} = \frac{6,962 - 100}{40,000 - 100}$$

$$= \frac{6,862}{39,900}$$

$$= 0.172$$

Calculating the equally distributed income index
$[0.494(0.045)^{-1} + 0.506(0.172)^{-1}]^{-1} = 0.072$

STEP THREE
Computing the GEM
$1/3(0.149 + 0.514 + 0.072)$
$= [1/3(0.735)]$
$= 0.245$

The human poverty index

Computing the human poverty index for developing countries

The human poverty index for developing countries (HPI-1) concentrates on deprivations in three essential dimensions of human life already reflected in the HDI—longevity, knowledge and a decent standard of living. The first deprivation relates to survival—vulnerability to death at a relatively early age. The second relates to knowledge—being excluded from the world of reading and communication. The third relates to a decent living standard in terms of overall economic provisioning.

In constructing the HPI-1, the deprivation in longevity is represented by the percentage of people not expected to survive to age 40 (P_1), and the deprivation in knowledge by the percentage of adults who are illiterate (P_2). The deprivation in living standard is represented by a composite (P_3) of three variables—the percentage of people without access to safe water (P_{31}), the percentage of people without access to health services (P_{32}) and the percentage of moderately and severely underweight children under five (P_{33}).

The composite variable P_3 is constructed by taking a simple average of the three variables P_{31}, P_{32} and P_{33}. Thus

$$P_3 = \frac{(P_{31} + P_{32} + P_{33})}{3}$$

Following technical note 1 in *Human Development Report 1997,* the formula for the HPI-1 is given by:

$$HPI\text{-}1 = [1/3(P_1^3 + P_2^3 + P_3^3)]^{1/3}$$

As an example, we compute the HPI-1 for Panama.

Country	P_1 (%)	P_2 (%)	P_{31} (%)	P_{32} (%)	P_{33} (%)
Panama	6.4	8.9	7.0	18.0	7.0

STEP ONE
Calculating P_3

$$P_3 = \frac{7 + 18 + 7}{3} = \frac{32}{3} = 10.7$$

STEP TWO
Constructing the HPI-1

$$
\begin{aligned}
HPI\text{-}1 &= [1/3(6.4^3 + 8.9^3 + 10.7^3)]^{1/3} \\
&= [1/3(262.144 + 704.97 + 1,225.04)]^{1/3} \\
&= [1/3(2,192.15)]^{1/3} \\
&= 730.72^{1/3} \\
&= 9.0
\end{aligned}
$$

Computing the human poverty index for industrialized countries

The human poverty index for industrialized countries (HPI-2) concentrates on deprivations in four dimensions of human life, quite similar to those reflected in the HDI—longevity, knowledge, a decent standard of living and social exclusion. The first deprivation relates to survival—vulnerability to death at a relatively early age. The second relates to knowledge—being deprived of the world of reading and communication. The third relates to a decent standard of living in terms of overall economic provisioning. And the fourth relates to non-participation or exclusion.

In constructing the HPI-2, the deprivation in longevity is represented by the percentage of people not expected to survive to age 60 (P_1), and the deprivation in knowledge by the percentage of people who are functionally illiterate as defined by the OECD (P_2). The deprivation in standard of living is represented by the percentage of people living below the income poverty line, set at 50% of the median dispos-

able personal income (P_3). And the fourth deprivation, in non-participation or exclusion, is measured by the rate of long-term (12 months or more) unemployment (P_4) of the labour force.

Following technical note 1 in *Human Development Report 1997,* the formula for the HPI-2 is given by:

$$HPI\text{-}2 = [1/4(P_1^3 + P_2^3 + P_3^3 + P_4^3)]^{1/3}$$

As an example, we compute the HPI-2 for the United States.

Country	P_1 (%)	P_2 (%)	P_3 (%)	P_4 (%)
United States	12.6	20.7	19.1	0.5

Constructing the HPI-2

$$
\begin{aligned}
HPI\text{-}2 &= [1/4(12.6^3 + 20.7^3 + 19.1^3 + 0.5^3)]^{1/3} \\
&= [1/4(2,000.4 + 8,869.7 + 6,967.9 + 0.125)]^{1/3} \\
&= [1/4(17,838.1)]^{1/3} \\
&= 4,459.5^{1/3} \\
&= 16.5
\end{aligned}
$$

HDI rank	Human development index (HDI) value			Difference in rank between 1998 and 1999 Reports [d]	Rank changes due to revised data [a]				Rank changes due to refined methodology
	1998 Report		1999 Report [c]		Life expectancy	Adult literacy	Gross enrolment	Income (PPP$)	
	New formula	Old formula [b]							
1 Canada	0.929	0.960	0.932	0	0	0	0	0	0
2 Norway	0.916	0.943	0.927	1	1	0	0	0	3
3 United States	0.923	0.943	0.927	1	1	0	-9	0	9
4 Japan	0.918	0.940	0.924	4	0	0	0	0	4
5 Belgium	..	0.933	0.923	7	-1	0	7	0	1
6 Sweden	0.917	0.936	0.923	4	0	0	8	0	-4
7 Australia	0.919	0.932	0.922	8	-1	0	13	0	-4
8 Netherlands	0.917	0.941	0.921	-1	2	0	1	0	-4
9 Iceland	0.908	0.942	0.919	-4	-2	0	-3	-1	2
10 United Kingdom	0.913	0.932	0.918	4	0	0	7	0	-3
11 France	0.913	0.946	0.918	-9	-4	0	-3	0	-2
12 Switzerland	..	0.930	0.914	4	1	0	-1	0	4
13 Finland	0.905	0.942	0.913	-7	2	0	-7	1	-3
14 Germany	..	0.925	0.906	5	0	0	4	0	1
15 Denmark	0.900	0.928	0.905	3	0	0	-2	0	5
16 Austria	0.901	0.933	0.904	-3	1	0	-6	0	2
17 Luxembourg	..	0.900	0.902	9	0	0	2	-1	8
18 New Zealand	0.898	0.939	0.901	-9	0	0	-4	0	-5
19 Italy	0.892	0.922	0.900	2	0	0	4	0	-2
20 Ireland	0.890	0.930	0.900	-3	0	0	-2	0	-1
21 Spain	0.889	0.935	0.894	-10	0	0	-3	0	-7
22 Singapore	0.873	0.896	0.888	6	-2	1	-1	0	8
23 Israel	..	0.913	0.883	-1	-1	0	2	-1	-1
24 Hong Kong, China (SAR)	0.875	0.909	0.880	1	0	0	-3	-1	5
25 Brunei Darussalam	..	0.889	0.878	10	-2	4	-4	-1	13
26 Cyprus	..	0.913	0.870	-3	1	0	-1	0	-3
27 Greece	0.859	0.924	0.867	-7	0	0	-2	1	-6
28 Portugal	0.850	0.892	0.858	5	1	2	4	0	-2
29 Barbados	..	0.909	0.857	-5	0	0	-1	1	-5
30 Korea, Rep. of	0.835	0.894	0.852	0	2	-3	2	2	-3
31 Bahamas	..	0.893	0.851	1	3	-8	1	0	5
32 Malta	..	0.899	0.850	-5	0	0	0	-1	-4
33 Slovenia	..	0.887	0.845	4	4	5	-3	0	-2
34 Chile	..	0.893	0.844	-3	-3	0	2	0	-2
35 Kuwait	..	0.848	0.833	19	1	2	0	2	14
36 Czech Republic	..	0.884	0.833	3	4	-1	3	0	-3
37 Bahrain	..	0.872	0.832	6	0	0	-2	1	7
38 Antigua and Barbuda	..	0.895	0.828	-9	-2	-1	-2	-1	-3
39 Argentina	0.821	0.888	0.827	-3	-2	0	0	1	-2
40 Uruguay	0.816	0.885	0.826	-2	2	1	0	1	-6
41 Qatar	..	0.840	0.814	16	1	0	-1	5	11
42 Slovakia	0.802	0.875	0.813	0	3	0	0	0	-3
43 United Arab Emirates	0.804	0.855	0.812	5	-2	-4	0	3	8
44 Poland	0.792	0.851	0.802	8	3	0	-1	10	-4
45 Costa Rica	0.800	0.889	0.801	-11	-6	0	-2	1	-4
46 Trinidad and Tobago	0.792	0.880	0.797	-6	-2	0	1	-1	-4
47 Hungary	..	0.857	0.795	0	1	0	3	0	-4
48 Venezuela	0.787	0.860	0.792	-2	-1	0	0	1	-2
49 Panama	..	0.868	0.791	-4	0	0	-1	1	-4
50 Mexico	..	0.855	0.786	-1	-2	1	1	2	-3

HDI rank	Human development index (HDI) value			Difference in rank between 1998 and 1999 Reports [d]	Rank changes due to revised data [a]				Rank changes due to refined methodology
	1998 Report		1999 Report [c]		Life expectancy	Adult literacy	Gross enrolment	Income (PPP$)	
	New formula	Old formula [b]							
51 Saint Kitts and Nevis	..	0.854	0.781	1	2	0	0	0	-3
52 Grenada	..	0.851	0.777	-1	-1	-3	0	-7	10
53 Dominica	..	0.079	0.770	12	0	0	1	30	17
54 Estonia	0.761	0.758	0.773	22	-1	0	1	17	5
55 Croatia	..	0.759	0.773	20	0	-1	2	15	8
56 Malaysia	0.755	0.834	0.768	4	2	1	1	3	-3
57 Colombia	..	0.850	0.768	-4	-2	2	1	2	-7
58 Cuba	..	0.729	0.765	26	-2	0	1	1	26
59 Mauritius	0.752	0.833	0.764	2	1	1	-1	4	-3
60 Belarus	0.757	0.783	0.763	8	-2	-1	0	5	6
61 Fiji	0.757	0.869	0.763	-17	0	0	0	-32	15
62 Lithuania	0.752	0.750	0.761	16	-4	1	2	6	11
63 Bulgaria	0.767	0.789	0.758	4	0	-1	2	-13	16
64 Suriname	..	0.796	0.757	1	-1	-1	0	2	1
65 Libyan Arab Jamahiriya	..	0.806	0.756	-1	5	1	-1	5	-11
66 Seychelles	..	0.845	0.755	-10	-1	-5	0	4	-8
67 Thailand	0.746	0.838	0.753	-8	-2	1	2	3	-12
68 Romania	0.740	0.767	0.752	6	1	-2	2	-2	7
69 Lebanon	..	0.796	0.749	-3	1	-5	0	13	-12
70 Samoa (Western)	..	0.694	0.747	23	4	0	-2	6	15
71 Russian Federation	0.747	0.769	0.747	1	1	-1	-2	-3	6
72 Ecuador	0.740	0.767	0.747	1	-1	0	-1	4	-1
73 Macedonia, TFYR	..	0.749	0.746	6	1	-1	2	-12	16
74 Latvia	0.735	0.704	0.744	17	0	0	1	7	9
75 Saint Vincent and the Grenadines	..	0.845	0.744	-20	1	2	-1	-27	5
76 Kazakhstan	..	0.695	0.740	16	0	0	-1	6	11
77 Philippines	0.728	0.677	0.740	20	2	0	0	7	11
78 Saudi Arabia	0.733	0.778	0.740	-8	1	4	0	1	-14
79 Brazil	0.728	0.809	0.739	-17	-1	-1	1	3	-19
80 Peru	0.731	0.729	0.739	5	0	0	-1	12	-6
81 Saint Lucia	..	0.839	0.737	-23	-4	1	0	-6	-14
82 Jamaica	..	0.735	0.734	1	0	0	-1	-6	8
83 Belize	..	0.807	0.732	-20	-1	1	-1	-18	-1
84 Paraguay	0.724	0.707	0.730	6	0	0	1	3	2
85 Georgia	..	0.633	0.729	22	0	-1	1	4	18
86 Turkey	..	0.782	0.728	-17	1	-1	0	8	-25
87 Armenia	..	0.674	0.728	11	0	0	-3	3	11
88 Dominican Republic	0.713	0.720	0.726	-1	0	0	-1	10	-10
89 Oman	..	0.771	0.725	-18	-1	6	-2	-1	-20
90 Sri Lanka	0.714	0.716	0.721	-1	1	0	1	-14	11
91 Ukraine	..	0.665	0.721	10	1	0	0	-4	13
92 Uzbekistan	..	0.659	0.720	11	0	-1	1	3	8
93 Maldives	..	0.683	0.716	1	1	0	1	1	-2
94 Jordan	..	0.729	0.715	-8	2	0	1	-9	-2
95 Iran, Islamic Rep. of	..	0.758	0.715	-18	1	3	1	4	-27
96 Turkmenistan	..	0.660	0.712	6	0	-1	-1	-1	9
97 Kyrgyzstan	..	0.633	0.702	11	2	-1	-1	2	9
98 China	0.680	0.650	0.701	7	0	0	0	6	1
99 Guyana	..	0.670	0.701	0	2	0	-2	2	-2
100 Albania	0.693	0.656	0.699	4	5	-2	3	-10	8

HDI rank	Human development index (HDI) value			Difference in rank between 1998 and 1999 Reports [d]	Rank changes due to revised data [a]				Rank changes due to refined methodology
	1998 Report		1999 Report [c]		Life expectancy	Adult literacy	Gross enrolment	Income (PPP$)	
	New formula	Old formula [b]							
101 South Africa	0.704	0.717	0.695	-13	-13	2	3	24	-29
102 Tunisia	0.676	0.744	0.695	-20	1	1	-1	0	-21
103 Azerbaijan	0.689	0.623	0.695	6	-1	0	-2	-1	10
104 Moldova, Rep. of	..	0.610	0.683	8	0	-3	2	-3	12
105 Indonesia	0.665	0.679	0.681	-10	1	0	0	-8	-3
106 Cape Verde	0.660	0.591	0.677	10	5	-2	3	3	1
107 El Salvador	..	0.604	0.674	6	-2	4	0	1	3
108 Tajikistan	..	0.575	0.665	9	0	0	0	-1	10
109 Algeria	0.655	0.746	0.665	-28	1	-2	0	-13	-14
110 Viet Nam	..	0.560	0.664	11	2	-4	5	1	7
111 Syrian Arab Republic	..	0.749	0.663	-31	1	1	-2	-29	-2
112 Bolivia	0.642	0.593	0.652	3	-1	0	0	2	2
113 Swaziland	0.634	0.597	0.644	1	1	-1	-1	3	-1
114 Honduras	0.635	0.573	0.641	4	0	0	-2	0	6
115 Namibia	0.656	0.644	0.638	-9	-2	2	0	10	-19
116 Vanuatu	..	0.559	0.627	7	3	0	-3	8	-1
117 Guatemala	0.617	0.615	0.624	-7	-4	2	-2	3	-6
118 Solomon Islands	..	0.560	0.623	4	1	0	-1	1	3
119 Mongolia	..	0.669	0.618	-19	4	0	-1	-29	7
120 Egypt	0.603	0.612	0.616	-9	2	0	0	-10	-1
121 Nicaragua	..	0.547	0.616	4	0	0	0	1	3
122 Botswana	0.632	0.678	0.609	-26	-8	2	0	9	-29
123 São Tomé and Principe	..	0.563	0.609	-3	-6	0	0	1	2
124 Gabon	..	0.568	0.607	-5	-5	2	1	27	-30
125 Iraq	..	0.538	0.586	1	3	-1	0	1	-2
126 Morocco	0.569	0.557	0.582	-2	2	3	0	-3	-4
127 Lesotho	0.582	0.469	0.582	6	-3	3	0	5	1
128 Myanmar	..	0.481	0.580	2	0	-2	3	-1	2
129 Papua New Guinea	..	0.507	0.570	-1	1	0	0	0	-2
130 Zimbabwe	0.570	0.507	0.560	-1	-2	0	0	2	-1
131 Equatorial Guinea	..	0.465	0.549	3	1	-2	0	4	0
132 India	..	0.451	0.545	6	1	0	0	5	0
133 Ghana	0.534	0.473	0.544	-1	3	-1	-2	-1	0
134 Cameroon	0.532	0.481	0.536	-3	-1	3	-1	-4	0
135 Congo	0.527	0.519	0.533	-8	-1	0	0	-7	0
136 Kenya	0.528	0.463	0.519	0	-2	0	0	2	0
137 Cambodia	..	0.422	0.514	2	0	0	0	2	0
138 Pakistan	0.495	0.453	0.508	-1	2	-1	0	-2	0
139 Comoros	0.504	0.411	0.506	1	0	0	0	1	0
140 Lao People's Dem. Rep.	0.475	0.465	0.491	-5	1	0	0	-6	0
141 Congo, Dem. Rep. of the	..	0.383	0.479	1	-2	-3	-1	6	1
142 Sudan	..	0.343	0.475	14	5	6	0	4	-1
143 Togo	0.458	0.380	0.469	0	-3	0	0	3	0
144 Nepal	0.447	0.351	0.463	7	1	7	1	-2	0
145 Bhutan	..	0.347	0.459	9	13	0	-2	-2	0
146 Nigeria	0.446	0.391	0.456	-5	-1	0	1	-5	0
147 Madagascar	..	0.348	0.453	5	-1	-1	2	4	1
148 Yemen	..	0.356	0.449	2	1	1	1	-2	1
149 Mauritania	0.435	0.361	0.447	-1	1	-2	-1	3	-2
150 Bangladesh	0.427	0.371	0.440	-4	3	-1	0	-6	0

TN1 Changes in HDI values and ranks

HDI rank	Human development index (HDI) value — 1998 Report — New formula	Old formula [b]	1999 Report [c]	Difference in rank between 1998 and 1999 Reports [d]	Rank changes due to revised data [a] — Life expectancy	Adult literacy	Gross enrolment	Income (PPP$)	Rank changes due to refined methodology
151 Zambia	0.430	0.378	0.431	-6	-3	-4	-1	0	2
152 Haiti	0.426	0.340	0.430	6	1	-1	-1	5	2
153 Senegal	0.412	0.342	0.426	4	5	1	0	0	-2
154 Côte d'Ivoire	0.414	0.368	0.422	-7	-8	-1	1	3	-2
155 Benin	0.407	0.378	0.421	-11	-1	-5	1	-7	1
156 Tanzania	..	0.358	0.421	-7	-5	1	-1	-1	-1
157 Djibouti	..	0.324	0.412	4	2	0	1	1	0
158 Uganda	0.386	0.340	0.404	1	1	1	0	-2	1
159 Malawi	0.397	0.334	0.399	1	-1	1	0	0	1
160 Angola	..	0.344	0.398	-5	-1	1	-1	-5	1
161 Guinea	0.383	0.277	0.398	5	1	2	1	4	-3
162 Chad	0.380	0.318	0.393	0	0	1	0	-2	1
163 Gambia	0.381	0.291	0.391	1	0	0	-1	3	-1
164 Rwanda	0.334	–	0.379	–	–	–	–	–	–
165 Central African Republic	0.378	0.347	0.378	-11	-7	-2	-2	0	0
166 Mali	0.356	0.236	0.375	5	2	3	2	-2	0
167 Eritrea	..	0.275	0.346	1	1	0	0	0	0
168 Guinea-Bissau	0.331	0.295	0.343	-4	0	-5	0	0	1
169 Mozambique	0.340	0.281	0.341	-3	-2	0	0	0	-1
170 Burundi	0.321	0.241	0.324	0	0	0	0	0	0
171 Burkina Faso	0.297	0.219	0.304	1	-1	0	0	1	1
172 Ethiopia	0.287	0.252	0.298	-3	-2	0	0	0	-1
173 Niger	0.291	0.207	0.298	0	1	0	0	-1	0
174 Sierra Leone	..	0.185	0.254	0	0	0	0	0	0

a. See the note on statistics for an explanation of the data revisions.
b. Ranks have been recalculated to exclude the Democratic People's Republic of Korea, since that country is not included in the 1997 HDI ranking (published in this year's Report).
c. Ranks have been recalculated to exclude Rwanda, since that country is not included in the 1995 HDI ranking (published in last year's Report).
d. A positive figure indicates that the rank has improved, a negative the opposite.
Source: Human Development Report Office.

HDI rank	Life expectancy at birth (years)		Infant mortality rate (per 1,000 live births)		Under-five mortality rate (per 1,000 live births)		People not expected to survive to age 60 (as % of total population)	Maternal mortality rate (per 100,000 live births)
	1970	1997	1970	1997	1970	1997	1997	1990
High human development	**70.6**	**77.0**	**25**	**7**	**32**	**8**	**11**	**26**
1 Canada	72.6	79.0	19	6	23	7	9	6
2 Norway	74.1	78.1	13	4	15	4	9	6
3 United States	70.7	76.7	20	7	26	8	13	12
4 Japan	72.2	80.0	14	4	21	6	8	18
5 Belgium	71.1	77.2	21	6	29	7	10	10
6 Sweden	74.4	78.5	11	4	15	4	9	7
7 Australia	71.1	78.2	17	5	20	6	9	9
8 Netherlands	73.7	77.9	13	5	15	6	9	12
9 Iceland	73.7	79.0	13	5	14	5	8	..
10 United Kingdom	71.7	77.2	18	6	23	7	10	9
11 France	71.9	78.1	18	5	24	5	11	15
12 Switzerland	72.9	78.6	15	5	18	5	10	6
13 Finland	70.1	76.8	13	4	16	4	11	11
14 Germany	70.8	77.2	22	5	26	5	11	22
15 Denmark	73.2	75.7	14	6	19	6	13	9
16 Austria	70.1	77.0	26	5	33	5	11	10
17 Luxembourg	70.3	76.7	19	5	26	7	11	..
18 New Zealand	71.4	76.9	17	7	20	7	11	25
19 Italy	71.5	78.2	30	5	33	6	9	12
20 Ireland	71.2	76.3	20	6	27	7	10	10
21 Spain	72.2	78.0	27	5	34	5	10	7
22 Singapore	68.8	77.1	22	4	27	4	11	10
23 Israel	71.2	77.8	24	6	27	6	9	7
24 Hong Kong, China (SAR)	71.1	78.5	..	..	..	..	9	7
25 Brunei Darussalam	66.7	75.5	58	8	78	10	11	..
26 Cyprus	70.8	77.8	29	8	33	9	10	..
27 Greece	71.7	78.1	38	7	54	8	9	10
28 Portugal	67.1	75.3	53	7	62	8	13	15
29 Barbados	68.5	76.4	40	11	54	12	12	..
30 Korea, Rep. of	60.1	72.4	43	6	54	6	17	130
31 Bahamas	66.2	73.8	38	18	49	21	18	..
32 Malta	69.9	77.2	25	9	32	10	8	..
33 Slovenia	69.4	74.4	25	5	29	6	15	13
34 Chile	61.9	74.9	77	11	96	13	14	65
35 Kuwait	65.9	75.9	49	12	59	13	10	29
36 Czech Republic	69.9	73.9	21	6	24	7	14	15
37 Bahrain	61.8	72.9	67	18	93	22	15	..
38 Antigua and Barbuda	..	..	..	17	..	21	..	..
39 Argentina	66.3	72.9	59	21	71	24	17	100
40 Uruguay	68.5	73.9	48	18	57	21	16	85
41 Qatar	60.9	71.7	71	16	93	20	16	..
42 Slovakia	70.2	73.0	25	10	29	11	16	..
43 United Arab Emirates	60.7	74.8	61	9	83	10	11	26
44 Poland	70.2	72.5	32	10	36	11	17	19
45 Costa Rica	66.7	76.0	58	12	77	14	12	60
Medium human development	**57.3**	**66.6**	**101**	**51**	**152**	**72**	**25**	**321**
46 Trinidad and Tobago	65.5	73.8	49	15	57	17	15	90
47 Hungary	69.3	70.9	36	10	39	11	22	30
48 Venezuela	64.7	72.4	47	21	61	25	17	120
49 Panama	65.1	73.6	48	18	71	20	15	55
50 Mexico	61.1	72.2	79	29	110	35	19	110

HDI rank	Life expectancy at birth (years)		Infant mortality rate (per 1,000 live births)		Under-five mortality rate (per 1,000 live births)		People not expected to survive to age 60 (as % of total population) 1997	Maternal mortality rate (per 100,000 live births) 1990
	1970	1997	1970	1997	1970	1997		
51 Saint Kitts and Nevis	..	..	..	30	..	37	..	..
52 Grenada	..	..	..	24	..	29	..	..
53 Dominica	..	..	..	17	..	20	..	..
54 Estonia	70.5	68.7	22	13	27	14	24	41
55 Croatia	69.1	72.6	34	8	42	9	16	..
56 Malaysia	61.3	72.0	46	10	63	11	16	80
57 Colombia	60.8	70.4	70	25	113	30	21	100
58 Cuba	69.5	75.7	34	7	43	8	13	95
59 Mauritius	62.2	71.4	64	20	86	23	19	120
60 Belarus	71.0	68.0	23	14	28	18	26	37
61 Fiji	63.9	72.7	50	20	61	24	15	..
62 Lithuania	71.4	69.9	25	13	30	15	23	36
63 Bulgaria	71.1	71.1	28	16	32	19	18	27
64 Suriname	63.3	70.1	52	24	65	30	20	..
65 Libyan Arab Jamahiriya	51.5	70.0	105	22	160	25	20	220
66 Seychelles	..	..	..	14	..	18	..	..
67 Thailand	58.3	68.8	74	31	102	38	26	200
68 Romania	68.5	69.9	46	22	57	26	21	130
69 Lebanon	64.1	69.9	40	30	50	37	19	300
70 Samoa (Western)	56.7	71.3	..	..	..	..	18	..
71 Russian Federation	68.7	66.6	30	20	38	25	30	75
72 Ecuador	57.7	69.5	94	30	140	39	22	150
73 Macedonia, TFYR	66.3	73.1	85	20	120	23	14	..
74 Latvia	70.3	68.4	22	16	27	20	25	40
75 Saint Vincent and the Grenadines	..	..	..	18	..	21	..	..
76 Kazakhstan	63.7	67.6	50	37	66	44	26	80
77 Philippines	56.9	68.3	60	32	90	41	22	280
78 Saudi Arabia	51.8	71.4	118	24	185	28	17	130
79 Brazil	58.7	66.8	95	37	135	44	27	220
80 Peru	53.5	68.3	115	44	178	56	23	280
81 Saint Lucia	..	..	..	24		29	..	..
82 Jamaica	68.3	74.8	47	10	62	11	13	120
83 Belize	66.4	74.7	56	35	77	43	14	..
84 Paraguay	65.4	69.6	57	27	76	33	20	160
85 Georgia	68.4	72.7	37	23	49	29	18	33
86 Turkey	56.4	69.0	150	40	201	45	20	180
87 Armenia	71.9	70.5	24	25	30	30	20	50
88 Dominican Republic	58.4	70.6	91	44	128	53	19	110
89 Oman	46.9	70.9	126	15	200	18	18	190
90 Sri Lanka	64.5	73.1	65	17	100	19	15	140
91 Ukraine	70.6	68.8	23	18	29	24	24	50
92 Uzbekistan	63.5	67.5	67	46	93	60	25	55
93 Maldives	49.9	64.5	121	53	188	74	28	..
94 Jordan	54.0	70.1	77	20	107	24	20	150
95 Iran, Islamic Rep. of	54.5	69.2	133	32	208	35	21	120
96 Turkmenistan	60.0	65.4	82	57	120	78	28	55
97 Kyrgyzstan	62.4	67.6	63	38	86	48	25	110
98 China	62.0	69.8	85	38	120	47	18	95
99 Guyana	59.6	64.4	81	59	101	82	28	..
100 Albania	66.9	72.8	68	34	82	40	14	65

HDI rank	Life expectancy at birth (years)		Infant mortality rate (per 1,000 live births)		Under-five mortality rate (per 1,000 live births)		People not expected to survive to age 60 (as % of total population)	Maternal mortality rate (per 100,000 live births)
	1970	1997	1970	1997	1970	1997	1997	1990
101 South Africa	52.8	54.7	80	49	108	65	51	230
102 Tunisia	53.7	69.5	135	27	201	33	20	170
103 Azerbaijan	68.4	69.9	42	34	54	45	22	22
104 Moldova, Rep. of	64.6	67.5	48	25	63	31	26	60
105 Indonesia	47.6	65.1	104	45	172	68	27	650
106 Cape Verde	56.5	68.9	87	54	123	73	21	..
107 El Salvador	57.4	69.1	105	31	160	36	23	300
108 Tajikistan	62.7	67.2	78	56	111	76	25	130
109 Algeria	53.0	68.9	123	34	192	39	19	160
110 Viet Nam	48.9	67.4	112	32	157	43	24	160
111 Syrian Arab Republic	55.5	68.9	90	27	129	33	21	180
112 Bolivia	45.8	61.4	144	69	243	96	33	650
113 Swaziland	45.9	60.2	140	66	209	94	35	..
114 Honduras	52.4	69.4	116	36	170	45	23	220
115 Namibia	47.5	52.4	104	58	155	75	52	370
116 Vanuatu	52.5	67.4	107	39	160	50	23	..
117 Guatemala	51.9	64.0	115	43	168	55	31	200
118 Solomon Islands	60.2	71.7	71	23	99	28	16	..
119 Mongolia	52.6	65.8	105	105	150	150	26	65
120 Egypt	50.9	66.3	157	54	235	73	23	170
121 Nicaragua	53.6	67.9	107	42	168	57	24	160
122 Botswana	51.6	47.4	98	39	139	49	68	250
123 São Tomé and Principe	..	..	..	61	..	78	..	..
124 Gabon	44.0	52.4	140	85	232	145	49	500
125 Iraq	54.9	62.4	90	94	127	122	32	310
126 Morocco	51.6	66.6	120	58	187	72	23	610
127 Lesotho	48.4	56.0	125	95	190	137	43	610
128 Myanmar	48.7	60.1	122	81	179	114	33	580
129 Papua New Guinea	46.4	57.9	90	79	130	112	41	930
130 Zimbabwe	50.3	44.1	86	53	138	80	75	570
131 Equatorial Guinea	39.8	50.0	165	109	281	172	49	..
132 India	49.1	62.6	130	71	206	108	30	570
133 Ghana	49.0	60.0	111	68	186	107	35	740
134 Cameroon	44.3	54.7	127	64	215	99	46	550
135 Congo	45.7	48.6	100	81	160	108	59	890
136 Kenya	49.7	52.0	96	57	156	87	56	650
137 Cambodia	43.9	53.4	155	106	244	167	47	900
138 Pakistan	49.2	64.0	118	95	183	136	27	340
139 Comoros	47.8	58.8	159	69	215	93	37	..
Low human development	42.8	50.6	147	106	241	169	52	1,057
140 Lao People's Dem. Rep.	40.2	53.2	145	99	218	122	45	650
141 Congo, Dem. Rep. of the	45.1	50.8	147	128	245	207	52	870
142 Sudan	42.6	55.0	107	73	177	115	43	660
143 Togo	44.2	48.8	128	78	216	125	59	640
144 Nepal	42.1	57.3	156	75	234	104	39	1,500
145 Bhutan	42.2	60.7	156	87	267	121	34	1,600
146 Nigeria	42.7	50.1	120	112	201	187	52	1,000
147 Madagascar	45.0	57.5	184	96	285	158	39	490
148 Yemen	40.9	58.0	175	76	303	100	38	1,400
149 Mauritania	42.5	53.5	150	120	250	183	44	930
150 Bangladesh	44.2	58.1	148	81	239	109	38	850

. . . TO LEAD A LONG AND HEALTHY LIFE . . .

HDI rank	Life expectancy at birth (years)		Infant mortality rate (per 1,000 live births)		Under-five mortality rate (per 1,000 live births)		People not expected to survive to age 60 (as % of total population)	Maternal mortality rate (per 100,000 live births)
	1970	1997	1970	1997	1970	1997	1997	1990
151 Zambia	46.3	40.1	109	112	181	202	80	940
152 Haiti	47.4	53.7	148	92	221	132	50	1,000
153 Senegal	40.6	52.3	164	72	279	124	47	1,200
154 Côte d'Ivoire	44.2	46.7	160	90	240	150	63	810
155 Benin	42.5	53.4	149	102	252	167	46	990
156 Tanzania, U. Rep. of	45.3	47.9	129	92	218	143	61	770
157 Djibouti	40.0	50.4	160	111	241	156	49	..
158 Uganda	46.3	39.6	110	86	185	137	76	1,200
159 Malawi	40.2	39.3	189	135	330	215	73	560
160 Angola	37.0	46.5	179	170	301	292	54	1,500
161 Guinea	36.5	46.5	197	126	345	201	54	1,600
162 Chad	38.0	47.2	149	118	252	198	56	1,500
163 Gambia	36.0	47.0	183	66	319	87	54	1,100
164 Rwanda	44.4	40.5	124	105	210	170	71	1,300
165 Central African Republic	42.3	44.9	149	113	248	173	65	700
166 Mali	41.9	53.3	221	145	391	239	43	1,200
167 Eritrea	43.3	50.8	150	73	225	116	52	1,400
168 Guinea-Bissau	36.0	45.0	186	130	316	220	58	910
169 Mozambique	41.9	45.2	163	130	281	208	61	1,500
170 Burundi	43.7	42.4	135	106	228	176	68	1,300
171 Burkina Faso	39.3	44.4	163	110	278	169	64	930
172 Ethiopia	40.0	43.3	159	111	239	175	66	1,400
173 Niger	38.3	48.5	191	191	320	320	52	1,200
174 Sierra Leone	34.4	37.2	206	182	363	316	70	1,800
All developing countries	54.5	64.4	111	64	170	94	28	491
Least developed countries	43.4	51.7	149	104	242	162	50	1,041
Sub-Saharan Africa	44.1	48.9	137	105	225	169	56	979
Arab States	50.6	65.1	125	53	192	70	26	396
East Asia	62.0	70.0	83	37	118	46	18	96
East Asia (excluding China)	61.0	72.8	46	15	59	20	16	114
South-East Asia and the Pacific	51.0	65.9	97	45	149	64	26	449
South Asia	49.0	62.7	131	72	207	106	30	551
South Asia (excluding India)	48.8	63.0	132	75	208	103	30	512
Latin America and the Caribbean	60.1	69.5	86	33	124	41	22	191
Eastern Europe and the CIS	68.8	68.6	37	26	48	33	25	62
Industrialized countries	71.4	77.7	20	6	26	7	11	13
World	59.1	66.7	98	58	149	85	25	437

Source: Columns 1, 2 and 7: UN 1998h; *columns 3 and 5:* UNICEF 1999b; *columns 4 and 6:* UNICEF 1999a; *column 8:* UNICEF 1998b.

HDI rank	Infants with low birth-weight (%) 1990-97 [a]	One-year-olds fully immunized Against tuber-culosis (%) 1995-97 [a]	One-year-olds fully immunized Against measles (%) 1995-97 [a]	Oral rehydration therapy use rate (%) 1990-97 [a]	AIDS cases (per 100,000 people) 1997 [b]	Tuber-culosis cases (per 100,000 people) 1996	Malaria cases (per 100,000 people) 1995	People with disabilities (as % of total population) 1985-92 [a,c]	Pregnant women with anaemia (%) 1975-91 [a,d]	Cigarette consumption per adult (1970-72 = 100) 1990-92	Doctors (per 100,000 people) 1993 [e]	Nurses (per 100,000 people) 1993 [e]
High human development	7	91	90	..	84.0	19.6	..	9.7	..	90	244	662
1 Canada	6	..	98 [f]	..	50.4	..	..	15.5	..	65	221	958
2 Norway	4	..	93 [f]	..	13.7	5.0	..	..	..	90	..	..
3 United States	7	..	89 [f]	..	225.3	7.9	0.3	12.0	..	72	245	878
4 Japan	7	91 [f]	94	..	1.2	33.5	..	2.3	..	110	177	641
5 Belgium	6	..	64	..	23.7	13.3	3.0	..	..	75	365	..
6 Sweden	5	12	96	..	17.6	5.6	..	12.0	..	91	299	1,048
7 Australia	6	..	87	..	40.5	..	3.4	15.6	..	79	..	..
8 Netherlands	..	..	96	..	29.6	10.8	2.0	11.5	..	90	..	..
9 Iceland	..	98	98	..	15.7	4.1	..	..	..	136	..	..
10 United Kingdom	7	99	95	..	25.9	10.7	..	14.2	..	68	164	..
11 France	5	83	97	..	81.0	13.1	1.7	..	..	114	280	392
12 Switzerland	5	..	..	..	83.8	10.6	..	..	..	79	301	..
13 Finland	4	100	98	..	5.2	12.6	..	17.0	..	87	269	2,184
14 Germany	..	..	75	..	20.7	14.4	..	8.4	..	97	319	..
15 Denmark	6	..	84	..	40.1	9.2	..	12.0	..	93	283	..
16 Austria	6	..	90	..	21.7	17.1	..	22.7	..	92	327	530
17 Luxembourg	..	58	91	..	29.3	9.9	..	..	..	67	213	..
18 New Zealand	6	20 [f]	100	..	17.1	8.7	..	13.0	..	82	210	1,249
19 Italy	5	..	94	..	71.5	7.2	..	2.7	..	107	..	..
20 Ireland	4	..	..	..	17.1	11.9	..	3.5	..	..	167	..
21 Spain	4	..	90 [f]	..	123.3	21.0	..	15.0	..	122	400	..
22 Singapore	7	98	89	..	9.1	21.8	9.4	0.4	57	64	147	416
23 Israel	7	..	94	..	8.1	6.4	..	..	..	111	459	671
24 Hong Kong, China (SAR)	..	..	..	..	4.6	..	..	0.8	..	111	..	..
25 Brunei Darussalam	..	99	98	..	..	..	15.3	..	..	..	..	..
26 Cyprus	..	..	90	..	7.0 [f]	3.2	0.1	2.3	..	..	231	425
27 Greece	6	70	90	..	16.5	..	..	..	..	..	387	278
28 Portugal	5	91	94	..	48.0	53.2	..	11.0	..	140	291	304
29 Barbados	10	..	92	..	290.8	1.1	..	..	29	..	113	323
30 Korea, Rep. of	9	90	85	..	0.2	68.7	0.3	..	..	127	127	232
31 Bahamas	..	..	93	..	891.3	20.7	..	..	12	..	141	258
32 Malta	..	96	51	..	11.6	7.4	..	..	..	..	250	1,189
33 Slovenia	..	98	92	..	3.2	28.2	..	..	..	..	219	686
34 Chile	5	98	92	..	13.4	28.0	..	..	32	86	108	42
35 Kuwait	7	..	95	..	1.4	23.7	38.8	0.4	..	..	178	468
36 Czech Republic	6	97	97	..	1.1	19.1	..	..	..	..	293	944
37 Bahrain	6	..	95	39	6.4	27.4	33.7	1.0	..	..	11	289
38 Antigua and Barbuda	8	..	93	..	..	7.6	..	..	..	..	76	233
39 Argentina	7	100	92	..	29.9	38.0	3.0	..	..	89	268	54
40 Uruguay	8	99	80	..	28.7	21.6	..	..	..	104	309	61
41 Qatar	..	99	87	71	14.9	46.0	85.1	0.2	..	..	143	354
42 Slovakia	..	90	98	..	0.3	28.0	..	..	..	..	325	..
43 United Arab Emirates	6	98	35	42	..	22.4	129.0	..	..	..	168	321
44 Poland	..	94	91	..	1.5	39.7	..	9.9	..	120	..	..
45 Costa Rica	7	91	99	31	32.8	4.4	..	..	..	72	126	95
Medium human development	17	94	86	75	17.0	75.2	627.4	2.7	..	162	108	175
46 Trinidad and Tobago	10	..	88	..	199.9	16.1	2.8	1.1	..	124	90	168
47 Hungary	9	100	100	..	2.8	43.2	..	15.7	..	97	337	..
48 Venezuela	9	89	68	..	30.4	25.0	73.4	3.8	52	93	194	77
49 Panama	8	99	92	94	52.5	41.0	27.3	1.4	..	83	119	98
50 Mexico	7	99	91	81	34.3	11.7	7.9	..	..	61	107	40

. . . TO LEAD A LONG AND HEALTHY LIFE . . .

HDI rank	Infants with low birth-weight (%) 1990-97 [a]	One-year-olds fully immunized Against tuber-culosis (%) 1995-97 [a]	One-year-olds fully immunized Against measles (%) 1995-97 [a]	Oral rehydration therapy use rate (%) 1990-97 [a]	AIDS cases (per 100,000 people) 1997 [b]	Tuber-culosis cases (per 100,000 people) 1996	Malaria cases (per 100,000 people) 1995	People with disabilities (as % of total population) 1985-92 [a,c]	Pregnant women with anaemia (%) 1975-91 [a,d]	Cigarette consumption per adult (1970-72 =100) 1990-92	Doctors (per 100,000 people) 1993 [e]	Nurses (per 100,000 people) 1993 [e]
51 Saint Kitts and Nevis	9	99	97	..	..	7.6	..	..	57	..	89	590
52 Grenada	9	..	92	..	..	..	1.1	..	63	..	50	239
53 Dominica	10	100	100	..	..	14.1	..	..	28	..	46	263
54 Estonia	..	99	88	..	1.2	35.5	..	..	..	..	312	636
55 Croatia	..	98	91	5	2.6	48.4	..	..	..	..	201	470
56 Malaysia	8	100	89	..	5.3	62.8	288.1	..	36	116	43	160
57 Colombia	9	98	76	53	21.5	24.7	126.4	1.2	8	93	105	49
58 Cuba	7	99	100	..	5.4	14.3	0.2	1.7	..	85	518	752
59 Mauritius	13	84	84	..	3.8	..	..	2.6	140	..	85	241
60 Belarus	..	98	74	..	0.2	53.9	..	..	..	..	379	1,160
61 Fiji	12	95	75	..	1.0	25.7	..	0.9	40	138	38	215
62 Lithuania	..	98	96	..	0.3	70.2	..	..	..	..	399	977
63 Bulgaria	6	97	93	..	0.6	36.8	..	0.4	..	127	333	652
64 Suriname	13	..	78	..	48.3 [g]	12.9	1,609.4	..	..	161	40	227
65 Libyan Arab Jamahiriya	7	99	92	49	0.3	25.2	0.6	..	..	..	137	366
66 Seychelles	10	100	100	..	..	20.2	..	..	..	..	104	417
67 Thailand	6	98	91	95	101.1	67.4	139.8	0.7	48	130	24	99
68 Romania	7	100	97	..	22.8	106.9	..	..	..	89	176	430
69 Lebanon	10	..	89	82	3.1 [g]	27.1	0.9	..	..	..	191	122
70 Samoa (Western)	6	99	99	..	..	21.8	..	..	..	..	38	186
71 Russian Federation	6	99	91	..	0.2	75.1	..	..	..	..	380	659
72 Ecuador	13	100	75	64	5.2	54.1	155.0	..	..	134	111	34
73 Macedonia, TFYR	..	97	98	..	1.1	36.7	..	..	..	..	219	334
74 Latvia	..	100	97	..	0.8	70.5	..	..	..	..	303	628
75 Saint Vincent and the Grenadines	8	98	100	..	..	..	..	..	20	..	46	187
76 Kazakhstan	..	99	92	31	0.1	84.8	..	..	..	..	360	874
77 Philippines	9	82	72	87	..	395.3	524.8	1.1	48	88	11	43
78 Saudi Arabia	7	99	87	58	1.7	..	99.6	..	23	175	166	348
79 Brazil	8	100	100	54	69.4	54.0	350.2	1.8	..	113	134	41
80 Peru	11	98	94	55	24.5	174.3	804.5	0.2	..	85	73	49
81 Saint Lucia	8	100	95	..	..	..	..	..	22	..	35	177
82 Jamaica	10	97	88	..	86.8	4.9	0.4	..	62	61	57	69
83 Belize	4	95	98	..	88.4	24.2	4,302.5	6.6	65	..	47	76
84 Paraguay	5	87	61	33	5.6	43.3	18.1	..	..	92	67	10
85 Georgia	..	76	95	14	0.4	67.9	..	..	..	..	436	863
86 Turkey	8	73	76	100	0.4	32.4	131.7	1.4	..	108	103	151
87 Armenia	7	72	92	33	0.2 [g]	26.0	..	..	..	..	312	831
88 Dominican Republic	13	88	80	39	48.7	75.4	22.7	..	..	111	77	20
89 Oman	8	96	98	61	5.6	10.0	80.8	..	..	..	120	290
90 Sri Lanka	25	96	94	34	0.4	30.1	786.3	0.4	..	93	23	112
91 Ukraine	..	95	97	..	0.7	45.7	..	..	..	..	429	1,211
92 Uzbekistan	..	97	88	37	(.)	52.2	..	..	..	..	335	1,032
93 Maldives	13	99	96	..	1.8	82.8	6.6	..	..	..	19	13
94 Jordan	7	24	90	41	0.9	8.0	3.3	0.5	..	165	158	224
95 Iran, Islamic Rep. of	10	99	96	37	..	22.4	106.4	..	..	102	..	..
96 Turkmenistan	5	97	100	98	(.)	49.9	..	..	..	..	353	1,195
97 Kyrgyzstan	..	99	85	98	0	89.1	..	..	..	..	310	879
98 China	9	96	96	85	(.)	38.1	..	4.9	..	260	115	88
99 Guyana	15	94	82	..	99.4 [g]	37.5	7,087.5	3.9	58	341	33	88
100 Albania	7	94	95	..	0.3	23.4	..	..	..	100	141	423

HDI rank	Infants with low birth-weight (%) 1990-97[a]	One-year-olds fully immunized Against tuber-culosis (%) 1995-97[a]	Against measles (%) 1995-97[a]	Oral rehydration therapy use rate (%) 1990-97[a]	AIDS cases (per 100,000 people) 1997[b]	Tuber-culosis cases (per 100,000 people) 1996	Malaria cases (per 100,000 people) 1995	People with disabilities (as % of total population) 1985-92[a,c]	Pregnant women with anaemia (%) 1975-91[a,d]	Cigarette consumption per adult (1970-72 = 100) 1990-92	Doctors (per 100,000 people) 1993[e]	Nurses (per 100,000 people) 1993[e]
101 South Africa	..	95	76	..	29.6 [g]	240.2	24.4	..	..	128	59	175
102 Tunisia	8	93	92	41	3.6	26.3	0.5	0.9	38	127	67	283
103 Azerbaijan	6	94	97	..	0.1	32.6	37.4	..	..	..	390	1,081
104 Moldova, Rep. of	4	99	99	..	0.4	66.8	..	..	..	..	356	1,020
105 Indonesia	8	100	92	97	..	12.3	728.8	1.1	74	103	12	67
106 Cape Verde	9	80	82	83	..	..	78.3	4.3	48	..	29	57
107 El Salvador	11	93	97	69	34.1	29.1	58.1	..	14	80	91	38
108 Tajikistan	..	99	95	..	0.0	28.2	105.3	..	..	..	210	738
109 Algeria	9	94	74	98	1.1	..	0.1	..	..	168	83	..
110 Viet Nam	17	96	96	..	1.3	99.4	886.3	5.7	..	..	..	..
111 Syrian Arab Republic	7	100	93	27	0.3	35.7	4.3	1.0	..	211	109	212
112 Bolivia	12	93	98	41	2.0	134.3	617.8	2.6	..	108	51	25
113 Swaziland	10	85	82	99	270.3	433.3	..	..	..	..	..	..
114 Honduras	9	98	89	32	107.1	71.8	1,022.1	..	..	..	22	17
115 Namibia	16	65	58	100	420.6	427.9	6,671.4	..	..	..	23	81
116 Vanuatu	7	60	59	..	..	72.8	4,808.8	..	87	..	..	..
117 Guatemala	15	87	74	22	17.9	34.1	236.0	3.8	..	..	90	30
118 Solomon Islands	20	73	68	..	..	73.8	30,269.6	..	30	56	..	141
119 Mongolia	7	96	91	..	0.0	119.7	..	..	..	..	268	452
120 Egypt	10	98	92	95	0.2	19.4	0.5	1.6	75	166	202	222
121 Nicaragua	9	100	94	54	3.6	66.0	1,525.6	..	..	106	82	56
122 Botswana	11	59	79	43	351.6	439.9	1,166.6	4.0	..	..	..	..
123 São Tomé and Principe	7	70	60	74	..	..	..	..	..	..	32	..
124 Gabon	..	72	32	25	120.9 [g]	80.5	..	..	..	..	19	56
125 Iraq	15	97	98	67	0.5	141.7	436.6	0.9	..	79	51	64
126 Morocco	9	94	92	29	1.4	120.3	0.7	1.6	..	135	34	94
127 Lesotho	11	46	43	84	114.3	221.3	..	..	..	..	5	33
128 Myanmar	24	94	88	96	3.9	51.2	1,481.2	0.4	60	167	28	43
129 Papua New Guinea	23	68	41	..	6.8	115.6	21,054.0	..	..	..	18	97
130 Zimbabwe	14	82	73	60	564.4	323.5	2,987.7	..	..	61	14	164
131 Equatorial Guinea	..	99	82	..	55.0 [g]	..	3,058.2	..	..	..	21	34
132 India	33	96	81	67	..	136.9	294.7	0.2	88	236	48	..
133 Ghana	8	72	59	93	102.1 [g]	57.6	6,472.3	..	..	61	4	..
134 Cameroon	13	53	43	43	69.1	22.5	1,631.2	..	..	274	7	..
135 Congo	16	29	18	41	372.4 [g]	..	..	..	..	102	27	49
136 Kenya	16	42	32	76	263.1	125.6	15,594.3	..	40	119	15	23
137 Cambodia	..	82	68	57	..	145.2	..	..	..	130	58	136
138 Pakistan	25	90	74	97	0.1	3.1	79.9	4.9	..	102	52	32
139 Comoros	8	55	49	32	2.8	22.5	30,030.2	..	..	..	10	33
Low human development	20	70	55	66	67.5	100.7	..	..	..	152	13	45
140 Lao People's Dem. Rep.	18	58	67	32	1.3	29.4	6,356.5	..	..	118	..	..
141 Congo, Dem. Rep. of the	15	91	63	90	80.0	98.3	..	..	..	123	..	..
142 Sudan	15	79	71	31	5.9	74.7	854.9	5.3	50	88	10	70
143 Togo	20	53	38	94	185.2	39.6	..	..	47	88	6	31
144 Nepal	..	96	85	29	0.8	105.4	44.6	3.0	..	341	5	5
145 Bhutan	..	92	84	85	0	67.2	1,225.6	..	30	..	20	6
146 Nigeria	16	29	38	86	14.4	23.7	..	..	65	128	21	142
147 Madagascar	5	64	39	23	0.2	89.7	..	..	..	170	24	55
148 Yemen	19	54	43	92	0.5 [g]	91.6	..	..	..	172	26	51
149 Mauritania	11	69	20	51	6.7 [g]	..	..	..	24	..	11	27
150 Bangladesh	50	91	62	61	(.)	52.6	126.6	0.8	58	194	18	5

... TO LEAD A LONG AND HEALTHY LIFE ...

9 Health profile

HDI rank	Infants with low birth-weight (%) 1990-97 [a]	One-year-olds fully immunized Against tuber-culosis (%) 1995-97 [a]	Against measles (%) 1995-97 [a]	Oral rehydration therapy use rate (%) 1990-97 [a]	AIDS cases (per 100,000 people) 1997 [b]	Tuber-culosis cases (per 100,000 people) 1996	Malaria cases (per 100,000 people) 1995	People with disabilities (as % of total population) 1985-92 [a,c]	Pregnant women with anaemia (%) 1975-91 [a,d]	Cigarette consumption per adult (1970-72 = 100) 1990-92	Doctors (per 100,000 people) 1993 [e]	Nurses (per 100,000 people) 1993 [e]
151 Zambia	13	81	69	57	530.1	481.8	32,687.5	1.6	..	86	..	..
152 Haiti	15	40	30	31	67.2 g	86.3	301.0	..	..	..	16	13
153 Senegal	4	80	65	39	22.6 g	99.6	..	..	53	244	7	35
154 Côte d'Ivoire	12	73	68	73	265.5 g	94.8	32.7	..	34	89	..	..
155 Benin	..	89	82	33	39.8	43.3	10,570.4	..	46	102	6	33
156 Tanzania, U. Rep. of	14	82	69	50	281.4 g	144.7	7,941.6	..	..	97	4	46
157 Djibouti	11	58	47	..	263.7	503.5	550.7	..	..	..	20	..
158 Uganda	13	84	60	49	249.0	140.5	..	..	..	100	4	28
159 Malawi	20	100	87	70	505.4	209.8	..	2.9	..	165	2	6
160 Angola	19	68	78	..	11.2 g	136.0	1,380.7	..	..	100	..	..
161 Guinea	13	69	56	31	44.0	58.9	7,048.7	..	..	..	15	3
162 Chad	..	36	17	29	109.7	28.1	..	..	..	..	2	6
163 Gambia	..	99	91	99	43.1	108.0	..	..	..	..	2	25
164 Rwanda	17	79	66	47	204.9 g	64.6	..	..	..	..	..	..
165 Central African Republic	15	94	46	100	205.4	..	3.8	..	..	..	6	45
166 Mali	16	76	56	29	35.1	35.9	..	2.8	50	..	4	9
167 Eritrea	13	67	53	38	101.6	158.2	..	..	..	..	2	..
168 Guinea-Bissau	20	82	51	..	74.0 g	155.6	..	..	..	93	18	45
169 Mozambique	20	79	57	49	33.5	102.7	..	..	58	124	..	..
170 Burundi	..	71	50	38	142.5	60.6	14,888.7	..	..	..	6	17
171 Burkina Faso	21	46	33	100	91.2 g	16.9	4,680.5	..	55	..	..	..
172 Ethiopia	16	90	52	95	35.9	301.2	..	3.8	..	150	4	8
173 Niger	15	44	42	85	30.7 g	..	8,697.7	..	57	155	3	17
174 Sierra Leone	11	38	26	..	4.6 g	75.6	..	..	45	176	..	..
All developing countries	18	88	79	74	28.9	78.7	883.1	..	..	160	76	85
Least developed countries	22	81	61	64	69.1	112.5	3,220.7	..	..	156	14	26
Sub-Saharan Africa	15	67	53	71	111.1	129.3	..	..	..	121	16	75
Arab States	11	88	82	65	2.2	61.7	174.0	..	..	159	111	180
East Asia	9	96	96	85	(.)	39.3	..	..	..	246	116	94
East Asia (excluding China)	9	91	86	..	0.7	71.3	0.3	..	..	127	134	243
South-East Asia and the Pacific	12	94	87	93	29.6	96.0	963.1	..	..	147	19	75
South Asia	32	95	80	67	..	107.3	251.3	..	..	134	44	..
South Asia (excluding India)	29	93	77	66	0.1	30.6	138.6	..	..	135	33	74
Latin America and the Caribbean	9	96	89	59	43.7	45.7	251.2	..	..	91	136	61
Eastern Europe and the CIS	..	97	92	..	1.8	61.3	..	..	..	..	356	813
Industrialized countries	6	..	90	..	99.1	14.8	..	..	..	88	253	..
World	17	89	80	74	39.7	68.5	..	..	..	115	122	241

a. Data refer to the most recent year available during the period specified in the column heading.
b. Data refer to the cumulative reported AIDS cases among adults and children.
c. For a definition of disability see the definitions of statistical terms.
d. Data refer to women aged 15-49.
e. Data refer to 1993 or a year around 1993.
f. Data refer to a year or period other than that specified in the column heading, differ from the standard definition or refer to only part of the country.
g. Data refer to a year prior to 1997.
Source: Columns 1-4: UNICEF 1999a; column 5: UNAIDS and WHO 1998b; columns 6, 7, 11 and 12: WHO 1998a; column 8: UN 1993; column 9: UN 1994; column 10: WHO 1997.

HDI rank	Adult literacy rate (%) 1997	Net enrolment ratio Primary (as % of relevant age group) 1997	Net enrolment ratio Secondary (as % of relevant age group) 1997	Tertiary science enrolment (as % of total tertiary) 1995 [a]	R&D scientists and technicians (per 1,000 people) 1990-96 [b]	Children not reaching grade 5 (%) 1992-95 [b]	Public education expenditure As % of GNP 1993-96 [b]	As % of total government expenditure 1993-96 [b]	Primary and secondary (as % of all levels) 1993-96 [b]	Higher (as % of all levels) 1993-96 [b]
High human development	..	99.3	94.0	..	3.8	..	5.1	12.5	..	..
1 Canada	..	99.9	95.2	..	3.7	..	7.0	13.5	61.5	35.3
2 Norway	..	99.9	97.6	19	5.1	0	7.5	..	53.5	27.9
3 United States	..	99.9	96.3	..	3.6	..	5.4	14.4	67.8	25.2
4 Japan	..	99.9	99.9	23	7.1	..	3.6	9.9	78.8	12.1
5 Belgium	..	99.9	99.9	25	4.0	..	3.2	..	68.0	20.3
6 Sweden	..	99.9	99.9	29	6.8	2	8.3	..	67.0	25.5
7 Australia	..	99.9	96.0	29	4.0	..	5.6	12.9	69.5	29.8
8 Netherlands	..	99.9	99.9	20	3.9	..	5.2	8.7	62.9	29.9
9 Iceland	..	99.9	87.5	..	4.4	1	5.4	..	72.7	17.7
10 United Kingdom	..	99.9	91.8	31	3.4	..	5.4	..	73.7	23.7
11 France	..	99.9	98.7	24	5.4	..	6.1	11.1	69.8	17.0
12 Switzerland	..	99.9	83.7	32	..	..	5.3	14.7	74.3	19.7
13 Finland	..	99.9	95.4	37	4.8	0	7.6	12.2	60.6	28.8
14 Germany	..	99.9	95.3	35	4.3	..	4.8	9.5	72.2	22.6
15 Denmark	..	99.9	94.8	24	5.2	0	8.2	13.1	61.2	22.8
16 Austria	..	99.9	97.3	29	2.4	..	5.7	10.6	68.8	21.6
17 Luxembourg	..	..	..	..	..	..	4.1	15.1	95.2	4.8
18 New Zealand	..	99.9	92.9	20	2.6	..	7.3	..	64.8	29.1
19 Italy	98.3	99.9	95.0	28	2.1	0	4.7	9.0	70.9	15.0
20 Ireland	..	99.9	99.9	31	2.4	..	5.8	..	66.0	23.8
21 Spain	97.2	99.9	91.9	..	1.6	1	4.9	12.8	74.8	15.1
22 Singapore	91.4	91.4	75.6	..	2.6	..	3.0	23.4	60.3	34.8
23 Israel	95.4	..	..	27	..	..	7.2	..	65.3	18.2
24 Hong Kong, China (SAR)	92.4	91.3	69.0	36	0.2	0	2.9	..	56.4	37.1
25 Brunei Darussalam	90.1	87.9	81.9	6	..	5	3.1	..	45.3	1.1
26 Cyprus	95.9	..	..	19	0.4	0	..	13.2	83.3	6.5
27 Greece	96.6	99.9	91.4	30	1.1	..	3.0	..	73.3	25.0
28 Portugal	90.8	99.9	89.7	30	1.4	..	5.5	..	77.9	16.4
29 Barbados	97.6	97.4	85.7	19	..	..	7.2	19.0	..	..
30 Korea, Rep. of	97.2	99.9	99.9	39	2.9	0	3.7	17.5	81.1	8.0
31 Bahamas	95.8	94.6	84.6	..	..	..	..	13.2	..	..
32 Malta	91.1	99.9	85.2	13	0.1	0	..	..	50.0	10.9
33 Slovenia	99.0 [c]	..	..	18	3.7	..	5.8	12.6	67.7	16.9
34 Chile	95.2	90.4	85.2	42	..	0	3.1	14.8	71.8	16.4
35 Kuwait	80.4	65.2	63.2	23	..	..	5.7	8.9	50.6	29.9
36 Czech Republic	..	99.9	99.9	36	1.9	..	5.4	..	69.4	15.1
37 Bahrain	86.2	98.2	87.2	39	..	1	..	12.8	73.1	..
38 Antigua and Barbuda	..	..	..	..	..	..	..	..	..	..
39 Argentina	96.5	99.9	76.9	30	0.8	..	3.5	12.6	61.4	21.0
40 Uruguay	97.5	94.3	83.8	..	0.7	2	3.3	15.5	61.6	19.6
41 Qatar	80.0	83.3	73.3	..	0.5	1	3.4	..	..	..
42 Slovakia	..	..	..	..	2.6	..	4.9	..	58.6	12.7
43 United Arab Emirates	74.8	82.0	77.8	..	..	2	..	16.7	..	..
44 Poland	99.0 [c]	99.4	86.5	29	1.8	2	5.2	..	63.0	14.6
45 Costa Rica	95.1	91.8	55.8	18	..	12	5.3	22.8	64.5	28.3
Medium human development	..	90.7	65.1	..	0.7	21	3.8	13.9	..	..
46 Trinidad and Tobago	97.8	99.9	71.5	45	..	..	3.7	11.6	80.0	..
47 Hungary	99.0 [c]	97.5	96.9	29	1.6	..	4.7	..	67.8	15.6
48 Venezuela	92.0	82.5	48.9	..	0.2	11	..	..	25.9	34.7
49 Panama	91.1	89.9	71.3	26	..	..	4.6	20.9	51.0	24.8
50 Mexico	90.1	99.9	66.1	33	0.3	14	4.9	23.0	73.9	17.2

. . . TO ACQUIRE KNOWLEDGE . . .

HDI rank	Adult literacy rate (%) 1997	Net enrolment ratio		Tertiary science enrolment (as % of total tertiary) 1995[a]	R&D scientists and technicians (per 1,000 people) 1990-96[b]	Children not reaching grade 5 (%) 1992-95[b]	Public education expenditure			
		Primary (as % of relevant age group) 1997	Secondary (as % of relevant age group) 1997				As % of GNP 1993-96[b]	As % of total government expenditure 1993-96[b]	Primary and secondary (as % of all levels) 1993-96[b]	Higher (as % of all levels) 1993-96[b]
51 Saint Kitts and Nevis	..	..	..	..	..	..	3.8	8.8	75.7	11.4
52 Grenada	..	..	..	..	..	..	..	..	..	..
53 Dominica	..	..	..	58	..	..	..	..	..	..
54 Estonia	..	99.9	86.1	34	2.6	4	7.3	22.3	50.7	17.9
55 Croatia	97.7	99.9	72.4	38	2.7	2	5.3	..	..	..
56 Malaysia	85.7	99.9	64.0	..	0.2	1	5.2	..	76.3	16.8
57 Colombia	90.9	89.4	76.4	31	..	27	4.4	19.0	72.0	19.2
58 Cuba	95.9	99.9	69.9	23	2.7	0	..	12.6	57.3	14.9
59 Mauritius	83.0	96.5	68.0	..	0.5	1	..	..	76.6	12.8
60 Belarus	99.0[c]	..	..	35	2.6	..	6.1	17.8	72.5	11.1
61 Fiji	91.8	99.9	84.2	..	0.2	..	..	..	..	..
62 Lithuania	99.0[c]	..	..	..	1.3	..	5.6	22.8	50.9	18.3
63 Bulgaria	98.2	97.9	77.6	25	2.6	..	3.3	7.0	52.4	18.0
64 Suriname	93.5	99.9	..	..	..	..	..	..	75.2	7.6
65 Libyan Arab Jamahiriya	76.5	99.9	99.9	..	..	..	..	..	..	..
66 Seychelles	..	..	..	45	..	0	7.6	16.3	59.7	13.1
67 Thailand	94.7	88.0	47.6	19	0.2	..	4.1	20.1	73.2	19.4
68 Romania	97.8	99.9	75.8	51	2.0	..	3.6	10.5	60.3	15.9
69 Lebanon	84.4	76.1	..	17	..	..	2.5	8.2	68.9	16.2
70 Samoa (Western)	..	96.5	..	14	..	14	..	..	..	..
71 Russian Federation	99.0[c]	99.9	87.6	49	4.2	..	4.1	9.6	..	..
72 Ecuador	90.7	99.9	50.9	..	0.3	15	3.5	13.0	74.4	21.3
73 Macedonia, TFYR	..	..	..	41	1.7	..	5.6	20.0	78.0	22.0
74 Latvia	99.0[c]	99.9	80.6	34	1.6	..	6.5	14.1	58.9	12.2
75 Saint Vincent and the Grenadines	..	..	..	..	..	..	..	..	..	..
76 Kazakhstan	..	..	..	42	..	..	4.7	..	60.4	12.5
77 Philippines	94.6	99.9	77.8	31	0.2	..	2.2	..	..	..
78 Saudi Arabia	73.4	60.1	58.7	..	..	11	..	17.0	82.2	17.8
79 Brazil	84.0	97.1	65.9	22	0.2	29	5.2	..	68.7	26.2
80 Peru	88.7	93.8	83.9	..	0.8	..	2.9	19.2	39.5	16.0
81 Saint Lucia	..	..	..	..	..	..	9.8	22.2	69.1	12.5
82 Jamaica	85.5	95.6	69.8	..	(.)	..	7.5	12.9	65.5	22.4
83 Belize	..	99.9	63.6	..	..	30	5.0	19.5	87.9	6.9
84 Paraguay	92.4	96.3	61.1	25	..	29	3.9	18.6	68.1	19.7
85 Georgia	..	89.0	75.9	48	..	..	..	..	45.1	18.5
86 Turkey	83.2	99.9	58.4	21	0.3	5	2.2	..	65.0	34.7
87 Armenia	..	..	..	..	..	..	2.0	10.3	63.0	13.2
88 Dominican Republic	82.6	91.3	78.5	..	..	..	2.0	13.4	62.0	13.0
89 Oman	67.1	67.7	66.6	..	..	4	..	17.8	98.8	..
90 Sri Lanka	90.7	99.9	76.0	..	0.2	17	3.4	8.9	74.8	9.3
91 Ukraine	..	..	..	..	3.9	..	7.2	..	65.2	10.7
92 Uzbekistan	..	..	..	..	2.0	..	8.1	21.1	69.9	9.7
93 Maldives	95.7	..	..	..	..	..	6.4	..	98.6	..
94 Jordan	87.2	..	..	28	0.1	2	7.3	19.8	64.5	33.0
95 Iran, Islamic Rep. of	73.3	90.0	81.2	37	0.7	10	..	..	83.0	1.2
96 Turkmenistan	..	..	..	..	..	..	..	..	..	..
97 Kyrgyzstan	..	99.5	77.8	28	0.8	..	5.7	23.5	68.0	14.1
98 China	82.9	99.9	70.0	37	0.6	6	2.3	11.9	68.3	15.6
99 Guyana	98.1	92.8	74.9	43	..	..	4.9	10.0	71.3	7.7
100 Albania	..	..	..	24	..	18	3.1	..	77.8	10.3

	Adult literacy rate (%) 1997	Net enrolment ratio		Tertiary science enrolment (as % of total tertiary) 1995 [a]	R&D scientists and technicians (per 1,000 people) 1990-96 [b]	Children not reaching grade 5 (%) 1992-95 [b]	Public education expenditure			
		Primary (as % of relevant age group) 1997	Secondary (as % of relevant age group) 1997				As % of GNP 1993-96 [b]	As % of total government expenditure 1993-96 [b]	Primary and secondary (as % of all levels) 1993-96 [b]	Higher (as % of all levels) 1993-96 [b]
HDI rank										
101 South Africa	84.0	99.9	94.9	57	1.2	..	7.9	23.9	71.6	14.3
102 Tunisia	67.0	99.9	74.3	24	0.4	9	6.7	17.4	79.7	18.5
103 Azerbaijan	..	..	..	38	..	..	3.3	21.3	63.9	7.5
104 Moldova, Rep. of	98.3	..	..	34	1.8	..	9.7	28.1	52.9	13.3
105 Indonesia	85.0	99.2	56.1	28	..	11	1.4	7.9	72.9	25.1
106 Cape Verde	71.0	99.9	36.6	..	..	..	..	..	..	..
107 El Salvador	77.0	89.1	36.4	25	0.3	23	2.2	..	67.5	7.2
108 Tajikistan	98.9	..	..	23	0.7	..	2.2	11.5	71.2	7.1
109 Algeria	60.3	96.0	68.5	52	..	6	5.2	16.4	95.3	..
110 Viet Nam	91.9	99.9	55.1	..	0.3	..	2.7	7.4	..	..
111 Syrian Arab Republic	71.6	94.7	42.3	29	..	6	4.2	13.6	71.7	25.9
112 Bolivia	83.6	97.4	40.0	..	0.4	..	5.6	11.1	57.7	27.7
113 Swaziland	77.5	94.6	81.5	22	..	13	7.3	18.1	62.8	26.6
114 Honduras	70.7	87.5	36.0	26	..	40	3.6	16.5	74.0	16.6
115 Namibia	79.8	91.4	80.7	5	..	21	9.1	25.6	76.0	9.4
116 Vanuatu	..	71.3	42.8	..	..	..	4.9	..	90.9	6.4
117 Guatemala	66.6	73.8	34.9	..	0.2	50	1.7	18.2	67.0	15.5
118 Solomon Islands	..	..	..	29	..	19	..	..	..	..
119 Mongolia	84.0	85.1	55.9	24	1.1	..	6.4	19.3	56.0	14.3
120 Egypt	52.7	95.2	75.1	15	0.7	..	..	..	66.7	33.3
121 Nicaragua	63.4	78.6	50.5	..	0.3	46	3.6	..	80.3	..
122 Botswana	74.4	80.1	88.8	24	..	10	10.4	20.2	..	..
123 São Tomé and Principe	..	..	..	..	..	..	..	..	..	..
124 Gabon	66.2	..	..	..	0.2	41	2.8	..	..	..
125 Iraq	..	74.6	42.9	..	..	..	..	..	..	..
126 Morocco	45.9	76.6	37.7	29	..	22	5.3	24.9	83.4	16.5
127 Lesotho	82.3	68.6	72.9	25	..	20	7.0	..	83.9	14.8
128 Myanmar	83.6	99.3	54.2	36	..	..	1.2	14.4	88.0	11.7
129 Papua New Guinea	73.7	78.9	..	..	..	27	..	..	..	..
130 Zimbabwe	90.9	93.1	59.2	23	..	21	..	..	78.1	17.3
131 Equatorial Guinea	79.9	79.3	68.5	..	..	..	1.8	5.6	..	..
132 India	53.5	77.2	59.7	..	0.3	41	3.4	11.6	66.0	13.7
133 Ghana	66.4	43.4	..	..	..	..	..	..	..	..
134 Cameroon	71.7	61.7	39.8	..	..	..	2.9	..	..	..
135 Congo	76.9	78.3	84.1	11	..	45	6.2	14.7	61.8	28.0
136 Kenya	79.3	65.0	61.1	..	..	..	6.6	16.7	78.5	15.8
137 Cambodia	..	99.9	38.8	..	..	51	2.9	..	..	..
138 Pakistan	40.9	..	..	..	0.1	..	3.0	8.1	77.3	13.2
139 Comoros	55.4	50.1	35.7	..	..	20	..	..	71.7	17.2
Low human development	..	56.6	28.4	..	..	36	..	..	..	..
140 Lao People's Dem. Rep.	58.6	73.0	63.4	45	..	47	2.5	..	78.0	7.9
141 Congo, Dem. Rep. of the	..	58.2	37.1	..	..	..	..	..	..	..
142 Sudan	53.3	..	..	..	..	..	..	9.0	69.8	21.1
143 Togo	53.2	82.3	58.3	16	..	..	4.7	24.7	72.8	24.7
144 Nepal	38.1	78.4	54.6	17	..	..	3.1	13.5	70.2	17.9
145 Bhutan	44.2	13.2	..	..	..	18	..	..	..	..
146 Nigeria	59.5	..	..	41	0.1	..	0.9	11.5	..	..
147 Madagascar	..	58.7	..	23	(.)	60	1.9	13.6	81.7	..
148 Yemen	42.5	..	..	..	..	..	6.1	20.8	..	..
149 Mauritania	38.4	62.9	..	8	..	36	..	..	74.7	21.2
150 Bangladesh	38.9	75.1	21.6	..	..	..	2.9	..	88.6	7.9

. . . TO ACQUIRE KNOWLEDGE . . .

HDI rank	Adult literacy rate (%) 1997	Net enrolment ratio Primary (as % of relevant age group) 1997	Net enrolment ratio Secondary (as % of relevant age group) 1997	Tertiary science enrolment (as % of total tertiary) 1995[a]	R&D scientists and technicians (per 1,000 people) 1990-96[b]	Children not reaching grade 5 (%) 1992-95[b]	Public education expenditure As % of GNP 1993-96[b]	As % of total government expenditure 1993-96[b]	Primary and secondary (as % of all levels) 1993-96[b]	Higher (as % of all levels) 1993-96[b]
151 Zambia	75.1	72.4	42.2	..	..	..	2.2	7.1	59.9	23.2
152 Haiti	45.0	19.4	34.2	..	..	..	..	..	..	..
153 Senegal	34.6	59.5	19.8	..	..	15	3.5	..	76.7	23.2
154 Côte d'Ivoire	42.6	58.3	34.1	26	..	25	5.0	..	82.6	17.4
155 Benin	33.9	67.6	28.2	19	0.2	39	3.2	15.2	79.3	18.8
156 Tanzania, U. Rep. of	71.6	47.4	..	39	..	17	..	..	..	..
157 Djibouti	48.3	31.9	19.6	..	..	21	..	..	..	..
158 Uganda	64.0	..	..	13	..	..	2.6	21.4	100.0	..
159 Malawi	57.7	98.5	72.6	18	..	..	5.5	..	67.7	20.5
160 Angola	..	34.7	31.2	..	..	..	..	..	..	..
161 Guinea	37.9	45.6	14.6	..	..	46	..	..	72.4	17.2
162 Chad	50.3	47.9	17.9	14	..	41	..	..	67.6	9.0
163 Gambia	33.1	65.9	33.3	..	..	20	..	21.2	80.5	12.9
164 Rwanda	63.0	78.3	..	..	(.)	..	..	..	..	..
165 Central African Republic	42.4	46.2	19.0	..	0.1	..	..	..	69.7	24.0
166 Mali	35.5	38.1	17.9	..	..	18	2.2	..	67.0	17.7
167 Eritrea	..	29.3	37.9	..	..	29	1.8	..	62.1	..
168 Guinea-Bissau	33.6	52.3	24.1	..	..	..	..	..	..	..
169 Mozambique	40.5	39.6	22.4	50	..	54	..	..	..	..
170 Burundi	44.6	35.6	17.1	..	0.1	..	3.2	18.3	79.4	17.1
171 Burkina Faso	20.7	32.3	12.8	18	..	25	3.6	11.1	..	..
172 Ethiopia	35.4	35.2	24.8	36	..	45	4.0	13.7	69.9	15.9
173 Niger	14.3	24.4	9.4	..	..	27	..	..	..	..
174 Sierra Leone	34.3	44.0	..	30	..	..	..	..	..	..
All developing countries	..	85.7	60.4	..	0.4	22	3.6	14.8	..	..
Least developed countries	..	60.4	31.2	..	..	..	..	..	..	..
Sub-Saharan Africa	..	56.2	41.4	..	..	34	5.4	..	..	..
Arab States	..	86.4	61.7	..	..	10	..	15.8	..	..
East Asia	..	99.8	71.0	..	0.6	6	2.7	13.6	..	..
East Asia (excluding China)	..	97.9	93.7	..	2.5	(.)	3.5	17.5	..	..
South-East Asia and the Pacific	..	97.8	58.3	..	..	14	3.0	..	..	..
South Asia	..	78.0	56.5	..	0.3	38	3.3	11.2	..	..
South Asia (excluding India)	..	80.9	45.2	..	..	..	3.0	..	..	..
Latin America and the Caribbean	..	93.3	65.3	..	0.4	23	4.5	17.9	..	..
Eastern Europe and the CIS	..	..	..	..	3.1	..	4.6	..	..	..
Industrialized countries	..	99.9	96.2	..	4.1	..	5.1	12.3	..	..
World	..	87.6	65.4	..	1.3	..	4.8	12.7	..	..

a. Data refer to enrolment in natural and applied sciences.

b. Data refer to the most recent year available during the period specified in the column heading.

c. Capped at 99.0%.

Source: Column 1: calculated on the basis of data from UNESCO 1999a; columns 2 and 3: UNESCO 1999d; column 4: UNESCO 1998c; columns 5, 7, 8 and 10: UNESCO 1998a; column 6: calculated on the basis of data from UNESCO 1999e; column 9: calculated on the basis of data from UNESCO 1998a.

HDI rank	GNP (US$ billions) 1997	GNP annual growth rate (%) 1975-95	GNP per capita (US$) 1997	GNP per capita annual growth rate (%) 1975-95	Average annual rate of inflation (%) 1985-96	1996
High human development	**24,193.6 T**	**2.7**	**23,999**	**1.9**	**4.7**	**2.1**
1 Canada	595.0	2.7	19,640	1.4	2.7	1.1
2 Norway	159.0	3.3	36,100	2.9	2.9	4.8
3 United States	7,783.1	2.5	29,080	1.5	3.2	2.6
4 Japan	4,812.1	3.5	38,160	2.9	1.0	-0.2
5 Belgium	272.4	2.0	26,730	1.9	2.9	1.7
6 Sweden	231.9	1.2	26,210	0.8	4.9	1.2
7 Australia	382.7	2.9	20,650	1.6	3.9	0.9
8 Netherlands	403.1	2.3	25,830	1.7	1.5	1.8
9 Iceland	7.1 [a]	3.1	26,470 [a]	2.1	11.0	1.7
10 United Kingdom	1,231.3	2.0	20,870	1.8	4.5	3.1
11 France	1,541.6	2.2	26,300	1.7	2.6	1.3
12 Switzerland	305.2	1.5	43,060	1.1	2.8	1.1
13 Finland	127.4	1.9	24,790	1.5	3.6	1.6
14 Germany	2,321.0	..	28,280	..	..	..
15 Denmark	184.3	2.0	34,890	1.9	3.1	2.6
16 Austria	225.4	2.4	27,920	2.1	2.9	2.6
17 Luxembourg	18.6 [a]	3.9	44,690 [a]	3.3	2.1	-0.8
18 New Zealand	59.5	1.4	15,830	0.6	5.2	2.3
19 Italy	1,160.4	2.4	20,170	2.3	5.9	4.8
20 Ireland	65.1	3.7	17,790	3.0	2.6	2.3
21 Spain	569.6	2.2	14,490	1.7	6.1	3.2
22 Singapore	101.8	7.8	32,810	5.8	3.1	1.4
23 Israel	94.4	4.5	16,180	2.1	..	..
24 Hong Kong, China (SAR)	163.8 T	7.6	25,200	5.7	7.6	5.4
25 Brunei Darussalam	..	..	..	..	..	..
26 Cyprus	..	..	..	..	..	..
27 Greece	122.4	2.4	11,640	1.7	14.3	8.5
28 Portugal	109.5	3.1	11,010	2.6	10.3	3.0
29 Barbados	..	2.0	..	1.7	..	..
30 Korea, Rep. of	485.2	8.3	10,550	7.0	6.0	3.4
31 Bahamas	..	4.5	..	2.5	..	..
32 Malta	3.5	5.7	9,330	5.1	..	..
33 Slovenia	19.5	..	9,840	..	..	..
34 Chile	70.5	5.5	4,820	3.8	16.0	2.9
35 Kuwait	..	1.3	..	-1.0	..	..
36 Czech Republic	54.0	..	5,240	..	11.5	9.1
37 Bahrain	5.2 [a]	..	8,640 [a]	..	0.3	2.7
38 Antigua and Barbuda	0.5	..	7,380	..	..	..
39 Argentina	319.3	1.4	8,950	-0.1	162.9	1.9
40 Uruguay	20.0	1.3	6,130	0.7	62.9	26.3
41 Qatar	..	1.0	..	-5.5	..	..
42 Slovakia	19.8	..	3,680	..	8.9	4.4
43 United Arab Emirates	..	4.2	..	-3.5	..	..
44 Poland	138.9	..	3,590	..	68.0	18.7
45 Costa Rica	9.3	3.7	2,680	0.9	17.8	16.2
Medium human development	**5,037.7 T**	**3.6**	**1,280**	**1.8**	**95.5**	**20.7**
46 Trinidad and Tobago	5.6	1.4	4,250	0.2	6.2	4.2
47 Hungary	45.8	0.9	4,510	1.1	18.9	21.2
48 Venezuela	79.3	1.7	3,480	-1.0	42.0	115.7
49 Panama	8.4	2.7	3,080	0.5	1.5	1.7
50 Mexico	348.6	2.8	3,700	0.6	40.7	28.7

. . . TO HAVE ACCESS TO THE RESOURCES NEEDED FOR A DECENT STANDARD OF LIVING . . .

HDI rank		GNP (US$ billions) 1997	GNP annual growth rate (%) 1975-95	GNP per capita (US$) 1997	GNP per capita annual growth rate (%) 1975-95	Average annual rate of inflation (%)	
						1985-96	1996
51	Saint Kitts and Nevis	0.3	..	6,260	..	..	..
52	Grenada	0.3	..	3,140	..	..	..
53	Dominica	0.2	3.7	3,040	3.6	4.5	2.2
54	Estonia	4.9	..	3,360	..	58.0	24.6
55	Croatia	19.3	..	4,060	..		
56	Malaysia	98.2	7.1	4,530	4.4	3.2	5.2
57	Colombia	87.1	4.2	2,180	2.0	24.6	18.7
58	Cuba	..	..	..	..	..	..
59	Mauritius	4.4	5.4	3,870	4.2	8.4	6.1
60	Belarus	22.1	..	2,150	..	..	49.4
61	Fiji	2.0	2.4	2,460	0.8	4.7	5.3
62	Lithuania	8.4	..	2,260	..	..	26.5
63	Bulgaria	9.8	..	1,170	..	46.1	121.0
64	Suriname	0.5	3.4	1,320	2.8	..	..
65	Libyan Arab Jamahiriya	..	..	..	..	..	..
66	Seychelles	0.5	4.1	6,910	2.9	3.2	2.5
67	Thailand	165.8	7.8	2,740	5.9	4.8	4.0
68	Romania	31.8	1.2	1,410	0.8	57.8	30.3
69	Lebanon	13.9	..	3,350	..	..	..
70	Samoa (Western)	0.2	..	1,140	..	6.2	6.4
71	Russian Federation	394.9	-0.4	2,680	-0.8	..	43.8
72	Ecuador	18.8	3.3	1,570	0.7	40.2	29.5
73	Macedonia, TFYR	2.2	..	1,100	..	..	..
74	Latvia	6.0	-0.9	2,430	-1.0	52.2	18.0
75	Saint Vincent and the Grenadines	0.3	5.4	2,420	4.5	..	..
76	Kazakhstan	21.3	..	1,350	..	..	38.9
77	Philippines	88.4	3.0	1,200	0.5	8.9	7.8
78	Saudi Arabia	143.4	2.4	7,150	-2.4	1.4	7.1
79	Brazil	784.0	3.5	4,790	1.5	569.8	17.2
80	Peru	63.7	1.8	2,610	-0.4	236.6	9.5
81	Saint Lucia	0.6	..	3,510	..	..	..
82	Jamaica	4.0	0.3	1,550	-0.9	26.5	21.4
83	Belize	0.6	5.8	2,670	3.0	4.0	6.3
84	Paraguay	10.2	4.3	2,000	1.2	23.2	11.3
85	Georgia	4.7	..	860	..	..	..
86	Turkey	199.3	3.9	3,130	1.7	65.6	78.3
87	Armenia	2.1	-2.0	560	-3.3	..	..
88	Dominican Republic	14.1	3.0	1,750	0.8	20.5	5.3
89	Oman	..	7.5	..	2.6	..	..
90	Sri Lanka	14.8	4.8	800	3.2	10.9	10.8
91	Ukraine	52.6	..	1,040	..	..	66.2
92	Uzbekistan	24.2	..	1,020	..	..	81.1
93	Maldives	0.3	..	1,180	..	8.6	5.2
94	Jordan	6.8	..	1,520	..	4.6	-2.0
95	Iran, Islamic Rep. of	108.6	1.2	1,780	-1.6	..	..
96	Turkmenistan	3.0	..	640	..	..	694.9
97	Kyrgyzstan	2.2	..	480	..	..	35.3
98	China	1,055.4	9.1	860	7.7	9.2	5.8
99	Guyana	0.7	-0.3	800	-0.9	..	..
100	Albania	2.5	..	760	..	29.4	14.6

HDI rank	GNP (US$ billions) 1997	GNP annual growth rate (%) 1975-95	GNP per capita (US$) 1997	GNP per capita annual growth rate (%) 1975-95	Average annual rate of inflation (%)	
					1985-96	1996
101 South Africa	130.2	1.7	3,210	-0.6	12.8	8.2
102 Tunisia	19.4	4.3	2,110	1.9	5.6	4.8
103 Azerbaijan	3.9	..	510	..	..	20.4
104 Moldova, Rep. of	2.0	..	460	..	..	..
105 Indonesia	221.5	7.1	1,110	5.1	8.6	8.5
106 Cape Verde	0.4	..	1,090	..	..	4.4
107 El Salvador	10.7	1.3	1,810	-0.3	14.6	6.4
108 Tajikistan	2.0	..	330	..	..	491.0
109 Algeria	43.9	2.7	1,500	-0.1	21.0	23.5
110 Viet Nam	24.0	..	310	..	85.4	6.1
111 Syrian Arab Republic	16.6	4.6	1,120	1.3	15.7	9.0
112 Bolivia	7.6	..	970	..	24.2	14.4
113 Swaziland	1.5	5.1	1,520	1.8	11.8	10.0
114 Honduras	4.4	3.7	740	0.5	14.8	21.2
115 Namibia	3.4	..	2,110	..	10.7	10.0
116 Vanuatu	0.2	..	1,340	..	6.2	2.9
117 Guatemala	16.6	2.5	1,580	-0.1	17.4	8.9
118 Solomon Islands	0.4	5.9	870	2.3	10.8	20.7
119 Mongolia	1.0	..	390	..	43.4	21.0
120 Egypt	72.2	6.6	1,200	4.1	14.8	9.1
121 Nicaragua	1.9	-1.2	410	-4.0	531.0	-4.4
122 Botswana	5.1	9.8	3,310	6.3	12.1	9.2
123 São Tomé and Principe	(.)	2.3	290	0.1	..	51.0
124 Gabon	4.8	0.2	4,120	-2.9	3.8	12.7
125 Iraq	..	..	..	..	..	..
126 Morocco	34.4	3.6	1,260	1.4	4.9	1.8
127 Lesotho	1.4	3.8	680	1.3	11.1	6.1
128 Myanmar	..	..	..	..	24.6	23.3
129 Papua New Guinea	4.2	3.0	930	0.7	5.5	5.4
130 Zimbabwe	8.2	1.8	720	-1.2	18.7	28.1
131 Equatorial Guinea	0.4	..	1,060	..	6.1	25.7
132 India	357.4	5.0	370	2.8	9.0	6.3
133 Ghana	7.0	2.4	390	-0.4	31.3	39.1
134 Cameroon	8.6	4.1	620	1.2	3.1	5.5
135 Congo	1.8	3.2	670	0.3	2.1	15.2
136 Kenya	9.7	4.0	340	0.5	12.2	8.8
137 Cambodia	3.2	..	300	..	..	6.8
138 Pakistan	64.6	6.0	500	3.1	9.2	10.5
139 Comoros	0.2	2.7	400	..	4.0	2.3
Low human development	177.8 T	2.3	274	-0.4	71.0	286.7
140 Lao People's Dem. Rep.	1.9	..	400	..	22.0	12.9
141 Congo, Dem. Rep. of the	5.2	-2.4	110	-5.4	636.4	613.1
142 Sudan	7.9	2.4	290	-0.2	..	..
143 Togo	1.5	1.6	340	-1.4	5.4	4.9
144 Nepal	4.9	4.3	220	1.6	11.0	7.8
145 Bhutan	0.3	..	430	..	..	..
146 Nigeria	33.4	2.5	280	-0.6	34.1	34.2
147 Madagascar	3.6	0.3	250	-2.3	20.1	17.9
148 Yemen	4.4	..	270	..	..	..
149 Mauritania	1.1	2.5	440	-0.2	6.5	3.6
150 Bangladesh	44.1	4.4	360	2.0	6.1	3.5

. . . TO HAVE ACCESS TO THE RESOURCES NEEDED FOR A DECENT STANDARD OF LIVING . . .

HDI rank	GNP (US$ billions) 1997	GNP annual growth rate (%) 1975-95	GNP per capita (US$) 1997	GNP per capita annual growth rate (%) 1975-95	Average annual rate of inflation (%) 1985-96	1996
151 Zambia	3.5	0.8	370	-2.2	74.4	22.5
152 Haiti	2.9	0.4	380	-1.5	16.6	21.2
153 Senegal	4.0	2.2	540	-0.5	4.4	3.7
154 Côte d'Ivoire	10.2	1.7	710	-1.8	3.2	3.7
155 Benin	2.2	3.6	380	0.5	5.6	6.7
156 Tanzania, U. Rep. of	6.6	..	210	..	..	..
157 Djibouti	..	..	..	..	..	..
158 Uganda	6.6	..	330	..	60.3	6.1
159 Malawi	2.1	2.5	210	-0.6	25.9	39.0
160 Angola	3.0	..	260	..	297.0	5,427.1
161 Guinea	3.8	..	550	..	..	2.5
162 Chad	1.6	3.0	230	0.4	4.0	14.1
163 Gambia	0.4	3.6	340	0	11.0	2.9
164 Rwanda	1.7	1.4	210	-0.5	11.2	10.5
165 Central African Republic	1.1	0.8	320	-1.5	3.1	-0.8
166 Mali	2.7	2.9	260	0.4	4.9	6.3
167 Eritrea	0.9	..	230	..	..	..
168 Guinea-Bissau	0.3	1.4	230	-1.3	62.5	48.1
169 Mozambique	2.4	..	140	..	50.9	41.9
170 Burundi	0.9	2.7	140	0.1	6.6	19.6
171 Burkina Faso	2.6	3.7	250	1.3	3.3	4.3
172 Ethiopia	6.5	..	110	..	5.0	1.5
173 Niger	2.0	1.5	200	-1.8	2.4	4.8
174 Sierra Leone	0.8	-0.7	160	-2.8	58.3	26.3
All developing countries	5,725.6 T	4.4	1,314	2.3	88.8	25.3
Least developed countries	136.2 T	2.3	260	-0.2	94.9	412.5
Sub-Saharan Africa	299.0 T	2.0	522	-0.9	44.7	168.8
Arab States	324.2 T	3.2	1,754	0.5	..	..
East Asia	1,705.4 T	8.8	1,330	7.3	8.0	5.1
East Asia (excluding China)	650.0 T	8.1	11,811	6.8	6.4	3.9
South-East Asia and the Pacific	711.8 T	6.6	1,556	4.4	6.4	6.0
South Asia	595.0 T	3.7	452	1.4	8.9	6.7
South Asia (excluding India)	237.6 T	2.2	670	-0.3	8.6	8.4
Latin America and the Caribbean	1,890.9 T	2.8	3,953	0.7	263.7	22.4
Eastern Europe and the CIS	897.8 T	..	2,249	..	..	40.6
Industrialized countries	22,785.7 T	2.6	27,174	1.9	3.0	2.0
World	29,409.1 T	2.8	5,257	1.1	17.8	7.9

a. Data refer to 1996.

Source: Columns 1 and 3: World Bank 1999b; *columns 2 and 4-6:* calculated on the basis of data from World Bank 1999b.

. . . TO HAVE ACCESS TO THE RESOURCES NEEDED FOR A DECENT STANDARD OF LIVING . . .

12 Macroeconomic structure

HDI rank	GDP (US$ billions) 1997	Agriculture (as % of GDP) 1997	Industry (as % of GDP) 1997	Services (as % of GDP) 1997	Consumption Private (as % of GDP) 1997	Consumption Government (as % of GDP) 1997	Gross domestic investment (as % of GDP) 1997	Gross domestic savings (as % of GDP) 1997	Tax revenue (as % of GDP) 1997	Central government expenditure (as % of GDP) 1997	Overall budget surplus/deficit (as % of GDP) 1997
High human development	23,120.9 T	2	..	64	63	16	21	22	26	29	-1.1
1 Canada	607.7	..	..	..	58 [a]	21 [a]	18 [a]	21 [a]	..	..	..
2 Norway	153.4	2 [a]	32 [a]	66 [a]	48 [a]	20 [a]	23 [a]	32 [a]	33 [a]	37 [a]	5.1 [a]
3 United Statea	7,834.0	2 [a]	27 [a]	71 [a]	68 [a]	16 [a]	18 [a]	16 [a]	20 [a]	22 [a]	-0.3
4 Japan	4,190.2	2 [a]	38 [a]	60 [a]	60 [a]	10 [a]	30 [a]	30 [a]	..	..	..
5 Belgium	242.5	1 [a]	..	78 [a]	63 [a]	15 [a]	18 [a]	22 [a]	..	..	..
6 Sweden	227.6	..	..	..	52 [a]	26 [a]	15 [a]	21 [a]	37 [a]	44 [a]	-1.3
7 Australia	393.5	3 [a]	26 [a]	71 [a]	63 [a]	17 [a]	20 [a]	21 [a]	23 [a]	26 [a]	0.4
8 Netherlands	360.3	..	..	..	60 [a]	14 [a]	20 [a]	26 [a]	43 [a]	48 [a]	-1.7
9 Iceland	7.3 [a]	..	..	..	61	21	18	18	27	32	-0.9 [a]
10 United Kingdom	1,286.5	2 [a]	31 [a]	67 [a]	64 [a]	21 [a]	16 [a]	15 [a]	..	..	..
11 France	1,392.5	2 [a]	26 [a]	72 [a]	61 [a]	19 [a]	17 [a]	20 [a]	39 [a]	47 [a]	-3.5
12 Switzerland	255.3	..	..	..	61 [a]	14 [a]	20 [a]	24 [a]	21 [a]	26 [a]	-1.2 [a]
13 Finland	119.8	4 [a]	34 [a]	62 [a]	53 [a]	22 [a]	17 [a]	25 [a]	28 [a]	40 [a]	-6.3 [a]
14 Germany	2,092.3	1 [a]	..	44 [a]	58 [a]	20 [a]	21 [a]	22 [a]	27 [a]	33 [a]	-1.4
15 Denmark	170.0	..	..	..	50 [a]	26 [a]	19 [a]	24 [a]	..	..	..
16 Austria	206.2	1 [a]	30 [a]	68 [a]	57 [a]	20 [a]	24 [a]	23 [a]	34 [a]	42 [a]	-4.1 [a]
17 Luxembourg	17.0 [a]	..	..	..	55 [a]	14 [a]	21 [a]	31 [a]	44 [a]	42 [a]	4.9 [a]
18 New Zealand	64.6	..	..	..	63 [a]	14 [a]	22 [a]	22 [a]	31 [a]	32 [a]	4.0
19 Italy	1,145.6	3 [a]	..	75 [a]	61 [a]	16 [a]	17 [a]	22 [a]	42 [a]	48 [a]	-3.1
20 Ireland	75.0	..	..	..	53 [a]	14 [a]	18 [a]	33 [a]	..	..	..
21 Spain	532.0	3 [a]	..	25 [a]	62 [a]	16 [a]	21 [a]	21 [a]	..	..	..
22 Singapore	96.3	(.)	35	65	39	9	37	51	16	17	11.6
23 Israel	98.1	..	..	..	62 [a]	29 [a]	22 [a]	9 [a]	37 [a]	48 [a]	0.4
24 Hong Kong, China (SAR)	171.4	(.)	15	84	61	9	34	31	..	..	..
25 Brunei Darussalam	5.3	..	..	..	..	..	..	..	..	..	..
26 Cyprus	8.2	..	..	..	..	..	..	..	..	..	..
27 Greece	122.9	..	..	..	75 [a]	14 [a]	19 [a]	11 [a]	20 [a]	33 [a]	-8.6 [a]
28 Portugal	102.1	..	..	..	65	18	24	..	31	42	-2.3 [a]
29 Barbados	..	..	..	..	..	..	..	..	.. ..	..	..
30 Korea, Rep. of	442.5	6	43	51	55	11	35	34	19	19	-1.4
31 Bahamas	3.8	..	..	..	..	..	..	..	..	..	..
32 Malta	3.3	..	..	..	64	21	25	15	29	42	-9.8
33 Slovenia	18.2	5	39	57	57	20	24	23	..	..	..
34 Chile	77.1	7	31	61	66	10	27	25	19	21	1.9
35 Kuwait	30.4	..	..	..	47	28	13	25	1	42	..
36 Czech Republic	52.0	..	..	..	51	20	34	28	33	36	-1.1
37 Bahrain	6.1 [a]	..	..	..	42	20	5	38	7	27	-5.5
38 Antigua and Barbuda	..	..	..	..	..	..	..	..	..	..	..
39 Argentina	325.0	7	33	61	78	3	20	18	11	14	-1.3
40 Uruguay	20.0	8	27	64	74	14	13	12	28	32	-1.3
41 Qatar	..	..	..	..	..	..	..	..	..	..	..
42 Slovakia	19.5	5	33	62	49	22	35	28	..	..	..
43 United Arab Emirates	..	..	..	..	..	..	..	..	..	..	..
44 Poland	135.7	..	..	..	64	18	22	18	35	41	-1.4
45 Costa Rica	9.5	15	23	62	63	12	27	25	23	31	-3.9 [a]
Medium human development	4,974.3 T	13	37	50	61	13	26	26	13	18	-1.9
46 Trinidad and Tobago	5.9	2	46	52	75	10	22	15	..	..	..
47 Hungary	45.7	6 [a]	34 [a]	60 [a]	63 [a]	10 [a]	27 [a]	27 [a]	33 [a]	43 [a]	-2.6
48 Venezuela	87.5	4	41	55	67	6	18	27	18	21	2.2
49 Panama	8.2	8 [a]	18 [a]	73 [a]	53 [a]	15 [a]	29 [a]	32 [a]	16 [a]	27 [a]	-0.7 [a]
50 Mexico	403.0	5	26	69	65	8	26	26	13	15	-0.2 [a]

. . . TO HAVE ACCESS TO THE RESOURCES NEEDED FOR A DECENT STANDARD OF LIVING . . .

12 Macroeconomic structure

HDI rank	GDP (US$ billions) 1997	Agriculture (as % of GDP) 1997	Industry (as % of GDP) 1997	Services (as % of GDP) 1997	Consumption Private (as % of GDP) 1997	Consumption Government (as % of GDP) 1997	Gross domestic investment (as % of GDP) 1997	Gross domestic savings (as % of GDP) 1997	Tax revenue (as % of GDP) 1997	Central government expenditure (as % of GDP) 1997	Overall budget surplus/ deficit (as % of GDP) 1997
51 Saint Kitts and Nevis	0.2	6	25	70	39	41	46	..	..	..	..
52 Grenada	0.3	10	20	70	70	17	33	..	..	..	..
53 Dominica	0.2	20	21	59	59	21	33	20	..	..	..
54 Estonia	4.7	7	28	65	59	23	30	18	30	32	2.4
55 Croatia	19.1	..	..	..	66 [a]	30 [a]	15 [a]	3 [a]	43 [a]	47 [a]	-0.5 [a]
56 Malaysia	98.5	12	47	41	45	11	43	44	19	20	3.0
57 Colombia	95.7	11	20	69	68	16	19	16	..	..	..
58 Cuba	..	..	..	..	..	..	..	..	..	..	..
59 Mauritius	4.4	9	33	58	64	12	28	24	18	24	-4.0
60 Belarus	22.6	14	44	42	59	19	26	22	29	34	-1.9 [a]
61 Fiji	2.1	18	26	56	73	16	12	11	21	30	-4.9 [a]
62 Lithuania	9.6	13	32	55	65	19	27	16	25	27	-1.9
63 Bulgaria	10.1	23	26	50	70	12	12	17	25	34	2.1
64 Suriname	..	..	..	..	..	..	..	..	..	..	..
65 Libyan Arab Jamahiriya	..	..	..	..	..	..	..	..	..	..	..
66 Seychelles	0.5	4	23	73	50	28	36	22	..	..	..
67 Thailand	153.9	11	40	49	54	10	35	36	16	19	-0.9
68 Romania	34.8	20	45	36	75	10	21	14	24	31	-4.0 [a]
69 Lebanon	15.0	12	27	61	101	16	27	-17	14	38	-20.6 [a]
70 Samoa (Western)	0.2	..	..	..	..	..	..	..	..	..	..
71 Russian Federation	447.0	8	37	55	63	12	22	25	..	..	..
72 Ecuador	19.8	12	35	53	67	12	20	21	..	..	..
73 Macedonia, TFYR	2.2	12	27	61	85	12	19	3	..	..	..
74 Latvia	5.5	7	31	62	67	23	20	10	29	32	0.9
75 Saint Vincent and the Grenadines	0.3	13	25	62	53	27	32	..	26	32	-2.1
76 Kazakhstan	22.2	12	27	61	81	5	16	13	..	..	..
77 Philippines	82.2	19	32	49	73	13	25	15	17	19	0.1
78 Saudi Arabia	140.4	6	45	49	35	30	20	35	..	..	..
79 Brazil	820.4	8	35	57	63	18	21	19	..	..	..
80 Peru	63.8	7	36	57	67	12	25	21	14	16	0.3
81 Saint Lucia	0.6	11	20	70	68	14	19	..	..	..	..
82 Jamaica	4.1	8	35	57	61	18	35	22	..	..	..
83 Belize	0.6	23	28	49	59	19	24	21	..	..	..
84 Paraguay	10.2	23	22	55	67	13	23	20	..	..	..
85 Georgia	5.2	32	23	45	95	9	7	-4	5	10	-2.7
86 Turkey	189.9	15	28	57	68	12	25	19	15	27	-8.4 [a]
87 Armenia	1.6	41	36	23	116	13	9	-29	..	..	..
88 Dominican Republic	15.0	12	32	55	70	8	25	22	14	16	-0.3 [a]
89 Oman	..	..	..	..	..	..	..	..	..	..	..
90 Sri Lanka	15.1	22	26	52	72	10	24	17	16	26	-4.5
91 Ukraine	49.7	12	40	48	62	22	20	16	..	..	..
92 Uzbekistan	25.0	31	27	42	61	21	19	19	..	..	..
93 Maldives	0.3	..	..	..	..	..	..	..	21	48	-4.9
94 Jordan	7.0	3	25	71	69	25	29	6	22	35	-1.4 [a]
95 Iran, Islamic Rep. of	..	..	..	..	..	..	..	..	..	..	..
96 Turkmenistan	4.4	..	..	..	..	..	..	..	..	..	..
97 Kyrgyzstan	1.8	45	23	33	69	17	22	14	..	..	..
98 China	902.0	19	49	32	46	12	38	43	5	8	-1.6 [a]
99 Guyana	0.8	..	..	..	59	18	32	23	..	..	..
100 Albania	2.5	63	18	19	103	11	12	-13	..	..	..

. . . TO HAVE ACCESS TO THE RESOURCES NEEDED FOR A DECENT STANDARD OF LIVING . . .

185

HDI rank	GDP (US$ billions) 1997	Agriculture (as % of GDP) 1997	Industry (as % of GDP) 1997	Services (as % of GDP) 1997	Consumption Private (as % of GDP) 1997	Consumption Government (as % of GDP) 1997	Gross domestic investment (as % of GDP) 1997	Gross domestic savings (as % of GDP) 1997	Tax revenue (as % of GDP) 1997	Central government expenditure (as % of GDP) 1997	Overall budget surplus/deficit (as % of GDP) 1997
101 South Africa	129.1	5	39	57	62	21	16	17	28	34	-3.8
102 Tunisia	18.9	13	29	58	60	16	27	24	25	33	-3.1 ª
103 Azerbaijan	4.4	22	18	60	83	8	28	10	..	..	..
104 Moldova, Rep. of	1.9	31	35	34	74	26	24	(.)	..	..	..
105 Indonesia	215.0	16	43	41	63	7	31	31	15	15	1.2 ª
106 Cape Verde	0.4	9	21	70	84	20	34	-4	..	..	..
107 El Salvador	11.3	13	28	60	86	9	15	4	..	..	..
108 Tajikistan	2.0	..	..	..	..	..	..	..	..	..	..
109 Algeria	47.1	11	49	39	51	14	26	35	31	30	3.0 ª
110 Viet Nam	24.8	26	31	43	70	9	29	21	..	..	..
111 Syrian Arab Republic	17.9	..	..	..	69	12	29	19	16	24	-0.2 ª
112 Bolivia	8.0	16	33	51	75	15	19	10	15	22	-2.3
113 Swaziland	1.3	19	42	40	53	27	34	19	..	..	..
114 Honduras	4.5	20	28	52	63	15	32	22	..	..	..
115 Namibia	3.3	11	33	56	55	31	20	14	..	..	..
116 Vanuatu	0.3	25	12	63	..	..	..	..	..	..	..
117 Guatemala	17.8	24	20	56	87	5	14	8	..	..	..
118 Solomon Islands	0.4	..	..	..	..	..	..	..	..	..	..
119 Mongolia	0.9	37	23	40	64	16	22	18	19	22	-6.6 ª
120 Egypt	75.6	18	32	51	77	10	18	13	..	..	..
121 Nicaragua	2.0	34	22	44	84	13	28	3	..	..	..
122 Botswana	5.1	3	48	49	28	27	26	45	16	39	9.4 ª
123 São Tomé and Principe	(.)	23	19	58	71	45	50	-16	..	..	..
124 Gabon	5.2	7	55	37	38	14	26	48	..	..	..
125 Iraq	..	..	..	..	..	..	..	..	..	..	..
126 Morocco	33.5	15	33	51	65	18	21	17	..	..	..
127 Lesotho	1.0	11	42	47	82	28	86	-10	31	40	1.0
128 Myanmar	..	59	10	31	..	..	13	12	4	10	-3.2 ª
129 Papua New Guinea	4.6	28	36	36	44	23	37	33	..	..	..
130 Zimbabwe	0.9	19	25	56	72	16	19	12	..	..	..
131 Equatorial Guinea	0.5	23	67	10	20	13	96	68	..	..	..
132 India	381.6	25	30	45	70	10	24	20	11	16	-4.9
133 Ghana	6.9	36	26	39	80	10	24	10	..	..	..
134 Cameroon	9.1	41	21	38	71	8	16	21	..	..	..
135 Congo	2.3	10	57	33	46	19	26	35	..	..	..
136 Kenya	10.2	29	16	56	72	17	19	11	23	29	-0.9 ª
137 Cambodia	3.0	51	15	34	87	9	16	4	..	..	..
138 Pakistan	61.7	25	25	50	78	12	15	10	13	23	-7.9
139 Comoros	0.2	39	13	49	89	14	21	-3	..	..	..
Low human development	191.6 T	32	30	38	76	10	18	15	..	..	..
140 Lao People's Dem. Rep.	1.8	52	21	26	81	7	29	11	..	..	..
141 Congo, Dem. Rep. of the	6.1	58	17	25	83	8	7	9	..	..	..
142 Sudan	10.2	..	..	..	..	..	..	..	..	..	..
143 Togo	1.5	42	21	37	80	10	16	10	..	..	..
144 Nepal	4.9	41	22	36	81	9	21	10	9	17	-4.1
145 Bhutan	0.4	38	38	25	39	29	43	32	6	33	-2.2
146 Nigeria	39.9	33	47	20	70	9	15	22	..	..	..
147 Madagascar	3.5	32	14	55	89	7	12	4	8	17	-1.3 ª
148 Yemen	5.7	18	49	34	68	19	21	13	13	39	-2.6
149 Mauritania	1.1	25	29	46	79	12	18	9	..	..	..
150 Bangladesh	41.4	24	27	49	81	4	21	15	..	..	..

... TO HAVE ACCESS TO THE RESOURCES NEEDED FOR A DECENT STANDARD OF LIVING ...

HDI rank	GDP (US$ billions) 1997	Agriculture (as % of GDP) 1997	Industry (as % of GDP) 1997	Services (as % of GDP) 1997	Consumption Private (as % of GDP) 1997	Government (as % of GDP) 1997	Gross domestic investment (as % of GDP) 1997	Gross domestic savings (as % of GDP) 1997	Tax revenue (as % of GDP) 1997	Central government expenditure (as % of GDP) 1997	Overall budget surplus/deficit (as % of GDP) 1997
151 Zambia	3.9	16	31	52	78	12	15	10	17	21	0.7 [a]
152 Haiti	2.8	30	20	50	97	7	10	-4	..	..	..
153 Senegal	4.5	18	22	59	77	10	19	13	..	..	..
154 Côte d'Ivoire	10.3	27	21	51	65	12	16	23	..	..	..
155 Benin	2.1	38	14	48	79	10	18	11	..	..	..
156 Tanzania, U. Rep. of	6.9	47	21	31	83	13	20	..	..	..	..
157 Djibouti	0.5	4	21	76	78	28	9	-6	..	..	..
158 Uganda	6.6	44	17	39	83	10	15	8	..	..	..
159 Malawi	2.5	36	18	46	85	13	12	2	..	..	..
160 Angola	7.7	9	62	29	30	43	25	27	..	..	..
161 Guinea	3.9	23	35	42	74	7	22	19	..	..	..
162 Chad	1.6	39	15	46	92	7	19	1	..	..	..
163 Gambia	0.4	30	15	55	85	11	18	4	..	..	..
164 Rwanda	1.9	37	26	36	99	9	11	-7	..	..	..
165 Central African Republic	1.0	54	18	28	84	9	9	7	..	..	..
166 Mali	2.5	49	17	34	74	12	23	14	..	..	..
167 Eritrea	0.7	9	30	61	85	33	41	-17	..	..	..
168 Guinea-Bissau	0.3	54	11	35	88	7	24	5	..	..	..
169 Mozambique	2.8	31	24	45	76	10	30	14	..	..	..
170 Burundi	1.0	53	17	30	83	15	7	3	13	24	-5.5
171 Burkina Faso	2.4	35	27	38	79	12	25	9	..	..	..
172 Ethiopia	6.4	55	7	38	80	11	19	9	..	..	..
173 Niger	1.9	38	18	44	83	14	11	3	..	..	..
174 Sierra Leone	0.8	50	21	29	98	10	-5	-8	10	18	-6.0
All developing countries	5,639.5 T	13	36	51	61	12	27	27	..	..	..
Least developed countries	143.3 T	33	25	42	79	11	20	11	..	..	..
Sub-Saharan Africa	304.3 T	20	34	46	66	17	18	17	..	..	..
Arab States	408.2 T	..	..	..	55	21	21	24	..	..	..
East Asia	1,516.8 T	13	44	43	50	11	37	39	10	12	-1.5
East Asia (excluding China)	614.8 T	4	36	60	56	11	35	33	19	19	-1.4
South-East Asia and the Pacific	688.3 T	13	40	47	56	10	34	34	16	17	2.3
South Asia	505.4 T	25	29	46	72	10	23	18	11	18	-5.2
South Asia (excluding India)	123.8 T	25	26	49	78	9	19	13	13	23	-7.0
Latin America and the Caribbean	2,018.4 T	8	32	60	67	12	22	21	..	..	..
Eastern Europe and the CIS	947.3 T	11	36	53	64	15	23	22	..	..	..
Industrialized countries	21,700.0 T	2 [a]	..	64 [a]	63 [a]	16 [a]	21 [a]	21 [a]	26 [a]	30 [a]	-1.2 [a]
World	28,286.8 T	..	..	..	..	..	..	..	..	..	..

Note: The percentage shares of agriculture, industry and services may not sum to 100 because of rounding

a. Data refer to 1996.

Source: Columns 1-11: World Bank 1999b.

... TO HAVE ACCESS TO THE RESOURCES NEEDED FOR A DECENT STANDARD OF LIVING ...

HDI rank	Public expenditure on education (as % of GNP)		Public expenditure on health		Military expenditure (as % of GDP)		Trade in conventional weapons (1990 prices)[a]				Total armed forces	
			As % of GNP	As % of GDP			Imports		Exports			Index (1985=100)
	1985	1996	1960	1995	1988	1996	US$ millions 1997	Index (1991=100) 1997	US$ millions 1997	Share (%) 1993-97[b]	Thousands 1997	1997
High human development	**5.1**	**5.1**	**..**	**6.1**	**3.6**	**2.3**	**..**	**..**	**..**	**..**	**5,421 T**	**79**
1 Canada	6.6	7.0	..	6.9	2.0	1.4	97	10	81	1.2	62	74
2 Norway	5.9	7.5	..	6.6	3.0	2.3	155	62	56	0.4	34	91
3 United States	4.9	5.4	..	6.5	5.8	3.6	656	148	10,840	46.9	1,448	67
4 Japan	..	3.6	..	5.6	1.0	0.1	584	24	3	0.1	236	97
5 Belgium	6.2	3.2	..	6.9	2.7	1.6	34	15	93	0.4	45	49
6 Sweden	7.7	8.3	..	7.1	2.5	2.4	123	..	273	0.8	53	81
7 Australia	5.6	5.6	..	5.8	2.7	2.3	215	85	318	0.4	57	82
8 Netherlands	6.4	5.2	..	6.8	2.9	2.0	93	31	504	1.9	57	54
9 Iceland	4.9	5.4	..	6.9	..	..	..	..	..	..	..	..
10 United Kingdom	4.9	5.4	..	5.9	4.2	3.0	71	8	2,631	8.3	214	65
11 France	5.8	6.1	..	8.0	3.8	3.0	160	16	3,343	6.9	381	82
12 Switzerland	4.8	5.3	..	6.9	1.8	1.5	391	166	72	0.3	26	132
13 Finland	5.4	7.6	..	5.8	1.5	1.6	492	502	..	..	31	85
14 Germany	..	4.8	..	8.1	2.9 [c]	1.7	..	..	569	6.3	347	73
15 Denmark	7.2	8.2	..	6.9	2.1	1.8	46	..	..	..	33	111
16 Austria	5.9	5.7	..	5.9	1.1	0.9	139	..	..	..	46	83
17 Luxembourg	3.8	4.1	..	6.2	1.3	0.7	..	..	..	..	1	114
18 New Zealand	4.7	7.3	..	5.7	2.2	1.2	343	..	..	..	10	77
19 Italy	5.0	4.7	..	5.4	2.3	1.9	552	484	408	1.6	325	84
20 Ireland	6.4	5.8	..	5.2	1.1	1.1	..	..	..	..	13	93
21 Spain	3.3	4.9	..	5.8	2.1	1.5	316	251	639	2.5	198	62
22 Singapore	4.4	3.0	1.0	1.5	4.7	4.3	108	34	..	..	70	127
23 Israel	7.0	7.2	..	..	13.0	8.7	41	3	335	1.0	175	123
24 Hong Kong, China (SAR)	2.8	2.9	..	2.3	..	..	..	..	..	..	..	..
25 Brunei Darussalam	2.1	3.1	..	0.8	6.2	..	..	..	..	..	5	122
26 Cyprus	3.7	..	0.6	..	3.9	3.4	110	..	..	..	10	100
27 Greece	2.9	3.0	..	4.4	5.2	4.5	715	126	..	..	162	81
28 Portugal	4.0	5.5	..	5.0	2.8	2.4	14	1	..	..	59	81
29 Barbados	6.1	7.2	3.0	4.4	..	..	..	..	..	..	1	60
30 Korea, Rep. of	4.5	3.7	0.2	1.9	4.0	3.2	1,077	273	12	0.1	672	112
31 Bahamas	4.0	..	..	2.5	..	..	..	..	..	..	1	180
32 Malta	3.4	..	..	..	1.3	0.1	..	..	..	..	2	250
33 Slovenia	..	5.8	..	7.1	..	1.6	..	..	..	..	10	..
34 Chile	4.4	3.1	2.0	2.3	2.3	1.6	180	212	..	..	94	93
35 Kuwait	4.9	5.7	..	3.5	8.2	11.9	411	67	..	..	15	128
36 Czech Republic	..	5.4	..	6.9	..	1.8	..	..	19	0.9	62	..
37 Bahrain	4.1	..	..	..	5.5	5.4	13	26	..	..	11	393
38 Antigua and Barbuda	2.7	..	..	3.7	..	..	..	..	..	..	0	200
39 Argentina	..	3.5	1.3	4.3	1.6	1.2	148	..	..	..	73	68
40 Uruguay	2.8	3.3	2.6	1.9	2.1	1.5	..	..	..	..	26	80
41 Qatar	4.1	3.4	..	..	..	..	286	..	29	0.1	12	197
42 Slovakia	..	4.9	..	6.1	..	2.3	..	..	..	..	41	..
43 United Arab Emirates	1.7	..	..	2.0	6.7 [d]	4.5	808	636	..	..	65	150
44 Poland	4.9	5.2	..	4.2	2.5	2.8	..	..	18	0.3	242	76
45 Costa Rica	4.5	5.3	3.0	6.0	0.5	..	..	..	..	..	..	..
Medium human development	**4.0**	**3.8**	**0.9**	**2.2**	**6.0**	**2.5**	**..**	**..**	**..**	**..**	**13,603 T**	**92**
46 Trinidad and Tobago	6.1	3.7	1.7	2.1	..	..	..	..	..	..	2	100
47 Hungary	5.5	4.7	..	4.9	3.4	1.6	..	..	..	..	49	46
48 Venezuela	5.1	..	2.6	1.0	1.5	1.0 [d]	..	..	..	..	56	114
49 Panama	4.6	4.6	3.0	4.7	2.1	1.2	..	..	..	..	..	..
50 Mexico	3.9	4.9	1.9	2.8	0.5	0.4	96	..	..	..	175	9

... TO HAVE ACCESS TO THE RESOURCES NEEDED FOR A DECENT STANDARD OF LIVING ...

	Public expenditure on education (as % of GNP)		Public expenditure on health		Military expenditure (as % of GDP)		Trade in conventional weapons (1990 prices) [a]				Total armed forces	
							Imports		Exports			Index (1985 = 100)
			As % of GNP	As % of GDP			US$ millions	Index (1991 = 100)	US$ millions	Share (%)	Thousands	
HDI rank	1985	1996	1960	1995	1988	1996	1997	1997	1997	1993-97 [b]	1997	1997
51 Saint Kitts and Nevis	5.8	3.8	..	3.1	..	..	..	..	..	..	..	..
52 Grenada	..	..	..	2.7	..	..	..	..	..	..	..	..
53 Dominica	5.0	..	..	3.9	..	..	..	..	..	..	..	..
54 Estonia	..	7.3	..	5.8	..	1.2	..	..	..	..	1	..
55 Croatia	..	5.3	..	8.5	..	14.5	37	..	..	..	58	..
56 Malaysia	6.6	5.2	1.1	1.3	2.5	2.4	1,346	..	..	..	112	101
57 Colombia	2.9	4.4	0.4	2.9	1.3	..	190	..	..	..	146	221
58 Cuba	6.3	..	3.0	7.9	..	..	..	..	..	..	60	37
59 Mauritius	3.8	..	1.5	2.2	0.2	0.3	..	..	..	..	..	..
60 Belarus	..	6.1	..	5.3	..	1.2	..	..	263	0.4	82	..
61 Fiji	6.0	..	..	..	2.2	..	..	..	..	..	4	133
62 Lithuania	5.3	5.6	..	5.1	..	0.5	..	..	..	..	5	..
63 Bulgaria	5.5	3.3	..	3.6	4.6	1.8	40	10	..	..	102	68
64 Suriname	9.4	..	..	2.0	..	..	..	..	..	..	2	90
65 Libyan Arab Jamahiriya	7.1	..	1.3	..	..	..	..	..	..	..	65	89
66 Seychelles	10.7	7.6	..	4.1	4.3	2.2	..	..	..	..	0	17
67 Thailand	3.8	4.1	0.4	2.0	2.7	1.9	1,031	164	..	..	266	113
68 Romania	2.2	3.6	..	3.6	3.3	3.5	12	32	..	..	227	120
69 Lebanon	..	2.5	..	..	..	6.3	10	..	..	..	55	317
70 Samoa (Western)	..	..	..	5.3	..	..	..	..	..	..	..	..
71 Russian Federation	3.2	4.1	..	4.3	15.8	3.7 [d]	..	..	3,466	13.5	1,240	..
72 Ecuador	3.7	3.5	0.4	2.0	2.0	..	..	..	..	..	57	134
73 Macedonia, TFYR	5.5	5.6	..	7.4	..	..	..	..	..	..	114	..
74 Latvia	3.4	6.5	..	4.4	..	0.8	..	..	..	..	5	..
75 Saint Vincent and the Grenadines	5.8	..	..	5.3	..	..	..	..	..	..	..	..
76 Kazakhstan	..	4.7	..	2.2	..	..	172	..	..	..	35	..
77 Philippines	1.4	2.2	0.4	..	1.9	1.6	47	..	..	..	111	96
78 Saudi Arabia	6.7	..	0.6	..	17.6	13.2 [d]	2,370	178	..	..	163	260
79 Brazil	3.8	5.2	0.6	1.9	1.4 [d]	1.9	384	233	28	0.1	315	114
80 Peru	2.9	2.9	1.1	2.2	2.0	1.3	258	..	..	..	125	98
81 Saint Lucia	5.5	9.8	..	2.5	..	..	..	..	..	..	..	..
82 Jamaica	5.7	7.5	2.0	..	..	..	..	..	..	..	3	157
83 Belize	..	5.0	..	6.0	1.3	..	..	..	..	..	1	183
84 Paraguay	1.5	3.9	0.5	1.8	1.0	1.3 [d]	..	..	..	..	20	140
85 Georgia	..	..	..	0.6	..	1.3	..	..	..	..	33	..
86 Turkey	1.8	2.2	0.8	2.4	3.0	4.3	1,276	134	..	..	639	101
87 Armenia	..	2.0	..	3.1	..	..	..	..	..	..	60	..
88 Dominican Republic	1.8	2.0	1.3	1.8	..	..	..	..	..	..	25	110
89 Oman	4.0	..	..	..	20.1	13.2	173	..	..	..	44	1,740
90 Sri Lanka	2.6	3.4	2.0	1.4	2.1	6.0 [d]	41	..	..	..	117	542
91 Ukraine	5.2	7.2	..	4.9	..	4.5	..	..	399	1.0	387	..
92 Uzbekistan	..	8.1	..	3.5	..	..	..	..	..	..	70	..
93 Maldives	4.4	6.4	..	..	..	..	..	..	..	..	..	..
94 Jordan	5.5	7.3	0.6	3.7	11.4	8.8	62	..	..	..	104	148
95 Iran, Islamic Rep. of	3.6	..	0.8	1.4	3.2	2.5	11	6	..	..	518	170
96 Turkmenistan	..	..	..	1.2	..	..	..	..	..	..	18	..
97 Kyrgyzstan	7.9	5.7	..	3.5	..	..	..	..	..	..	12	..
98 China	2.5	2.3	1.3	..	1.6	1.1	1,816	1,203	170	3.1	2,840	73
99 Guyana	9.8	4.9	..	4.3	3.3	0.8	..	..	..	..	2	24
100 Albania	..	3.1	..	2.5	5.6	1.5	..	..	..	..	54	134

... TO HAVE ACCESS TO THE RESOURCES NEEDED FOR A DECENT STANDARD OF LIVING ...

HDI rank	Public expenditure on education (as % of GNP)		Public expenditure on health		Military expenditure (as % of GDP)		Trade in conventional weapons (1990 prices)[a]				Total armed forces	
			As % of GNP	As % of GDP			Imports		Exports			Index
							US$ millions	Index (1991 = 100)	US$ millions	Share (%)	Thousands	(1985 = 100)
	1985	1996	1960	1995	1988	1996	1997	1997	1997	1993-97[b]	1997	1997
101 South Africa	6.0	7.9	0.5	..	4.3	2.1	8	..	1	0.1	79	75
102 Tunisia	5.8	6.7	1.6	..	2.7	1.8	37	..	..	..	35	100
103 Azerbaijan	5.7	3.3	..	1.1	..	..	..	..	..	..	67	..
104 Moldova, Rep. of	..	9.7	..	5.8	..	0.8	..	..	392	0.5	11	..
105 Indonesia	..	1.4	0.3	0.7	1.7	1.3	171	72	13	0.1	284	102
106 Cape Verde	3.6	..	..	3.3	1.8	..	..	..	..	..	1	14
107 El Salvador	3.1	2.2	0.9	2.4	2.8	0.9	..	..	..	..	28	68
108 Tajikistan	..	2.2	..	5.8	..	..	..	..	..	..	9	..
109 Algeria	8.5	5.2	1.2	..	1.9	3.4	..	..	..	..	124	73
110 Viet Nam	..	2.7	..	..	..	..	84	..	..	..	492	48
111 Syrian Arab Republic	6.1	4.2	0.4	..	7.9	6.7	..	..	..	..	320	80
112 Bolivia	2.1	5.6	0.4	3.8	1.7	1.1	..	..	..	..	34	121
113 Swaziland	5.9	7.3	..	3.0	1.1	2.3	..	..	..	..	..	..
114 Honduras	4.2	3.6	1.0	2.8	1.6	1.1 [d]	..	..	..	..	19	113
115 Namibia	..	9.1	..	4.2	..	2.3	..	..	..	..	6	..
116 Vanuatu	..	4.9	..	..	..	..	..	..	..	..	..	..
117 Guatemala	1.8	1.7	0.6	1.8	1.6	0.8	..	..	..	..	41	128
118 Solomon Islands	4.7	..	..	4.9	..	..	..	..	..	..	..	..
119 Mongolia	7.8	6.4	..	4.3	8.7	2.2	..	..	..	..	9	27
120 Egypt	6.3	..	0.6	1.7	4.5	..	867	70	..	..	450	101
121 Nicaragua	6.8	3.6	0.4	5.3	8.7	1.6	..	..	..	..	17	27
122 Botswana	6.8	10.4	1.5	..	4.4	3.2	..	..	..	..	8	188
123 São Tomé and Principe	4.6	..	..	6.2	..	..	..	..	..	..	..	..
124 Gabon	4.5	2.8	0.5	0.6	..	..	..	..	..	..	5	196
125 Iraq	4.0	..	1.0	..	..	..	..	..	..	..	388	75
126 Morocco	6.3	5.3	1.0	..	4.1	3.9	104	117	..	..	196	132
127 Lesotho	4.3	7.0	1.0	3.7	3.1	..	..	..	..	..	2	100
128 Myanmar	..	1.2	0.7	0.4	2.2	..	100	44	..	..	429	231
129 Papua New Guinea	..	..	..	2.8	1.4	..	..	..	..	..	4	134
130 Zimbabwe	9.1	..	1.2	1.7	6.2	2.7	..	..	..	..	39	95
131 Equatorial Guinea	..	1.8	..	..	..	..	..	..	..	..	1	59
132 India	3.4	3.4	0.5	0.7	3.4	2.5	1,085	73	..	..	1,145	91
133 Ghana	2.6	..	1.1	1.6	0.4	0.6	..	..	..	..	7	46
134 Cameroon	3.1	2.9	1.0	1.0	1.4	..	..	..	..	..	13	180
135 Congo	5.1	6.2	1.6	1.8	..	..	..	..	..	..	10	115
136 Kenya	6.4	6.6	1.5	..	2.7	..	..	..	..	..	24	177
137 Cambodia	..	2.9	..	0.7	..	4.7	..	..	..	..	141	401
138 Pakistan	2.5	3.0	0.3	0.8	6.5	5.6 [d]	572	95	..	..	587	122
139 Comoros	4.1	..	..	1.1	..	..	..	..	..	..	..	..
Low human development	2.7	..	0.8	1.2	2.9	..	..	..	..	..	1,091 T	114
140 Lao People's Dem. Rep.	..	2.5	0.5	1.3	..	..	..	..	..	..	29	54
141 Congo, Dem. Rep. of the	1.0	..	..	..	..	..	..	..	..	..	40	83
142 Sudan	..	..	1.0	..	2.0	1.6	..	..	..	..	80	141
143 Togo	5.0	4.7	1.3	1.6	3.1	..	..	..	..	..	7	194
144 Nepal	2.6	3.1	0.2	1.2	0.9	0.8	..	..	..	..	46	184
145 Bhutan	..	..	..	2.3	..	..	..	..	..	..	..	..
146 Nigeria	..	0.9	0.3	0.3	1.2	0.7	..	..	..	..	77	82
147 Madagascar	2.9	1.9	1.4	1.1	1.4	0.8	..	..	..	..	21	100
148 Yemen	..	6.1	..	1.0	..	..	..	..	..	..	66	103
149 Mauritania	..	..	0.5	1.8	4.5	..	..	..	..	..	16	185
150 Bangladesh	1.9	2.9	..	1.2	1.7	..	13	10	..	..	121	133

. . . TO HAVE ACCESS TO THE RESOURCES NEEDED FOR A DECENT STANDARD OF LIVING . . .

HDI rank	Public expenditure on education (as % of GNP)		Public expenditure on health		Military expenditure (as % of GDP)		Trade in conventional weapons (1990 prices) [a]				Total armed forces	
			As % of GNP	As % of GDP			Imports		Exports			Index (1985 = 100)
							US$ millions	Index (1991 = 100)	US$ millions	Share (%)	Thousands	
	1985	1996	1960	1995	1988	1996	1997	1997	1997	1993-97 [b]	1997	1997
151 Zambia	4.7	2.2	1.0	2.9	..	1.1 [d]	..	..	..	..	22	133
152 Haiti	1.2	..	1.0	1.3	..	..	..	..	..	..	..	..
153 Senegal	..	3.5	1.5	1.2	2.0	..	..	..	..	..	13	133
154 Côte d'Ivoire	..	5.0	1.5	1.4	1.2	..	..	..	..	..	8	64
155 Benin	..	3.2	1.5	1.8	2.3	..	..	..	..	..	5	107
156 Tanzania, U. Rep. of	4.4	..	0.5	2.5	1.8	..	..	..	..	..	35	86
157 Djibouti	2.7	..	..	..	..	..	..	..	..	..	10	320
158 Uganda	3.5	2.6	0.7	1.6	1.8	3.8	..	..	..	..	55	275
159 Malawi	3.5	5.5	0.2	2.3	1.5	0.8	..	..	..	..	5	94
160 Angola	5.1	..	..	..	13.0	..	..	..	..	..	111	223
161 Guinea	..	..	1.0	1.2	..	..	..	..	..	..	10	98
162 Chad	..	..	0.5	2.7	..	..	..	..	..	..	25	208
163 Gambia	3.2	..	..	1.7	0.8	1.4	..	..	..	..	1	160
164 Rwanda	3.1	..	0.5	..	1.5	..	..	..	..	..	55	1,058
165 Central African Republic	2.8	..	1.3	1.9	..	1.1	..	..	..	..	3	117
166 Mali	3.7	2.2	1.0	2.0	2.4	..	..	..	..	..	7	151
167 Eritrea	..	1.8	..	1.1	..	..	53	..	..	..	46	..
168 Guinea-Bissau	3.2	..	..	1.1	..	..	..	..	..	..	7	85
169 Mozambique	4.2	..	..	..	9.2	3.4	..	..	..	..	6	39
170 Burundi	2.5	3.2	0.8	1.0	3.2	4.9	..	..	..	..	19	356
171 Burkina Faso	..	3.6	0.6	4.7	2.6	..	..	..	..	..	6	145
172 Ethiopia	3.0	4.0	0.7	1.7	9.8	1.8	..	..	..	..	120	55
173 Niger	..	..	0.2	1.6	0.8	..	..	..	..	..	5	241
174 Sierra Leone	1.9	..	..	..	0.5	1.8	..	..	..	..	15	484
All developing countries	3.9	3.6	0.9	1.8	3.1	2.4	..	..	..	..	13,107 T	95
Least developed countries	2.7	..	..	1.6	..	..	..	..	..	..	1,566 T	147
Sub-Saharan Africa	4.9	5.4	0.7	1.4	3.7	..	..	..	..	..	934 T	126
Arab States	5.9	..	1.0	..	8.2	..	..	..	..	..	2,201 T	103
East Asia	3.0	2.7	1.0	..	2.5	1.7	..	..	..	..	3,521 T	78
East Asia (excluding China)	4.0	3.5	0.2	2.0	4.0	3.2	..	..	..	..	681 T	108
South-East Asia and the Pacific	..	3.0	0.5	1.3	2.4	2.0	..	..	..	..	1,945 T	92
South Asia	3.3	3.3	0.5	0.9	3.5	2.9	..	..	..	..	2,534 T	116
South Asia (excluding India)	3.3	3.0	..	1.3	3.6	..	..	..	..	..	1,389 T	150
Latin America and the Caribbean	3.9	4.5	1.2	2.5	1.3	1.3	..	..	..	..	1,322 T	87
Eastern Europe and the CIS	..	4.6	..	4.5	..	3.2	..	..	..	..	2,996 T	..
Industrialized countries	5.2	5.1	..	6.3	3.6	2.3	..	..	..	..	4,013 T	74
World	4.9	4.8	..	5.5	4.0	2.4	..	..	..	..	20,115 T	89

a. Figures are trend-indicator values.

b. Calculated using the 1993-97 total for suppliers of conventional weapons as defined by SIPRI 1998.

c. Data refer to the Federal Republic of Germany before reunification.

d. Data refer to estimates deemed uncertain by SIPRI 1998.

Source: Columns 1 and 2: UNESCO 1998a; column 3: UN 1993 and World Bank 1993; column 4: World Bank 1999b; columns 5-7 and 9: SIPRI 1998; columns 8 and 10: calculated on the basis of data from SIPRI 1998; columns 11 and 12: IISS 1998.

HDI rank	Net official development assistance (ODA) disbursed			ODA as % of central government budget	ODA per capita of donor country (1996 US$)		Multi-lateral ODA as % of GNP	Share of ODA through NGOs [b] (%)	Aid by NGOs as % of GNP		Aid to least developed countries (as % of total)	
	Total [a] (US$ millions)	As % of GNP										
	1997	1986/87	1997	1992/93	1986/87	1996/97	1996/97	1995/96	1986/87	1996/97	1986/87	1997
1 Canada	2,045	0.48	0.34	1.6	89	64	0.11	8.5	0.05	0.04	32	23
2 Norway	1,306	1.13	0.86	1.7	294	308	0.25	..	0.08	0.07	41	39
3 United States	6,878	0.21	0.09	1.8	52	30	0.03	8.6	0.04	0.03	18	20
4 Japan	9,358	0.30	0.22	1.4	83	79	0.05	2.1	0.00	0.01	27	19
5 Belgium	764	0.48	0.31	..	107	88	0.06	0.3	0.01	0.02	50	27
6 Sweden	1,731	0.87	0.79	..	225	222	0.20	6.0	0.07	0.01	39	30
7 Australia	1,061	0.40	0.28	1.3	70	59	0.07	0.6	0.02	0.03	19	19
8 Netherlands	2,947	0.99	0.81	..	203	212	0.17	9.2	0.08	0.01	34	27
10 United Kingdom	3,433	0.29	0.26	..	49	55	0.06	2.0	0.03	0.03	31	22
11 France	6,307	0.58	0.45	..	131	125	0.05	0.2	0.01	0.00	27	22
12 Switzerland	911	0.30	0.34	3.1	124	148	0.11	5.8	0.05	0.04	39	33
13 Finland	379	0.48	0.33	1.5	105	81	0.12	0.7	0.04	0.00	44	24
14 Germany	5,857	0.41	0.28	..	90	87	0.06	2.6	0.06	0.05	28	19
15 Denmark	1,637	0.88	0.97	2.5	250	342	0.35	0.5	0.02	0.02	38	30
16 Austria	527	0.19	0.26	0.7	45	72	0.04	0.5	0.02	0.02	19	17
17 Luxembourg	95	0.17	0.55	..	54	226	0.07	12.5	0.00	0.03	..	29
18 New Zealand	154	0.28	0.26	0.4	43	38	0.05	2.0 [c]	0.02	0.03	20	23
19 Italy	1,266	0.37	0.11	0.6	67	33	0.05	1.0	0.00	0.00	50	26
20 Ireland	187	0.23	0.31	..	22	51	0.04	0.1	0.10	0.10	36	48
21 Spain	1,234	0.08	0.23	1.0	10	34	0.02	..	0.00	0.02	15	16
28 Portugal	250	0.10	0.25	..	6	25	0.02	0.8	0.00	0.00	..	66
DAC total [d]	48,324 T	0.33	0.22	..	75	66	0.05	3.4	0.03	0.02	28	23

Note: DAC refers to the Development Assistance Committee of the OECD.

a. Some non-DAC countries and areas also provide ODA. Net ODA disbursed in 1997 by the Czech Republic, Iceland, Kuwait, Saudi Arabia and Taiwan (province of China) totalled $1,032 million.

b. On a disbursements basis.

c. Data refer to 1994.

d. Totals are as calculated in OECD 1999a.

Source: Columns 1-12: OECD 1999a.

... TO HAVE ACCESS TO THE RESOURCES NEEDED FOR A DECENT STANDARD OF LIVING ...

15 Aid and debt by recipient country

	Net official development assistance (ODA) received (net disbursements)						External debt				Debt service ratio (debt service as % of exports of goods and services)	
	Total (US$ millions)		As % of GNP		Per capita (US$)		Total (US$ millions)		As % of GNP			
HDI rank	1991	1997	1991	1997	1991	1997	1985	1997	1985	1997	1985	1997
High human development	5,476 T	2,539 T	0.7	0.1	31.9	15.4	174,074.4 T	393,373.5 T	55.7	36.0	33.0	13.5
22 Singapore	8	1 [a]	( )	(.)	2.9	0.4	..	..	..	..	..	..
23 Israel	1,750	1,192 [a]	3.0	1.2	353.6	240.7	..	..	..	..	..	..
24 Hong Kong, China (SAR)	36	8 [a]	(.)	(.)	6.3	1.4	..	..	..	..	..	..
25 Brunei Darussalam	4	(.) [a]	0.1	..	15.1	1.1	..	..	..	..	..	..
26 Cyprus	40	49 [a]	0.7	0.6	57.6	70.6	..	..	..	..	..	..
27 Greece	..	..	..	..	..	..	..	..	..	..	..	..
29 Barbados	2	3	0.1	..	7.7	11.5	457.2	644.3	38.4	..	6.3	7.5 [b]
30 Korea, Rep. of	55	-160	(.)	(.)	1.3	-3.7	54,585.3	143,372.5	59.9	32.8	27.8	8.6
31 Bahamas	2	3 [a]	0.1	..	7.7	11.6	..	..	..	..	..	..
32 Malta	21	22	0.8	0.7	58.7	61.5	185.4	1,033.9	16.8	30.6	1.9	2.1
33 Slovenia	..	97	..	0.5	..	48.5	..	4,762.1	..	26.0	..	3.9
34 Chile	126	136	0.4	0.2	9.5	10.2	20,383.9	31,440.1	141.7	42.4	48.4	20.4
35 Kuwait	5	2 [a]	(.)	(.)	3.7	1.5	..	..	..	..	..	..
36 Czech Republic	231 [a]	107 [a]	1.0	0.2	22.4	10.4	3,459.3	21,456.3	12.6	41.8	..	14.1
37 Bahrain	44	84	1.2	1.6	86.6	165.4	1,264.0	7,084.0 [b]	37.6	138.4 [b]	..	..
38 Antigua and Barbuda	7	4	1.8	0.8	109.0	62.3	59.0	280.0 [b]	31.4	59.7 [b]	..	..
39 Argentina	300	222	0.2	0.1	9.1	6.7	50,945.9	123,221.4	60.9	38.7	60.1	58.7
40 Uruguay	52	57	0.5	0.3	16.6	18.2	3,919.4	6,652.0	89.3	33.6	42.6	15.4
41 Qatar	2	1 [a]	(.)	..	3.9	2.0	..	..	..	..	..	..
42 Slovakia	115 [a]	67 [a]	1.1	0.3	21.8	12.7	1,107.6	9,989.0	8.2	51.7	..	12.2
43 United Arab Emirates	-6	4 [a]	(.)	..	-3.0	2.0	..	..	..	..	..	..
44 Poland	2,508 [a]	641 [a]	3.4	0.5	65.6	16.8	33,307.1	39,889.5	48.6	29.5	15.5	6.1
45 Costa Rica	174	..	3.2	..	56.3	..	4,400.3	3,548.4	121.0	38.1	41.5	11.8
Medium human development	34,101 T	24,130 T	1.2	0.6	9.3	6.2	734,448.7 T	1,720,856.1 T	35.3	32.9	26.0	18.0
46 Trinidad and Tobago	-2	33	(.)	0.6	-1.6	26.5	1,448.2	2,161.5	20.6	38.8	10.2	19.6
47 Hungary	626 [a]	152 [a]	2.0	0.3	60.5	14.7	13,956.5	24,373.4	70.6	55.0	39.3	29.7
48 Venezuela	31	28	0.1	(.)	1.6	1.4	35,333.7	35,541.5	58.4	41.6	25.0	31.3
49 Panama	102	124	1.9	1.5	41.7	50.7	4,758.5	6,338.0	91.4	75.4	7.3	16.4
50 Mexico	278	108	0.1	(.)	3.3	1.3	96,861.9	149,689.9	56.1	38.4	43.7	32.4
51 Saint Kitts and Nevis	7	7	4.4	2.7	167.5	167.5	12.8	62.0	16.7	24.3	1.8	3.9
52 Grenada	16	8	6.8	2.7	170.9	85.5	52.2	105.3	42.4	34.9	10.7	5.7 [b]
53 Dominica	17	14	9.8	6.2	236.1	194.4	54.3	161.4	55.8	43.5	7.6	8.2
54 Estonia	15 [a]	65 [a]	0.3	1.4	9.6	41.5	..	658.4	..	14.5	..	1.4
55 Croatia	..	44	..	0.2	..	9.2	..	6,841.5	..	35.2	..	11.9
56 Malaysia	290	-241	0.7	-0.3	15.5	-12.9	20,269.1	47,228.2	69.9	50.5	30.4	7.5
57 Colombia	123	274	0.3	0.3	3.4	7.7	14,245.5	31,777.4	42.9	34.4	41.9	26.6
58 Cuba	38	67	..	..	3.5	6.2	20,082.0	35,344.0 [b]	..	..	..	..
59 Mauritius	68	42	2.4	1.0	63.8	39.4	628.8	2,471.6	61.1	56.7	24.3	10.9
60 Belarus	187 [a]	43 [a]	0.5	0.2	18.2	4.2	..	1,161.5	..	5.2	..	1.8
61 Fiji	45	44	3.1	2.2	60.3	59.0	443.7	213.4	40.5	10.5	11.7	3.0
62 Lithuania	4 [a]	102 [a]	(.)	1.1	1.1	27.3	..	1,540.5	..	16.4	..	6.0
63 Bulgaria	316 [a]	206 [a]	3.2	2.1	36.6	23.9	3,851.5	9,858.3	22.0	101.3	10.2	14.4
64 Suriname	44	77	12.6	11.4	108.9	190.6	57.0	118.0 [b]	6.1	17.5 [b]	..	..
65 Libyan Arab Jamahiriya	26	9	..	..	5.7	2.0	4,759.0	3,363.0 [b]	17.4	..	..	..
66 Seychelles	23	15	6.3	2.8	325.1	212.0	97.2	149.1	59.6	28.2	7.9	4.0
67 Thailand	722	626	0.7	0.4	12.8	11.1	17,545.5	93,415.7	45.9	62.6	31.9	15.4
68 Romania	321 [a]	197 [a]	1.1	0.6	13.8	8.5	7,008.0	10,442.1	..	30.2	18.7	15.7
69 Lebanon	132	239	2.7	1.6	35.6	64.5	869.5	5,036.2	..	32.8	..	14.4
70 Samoa (Western)	57	28	38.2	14.4	351.7	172.8	76.1	156.3	88.8	80.1	15.1	3.8

... TO HAVE ACCESS TO THE RESOURCES NEEDED FOR A DECENT STANDARD OF LIVING ...

193

HDI rank	Net official development assistance (ODA) received (net disbursements)						External debt				Debt service ratio (debt service as % of exports of goods and services)	
	Total (US$ millions)		As % of GNP		Per capita (US$)		Total (US$ millions)		As % of GNP			
	1991	1997	1991	1997	1991	1997	1985	1997	1985	1997	1985	1997
71 Russian Federation	564 [a]	718 [a]	0.1	0.2	3.8	4.8	28,296.4	125,645.2	..	28.7	..	6.5
72 Ecuador	238	172	2.2	0.9	22.7	16.4	8,702.8	14,918.4	58.9	79.4	33.0	31.0
73 Macedonia, TFYR	..	149	..	6.8	..	77.8	..	1,542.5	..	70.8	..	8.8
74 Latvia	3 [a]	81 [a]	(.)	1.5	1.1	30.4	..	503.3	..	9.0	..	4.4
75 Saint Vincent and the Grenadines	14	6	7.0	2.2	129.6	55.6	24.8	257.8	22.3	94.8	3.8	8.3 [b]
76 Kazakhstan	112	131	0.4	0.6	6.8	8.0	..	4,278.0	..	19.5	..	6.5
77 Philippines	1,053	689	2.3	0.8	16.4	10.8	26,637.3	45,433.3	89.1	53.0	31.6	9.2
78 Saudi Arabia	45	15	(.)	(.)	2.8	0.9	14,181.0	19,222.0 [b]	14.6	13.5 [b]	..	..
79 Brazil	183	487	(.)	0.1	1.2	3.2	104,000.0	193,662.8	49.1	24.1	39.1	57.4
80 Peru	614	488	2.2	0.8	27.9	22.2	12,879.3	30,495.7	72.9	48.8	27.7	30.9
81 Saint Lucia	22	24	5.5	4.1	146.7	160.0	23.1	151.7	10.8	25.7	1.2	3.3 [b]
82 Jamaica	162	71	4.9	1.8	66.8	29.3	4,102.9	3,912.9	225.6	97.7	37.6	16.2
83 Belize	21	14	5.0	2.3	108.1	72.1	118.3	383.4	59.4	62.2	11.6	9.2
84 Paraguay	146	116	2.4	1.2	33.6	26.7	1,816.9	2,052.5	58.0	20.8	19.7	5.0
85 Georgia	(.)	246	(.)	4.7	(.)	45.0	..	1,445.5	..	27.4	..	6.4
86 Turkey	1,623	-1	1.1	(.)	28.3	(.)	26,012.6	91,205.4	38.4	47.1	35.0	18.4
87 Armenia	3	168	0.1	9.6	0.8	46.5	..	665.5	..	38.0	..	5.8
88 Dominican Republic	67	76	0.9	0.5	9.2	10.5	3,502.4	4,238.7	73.8	29.0	19.0	6.2
89 Oman	15	20	0.2	..	8.5	11.4	2,329.4	3,601.7	26.3	..	5.4	5.9
90 Sri Lanka	891	345	10.1	2.3	51.7	20.0	..	7,638.1	59.5	51.2	16.5	6.4
91 Ukraine	368 [a]	176 [a]	0.4	0.4	7.1	3.4	..	10,901.3	..	22.2	..	6.6
92 Uzbekistan	..	130	..	0.5	..	6.2	..	2,760.5	..	11.2	..	12.9
93 Maldives	35	26	23.4	8.4	159.9	118.8	83.1	160.3	116.3	51.8	11.3	6.7
94 Jordan	921	462	23.8	6.8	259.8	130.3	4,021.9	8,234.1	78.7	121.0	17.2	11.1
95 Iran, Islamic Rep. of	194	196	..	0.2	3.5	3.5	6,057.0	11,816.4	3.4	9.6	4.1	32.2
96 Turkmenistan	..	11	..	0.4	..	2.9	..	1,771.2	..	62.5	..	34.7
97 Kyrgyzstan	..	240	..	14.1	..	53.9	..	928.2	..	54.4	..	6.3
98 China	1,999	2,040	0.5	0.2	1.7	1.8	16,696.0	146,697.0	5.5	16.6	8.3	8.6
99 Guyana	130	272	60.9	39.9	162.4	339.9	1,496.5	1,610.6	388.8	236.0	27.7	17.6
100 Albania	324	155	29.2	6.2	99.4	47.5	..	706.0	..	28.1	..	7.1
101 South Africa	..	497	..	0.4	..	13.8	..	25,221.6	..	20.0	..	12.8
102 Tunisia	357	194	2.8	1.1	42.8	23.3	4,884.1	11,322.7	60.6	62.8	25.0	16.0
103 Azerbaijan	..	182	..	4.2	..	25.1	..	503.7	..	11.7	..	6.8
104 Moldova, Rep. of	..	63	..	3.5	..	14.5	..	1,039.8	..	57.4	..	10.9
105 Indonesia	1,874	832	1.5	0.4	10.3	4.6	36,715.2	136,173.5	44.4	65.3	28.8	30.0
106 Cape Verde	106	110	33.1	26.2	305.1	316.6	97.4	220.0	94.9	52.5	9.5	5.5
107 El Salvador	294	294	5.6	2.6	56.5	56.5	1,850.8	3,281.8	49.8	29.4	24.0	7.0
108 Tajikistan	..	101	..	5.0	..	18.5	..	901.1	..	44.6	..	4.6
109 Algeria	340	248	0.8	0.6	13.3	9.7	18,259.9	30,920.6	32.4	69.0	35.6	27.2
110 Viet Nam	238	997	2.5	4.1	3.5	14.7	..	21,629.3	..	89.4	..	7.8
111 Syrian Arab Republic	381	199	3.1	1.2	30.4	15.9	10,842.8	20,864.7	66.5	126.4	12.3	9.3
112 Bolivia	513	717	10.1	9.2	76.2	106.5	4,804.6	5,247.5	167.3	67.6	49.5	32.5
113 Swaziland	54	27	5.4	1.9	68.0	34.0	243.1	368.2	60.8	25.4	9.9	2.5
114 Honduras	303	308	10.6	6.7	60.3	61.3	2,730.2	4,697.8	78.5	102.8	24.7	20.9
115 Namibia	184	166	6.9	5.0	132.7	119.7	30.0	85.0 [b]	2.6	2.6 [b]	..	..
116 Vanuatu	53	27	30.7	11.6	349.8	178.2	15.8	47.9	13.0	20.5	1.4	1.5
117 Guatemala	199	302	2.1	1.7	22.2	33.7	2,677.5	4,085.7	28.0	23.2	28.1	9.9
118 Solomon Islands	35	42	15.2	11.4	105.2	126.3	65.5	135.4	42.6	36.9	4.5	2.4
119 Mongolia	70	248	..	25.2	31.0	109.7	..	717.9	..	72.9	..	11.7
120 Egypt	5,025	1,947	15.5	2.5	93.7	36.3	36,102.1	29,849.1	115.0	39.0	25.8	9.0

... TO HAVE ACCESS TO THE RESOURCES NEEDED FOR A DECENT STANDARD OF LIVING ...

HDI rank	Net official development assistance (ODA) received (net disbursements) Total (US$ millions) 1991	1997	As % of GNP 1991	1997	Per capita (US$) 1991	1997	External debt Total (US$ millions) 1985	1997	As % of GNP 1985	1997	Debt service ratio (debt service as % of exports of goods and services) 1985	1997
121 Nicaragua	841	421	..	..	..	..	5,758.4	5,677.4	229.0	305.6	18.4	31.7
122 Botswana	136	125	3.4	2.6	103.4	95.1	351.1	562.0	31.6	11.5	5.4	5.2 b
123 São Tomé and Principe	52	34	98.5	87.5	439.4	287.3	62.6	260.7	187.8	671.2	29.2	52.0
124 Gabon	143	40	2.0	0.9	144.4	40.4	1,200.2	4,284.5	39.0	95.7	11.6	13.1
125 Iraq	552	281	..	..	29.6	15.1	12,839.0	21,912.0 b	29.0	..	..	..
126 Morocco	1,232	462	4.6	1.4	50.2	18.8	15,779.2	19,320.8	130.4	59.5	34.6	26.6
127 Lesotho	126	93	13.1	7.3	71.5	52.8	175.3	659.8	36.7	51.9	6.8	6.4
128 Myanmar	179	45	..	..	4.4	1.1	3,097.6	5,074.1	..	..	52.5	8.0
129 Papua New Guinea	397	349	10.8	8.6	101.1	88.9	2,112.2	2,272.5	90.4	56.3	32.5	15.0
130 Zimbabwe	393	327	4.7	3.9	39.2	32.6	2,414.6	4,961.3	43.9	58.5	29.0	22.0
131 Equatorial Guinea	63	24	51.7	4.9	174.8	66.6	132.3	283.2	175.7	57.8	..	1.4
132 India	2,745	1,678	1.1	0.4	3.2	1.9	40,950.7	94,404.2	19.2	24.9	22.7	19.6
133 Ghana	882	493	13.6	7.3	57.6	32.2	2,256.5	5,982.0	51.0	88.6	23.6	29.5
134 Cameroon	519	501	4.5	5.9	44.0	42.5	3,174.2	9,292.9	40.2	109.2	23.4	20.4
135 Congo	134	268	5.9	14.7	58.6	117.3	3,050.4	5,070.8	150.7	278.4	34.4	6.2
136 Kenya	921	457	12.1	4.6	37.9	18.8	4,177.6	6,485.8	70.7	64.7	38.6	21.5
137 Cambodia	91	372	5.6	12.2	10.2	41.7	..	2,128.7	..	69.9	..	1.1
138 Pakistan	1,371	597	3.1	1.0	12.4	5.4	13,464.9	29,664.5	46.1	47.5	24.9	35.2
139 Comoros	65	28	26.4	14.5	146.6	63.1	134.2	197.4	118.4	101.9	8.9	3.9
Low human development	15,809 T	13,285 T	12.3	10.5	34.2	28.2	98,339.3 T	173,123.7 T	69.2	93.4	26.0	13.1
140 Lao People's Dem. Rep.	143	341	13.9	19.5	34.6	82.4	618.7	2,319.9	26.1	132.4	9.2	6.5
141 Congo, Dem. Rep. of the	476	168	5.7	3.2	12.3	4.4	6,170.7	12,329.6	93.0	232.3	24.8	0.9
142 Sudan	881	187	7.9	2.1	35.9	7.6	8,955.2	16,326.1	75.1	182.4	12.8	9.2
143 Togo	202	124	12.9	8.6	55.6	34.1	935.3	1,339.0	128.9	92.6	27.3	8.1
144 Nepal	453	414	12.0	8.4	23.5	21.5	589.9	2,397.7	22.2	48.6	6.8	6.9
145 Bhutan	64	70	29.0	21.3	103.6	113.3	8.8	89.3	5.6	27.2	0.0	5.1
146 Nigeria	263	202	11.5	11.0	32.9	25.3	18,643.3	28,455.1	68.1	75.6	32.7	7.8
147 Madagascar	456	838	18.4	24.3	38.3	70.5	2,529.3	4,104.7	92.7	119.2	41.7	27.0
148 Yemen	300	366	6.2	7.3	22.4	27.3	3,338.9	3,856.3	..	76.7	..	2.6
149 Mauritania	220	250	20.6	23.9	105.6	120.0	1,453.9	2,453.2	230.5	234.7	25.3	24.2
150 Bangladesh	1,889	1,009	6.0	2.3	16.8	9.0	6,869.7	15,125.3	31.8	35.1	22.4	10.6
151 Zambia	883	618	29.5	16.9	110.1	77.0	4,575.8	6,757.8	230.4	184.6	14.4	19.9
152 Haiti	182	332	5.5	11.8	27.6	50.4	717.4	1,057.2	36.1	37.7	10.2	15.9
153 Senegal	639	427	12.0	9.6	85.1	56.9	2,566.0	3,670.6	104.7	82.9	20.8	15.3
154 Côte d'Ivoire	633	444	6.9	4.7	52.8	37.0	9,658.9	15,608.6	153.4	165.3	34.8	27.4
155 Benin	268	225	14.5	10.7	54.9	46.1	853.7	1,624.3	83.3	76.9	12.9	9.1
156 Tanzania, U. Rep. of	1,081	963	24.9	13.0	41.1	36.6	9,107.1	7,177.1	..	97.2	40.0	12.9
157 Djibouti	108	87	23.8	17.5	202.7	163.3	144.0	283.6	..	57.1	..	3.1
158 Uganda	667	840	20.4	12.8	39.5	49.7	1,231.9	3,707.9	35.5	56.5	38.0	22.1
159 Malawi	525	350	24.3	14.1	60.0	40.0	1,020.7	2,206.0	94.6	89.0	39.8	12.4
160 Angola	280	436	2.8	9.9	29.2	45.5	2,993.0	10,159.8	47.7	231.8	6.4	15.9
161 Guinea	382	382	13.5	10.3	64.5	64.5	1,465.5	3,520.4	..	95.3	..	21.5
162 Chad	266	225	15.0	14.3	45.2	38.2	216.5	1,026.5	22.0	65.2	17.5	12.5
163 Gambia	103	40	34.1	10.0	107.2	41.6	245.1	430.1	113.7	107.6	10.3	11.6
164 Rwanda	364	592	19.1	32.0	50.9	82.8	365.6	1,110.9	21.4	60.0	10.4	13.3
165 Central African Republic	175	92	12.6	9.2	58.1	30.5	343.5	885.3	40.1	88.2	14.2	6.2
166 Mali	458	455	19.2	18.4	52.6	52.3	1,456.1	2,945.1	119.8	119.2	17.3	10.5
167 Eritrea	..	123	..	14.8	..	38.2	..	75.5	..	9.1	..	0.1
168 Guinea-Bissau	116	125	48.3	49.7	117.0	126.0	318.4	921.3	199.6	366.5	51.9	17.3
169 Mozambique	1,070	963	57.3	37.4	74.2	66.8	2,870.5	5,990.6	81.8	232.9	34.5	18.6
170 Burundi	259	119	22.4	12.6	46.2	21.2	455.1	1,065.5	40.2	112.6	20.4	29.0

HDI rank	Net official development assistance (ODA) received (net disbursements)						External debt				Debt service ratio (debt service as % of exports of goods and services)	
	Total (US$ millions)		As % of GNP		Per capita (US$)		Total (US$ millions)		As % of GNP			
	1991	1997	1991	1997	1991	1997	1985	1997	1985	1997	1985	1997
171 Burkina Faso	424	370	15.3	15.5	46.6	40.7	511.1	1,297.1	35.9	54.3	10.1	11.8
172 Ethiopia	1,097	637	20.6	10.1	20.7	12.0	5,205.7	10,078.5	78.1	159.0	28.4	9.5
173 Niger	377	341	28.7	18.4	95.6	86.5	1,194.9	1,579.1	85.5	86.3	33.7	19.5
174 Sierra Leone	105	130	13.9	16.0	25.7	31.8	709.1	1,148.7	60.4	141.4	14.7	21.2
All developing countries	47,918 T c	34,469 T c	1.9	0.9	12.5	9.0	915,690.6 T	2,001,755.0 T	39.9	36.0	28.7	18.4
Least developed countries	15,136 T	13,041 T	13.2	11.1	33.7	29.1	71,411.0 T	134,713.2 T	62.4	92.3	20.5	12.4
Sub-Saharan Africa	15,658 T	13,726 T	12.3	6.7	42.6	33.5	95,328.2 T	198,224.2 T	74.0	66.3	25.2	13.7
Arab States	10,360 T	4,807 T	4.0	..	49.2	20.7	138,570.0 T	201,196.9 T	41.6	45.7	..	..
East Asia	2,160 T	2,136 T	0.3	0.1	1.7	1.6	71,281.3 T	290,787.4 T	18.0	22.0	18.5	8.6
East Asia (excluding China)	161 T	96 T	(.)	(.)	1.9	-3.1	54,585.3 T	144,090.4 T	59.9	32.9	27.8	8.6
South-East Asia and the Pacific	5,189 T	4,152 T	1.4	0.5	13.9	9.2	107,596.7 T	356,228.2 T	56.2	61.3	30.5	14.7
South Asia	7,642 T	4,335 T	1.9	0.7	6.5	3.7	68,024.1 T	161,295.8 T	15.8	25.7	15.8	19.9
South Asia (excluding India)	4,897 T	2,657 T	5.2	1.9	15.5	8.4	27,073.4 T	66,891.6 T	12.8	26.8	10.9	20.5
Latin America and the Caribbean	5,246 T	5,265 T	0.5	0.5	10.2	11.4	408,877.7 T	702,817.1 T	58.3	33.9	38.1	35.6
Eastern Europe and the CIS	5,697 T	4,272 T	0.6	0.4	16.9	10.0	..	284,564.4 T	..	30.5	..	9.8
Industrialized countries	..	..	..	..	..	..	..	..	..	..	..	..
World	..	..	..	..	..	..	..	..	..	..	..	..

a. Data refer to net official aid.

b. Data refer to 1996.

c. The total differs from that in OECD 1999b because it does not include net ODA to countries unspecified in that source, to Eastern European countries and to other developing countries not included in this table.

Source: Columns 1 and 2: OECD 1999b; *columns 3-6:* calculated on the basis of data from OECD 1999b, UN 1998h and World Bank 1999b; *columns 7-12:* World Bank 1999b.

. . . TO HAVE ACCESS TO THE RESOURCES NEEDED FOR A DECENT STANDARD OF LIVING . . .

HDI rank	Total population (millions)			Annual population growth rate (%)		Urban population (as % of total)			Dependency ratio (%)		Population aged 65 and above (as % of total)		Total fertility rate		Contraceptive prevalence rate (%)
	1975	1997	2015	1975-1997	1997-2015	1975	1997	2015	1997	2015	1997	2015	1975	1997	1990-98[a]
High human development	872.4 T	1,018.2 T	1,088.3 T	0.7	0.4	72.9	77.9	82.2	49.6	51.5	13.6	17.1	2.1	1.7	..
1 Canada	23.2	30.3	35.3	1.2	0.9	75.6	76.8	79.8	47.2	48.7	12.3	16.2	1.8	1.6	73 [b]
2 Norway	4.0	4.4	4.7	0.4	0.4	68.2	73.6	78.0	54.5	54.8	15.8	18.0	2.0	1.9	76 [b]
3 United States	220.2	271.8	307.7	1.0	0.7	73.7	76.6	81.0	52.7	49.8	12.5	14.7	1.8	2.0	71
4 Japan	111.5	126.0	126.1	0.6	(.)	75.7	78.4	82.0	44.8	64.3	15.6	24.6	1.9	1.4	59
5 Belgium	9.8	10.1	10.1	0.2	(.)	94.9	97.1	98.0	51.0	51.6	16.2	19.1	1.8	1.6	79
6 Sweden	8.2	8.9	9.1	0.4	0.1	82.7	83.2	85.2	56.5	57.5	17.5	21.8	1.7	1.6	78
7 Australia	13.9	18.3	21.5	1.3	0.9	85.9	84.6	86.0	50.1	50.3	12.1	15.2	2.3	1.8	76 [b]
8 Netherlands	13.7	15.6	15.9	0.6	0.1	88.4	89.1	90.9	46.7	49.2	13.4	18.5	1.7	1.5	80
9 Iceland	0.2	0.3	0.3	1.0	0.8	86.6	91.9	93.8	54.4	51.4	11.3	13.7	2.5	2.1	..
10 United Kingdom	56.2	58.5	59.6	0.2	0.1	88.7	89.3	90.8	54.1	54.1	15.9	18.7	1.8	1.7	82
11 France	52.7	58.5	61.1	0.5	0.2	73.0	75.0	79.4	52.9	55.5	15.4	18.4	2.0	1.7	75
12 Switzerland	6.3	7.3	7.6	0.6	0.3	55.7	61.6	68.3	47.2	49.6	14.5	18.7	1.6	1.5	71 [b]
13 Finland	4.7	5.1	5.3	0.4	0.1	58.3	63.9	70.9	49.7	56.9	14.5	20.1	1.6	1.7	80 [b]
14 Germany	78.7	82.1	81.6	0.2	(.)	81.2	86.9	89.9	46.6	49.7	15.7	20.3	1.5	1.3	75
15 Denmark	5.1	5.3	5.3	0.2	0.1	81.8	85.4	87.8	48.7	54.4	15.2	19.2	1.8	1.7	78 [b]
16 Austria	7.6	8.1	8.3	0.3	0.2	65.2	64.4	68.5	47.6	46.8	14.7	17.8	1.8	1.4	71 [b]
17 Luxembourg	0.4	0.4	0.5	0.6	0.6	73.7	90.0	94.0	47.0	50.4	14.0	17.0	1.7	1.7	..
18 New Zealand	3.1	3.8	4.4	0.9	0.8	82.8	86.3	89.4	52.9	51.8	11.6	14.1	2.4	2.0	70 [b]
19 Italy	55.4	57.4	54.4	0.2	-0.3	65.6	66.7	70.7	46.8	53.0	17.3	22.6	2.1	1.2	78 [b]
20 Ireland	3.2	3.7	4.2	0.6	0.7	53.6	57.9	63.9	51.3	52.5	11.4	13.6	3.7	1.9	..
21 Spain	35.6	39.6	38.5	0.5	-0.2	69.6	76.9	81.3	46.0	48.1	16.1	19.7	2.8	1.2	59 [b]
22 Singapore	2.3	3.4	4.0	1.9	0.9	100.0	100.0	100.0	40.8	41.3	6.6	12.4	2.1	1.7	74 [b]
23 Israel	3.5	5.9	7.6	2.4	1.4	86.6	90.9	92.6	61.9	52.4	9.7	11.3	3.6	2.7	..
24 Hong Kong, China (SAR)	4.4	6.5	7.7	1.8	0.9	89.7	95.3	96.7	40.2	38.4	10.1	13.7	2.5	1.3	..
25 Brunei Darussalam	0.2	0.3	0.4	3.0	1.6	62.0	70.5	78.7	57.8	42.5	3.0	6.6	4.8	2.8	..
26 Cyprus	0.6	0.8	0.9	1.0	0.7	43.4	55.2	64.6	55.9	51.9	11.3	14.9	2.3	2.0	..
27 Greece	9.0	10.6	10.4	0.7	-0.1	55.3	59.5	65.1	48.6	52.4	16.7	21.4	2.3	1.3	..
28 Portugal	9.1	9.9	9.7	0.4	-0.1	27.7	36.5	46.6	47.4	48.3	15.1	18.2	2.6	1.4	66 [b]
29 Barbados	0.2	0.3	0.3	0.4	0.4	38.6	48.4	58.4	50.5	39.6	11.1	11.3	2.4	1.5	55 [b]
30 Korea, Rep. of	35.3	45.7	51.1	1.2	0.6	48.0	83.5	92.2	40.0	41.4	6.0	10.6	3.4	1.7	79
31 Bahamas	0.2	0.3	0.4	2.0	1.4	73.4	87.4	91.5	56.0	48.5	5.0	7.7	3.3	2.6	62 [b]
32 Malta	0.3	0.4	0.4	1.0	0.6	80.4	89.8	92.6	48.2	54.2	11.3	16.5	2.0	1.9	..
33 Slovenia	1.7	2.0	1.9	0.6	-0.2	42.4	51.8	58.8	43.6	44.7	12.8	17.6	2.2	1.3	..
34 Chile	10.3	14.6	17.9	1.6	1.1	78.4	84.2	86.9	56.2	50.0	6.8	9.7	3.2	2.4	43 [b]
35 Kuwait	1.0	1.7	2.6	2.5	2.3	83.8	97.3	98.2	64.6	44.4	1.8	5.6	6.3	2.9	35 [b]
36 Czech Republic	10.0	10.3	9.9	0.1	-0.2	57.8	65.7	70.7	45.1	46.0	13.3	18.4	2.3	1.2	69
37 Bahrain	0.3	0.6	0.8	3.5	1.5	79.2	91.2	95.0	50.8	36.6	2.8	6.2	5.5	2.9	62
38 Antigua and Barbuda	0.1	0.1	0.1	0.5	0.5	34.2	36.2	43.3	..	..	..	..	..	..	53 [b]
39 Argentina	26.0	35.7	43.5	1.4	1.1	80.7	88.6	91.9	61.0	54.5	9.5	10.7	3.4	2.6	74 [b]
40 Uruguay	2.8	3.3	3.7	0.7	0.7	83.1	90.7	93.2	59.9	56.3	12.6	13.4	3.0	2.4	84
41 Qatar	0.2	0.6	0.7	5.6	1.4	82.9	91.8	94.2	39.8	49.5	1.6	9.1	6.4	3.7	32 [b]
42 Slovakia	4.7	5.4	5.5	0.6	0.1	46.3	59.7	68.0	48.2	42.1	11.0	13.5	2.5	1.4	74
43 United Arab Emirates	0.5	2.3	3.0	7.2	1.5	65.4	84.8	88.8	46.2	48.1	2.0	9.3	5.9	3.4	28
44 Poland	34.0	38.7	39.3	0.6	0.1	55.4	64.4	71.4	49.0	44.5	11.4	14.3	2.2	1.5	75 [b]
45 Costa Rica	2.0	3.7	5.2	3.0	1.9	41.3	50.3	60.3	62.6	52.0	4.8	7.1	4.0	2.8	75
Medium human development	2,789.4 T	4,089.4 T	4,996.1 T	1.8	1.1	29.7	41.2	51.6	58.5	46.6	5.7	7.3	4.5	2.6	..
46 Trinidad and Tobago	1.0	1.3	1.4	1.1	0.6	63.0	72.7	79.3	53.3	41.4	6.4	9.5	3.4	1.7	53 [b]
47 Hungary	10.5	10.2	9.4	-0.2	-0.4	52.8	65.5	73.2	47.0	45.5	14.3	17.2	2.1	1.4	73 [b]
48 Venezuela	12.7	22.8	30.9	2.7	1.7	75.8	86.5	90.4	65.6	51.7	4.2	6.5	4.6	3.0	49 [b]
49 Panama	1.7	2.7	3.5	2.1	1.3	49.0	56.5	64.9	61.1	48.6	5.4	7.8	4.4	2.6	58 [b]
50 Mexico	59.1	94.3	119.2	2.1	1.3	62.8	73.8	77.9	63.8	49.4	4.4	6.8	5.8	2.8	53 [b]

HDI rank	Total population (millions)			Annual population growth rate (%)		Urban population (as % of total)			Dependency ratio (%)		Population aged 65 and above (as % of total)		Total fertility rate		Contraceptive prevalence rate (%)
	1975	1997	2015	1975-1997	1997-2015	1975	1997	2015	1997	2015	1997	2015	1975	1997	1990-98 [a]
51 Saint Kitts and Nevis	(.)	(.)	(.)	-0.6	-0.5	35.0	33.9	39.3	..	..	..	..	..	..	41 [b]
52 Grenada	0.1	0.1	0.1	0.1	0.4	32.6	36.6	47.2	..	..	..	..	..	..	54
53 Dominica	0.1	0.1	0.1	-0.1	0.1	55.3	70.0	76.0	..	..	..	..	..	..	50 [b]
54 Estonia	1.4	1.4	1.2	(.)	-0.9	67.6	73.5	78.7	48.4	43.7	13.2	16.4	2.1	1.3	70
55 Croatia	4.3	4.5	4.3	0.2	-0.2	45.1	56.5	64.4	46.5	50.2	13.6	17.6	2.0	1.6	..
56 Malaysia	12.3	21.0	27.5	2.5	1.5	37.7	55.1	66.2	64.6	46.6	4.0	6.4	4.5	3.2	48 [b]
57 Colombia	25.4	40.0	53.2	2.1	1.6	60.7	73.6	80.0	62.2	50.1	4.6	6.4	4.6	2.8	72
58 Cuba	9.3	11.1	11.6	0.8	0.3	64.2	76.7	82.7	45.4	44.0	9.2	14.1	2.6	1.6	82
59 Mauritius	0.9	1.1	1.3	1.1	0.8	43.4	40.7	48.6	48.5	42.0	6.1	8.5	3.1	1.9	75
60 Belarus	9.4	10.4	9.8	0.5	-0.3	50.3	72.5	80.4	50.5	44.0	13.0	14.2	2.1	1.4	50
61 Fiji	0.6	0.8	1.0	1.4	1.3	36.7	41.2	50.5	60.2	49.4	4.1	7.3	4.0	2.7	32 [b]
62 Lithuania	3.3	3.7	3.5	0.5	-0.3	55.7	73.1	80.1	50.3	45.0	12.6	15.8	2.2	1.4	..
63 Bulgaria	8.7	8.4	7.5	-0.2	-0.6	57.5	69.0	75.4	48.5	46.3	15.1	18.4	2.2	1.2	76 [b]
64 Suriname	0.4	0.4	0.5	0.6	0.8	44.8	50.3	60.8	61.5	42.3	5.2	5.9	4.6	2.2	..
65 Libyan Arab Jamahiriya	2.4	5.2	7.6	3.5	2.1	60.9	86.4	90.3	75.0	55.7	3.0	4.8	7.5	3.8	..
66 Seychelles	0.1	0.1	0.1	1.1	1.0	33.3	56.1	67.3	..	..	..	..	..	..	..
67 Thailand	41.4	59.7	68.9	1.7	0.8	15.1	20.6	29.3	47.3	41.2	5.3	8.5	4.6	1.7	74
68 Romania	21.2	22.5	21.1	0.3	-0.4	46.2	56.8	65.4	46.6	40.8	12.4	15.4	2.6	1.2	57
69 Lebanon	2.8	3.1	3.9	0.6	1.3	67.0	88.5	92.6	64.9	43.5	5.7	5.9	4.5	2.7	63
70 Samoa (Western)	0.2	0.2	0.2	0.6	1.8	21.0	21.1	26.7	76.7	57.6	4.4	4.8	6.5	4.2	21
71 Russian Federation	134.2	147.7	142.9	0.4	-0.2	66.4	76.6	82.0	47.5	42.6	12.2	13.7	1.9	1.3	..
72 Ecuador	6.9	11.9	15.9	2.5	1.6	42.4	60.4	70.6	66.3	50.0	4.5	6.2	5.7	3.1	57
73 Macedonia, TFYR	1.7	2.0	2.2	0.8	0.5	50.6	60.7	68.5	49.7	50.0	9.3	12.6	2.8	2.1	..
74 Latvia	2.5	2.5	2.1	(.)	-1.0	65.4	73.4	78.9	49.9	45.8	13.6	16.8	2.0	1.3	..
75 Saint Vincent and the Grenadines	0.1	0.1	0.1	0.9	0.6	20.6	50.9	68.0	..	..	..	..	..	..	58 [b]
76 Kazakhstan	14.1	16.4	16.9	0.7	0.2	52.2	60.4	68.4	56.3	46.8	7.0	8.4	3.2	2.3	59
77 Philippines	43.0	71.4	96.7	2.3	1.7	35.6	56.0	67.8	70.0	51.4	3.5	5.0	5.1	3.6	40
78 Saudi Arabia	7.3	19.5	32.6	4.6	2.9	58.4	84.1	89.7	78.5	69.1	2.8	4.4	7.3	5.8	..
79 Brazil	108.2	163.7	200.7	1.9	1.1	61.2	79.6	86.5	55.0	46.0	4.9	7.2	4.5	2.3	77
80 Peru	15.2	24.4	31.9	2.2	1.5	61.5	71.6	77.9	65.2	49.7	4.5	6.5	5.6	3.0	64
81 Saint Lucia	0.1	0.1	0.2	1.4	1.3	38.6	37.3	43.6	..	..	..	..	..	..	47 [b]
82 Jamaica	2.0	2.5	2.9	1.0	0.9	44.1	54.7	63.5	65.2	47.1	7.1	7.5	4.4	2.5	65
83 Belize	0.1	0.2	0.3	2.4	2.0	50.2	46.4	51.0	82.8	51.0	4.3	4.4	6.3	3.7	47
84 Paraguay	2.7	5.1	7.8	3.0	2.4	39.0	53.9	65.0	79.8	62.1	3.5	4.3	5.3	4.2	51
85 Georgia	4.9	5.1	5.1	0.2	(.)	49.5	59.3	67.7	54.2	50.1	12.0	13.8	2.5	1.9	..
86 Turkey	40.0	63.4	80.3	2.1	1.3	41.6	71.9	84.5	54.2	45.5	5.4	7.2	4.7	2.5	63
87 Armenia	2.8	3.6	3.8	1.0	0.4	63.0	69.1	75.0	54.0	42.4	7.9	9.6	2.7	1.7	60
88 Dominican Republic	5.0	8.1	10.3	2.2	1.3	45.3	63.3	72.8	62.7	49.0	4.2	6.6	5.1	2.8	64
89 Oman	0.9	2.3	4.1	4.5	3.3	19.6	79.5	92.8	91.4	81.7	2.5	3.7	7.2	5.9	40
90 Sri Lanka	13.6	18.3	21.9	1.4	1.0	22.0	22.6	32.0	52.4	47.5	6.3	9.3	3.9	2.1	66
91 Ukraine	49.0	51.1	47.9	0.2	-0.4	58.3	71.1	78.0	49.9	45.4	14.0	16.2	2.0	1.4	..
92 Uzbekistan	14.0	23.2	29.9	2.3	1.4	39.1	41.6	50.1	77.0	50.8	4.5	4.6	5.5	3.4	56
93 Maldives	0.1	0.3	0.4	3.0	2.6	18.0	27.4	36.3	92.5	68.0	3.5	3.3	7.0	5.4	17
94 Jordan	2.6	6.1	9.9	4.0	2.7	55.3	72.6	79.8	83.0	67.0	2.9	3.4	7.6	4.9	53
95 Iran, Islamic Rep. of	33.3	64.6	83.1	3.1	1.4	45.8	60.0	68.8	78.8	46.1	4.1	4.8	6.4	2.8	73
96 Turkmenistan	2.5	4.2	5.6	2.4	1.5	47.6	45.0	52.4	76.1	48.8	4.2	4.4	5.7	3.6	..
97 Kyrgyzstan	3.3	4.6	5.5	1.5	0.9	37.9	39.2	47.9	73.0	48.8	5.9	5.8	4.3	3.2	60
98 China	927.8	1,244.2	1,417.7	1.3	0.7	17.3	31.9	45.9	47.8	40.6	6.4	9.3	3.9	1.8	83
99 Guyana	0.7	0.8	1.0	0.6	0.7	30.0	36.4	48.0	55.3	41.3	4.1	5.7	4.3	2.3	..
100 Albania	2.4	3.1	3.5	1.2	0.6	32.8	37.9	47.6	57.2	45.3	5.7	8.2	4.4	2.5	..

HDI rank	Total population (millions)			Annual population growth rate (%)		Urban population (as % of total)			Dependency ratio (%)		Population aged 65 and above (as % of total)		Total fertility rate		Contraceptive prevalence rate (%)
	1975	1997	2015	1975-1997	1997-2015	1975	1997	2015	1997	2015	1997	2015	1975	1997	1990-98 [a]
101 South Africa	24.7	38.8	43.4	2.1	0.6	48.0	49.7	56.3	64.4	53.6	3.5	4.0	4.6	3.3	50 [b]
102 Tunisia	5.7	9.2	11.6	2.2	1.3	49.9	63.4	73.5	61.7	45.4	5.7	6.1	5.9	2.6	60
103 Azerbaijan	5.7	7.6	8.8	1.4	0.8	51.5	56.3	64.0	59.3	41.3	6.3	7.7	3.9	2.0	..
104 Moldova, Rep. of	3.8	4.4	4.5	0.6	0.1	35.8	53.1	63.9	53.3	43.1	9.5	10.8	2.5	1.8	..
105 Indonesia	135.7	203.4	250.4	1.9	1.2	19.4	37.4	52.4	57.3	44.9	4.5	6.3	4.9	2.6	55
106 Cape Verde	0.3	0.4	0.6	1.7	2.1	21.4	57.7	73.5	82.6	54.0	4.6	3.2	6.8	3.6	27
107 El Salvador	4.1	5.9	8.0	1.7	1.7	40.4	45.6	53.6	70.3	55.3	4.8	6.1	5.9	3.2	53
108 Tajikistan	3.4	5.9	7.8	2.5	1.5	35.5	32.4	40.1	85.7	56.5	4.4	4.3	6.3	4.2	..
109 Algeria	16.0	29.4	41.2	2.8	1.9	40.3	57.2	67.5	71.7	51.2	3.6	4.4	7.3	3.8	57
110 Viet Nam	48.0	76.4	96.6	2.1	1.3	18.8	19.5	24.3	68.3	43.0	5.1	5.3	5.8	2.6	65
111 Syrian Arab Republic	7.4	14.9	22.6	3.2	2.3	45.1	53.1	62.1	86.2	58.0	3.0	3.4	7.5	4.0	36
112 Bolivia	4.8	7.8	11.2	2.3	2.1	41.5	62.3	73.7	79.0	62.7	3.9	4.9	6.1	4.4	45
113 Swaziland	0.5	0.9	1.5	3.0	2.6	14.0	33.0	47.2	86.0	68.9	2.6	3.5	6.5	4.7	21 [b]
114 Honduras	3.0	6.0	9.0	3.2	2.3	32.1	45.0	56.1	86.1	60.2	3.3	4.3	6.8	4.3	50
115 Namibia	0.9	1.6	2.0	2.7	1.3	20.6	38.0	53.2	84.3	74.5	3.8	3.1	6.0	4.9	29
116 Vanuatu	0.1	0.2	0.3	2.5	2.3	15.7	19.3	27.0	85.9	63.0	3.4	4.1	5.9	4.3	15
117 Guatemala	6.0	10.5	16.4	2.6	2.5	36.7	39.4	48.3	92.2	69.9	3.4	3.8	6.4	4.9	31
118 Solomon Islands	0.2	0.4	0.7	3.5	2.8	9.1	18.0	28.6	87.6	68.9	2.9	3.8	7.2	4.9	25
119 Mongolia	1.4	2.5	3.3	2.6	1.5	48.7	61.9	70.5	69.6	43.5	3.8	4.5	7.0	2.6	59
120 Egypt	38.8	64.7	85.2	2.3	1.5	43.5	45.1	53.5	70.1	47.3	4.0	5.2	5.3	3.4	55
121 Nicaragua	2.5	4.7	7.3	2.9	2.5	50.3	63.2	71.3	89.2	64.3	3.0	3.8	6.5	4.4	49
122 Botswana	0.8	1.5	2.0	3.3	1.4	12.0	66.1	88.7	83.7	64.7	2.4	2.4	6.5	4.4	48
123 São Tomé and Principe	0.1	0.1	0.2	2.5	1.8	26.9	44.5	56.2	..	..	..	..	..	..	10 [b]
124 Gabon	0.6	1.1	1.7	3.0	2.1	29.2	52.2	66.2	82.4	77.9	5.9	5.4	4.3	5.4	..
125 Iraq	11.0	21.2	34.1	3.0	2.7	61.4	75.5	81.6	82.8	69.0	3.0	4.0	6.8	5.3	18 [b]
126 Morocco	17.3	26.9	34.8	2.0	1.4	37.7	53.3	64.3	61.8	46.2	4.3	5.3	6.3	3.1	59
127 Lesotho	1.2	2.0	2.9	2.4	2.0	10.8	25.6	38.9	79.3	72.7	4.1	4.5	5.8	4.8	23
128 Myanmar	30.4	43.9	53.5	1.7	1.1	23.9	26.5	36.7	52.8	42.7	4.5	6.0	5.5	2.4	33
129 Papua New Guinea	2.7	4.5	6.5	2.3	2.1	11.9	16.6	23.7	73.0	61.2	3.0	3.7	6.0	4.6	26
130 Zimbabwe	6.1	11.2	13.6	2.8	1.1	19.6	33.2	45.9	83.7	56.3	2.8	2.4	6.8	3.8	48
131 Equatorial Guinea	0.2	0.4	0.6	2.9	2.4	27.1	44.7	61.4	89.7	77.2	4.0	3.7	5.7	5.6	..
132 India	620.7	966.2	1,211.7	2.0	1.3	21.3	27.4	35.9	65.0	47.3	4.7	6.4	5.1	3.1	41
133 Ghana	9.8	18.7	29.8	3.0	2.6	30.1	36.8	47.8	89.9	73.3	3.1	3.7	6.5	5.2	20
134 Cameroon	7.5	13.9	21.5	2.8	2.4	26.9	46.4	58.9	90.4	79.8	3.6	3.5	6.4	5.3	16
135 Congo	1.4	2.7	4.4	2.9	2.8	34.8	60.2	70.1	97.7	84.9	3.3	2.8	6.3	6.1	..
136 Kenya	13.7	28.4	37.6	3.4	1.6	12.9	30.4	44.5	91.8	62.1	3.0	2.5	8.2	4.5	33
137 Cambodia	7.1	10.5	14.4	1.8	1.8	10.3	21.6	32.9	83.1	58.8	3.0	4.0	4.5	4.6	13
138 Pakistan	74.7	144.0	222.6	3.0	2.4	26.4	35.4	46.7	83.8	64.0	3.1	3.8	7.0	5.0	17
139 Comoros	0.3	0.6	1.0	3.2	2.5	21.2	31.5	42.6	86.3	66.5	2.6	3.2	7.0	4.8	21
Low human development	355.6 T	636.1 T	955.8 T	2.7	2.3	15.6	27.5	39.0	88.4	73.6	3.0	3.2	6.8	5.2	..
140 Lao People's Dem. Rep.	3.0	5.0	7.8	2.3	2.5	11.4	21.8	32.7	90.9	75.1	3.2	3.8	6.5	5.8	19
141 Congo, Dem. Rep. of the	23.3	48.0	80.3	3.3	2.9	29.5	29.2	39.3	101.8	89.2	2.8	2.8	6.4	6.4	8
142 Sudan	16.0	27.7	39.8	2.5	2.0	18.9	33.3	48.7	78.9	64.7	3.0	4.2	6.7	4.6	8
143 Togo	2.3	4.3	6.7	2.9	2.6	16.3	31.7	42.5	96.8	81.5	3.1	3.0	6.6	6.1	24
144 Nepal	12.8	22.3	32.7	2.6	2.1	5.0	10.9	18.1	84.1	63.2	3.6	4.1	6.3	4.5	30
145 Bhutan	1.2	1.9	3.1	2.3	2.6	3.5	6.5	11.6	87.6	75.1	4.0	4.4	5.9	5.5	19
146 Nigeria	57.0	103.9	153.3	2.8	2.2	23.4	41.3	55.4	88.7	74.2	3.0	3.4	6.9	5.2	6
147 Madagascar	7.8	14.6	23.4	2.9	2.6	16.1	27.6	39.3	89.7	71.2	3.0	3.1	6.6	5.4	19
148 Yemen	7.0	16.3	29.6	3.9	3.4	16.4	35.3	49.2	100.7	85.7	2.4	2.3	7.6	7.6	21
149 Mauritania	1.4	2.5	3.9	2.7	2.6	20.3	54.0	68.6	89.4	75.0	3.2	3.4	6.5	5.5	4
150 Bangladesh	76.6	122.7	161.5	2.2	1.5	9.3	19.4	30.8	69.9	50.0	3.2	4.3	6.8	3.1	49

HDI rank	Total population (millions)			Annual population growth rate (%)		Urban population (as % of total)			Dependency ratio (%)		Population aged 65 and above (as % of total)		Total fertility rate		Contraceptive prevalence rate (%)
	1975	1997	2015	1975-1997	1997-2015	1975	1997	2015	1997	2015	1997	2015	1975	1997	1990-98 [a]
151 Zambia	4.8	8.6	12.8	2.6	2.3	34.8	43.6	51.5	100.7	78.5	2.3	1.8	7.1	5.6	26
152 Haiti	4.9	7.8	10.4	2.1	1.6	21.7	33.0	44.8	84.9	63.5	3.6	3.9	5.8	4.4	18
153 Senegal	4.8	8.8	13.7	2.8	2.5	34.2	45.0	56.5	90.9	75.5	2.5	2.7	7.0	5.6	13
154 Côte d'Ivoire	6.8	14.1	20.0	3.4	2.0	32.1	44.7	55.7	89.3	71.0	2.8	3.1	7.4	5.1	11
155 Benin	3.0	5.6	8.9	2.8	2.6	21.9	39.9	53.0	100.1	78.8	2.9	2.8	7.1	5.8	37
156 Tanzania, U. Rep. of	15.9	31.4	47.2	3.1	2.3	10.1	25.7	38.3	94.1	78.8	2.6	2.7	6.8	5.5	18
157 Djibouti	0.2	0.6	0.9	5.1	1.9	68.5	82.7	86.3	79.8	68.8	3.2	4.3	6.7	5.3	..
158 Uganda	11.2	20.0	34.5	2.7	3.1	8.3	13.2	20.7	107.9	94.7	2.2	1.7	6.9	7.1	15
159 Malawi	5.2	10.1	15.8	3.0	2.5	7.7	14.2	22.7	99.7	86.1	2.7	2.5	7.5	6.8	22
160 Angola	6.1	11.7	19.7	3.0	2.9	17.8	32.3	44.1	102.3	88.0	2.9	2.9	6.7	6.8	8
161 Guinea	4.1	7.3	10.5	2.6	2.0	16.3	30.6	42.9	91.3	73.8	2.7	3.0	7.0	5.5	29
162 Chad	4.0	7.1	11.2	2.6	2.6	15.6	22.8	30.9	97.5	83.1	3.4	3.1	6.6	6.1	4
163 Gambia	0.5	1.2	1.8	3.6	2.4	17.0	30.4	42.5	77.6	69.2	3.0	3.9	6.5	5.2	12
164 Rwanda	4.4	6.0	10.5	1.4	3.2	4.0	5.8	8.9	94.9	77.1	2.3	2.4	8.5	6.2	..
165 Central African Republic	2.1	3.4	4.8	2.3	1.9	33.7	39.9	49.7	88.2	74.3	3.9	3.4	5.8	4.9	15
166 Mali	6.2	10.4	16.7	2.4	2.6	16.2	28.1	40.1	101.8	86.6	3.6	3.8	7.1	6.6	7
167 Eritrea	2.1	3.4	5.5	2.3	2.7	12.2	17.7	26.2	89.4	75.5	2.8	3.4	6.4	5.7	8
168 Guinea-Bissau	0.6	1.1	1.6	2.7	2.0	16.0	22.5	31.7	88.0	81.4	4.1	3.9	5.5	5.8	1 [b]
169 Mozambique	10.5	18.4	25.2	2.6	1.8	8.6	36.5	51.5	92.8	84.5	3.3	2.6	6.5	6.3	6
170 Burundi	3.7	6.4	9.5	2.5	2.2	3.2	8.1	14.5	97.1	75.2	2.8	2.3	6.8	6.3	9 [b]
171 Burkina Faso	6.1	11.0	18.1	2.7	2.8	6.3	16.9	27.4	100.6	88.1	2.6	2.4	7.8	6.6	8
172 Ethiopia	32.2	58.2	90.9	2.7	2.5	9.5	16.3	25.8	95.5	86.6	2.9	2.7	6.8	6.3	4
173 Niger	4.8	9.8	16.7	3.3	3.0	10.6	19.1	29.1	103.4	87.5	2.5	2.6	8.1	6.8	4
174 Sierra Leone	2.9	4.4	6.7	1.9	2.3	21.4	34.6	46.7	88.9	80.3	2.9	3.0	6.5	6.1	4 [b]
All developing countries	2,928.0 T	4,502.9 T	5,750.8 T	2.0	1.4	26.1	38.4	49.1	62.5	50.7	4.9	6.4	5.0	3.0	..
Least developed countries	327.2 T	568.4 T	843.6 T	2.5	2.2	14.2	23.8	34.6	84.8	70.8	3.2	3.4	6.6	5.0	..
Sub-Saharan Africa	303.1 T	555.4 T	834.0 T	2.8	2.3	21.0	32.4	43.2	91.4	77.6	3.0	3.0	6.7	5.5	..
Arab States	137.4 T	252.4 T	365.1 T	2.8	2.1	42.1	55.6	65.7	74.3	57.4	3.6	4.5	6.4	4.1	..
East Asia	968.9 T	1,299.0 T	1,479.8 T	1.3	0.7	18.8	34.1	47.8	47.5	40.6	6.5	9.4	3.9	1.8	..
East Asia (excluding China)	41.1 T	54.8 T	62.0 T	1.3	0.7	52.5	83.9	91.4	41.2	41.1	6.5	10.6	3.5	1.7	..
South-East Asia and the Pacific	327.1 T	501.1 T	629.0 T	2.0	1.3	22.3	34.8	46.3	60.0	45.8	4.5	6.1	5.0	2.7	..
South Asia	833.1 T	1,340.3 T	1,737.0 T	2.2	1.5	21.4	28.9	38.4	68.1	49.8	4.5	5.8	5.4	3.3	..
South Asia (excluding India)	212.4 T	374.1 T	525.3 T	2.6	1.9	21.6	32.7	43.8	76.5	55.8	3.6	4.4	6.6	3.8	..
Latin America and the Caribbean	317.9 T	490.4 T	624.9 T	2.0	1.4	61.2	74.2	79.9	61.5	50.2	5.2	7.1	4.7	2.7	..
Eastern Europe and the CIS	353.8 T	398.8 T	399.9 T	0.5	(.)	57.5	66.6	72.2	51.2	44.7	11.4	13.0	2.4	1.6	..
Industrialized countries	735.5 T	842.0 T	889.4 T	0.6	0.3	74.9	77.8	81.6	49.7	52.7	14.5	18.3	1.9	1.6	..
World	4,017.4 T	5,743.7 T	7,040.2 T	1.6	1.1	37.8	46.1	54.4	59.6	50.6	6.8	8.3	4.1	2.7	..

a. Data refer to the most recent year available during the period specified in the column heading.

b. Data refer to a year or period other than that specified in the column heading, differ from the standard definition or refer to only part of the country.

Source: Columns 1-3, 13 and 14: UN 1998h; *columns 4, 5 and 9-12:* calculated on the basis of data from UN 1998h; *columns 6-8:* UN 1996b; *column 15:* UNICEF 1999a.

17 Energy use

HDI rank	Electricity consumption: Total (millions of kilowatt-hours) 1996	Index (1980 = 100) 1996	Per capita (kilowatt-hours) 1980	Per capita (kilowatt-hours) 1996	Traditional fuel consumption (as % of total) 1980	Traditional fuel consumption (as % of total) 1995	Commercial energy use: Total (1,000 metric tons) 1980	Commercial energy use: Total (1,000 metric tons) 1996	Per capita (kilograms) 1980	Per capita (kilograms) 1996	GDP output per kilogram (US$)[a] 1980	GDP output per kilogram (US$)[a] 1996	Net commercial energy imports (as % of energy consumption) 1980	Net commercial energy imports (as % of energy consumption) 1996
High human development	8,644,140 T	159	6,361	8,550	..	..	4,034,488 T	5,015,657 T	4,468	4,977	2.8	3.2	25	22
1 Canada	620,441	177	14,243	20,904	1	1	193,000	236,170	7,848	7,880	2.1	2.5	-7	-51
2 Norway	103,732	125	20,327	23,030	1	1	18,819	23,150	4,600	5,284	5.1	6.7	-196	-799
3 United States	3,496,590	147	10,334	12,977	1	4	1,811,650	2,134,960	7,973	8,051	2.7	3.4	14	21
4 Japan	1,012,145	175	4,944	8,074	(.)	1	346,491	510,359	2,967	4,058	9.3	10.5	88	80
5 Belgium	80,300	159	5,125	7,904	(.)	1	46,100	56,399	4,682	5,552	4.6	4.9	84	79
6 Sweden	144,837	150	11,655	16,423	4	3	40,984	52,507	4,932	5,944	4.5	4.5	61	39
7 Australia	177,326	184	6,599	9,820	2	4	70,372	100,612	4,790	5,494	3.3	3.7	-22	-88
8 Netherlands	95,676	148	4,560	6,143	(.)	(.)	65,000	75,797	4,594	4,885	4.4	5.4	-11	3
9 Iceland	5,131	163	13,838	18,934	..	..	1,469	2,270	6,445	8,408	3.5	3.2	43	38
10 United Kingdom	364,725	129	5,020	6,249	(.)	1	201,299	234,719	3,574	3,992	4.0	4.8	2	-14
11 France	438,233	176	4,615	7,508	1	1	190,111	254,196	3,528	4,355	6.1	6.1	76	49
12 Switzerland	56,111	151	5,855	7,734	1	2	20,861	25,622	3,301	3,622	12.1	12.0	66	59
13 Finland	79,529	199	8,351	15,515	4	6	25,413	31,482	5,316	6,143	3.7	4.1	73	57
14 Germany	541,113	..	..	6,605	..	1	360,441	349,552	4,603	4,267	..	7.0	48	60
15 Denmark	39,328	152	5,054	7,510	(.)	4	19,734	22,870	3,852	4,346	6.8	8.2	95	23
16 Austria	55,787	148	4,988	6,882	1	3	23,450	27,187	3,105	3,373	7.1	8.7	67	71
17 Luxembourg	6,211	165	10,330	15,075	(.)	..	3,643	3,445	9,983	8,291	2.4	5.2	99	99
18 New Zealand	35,932	163	7,061	9,976	(.)	1	9,251	16,295	2,972	4,388	4.7	3.8	41	17
19 Italy	278,796	147	3,357	4,870	1	2	138,629	161,140	2,456	2,808	6.0	6.8	86	82
20 Ireland	19,044	180	3,106	5,358	(.)	(.)	8,484	11,961	2,495	3,293	4.0	5.9	78	71
21 Spain	173,280	161	2,872	4,368	1	1	68,583	101,411	1,834	2,583	5.7	5.6	77	68
22 Singapore	23,458	343	2,836	6,932	..	..	6,054	23,851	2,653	7,835	4.6	3.8	..	100
23 Israel	32,161	260	3,187	5,678	(.)	..	8,609	16,185	2,220	2,843	5.1	5.6	98	96
24 Hong Kong, China (SAR)	35,687	289	2,449	5,764	1	..	5,681	12,190	1,127	1,931	10.0	12.0	99	100
25 Brunei Darussalam	1,575	336	2,430	5,250	5	..	348	3,347	1,806	11,118	16.5	1.5	-5,263	-470
26 Cyprus	2,592	251	1,692	3,429	(.)	..	945	2,122	1,546	2,868	..	..	99	99
27 Greece	48,586	209	2,413	4,632	3	1	15,960	24,389	1,655	2,328	5.7	4.8	77	64
28 Portugal	34,643	203	1,750	3,532	1	1	10,291	19,148	1,054	1,928	6.8	5.6	86	87
29 Barbados	650	196	1,333	2,490	17	..	..	..	..	..	..	..	..	..
30 Korea, Rep. of	227,554	568	1,051	5,022	6	1	43,756	162,874	1,148	3,576	3.1	3.0	72	86
31 Bahamas	1,340	157	4,062	4,718	..	..	..	..	..	..	..	..	..	..
32 Malta	1,514	287	1,627	4,103	..	..	402	894	1,105	2,398	4.3	3.8	..	..
33 Slovenia	11,109	..	..	5,774	..	1	4,313	6,167	2,269	3,098	..	3.1	62	55
34 Chile	31,278	266	1,054	2,169	14	13	9,525	20,456	855	1,419	2.8	3.1	41	62
35 Kuwait	25,925	275	6,849	15,368	..	..	9,564	13,859	6,956	8,167	2.4	..	-884	-712
36 Czech Republic	60,974	..	..	5,948	..	1	46,910	40,404	4,585	3,917	..	1.3	9	22
37 Bahrain	5,016	302	4,784	8,800	..	..	3,324	6,555	9,951	10,943	1.2	0.9	-54	-17
38 Antigua and Barbuda	98	163	984	1,485	..	..	..	..	..	..	..	..	..	..
39 Argentina	73,109	..	..	2,076	7	4	41,868	58,921	1,490	1,673	5.7	5.0	7	-27
40 Uruguay	6,538	193	1,163	2,041	20	25	2,637	2,955	905	912	5.8	6.4	75	65
41 Qatar	6,340	261	10,616	11,362	(.)	..	4,796	8,733	20,945	12,602	..	..	-481	-239
42 Slovakia	28,800	..	..	5,386	..	1	20,810	17,449	4,175	3,266	..	1.1	84	72
43 United Arab Emirates	19,250	306	6,204	8,518	..	..	8,576	32,336	8,222	13,155	..	..	-995	-360
44 Poland	136,679	112	3,419	3,541	(.)	1	124,806	108,411	3,508	2,807	0.9	1.2	2	6
45 Costa Rica	4,997	227	964	1,428	33	11	1,527	2,248	669	657	3.7	4.0	50	67
Medium human development	4,637,147 T	283	424	1,147	..	..	2,707,998 T	3,988,626 T	902	1,007	0.9	0.9	-34	-29
46 Trinidad and Tobago	4,541	221	1,900	3,501	2	1	3,873	7,887	3,580	6,081	1.3	0.7	-239	-72
47 Hungary	36,414	116	2,920	3,624	2	2	28,895	25,470	2,699	2,499	1.6	1.8	48	50
48 Venezuela	72,529	202	2,379	3,251	1	1	35,026	54,962	2,321	2,463	1.7	1.4	-280	-253
49 Panama	3,978	219	930	1,486	27	18	1,865	2,280	957	853	2.8	3.6	72	67
50 Mexico	162,625	241	999	1,754	4	4	98,904	141,384	1,464	1,525	2.3	2.1	-51	-51

HDI rank	Electricity consumption Total (millions of kilowatt-hours) 1996	Index (1980 = 100) 1996	Per capita (kilowatt-hours) 1980	Per capita (kilowatt-hours) 1996	Traditional fuel consumption (as % of total) 1980	Traditional fuel consumption (as % of total) 1995	Commercial energy use (oil equivalent) Total (1,000 metric tons) 1980	Total 1996	Per capita (kilograms) 1980	Per capita 1996	GDP output per kilogram (US$)[a] 1980	GDP output per kilogram 1996	Net commercial energy imports (as % of energy consumption) 1980	Net 1996
51 Saint Kitts and Nevis	88	..	..	2,146	..	..	..	..	..	..	..	..	..	..
52 Grenada	95	380	281	1,033	..	..	..	..	..	..	..	..	..	..
53 Dominica	37	336	149	521	..	..	..	..	..	..	..	..	..	..
54 Estonia	8,243	..	..	5,604	..	2	..	5,621	..	3,834	..	0.9	..	31
55 Croatia	12,878	..	..	2,861	..	3	..	6,765	..	1,418	..	2.8	..	42
56 Malaysia	52,986	521	740	2,575	14	6	11,128	41,209	809	1,950	2.9	2.3	-50	-69
57 Colombia	44,769	217	778	1,228	21	22	19,127	31,393	672	799	2.4	2.6	5	-113
58 Cuba	13,236	132	1,029	1,201	28	22	14,570	15,953	1,501	1,448	..	..	73	58
59 Mauritius	1,255	269	482	1,112	44	38	..	..	..	..	..	..	..	..
60 Belarus	32,271	..	..	3,119	..	1	2,385	24,566	247	2,386	..	0.8	-8	87
61 Fiji	545	176	489	684	32	52	..	..	..	..	..	..	..	..
62 Lithuania	11,630	..	..	3,120	..	6	11,701	8,953	3,428	2,414	..	0.8	95	53
63 Bulgaria	42,267	109	4,371	4,991	1	1	28,673	22,605	3,235	2,705	0.4	0.5	73	54
64 Suriname	1,621	103	4,442	3,752	1	..	..	..	..	..	..	..	..	..
65 Libyan Arab Jamahiriya	18,300	379	1,588	3,272	2	1	7,173	14,911	2,357	2,935	..	..	-1,248	-421
66 Seychelles	128	256	794	1,730	..	..	..	..	..	..	..	..	..	..
67 Thailand	92,183	581	340	1,570	48	33	22,740	79,987	487	1,333	2.3	2.2	51	45
68 Romania	62,157	91	3,061	2,744	1	22	64,694	45,824	2,914	2,027	0.6	0.7	19	32
69 Lebanon	5,795	206	1,056	1,879	4	3	2,483	4,747	827	1,164	..	..	93	96
70 Samoa (Western)	65	167	252	392	..	..	..	..	..	..	..	..	..	..
71 Russian Federation	827,700	..	..	5,588	..	1	764,349	615,899	5,499	4,169	..	0.5	2	-54
72 Ecuador	9,260	275	423	792	26	15	5,191	8,548	652	731	2.4	2.1	-126	-156
73 Macedonia, TFYR	6,489	..	..	2,985	..	6	..	..	..	..	..	..	..	..
74 Latvia	6,351	..	..	2,536	..	18	566	4,171	223	1,674	16.0	1.5	54	76
75 Saint Vincent and the Grenadines	66	244	276	584	..	..	..	..	..	..	..	..	..	..
76 Kazakhstan	65,502	..	..	3,894	..	(.)	76,799	43,376	5,163	2,724	..	0.5	0	-44
77 Philippines	34,775	193	373	502	36	32	21,212	37,992	439	528	2.7	2.1	50	55
78 Saudi Arabia	104,118	551	1,969	5,528	..	..	35,357	92,243	3,773	4,753	3.0	1.4	-1,408	-415
79 Brazil	326,373	234	1,145	2,026	41	31	108,997	163,374	896	1,012	4.7	4.4	43	31
80 Peru	20,038	200	579	837	19	25	11,700	13,933	675	582	4.1	4.3	-25	11
81 Saint Lucia	115	198	504	799	..	..	..	..	..	..	..	..	..	..
82 Jamaica	6,038	340	834	2,424	6	8	2,378	3,718	1,115	1,465	1.3	1.1	91	85
83 Belize	177	328	370	808	53	40	..	..	..	..	..	..	..	..
84 Paraguay	7,938	1,092	233	1,601	66	51	2,094	4,285	672	865	2.8	2.1	23	-56
85 Georgia	7,315	..	..	1,344	..	1	4,474	1,576	882	291	2.7	2.1	-5	55
86 Turkey	90,695	368	554	1,468	18	4	31,314	65,520	704	1,045	2.8	2.8	45	59
87 Armenia	6,214	..	..	1,708	..	..	1,070	1,790	346	474	..	1.7	-18	59
88 Dominican Republic	6,847	206	582	860	30	12	3,464	5,191	608	652	2.2	2.5	62	72
89 Oman	8,979	938	847	3,901	..	..	1,387	4,848	1,260	2,231	2.8	..	-994	-876
90 Sri Lanka	4,366	262	113	241	54	51	4,493	6,792	305	371	1.5	2.0	29	38
91 Ukraine	179,709	..	..	3,482	..	(.)	97,893	153,937	1,956	3,012	..	0.5	-12	49
92 Uzbekistan	46,510	..	..	2,004	..	..	4,821	42,406	302	1,826	..	0.5	4	-12
93 Maldives	63	1,575	25	240	..	..	..	..	..	..	..	..	..	..
94 Jordan	6,058	566	366	1,085	(.)	..	1,714	4,487	786	1,040	2.2	1.5	100	96
95 Iran, Islamic Rep. of	82,600	369	570	1,180	2	1	38,918	89,340	995	1,491	1.4	..	-116	-147
96 Turkmenistan	7,300	..	..	1,757	..	..	7,948	12,164	2,778	2,646	..	0.3	-1	-168
97 Kyrgyzstan	11,400	..	..	2,551	..	..	1,717	2,952	473	645	..	1.2	-27	51
98 China	1,078,910	359	307	891	8	6	593,109	1,096,800	604	902	0.3	0.7	-3	(.)
99 Guyana	342	83	545	408	23	35	..	..	..	..	..	..	..	..
100 Albania	6,126	191	1,204	1,801	11	11	3,049	1,188	1,142	362	0.8	2.2	-12	9

. . . WHILE PRESERVING IT FOR FUTURE GENERATIONS . . .

17 Energy use

	Electricity consumption				Traditional fuel consumption (as % of total)		Commercial energy use (oil equivalent)						Net commercial energy imports (as % of energy consumption)	
	Total (millions of kilowatt-hours)	Index (1980 = 100)	Per capita (kilowatt-hours)				Total (1,000 metric tons)		Per capita (kilograms)		GDP output per kilogram (US$)[a]			
HDI rank	1996	1996	1980	1996	1980	1995	1980	1996	1980	1996	1980	1996	1980	1996
101 South Africa	188,237	188	3,025	3,888	4	4	65,355	99,079	2,370	2,482	1.7	1.4	-12	-29
102 Tunisia	7,851	281	434	857	15	14	3,900	6,676	611	735	2.7	2.9	-79	6
103 Azerbaijan	17,530	..	..	2,308	..	..	15,002	11,862	2,433	1,570		0.3	1	-21
104 Moldova, Rep. of	7,728	..	..	1,739	..	..	..	4,601	..	1,064	..	0.6	106	99
105 Indonesia	73,794	518	94	368	52	32	59,561	132,419	402	672	1.3	1.6	-116	-66
106 Cape Verde	41	256	55	104	..	..	..	..	..	..	..	..	..	..
107 El Salvador	3,473	225	339	599	50	44	2,540	4,058	554	700	2.9	2.4	25	36
108 Tajikistan	15,320	..	..	2,581	..	..	1,650	3,513	416	594	..	0.5	-20	62
109 Algeria	20,378	286	381	708	3	2	12,410	24,150	665	842	2.5	1.8	-440	-381
110 Viet Nam	16,320	388	78	217	53	45	19,348	33,750	360	448	..	0.7	7	-14
111 Syrian Arab Republic	17,278	458	433	1,186	(.)	..	5,348	14,541	614	1,002	1.7	1.2	-78	-132
112 Bolivia	3,227	206	292	425	19	13	2,335	3,633	436	479	2.3	1.9	-84	-44
113 Swaziland	..	..	..	..	..	..	..	..	..	..	..	..	..	..
114 Honduras	2,819	305	259	485	54	50	1,877	2,925	526	503	1.4	1.4	30	40
115 Namibia	..	..	..	..	..	..	..	..	..	..	..	..	..	..
116 Vanuatu	30	150	171	172	13	..	..	..	..	..	..	..	..	..
117 Guatemala	3,500	209	242	320	53	61	3,754	5,224	550	510	2.9	2.9	33	23
118 Solomon Islands	32	152	93	82	14	60	..	..	..	..	..	..	..	..
119 Mongolia	2,975	160	1,119	1,183	14	4	..	..	..	..	..	..	..	..
120 Egypt	50,660	267	433	801	5	4	15,970	37,790	391	638	1.8	1.6	-114	-58
121 Nicaragua	1,923	182	380	454	48	43	1,562	2,391	535	525	1.3	1.0	42	37
122 Botswana	..	..	..	..	36	..	..	..	..	..	..	..	..	..
123 São Tomé and Principe	15	167	96	111	..	..	..	..	..	..	..	..	..	..
124 Gabon	949	179	767	858	36	32	1,493	1,578	2,160	1,403	2.4	3.3	-532	-1,149
125 Iraq	29,660	260	878	1,439	(.)	(.)	12,030	25,027	925	1,174	..	..	-1,036	-30
126 Morocco	13,228	269	254	490	5	5	4,778	8,822	247	329	4.5	4.2	82	90
127 Lesotho	..	..	..	..	..	..	..	..	..	..	..	..	..	..
128 Myanmar	4,256	286	44	93	66	65	9,430	12,767	279	294	..	..	-1	7
129 Papua New Guinea	1,790	143	406	407	64	63	..	..	..	..	..	..	..	..
130 Zimbabwe	10,991	151	1,020	961	34	37	6,511	10,442	929	929	0.7	0.7	13	16
131 Equatorial Guinea	20	111	83	49	84	67	..	..	..	..	..	..	..	..
132 India	433,914	364	173	459	35	23	242,024	450,287	352	476	0.6	0.8	8	13
133 Ghana	5,808	119	451	326	68	79	4,071	6,657	379	380	1.0	1.0	19	16
134 Cameroon	2,753	190	168	203	69	80	3,687	5,000	426	369	1.7	1.7	-58	-100
135 Congo	553	339	98	207	56	51	845	1,205	506	457	1.5	1.9	-370	-854
136 Kenya	3,920	217	109	141	75	78	9,791	13,279	589	476	0.6	0.7	19	15
137 Cambodia	201	201	15	20	71	90	..	..	..	..	..	..	..	..
138 Pakistan	56,946	380	176	407	27	20	25,479	55,903	308	446	1.0	1.1	18	26
139 Comoros	17	170	26	27	..	..	..	..	..	..	..	..	..	..
Low human development	56,748 T	162	86	91	..	..	138,686 T	202,853 T	420	400	..	..	-68	-63
140 Lao People's Dem. Rep.	517	238	68	103	87	90	..	..	..	..	..	..	..	..
141 Congo, Dem. Rep. of the	4,420	102	161	94	80	91	8,706	13,799	322	305	1.0	0.5	(.)	1
142 Sudan	1,338	153	47	49	76	83	8,169	10,787	437	397	0.5	0.7	13	12
143 Togo	408	211	74	97	38	70	..	..	..	..	..	..	..	..
144 Nepal	1,243	499	17	56	95	91	4,663	6,974	322	320	0.5	0.7	3	9
145 Bhutan	261	1,186	17	144	100	81	..	..	..	..	..	..	..	..
146 Nigeria	14,820	209	98	129	64	68	52,846	82,669	743	722	0.4	0.4	-181	-106
147 Madagascar	683	156	48	44	77	86	..	..	..	..	..	..	..	..
148 Yemen	..	..	..	..	..	2	1,424	2,936	167	187	..	1.3	96	-519
149 Mauritania	153	165	60	66	1	..	..	..	..	..	..	..	..	..
150 Bangladesh	12,404	468	30	103	68	49	14,920	23,928	172	197	1.3	1.7	11	10

. . . WHILE PRESERVING IT FOR FUTURE GENERATIONS . . .

HDI rank	Electricity consumption Total (millions of kilowatt-hours) 1996	Index (1980 = 100) 1996	Per capita (kilowatt-hours) 1980	1996	Traditional fuel consumption (as % of total) 1980	1995	Commercial energy use (oil equivalent) Total (1,000 metric tons) 1980	1996	Per capita (kilograms) 1980	1996	GDP output per kilogram (US$)[a] 1980	1996	Net commercial energy imports (as % of energy consumption) 1980	1996
151 Zambia	6,315	98	1,125	763	55	73	4,551	5,790	793	628	0.7	0.6	8	7
152 Haiti	633	201	59	87	82	87	2,099	1,968	392	268	1.5	1.4	11	19
153 Senegal	1,160	183	115	136	49	55	1,921	2,588	347	302	1.6	1.8	46	39
154 Côte d'Ivoire	1,918	109	214	137	53	54	3,662	5,301	447	382	2.3	2.0	34	10
155 Benin	270	221	35	49	85	89	1,363	1,920	394	341	0.9	1.1	11	-2
156 Tanzania, U. Rep. of	1,737	227	41	56	84	91	10,280	13,798	553	453	..	0.3	8	5
157 Djibouti	185	158	416	300	..	..	..	..	..	..	..	..	..	..
158 Uganda	678	186	28	33	87	90	..	..	..	..	..	..	..	..
159 Malawi	873	213	66	89	89	90	..	..	..	..	..	..	..	..
160 Angola	1,885	126	214	169	47	69	4,538	6,017	647	532	..	0.9	-149	-573
161 Guinea	541	142	85	72	68	72	..	..	..	..	..	..	..	..
162 Chad	90	191	10	14	87	98	..	..	..	..	..	..	..	..
163 Gambia	76	169	70	67	80	79	..	..	..	..	..	..	..	..
164 Rwanda	175	105	32	32	85	88	..	..	..	..	..	..	..	..
165 Central African Republic	104	153	29	31	91	89	..	..	..	..	..	..	..	..
166 Mali	335	319	15	30	85	90	..	..	..	..	..	..	..	..
167 Eritrea	..	..	..	..	..	..	..	..	..	..	..	..	..	..
168 Guinea-Bissau	43	307	18	39	76	57	..	..	..	..	..	..	..	..
169 Mozambique	1,168	27	364	66	73	91	8,386	7,813	693	481	0.2	0.3	-2	7
170 Burundi	149	355	10	24	93	94	..	..	..	..	..	..	..	..
171 Burkina Faso	223	197	16	21	91	87	..	..	..	..	..	..	..	..
172 Ethiopia	1,329	193	18	22	92	91	11,157	16,566	296	284	..	0.4	5	6
173 Niger	373	171	39	39	78	78	..	..	..	..	..	..	..	..
174 Sierra Leone	241	120	62	56	64	86	..	..	..	..	..	..	..	..
All developing countries	3,742,248 T	310	366	845	..	..	1,869,600 T	3,502,685 T	599	825	1.1	1.1	-67	-33
Least developed countries	43,590 T	159	76	81	..	..	89,687 T	125,062 T	321	303	..	..	-1	-33
Sub-Saharan Africa	254,854 T	173	381	399	..	..	199,164 T	293,499 T	739	687	..	0.8	-58	-60
Arab States	340,359 T	346	688	1,574	..	..	138,402 T	313,448 T	888	1,290	3.2	..	-715	-275
East Asia	1,345,126 T	379	346	1,061	..	..	642,546 T	1,271,864 T	627	1,004	0.4	0.8	3	12
East Asia (excluding China)	266,216 T	491	1,211	4,932	..	..	49,437 T	175,064 T	1,145	3,376	2.1	2.0	75	87
South-East Asia and the Pacific	302,527 T	413	201	615	..	..	149,820 T	365,322 T	432	774	1.3	1.3	-48	-15
South Asia	591,797 T	367	173	445	..	..	330,497 T	633,224 T	357	490	1.0	1.0	-5	-8
South Asia (excluding India)	157,883 T	376	172	410	..	..	88,473 T	182,937 T	372	527	1.8	1.0	-42	-61
Latin America and the Caribbean	814,298 T	229	990	1,697	..	..	376,913 T	557,686 T	1,062	1,163	1.8	1.7	-24	-35
Eastern Europe and the CIS	1,654,616 T	..	..	4,153	..	..	1,312,527 T	1,211,670 T	3,672	3,047	..	0.6	7	-16
Industrialized countries	7,941,171 T	155	6,988	9,491	..	..	3,699,046 T	4,492,781 T	4,889	5,388	2.9	3.4	31	26
World	13,338,035 T	183	1,568	2,370	..	..	6,881,172 T	9,207,136 T	1,625	1,681	2.0	2.2	..	..

a. Estimated real GDP (at 1987 prices) divided by kilograms of oil equivalent of commercial energy use.

Source: Columns 1-4: UN 1997a and 1998c; columns 5-6: WRI 1998; columns 7-14: World Bank 1999b.

... WHILE PRESERVING IT FOR FUTURE GENERATIONS ...

18 Profile of environmental degradation

HDI rank	Internal renewable water resources per capita (cubic metres per year) 1998	Annual fresh water withdrawals		Average annual rate of deforestation (%)		Printing and writing paper consumed (metric tons per 1,000 people) 1996	CO₂ emissions			SO₂ emissions per capita (kilograms) 1995
		As % of water resources 1987-95 [a]	Per capita (cubic metres) 1987-95 [a]	1980-90 [h]	1990-95 [b]		Total (millions of metric tons) 1996	Share of world total (%) 1996	Per capita (metric tons) 1996	
High human development	**9,714**	**9.6**	**997**	**..**	**..**	**92.4**	**11,878.7 T**	**49.7**	**11.7**	**49.2**
1 Canada	94,373	1.6	1,602		-0.1	101.3	410.0	1.7	13.8	91.2 [c]
2 Norway	87,691	0.5 [d]	488 [d]	..	-0.3	94.8	67.1	0.3	15.4	8.0 [e]
3 United States	8,983	19.0	1,839	..	-0.3	136.8	5,309.7	22.2	19.7	63.2
4 Japan	4,344	16.6	735	..	0.1	114.9	1,169.6	4.9	9.3	..
5 Belgium	822	107.5	917	..	..	161.4	106.2	0.4	10.5	25.0 [c]
6 Sweden	19,858	1.7	341	..	..	115.3	54.2	0.2	6.2	..
7 Australia	18,596	4.3	933	..	0.0	91.3	307.1	1.3	17.0	..
8 Netherlands	635	78.1	518	..	0.0	86.5	155.4	0.6	10.0	..
9 Iceland	606,498	0.1	636	..	0.0	41.7	2.2	(.)	8.1	29.6
10 United Kingdom	1,219	16.6	204	..	-0.5	104.6	557.9	2.3	9.5	40.4
11 France	3,065	21.0	665	..	-1.1	71.1	362.4	1.5	6.2	17.0 [f]
12 Switzerland	5,802	2.8	173	..	0.0	110.1	44.3	0.2	6.1	4.8
13 Finland	21,334	2.0	440	..	0.1	240.1	59.3	0.2	11.6	18.8
14 Germany	1,165	48.2	580	..	0.0	85.8	862.6	3.6	10.5	36.8 [c]
15 Denmark	2,092	10.9	233	..	0.0	115.4	56.7	0.2	10.8	28.7
16 Austria	6,857	4.2	304	..	0.0	84.2	59.4	0.2	7.3	8.0 [c, f]
17 Luxembourg	..	..	..	..	..	..	8.3	(.)	20.2	19.5
18 New Zealand	88,859	0.6	589	..	-0.6	20.4	29.8	0.1	8.3	..
19 Italy	2,785	35.3	986	..	-0.1	59.0	403.9	1.7	7.1	26.1 [e, f]
20 Ireland	13,187	1.7 [d]	233 [d]	..	-2.6	55.7	35.0	0.1	9.8	46.4 [f]
21 Spain	2,775	27.9	781	..	0.0	51.4	232.9	1.0	5.9	53.3 [e]
22 Singapore	172	31.7 [d]	84 [d]	0.0	0.0	67.9	65.9	0.3	19.5	..
23 Israel	289	108.8	407	..	0.0	52.0	52.4	0.2	9.3	51.6
24 Hong Kong, China (SAR)	..	..	..	..	..	127.9	23.1	0.1	3.7	..
25 Brunei Darussalam	..	..	..	..	..	2.1	5.1	(.)	16.9	..
26 Cyprus	..	..	..	..	..	22.6	5.4	(.)	7.1	63.0
27 Greece	4,279	11.2 [d]	523 [d]	..	-2.3	24.5	80.7	0.3	7.7	50.2 [g]
28 Portugal	3,878	19.2	738	..	-0.9	36.9	48.0	0.2	4.9	27.5 [c]
29 Barbados	..	..	..	..	..	13.4	0.8	(.)	3.2	..
30 Korea, Rep. of	1,434	41.7	632	-2.0	0.2	58.6	408.7	1.7	9.0	..
31 Bahamas	..	..	..	..	..	5.6	1.7	(.)	6.0	..
32 Malta	..	..	..	..	..	36.6	1.8	(.)	4.8	..
33 Slovenia	..	..	..	..	0.0	30.1	13.1	0.1	6.8	88.9
34 Chile	31,570	3.6 [d]	1,625 [d]	0.1	0.4	16.1	48.9	0.2	3.4	..
35 Kuwait	11	2,690.0	307	-33.8	0.0	14.6	42.7	0.2	25.3	..
36 Czech Republic	5,694	4.7	266	..	0.0	34.6	126.9	0.5	12.4	105.6
37 Bahrain	..	..	..	..	..	13.2	10.6	(.)	18.6	..
38 Antigua and Barbuda	..	..	..	..	..	3.6	0.3	(.)	4.9	..
39 Argentina	19,212	4.0 [d]	1,043 [d]	0.6	0.3	16.5	130.1	0.5	3.7	..
40 Uruguay	18,215	1.1 [d]	241 [d]	-0.2	0.0	11.3	5.7	(.)	1.8	..
41 Qatar	..	..	..	..	..	3.0	29.2	0.1	52.3	..
42 Slovakia	5,745	5.8	337	..	-0.1	14.8	39.7	0.2	7.4	44.4 [c]
43 United Arab Emirates	64	1,405.3	954	-46.6	0.0	19.1	82.0	0.3	36.3	..
44 Poland	1,278	24.9	321	..	-0.1	19.3	357.4	1.5	9.3	60.6
45 Costa Rica	26,027	1.4 [d]	780 [d]	2.8	3.1	6.1	4.7	(.)	1.4	..
Medium human development	**6,410**	**7.5**	**596**	**..**	**..**	**5.1**	**10,387.4 T**	**43.4**	**2.8**	**..**
46 Trinidad and Tobago	3,869	2.9 [d]	148 [d]	1.6	1.6	7.5	22.3	0.1	17.2	..
47 Hungary	604	113.6	660	..	-0.5	23.4	59.6	0.2	6.0	68.3
48 Venezuela	36,830	0.5 [d]	382 [d]	1.1	1.1	10.0	144.7	0.6	6.5	..
49 Panama	52,042	0.9 [d]	755 [d]	1.9	2.2	8.6	6.7	(.)	2.5	..
50 Mexico	3,729	21.7	915	-0.4	0.9	9.4	348.7	1.5	3.7	..

HDI rank	Internal renewable water resources per capita (cubic metres per year) 1998	Annual fresh water withdrawals		Average annual rate of deforestation (%)		Printing and writing paper consumed (metric tons per 1,000 people) 1996	CO₂ emissions			SO₂ emissions per capita (kilograms) 1995
		As % of water resources 1987-95 [a]	Per capita (cubic metres) 1987-95 [a]	1980-90 [b]	1990-95 [b]		Total (millions of metric tons) 1996	Share of world total (%) 1996	Per capita (metric tons) 1996	
51 Saint Kitts and Nevis	..	..	..	..	..	3.9	0.1	(.)	2.5	..
52 Grenada	..	..	..	..	..	0.8	0.2	(.)	1.8	..
53 Dominica	..	..	..	..	..	1.2	0.1	(.)	1.1	..
54 Estonia	8,946	25.6	2,102	..	-1.0	28.4	16.4	0.1	11.2	..
55 Croatia	13,663	..	..	..	0.0	14.4	17.6	0.1	3.9	13.5
56 Malaysia	21,259	2.1 [d]	768 [d]	2.1	2.4	25.3	119.3	0.5	5.8	..
57 Colombia	28,393	0.5	174	0.6	0.5	7.9	65.4	0.3	1.8	..
58 Cuba	3,104	23.5 [d]	870 [d]	0.2	1.2	1.6	31.2	0.1	2.8	..
59 Mauritius	1,915	16.3 [d]	410 [d]	-1.2	0.0	10.5	1.7	(.)	1.5	..
60 Belarus	5,047	5.8	294	..	-1.0	0.2	61.8	0.3	6.0	31.5
61 Fiji	34,732	0.1	42	-0.2	0.4	7.5	0.8	(.)	1.0	..
62 Lithuania	3,720	31.9	1,185	..	-0.6	6.4	13.9	0.1	3.7	28.8
63 Bulgaria	2,146	77.2	1,574	..	..	4.2	55.4	0.2	6.5	178.2
64 Suriname	452,489	0.2	1,192	0.1	0.1	2.1	2.1	(.)	4.9	..
65 Libyan Arab Jamahiriya	100	766.7	880	-3.2	0.0	0.3	40.6	0.2	7.3	..
66 Seychelles	..	..	..	..	0.0	3.4	0.2	(.)	2.3	..
67 Thailand	1,845	29.0	602	3.1	2.6	16.1	205.7	0.9	3.5	..
68 Romania	1,639	70.3	1,139	..	..	5.5	119.5	0.5	5.3	40.1 [c]
69 Lebanon	1,315	30.8	444	0.7	8.1	13.2	14.2	0.1	4.6	..
70 Samoa (Western)	..	..	..	..	..	2.2	0.1	(.)	0.8	..
71 Russian Federation	29,009	2.7	787	..	0.0	4.7	1,582.1	6.6	10.7	25.8 [c,h]
72 Ecuador	25,791	1.8	581	1.7	1.6	2.9	24.5	0.1	2.1	..
73 Macedonia, TFYR	..	..	..	..	..	5.0	12.7	0.1	5.9	..
74 Latvia	7,029	4.1	261	..	-0.9	5.2	9.3	(.)	3.7	15.1
75 Saint Vincent and the Grenadines	..	..	..	..	..	0.5	0.1	(.)	1.1	..
76 Kazakhstan	6,728	33.4	2,281	..	-1.9	(.)	174.1	0.7	10.4	..
77 Philippines	4,476	9.1 [d]	686 [d]	3.3	3.5	5.2	64.7	0.3	0.9	..
78 Saudi Arabia	119	709.1	1,003	0.7	0.8	4.0	268.3	1.1	14.2	..
79 Brazil	31,424	0.7	246	0.6	0.5	13.0	273.8	1.1	1.7	..
80 Peru	1,613	15.3	300	0.3	0.3	4.2	26.2	0.1	1.1	..
81 Saint Lucia	..	..	..	..	..	7.4	0.2	(.)	1.3	..
82 Jamaica	3,269	3.9 [d]	159 [d]	7.1	7.5	7.4	10.1	(.)	4.0	..
83 Belize	69,565	0.1	109	0.3	0.3	1.4	0.4	(.)	1.6	..
84 Paraguay	18,001	0.5	112	2.5	2.6	3.2	3.7	(.)	0.7	..
85 Georgia	10,556	7.0	735	..	0.0	(.)	3.0	(.)	0.6	..
86 Turkey	3,074	16.1	544	..	0.0	11.2	178.6	0.7	2.9	7.1 [g]
87 Armenia	3,069	34.0	1,082	..	-2.7	(.)	3.7	(.)	1.0	..
88 Dominican Republic	2,430	14.9	446	-1.8	1.6	4.9	12.9	0.1	1.6	..
89 Oman	393	124.2	656	..	0.0	0.8	15.2	0.1	6.6	..
90 Sri Lanka	2,341	14.6 [d]	503 [d]	1.0	1.1	3.2	7.1	(.)	0.4	..
91 Ukraine	3,838	17.7	670	..	-0.1	0.2	397.9	1.7	7.7	31.8
92 Uzbekistan	1,307	261.0	4,100	..	-2.6	0.1	95.1	0.4	4.1	..
93 Maldives	..	..	..	..	0.0	3.9	0.3	(.)	1.1	..
94 Jordan	114	144.7	201	-0.3	2.5	7.2	13.8	0.1	2.5	..
95 Iran, Islamic Rep. of	1,755	54.6	1,079	1.8	1.8	4.1	267.1	1.1	3.8	..
96 Turkmenistan	232	2,280.0	6,367	..	0.0	(.)	34.3	0.1	8.3	..
97 Kyrgyzstan	10,503	23.4	2,511	..	0.0	0.7	6.1	(.)	1.4	..
98 China	2,231	16.4 [d]	461 [d]	-0.6	0.1	6.1	3,369.0	14.1	2.8	..
99 Guyana	281,542	0.6	1,819	..	..	1.6	1.0	(.)	1.1	..
100 Albania	2,903	2.0 [d]	94 [d]	..	0.0	4.2	1.9	(.)	0.6	..

... WHILE PRESERVING IT FOR FUTURE GENERATIONS ...

HDI rank	Internal renewable water resources per capita (cubic metres per year) 1998	Annual fresh water withdrawals — As % of water resources 1987-95 [a]	Annual fresh water withdrawals — Per capita (cubic metres) 1987-95 [a]	Average annual rate of deforestation (%) 1980-90 [b]	Average annual rate of deforestation (%) 1990-95 [b]	Printing and writing paper consumed (metric tons per 1,000 people) 1996	CO_2 emissions — Total (millions of metric tons) 1996	CO_2 emissions — Share of world total (%) 1996	CO_2 emissions — Per capita (metric tons) 1996	SO_2 emissions per capita (kilograms) 1995
101 South Africa	1,011	29.7	359	0.1	0.2	17.2	293.2	1.2	6.9	..
102 Tunisia	371	87.3	376	-0.9	0.5	6.1	16.2	0.1	1.8	..
103 Azerbaijan	1,657	123.6	2,235	..	0.0	(.)	30.1	0.1	4.0	..
104 Moldova, Rep. of	519	160.2	853	..	0.0	1.6	12.1	0.1	2.7	13.8
105 Indonesia	12,251	0.7	96	0.8	1.0	7.2	245.5	1.0	1.2	..
106 Cape Verde	..	..	..	..	..	0.3	0.1	(.)	0.3	..
107 El Salvador	3,128	5.3 [d]	244 [d]	2.3	3.3	6.6	4.1	(.)	0.7	..
108 Tajikistan	10,031	20.4	2,438	..	0.0	(.)	5.9	(.)	1.0	..
109 Algeria	460	32.4	180	1.2	1.2	2.9	94.5	0.4	3.3	..
110 Viet Nam	4,827	7.7	416	0.9	1.4	1.4	37.7	0.2	10.8	..
111 Syrian Arab Republic	456	205.9	1,069	2.5	2.2	1.0	44.4	0.2	3.1	..
112 Bolivia	37,703	0.4	201	0.8	1.2	1.8	10.1	(.)	1.3	..
113 Swaziland	2,836	24.9 [d]	1,171 [d]	0.0	0.0	..	0.3	(.)	0.4	..
114 Honduras	9,015	2.8	294	2.1	2.3	2.7	4.0	(.)	0.7	..
115 Namibia	3,751	4.0	179	0.3	0.3	..	..	..	..	..
116 Vanuatu	..	..	..	..	..	0.1	0.1	(.)	0.4	..
117 Guatemala	10,033	0.6 [d]	139 [d]	1.7	2.0	3.6	6.8	(.)	0.6	..
118 Solomon Islands	107,194	0.0	0	0.2	0.2	(.)	0.2	(.)	0.4	..
119 Mongolia	9,375	2.2	271	0.0	0.0	0.5	8.9	(.)	3.5	..
120 Egypt	43	1,967.9	921	-1.8	0.0	2.7	98.0	0.4	1.5	..
121 Nicaragua	39,203	0.5 [d]	368 [d]	1.4	2.5	0.1	2.9	(.)	0.7	..
122 Botswana	1,870	3.9	84	0.5	0.5	..	2.1	(.)	1.4	..
123 São Tomé and Principe	..	..	..	..	..	..	0.1	(.)	0.6	..
124 Gabon	140,171	(.)	70	0.6	0.5	0.4	3.7	(.)	3.3	..
125 Iraq	1,615	121.6	2,368	0.0	0.0	4.3	91.5	0.4	4.4	..
126 Morocco	1,071	36.2	433	0.3	0.3	2.3	27.9	0.1	1.0	..
127 Lesotho	2,395	1.0	30	-14.6	0.0	..	..	..	..	..
128 Myanmar	22,719	0.4	101	1.2	1.4	0.4	7.3	(.)	0.2	..
129 Papua New Guinea	174,055	(.)	28	-0.1	0.4	0.2	2.4	(.)	0.6	..
130 Zimbabwe	1,182	8.7	136	0.7	0.6	0.2	18.4	0.1	1.6	..
131 Equatorial Guinea	69,767	(.)	15	0.4	0.5	..	0.1	(.)	0.4	..
132 India	1,896	20.5 [d]	612 [d]	-1.1	0.0	2.0	999.0	4.2	1.1	..
133 Ghana	1,607	1.0 [d]	35 [d]	1.3	1.3	0.3	4.1	(.)	0.2	..
134 Cameroon	18,711	0.2	38	0.6	0.6	0.5	3.5	(.)	0.3	..
135 Congo	78,668	(.)	20	0.2	0.2	0.1	5.0	(.)	1.9	..
136 Kenya	696	10.2	87	0.4	0.3	1.5	6.8	(.)	0.3	..
137 Cambodia	8,195	0.6	66	2.4	1.6	0.1	0.5	(.)	(.)	..
138 Pakistan	1,678	62.7	1,269	3.1	2.9	1.8	94.5	0.4	0.7	..
139 Comoros	..	..	..	..	..	0.7	0.1	(.)	0.1	..
Low human development	7,302	1.7	158	..	..	0.4	176.5 T	0.7	0.3	..
140 Lao People's Dem. Rep.	50,392	0.4	259	..	..	0.1	0.3	(.)	0.1	..
141 Congo, Dem. Rep. of the	19,001	(.)	10	0.7	0.7	(.)	2.3	(.)	(.)	..
142 Sudan	1,227	50.9	666	1.0	0.8	0.2	3.5	(.)	0.1	..
143 Togo	2,594	0.8	28	1.6	1.4	0.2	0.8	(.)	0.2	..
144 Nepal	7,338	1.6	154	0.9	1.1	0.1	1.6	(.)	0.1	..
145 Bhutan	49,557	(.)	13	0.6	0.3	(.)	0.3	(.)	0.2	..
146 Nigeria	1,815	1.6	41	1.6	0.9	0.3	83.5	0.3	0.7	..
147 Madagascar	20,614	4.8	1,579	0.9	0.8	0.3	1.2	(.)	0.1	..
148 Yemen	243	..	..	0.0	0.0	0.1	17.0	0.1	1.1	..
149 Mauritania	163	407.5 [d]	923 [d]	0.0	0.0	0.2	3.0	(.)	1.3	..
150 Bangladesh	10,940	1.7	217	1.8	0.9	1.3	23.0	0.1	0.2	..

18 Profile of environmental degradation	Internal renewable water resources per capita (cubic metres per year) 1998	Annual fresh water withdrawals		Average annual rate of deforestation (%)		Printing and writing paper consumed (metric tons per 1,000 people) 1996	CO$_2$ emissions			SO$_2$ emissions per capita (kilograms) 1995
		As % of water resources 1987-95 [a]	Per capita (cubic metres) 1987-95 [a]	1980-90 [b]	1990-95 [b]		Total (millions of metric tons) 1996	Share of world total (%) 1996	Per capita (metric tons) 1996	
HDI rank										
151 Zambia	9,229	2.1	216	0.9	0.8	1.9	2.4	(.)	0.3	..
152 Haiti	1,460	0.4	7	4.3	3.5	0.3	1.1	(.)	0.2	..
153 Senegal	2,933	5.2	202	0.6	0.7	0.2	3.1	(.)	0.4	..
154 Côte d'Ivoire	5,265	0.9	67	7.7	0.6	0.8	13.1	0.1	0.9	..
155 Benin	1,751	1.4	28	1.4	1.2	0.1	0.7	(.)	0.1	..
156 Tanzania, U. Rep. of	2,485	1.5	40	1.1	1.0	0.5	2.4	(.)	0.1	..
157 Djibouti	..	..	..	..	..	(.)	0.4	(.)	0.6	..
158 Uganda	1,829	0.5 [d]	20 [d]	0.9	0.9	0.1	1.0	(.)	(.)	..
159 Malawi	1,690	5.3	98	1.2	1.6	0.1	0.7	(.)	0.1	..
160 Angola	15,376	0.3	57	0.6	1.0	0.1	5.1	(.)	0.4	..
161 Guinea	29,454	0.3	142	1.1	1.1	(.)	1.1	(.)	0.2	..
162 Chad	2,176	1.2	34	0.7	0.8	(.)	0.1	(.)	(.)	..
163 Gambia	2,513	0.7 [d]	30 [d]	1.1	0.9	0.1	0.2	(.)	0.2	..
164 Rwanda	965	12.2	135	-1.7	0.2	0.1	0.5	(.)	0.1	..
165 Central African Republic	40,413	0.1	26	0.4	0.4	0.1	0.2	(.)	0.1	..
166 Mali	5,071	2.3	162	0.8	1.0	0.1	0.5	(.)	(.)	..
167 Eritrea	789	..	..	..	0.0	..	0.1	(.)	11.2	..
168 Guinea-Bissau	14,109	0.1	17	-0.8	0.4	(.)	0.2	(.)	0.2	..
169 Mozambique	5,350	0.6	40	0.7	0.7	(.)	1.0	(.)	0.1	..
170 Burundi	546	2.8	20	-2.2	0.4	0.1	0.2	(.)	(.)	..
171 Burkina Faso	1,535	2.2	39	0.7	0.7	(.)	1.0	(.)	0.1	..
172 Ethiopia	1,771	2.0	51	..	0.5	0.1	3.4	(.)	(.)	..
173 Niger	346	14.3	69	0.0	0.0	0.1	1.1	(.)	0.1	..
174 Sierra Leone	34,957	0.2	98	2.8	3.0	0.4	0.4	(.)	0.1	..
All developing countries	6,055	6.2	492	..	..	5.5	8,716.2 T	36.4	2.1	..
Least developed countries	9,731	1.4	175	..	..	0.4	85.8 T	0.4	0.2	..
Sub-Saharan Africa	6,363	1.5	125	..	..	1.6	468.8 T	2.0	0.9	..
Arab States	554	129.2	926	..	..	2.9	909.8 T	3.8	3.7	..
East Asia	2,217	16.9	466	..	..	8.5	3,809.8 T	15.9	3.0	..
East Asia (excluding China)	1,855	31.0	613	..	..	64.1	440.7 T	1.8	8.2	..
South-East Asia and the Pacific	11,860	2.0	317	..	..	7.3	755.5 T	3.2	3.1	..
South Asia	2,860	16.4	658	..	..	2.0	1,392.9 T	5.8	1.0	..
South Asia (excluding India)	5,338	12.6	777	..	..	2.0	393.8 T	1.6	1.0	..
Latin America and the Caribbean	21,504	1.9	507	..	..	9.8	1,195.4 T	5.0	2.5	..
Eastern Europe and the CIS	13,179	8.2	1,122	..	..	6.3	3,249.6 T	13.6	8.2	40.3
Industrialized countries	9,817	10.3	1,058	..	..	104.6	10,476.9 T	43.8	12.5	47.5
World	6,918 [i]	7.3	626 [i]	..	..	20.1	22,442.6 T	93.8 [j]	4.1	..

a. Data refer to the most recent year available during the period specified in the column heading.

b. A positive number indicates a loss of forest area, a negative number a gain.

c. Data refer to 1994.

d. Data refer to an earlier year or period than that specified in the column heading.

e. Data refer to 1993.

f. Provisional.

g. Data refer to 1990.

h. Data refer to only part of the country.

i. WRI 1998.

j. The world total is less than 100% because of the omission of data for countries not reported on and because the global total used in this calculation includes other emissions not included in national totals, such as emissions from bunker fuels and oxidation of non-fuel hydrocarbon products.

Source: Columns 1-5: WRI 1998; column 6: UNESCO 1998a; columns 7-9: calculated on the basis of data from CDIAC 1999a and 1999b; column 10: UNECE 1999a.

HDI rank	Major protected areas (as % of national territory)[a] 1998	Spent fuel produced (metric tons of heavy metal)[b] 1996	Hazardous waste produced (1,000 metric tons) 1991-94[c,d]	Municipal waste generated (kilograms per person) 1991-97[d]	Population served — By municipal waste services (%) 1992-95[d]	Population served — By public sanitation services (%) 1992-95[d]	Waste recycling (as % of apparent consumption) — Paper and cardboard 1992-95[d]	Waste recycling (as % of apparent consumption) — Glass 1992-95[d]
High human development	**12.5**	**8,044 T**	**255,385 T**	**536**	**99**	**84**	**43**	**42**
1 Canada	9.5	1,000	5,896	630	100	91	33	17
2 Norway	24.2	..	500	590	98	73	11	75
3 United States	18.9	2,300	213,620	720	100	..	35	23
4 Japan	6.8	852	..	400	100	..	51	56
5 Belgium	2.6	123	776	480	100	..	12	67
6 Sweden	4.7	235	..	440	100	95	54	61
7 Australia	8.7	..	426	690 [e]	..	..	50 [e]	36
8 Netherlands	11.5	14	1,520	570	100	98	77	80
9 Iceland	9.4	..	6	570	99	90	30 [e]	75
10 United Kingdom	19.8	781	1,844	480	100	97	35	27
11 France	11.6	1,264	7,000 [e]	590	100	81	38	50
12 Switzerland	17.3	64	854	600	99	94	61	85
13 Finland	8.3	68	559	410	75	77	57	50
14 Germany	26.4	450	9,100	400	100	92	67	75
15 Denmark	31.8	..	250	540	100	..	44	63
16 Austria	28.2	..	550	510	99	76	65	76
17 Luxembourg	13.9	..	180	460	100	88	..	..
18 New Zealand	23.4	..	110	350	..	..	..	..
19 Italy	7.1	..	2,708	470	..	..	29	53
20 Ireland	0.8	..	248	430	..	68	12	39
21 Spain	8.3	158	1,708 [e]	370	..	62	52	32
23 Israel	14.9 [f,g]	..	..	..	..	..	..	..
27 Greece	2.5	..	450	340	100	51	19	20
28 Portugal	6.5	..	..	350	89	55	37	42
32 Malta	..	..	..	..	..	..	..	..
33 Slovenia	5.7 [f,g]	..	..	..	..	..	..	..
36 Czech Republic	15.5	45	1,867	310	85	73	..	..
42 Slovakia	21.3 [f]	..	1,347	..	..	52	..	..
44 Poland	9.3	..	3,866	320	..	..	..	..
Medium human development	**3.2**	**..**	**..**	**..**	**..**	**..**	**..**	**..**
47 Hungary	6.8	55	3,537	500	85	43	..	..
54 Estonia	12.0 [f,g]	..	..	..	..	..	..	..
55 Croatia	6.7 [f,g]	..	..	..	..	..	..	..
60 Belarus	4.2 [f,g]	..	..	..	..	..	..	..
62 Lithuania	10.0 [f,g]	..	..	..	..	..	..	..
63 Bulgaria	4.4 [f,g]	..	..	..	..	..	..	..
68 Romania	4.7 [f,g]	..	..	..	..	..	..	..
71 Russian Federation	3.1 [f,g]	..	..	..	..	..	..	..
73 Macedonia, TFYR	7.1 [f,g]	..	..	..	..	..	..	..
74 Latvia	12.5 [f,g]	..	..	..	..	..	..	..
76 Kazakhstan	2.7 [f,g]	..	..	..	..	..	..	..
85 Georgia	2.8 [f,g]	..	..	..	..	..	..	..
87 Armenia	7.6 [f,g]	..	..	..	..	..	..	..
91 Ukraine	1.6 [f,g]	..	..	..	..	..	..	..
92 Uzbekistan	2.1 [f,g]	..	..	..	..	..	..	..
96 Turkmenistan	4.2 [f,g]	..	..	..	..	..	..	..
97 Kyrgyzstan	3.6 [f,g]	..	..	..	..	..	..	..
100 Albania	2.8 [f,g]	..	..	..	..	..	..	..
103 Azerbaijan	5.5 [f,g]	..	..	..	..	..	..	..
104 Moldova, Rep. of	1.2 [f,g]	..	..	..	..	..	..	..
108 Tajikistan	4.2 [f,g]	..	..	..	..	..	..	..

HDI rank	Major protected areas (as % of national territory) [a] 1998	Spent fuel produced (metric tons of heavy metal) [b] 1996	Hazardous waste produced (1,000 metric tons) 1991-94 [c, d]	Municipal waste generated (kilograms per person) 1991-97 [d]	Population served		Waste recycling (as % of apparent consumption)	
					By municipal waste services (%) 1992-95 [d]	By public sanitation services (%) 1992-95 [d]	Paper and cardboard 1992-95 [d]	Glass 1992-95 [d]
All developing countries	..	..	..	..	..	..	..	..
Eastern Europe and the CIS	3.3 [f, g]	..	..	..	..	..	..	..
Industrialized countries	12.5	7,999 T	248,305 T	549	100	84	..	..
World	..	..	..	..	..	..	..	..

Note: This table includes industrialized countries and Eastern Europe and the CIS only.

a. National classifications may differ. Includes only areas greater than 10 square kilometres except for islands. World Conservation Union (IUCN) management categories I-VI, except where otherwise noted.

b. Spent fuel arising in nuclear power plants.

c. Waste, generated mainly by industrial activities, that may lead to toxic contamination of soil, water and air if not properly managed.

d. Data refer to the most recent year available during the period specified in the column heading.

e. Data refer to an earlier year or period than that specified in the column heading.

f. Data refer to 1996.

g. IUCN categories I-V.

Source: Column 1: OECD 1997c and forthcoming and WRI 1998; *columns 2 and 4:* OECD forthcoming; *columns 3 and 5-8:* OECD 1997c.

. . . WHILE PRESERVING IT FOR FUTURE GENERATIONS . . .

| | Daily per capita supply of calories | | Daily per capita supply of protein | | Daily per capita supply of fat | | Food production per capita index (1989-91 = 100) | Food imports (as % of merchandise imports) | Food aid in cereals (thousands of metric tons) | Food consumption (as % of total household consumption) |
| | | | Total [a] (grams) | Change (%) | Total [a] (grams) | Change (%) | | | | |
HDI rank	1970	1996	1996	1970-96	1996	1970-96	1997	1997	1994-95 [b]	1980-85 [c]
High human development	3,000	3,347	102.7	13.0	127.6	32.3	106	8	..	..
1 Canada	2,942	3,056	98.2	3.4	120.2	3.6	113	6	..	..
2 Norway	2,944	3,350	108.9	25.2	136.8	137.1	100	7	..	..
3 United States	2,933	3,642	111.4	16.0	140.5	19.1	117	5	..	..
4 Japan	2,527	2,905	96.7	16.5	82.5	50.0	96	15	..	..
5 Belgium	..	3,543	102.0	8.5	158.3	19.9	..	..	..	..
6 Sweden	2,816	3,160	100.8	14.5	131.8	12.6	97	7	..	..
7 Australia	3,111	3,001	103.5	0.5	112.2	0.2	129	5	..	..
8 Netherlands	2,998	3,259	103.7	48.1	141.0	6.8	108	11	..	..
9 Iceland	2,818	3,104	111.2	-8.1	116.4	0.3	93	10	..	..
10 United Kingdom	3,242	3,237	94.5	2.7	140.2	-0.6	99	9	..	..
11 France	3,263	3,551	114.5	10.1	164.2	29.3	105	10	..	..
12 Switzerland	3,464	3,280	88.5	-1.7	143.3	-4.5	96	6	..	..
13 Finland	3,074	2,916	95.1	6.9	125.5	-0.4	94	7	..	..
14 Germany	3,135	3,330	95.1	8.1	144.9	12.3	93	9	..	..
15 Denmark	3,134	3,808	106.4	36.4	181.2	9.8	102	13	..	..
16 Austria	3,204	3,343	96.3	7.0	157.6	26.1	98	6	..	..
17 Luxembourg	..	..	..	..	..	..	..	..	..	..
18 New Zealand	3,006	3,405	104.5	7.7	131.0	5.7	124	8	..	..
19 Italy	3,395	3,504	109.2	12.6	145.1	29.6	97	11	..	..
20 Ireland	3,424	3,636	113.4	7.0	130.2	3.3	108	8	..	..
21 Spain	2,723	3,295	106.9	27.3	142.2	51.3	104	12	..	..
22 Singapore	..	..	..	..	..	..	35	4	..	..
23 Israel	2,986	3,272	107.5	7.5	115.2	12.9	116	7	..	..
24 Hong Kong, China (SAR)	2,743	3,282	99.7	17.3	136.5	40.3	58	6	..	..
25 Brunei Darussalam	2,331	2,886	85.5	58.3	89.0	107.0	100	..	..	..
26 Cyprus	3,102	3,341	105.7	21.5	135.3	12.6	107	27	..	..
27 Greece	3,104	3,575	113.4	13.4	150.3	33.1	96	15	..	..
28 Portugal	2,850	3,658	112.0	36.6	130.9	67.8	102	13	..	..
29 Barbados	2,805	3,207	87.9	11.3	104.0	21.0	109	18	..	..
30 Korea, Rep. of	2,793	3,336	80.2	22.5	81.5	226.0	123	6	..	35
31 Bahamas	2,575	2,443	74.7	-4.2	80.2	-6.1	123	..	..	..
32 Malta	3,102	3,417	109.8	15.6	116.1	18.5	136	11	..	..
33 Slovenia	..	3,117	102.3	..	99.7	..	103	7	..	..
34 Chile	2,619	2,810	78.9	14.3	82.0	39.1	131	7	2	29
35 Kuwait	..	3,075	98.3	31.1	97.1	38.3	157	16	..	..
36 Czech Republic	..	3,177	94.7	..	114.2	..	81	7	..	..
37 Bahrain	..	..	..	..	..	..	117	12	..	..
38 Antigua and Barbuda	2,489	2,365	86.7	35.5	90.0	8.4	95	..	..	..
39 Argentina	3,340	3,136	96.5	-5.4	112.5	2.7	127	5	..	35
40 Uruguay	3,041	2,830	89.0	-2.2	105.2	-6.3	136	10	..	31
41 Qatar	..	..	..	..	..	..	137	..	..	..
42 Slovakia	..	3,030	77.9	..	101.3	..	73	8	..	..
43 United Arab Emirates	3,196	3,366	104.8	..	108.3	40.7	190	..	..	..
44 Poland	3,416	3,344	99.3	-4.5	110.8	5.5	80	8	..	..
45 Costa Rica	2,391	2,822	74.3	28.1	77.5	36.4	130	13	2	33
Medium human development	2,123	2,695	69.6	33.7	60.9	99.7	130	9	4,190 T	..
46 Trinidad and Tobago	2,464	2,751	63.1	-1.4	74.6	20.8	111	10	..	19
47 Hungary	3,311	3,402	88.8	-3.5	142.0	22.4	81	5	..	..
48 Venezuela	..	2,398	61.3	3.9	65.8	24.0	121	16	..	23
49 Panama	2,236	2,556	64.2	8.8	71.1	39.1	103	10	..	38
50 Mexico	2,698	3,137	82.2	17.4	85.8	47.7	120	6	44	35 [d, e]

HDI rank	Daily per capita supply of calories		Daily per capita supply of protein		Daily per capita supply of fat		Food production per capita index (1989-91 = 100)	Food imports (as % of merchandise imports)	Food aid in cereals (thousands of metric tons)	Food consumption (as % of total household consumption)
			Total[a] (grams)	Change (%)	Total[a] (grams)	Change (%)				
	1970	1996	1996	1970-96	1996	1970-96	1997	1997	1994-95[b]	1980-85[c]
51 Saint Kitts and Nevis	1,762	2,240	62.8	57.0	77.2	40.4	127	19	..	..
52 Grenada	2,185	2,731	71.4	21.0	93.9	40.3	96	26	..	..
53 Dominica	2,012	3,093	82.9	65.8	90.7	92.4	80	28	7	..
54 Estonia	..	3,004	101.3	..	105.6	..	48	16	..	..
55 Croatia	..	2,458	64.7	..	69.3	..	59	10	..	..
56 Malaysia	2,518	2,899	74.4	45.9	78.7	40.9	127	5	(.)	23 [d]
57 Colombia	2,042	2,800	66.6	38.8	71.9	71.7	111	11	15	29
58 Cuba	2,619	2,357	52.1	-24.5	45.4	-34.0	64	..	3	..
59 Mauritius	2,322	2,952	77.5	55.0	82.1	64.2	109	15	..	24
60 Belarus	3,091	3,101	91.0	..	90.4	..	59	..	57	..
61 Fiji	2,380	3,038	73.3	35.7	112.5	78.8	108	..	..	..
62 Lithuania	..	2,805	93.3	..	65.0	..	74	11	..	..
63 Bulgaria	3,451	2,756	81.0	-15.6	91.9	8.1	59	..	..	..
64 Suriname	2,177	2,578	61.0	8.9	49.8	13.4	86	..	17	..
65 Libyan Arab Jamahiriya	2,439	3,132	71.8	19.7	112.6	50.1	101	..	..	..
66 Seychelles	1,826	2,424	74.5	52.0	72.1	100.7	141	20	..	..
67 Thailand	2,148	2,334	52.2	2.4	43.9	51.2	107	5	3	30
68 Romania	3,105	2,943	91.1	1.2	81.8	12.1	105	6	..	..
69 Lebanon	2,330	3,279	82.6	40.0	107.4	67.6	119	..	7	..
70 Samoa (Western)	..	..	..	..	..	..	94	..	..	..
71 Russian Federation	..	2,704	85.9	..	74.1	..	71	19	10	..
72 Ecuador	2,175	2,592	55.2	8.2	99.5	99.0	137	9	32	30
73 Macedonia, TFYR	..	2,336	63.6	..	71.1	..	96	..	..	..
74 Latvia	1,986	2,861	91.1	..	83.1	..	45	13	..	..
75 Saint Vincent and the Grenadines	2,295	2,434	60.3	11.7	65.4	8.7	81	..	..	..
76 Kazakhstan	..	3,007	96.8	..	58.8		72	..	..	..
77 Philippines	1,670	2,356	54.6	24.1	47.8	44.4	123	8	44	51
78 Saudi Arabia	1,872	2,735	77.9	62.3	74.4	125.4	90	18	..	..
79 Brazil	2,398	2,938	74.1	21.5	81.5	73.2	128	9	33	35
80 Peru	2,207	2,310	61.1	3.6	48.4	27.5	139	14	348	35
81 Saint Lucia	..	2,822	86.4	66.2	75.5	30.6	75	26	3	..
82 Jamaica	2,483	2,575	61.7	-7.9	71.4	16.7	119	15	46	36
83 Belize	2,265	2,862	63.5	9.5	74.0	17.3	148	20	..	..
84 Paraguay	2,591	2,485	74.8	2.5	75.7	23.9	119	21	1	30
85 Georgia	..	2,184	63.8	..	38.1	..	73	..	388	..
86 Turkey	2,991	3,568	100.9	12.1	100.4	35.3	105	5	..	40
87 Armenia	..	2,147	60.0	..	50.7	..	84	..	356	..
88 Dominican Republic	1,988	2,316	51.3	16.6	74.1	51.5	113	..	2	46
89 Oman	..	..	..	..	..	..	101	17	..	..
90 Sri Lanka	2,229	2,263	48.8	10.9	48.4	-1.3	115	..	342	43
91 Ukraine	..	2,753	80.3	..	70.2	..	68	..	..	..
92 Uzbekistan	..	2,550	76.0	..	63.7	..	96	..	..	..
93 Maldives	1,428	2,495	85.1	57.6	49.0	32.3	113	..	3	..
94 Jordan	2,415	2,681	69.2	4.8	79.4	32.3	151	..	111	35
95 Iran, Islamic Rep. of	1,994	2,824	74.5	35.5	65.1	51.6	136	..	..	37
96 Turkmenistan	..	2,563	71.5	..	77.5	..	99	..	50	..
97 Kyrgyzstan	..	2,489	82.0	..	47.7	..	124	21	19	..
98 China	2,000	2,844	76.0	58.3	65.9	186.3	163	5	..	61 [d, e]
99 Guyana	2,224	2,392	63.5	11.4	46.4	-5.1	185	..	30	..
100 Albania	2,434	2,523	88.8	26.9	77.9	49.8	..	27	34	..

... ENSURING HUMAN SECURITY ...

HDI rank	Daily per capita supply of calories		Daily per capita supply of protein		Daily per capita supply of fat		Food production per capita index (1989-91 = 100)	Food imports (as % of merchandise imports)	Food aid in cereals (thousands of metric tons)	Food consumption (as % of total household consumption)
			Total[a] (grams)	Change (%)	Total[a] (grams)	Change (%)				
	1970	1996	1996	1970-96	1996	1970-96	1997	1997	1994-95[b]	1980-85[c]
101 South Africa	2,807	2,933	73.3	-0.9	79.5	15.6	100	6	..	34
102 Tunisia	2,221	3,250	87.6	43.6	84.9	49.2	105	11	22	37
103 Azerbaijan	..	2,139	62.6	..	40.5	..	58	..	379	
104 Moldova, Rep. of	..	2,562	66.8	..	53.9	..	57	..	58	..
105 Indonesia	1,859	2,930	67.8	73.8	58.9	103.5	124	9	15	48
106 Cape Verde	1,475	3,135	63.1	61.8	108.6	229.2	96	..	65	..
107 El Salvador	1,827	2,515	62.8	33.6	53.4	40.0	112	17	7	33
108 Tajikistan	..	2,129	58.5	..	40.1	..	68	..	97	..
109 Algeria	1,798	3,020	80.6	70.8	71.0	97.7	108	32	23	..
110 Viet Nam	2,122	2,502	57.9	13.5	35.1	59.5	135	..	64	..
111 Syrian Arab Republic	2,317	3,339	86.7	35.5	92.1	50.8	133	..	59	..
112 Bolivia	2,000	2,170	56.4	12.8	50.0	16.3	134	9	175	33[d]
113 Swaziland	2,346	2,529	61.7	-5.1	42.7	-0.4	93	..	1	..
114 Honduras	2,177	2,368	55.4	0.7	60.1	46.7	110	18	73	39
115 Namibia	2,149	2,168	59.0	15.7	36.6	-16.3	126	..	..	..
116 Vanuatu	2,412	2,624	55.6	-17.0	96.7	7.3	103	..	..	..
117 Guatemala	2,100	2,191	55.6	-0.7	42.0	10.6	118	13	144	36
118 Solomon Islands	2,150	2,103	42.9	-23.4	39.3	-10.9	107	16	..	..
119 Mongolia	2,279	2,098	70.7	-13.8	76.7	-9.4	82	14	12	..
120 Egypt	2,352	3,289	87.9	37.3	57.5	22.5	133	26	179	49
121 Nicaragua	2,411	2,328	51.5	-28.5	47.2	2.4	128	14	33	..
122 Botswana	2,101	2,272	72.3	-4.9	57.3	30.1	102	..	7	25
123 São Tomé and Principe	..	2,156	43.6	..	69.9	6.3	122	..	6	..
124 Gabon	2,118	2,517	69.8	14.4	49.7	27.1	107	19	..	..
125 Iraq	2,254	2,252	45.2	-25.9	86.3	100.2	90	..	68	..
126 Morocco	2,404	3,244	85.8	32.0	65.1	51.6	95	17	13	38
127 Lesotho	..	2,209	62.2	2.0	32.9	36.7	101	..	15	..
128 Myanmar	1,997	2,752	71.8	38.1	42.3	27.8	131	..	5	..
129 Papua New Guinea	1,920	2,253	47.5	18.8	47.8	45.2	107	..	..	..
130 Zimbabwe	2,222	2,083	49.9	-19.5	53.5	4.8	106	7	4	40
131 Equatorial Guinea	..	..	..	..	..	..	98	..	3	..
132 India	2,078	2,415	58.6	14.9	44.2	47.3	119	5	264	52
133 Ghana	2,121	2,560	49.4	-5.0	34.5	-18.3	148	..	101	50[d]
134 Cameroon	2,280	2,175	51.0	-16.4	45.5	-2.8	119	14	2	24
135 Congo	1,996	2,107	40.8	13.3	56.2	30.4	116	..	12	37
136 Kenya	2,180	1,971	51.5	-19.5	47.4	39.1	105	17	102	38
137 Cambodia	2,059	1,974	45.3	-5.6	32.6	72.1	126	..	64	..
138 Pakistan	2,198	2,408	59.9	10.9	65.6	92.9	134	19	103	37
139 Comoros	1,848	1,824	42.1	20.3	41.1	2.8	118	..	10	..
Low human development	2,147	2,145	51.0	-4.4	38.7	22.5	117	..	3,459 T	..
140 Lao People's Dem. Rep.	2,154	2,143	51.6	-7.9	24.1	5.1	113	..	10	..
141 Congo, Dem. Rep. of the	2,158	1,815	29.7	-19.7	29.6	-13.1	104	..	83	..
142 Sudan	2,167	2,391	73.5	20.5	72.5	..	146	17	132	60[d]
143 Togo	2,261	2,155	52.7	3.3	42.3	24.9	138	..	8	..
144 Nepal	1,933	2,339	60.0	-31.0	35.1	35.1	116	14	21	57
145 Bhutan	..	..	..	..	..	..	107	..	4	..
146 Nigeria	2,254	2,609	56.3	12.6	66.3	24.9	136	..	..	48
147 Madagascar	2,406	2,001	45.7	-25.1	31.3	-5.0	107	15	26	59
148 Yemen	1,763	2,041	54.3	6.5	38.2	31.8	121	..	..	..
149 Mauritania	1,868	2,653	78.3	5.8	64.1	23.3	105	..	22	..
150 Bangladesh	2,177	2,105	45.0	..	23.2	55.0	111	17	888	59

HDI rank	Daily per capita supply of calories		Daily per capita supply of protein		Daily per capita supply of fat		Food production per capita index (1989-91 = 100)	Food imports (as % of merchandise imports)	Food aid in cereals (thousands of metric tons)	Food consumption (as % of total household consumption)
			Total [a] (grams)	Change (%)	Total [a] (grams)	Change (%)				
	1970	1996	1996	1970-96	1996	1970-96	1997	1997	1994-95 [b]	1980-85 [c]
151 Zambia	2,140	1,939	51.1	-20.2	28.8	-29.9	94	..	11	36
152 Haiti	..	1,855	41.1	..	31.7	..	92	..	117	..
153 Senegal	2,546	2,394	67.6	4.0	67.2	-0.1	112	..	16	49
154 Côte d'Ivoire	2,428	2,421	51.0	-3.8	42.9	..	115	17	56	39
155 Benin	1,964	2,415	57.3	19.4	42.9	..	127	..	15	37
156 Tanzania, U. Rep. of	1,749	2,028	50.8	-40.9	30.6	13.5	94	..	118	64
157 Djibouti	1,842	1,920	39.0	-7.1	53.9	46.1	83	..	23	..
158 Uganda	2,294	2,110	46.1	-19.1	28.8	-20.1	110	..	62	..
159 Malawi	2,340	2,097	55.9	-24.5	28.9	-35.8	100	..	204	30
160 Angola	2,071	1,983	43.3	-5.9	39.7	13.7	133	..	..	..
161 Guinea	2,212	2,099	44.0	-8.3	47.2	-15.6	133	..	29	..
162 Chad	2,183	1,972	56.7	-11.4	55.1	14.7	119	..	14	..
163 Gambia	2,108	2,332	46.8	-16.4	56.8	9.0	84	..	2	..
164 Rwanda	..	2,142	47.5	..	25.1	..	81	..	269	29
165 Central African Republic	2,378	1,938	44.7	27.7	63.9	13.8	124	12	1	..
166 Mali	2,095	2,027	60.8	3.1	42.3	..	127	..	17	57
167 Eritrea	..	1,585	49.3	..	20.5	..	107	..	140	..
168 Guinea-Bissau	1,989	2,381	47.7	10.9	57.3	-4.2	112	..	2	..
169 Mozambique	1,886	1,799	34.5	-1.4	32.5	12.2	133	22	320	..
170 Burundi	2,094	1,708	54.2	-25.8	11.9	-20.3	96	..	48	..
171 Burkina Faso	1,762	2,137	63.5	17.6	48.5	61.3	123	..	19	..
172 Ethiopia	..	1,845	58.6	..	22.3	..	..	..	720	49
173 Niger	1,992	2,116	62.2	11.1	31.5	..	121	..	32	..
174 Sierra Leone	2,419	2,002	43.7	-5.0	55.5	-13.8	97	..	30	56
All developing countries	2,129	2,628	66.4	30.1	57.7	92.9	132	..	6,203 T	..
Least developed countries	2,090	2,095	51.4	-3.3	33.3	24.3	115	..	3,558 T	..
Sub-Saharan Africa	2,226	2,205	52.7	-5.7	44.8	9.5	116	..	2,592 T	..
Arab States	2,206	2,907	77.4	27.2	70.2	51.1	120	..	636 T	..
East Asia	2,033	2,862	76.5	56.7	66.8	186.7	161	..	..	..
East Asia (excluding China)	2,770	3,273	88.7	20.5	87.7	195.6	113	..	..	..
South-East Asia and the Pacific	1,957	2,659	62.3	41.7	50.3	70.6	123	..	205 T	..
South Asia	2,094	2,402	58.2	14.7	45.5	51.7	120	..	1,625 T	..
South Asia (excluding India)	2,144	2,369	57.0	13.6	48.8	63.7	125	..	1,361 T	..
Latin America and the Caribbean	2,491	2,812	72.4	14.8	77.8	48.9	122	..	1,134 T	..
Eastern Europe and the CIS	..	2,800	85.0	..	78.2	..	76	..	..	..
Industrialized countries	2,986	3,377	104.8	14.0	133.1	24.6	106	..	..	..
World	2,336	2,751	73.5	26.5	70.4	79.0	124	..	..	..

a. Amount available for human consumption. Per capita supply represents the average supply available for the population as a whole and does not necessarily indicate what is actually consumed by individuals.
b. The time reference for food aid is the crop year, July to June.
c. Data refer to the most recent year available during the period specified in the column heading.
d. Data refer to a year or period other than that specified in the column heading.
e. Includes beverages and tobacco.
Source: Column 1: FAO 1997; column 2: FAO 1998; columns 3 and 5: FAO 1999; columns 4 and 6: calculated on the basis of data from FAO 1999; columns 7-9: World Bank 1999b; column 10: World Bank 1993.

. . . ENSURING HUMAN SECURITY . . .

HDI rank	Unemployed people (thousands) 1997	Total unemploy-ment rate (%) 1997	Incidence of long-term unemployment [a] (as % of total unemployment)		Discouraged workers (as % of total labour force) 1993	Involuntary part-time workers (as % of total labour force) 1993	Unemployment benefits expenditure (as % of total government expenditure) 1991
			Female 1997	Male 1997			
High human development	32,495 T	7.8	26.0	29.2	1.2	3.6	2.0
1 Canada	1,414	9.3	10.2	14.5	0.9	5.5	8.1
2 Norway	93	4.1	11.1	14.0	1.2	..	2.2
3 United States	6,739	5.0	8.0	9.4	0.9	5.0	1.5
4 Japan	2,300	3.5	11.8	28.8	2.2	1.9	0.7
5 Belgium	375	9.0	61.5	59.4	1.5	3.8	5.8
6 Sweden	367 [b]	8.0	26.9	31.8	2.0	6.2	0.8
7 Australia	791	8.5	27.5	33.1	1.6	6.9	4.0
8 Netherlands	422	5.6	48.5	49.9	0.6	5.6	4.5
9 Iceland	6	3.8	12.0	20.0	..	..	..
10 United Kingdom	2,034	7.1	27.8	44.9	0.6	3.2	1.7
11 France	3,192	12.4	43.3	39.1	0.2	4.8	3.2
12 Switzerland	162	4.2	32.8	25.5	..	..	0.4
13 Finland	367	14.5	28.2	33.9	1.5	2.9	3.6
14 Germany	4,308	9.8	..	..	..	1.5	3.0
15 Denmark	174	5.4	27.9	26.3	1.6	4.8	5.5
16 Austria	165	5.2	28.4	28.9	..	..	1.8
17 Luxembourg	6 [b]	..	..	..	..	..	..
18 New Zealand	121	7.2	16.1	22.2	1.0	6.3	..
19 Italy	2,805	12.5	66.2	66.5	2.6	2.3	1.0
20 Ireland	159	10.5	46.9	63.3	0.5	3.3	6.3
21 Spain	3,357	20.9	60.4	49.9	0.2	1.0	7.0
23 Israel	170	7.7 [c]	..	..	..	..	..
27 Greece	440	9.8	62.2	45.8	0.3	3.1	..
28 Portugal	..	6.9	57.7	53.4	0.1	1.8	..
32 Malta	7 [b]	5.0 [b, c]	..	..	..	..	..
33 Slovenia	69	7.1 [c]	..	..	..	..	..
36 Czech Republic	242	4.7	29.9	31.3	..	..	..
42 Slovakia	287	11.6 [c]	..	..	..	..	..
44 Poland	1,923	11.5	41.9	33.5	..	..	..
Medium human development	12,399 T	7.9	..	..	..	..	..
47 Hungary	349	8.7	49.2	52.6	..	..	..
54 Estonia	16 [d]	10.0 [c, d]	..	..	..	..	..
55 Croatia	278 [b]	..	..	..	..	..	..
60 Belarus	126	2.7 [c]	..	..	..	..	..
62 Lithuania	256	14.1 [c]	..	..	..	..	..
63 Bulgaria	505 [b]	13.7 [b, c]	..	..	..	..	..
68 Romania	706	6.0 [c]	..	..	..	..	..
71 Russian Federation	6,788 [d]	9.3 [c, d]	..	..	..	..	..
73 Macedonia, TFYR	253 [e]	..	..	..	..	..	..
74 Latvia	171	14.4 [c]	..	..	..	..	..
76 Kazakhstan	282 [b, d]	4.1 [b, c, d]	..	..	..	..	..
85 Georgia	..	..	..	..	..	..	..
87 Armenia	..	..	..	..	..	..	..
91 Ukraine	2,330	8.9 [c]	..	..	..	..	..
92 Uzbekistan	31 [f]	0.4 [c, f]	..	..	..	..	..
96 Turkmenistan	..	..	..	..	..	..	..
97 Kyrgyzstan	55 [b]	..	..	..	..	..	..
100 Albania	140 [g]	9.1 [c, g]	..	..	..	..	..
103 Azerbaijan	38 [b]	1.3 [b, c]	..	..	..	..	..
104 Moldova, Rep. of	23 [b, d]	..	..	..	..	..	..
108 Tajikistan	51 [b]	2.7 [b, c]	..	..	..	..	..

HDI rank	Unemployed people (thousands) 1997	Total unemployment rate (%) 1997	Incidence of long-term unemployment[a] (as % of total unemployment)		Discouraged workers (as % of total labour force) 1993	Involuntary part-time workers (as % of total labour force) 1993	Unemployment benefits expenditure (as % of total government expenditure) 1991
			Female 1997	Male 1997			
All developing countries	..	..	..	..	..	..	..
Eastern Europe and the CIS	14,920 T	8.2	..	..	..	..	..
Industrialized countries	29,974 T	7.7	25.0	28.9	..	..	..
World	..	..	..	..	..	..	..

Note: This table includes industrialized countries and Eastern Europe and the CIS only.

a. Data refer to unemployment lasting 12 months or longer.

b. Data refer to registered unemployment.

c. ILO, *Yearbook of Labour Statistics 1998.*

d. Date refer to 1996.

e. Includes only those applying for work.

f. Data refer to 1995.

g. Data refer to 1991.

Source: Column 1: ILO, *Yearbook of Labour Statistics 1998; column 2:* OECD 1998b and ILO, *Yearbook of Labour Statistics 1998; columns 3 and 4:* OECD 1998b; *columns 5 and 6:* OECD 1997b; *column 7:* ILO 1995.

	Elections for lower or single house		Elections for upper house or senate		Voter turnout	Political parties represented	
HDI rank	Date of latest elections	Members elected (E) or appointed (A)	Date of latest elections	Members elected (E) or appointed (A)	at latest elections (%) [a]	In lower or single house	In upper house or senate
High human development							
1 Canada	06 1997	E	1994 [b]	A	69	5 [c]	2 [c]
2 Norway	09 1997	E	..	..	78	7 [c]	..
3 United States	11 1998	E	11 1998	E	36	2 [c]	2
4 Japan	10 1996	E	07 1998	E	59	7 [c]	9 [c]
5 Belgium	05 1995	E	05 1995	E/A	91	11	10
6 Sweden	09 1998	E	..	..	81	7	..
7 Australia	10 1998	E	10 1998	E	95	3 [c]	5 [c]
8 Netherlands	05 1998	E	05 1995	E	73	9	7 [c]
9 Iceland	04 1995	E	..	..	87	6	..
10 United Kingdom	05 1997	E	1997 [b]	A	72	10 [c]	3 [c]
11 France	05 1997	E	09 1998	E	71	9	8 [c]
12 Switzerland	10 1995	E	10 1995	E	42	11 [c]	6
13 Finland	03 1995	E	..	..	68	7 [c]	..
14 Germany	09 1998	E	1997 [b]	A	82	5	†
15 Denmark	03 1998	E	..	..	86	10	..
16 Austria	12 1995	E	11 1994 [b]	E	86	5	3
17 Luxembourg	06 1994	E	..	..	88 [d]	5	..
18 New Zealand	10 1996	E	..	..	88	6	..
19 Italy	04 1996	E	04 1996	E + A	83	4 [c]	6 [c]
20 Ireland	06 1997	E	08 1997	E + A	66	7 [c]	5 [c]
21 Spain	03 1996	E	03 1996	E	77	8 [c]	4 [c]
22 Singapore	01 1997	E + A	..	..	41	3	..
23 Israel	05 1996	E	..	..	79	11	..
25 Brunei Darussalam [e]	–	–	–	–	–	–	–
26 Cyprus	05 1996	E	..	..	93	5	..
27 Greece	09 1996	E	..	..	76	5	..
28 Portugal	10 1995	E	..	..	67	4	..
29 Barbados	01 1999	E	01 1999	A	†	†	†
30 Korea, Rep. of	04 1996	E	..	..	64	4 [c]	..
31 Bahamas	03 1997	E	03 1997	A	68 [d]	2	2
32 Malta	09 1998	E	..	..	95	2	..
33 Slovenia	11 1996	E	..	..	74	8	..
34 Chile	12 1997	E	12 1997	E + A	86	7 [c]	6 [c]
35 Kuwait	10 1996	E	..	..	80	0	..
36 Czech Republic	06 1998	E	11 1998	E	74	5	4
37 Bahrain	12 1973 [f]	E	–	–	–	–	–
38 Antigua and Barbuda	03 1994	E	03 1994	A	62 [d]	3	3 [c]
39 Argentina	10 1997	E	12 1995	E	78	6 [c]	4 [c]
40 Uruguay	11 1994	E	11 1994	E	91	3 [c]	3 [c]
41 Qatar [e]	–	–	–	–	–	–	–
42 Slovakia	09 1998	E	..	..	84	6	..
43 United Arab Emirates	12 1997	A	..	..	–	–	..
44 Poland	09 1997	E	09 1997	E	48	6	6
45 Costa Rica	02 1998	E	..	..	70	7	..
Medium human development							
46 Trinidad and Tobago	11 1995	E	11 1995	A	63	3	2 [c]
47 Hungary	05 1998	E	..	..	56	6 [c]	..
48 Venezuela	11 1998	E	11 1998	E	†	8 [c]	5 [c]
49 Panama	05 1994	E	..	..	74	4 [c]	..
50 Mexico	07 1997	E	07 1997	E	57	5 [c]	5 [c]

22 Profile of political life

HDI rank	Elections for lower or single house		Elections for upper house or senate		Voter turnout at latest elections (%)[a]	Political parties represented	
	Date of latest elections	Members elected (E) or appointed (A)	Date of latest elections	Members elected (E) or appointed (A)		In lower or single house	In upper house or senate
51 Saint Kitts and Nevis	07 1995	E + A	..	..	68 [d]	4	..
52 Grenada	01 1999	E	01 1999	A	57	1	†
53 Dominica	06 1995	E + A	..	..	75 [d]	3	..
54 Estonia	03 1995	E	..	..	70	7	..
55 Croatia	10 1995	E	04 1997	E + A	69	5 [c]	6
56 Malaysia	04 1995	E	03 1998	E + A	72	5	†
57 Colombia	03 1998	E	03 1998	E	45	2 [c]	2 [c]
58 Cuba	01 1998	E	..	..	98	1	..
59 Mauritius	12 1995	E + A	..	..	80	5	..
60 Belarus	11 1996 [g]	A	11 1996	A	–	†	†
61 Fiji	02 1994	E	02 1994	A	75 [d]	6 [c]	†
62 Lithuania	10 1996	E	..	..	53	6 [c]	..
63 Bulgaria	04 1997	E	..	..	68	5	..
64 Suriname	05 1996	E	..	..	67 [d]	5	..
65 Libyan Arab Jamahiriya	03 1997	E	..	..	†	1	..
66 Seychelles	03 1998	E	..	..	87	3	..
67 Thailand	11 1996	E	03 1996	A	62	11	†
68 Romania	11 1996	E	11 1996	E	76	7	6
69 Lebanon	08 1996	E	..	..	44	10 [c]	..
70 Samoa (Western)	04 1996	E	..	..	86	2 [c]	..
71 Russian Federation	12 1995	E	–	A	–	9 [c]	†
72 Ecuador	05 1998	E	..	..	†	8 [c]	..
73 Macedonia, TFYR	10 1998	E	..	..	73	7 [c]	..
74 Latvia	10 1998	E	..	..	72	6	..
75 Saint Vincent and the Grenadines	06 1998	E + A	..	..	†	2	..
76 Kazakhstan	12 1995	E	12 1995	E + A	76	6 [c]	4 [c]
77 Philippines	05 1998	E	05 1998	E	79	5 [c]	2 [c]
78 Saudi Arabia [e]	–	–	–	–	–	–	–
79 Brazil	10 1998	E	10 1998	E	†	12 [c]	9
80 Peru	04 1995	E	..	..	63 [d]	13	..
81 Saint Lucia	05 1997	E	05 1997	A	66	2	2 [c]
82 Jamaica	12 1997	E	12 1997	A	65	2	†
83 Belize	08 1998	E	08 1998	A	90	2	2 [c]
84 Paraguay	05 1998	E	05 1998	E	80	2	2 [c]
85 Georgia	11 1995	E	..	..	68	12 [c]	..
86 Turkey	12 1995	E	..	..	85	5	..
87 Armenia	07 1995	E	..	..	56	8 [c]	..
88 Dominican Republic	05 1998	E	05 1998	E	66	3	3
89 Oman [e]	–	–	–	–	–	–	–
90 Sri Lanka	08 1994	E	..	..	76	7 [c]	..
91 Ukraine	03 1998	E	..	..	70	9 [c]	..
92 Uzbekistan	12 1994	E	..	..	94	2 [c]	..
93 Maldives	12 1994	E + A	..	..	75 [d]	–	..
94 Jordan	11 1997	E	11 1997	A	47	†	†
95 Iran, Islamic Rep. of	03 1996	E	..	..	77	2 [c]	..
96 Turkmenistan	12 1994	E	..	..	100	1	..
97 Kyrgyzstan	02 1995	E	02 1995	E	61	†	†
98 China	11 1997	E	..	..	†	1	..
99 Guyana	12 1997	E	..	..	98	5 [c]	..
100 Albania	06 1997	E	..	..	73	6 [c]	..

	Elections for lower or single house		Elections for upper house or senate		Voter turnout at latest elections (%) [a]	Political parties represented	
HDI rank	Date of latest elections	Members elected (E) or appointed (A)	Date of latest elections	Members elected (E) or appointed (A)		In lower or single house	In upper house or senate
101 South Africa	04 1994	E	04 1994	E	87	7	5
102 Tunisia	03 1994	E	..	..	95	5	..
103 Azerbaijan	11 1995	E	..	..	86	9 [c]	..
104 Moldova, Rep. of	03 1998	E	..	..	72	4	..
105 Indonesia	05 1997	E + A	..	..	89	3	..
106 Cape Verde	12 1995	E	..	..	77	3	..
107 El Salvador	03 1997	E	..	..	89	9	..
108 Tajikistan	02 1995	E	..	..	84	4	..
109 Algeria	06 1997	E	12 1997	E + A	66	10 [c]	4
110 Viet Nam	07 1997	E	..	..	100	1 [c]	..
111 Syrian Arab Republic	11 1998	E	..	..	82	1 [c]	..
112 Bolivia	06 1997	E	06 1997	E	70	7	5
113 Swaziland	10 1998	E + A	09 1993	E + A	†	–	–
114 Honduras	11 1997	E	..	..	73 [d]	5	..
115 Namibia	12 1994	E	11 1992	E	76	5	†
116 Vanuatu	03 1998	E	..	..	75	3 [c]	..
117 Guatemala	11 1995	E	..	..	†	7	..
118 Solomon Islands	08 1997	E	..	..	64 [d]	2	..
119 Mongolia	06 1996	E	..	..	88	4 [c]	..
120 Egypt	11 1995	E + A	..	..	48	6 [c]	..
121 Nicaragua	10 1996	E	..	..	77	4 [c]	..
122 Botswana	10 1994	E	..	..	77 [d]	2	..
123 São Tomé and Principe	11 1998	E	..	..	65	3	..
124 Gabon	12 1996	E	01 1997	E	†	7 [c]	6 [c]
125 Iraq	03 1996	E	..	..	94	4 [c]	..
126 Morocco	11 1997	E	12 1997	E	58	15	13
127 Lesotho	05 1998	E	05 1998	A	74	2	†
128 Myanmar	04 1990 [h]	E	–	–	–	–	–
129 Papua New Guinea	06 1997	E	..	..	81 [d]	9 [c]	..
130 Zimbabwe	04 1995	E + A	..	..	57	2	..
131 Equatorial Guinea	11 1993	E	..	..	I	4	..
132 India	02 1998	E + A	03 1998	E + A	62	15 [c]	8 [c]
133 Ghana	12 1996	E	..	..	65	4	..
134 Cameroon	05 1997	E	..	..	76	4 [c]	..
135 Congo	01 1998 [i]	A	–	–	–	–	–
136 Kenya	12 1997	E + A	..	..	65	10	..
137 Cambodia	07 1998	E	..	..	†	3	..
138 Pakistan	02 1997	E	03 1997	E	35	4 [c]	9 [c]
139 Comoros	12 1996	E	..	..	20	2 [c]	..
Low human development							
140 Lao People's Dem. Rep.	12 1997	E	..	..	99	1 [c]	..
141 Congo, Dem. Rep. of the	10 1993 [j]	E	..	..	..	..	..
142 Sudan	03 1996	E	..	..	55	–	..
143 Togo	02 1994	E	..	..	65	5	..
144 Nepal	11 1994	E	06 1997	E + A	62	5 [c]	4
145 Bhutan	1998	E + A	..	..	–	–	..
146 Nigeria	02 1999	E	02 1999	E	†	†	†
147 Madagascar	05 1998	E	..	..	†	9 [c]	..
148 Yemen	04 1997	E	..	..	61	5 [c]	..
149 Mauritania	10 1996	E	04 1996	E	39 [d]	3 [c]	3
150 Bangladesh	06 1996	E	..	..	74	4 [c]	..

HDI rank	Elections for lower or single house		Elections for upper house or senate		Voter turnout at latest elections (%) [a]	Political parties represented	
	Date of latest elections	Members elected (E) or appointed (A)	Date of latest elections	Members elected (E) or appointed (A)		In lower or single house	In upper house or senate
151 Zambia	11 1996	E + A	..	..	40	4 [c]	..
152 Haiti	06 1995	E	04 1997	E	31	6 [c]	†
153 Senegal	01 1999	E	01 1999	E + A	41	6	†
154 Côte d'Ivoire	11 1995	E	..	..	71 [d]	2	..
155 Benin	03 1995	E	..	..	76	6 [c]	..
156 Tanzania, U. Rep. of	10 1995	E + A	..	..	77 [d]	5	..
157 Djibouti	12 1997	E	..	..	57	1	..
158 Uganda	06 1996	E	..	..	59 [d]	–	..
159 Malawi	05 1994	E	..	..	80	3	..
160 Angola	09 1992	E	..	..	91	12	..
161 Guinea	06 1995	E	..	..	62	5 [c]	..
162 Chad	01 1997	E	..	..	49	10	..
163 Gambia	01 1997	E + A	..	..	69	4 [c]	..
164 Rwanda	11 1994 [i]	A	–	–	–	8	–
165 Central African Republic	11 1998	E	..	..	†	3 [c]	..
166 Mali	07 1997	E	..	..	22	8	..
167 Eritrea	02 1994	E	..	..	†	†	..
168 Guinea-Bissau	07 1994	E	..	..	45 [d]	5	..
169 Mozambique	10 1994	E	..	..	88	3	..
170 Burundi	06 1993	E	..	..	..	2	91
171 Burkina Faso	05 1997	E	12 1995	E + A	45	4	†
172 Ethiopia	05 1995	E	05 1995	E	85 [d]	1 [c]	†
173 Niger	11 1996	E	..	..	39	7 [c]	..
174 Sierra Leone	02 1996 [k]	–	–	–	–	–	–

† No information or confirmation available.

Note: Information is as of February 1999.

a. For lower or single house.

b. Data valid as of 1997.

c. There are also independent and other parties not sufficiently represented to constitute a parliamentary group.

d. Average turnout in the 1990s. No official data available. The figures are from IDEA 1997.

e. The country has never had a parliament.

f. First legislature of Bahrain dissolved by decree of the emir on 26 August 1975.

g. Following a referendum held on 24 November 1996, the Supreme Council elected in November-December 1995 was replaced by a bicameral National Assembly comprising some of the members of the former Supreme Council.

h. The Parliament elected in 1990 has never been convened nor authorized to sit, and many of its members were detained or forced into exile.

i. Transitional appointed unicameral Parliament created by decree.

j. Transitional unicameral Parliament dissolved following change of regime in May 1997.

k. Unicameral Parliament dissolved following a military coup d'etat on 25 April 1997.

Source: IPU 1999b.

HDI rank	Prisoners (per 100,000 people) 1994	Juvenile prisoners (as % of total prisoners) 1994	Intentional homicides (per 100,000 people) 1994	Drug crimes (per 100,000 people) 1994	Recorded rapes (thousands) 1994
High human development	..	..	..	..	..
1 Canada	419.3	..	1.9	207.1	31.7
2 Norway	272.2	(.)	2.1	533.4	0.4
3 United States	207.7	..	..	..	102.2
4 Japan	38.5	..	1.0	18.4	1.6
5 Belgium	169.0	3.6	3.1	148.0	0.9
6 Sweden	161.7	0.2	9.5	350.5	1.8
7 Australia	129.4 [a]	..	3.6	398.4 [a]	14.0
8 Netherlands	182.4 [a]	..	14.8 [a]	39.4 [a]	1.3 [a]
9 Iceland	..	..	..	..	..
10 United Kingdom	..	..	..	..	..
11 France	138.3 [a]	..	4.7	93.1	6.5
12 Switzerland	..	..	2.3	563.2	0.3
13 Finland	171.3	..	10.1	116.5	0.4
14 Germany	..	..	..	..	5.1 [a]
15 Denmark	289.5	1.3	4.9	270.9 [a]	0.5
16 Austria	216.2	..	2.4	148.4	0.6
17 Luxembourg	..	..	7.6 [a]	196.6 [a]	(.)
18 New Zealand	187.4 [a]	..	..	..	..
19 Italy	177.2	1.4	4.7	67.3	0.9
20 Ireland	182.6 [a]	..	0.7	128.6	0.2
21 Spain	156.7 [a]	..	1.6	65.5 [a]	1.2
22 Singapore	631.0	1.2	1.6	56.4	0.1
23 Israel	195.7	0.8	6.2	169.8	0.6
24 Hong Kong, China (SAR)	262.8	17.4	1.5	76.1	0.1
25 Brunei Darussalam	314.5	8.0	..	..	..
26 Cyprus	66.5	12.2	1.5	18.6	(.)
27 Greece	46.5	5.9	2.5	24.2	0.3
28 Portugal	79.6	6.9	4.1 [a]	60.2 [a]	0.3 [a]
29 Barbados	..	..	11.8 [a]	217.7 [a]	0.1 [a]
30 Korea, Rep. of	64.4	23.4	1.5	3.9	6.2
31 Bahamas	..	..	85.5	282.6	0.2
32 Malta	171.6	1.3	2.4	66.8	(.)
33 Slovenia	89.8	2.2	4.9	20.7	0.2
34 Chile	931.7	..	2.4	63.0	1.0
35 Kuwait	..	..	10.9	134.0	(.)
36 Czech Republic	159.7	7.5	2.1 [a]	..	0.9 [a]
37 Bahrain	..	..	1.0 [a]	34.1 [a]	(.) [a]
38 Antigua and Barbuda	..	..	..	..	..
39 Argentina	..	..	7.5 [a]	..	..
40 Uruguay	..	..	5.8	44.9	..
41 Qatar	528.7	4.5	1.9	2.9	0
42 Slovakia	165.7	..	2.4	1.6	0.2
43 United Arab Emirates	..	..	..	..	..
44 Poland	196.9	..	3.1	10.4	2.0
45 Costa Rica	226.2	..	8.4	12.7	0.3
Medium human development	..	..	..	..	..
46 Trinidad and Tobago	..	..	6.8 [a]	244.0 [a]	0.2 [a]
47 Hungary	177.6	..	4.3	2.5	0.8
48 Venezuela	..	..	..	33.9 [a]	2.9 [a]
49 Panama	197.5	..	..	116.0	0.3
50 Mexico	..	..	..	..	..

HDI rank	Prisoners (per 100,000 people) 1994	Juvenile prisoners (as % of total prisoners) 1994	Intentional homicides (per 100,000 people) 1994	Drug crimes (per 100,000 people) 1994	Recorded rapes (thousands) 1994
51 Saint Kitts and Nevis	–	..	..	..	..
52 Grenada	..	..	..	..	..
53 Dominica	..	..	..	..	..
54 Estonia	302.3	7.7	24.4	2.2	3.0
55 Croatia	29.2	0.9	7.5	18.1	0.1
56 Malaysia	302.8	0.7	2.0	54.0	1.0
57 Colombia	82.4	..	75.9	38.7	1.9
58 Cuba	..	..	..	..	..
59 Mauritius	248.0	1.6	3.0	168.3	(.)
60 Belarus	206.6	6.6	9.2	13.9	0.7
61 Fiji	..	..	4.8	..	0.1
62 Lithuania	247.1	2.8	14.2	9.1	0.2
63 Bulgaria	54.5	3.0	10.5	..	0.9
64 Suriname	..	..	..	..	..
65 Libyan Arab Jamahiriya	..	..	..	..	..
66 Seychelles	–	..	..	..	..
67 Thailand	..	..	9.7 [a]	28.4 [a]	2.5 [a]
68 Romania	112.0 [a]	..	5.8	1.2	1.4
69 Lebanon	..	..	..	38.3	0.1
70 Samoa (Western)	165.3	12.4	2.4	56.7	(.)
71 Russian Federation	1,538.9	..	21.8	50.4	14.0
72 Ecuador	..	..	17.7	141.6	0.9
73 Macedonia, TFYR	86.4	1.8	..	6.0	(.)
74 Latvia	768.0	..	14.7	10.9	0.1
75 Saint Vincent and the Grenadines	..	..	9.8 [a]	..	0.1
76 Kazakhstan	..	..	15.0	56.4	1.9
77 Philippines	6.2	..	..	..	2.5
78 Saudi Arabia	..	..	..	..	..
79 Brazil	..	..	..	..	..
80 Peru	79.5	..	..	..	..
81 Saint Lucia	..	..	..	..	..
82 Jamaica	86.9	6.6	27.1	231.1	1.1
83 Belize	..	..	..	..	..
84 Paraguay	..	..	18.5	2.5	0.1
85 Georgia	143.5	0.9	12.8	20.8	(.)
86 Turkey	100.6	1.7	..	3.9	0.5
87 Armenia	111.7	1.5	5.8	0.7 [a]	(.)
88 Dominican Republic	..	..	..	..	..
89 Oman	..	..	..	..	..
90 Sri Lanka	419.5 [a]	..	11.5 [a]	..	0.4 [a]
91 Ukraine	108.2	5.9	8.9	55.3	1.7
92 Uzbekistan	..	..	..	..	..
93 Maldives	277.9 [a]	..	0.5 [a]	3.7 [a]	(.) [a]
94 Jordan	..	..	7.1	4.1 [a]	(.)
95 Iran, Islamic Rep. of	..	..	..	..	..
96 Turkmenistan	..	..	..	..	..
97 Kyrgyzstan	251.5	1.8	12.0	56.0	0.4
98 China	..	..	..	0.3	44.1
99 Guyana	536.9	..	18.0	252.4	0.1
100 Albania	..	..	..	..	..

HDI rank	Prisoners (per 100,000 people) 1994	Juvenile prisoners (as % of total prisoners) 1994	Intentional homicides (per 100,000 people) 1994	Drug crimes (per 100,000 people) 1994	Recorded rapes (thousands) 1994
101 South Africa	462.0	..	..	..	..
102 Tunisia	..	..	..	..	..
103 Azerbaijan	..	..	8.0	29.4	0.1
104 Moldova, Rep. of	121.2	2.3	8.6	6.5	0.3
105 Indonesia	30.4	31.4	0.8	0.3	1.7
106 Cape Verde	..	..	..	..	..
107 El Salvador	260.0	18.6	..	..	..
108 Tajikistan	..	..	3.2 [a]	..	0.1 [a]
109 Algeria	..	..	..	..	..
110 Viet Nam	..	..	..	..	..
111 Syrian Arab Republic	..	..	2.8	18.5	0.1
112 Bolivia	..	..	..	1.6	2.3
113 Swaziland	967.0	11.6	31.1	55.9	0.5
114 Honduras	..	..	..	..	..
115 Namibia	..	..	..	..	..
116 Vanuatu	22.1 [a]	..	0.6 [a]	..	(.) [a]
117 Guatemala	..	..	30.1	..	..
118 Solomon Islands	..	..	..	..	..
119 Mongolia	..	..	..	..	..
120 Egypt	64.5	..	1.3	143.9	(.)
121 Nicaragua	105.0	..	23.3	24.3	1.3
122 Botswana	230.8 [a]	..	11.7 [a]	73.8 [a]	0.6 [a]
123 São Tomé and Principe	66.8	..	133.7	..	..
124 Gabon	..	..	..	..	..
125 Iraq	..	..	13.2	(.)	0.3
126 Morocco	..	..	1.1	55.0	0.9
127 Lesotho	246.7	20.6	70.4	6.4	0.9
128 Myanmar	..	..	0.6 [a]	11.3 [a]	0.8 [a]
129 Papua New Guinea	..	..	..	..	..
130 Zimbabwe		..	9.4	98.8	3.1
131 Equatorial Guinea	..	..	..	..	..
132 India	..	..	7.5	2.2	13.2
133 Ghana	65.8 [a]	..	..	..	..
134 Cameroon	..	..	..	..	..
135 Congo	..	..	..	..	..
136 Kenya	..	..	..	..	..
137 Cambodia	..	..	..	..	..
138 Pakistan	..	..	..	..	..
139 Comoros	..	..	..	..	..
Low human development	..	..	..	..	..
140 Lao People's Dem. Rep.	..	..	..	..	..
141 Congo, Dem. Rep. of the	..	..	..	..	..
142 Sudan	282.6	0.8	3.2	5.9	0.6
143 Togo	..	..	..	..	..
144 Nepal	..	..	..	1.1 [a]	0.1 [a]
145 Bhutan	..	..	..	..	..
146 Nigeria	..	..	1.9	..	2.4
147 Madagascar	260.1	2.4	0.5	2.5	0.1
148 Yemen	..	..	..	..	..
149 Mauritania	..	..	..	..	..
150 Bangladesh	..	..	..	..	..

HDI rank	Prisoners (per 100,000 people) 1994	Juvenile prisoners (as % of total prisoners) 1994	Intentional homicides (per 100,000 people) 1994	Drug crimes (per 100,000 people) 1994	Recorded rapes (thousands) 1994
151 Zambia	439.7	0.1	..	3.9	0.3
152 Haiti	..	..	..	..	..
153 Senegal	..	..	..	..	..
154 Côte d'Ivoire	..	..	..	..	..
155 Benin	..	..	..	..	..
156 Tanzania, U. Rep. of	..	..	..	..	..
157 Djibouti	..	..	..	..	..
158 Uganda	108.0	1.0	..	..	..
159 Malawi	..	..	..	..	..
160 Angola	..	..	..	..	..
161 Guinea	..	..	..	..	..
162 Chad	..	..	..	..	..
163 Gambia	..	..	..	..	..
164 Rwanda	87.0 [a]	..	..	9.1 [a]	0.7 [a]
165 Central African Republic	..	..	..	..	..
166 Mali	..	..	..	..	..
167 Eritrea	..	..	..	..	..
168 Guinea-Bissau	..	..	..	..	..
169 Mozambique	..	..	..	..	..
170 Burundi	..	..	..	..	..
171 Burkina Faso	..	..	..	..	..
172 Ethiopia	48.9 [a]	..	6.1 [a]	..	0.3 [a]
173 Niger	..	..	..	..	..
174 Sierra Leone	..	..	..	..	..
All developing countries	..	..	..	..	..
Least developed countries	..	..	..	..	..
Sub-Saharan Africa	..	..	..	..	..
Arab States	..	..	..	..	..
East Asia	..	..	..	..	..
East Asia (excluding China)	..	..	..	..	..
South-East Asia and the Pacific	..	..	..	..	..
South Asia	..	..	..	..	..
South Asia (excluding India)	..	..	..	..	..
Latin America and the Caribbean	..	..	..	..	..
Eastern Europe and the CIS	..	..	..	..	..
Industrialized countries	..	..	..	..	..
World	..	..	..	..	..

a. Data refer to 1990.

Source: Columns 1 and 3-5: UN 1999b; *column 2:* calculated on the basis of data from UN 1999b.

HDI rank	Injuries and deaths from road accidents (per 100,000 people) 1997	Suicides (per 100,000 people) Male 1990-95[a]	Suicides (per 100,000 people) Female 1990-95[a]	Divorces (as % of marriages) 1996	Births to mothers under 20 (%) 1991-97[a]	People killed or affected by disasters (annual average; thousands) 1969-93	Refugees By country of asylum (thousands) 1997	Refugees By country of origin (thousands) 1997
High human development	750	19.0	5.6	40	6.9	1,149 T	2,801.2 T	..
1 Canada	741	21.5	5.4	45	6.3	20	121.4	..
2 Norway	276	17.7	6.9	43	2.9	(.)	57.0	..
3 United States	1,266	19.8	4.5	49	13.1	31	547.1	..
4 Japan	..	..	..	..	1.3	141	2.1	..
5 Belgium	700	26.8	11.6	56	2.9	0	36.1	..
6 Sweden	246	21.5	9.2	64	2.0	(.)	187.0	..
7 Australia	..	21.0	4.7	..	4.9	3	60.2	..
8 Netherlands	82	13.1	6.5	41	1.3	1	118.7	..
9 Iceland	552	..	..	39	5.2	0	0.3	1.1
10 United Kingdom	559	11.7	3.2	53	6.9	0	102.7	..
11 France	304	31.5	10.7	43	1.9	34	147.3	..
12 Switzerland	384	..	..	40	1.3	0	83.2	..
13 Finland	183	43.4	11.8	56	2.6	(.)	11.7	..
14 Germany	621	23.2	8.7	41	2.6	5	1,049.0	..
15 Denmark	192	24.2	11.2	35	2.0	(.)	57.0	..
16 Austria	651	34.2	11.0	38	3.9	(.)	84.4	..
17 Luxembourg	374	..	..	39	2.0	..	0.7	..
18 New Zealand	..	..	..	..	7.5	2	1.9	..
19 Italy	483	12.7	4.0	12	2.3	76	73.4	..
20 Ireland	371	14.6	3.7	..	5.4	0	0.4	..
21 Spain	330	12.7	3.7	17	3.3	32	5.6	..
22 Singapore	..	16.3	10.5	..	1.5	(.)	..	..
23 Israel	810	9.4	3.6	26	3.8	(.)	..	..
24 Hong Kong, China (SAR)	..	14.3	9.2	..	1.9	2	1.2	..
25 Brunei Darussalam	..	..	..	..	6.3	..	..	..
26 Cyprus	603	..	..	13	3.8	0	..	..
27 Greece	330	5.9	1.2	18	4.7	29	5.5	..
28 Portugal	694	12.2	4.4	21	7.1	2	0.3	..
29 Barbados	..	..	..	..	..	(.)	..	..
30 Korea, Rep. of	..	14.5	6.7	..	0.9	81	..	..
31 Bahamas	..	..	..	..	13.8	(.)	0.1	..
32 Malta	203	..	..	..	4.8	..	0.3	..
33 Slovenia	453	45.3	12.6	26	4.3	..	5.1	3.3
34 Chile	..	10.2	1.4	..	15.0	168	0.3	8.2
35 Kuwait	..	..	..	..	4.0	..	3.8	..
36 Czech Republic	371	25.6	8.5	61	9.0	(.)	1.7	0.5
37 Bahrain	..	..	..	..	3.2	(.)	..	..
38 Antigua and Barbuda	..	..	..	..	15.8	..	..	..
39 Argentina	..	10.6	2.9	..	15.7	511	10.5	..
40 Uruguay	..	..	..	..	15.6	1	0.1	..
41 Qatar	..	..	..	..	3.8	..	..	..
42 Slovakia	249	23.4	4.6	34	12.3	..	0.7	..
43 United Arab Emirates	..	..	..	..	..	(.)	0.5	..
44 Poland	234	24.3	4.7	19	7.8	1	0.8	1.2
45 Costa Rica	..	8.0	1.8	..	18.4	10	23.1	..
Medium human development	..	..	..	..	..	98,605 T	5,433.7 T	2,684.4 T
46 Trinidad and Tobago	..	17.4	5.0	..	13.7	2	..	..
47 Hungary	257	50.6	16.7	46	11	(.)	5.9	8.2
48 Venezuela	..	8.3	1.9	..	19.9	5	0.3	..
49 Panama	..	..	..	..	18.9	7	0.6	..
50 Mexico	..	5.4	1.0	..	15.7	88	31.9	..

HDI rank	Injuries and deaths from road accidents (per 100,000 people) 1997	Suicides (per 100,000 people)		Divorces (as % of marriages) 1996	Births to mothers under 20 (%) 1991-97 [a]	People killed or affected by disasters (annual average; thousands) 1969-93	Refugees	
		Male 1990-95 [a]	Female 1990-95 [a]				By country of asylum (thousands) 1997	By country of origin (thousands) 1997
51 Saint Kitts and Nevis	..	..	..	..	16.7	..	..	..
52 Grenada	..	..	..	..	..	..	..	..
53 Dominica	..	..	..	..	..	..	..	..
54 Estonia	146	67.6	16	..	12.9	..	..	0.8
55 Croatia	378	29.7	9.8	15	5.6	..	68.9	342
56 Malaysia	..	..	..	..	3.2	15	5.3	..
57 Colombia	..	5.5	1.5	..	..	243	0.2	1.2
58 Cuba	..	25.6	14.9	..	15.4	62	1.3	1.7
59 Mauritius	..	21.1	5.9	..	10.6	40	..	..
60 Belarus	86	..	..	68	14.0	2	0.1	0.1
61 Fiji	..	..	..	..	..	51	..	..
62 Lithuania	187	79.1	15.6	55	12.1	..	..	0.3
63 Bulgaria	94	..	..	28	22.6	(.)	0.4	0.4
64 Suriname	..	..	..	..	16.6	0	..	..
65 Libyan Arab Jamahiriya	..	..	..	..	..	(.)	8.5	..
66 Seychelles	..	..	..	..	16.2	..	..	..
67 Thailand	..	5.6	2.4	..	13.0	481	169.2	..
68 Romania	46	20.3	4.6	24	16.5	58	0.6	4.6
69 Lebanon	..	..	..	..	..	2	3.1	5.5
70 Samoa (Western)	..	..	..	..	..	(.)	..	..
71 Russian Federation	139	72.9	13.7	65	17.5	2	237.7	3.9
72 Ecuador	..	..	..	..	17.2	62	0.2	..
73 Macedonia, TFYR	170	..	..	5	10.0	(.)	3.5	12.3
74 Latvia	211	70.8	14.7	63	10.5	..	..	1.6
75 Saint Vincent and the Grenadines	..	..	..	..	20.5	0	..	..
76 Kazakhstan	95	48.9	9.4	39	12.6	1	15.6	40.2
77 Philippines	..	..	..	..	6.2	2,051	0.3	..
78 Saudi Arabia	..	..	..	..	..	0	5.8	..
79 Brazil	..	..	..	..	18.0	1,879	2.3	..
80 Peru	..	..	..	..	..	514	0.8	2.4
81 Saint Lucia	..	..	..	..	..	..	..	..
82 Jamaica	..	..	..	..	..	54	..	..
83 Belize	..	..	..	..	17.7	4	8.4	..
84 Paraguay	..	..	..	..	4.5	18	0.1	..
85 Georgia	49	..	..	12	19.7	4	0.2	46.2
86 Turkey	176	..	..	6	12	33	2.4	36.5
87 Armenia	48	..	..	18	20.8	52	219.0	201.0
88 Dominican Republic	..	..	..	..	..	102	0.6	..
89 Oman	..	..	..	..	..	0	..	..
90 Sri Lanka	..	..	..	..	8.3	579	..	93.6
91 Ukraine	94	..	..	63	19.9	16	4.6	2.6
92 Uzbekistan	58	..	..	12	10.9	2	3.2	68.7
93 Maldives	..	..	..	..	14.8	1	..	..
94 Jordan	..	..	..	..	..	1	0.7	..
95 Iran, Islamic Rep. of	..	..	..	..	11.7	73	1,982.6	56.8
96 Turkmenistan	..	..	..	18	..	..	15.8	..
97 Kyrgyzstan	96	21.2	6.1	25	10.6	6	15.3	16.3
98 China	..	..	..	..	..	23,655	291.5	119.8
99 Guyana	..	..	..	..	..	11	..	..
100 Albania	19	..	..	7	2.9	..	..	0.8

HDI rank	Injuries and deaths from road accidents (per 100,000 people) 1997	Suicides (per 100,000 people) Male 1990-95[a]	Suicides (per 100,000 people) Female 1990-95[a]	Divorces (as % of marriages) 1996	Births to mothers under 20 (%) 1991-97[a]	People killed or affected by disasters (annual average; thousands) 1969-93	Refugees By country of asylum (thousands) 1997	Refugees By country of origin (thousands) 1997
101 South Africa	..	..	..	..	..	263	6.5	..
102 Tunisia	..	..	..	..	2.9	19	0.5	0.3
103 Azerbaijan	38	11	0.2	15	..	(.)	233.7	234.2
104 Moldova, Rep. of	104	29.7	8.3	52	19.8	..	..	4.5
105 Indonesia	..	..	..	..	..	316	..	8.2
106 Cape Verde	..	..	..	..	14.7	0	..	..
107 El Salvador	..	..	..	..	20.2	65	0.1	13.4
108 Tajikistan	37	5.1	2.3	13	9.8	3	2.2	75.7
109 Algeria	..	..	..	..	..	..	170.7	0.3
110 Viet Nam	..	..	..	..	..	1,579	15.0	316.6
111 Syrian Arab Republic	..	..	..	..	..	5	22.7	3.4
112 Bolivia	..	..	..	..	..	162	0.3	..
113 Swaziland	..	..	..	..	..	62	0.6	..
114 Honduras	..	..	..	..	..	49	..	0.2
115 Namibia	..	..	..	..	..	10	2.5	..
116 Vanuatu	..	..	..	..	..	7	..	..
117 Guatemala	..	..	..	..	17.3	158	1.5	32.2
118 Solomon Islands	..	..	..	..	..	9	0.8	..
119 Mongolia	..	..	..	..	..	4	..	..
120 Egypt	..	..	..	..	2.3	3	6.4	..
121 Nicaragua	..	..	..	..	..	59	0.5	19.6
122 Botswana	..	..	..	..	..	171	0.3	..
123 São Tomé and Principe	..	..	..	..	..	8	..	..
124 Gabon	..	..	..	..	..	0	0.9	..
125 Iraq	..	..	..	..	..	..	104.0	630.7
126 Morocco	..	..	..	..	9.2	17	0.1	0.1
127 Lesotho	..	..	..	..	..	34	..	..
128 Myanmar	..	..	..	..	..	239	..	132.3
129 Papua New Guinea	..	..	..	..	..	8	8.2	0.8
130 Zimbabwe	..	..	..	..	14.5	184	0.8	..
131 Equatorial Guinea	..	..	..	..	..	(.)	..	0.1
132 India	..	..	..	..	..	63,271	223.1	..
133 Ghana	..	..	..	..	..	501	22.9	13.3
134 Cameroon	..	..	..	..	..	41	47.1	1.3
135 Congo	..	..	..	..	..	(.)	20.6	20.7
136 Kenya	..	..	..	..	..	142	232.1	8.7
137 Cambodia	..	..	..	..	..	42	..	100.0
138 Pakistan	..	..	..	..	8.0	983	1,202.7	0.3
139 Comoros	..	..	..	..	..	15	..	..
Low human development	..	..	..	..	..	19,409 T	3,023.0 T	2,490.2 T
140 Lao People's Dem. Rep.	..	..	..	..	..	192	..	15.8
141 Congo, Dem. Rep. of the	..	..	..	..	..	33	297.5	165.7
142 Sudan	..	..	..	..	..	987	374.4	351.3
143 Togo	..	..	..	..	..	24	12.7	6.4
144 Nepal	..	..	..	..	..	252	129.2	..
145 Bhutan	..	..	..	..	..	..	..	108.7
146 Nigeria	..	..	..	..	..	125	9.0	1.0
147 Madagascar	..	..	..	..	..	255	..	..
148 Yemen	..	..	..	..	..	121	38.5	1.2
149 Mauritania	..	..	..	..	..	253	..	68.8
150 Bangladesh	..	..	..	..	..	10,928	21.6	41.2

HDI rank	Injuries and deaths from road accidents (per 100,000 people) 1997	Suicides (per 100,000 people) Male 1990-95 [a]	Suicides (per 100,000 people) Female 1990-95 [a]	Divorces (as % of marriages) 1996	Births to mothers under 20 (%) 1991-97 [a]	People killed or affected by disasters (annual average; thousands) 1969-93	Refugees By country of asylum (thousands) 1997	Refugees By country of origin (thousands) 1997
151 Zambia	..	..	..	..	..	103	165.1	..
152 Haiti	..	..	..	..	..	160	..	2.7
153 Senegal	..	..	..	..	..	291	57.2	17.1
154 Côte d'Ivoire	..	..	..	..	..	0	208.5	..
155 Benin	..	..	..	..	..	136	2.9	..
156 Tanzania, U. Rep. of	..	..	..	..	..	141	570.4	..
157 Djibouti	..	..	..	..	..	28	23.6	8.0
158 Uganda	..	..	..	..	..	57	188.5	50.5
159 Malawi	..	..	..	..	..	460	0.3	..
160 Angola	..	..	..	..	..	..	9.4	262.7
161 Guinea	..	..	..	..	..	1	435.3	0.4
162 Chad	..	..	..	..	..	283	0.3	54.7
163 Gambia	..	..	..	..	..	29	7.3	..
164 Rwanda	..	..	..	..	..	164	34.2	63.6
165 Central African Republic	..	..	..	..	..	1	38.6	..
166 Mali	..	..	..	..	..	209	12.6	10.4
167 Eritrea	..	..	..	..	..	0	2.6	315.6
168 Guinea-Bissau	..	..	..	..	..	0	15.9	0.9
169 Mozambique	..	..	..	..	..	1,180	0.1	33.6
170 Burundi	..	..	..	..	..	0	22.0	515.8
171 Burkina Faso	..	..	..	..	..	279	1.8	..
172 Ethiopia	..	..	..	..	..	2,402	323.1	63.4
173 Niger	..	..	..	..	..	313	7.4	2.5
174 Sierra Leone	..	..	..	..	..	1	13.0	328.2
All developing countries	..	..	..	..	..	..	7,669.6 T	..
Least developed countries	..	..	..	..	..	..	2,749.1 T	2,704.5 T
Sub-Saharan Africa	..	..	..	..	..	..	2,770.0 T	2,005.4 T
Arab States	..	..	..	..	..	..	763.3 T	..
East Asia	..	..	..	..	..	..	292.7 T	119.8 T
East Asia (excluding China)	..	..	..	..	..	..	..	..
South-East Asia and the Pacific	..	..	..	..	..	..	..	..
South Asia	..	..	..	..	..	..	3,559.2 T	..
South Asia (excluding India)	..	..	..	..	..	..	3,336.1 T	300.6 T
Latin America and the Caribbean	..	..	..	..	..	..	83.2 T	..
Eastern Europe and the CIS	138	51.9	10.5	48	..	..	835.0 T	1,069.4 T
Industrialized countries	789	19.5	5.7	41	..	..	2,753.3 T	..
World	..	..	..	..	..	..	11,975.5 T [b]	..

a. Data refer to the most recent year available during the period specified in the column heading.

b. Data refer to estimate by UNHCR 1998.

Source: Column 1: calculated on the basis of data from UNECE 1999b; *columns 2 and 3:* WHO 1998b; *column 4:* UNECE 1999a; *column 5:* UN 1999a; *column 6:* International Federation of Red Cross and Red Crescent Societies 1995; *columns 7 and 8:* UNHCR 1998.

	Female adult literacy			Female primary net enrolment			Female secondary net enrolment			Female tertiary students			Female tertiary science enrolment (as % of female tertiary students) [a]
	Rate (%)	Index (1985 = 100)	As % of male rate	Ratio (as % of relevant age group)	Index (1985 = 100)	As % of male ratio	Ratio (as % of relevant age group)	Index (1985 = 100)	As % of male ratio	Per 100,000 women	Index (1985 = 100)	As % of males	
HDI rank	1997	1997	1997	1997	1997	1997	1997	1997	1997	1996	1996	1996	1995
High human development	..	..	..	99.3	101	100	94.5	106	101	4,227	134	105	24
1 Canada	..	..	..	99.9	100	100	94.4	103	98	6,329	93	112	..
2 Norway	..	..	..	99.9	103	100	98.0	112	101	4,564	195	121	27
3 United States	..	..	..	99.9	106	100	96.2	100	100	5,844	112	121	..
4 Japan	..	..	..	99.9	100	100	99.9	104	100	..	..	..	13
5 Belgium	..	..	..	99.9	100	100	99.9	100	100	..	..	..	24
6 Sweden	..	..	..	99.9	100	100	99.9	117	100	..	..	..	27
7 Australia	..	..	..	99.9	100	100	96.0	108	100	5,608	250	102	25
8 Netherlands	..	..	..	99.9	100	100	99.9	100	100	2,986	132	89	17
9 Iceland	..	..	..	99.9	100	100	88.1	115	101	..	..	..	..
10 United Kingdom	..	..	..	99.9	100	100	93.2	103	103	3,102	192	98	24
11 France	..	..	..	99.9	100	100	98.6	99	100	3,850	169	115	30
12 Switzerland	..	..	..	99.9	100	100	80.3	106	92	1,541	146	59	15
13 Finland	..	..	..	99.9	100	100	96.2	103	102	4,303	174	106	23
14 Germany	..	..	..	99.9	100	100	94.9	112	99	2,287	..	77	21
15 Denmark	..	..	..	99.9	100	100	95.4	112	101	3,468	157	119	28
16 Austria	..	..	..	99.9	100	100	97.1	108	99	2,816	142	90	26
17 Luxembourg	..	..	..	..	..	..	..	..	..	..	..	..	..
18 New Zealand	..	..	..	99.9	100	100	94.0	107	102	4,990	187	124	31
19 Italy	97.8	102	99	99.9	100	100	96.0	136	102	3,197	171	106	33
20 Ireland	..	..	..	99.9	100	100	99.9	103	100	3,656	213	102	33
21 Spain	96.2	103	98	99.9	100	100	93.0	104	102	4,164	178	108	..
22 Singapore	87.0	111	91	90.5	93	98	74.8	112	98	2,250	201	81	..
23 Israel	93.4	104	96	..	..	..	..	..	..	..	..	..	32
24 Hong Kong, China (SAR)	88.4	110	92	93.2	95	104	71.5	97	107	..	..	..	19
25 Brunei Darussalam	86.0	118	92	88.5	113	101	83.9	100	105	640	..	156	36
26 Cyprus	93.5	108	95	..	..	..	..	..	..	1,130	205	69	28
27 Greece	94.9	107	97	99.9	100	100	93.1	114	104	2,998	170	91	27
28 Portugal	88.3	110	94	99.9	100	100	91.0	151	103	..	..	..	38
29 Barbados	97.0	102	99	94.5	95	95	83.1	105	94	2,965	..	138	44
30 Korea, Rep. of	95.5	105	97	99.9	100	100	99.9	116	100	4,182	196	60	16
31 Bahamas	96.4	102	101	99.9	101	113	95.9	103	130	..	..	..	..
32 Malta	91.7	106	101	99.9	103	100	83.3	101	96	..	..	..	21
33 Slovenia	99.0 [b]	100	100	..	..	..	..	..	..	2,985	185	119	29
34 Chile	94.9	103	100	89.2	98	97	87.2	115	105	2,291	163	82	29
35 Kuwait	77.5	113	93	64.0	75	96	63.2	74	100	2,590	151	134	43
36 Czech Republic	..	..	..	99.9	100	100	99.9	108	100	..	..	..	25
37 Bahrain	80.7	121	90	98.8	99	101	90.8	93	108	..	..	..	42
38 Antigua and Barbuda	..	..	..	..	..	..	..	..	..	..	..	..	..
39 Argentina	96.5	102	100	99.9	103	100	79.8	107	108	..	..	..	36
40 Uruguay	97.8	102	101	94.8	107	101	88.7	110	112	..	..	..	..
41 Qatar	81.2	114	102	84.5	88	103	72.0	90	97	3,278	116	531	44
42 Slovakia	..	..	..	..	..	..	..	..	..	1,864	..	96	..
43 United Arab Emirates	76.8	115	104	81.3	103	98	79.9	153	105	1,721	200	608	..
44 Poland	99.0 [b]	101	100	99.3	100	100	88.5	113	105	2,058	155	121	31
45 Costa Rica	95.1	103	100	92.5	110	102	56.9	109	104	..	..	..	..
Medium human development	..	..	..	88.5	109	95	59.9	129	86	662	..	71	..
46 Trinidad and Tobago	97.0	103	98	99.9	103	100	72.2	97	102	685	159	81	34
47 Hungary	99.0 [b]	101	100	96.7	99	99	98.2	134	103	1,965	202	104	28
48 Venezuela	91.6	106	99	83.6	96	103	54.2	181	124	..	..	..	..
49 Panama	90.4	105	99	90.2	100	101	71.7	111	101	..	..	..	36
50 Mexico	87.9	107	95	99.9	100	100	64.0	104	94	..	..	..	26

HDI rank	Female adult literacy			Female primary net enrolment			Female secondary net enrolment			Female tertiary students			Female tertiary science enrolment (as % of female tertiary students)[a]
	Rate (%) 1997	Index (1985 = 100) 1997	As % of male rate 1997	Ratio (as % of relevant age group) 1997	Index (1985 = 100) 1997	As % of male ratio 1997	Ratio (as % of relevant age group) 1997	Index (1985 = 100) 1997	As % of male ratio 1997	Per 100,000 women 1996	Index (1985 = 100) 1996	As % of males 1996	1995
51 Saint Kitts and Nevis	..	..	..	..	..	..	..	..	..	..	..	..	..
52 Grenada	..	..	..	..	..	..	..	..	..	..	..	..	..
53 Dominica	..	..	..	..	..	..	..	..	..	..	..	..	28
54 Estonia	..	..	..	99.9	100	100	87.4	87	103	2,982	168	102	25
55 Croatia	96.4	105	97	99.9	100	100	73.0	88	102	1,875	..	97	27
56 Malaysia	81.0	118	90	99.9	100	100	68.5	129	115	..	..	..	..
57 Colombia	90.8	105	100	89.4	132	100	78.2	126	105	1,820	142	106	32
58 Cuba	95.9	102	100	99.9	107	100	72.6	96	108	1,223	48	152	35
59 Mauritius	79.2	111	91	96.6	97	100	69.9	141	106	578	696	95	..
60 Belarus	98.5	105	99	..	..	..	..	..	..	3,323	..	110	..
61 Fiji	89.4	108	95	99.9	103	100	84.4	130	100	..	..	..	..
62 Lithuania	99.0 b	103	100	..	..	..	..	..	..	2,524	77	131	..
63 Bulgaria	97.6	103	99	99.2	102	103	75.4	78	95	3,721	270	151	45
64 Suriname	91.6	..	..	99.9	106	100	..	..	..	..	..	..	..
65 Libyan Arab Jamahiriya	62.9	154	71	99.9	106	100	99.9	122	100	..	..	..	..
66 Seychelles	..	..	..	..	..	..	..	..	..	..	..	..	33
67 Thailand	92.8	107	96	89.2	101	103	46.9	191	97	..	..	..	23
68 Romania	96.7	104	98	99.9	115	100	76.3	80	101	1,892	304	109	38
69 Lebanon	78.3	115	86	74.9	99	97	..	..	..	2,605	..	92	37
70 Samoa (Western)	..	..	..	96.8	98	101	..	..	..	..	..	..	26
71 Russian Federation	98.8	104	99	99.9	107	100	90.7	91	107	..	..	..	34
72 Ecuador	88.8	108	96	99.9	104	100	51.3	79	101	..	..	..	..
73 Macedonia, TFYR	..	..	..	..	..	..	..	..	..	1,552	..	121	38
74 Latvia	99.0 b	101	100	99.9	100	100	80.5	87	100	2,467	128	125	28
75 Saint Vincent and the Grenadines	..	..	..	..	..	..	..	..	..	..	..	..	..
76 Kazakhstan	..	..	..	..	..	..	..	..	..	3,032	..	118	..
77 Philippines	94.3	105	99	99.9	102	100	78.5	118	102	3,404	..	133	27
78 Saudi Arabia	62.5	152	77	58.0	137	93	52.9	127	82	1,528	190	109	..
79 Brazil	83.9	109	100	94.3	121	94	67.0	136	103	..	..	..	34
80 Peru	83.7	111	89	93.3	98	99	81.1	106	94	..	..	..	..
81 Saint Lucia	..	..	..	..	..	..	..	..	..	..	..	..	..
82 Jamaica	89.6	106	110	95.7	97	100	72.1	111	107	658	160	75	..
83 Belize	..	..	..	99.9	112	100	62.6	105	97	..	..	..	..
84 Paraguay	91.1	106	97	97.0	107	101	60.1	164	97	1,098	..	110	42
85 Georgia	..	..	..	88.6	99	99	75.3	75	99	2,970	..	98	40
86 Turkey	73.9	115	80	98.1	101	98	48.5	134	72	..	..	..	28
87 Armenia	..	..	..	..	..	..	..	..	..	1,066	..	121	..
88 Dominican Republic	82.3	108	99	93.6	94	105	82.1	141	109	..	..	..	..
89 Oman	55.0	206	72	66.7	105	97	65.1	319	96	524	970	97	..
90 Sri Lanka	87.6	107	93	99.9	100	100	79.3	112	109	388	129	69	..
91 Ukraine	..	..	..	..	..	..	..	..	..	..	..	..	..
92 Uzbekistan	..	..	..	..	..	..	..	..	..	..	..	..	..
93 Maldives	95.6	104	100	..	..	..	..	..	..	..	..	..	..
94 Jordan	81.8	130	89	..	..	..	..	..	..	2,492	132	96	35
95 Iran, Islamic Rep. of	65.8	169	81	89.2	120	98	75.8	168	88	1,192	544	60	20
96 Turkmenistan	..	..	..	..	..	..	..	..	..	..	..	..	..
97 Kyrgyzstan	..	..	..	99.3	99	100	78.7	79	102	..	..	..	38
98 China	74.5	122	82	99.9	114	100	65.1	145	88	327	164	54	..
99 Guyana	97.5	103	99	93.0	93	100	76.4	104	104	886	319	87	24
100 Albania	..	..	..	..	..	..	..	..	..	1,167	108	136	40

... AND ACHIEVING EQUALITY FOR ALL WOMEN AND MEN

HDI rank	Female adult literacy			Female primary net enrolment			Female secondary net enrolment			Female tertiary students			Female tertiary science enrolment (as % of female tertiary students)[a]
	Rate (%) 1997	Index (1985 = 100) 1997	As % of male rate 1997	Ratio (as % of relevant age group) 1997	Index (1985 = 100) 1997	As % of male ratio 1997	Ratio (as % of relevant age group) 1997	Index (1985 = 100) 1997	As % of male ratio 1997	Per 100,000 women 1996	Index (1985 = 100) 1996	As % of males 1996	1995
101 South Africa	83.2	107	98	99.9	123	100	96.9	140	104	..	..	..	38
102 Tunisia	55.8	143	72	99.9	114	100	72.4	167	95	1,201	293	82	28
103 Azerbaijan	..	..	..	..	..	..	..	..	..	1,472	59	94	
104 Moldova, Rep. of	97.4	106	98	..	..	..	..	..	..	2,216	..	111	..
105 Indonesia	79.5	119	88	98.6	103	99	53.4	115	91	812	..	53	23
106 Cape Verde	62.5	132	76	99.9	107	100	35.5	125	94	..	..	..	..
107 El Salvador	74.2	114	93	89.1	128	100	36.7	114	102	1,907	146	97	28
108 Tajikistan	98.3	104	99	..	..	..	..	..	..	1,191	68	47	13
109 Algeria	47.7	146	66	92.6	117	93	64.0	151	88	1,000	197	68	35
110 Viet Nam	89.0	110	94	99.9	114	100	54.2	119	97	..	..	..	..
111 Syrian Arab Republic	56.5	139	65	90.6	98	92	39.4	79	87	..	..	..	30
112 Bolivia	76.8	119	85	94.9	115	95	37.1	89	86	..	..	..	..
113 Swaziland	76.3	119	97	95.3	118	102	78.8	128	93	542	..	72	16
114 Honduras	70.2	112	99	88.6	95	103	37.9	77	111	..	..	..	26
115 Namibia	78.5	117	97	94.0	98	106	83.9	113	108	894	..	154	31
116 Vanuatu	..	..	..	69.2	96	95	38.8	111	84	..	..	..	..
117 Guatemala	58.9	119	79	70.2	115	91	31.7	122	83	..	..	..	..
118 Solomon Islands	..	..	..	..	..	..	..	..	..	..	..	..	31
119 Mongolia	78.6	115	88	87.5	88	106	63.7	69	132	2,432	92	226	53
120 Egypt	40.5	139	63	90.6	122	91	70.1	158	88	1,472	142	64	27
121 Nicaragua	63.4	106	100	80.2	106	104	52.6	102	108	1,261	124	105	..
122 Botswana	76.9	118	107	82.6	87	106	91.3	195	106	555	354	87	26
123 São Tomé and Principe	..	..	..	..	..	..	..	..	..	..	..	..	..
124 Gabon	56.8	157	75	..	..	..	..	..	..	..	..	..	..
125 Iraq	..	..	..	69.6	80	88	33.8	74	66	..	..	..	..
126 Morocco	32.7	164	55	67.2	137	78	31.9	103	74	..	..	..	28
127 Lesotho	92.5	107	129	74.3	90	118	80.3	93	122	238	203	116	21
128 Myanmar	78.8	112	89	98.5	131	99	53.0	149	96	..	..	..	61
129 Papua New Guinea	64.7	125	79	72.5	121	85	..	..	..	209	294	50	..
130 Zimbabwe	87.6	112	93	92.2	92	98	56.3	111	91	373	..	41	14
131 Equatorial Guinea	70.1	133	77	79.9	80	102	64.8	92	90	..	..	..	..
132 India	39.4	134	59	71.0	111	86	48.0	133	68	481	134	61	..
133 Ghana	56.5	..	..	41.8	107	93	..	..	..	..	..	..	..
134 Cameroon	64.6	147	82	59.1	86	92	34.7	90	77	..	..	..	..
135 Congo	69.8	145	83	75.8	77	94	74.3	74	79	..	..	..	..
136 Kenya	71.8	..	..	66.6	86	105	57.4	102	89	..	..	..	..
137 Cambodia	..	..	..	99.9	100	100	30.9	109	66	30	..	18	..
138 Pakistan	25.4	151	46	..	..	..	..	..	..	..	..	..	..
139 Comoros	48.2	107	77	45.4	85	83	32.2	100	82	..	..	..	..
Low human development	..	..	..	50.4	117	80	21.1	116	60	..	..	..	..
140 Lao People's Dem. Rep.	46.8	142	66	69.2	104	90	52.9	113	72	151	141	42	11
141 Congo, Dem. Rep. of the	..	..	..	47.8	91	70	28.6	99	63	..	..	..	..
142 Sudan	41.3	171	63	..	..	..	..	..	..	..	..	..	..
143 Togo	38.3	166	56	70.2	144	74	40.0	167	52	107	228	20	5
144 Nepal	20.7	204	37	62.5	167	67	39.7	187	58	..	..	..	..
145 Bhutan	30.3	161	52	12.3	119	88	..	..	..	..	..	..	..
146 Nigeria	50.8	170	74	..	..	..	..	..	..	..	..	..	..
147 Madagascar	..	..	..	59.4	82	102	..	..	..	156	57	81	31
148 Yemen	21.0	243	32	..	..	..	..	..	..	105	..	14	..
149 Mauritania	27.8	133	56	59.8	212	91	..	..	..	129	..	21	15
150 Bangladesh	27.4	138	55	69.6	149	87	15.6	125	58	..	..	..	..

HDI rank	Female adult literacy			Female primary net enrolment			Female secondary net enrolment			Female tertiary students			Female tertiary science enrolment (as % of female tertiary students)[a]
	Rate (%) 1997	Index (1985 = 100) 1997	As % of male rate 1997	Ratio (as % of relevant age group) 1997	Index (1985 = 100) 1997	As % of male ratio 1997	Ratio (as % of relevant age group) 1997	Index (1985 = 100) 1997	As % of male ratio 1997	Per 100,000 women 1996	Index (1985 = 100) 1996	As % of males 1996	1995
151 Zambia	67.5	127	81	71.7	84	98	34.9	104	71	..	..	..	..
152 Haiti	43.4	135	90	19.9	39	105	33.2	75	95	..	..	..	..
153 Senegal	24.8	165	56	53.6	136	82	15.5	120	65	..	..	..	..
154 Côte d'Ivoire	33.7	191	66	50.3	114	76	23.6	84	53	..	..	..	10
155 Benin	20.9	165	44	50.4	140	59	18.3	104	48	94	134	23	11
156 Tanzania, U. Rep. of	62.0	146	76	48.0	85	102	..	..	..	14	233	19	9
157 Djibouti	35.0	155	56	27.4	104	75	15.6	103	66	23	..	77	..
158 Uganda	53.0	143	71	..	..	..	..	..	..	99	309	47	17
159 Malawi	43.4	137	60	99.7	244	102	53.9	211	59	34	179	41	15
160 Angola	..	..	..	34.1	70	97	28.0	73	82	..	..	..	..
161 Guinea	23.9	173	46	33.2	189	58	6.9	73	31	24	47	13	..
162 Chad	37.1	155	58	35.2	185	58	9.6	135	37	14	233	15	3
163 Gambia	26.4	173	66	58.2	119	79	25.1	244	60	..	..	..	..
164 Rwanda	55.6	154	79	78.6	134	101	..	..	..	..	..	..	..
165 Central African Republic	30.1	191	53	37.8	80	69	12.7	68	50	..	..	..	..
166 Mali	28.3	222	65	31.2	217	69	12.9	222	56	..	..	..	..
167 Eritrea	..	..	..	27.9	..	91	34.3	..	83	22	..	13	..
168 Guinea-Bissau	18.3	198	37	38.8	111	59	16.4	162	51	..	..	..	..
169 Mozambique	25.0	172	44	34.3	73	76	17.1	74	62	19	380	31	21
170 Burundi	36.1	169	67	32.9	93	86	14.1	155	70	..	..	..	..
171 Burkina Faso	11.2	195	36	25.2	148	64	9.4	196	58	37	154	29	8
172 Ethiopia	29.2	187	70	27.0	110	62	17.5	109	55	24	100	24	11
173 Niger	7.2	188	33	18.5	108	61	6.5	163	53	..	..	..	..
174 Sierra Leone	20.0	179	42	38.8	88	79	..	..	..	..	..	..	31
All developing countries	62.9	122	79	82.9	108	94	54.8	128	83	..	..	..	..
Least developed countries	38.1	141	65	54.8	116	83	24.6	119	66	..	..	..	..
Sub-Saharan Africa	49.6	144	75	51.8	101	85	35.8	111	76	..	..	..	..
Arab States	46.4	150	66	82.1	113	91	56.8	130	85	1,287	..	73	30
East Asia	75.4	121	83	99.8	113	100	66.4	143	88	472	171	57	..
East Asia (excluding China)	94.0	105	96	98.3	99	101	94.5	111	102	4,084	189	61	18
South-East Asia and the Pacific	84.4	113	91	97.5	106	99	56.9	126	95	..	..	..	28
South Asia	38.6	137	59	72.1	116	86	46.0	135	70	526	149	61	..
South Asia (excluding India)	36.2	144	60	76.1	134	89	39.2	147	78	..	..	..	..
Latin America and the Caribbean	86.2	108	98	92.4	108	98	65.8	116	101	..	..	..	32
Eastern Europe and the CIS	..	..	..	..	..	..	..	..	..	2,234	..	112	33
Industrialized countries	..	..	..	99.9	102	100	96.3	106	100	4,486	130	110	23
World	..	..	..	85.2	107	95	60.8	119	87	..	..	..	..

a. Data refer to enrolment in natural and applied sciences.
b. Capped at 99.0%.
Source: Columns 1-3: calculated on the basis of data from UNESCO 1999a; columns 4 and 7: UNESCO 1999d; columns 5, 6, 8 and 9: calculated on the basis of data from UNESCO 1999d; column 10: UNESCO 1998a; columns 11 and 12: calculated on the basis of data from UNESCO 1998a; column 13: UNESCO 1998c.

. . . AND ACHIEVING EQUALITY FOR ALL WOMEN AND MEN

	Female economic activity rate (age 15+)			Unemployment rate (%)				Female unpaid family workers (as % of total)
				Total [a] (age 15-64)		Youth (age 15-24)		
	Rate (%)	Index (1985 = 100)	As % of male rate	Female	Male	Female	Male	
HDI rank	1997	1997	1997	1997	1997	1997	1997	1990-97 [b]
High human development	**41.2**	**119.0**	**71.5**	**8.3**	**7.1**	**16**	**15**	**..**
1 Canada	47.9	122.7	81.4	9.2	9.4	16	18	74
2 Norway	47.1	123.5	83.8	4.3 [c]	4.0 [c]	11 [d]	10 [d]	63
3 United States	45.7	117.1	81.1	5.1 [c]	4.9 [c]	11 [d]	12 [d]	62
4 Japan	43.3	118.4	67.3	3.6	3.5	6	7	83
5 Belgium	32.9	123.8	65.3	11.6	7.1	26	18	86
6 Sweden	51.2	116.6	90.0	7.5	8.5	14 [d]	16 [d]	60
7 Australia	43.6	129.5	75.4	8.2	8.8	15	17	58
8 Netherlands	36.9	148.2	65.5	7.2	4.4	10	9	82
9 Iceland	50.9	117.4	83.2	4.4 [c]	3.3 [c]	7 [d]	8 [d]	..
10 United Kingdom	42.6	117.5	74.3	5.8 [c]	8.2 [c]	11 [d]	16 [d]	72
11 France	39.1	112.6	76.5	10.9	14.2	25	33	..
12 Switzerland	42.5	122.9	65.7	3.9	4.4	4	8	71
13 Finland	47.3	104.2	87.3	15.1	13.9	27	23	33
14 Germany	41.1	112.5	69.5	11.0	9.0	10	10	82
15 Denmark	51.2	111.2	84.7	6.5	4.6	10	7	95
16 Austria	37.0	107.4	65.3	5.3	5.1	7	8	66
17 Luxembourg	31.0	116.6	56.4	..	..	..	..	90
18 New Zealand	43.6	149.8	78.1	7.3	7.2	15	15	64
19 Italy	32.9	128.2	58.1	16.8	9.8	40	29	58
20 Ireland	27.7	132.6	50.8	10.4	10.6	15	17	40
21 Spain	31.1	150.1	55.5	28.4 [c]	16.2 [c]	46 [d]	33 [d]	62
22 Singapore	39.4	120.5	64.8	..	..	..	..	75
23 Israel	34.1	135.0	66.9	..	..	..	..	77
24 Hong Kong, China (SAR)	39.9	113.3	62.5	..	..	..	..	..
25 Brunei Darussalam	32.2	178.6	58.8	..	..	..	..	44
26 Cyprus	37.1	115.0	62.5	..	..	..	..	97
27 Greece	31.3	146.2	57.3	15.1	6.4	41	22	75
28 Portugal	42.4	119.8	71.9	7.9	6.2	18	11	58
29 Barbados	46.9	126.1	80.3	..	..	..	..	..
30 Korea, Rep. of	41.2	129.4	70.1	2.4	2.9	7	9	89
31 Bahamas	49.2	134.2	85.1	..	..	..	..	72
32 Malta	20.0	132.8	36.1	..	..	..	..	..
33 Slovenia	45.4	102.0	81.5	..	..	..	..	62
34 Chile	25.9	145.7	47.5	..	..	..	..	48
35 Kuwait	24.8	224.3	49.9	..	..	..	..	4
36 Czech Republic	51.3	107.9	86.2	5.8	3.8	10	7	76
37 Bahrain	20.7	200.1	33.1	..	..	..	..	..
38 Antigua and Barbuda	..	..	..	..	..	..	..	..
39 Argentina	24.9	120.0	45.3	..	..	..	..	55
40 Uruguay	36.2	151.1	66.2	..	..	..	..	68
41 Qatar	22.1	273.4	30.7	..	..	..	..	4
42 Slovakia	49.9	112.8	86.8	..	..	..	..	66
43 United Arab Emirates	18.9	216.0	28.1	..	..	..	..	..
44 Poland	45.5	99.0	81.4	13.5	9.8	28	22	56
45 Costa Rica	24.1	165.5	44.4	..	..	..	..	36
Medium human development	**40.2**	**110.9**	**69.0**	**..**	**..**	**..**	**..**	**..**
46 Trinidad and Tobago	30.6	123.9	56.3	..	..	..	..	68
47 Hungary	40.5	101.0	73.6	7.7	9.5	15	17	72
48 Venezuela	27.2	147.0	51.9	..	..	..	..	42
49 Panama	28.8	135.8	53.9	..	..	..	..	19
50 Mexico	25.7	146.6	47.0	4.9	3.0	8	6	45

HDI rank	Female economic activity rate (age 15+)			Unemployment rate (%)				Female unpaid family workers (as % of total)
				Total [a] (age 15-64)		Youth (age 15-24)		
	Rate (%) 1997	Index (1985 = 100) 1997	As % of male rate 1997	Female 1997	Male 1997	Female 1997	Male 1997	1990-97 [b]
51 Saint Kitts and Nevis	..	..	..	..	..	..	..	..
52 Grenada	..	..	..	..	..	..	..	..
53 Dominica	..	..	..	..	..	..	..	50
54 Estonia	50.9	97.6	85.3	..	..	..	..	..
55 Croatia	39.9	108.6	73.1	..	..	..	..	74
56 Malaysia	30.5	116.9	60.6	..	..	..	..	71
57 Colombia	32.1	185.2	60.2	..	..	..	..	70
58 Cuba	37.8	155.3	63.4	..	..	..	..	..
59 Mauritius	27.2	151.1	46.9	..	..	..	..	48
60 Belarus	47.8	97.2	84.4	..	..	..	..	..
61 Fiji	22.7	202.5	41.7	..	..	..	..	21
62 Lithuania	46.9	94.9	82.6	..	..	..	..	..
63 Bulgaria	47.8	102.1	88.6	..	..	..	..	..
64 Suriname	23.8	153.8	47.9	..	..	..	..	42
65 Libyan Arab Jamahiriya	13.0	106.2	30.2	..	..	..	..	..
66 Seychelles	..	..	..	..	..	..	..	..
67 Thailand	55.5	112.0	86.3	..	..	..	..	69
68 Romania	41.5	93.5	77.6	..	..	..	..	67
69 Lebanon	19.2	152.6	38.7	..	..	..	..	..
70 Samoa (Western)	..	..	..	..	..	..	..	31
71 Russian Federation	48.1	96.1	83.6	..	..	..	..	..
72 Ecuador	20.7	160.3	37.6	..	..	..	..	63
73 Macedonia, TFYR	38.3	122.4	71.0	..	..	..	..	59
74 Latvia	50.3	95.4	85.0	..	..	..	..	..
75 Saint Vincent and the Grenadines	..	..	..	..	..	..	..	42
76 Kazakhstan	43.7	100.9	82.7	..	..	..	..	91
77 Philippines	31.4	114.3	60.8	..	..	..	..	56
78 Saudi Arabia	10.6	216.6	21.1	..	..	..	..	..
79 Brazil	32.1	144.7	53.4	..	..	..	..	52
80 Peru	22.1	146.8	43.0	..	..	..	..	59
81 Saint Lucia	..	..	..	..	..	..	..	..
82 Jamaica	48.0	117.1	86.4	..	..	..	..	..
83 Belize	15.7	123.8	30.9	..	..	..	..	13
84 Paraguay	22.0	111.6	42.4	..	..	..	..	58
85 Georgia	43.6	93.2	79.8	..	..	..	..	..
86 Turkey	34.9	114.9	59.6	6.2	7.7	15	14	68
87 Armenia	46.0	105.2	88.3	..	..	..	..	..
88 Dominican Republic	26.1	140.8	44.1	..	..	..	..	..
89 Oman	8.7	214.0	20.4	..	..	..	..	..
90 Sri Lanka	30.5	151.3	55.4	..	..	..	..	53
91 Ukraine	45.6	93.3	81.9	..	..	..	..	66
92 Uzbekistan	38.2	100.1	85.7	..	..	..	..	..
93 Maldives	35.5	94.2	78.2	..	..	..	..	29
94 Jordan	13.6	188.3	31.0	..	..	..	..	..
95 Iran, Islamic Rep. of	15.8	127.1	35.6	..	..	..	..	44
96 Turkmenistan	38.4	100.3	82.1	..	..	..	..	..
97 Kyrgyzstan	39.1	99.1	85.1	..	..	..	..	..
98 China	55.7	113.8	87.3	..	..	..	..	..
99 Guyana	28.1	171.1	48.9	..	..	..	..	..
100 Albania	41.5	114.9	73.0	..	..	..	..	..

. . . AND ACHIEVING EQUALITY FOR ALL WOMEN AND MEN

HDI rank	Female economic activity rate (age 15+)			Unemployment rate (%)				Female unpaid family workers (as % of total)
	Rate (%) 1997	Index (1985 = 100) 1997	As % of male rate 1997	Total [a] (age 15-64)		Youth (age 15-24)		1990-97 [b]
				Female 1997	Male 1997	Female 1997	Male 1997	
101 South Africa	29.4	111.9	59.4	..	..	..	..	..
102 Tunisia	24.1	119.8	46.1	..	..	..	..	49
103 Azerbaijan	37.9	92.9	76.2	..	..	..	..	..
104 Moldova, Rep. of	45.9	92.2	86.4	..	..	..	..	..
105 Indonesia	37.9	136.9	66.9	..	..	..	..	71
106 Cape Verde	29.5	143.0	56.8	..	..	..	..	54
107 El Salvador	28.9	162.8	52.3	..	..	..	..	30
108 Tajikistan	33.7	93.0	78.7	..	..	..	..	..
109 Algeria	16.9	153.0	36.0	..	..	..	..	6
110 Viet Nam	49.4	111.2	93.9	..	..	..	..	..
111 Syrian Arab Republic	16.3	119.6	36.5	..	..	..	..	48
112 Bolivia	30.1	121.8	59.3	..	..	..	..	62
113 Swaziland	26.1	110.3	55.5	..	..	..	..	60
114 Honduras	22.7	133.3	45.1	..	..	..	..	31
115 Namibia	33.5	97.6	68.1	..	..	..	..	69
116 Vanuatu	..	..	..	..	..	..	..	..
117 Guatemala	20.1	129.4	38.7	..	..	..	..	13
118 Solomon Islands	49.4	98.5	92.8	..	..	..	..	..
119 Mongolia	46.1	108.4	88.5	..	..	..	..	..
120 Egypt	22.2	117.9	43.2	..	..	..	..	42
121 Nicaragua	27.3	145.6	53.2	..	..	..	..	..
122 Botswana	39.6	94.9	81.0	..	..	..	..	35
123 São Tomé and Principe	..	..	..	..	..	..	..	..
124 Gabon	40.9	88.3	78.3	..	..	..	..	..
125 Iraq	10.4	109.2	24.0	..	..	..	..	50
126 Morocco	27.1	112.5	53.1	..	..	..	..	..
127 Lesotho	29.7	96.3	56.8	..	..	..	..	39
128 Myanmar	45.7	103.0	76.3	..	..	..	..	..
129 Papua New Guinea	42.5	98.5	76.9	..	..	..	..	..
130 Zimbabwe	40.7	102.9	78.8	..	..	..	..	..
131 Equatorial Guinea	29.2	94.4	53.6	..	..	..	..	..
132 India	29.0	95.0	50.3	..	..	..	..	..
133 Ghana	47.3	98.8	100.9	..	..	..	..	..
134 Cameroon	30.4	100.2	59.9	..	..	..	..	..
135 Congo	35.1	100.5	73.3	..	..	..	..	..
136 Kenya	46.8	108.0	85.9	..	..	..	..	..
137 Cambodia	52.3	93.9	101.3	..	..	..	..	..
138 Pakistan	20.8	123.3	40.3	..	..	..	..	33
139 Comoros	39.1	98.8	75.9	..	..	..	..	..
Low human development	38.2	99.0	72.4	..	..	..	..	..
140 Lao People's Dem. Rep.	44.7	94.9	86.9	..	..	..	..	..
141 Congo, Dem. Rep. of the	36.0	92.9	75.3	..	..	..	..	..
142 Sudan	22.8	115.6	41.0	..	..	..	..	..
143 Togo	32.8	96.9	65.4	..	..	..	..	..
144 Nepal	37.9	98.3	69.6	..	..	..	..	61
145 Bhutan	38.8	94.7	66.7	..	..	..	..	..
146 Nigeria	28.4	95.7	55.8	..	..	..	..	46
147 Madagascar	41.8	96.1	80.5	..	..	..	..	..
148 Yemen	17.8	97.9	39.0	..	..	..	..	..
149 Mauritania	40.0	93.5	76.6	..	..	..	..	38
150 Bangladesh	44.4	107.8	77.2	..	..	..	..	71

. . . AND ACHIEVING EQUALITY FOR ALL WOMEN AND MEN

HDI rank	Female economic activity rate (age 15+)			Unemployment rate (%)				Female unpaid family workers (as % of total)
				Total [a] (age 15-64)		Youth (age 15-24)		
	Rate (%) 1997	Index (1985 = 100) 1997	As % of male rate 1997	Female 1997	Male 1997	Female 1997	Male 1997	1990-97 [b]
151 Zambia	37.3	100.4	80.0	..	..	..	..	54
152 Haiti	37.3	90.1	72.8	..	..	..	..	37
153 Senegal	38.1	98.3	74.3	..	..	..	..	..
154 Côte d'Ivoire	26.8	101.4	51.1	..	..	..	..	51
155 Benin	42.5	95.6	90.2	..	..	..	..	40
156 Tanzania, U. Rep. of	50.1	99.8	95.2	..	..	..	..	..
157 Djibouti	..	..	..	..	..	..	..	22
158 Uganda	47.0	95.7	89.9	..	..	..	..	72
159 Malawi	46.7	94.6	93.6	..	..	..	..	..
160 Angola	42.0	91.9	84.3	..	..	..	..	..
161 Guinea	45.3	93.5	90.5	..	..	..	..	..
162 Chad	42.4	99.5	78.3	..	..	..	..	..
163 Gambia	45.2	99.4	79.8	..	..	..	..	..
164 Rwanda	51.5	103.8	93.2	..	..	..	..	53
165 Central African Republic	43.9	90.1	82.5	..	..	..	..	55
166 Mali	44.6	95.0	83.6	..	..	..	..	53
167 Eritrea	47.0	97.9	88.8	..	..	..	..	..
168 Guinea-Bissau	37.4	95.2	65.7	..	..	..	..	..
169 Mozambique	49.7	93.2	91.6	..	..	..	..	..
170 Burundi	51.3	96.5	91.5	..	..	..	..	60
171 Burkina Faso	46.4	90.0	86.8	..	..	..	..	66
172 Ethiopia	35.6	94.7	69.7	..	..	..	..	..
173 Niger	41.4	94.5	77.6	..	..	..	..	24
174 Sierra Leone	26.6	98.9	55.2	..	..	..	..	74
All developing countries	39.3	111.3	68.0	..	..	..	..	..
Least developed countries	41.1	99.7	76.5	..	..	..	..	..
Sub-Saharan Africa	37.8	97.7	73.9	..	..	..	..	..
Arab States	19.2	123.7	38.6	..	..	..	..	..
East Asia	55.1	114.2	86.6	..	..	..	..	..
East Asia (excluding China)	41.2	126.1	69.7	..	..	..	..	..
South-East Asia and the Pacific	41.7	118.6	74.1	..	..	..	..	..
South Asia	29.1	99.4	51.7	..	..	..	..	..
South Asia (excluding India)	29.5	114.2	55.9	..	..	..	..	..
Latin America and the Caribbean	28.8	140.0	51.3	..	..	..	..	..
Eastern Europe and the CIS	45.6	97.3	82.4	..	..	..	..	..
Industrialized countries	41.9	119.4	72.6	8.5	7.3	16	16	..
World	40.2	111.3	69.8	..	..	..	..	..

a. Data refer to the number of unemployed divided by the labour force.
b. Data refer to the most recent year available during the period specified in the column heading.
c. Data refer to the age group 16-64.
d. Data refer to the age group 16-24.
Source: Columns 1-3: calculated on the basis of data from ILO 1996; columns 4-7: OECD 1998b; column 8: ILO 1998.

. . . AND ACHIEVING EQUALITY FOR ALL WOMEN AND MEN

| | | Burden of work | | | Time allocation (%) | | | | | |
| | | Work time (minutes per day) | | | Total work time | | Market activities | | Non-market activities | |
	Year	Females	Males	Females as % of males	Market activities	Non-market activities	Females	Males	Females	Males
Selected developing countries										
Urban										
Colombia	1983	399	356	112	49	51	24	77	76	23
Indonesia	1992	398	366	109	60	40	35	86	65	14
Kenya	1986	590	572	103	46	54	41	79	59	21
Nepal	1978	579	554	105	58	42	25	67	75	33
Venezuela	1983	440	416	106	59	41	30	87	70	13
Average		481	453	106	54	46	31	79	69	21
Rural										
Bangladesh	1990	545	496	110	52	48	35	70	65	30
Guatemala	1977	678	579	117	59	41	37	84	63	16
Kenya	1988	676	500	135	56	44	42	76	58	24
Nepal	1978	641	547	117	56	44	46	67	54	33
Highlands	1978	692	586	118	59	41	52	66	48	34
Mountains	1978	649	534	122	56	44	48	65	52	35
Rural hills	1978	583	520	112	52	48	37	70	63	30
Philippines	1975-77	546	452	121	73	27	29	84	71	16
Average		617	515	120	59	41	38	76	62	24
National										
Korea, Rep. of	1990	488	480	102	45	55	34	56	66	44
Average for selected developing countries		544	483	113	54	46	34	76	66	24
Selected industrialized countries										
Australia	1992	443	443	100	44	56	28	61	72	39
Austria	1992	438	393	111	49	51	31	71	69	29
Canada	1992	429	430	100	52	48	39	65	61	35
Denmark	1987	449	458	98	68	32	58	79	42	21
Finland	1987/88	430	410	105	51	49	39	64	61	36
France	1985/86	429	388	111	45	55	30	62	70	38
Germany	1991/92	440	441	100	44	56	30	61	70	39
Israel	1991/92	375	377	99	51	49	29	74	71	26
Italy	1988/89	470	367	128	45	55	22	77	78	23
Netherlands	1987	377	345	109	35	65	19	52	81	48
Norway	1990/91	445	412	108	50	50	38	64	62	36
United Kingdom	1985	413	411	100	51	49	37	68	63	32
United States	1985	453	428	106	50	50	37	63	63	37
Average for selected industrialized countries		430	408	105	49	51	34	66	66	34

Note: Market activities refer to market-oriented production activities as defined by the 1993 revised UN System of National Accounts.
Source: UNDP 1995.

HDI rank	Year women received right		Year first woman elected (E) or nominated (N) to parliament	Women in government		
	To vote [a]	To stand for elections [a]		At all levels [b] (%) 1996	At ministerial level [b] (%) 1996	At sub-ministerial level [b] (%) 1996
High human development	..	..	..	..	..	..
1 Canada	1950	1960	1921 E	17.7	18.5	17.6
2 Norway	1913	1913	1911 N	24.1	28.6	22.7
3 United States	1920	1788	1917 E	33.1	14.3	34.5
4 Japan	1947	1947	1946 E	9.3	5.9	10.1
5 Belgium	1948	1948	1921 N	6.6	11.1	4.6
6 Sweden	1921	1921	1921 E	30.8	38.1	27.3
7 Australia	1962	1962	1943 E	22.6	14.7	25.9
8 Netherlands	1919	1917	1918 E	16.7	23.5	14.3
9 Iceland	1915	1915	1922 E	8.2	15.4	6.7
10 United Kingdom	1928	1928	1918 E	6.9	8.3	6.6
11 France	1944	1944	1945 E	10.8	14.7	9.7
12 Switzerland	1971	1971	1971 E	7.1	15.4	5.9
13 Finland	1906	1906	1907 E	20.4	36.4	15.5
14 Germany	1918	1918	1919 E	6.1	10.7	5.3
15 Denmark	1915	1915	1918 E	13.9	29.2	10.3
16 Austria	1918	1918	1919 E	6.8	23.5	4.0
17 Luxembourg	1919	1919	1919	17.8	28.6	12.9
18 New Zealand	1893	1919	1933 E	26.4	9.1	28.9
19 Italy	1945	1945	1946 E	7.1	3.6	8.2
20 Ireland	1928	1928	1918 E	11.7	21.4	8.4
21 Spain	1931	1931	1931 E	15.4	16.7	15.1
22 Singapore	1947	1947	1963 E	7.2	0.0	9.6
23 Israel	1948	1948	1949 E	10.6	13.0	9.7
24 Hong Kong, China (SAR)	..	..	..	..	..	..
25 Brunei Darussalam	– [c]	– [c]	– [c]	2.3	0.0	16.7
26 Cyprus	1960	1960	1963 E	5.3	7.7	4.0
27 Greece	1952	1952	1952 E	8.9	0.0	13.2
28 Portugal	1976	1976	1934 E	17.1	11.5	18.1
29 Barbados	1950	1950	1966 N	25.5	30.8	23.5
30 Korea, Rep. of	1948	1948	1948 E	1.0	3.0	0.6
31 Bahamas	1964	1964	1977 N	30.3	18.8	34.0
32 Malta	1947	1947	1966 E	3.0	0.0	3.9
33 Slovenia	1945	1945	1992 E	16.9	9.1	19.7
34 Chile	1949	1949	1951 E	10.3	14.3	8.5
35 Kuwait	– [c]	– [c]	– [c]	4.9	0.0	6.7
36 Czech Republic	1920	1920	1992 E	10.6	0.0	12.6
37 Bahrain	1973 †	1973 †	..	0.0	0.0	0.0
38 Antigua and Barbuda	1951	1951	1984 N	26.7	0.0	42.1
39 Argentina	1947	1947	1951 E	5.2	0.0	5.6
40 Uruguay	1932	1932	1942 E	13.7	6.7	16.7
41 Qatar	– [c]	– [c]	– [c]	0.0	0.0	0.0
42 Slovakia	1920	1920	1992 E	15.6	15.0	15.7
43 United Arab Emirates	1997 †	1997 †	– [d]	0.0	0.0	0.0
44 Poland	1918	1918	1919 E	9.8	8.3	10.1
45 Costa Rica	1949	1949	1953 E	27.2	11.1	35.2
Medium human development	..	..	..	..	..	..
46 Trinidad and Tobago	1946	1946	1962 E + N	13.8	16.0	12.5
47 Hungary	1953	1958	1945 E	6.9	5.6	7.1
48 Venezuela	1946	1946	1948 E	14.5	11.1	17.9
49 Panama	1946	1946	1946 E	9.4	16.7	6.5
50 Mexico	1947	1953	1952 N	7.5	15.8	5.9

	Year women received right		Year first woman elected (E) or nominated (N) to parliament	Women in government		
				At all levels [b] (%)	At ministerial level [b] (%)	At sub-ministerial level [b] (%)
HDI rank	To vote [a]	To stand for elections [a]		1996	1996	1996
51 Saint Kitts and Nevis	1951	1951	1984 E	16.7	0.0	25.0
52 Grenada	1951	1951	1976 E + N	22.5	21.4	23.1
53 Dominica	1951	1951	1980 E	25.0	18.2	26.5
54 Estonia	1918	1918	1919 E	14.3	0.0	16.8
55 Croatia	1945	1945	1992 E	19.0	11.5	21.1
56 Malaysia	1957	1957	1959 E	8.1	6.1	9.0
57 Colombia	1954	1954	1954 N	20.5	12.5	22.6
58 Cuba	1934	1934	1940 E	9.1	2.7	11.9
59 Mauritius	1956	1956	1976 E	9.8	0.0	12.6
60 Belarus	1919	1919	1990 E	6.6	5.3	7.0
61 Fiji	1963	1963	1970 N	14.5	4.8	18.2
62 Lithuania	1921	1921	1920 N	7.3	0.0	6.8
63 Bulgaria	1944	1944	1945 E	14.6	4.8	16.2
64 Suriname	1948	1948	1975 E	11.3	0.0	17.6
65 Libyan Arab Jamahiriya	1964	1964	– [c]	3.4	4.5	0.0
66 Seychelles	1948	1948	1976 E + N	20.8	33.3	18.3
67 Thailand	1932	1932	1948 N	2.1	0.0	2.6
68 Romania	1946	1946	1946 E	3.3	0.0	4.1
69 Lebanon	1952	1952	1991 N	0.0	0.0	0.0
70 Samoa (Western)	1990	1990	1976 N	9.1	7.7	9.5
71 Russian Federation	1918	1918	1993 E	2.6	2.4	2.6
72 Ecuador	1967	1967	1956 E	3.4	6.2	2.8
73 Macedonia, TFYR	1946	1946	1990 E	20.0	8.7	25.0
74 Latvia	1918	1918	†	17.6	11.1	19.0
75 Saint Vincent and the Grenadines	1951	1951	1979 E	19.2	20.0	18.8
76 Kazakhstan	1993	1993	1990 E	2.1	2.6	1.7
77 Philippines	1937	1937	1941 E	22.8	4.5	25.3
78 Saudi Arabia	– [c]	– [c]	– [c]	0.0	0.0	0.0
79 Brazil	1934	1934	1933 E	13.7	4.3	15.1
80 Peru	1955	1955	1956 E	13.2	5.6	15.5
81 Saint Lucia	1924	1924	1979 N	5.0	9.1	0.0
82 Jamaica	1944	1944	1944 E	14.3	5.6	18.4
83 Belize	1954	1954	1984 E + N	6.0	0.0	8.8
84 Paraguay	1961	1961	1963 E	4.3	6.7	3.7
85 Georgia	1921	1921	1992 E	3.4	0.0	4.7
86 Turkey	1930	1934	1935 N	5.0	2.9	5.6
87 Armenia	1921	1921	1990 E	2.1	0.0	2.9
88 Dominican Republic	1942	1942	1942 E	9.8	4.0	11.9
89 Oman	– [c]	– [c]	– [c]	3.6	0.0	4.1
90 Sri Lanka	1931	1931	1947 E	10.2	13.0	9.6
91 Ukraine	1919	1919	1990 E	1.7	0.0	2.2
92 Uzbekistan	1938	1938	1990 E	1.3	2.6	0.0
93 Maldives	1932	1932	1979 E	13.0	5.6	14.1
94 Jordan	1974	1974	1989 N	3.4	6.1	0.0
95 Iran, Islamic Rep. of	1963	1963	1963 E + N	0.4	0.0	0.5
96 Turkmenistan	1927	1927	1990 E	2.2	3.1	0.0
97 Kyrgyzstan	1918	1918	1990 E	11.4	10.5	12.0
98 China	1949	1949	1954 E	4.3	6.1	3.9
99 Guyana	1953	1945	1968 E	14.6	5.6	20.0
100 Albania	1920	1920	1945 E	11.8	5.3	14.0

... AND ACHIEVING EQUALITY FOR ALL WOMEN AND MEN

	Year women received right		Year first woman elected (E) or nominated (N) to parliament	Women in government		
				At all levels [b] (%)	At ministerial level [b] (%)	At sub-ministerial level [b] (%)
HDI rank	To vote [a]	To stand for elections [a]		1996	1996	1996
101 South Africa	1930	1930	1933 E	7.0	1.0	7.5
102 Tunisia	1959	1959	1959 E	7.9	2.9	10.9
103 Azerbaijan	1921	1921	1990 E	7.1	7.7	6.9
104 Moldova, Rep. of	1993	1993	1990 E	4.3	0.0	7.0
105 Indonesia	1945	1945	1950 N	1.9	3.6	1.6
106 Cape Verde	1975	1975	1975 E	11.1	13.3	8.3
107 El Salvador	1939	1961	1961 E	26.8	6.2	27.0
108 Tajikistan	1924	1924	1990 E	3.8	3.7	3.9
109 Algeria	1962	1962	1962 N	4.8	0.0	8.3
110 Viet Nam	1946	1946	1976 E	5.3	7.0	4.4
111 Syrian Arab Republic	1953	1953	1973 E	3.9	6.8	1.7
112 Bolivia	1952	1952	1966 E	7.3	0.0	8.3
113 Swaziland	1968	1968	1972 E + N	7.5	0.0	13.6
114 Honduras	1955	1955	1957	14.1	10.0	15.9
115 Namibia	1989	1989	1989 E	11.4	8.7	12.3
116 Vanuatu	1975	1975	1987 E	0.0	0.0	0.0
117 Guatemala	1946	1946	1956 E	16.7	13.3	22.2
118 Solomon Islands	1974 †	1974 †	1993 E	0.0	0.0	0.0
119 Mongolia	1924	1924	1951 E	1.7	0.0	2.6
120 Egypt	1956	1956	1957 E	4.0	3.1	4.5
121 Nicaragua	1955	1955	1972 E	17.4	15.8	17.9
122 Botswana	1965	1965	1979 E	13.5	7.7	15.4
123 São Tomé and Principe	1975	1975	1975 E	7.7	0.0	16.7
124 Gabon	1956	1956	1961 E	7.7	3.3	11.4
125 Iraq	1980	1980	1980 E	0.0	0.0	0.0
126 Morocco	1963	1963	1993 E	0.9	0.0	1.4
127 Lesotho	1965	1965	1965 N	14.6	0.0	18.2
128 Myanmar	1935	1946	1947 E	0.0	0.0	0.0
129 Papua New Guinea	1964	1963 †	1977 E	4.3	0.0	7.0
130 Zimbabwe	1957	1978	1980 E + N	11.6	8.3	14.0
131 Equatorial Guinea	1963	1963	1968 E	4.9	4.8	5.0
132 India	1950	1950	1952 E	5.8	3.2	6.2
133 Ghana	1954	1954	1960 N†	9.6	10.3	9.4
134 Cameroon	1946	1946	1960 E	4.5	2.6	5.3
135 Congo	1963	1963	1963 E	6.5	7.4	5.3
136 Kenya	1963	1963	1969 E + N	5.8	3.4	6.6
137 Cambodia	1955	1955	1958 E	2.4	0.0	3.1
138 Pakistan	1947	1947	1973 E	2.6	4.0	2.2
139 Comoros	1956	1956	1993 E	2.7	6.2	0.0
Low human development	..	..	..	..	..	..
140 Lao People's Dem. Rep.	1958	1958	1958 E	3.7	0.0	6.4
141 Congo, Dem. Rep. of the	1967	1970	1970 E	3.4	8.0	0.0
142 Sudan	1964	1964	1964 E	1.7	2.4	1.3
143 Togo	1945	1945	1961 E	3.0	4.3	0.0
144 Nepal	1951	1951	1952 N	0.0	0.0	0.0
145 Bhutan	1953	1953	1975 E	5.3	12.5	0.0
146 Nigeria	1958 †	1958 †	– [e]	6.2	7.7	5.6
147 Madagascar	1959	1959	1965 E	1.8	0.0	3.3
148 Yemen	1967 [f]	1967 [f]	1990 E †	0.0	0.0	0.0
149 Mauritania	1961	1961	1975 E	5.4	3.6	5.9
150 Bangladesh	1972	1972	1973 E	1.9	7.7	0.0

. . . AND ACHIEVING EQUALITY FOR ALL WOMEN AND MEN

	Year women received right		Year first woman elected (E) or nominated (N) to parliament	Women in government		
				At all levels [b] (%)	At ministerial level [b] (%)	At sub-ministerial level [b] (%)
HDI rank	To vote [a]	To stand for elections [a]		1996	1996	1996
151 Zambia	1962	1962	1964 E + N	8.4	7.7	8.6
152 Haiti	1950	1950	1961 E	22.2	29.4	15.8
153 Senegal	1945	1945	1963 E	5.6	6.7	4.2
154 Côte d'Ivoire	1952	1952	1965 E	7.1	8.3	6.8
155 Benin	1956	1956	1979 E	14.9	19.0	13.3
156 Tanzania, U. Rep. of	1959	1959	– [e]	9.6	10.5	8.9
157 Djibouti	1946	1986	– [d]	0.9	0.0	1.0
158 Uganda	1962	1962	1962 N	8.9	10.7	8.1
159 Malawi	1961	1961	1964 E	4.3	3.6	4.7
160 Angola	1975	1975	1980 E	4.9	10.7	1.8
161 Guinea	1958	1958	1963 E	13.0	15.0	11.5
162 Chad	1958	1958	1962 E	4.3	8.7	0.0
163 Gambia	1960	1960	1982 E †	18.9	18.8	19.0
164 Rwanda	1961	1961	1965 †	10.7	8.3	12.5
165 Central African Republic	1986	1986	1987 E	4.9	8.0	2.4
166 Mali	1956	1956	1964 E	6.2	10.0	0.0
167 Eritrea	1955 †	1955 †	1994 E	7.8	18.8	4.2
168 Guinea-Bissau	1977	1977	1972 N	11.9	8.0	13.2
169 Mozambique	1975	1975	1977 E	12.8	4.0	14.7
170 Burundi	1961	1961	1982 E	5.4	10.3	0.0
171 Burkina Faso	1958	1958	1978 E	11.5	9.1	11.9
172 Ethiopia	1955	1955	1957 E	8.9	6.7	9.6
173 Niger	1948	1948	1989 E	10.9	14.3	10.0
174 Sierra Leone	1961	1961	– [e]	5.9	3.8	6.5

† No information or confirmation available.

a. Refers to year in which right to election or representation on a universal and equal basis was recognized. In some countries confirmation and constitutional rights came later.

b. Including elected heads of state and governors of central banks. For countries for which the value is zero, no female ministers were reported by the United Nations Division for the Advancement of Women; this information could not be reconfirmed by the Human Development Report Office.

c. Women's right to vote and to stand for election has not been recognized.

d. The country has not yet elected or nominated a woman to the national parliament.

e. Exact date when a woman was first elected or nominated to parliament is not available.

f. Refers to the former People's Democratic Republic of Yemen.

Source: Columns 1-3: IPU 1999b; columns 4-6: UN 1996a.

... AND ACHIEVING EQUALITY FOR ALL WOMEN AND MEN

	International covenant on economic, social and cultural rights 1966	International covenant on civil and political rights 1966	International convention on the elimination of all forms of racial discrimination 1966	Convention on the prevention and punishment of the crime of genocide 1948	Convention on the rights of the child 1989	Convention on the elimination of all forms of discrimination against women 1979	Convention against torture and other cruel, inhuman or degrading treatment or punishment 1984	Convention relating to the status of refugees 1951
Afghanistan	●	●	●	●	●	○	●	
Albania	●	●	●	●	●	●	●	●
Algeria	●	●	●	●	●	●	●	●
Andorra					●	●	●	
Angola	●	●			●			●
Antigua and Barbuda			●	●	●	●	●	
Argentina	●	●	●	●	●	●	●	●
Armenia	●	●	●	●	●	●	●	●
Australia	●	●	●	●	●	●	●	●
Austria	●	●	●	●	●	●	●	●
Azerbaijan	●	●	●	●	●	●	●	●
Bahamas			●	●	●	●	●	●
Bahrain			●	●	●		●	
Bangladesh	●		●	●	●	●	●	
Barbados	●	●	●	●	●	●		
Belarus	●	●	●	●	●	●	●	
Belgium	●	●	●	●	●	●	○	●
Belize		●		●	●	●	●	●
Benin	●	●	○		●	●	●	●
Bhutan			○		●			
Bolivia	●	●	●	○	●	●	○	●
Bosnia and Herzegovina	●	●	●	●	●	●	●	●
Botswana			●		●	●		●
Brazil	●	●	●	●	●	●	●	●
Brunei Darussalam					●			
Bulgaria	●	●	●	●	●	●	●	●
Burkina Faso	●	●	●	●	●	●	●	●
Burundi	●	●	●	●	●	●	●	●
Cambodia	●	●	●	●	●	●		●
Cameroon	●	●	●		●	●	●	●
Canada	●	●	●	●	●	●	●	●
Cape Verde	●	●	●		●	●	●	
Central African Republic	●	●	●		●	●		●
Chad	●	●	●		●	●	●	●
Chile	●	●	●	●	●	●	●	●
China	○	○	●	●	●	●	●	
Colombia	●	●	●	●	●	●	●	●
Comoros					●	●		
Congo	●	●	●		●	●		●
Congo, Dem. Rep. of the	●	●	●	●	●	●		●
Cook Islands					●			
Costa Rica	●	●	●	●	●	●	●	●
Côte d'Ivoire	●	●	●	●	●	●	●	●
Croatia	●	●	●	●	●	●	●	●
Cuba			●	●	●	●	●	
Cyprus	●	●	●	●	●	●	●	●
Czech Republic	●	●	●	●	●	●	●	●
Denmark	●	●	●	●	●	●	●	●
Djibouti					●	●		●
Dominica	●	●			●	●		●

	International covenant on economic, social and cultural rights 1966	International covenant on civil and political rights 1966	International convention on the elimination of all forms of racial discrimination 1966	Convention on the prevention and punishment of the crime of genocide 1948	Convention on the rights of the child 1989	Convention on the elimination of all forms of discrimination against women 1979	Convention against torture and other cruel, inhuman or degrading treatment or punishment 1984	Convention relating to the status of refugees 1951
Dominican Republic	●	●	●	○	●	●	○	●
Ecuador	●	●	●	●	●	●	●	●
Egypt	●	●	●	●	●	●	●	●
El Salvador	●	●	●	●	●	●	●	●
Equatorial Guinea	●	●			●	●		●
Eritrea					●	●		
Estonia	●	●	●	●	●	●	●	●
Ethiopia	●	●	●	●	●	●	●	●
Fiji			●	●	●	●		●
Finland	●	●	●	●	●	●	●	●
France	●	●	●	●	●	●	●	●
Gabon	●	●	●	●	●	●	○	●
Gambia	●	●	●	●	●	●	○	●
Georgia	●	●	●	●	●	●	●	●
Germany	●	●	●	●	●	●	●	●
Ghana			●	●	●	●	●	●
Greece	●	●	●	●	●	●	●	●
Grenada	●	●	○		●	●		●
Guatemala	●	●	●	●	●	●	●	●
Guinea	●	●	●	●	●	●	●	●
Guinea-Bissau	●				●	●		
Guyana	●	●	●		●	●	●	●
Haiti		●	●	●	●	●		●
Holy See			●		●			●
Honduras	●	●			●	●	●	●
Hungary	●	●	●	●	●	●	●	●
Iceland	●	●	●	●	●	●	●	●
India	●	●	●	●	●	●	○	
Indonesia					●	●	●	
Iran, Islamic Rep. of	●	●	●	●	●			●
Iraq	●	●	●	●	●	●		
Ireland	●	●	○	●	●	●	●	●
Israel	●	●	●	●	●	●	●	●
Italy	●	●	●	●	●	●	●	●
Jamaica	●	●	●	●	●	●		
Japan	●	●	●		●	●		●
Jordan	●	●	●	●	●	●	●	
Kazakhstan			●	●	●	●	●	●
Kenya	●	●			●	●	●	●
Kiribati					●			
Korea, Dem. People's Rep. of	●	●		●	●	●		
Korea, Rep. of	●	●	●		●	●	●	●
Kuwait	●	●	●		●	●	●	
Kyrgyzstan	●	●	●	●	●	●		
Lao People's Dem. Rep.			●	●	●	●		
Latvia	●	●	●	●	●	●	●	●
Lebanon	●	●	●	●	●	●		
Lesotho	●	●	●	●	●	●		●
Liberia	○	○	●	●	●	●		●
Libyan Arab Jamahiriya	●	●	●	●	●	●	●	

243

	International covenant on economic, social and cultural rights 1966	International covenant on civil and political rights 1966	International convention on the elimination of all forms of racial discrimination 1966	Convention on the prevention and punishment of the crime of genocide 1948	Convention on the rights of the child 1989	Convention on the elimination of all forms of discrimination against women 1979	Convention against torture and other cruel, inhuman or degrading treatment or punishment 1984	Convention relating to the status of refugees 1951
Liechtenstein	●	●		●	●	●	●	●
Lithuania	●	●		●	●	●	●	●
Luxembourg	●	●	●	●	●	●	●	●
Macedonia, TFYR	●	●	●	●	●	●	●	
Madagascar	●	●	●		●	●		●
Malawi	●	●	●		●	●	●	●
Malaysia				●	●	●		
Maldives			●	●	●	●		
Mali	●	●	●	●	●	●		●
Malta	●	●	●		●	●	●	●
Marshall Islands					●			
Mauritania			●		●			●
Mauritius	●	●	●		●	●	●	
Mexico	●	●	●	●	●	●	●	
Micronesia, Fed. States of					●			
Moldova, Rep. of	●	●	●	●	●	●		
Monaco	●	●	●	●	●		●	●
Mongolia	●	●	●	●	●	●		
Morocco	●	●	●	●	●	●	●	●
Mozambique		●		●	●	●	●	●
Myanmar				●	●	●		
Namibia	●	●	●	●	●	●	●	
Nauru					●			
Nepal	●	●	●	●	●	●	●	
Netherlands	●	●	●	●	●	●	●	●
New Zealand	●	●	●	●	●	●	●	●
Nicaragua	●	●	●	●	●	●	○	●
Niger	●	●	●		●	●		●
Nigeria	●	●	●		●	●	○	●
Niue					●			
Norway	●	●	●	●	●	●	●	●
Oman					●			
Pakistan			●	●	●	●		
Palau					●			
Panama	●	●	●	●	●	●	●	●
Papua New Guinea			●	●	●	●		●
Paraguay	●	●		○	●	●	●	●
Peru	●	●	●	●	●	●	●	●
Philippines	●	●	●	●	●	●	●	●
Poland	●	●	●	●	●	●	●	●
Portugal	●	●	●	●	●	●	●	●
Qatar					●			
Romania	●	●	●	●	●	●	●	●
Russian Federation	●	●	●	●	●	●	●	●
Rwanda	●	●	●	●	●	●		●
Saint Kitts and Nevis					●	●		
Saint Lucia			●		●	●		
Saint Vincent and the Grenadines	●	●	●		●	●		●
Samoa (Western)					●	●		●
San Marino	●	●			●			

29 Status of selected international human rights instruments

	International covenant on economic, social and cultural rights 1966	International covenant on civil and political rights 1966	International convention on the elimination of all forms of racial discrimination 1966	Convention on the prevention and punishment of the crime of genocide 1948	Convention on the rights of the child 1989	Convention on the elimination of all forms of discrimination against women 1979	Convention against torture and other cruel, inhuman or degrading treatment or punishment 1984	Convention relating to the status of refugees 1951
São Tomé and Principe	○	○			●	○		●
Saudi Arabia			●	●	●		●	
Senegal	●	●	●	●	●	●	●	●
Seychelles	●	●	●	●	●	●	●	●
Sierra Leone	●	●	●		●	●	○	●
Singapore				●	●	●		●
Slovakia	●	●	●	●	●	●	●	●
Slovenia	●	●	●	●	●	●	●	●
Solomon Islands	●		●		●			●
Somalia	●	●	●				●	●
South Africa	○	●	●	●	●	●	●	●
Spain	●	●	●	●	●	●	●	●
Sri Lanka	●	●	●	●	●	●	●	●
Sudan	●	●	●		●		○	●
Suriname	●	●	●		●	●		●
Swaziland			●		●			
Sweden	●	●	●	●	●	●	●	●
Switzerland	●	●	●	●	●		●	●
Syrian Arab Republic	●	●	●	●	●			●
Tajikistan	●	●	●		●	●	●	●
Tanzania, U. Rep. of	●	●	●		●	●		●
Thailand					●	●		
Togo	●	●	●	●	●	●	●	●
Tonga			●	●	●			
Trinidad and Tobago	●	●	●		●	●		
Tunisia	●	●	●		●	●	●	●
Turkey			○	●	●	●	●	●
Turkmenistan	●	●	●		●	●		
Tuvalu					●			●
Uganda	●	●	●	●	●	●	●	●
Ukraine	●	●	●	●	●	●	●	
United Arab Emirates			●		●			
United Kingdom	●	●	●	●	●	●	●	●
United States	○	●	●	●	○	○	●	
Uruguay	●	●	●	●	●	●	●	●
Uzbekistan	●	●	●		●	●	●	
Vanuatu					●	●		
Venezuela	●	●	●	●	●	●	●	●
Viet Nam	●	●	●	●	●	●		
Yemen	●	●	●	●	●	●	●	●
Yugoslavia	●	●	●	●	●	●	●	●
Zambia	●	●	●		●	●	●	●
Zimbabwe	●	●	●	●	●	●		●
Total states parties	141	144	153	129	191	163	111	133
Signatures not followed by ratification	5	3	5	3	1	3	10	0
States that have not ratified and signed	47	46	35	61	1	27	72	60

● Ratification, accession, approval, notification or succession, acceptance or definitive signature.

○ Signature not yet followed by ratification.

Note: Status as of 1 February 1999.

Source: UN 1999c.

	Total population (thousands) 1997	Life expectancy at birth (years) 1997	Infant mortality rate (per 1,000 live births) 1997	Under-five mortality rate (per 1,000 live births) 1997	Total fertility rate 1997	Adult literacy rate (%) 1997	GNP Total (US$ millions) 1997	GNP Per capita (US$) 1997	Daily per capita supply of calories 1996	Population without access to safe water (%) 1990-97 [a]	Refugees by country of origin (thousands) 1997
Afghanistan	20,893	45.5	165	257	6.9	33.4	4,141 [b]	250 [b]	1,676	88	2,647.6
Andorra	70	..	5	6	..	..	..	..	..	..	..
Bosnia and Herzegovina	3,520	73.3	14	16	1.4	..	..	..	2,277	..	391.2
Korea, Dem. People's Rep. of	22,981	72.2	23	30	2.1	..	..	..	2,271	19	..
Liberia	2,402	47.3	157	235	6.3	48.4	1,120 [c]	490 [c]	2,161	54	486.7
Liechtenstein	32	..	6	7	..	..	..	..	..	..	..
Marshall Islands	58	..	63	92	..	..	97	1,610	..	18	..
Micronesia, Fed. States of	112	..	20	24	..	..	213	1,910	..	78	..
Monaco	33	..	5	5	..	..	..	..	..	..	..
Palau	18	..	28	34	..	..	149 [d]	11,220 [d]	..	12	..
San Marino	26	..	5	6	..	..	..	..	..	..	..
Somalia	8,821	47.0	125	211	7.3	..	961 [e]	210 [e]	1,532	74	524.4
Yugoslavia	10,628	72.8	18	21	1.8	..	..	..	3,101	24	66.7

Note: The table presents data for countries not included in the main indicator tables.

a. Data refer to the most recent year available during the period specified in the column heading.

b. Data refer to 1981.

c. Data refer to 1987.

d. Data refer to 1984.

e. Data refer to 1990.

Source: Columns 1, 2 and 5: UN 1998h; *columns 3, 4 and 10:* UNICEF 1999a; *column 6:* calculated on the basis of data from UNESCO 1999a; *columns 7 and 8:* World Bank 1999b; *column 9:* FAO 1998; *column 11:* UNHCR 1998.

The *Human Development Report* has presented data on broad aspects of human development since its inception in 1990. This has required a wide array of statistics that reflect people's well-being and the opportunities that they actually enjoy.

This year's Report introduces important improvements in the selection, use and presentation of statistics. Greater attention has been paid to coordinating with international statistical bodies, to harmonizing the selection of indicators with data reported by them and to ensuring that the most up-to-date estimates have been used. In most cases the time lag between the reference date of key indicators and the date of the Report's release has been narrowed from three years to two.

For the first time the indicator tables are organized into categories to better reflect the different dimensions of human development: levels and trends of human development (including the composite indices—the HDI, GDI, GEM, HPI-1 and HPI-2), health and survival, education, economic resources, sustainability, human security and gender equality. Unlike in earlier years, data for developing and industrialized countries are presented together rather than in separate tables. In all but a few tables all countries are included, to ease comparisons across countries and across regions or country groups.

As a standard practice, this year's Report, like earlier ones, relies on national estimates reported by the United Nations and its agencies and by other internationally recognized organizations, and thus on a set of standardized and consistent data produced by these offices. The few exceptions in which data from other sources have been used are noted. This year's Report continues the practice of documenting as thoroughly as possible the international statistical sources used.

DATA STANDARDS AND METHODOLOGY

Even when standardized international sources are used, a number of problems remain for any user of statistical data. First, despite the considerable efforts of international organizations to collect, process and disseminate social and economic statistics and to standardize definitions and data collection methods, limitations remain in the coverage, consistency and comparability of data across time and countries. Second, significant shifts and breaks in statistical series can occur when statistical bodies and research institutions update or improve their estimates using new sources of data, such as censuses and surveys.

Such concerns arise in preparing the human development index (HDI). For example, for the 1998 revision of the United Nations database *World Population Prospects 1950–2050* (UN 1998h), released on 24 November 1998, the United Nations Population Division derived population estimates and projections from the most recently available population censuses—supplemented with information from national survey data—using specialized demographic techniques. It made significant adjustments to the 1996 revision to continue to incorporate the demographic impact of HIV/AIDS and to accommodate the extensive migratory movements within Europe and elsewhere and the rapid growth in the number of refugees in Africa and other parts of the world (UN 1998h).[1] It also incorporated newly available data reflecting the continuing changes in the demographic profiles of countries in Eastern Europe and the Commonwealth of Independent States (CIS).

Changes in the population estimates have an effect on other indicators—such as adult literacy rates and enrolment ratios for different levels of schooling published by UNESCO. Thus readers must take into account the potential for fluctuation in both literacy rates and enrolment ratios when making comparisons across time and countries.

The adult literacy rates presented in this Report are new estimates from UNESCO's 1998 literacy assessment. They improve on results from the 1994 assessment used in earlier Reports by incorporating the 1998 revision of the United Nations population estimates and new literacy statistics collected through national population censuses, and through refinement of the estimation procedures.

The gross enrolment ratio is defined as the ratio of the number of children enrolled in a schooling level to the number of children in the relevant age group. The age group indicator depends on the estimates of age- and sex-specific populations published by the United Nations Population Division. Data on enrolment are affected by the methodology and timing used by the administrative registries, population censuses and education surveys at the national level. In addition, independent of the variations in population estimates and enrolment data, UNESCO may periodically revise the methodology used for its projections and estimations of enrolment.

Estimates of income used in the HDI are GDP converted to international dollars by using purchasing power parities (PPP) established by the World Bank, based on the results of surveys by the International Comparison Programme (ICP). Revision and updating of the PPP-based income estimates lead to fluctuations across time and country series. The real GDP per capita (PPP$) estimates used in this year's Report integrate the 1997 results from the ICP. For some countries the new estimates differ considerably from earlier published estimates, largely because of the revised national currency–based estimates used to extrapolate the latest (1993) PPP estimates to the reference year (1997), because of new PPP estimates, or both. For countries not covered by the World Bank, PPP estimates provided by Alan Heston and Robert Summers (1999) of the University of Pennsylvania are used.

Another issue is uneven data availability and data quality across country groups. Some indicators—literacy, for example—are well documented in the developing countries but less so in the industrialized countries, or vice versa. Another example is crime data made available by the United Nations Crime Prevention and Criminal Justice Division through the Fifth United Nations Survey of Crime Trends and Operations of Criminal Justice Systems (1990–94). The availability and reliability of these crime data depend heavily on a country's law enforcement and reporting systems. In such cases the Report presents the limited data available, primarily from official national reporting systems and compiled by the United Nations, with the caveat that these data may not be readily used for international comparisons.

The transition in the countries of Eastern Europe and the CIS has led to a break in most of their statistical series, so the data available for recent years present problems of reliability, consistency and comparability at the international level and are often subject to revision.

The quality of data also suffers in countries in which there is a war or civil strife. Where the availability and quality of estimates have become extremely limited, reporting of the data in the *Human Development Report* has been interrupted, as for Afghanistan, the Democratic People's Republic of Korea, Liberia and Somalia. But other countries, such as Rwanda, have been reintroduced in the Report as data have become available.

IMPROVING HUMAN DEVELOPMENT STATISTICS

A major goal of the Report is to encourage national governments, international bodies and policy-makers to improve statistical indicators of human development.

The importance of strengthening data collection and reporting to monitor progress in human development at the national and international levels cannot be overstated. As the frequent use of the symbol for unavailable data in the indicator tables in this Report demonstrates, there are many gaps in the coverage of human development data. Lack of data is a particular constraint in monitoring gender equality and poverty eradication. Coverage of the gender-related development index (GDI) is limited to 143 countries, the gender empowerment measure (GEM) to 102 countries and the human poverty index (HPI-1 and HPI-2) to 92 developing and 17 industrialized countries.

Reliable data are essential for assessing the progress towards national goals in poverty reduction, gender equality, environmental sustainability and many other priorities for human development. Internationally comparable series help national bodies compare achievements with progress in other countries. They aid in international monitoring of progress towards the goals of the global United Nations conferences. And they are necessary for policy analysis.

The Human Development Report team, in striving to overcome the shortcomings of data on important human development issues, has received valuable and generous assistance from many colleagues in international and national organizations. They have made special efforts to provide additional data and guidance in their fields of specialization, especially for the purpose of constructing time series and improving the consistency and comparability of human development indicators across countries.

COUNTRY CLASSIFICATION

The main criterion for classifying countries is the HDI. Countries are classified into three groups: high human development, with HDI values of 0.800 and above; medium human development, with HDI values of 0.500–0.799; and low human development, with HDI values below 0.500.

For analytical purposes and statistical convenience, aggregate measures of statistical indicators are calculated for three major groups of countries: all developing countries, Eastern Europe and the CIS, and industrialized countries. These designations do not necessarily express a judgement about the development stage reached by a particular country or area. Developing countries are further classified into the following regions: Arab States, East Asia, Latin America and the Caribbean (including Mexico), South Asia, South-East Asia and the Pacific, Southern Europe and Sub-Saharan Africa. This regional classification is consistent with the Regional Bureaux of UNDP. For analytical purposes, aggregate measures for East Asia and South Asia are also computed after excluding China and India because the magnitudes of their population, GDP and other measures overwhelm those of the smaller countries in the regions. Unless otherwise noted, aggregate measures for the world presented at the end of each indicator table reflect the aggregate for all the countries covered in this Report.

The term *country* as used in the text and tables refers, as appropriate, to territories or areas.

INDICATOR TABLES

In the indicator tables countries and areas are ranked in descending order by their HDI value. To locate a country in the tables, readers can refer to the key to countries, which lists countries alphabetically with their HDI rank.

Where estimates have been calculated using established international statistical series, the estimates are footnoted and the sources given in the notes at the end of each table. These notes also give the data sources for each column. The first source listed is the main international source for the indicator. The indicator tables no longer include estimates derived from sources other than the documented sources, except for table 1 (HDI). Short citations of sources are given, corresponding to the full references in the list of data sources used in preparing the indicator tables.

Not all countries have been included in the indicator tables, owing to lack of comparable data. For United Nations member countries not included in the main indicator tables, basic human development indicators are presented in table 30.

Unless otherwise stated, aggregate data for the human development and regional groups of countries are weighted by population subgroups or other appropriate indicators. Aggregates are not presented in cases where there were no data for the majority of countries in a group or appropriate weighting procedures were unavailable. Where appropriate, aggregate data are presented as the sum for the region rather than as a weighted average. To present a consistent set of aggregates, summary measures calculated for the variables used in the HDI for the universe of 174 countries, and in the GDI for the universe of 143 countries, have been used throughout the Report. For other indicators the summary measures presented have been calculated on the basis of the majority of countries for which data are available.

Unless otherwise indicated, multiyear averages of growth rates are expressed as compound annual rates of change. Year-to-year growth rates are expressed as annual percentage changes.

In the absence of the phrase annual, annual rate or growth rate, a dash between two years indicates that the data were collected during one of the years shown, such as 1993–97. A slash between two years indicates an average for the years shown, such as 1996/97. The following signs have been used:

.. Data not available.

(.) Less than half the unit shown.

(..) Less than one-tenth the unit shown.

< Less than.

— Not applicable.

T Total.

NOTE

1. The 1998 revision gives special attention to the demographic impact of HIV/AIDS in the population estimates and projections for developing countries with a population of at least one million and an adult HIV prevalence of 2% or more, or with very large populations of infected adults. The number of such countries covered has increased from 28 in the 1996 revision to 34 in the 1998 revision: Benin, Botswana, Brazil, Burkina Faso, Burundi, Cambodia, Cameroon, the Central African Republic, Chad, the Congo, the Democratic Republic of the Congo, Côte d'Ivoire, Eritrea, Ethiopia, Gabon, Guinea-Bissau, Haiti, India, Kenya, Lesotho, Liberia, Malawi, Mozambique, Namibia, Nigeria, Rwanda, Sierra Leone, South Africa, Thailand, Togo, Uganda, the United Republic of Tanzania, Zambia and Zimbabwe.

Primary statistical references

CDIAC (Carbon Dioxide Information Analysis Center). 1999a. "CO$_2$ Emissions." [http://www.cdiac.esd.ornl.gov/ftp/ndp030/global96.ems]. February 1999.

———. 1999b. "CO$_2$ Emissions." [http://www.cdiac.esd.ornl.gov/ftp/ndp030/nation96.ems]. February 1999.

FAO (Food and Agriculture Organization of the United Nations). 1997. Correspondence on daily per capita calorie supply. July. Rome.

———. 1998. "Daily Per Capita Supply of Calories." [http://www.fao.org/NEWS/1998/981204-e.htm]. February 1999.

———. 1999. "Food Balance Sheets." [http://www.apps.fao.org/lim500/nph-wrap.pl?FoodBalanceSheet&Domain=FoodBalanceSheet]. February 1999.

Heston, Alan, and Robert Summers. 1999. Data on real GDP per capita (PPP$). March. University of Pennsylvania, Department of Economics, Philadelphia.

IISS (International Institute for Strategic Studies). 1998. *The Military Balance 1998–99*. London: Oxford University Press.

IDEA (Institute for Democracy and Electoral Assistance). 1997. *Voter Turnout from 1945 to 1997: A Global Report*. Stockholm.

ILO (International Labour Office). 1995. *World Labour Report 1995*. Geneva.

———.1996. *Estimates and Projections of the Economically Active Population, 1950–2010*. 4th ed. Diskette. Geneva.

———.1998. *Labour Statistics Database*. Geneva.

———. Various years. *Yearbook of Labour Statistics*. Geneva.

International Federation of Red Cross and Red Crescent Societies. 1995. *World Disasters Report 1995*. Geneva.

IPU (Inter-Parliamentary Union). 1999a. "Women in Parliaments." [http://www.ipu.org/wmn-e/classif.htm]. February 1999.

———. 1999b. Correspondence on date of latest elections, political parties represented and women's rights to vote and to stand for election. February. Geneva.

ITU (International Telecommunication Union). 1997. *World Telecommunication Indicators*. Database. Geneva.

Lipton, Michael. 1996. "Poverty-Basic and Annex Tables: Notes on Method." Background Paper for the *Human Development Report 1997*. United Nations Development Programme, Human Development Report Office, New York.

Milanovic, Branko. 1998. *Income, Inequality and Poverty during the Transition from Planned to Market Economy*. Washington, DC: World Bank.

Network Wizards. 1998a. "Internet Domain Survey July 1998." [http://www.nw.com]. March 1999.

OECD (Organisation for Economic Co-operation and Development). 1997a. *Education Policy Analysis*. Paris.

———.1997b. *Employment Outlook*. Paris.

———. 1997c. *Environmental Data: Compendium 1997*. Paris.

———.1998b. *Employment Outlook*. Paris.

———. 1999a. *Development Co-operation 1998 Report*. Development Assistance Committee Report. Paris.

———. 1999b. *Geographical Distribution of Financial Flows to Aid Recipients*. Paris.

———. Forthcoming. *Environmental Data: Compendium 1999*. Paris.

Psacharopoulos, George, and Zafiris Tzannatos, eds. 1992. *Case Studies on Women's Employment and Pay in Latin America*. Washington, DC: World Bank.

SIPRI (Stockholm International Peace Research Institute). 1998. *SIPRI Yearbook 1998*. New York: Oxford University Press.

Smeeding, Timothy. 1997. "Financial Poverty in Developed Countries: The Evidence from the Luxembourg Income Study." *Human Development Papers 1997: Poverty and Human Development*. New York: United Nations Development Programme.

Standard & Poor's. 1999. Email correspondence on sovereign ratings history. 9 March.

UN (United Nations). 1993. "Statistical Chart on World Families." Statistics Division and the Secretariat for the International Year of the Family. New York.

———.1994. *Women's Indicators and Statistics Database*. Version 3. CD-ROM. Statistics Division. New York.

———. 1995. *The World's Women 1970–95: Trends and Statistics.* New York.

———.1996a. "Factsheet on Women in Government as at January 1996." Division for the Advancement of Women. New York.

———. 1996b. *World Urbanization Prospects: The 1996 Revision.* Database. Population Division. New York.

———.1997a. *Energy Statistics Yearbook 1995.* New York.

———.1998c. *Energy Statistics Yearbook 1996.* New York.

———. 1998h. *World Population Prospects 1950–2050: The 1998 Revision.* Database. Population Division. New York.

———.1999a. *Demographic Yearbook 1997.* New York.

———.1999b. *Fifth United Nations Survey of Crime Trends and Operations of Criminal Justice Systems.* United Nations Office at Vienna, Crime Prevention and Criminal Justice Division. Vienna. [http://www.ifs.univie.ac.at/~uncjin/wcs]. March 1999.

———. 1999c. "Multilateral Treaties Deposited with the Secretary-General." New York. [http://www.un.org/Depts/Treaty]. March 1999.

UNAIDS (Joint United Nations Programme on HIV/AIDS) and WHO (World Health Organization). 1998b. *Report on the Global HIV/AIDS Epidemic.* Geneva. [http://www.who.org/emc_hiv/global_report/data/globrep_e.pdf].

UNCTAD (United Nations Conference on Trade and Development). 1999. Email correspondence on unpublished data on foreign direct investment. Division on Transnational Corporations and Investment. 20 January. New York and Geneva.

UNDP (United Nations Development Programme). 1995. *Human Development Report 1995.* New York: Oxford University Press.

UNECE (United Nations Economic Commission for Europe). 1999a. *Trends in Europe and North America 1998–99.* New York and Geneva.

———. 1999b. Correspondence on injuries and deaths from road accidents. March. New York and Geneva.

UNESCO (United Nations Educational, Scientific and Cultural Organization). 1996. Correspondence on gross enrolment ratios. December. Paris.

———. 1997. Correspondence on gross enrolment ratios. November. Paris.

———.1998a. *Statistical Yearbook 1998.* Paris.

———.1998c. *World Education Report 1998.* Paris.

———. 1999a. Correspondence on adult literacy rates. January. Paris.

———. 1999b. Correspondence on gross enrolment ratios. April. Paris.

———.1999d. Correspondence on net enrolment ratios. February. Paris.

———. 1999e. Correspondence on rate of survival to grade 5 of primary education. February. Paris.

UNHCR (United Nations High Commissioner for Refugees). 1998. *Refugees and Others of Concern to UNHCR: 1997, Statistical Overview.* Geneva.

UNICEF (United Nations Children's Fund). 1998b. *The State of the World's Children 1998.* New York: Oxford University Press.

———.1999a. *The State of the World's Children 1999.* New York: Oxford University Press.

———.1999b. Correspondence on infant mortality and under-five mortality rates. February. New York.

WHO (World Health Organization). 1997. *Tobacco or Health: A Global Status Report.* Geneva.

———.1998a. *The World Health Report 1998.* Geneva.

———. 1998b. *World Health Statistics Annual 1996.* Geneva.

World Bank. 1993. *World Development Report 1993: Investing in Health.* New York: Oxford University Press.

———.1995. *World Development Report 1995: Workers in an Integrating World.* New York: Oxford University Press.

———.1996. *World Bank Atlas 1996.* Washington, DC.

———. 1997a. *World Development Indicators 1997.* Washington, DC.

———. 1997b. *World Development Indicators 1997.* CD-ROM. Washington, DC.

———. 1998c. *World Development Indicators 1998.* CD-ROM. Washington, DC.

———. 1999b. *World Development Indicators 1999.* CD-ROM. Washington, DC.

———.1999e. Correspondence on the percentage of population with access to health services. Development Economics Data Group. March. Washington, DC.

———.1999f. Correspondence on unpublished World Bank data on GDP per capita (PPP$) for 1997. Development Economics Data Group. February. Washington, DC.

WRI (World Resources Institute). 1998. *World Resources 1998–99.* New York: Oxford University Press.

Definitions of statistical terms

Administrators and managers Includes legislators, senior government administrators, traditional chiefs and heads of villages and administrators of special interest organizations. It also includes corporate managers such as chief executives and general managers as well as specialized managers and managing supervisors, according to the International Standard Classification of Occupations (ISCO-1968).

Bank and trade-related lending Covers commercial bank lending and other private credit.

Budget deficit or surplus Central government current and capital revenue and official grants received, less total expenditure and lending minus repayments.

Carbon dioxide (CO_2) emissions Anthropogenic (human-originated) carbon dioxide emissions stemming from the burning of fossil fuels and the production of cement. Emissions are calculated from data on the consumption of solid, liquid and gaseous fuels and gas flaring.

Children reaching grade 5 The percentage of children starting primary school who eventually attain grade 5 (grade 4 if the duration of primary school is four years). The estimate is based on the Reconstructed Cohort Method, which uses data on enrolment and repeaters for two consecutive years.

Cigarette consumption per adult The sum of production and imports minus exports of cigarettes divided by the population aged 15 years and older.

Commercial energy use The domestic primary commercial energy supply. It is calculated as local production plus imports and stock changes, minus exports and international marine bunkers.

Contraceptive prevalence rate The percentage of married women of child-bearing age (15–49) who are using, or whose husbands are using, any form of contraception, whether modern or traditional.

Current account balance The difference between (a) exports of goods and services as well as inflows of unrequited transfers but exclusive of foreign aid and (b) imports of goods and services as well as all unrequited transfers to the rest of the world.

Daily per capita calorie supply The calorie equivalent of the net food supply (local production plus imports minus exports) in a country, divided by the population, per day.

Deforestation The permanent clearing of forest-land for all agricultural uses and for settlements. It does not include other alterations such as selective logging.

Dependency ratio The ratio of the population defined as dependent—those under 15 and over 65—to the working-age population, aged 15–64.

Disability A restriction or lack of ability (resulting from impairment) to perform an activity in the manner or within the range considered normal for a human being. Impairment is defined as any loss of psychological, physiological or anatomical structure and function.

Disbursement Records the actual international transfer of financial resources or of goods or services, valued at the cost to the donor.

Discouraged workers Individuals who would like to work and are available for work, but are not actively seeking it because of a stated belief that no suitable job is available or because they do not know where to get jobs.

Doctors Physicians and all graduates of any faculty or school of medicine in any medical field (including practice, teaching, administration and research).

Drug crimes Any crimes involving drugs, including the illicit brokerage, cultivation, delivery, distribution, extraction, exportation or importation, offering for sale, production, purchase, manufacture, sale, traffic, transportation or use of narcotic drugs.

Economically active population All men or women who supply labor for the production of economic goods and services during a specified period.

Education expenditure Expenditure on the provision, management, inspection and support of pre-primary, primary and secondary schools; universities and colleges; vocational, technical and other training institutions; and general administration and subsidiary services.

Electricity consumption The production of heat and power plants less own use and distribution losses.

Enrolment The *gross enrolment ratio* is the number of students enrolled in a level of education, regardless of age, as a percentage of the population of official school age for that level. The *net enrolment ratio* is the number of children of official school age (as defined by the education system) enrolled in school as a percentage of the number of children of official school age in the population.

Exports of goods and services The value of all goods and non-factor services provided to the rest of the world, including merchandise freight, insurance, travel and other non-factor services.

External debt Debt owed by a country to non-residents repayable in foreign currency, goods or services.

Food aid in cereals The quantity of cereals provided by donor countries and international organizations, including the World Food Programme and the International Wheat Council, as reported for a crop year.

Foreign direct investment An investment in a country involving a long-term relationship and control of an enterprise by non-residents. It is the sum of equity capital, reinvestment of earnings, other long-term capital and short-term capital as shown in the balance of payments.

Fresh water withdrawals Total water withdrawals, not counting evaporation losses from storage basins. Withdrawals also include water from desalination plants in countries where they are a significant source of water withdrawals.

Gini coefficient Measures the extent to which the distribution of income (or, in some cases, consumption expenditures) among individuals or households within an economy deviates from a perfectly equal distribution. The coefficient ranges from 0—meaning perfect equality—to 1—complete inequality.

Government consumption Includes all current expenditures for purchases of goods and services by all levels of government, excluding most government enterprises.

Gross domestic investment Outlays on additions to the fixed assets of the economy plus net changes in the level of inventories.

Gross domestic product (GDP) The total output of goods and services for final use produced by an economy by both residents and non-residents, regardless of the allocation to domestic and foreign claims. It does not include deductions for depreciation of physical capital or depletion and degradation of natural resources.

Gross national product (GNP) Comprises GDP plus net factor income from abroad, which is the income residents receive from abroad for factor services (labour and capital), less similar payments made to non-residents who contribute to the domestic economy.

Homicides Intentional deaths purposely inflicted by another person.

Immunization coverage The percentage of children under one year of age receiving antigens used in the Universal Child Immunization (UCI) Programme.

Income or expenditure share The distribution of income or expenditure accruing to percentile groups of households ranked by total household income, per capita income or expenditure.

Infant mortality rate The probability of dying between birth and exactly one year of age times 1,000.

Infants with low birth-weight The percentage of babies born weighing less than 2,500 grams.

Inflation A fall in the purchasing power of money reflected in a persistent increase in the general level of prices as generally measured by the retail price index.

Internet host A computer system connected to the Internet—either a single terminal directly connected, or a computer that allows multiple users to access network services through it.

Life expectancy at birth The number of years a newborn infant would live if prevailing patterns of mortality at the time of birth were to stay the same throughout the child's life.

Literacy rate (adult) The percentage of people aged 15 and above who can, with understanding, both read and write a short, simple statement on their everyday life.

Maternal mortality rate The annual number of deaths of women from pregnancy-related causes per 100,000 live births.

Military expenditure All expenditure of the defence ministry and other ministries on recruiting and training of military personnel as well as construction and the purchase of military supplies and equipment. Military assistance is included in the expenditures of the donor country.

Municipal waste Waste collected by municipalities or by their order that has been generated by households, commercial activities, office buildings, schools, government buildings and small businesses.

National poverty line The poverty line deemed appropriate for a country by its authorities.

Official development assistance (ODA) Grants or loans to countries or territories that are undertaken by the official sector, with promotion of economic development and welfare as the main objective, at concessional financial terms.

Portfolio investment flows (net) Non-debt-creating portfolio equity flows (the sum of country funds, depository receipts and direct purchases of shares by foreign investors) and portfolio debt flows (bond issues purchased by foreign investors).

Primary education Education at the first level (level 1), the main function of which is to provide the basic elements of education.

Private consumption The market value of all goods and services, including durable products, purchased or received as income in kind by households and non-profit institutions.

Professional and technical workers Physical scientists; architects and engineers; aircraft and ship's officers; life scientists; medical, dental, veterinary and related workers; statisticians, mathematicians and systems analysts; economists; accountants; jurists; teachers; workers in religion; authors and journalists; sculptors, painters, photographers and related creative artists; composers and performing artists; athletes and sportsmen; and professional, technical and related workers not elsewhere classified, according to the International Standard Classification of Occupations (ISCO-1968).

Protected areas Totally or partially protected areas of at least 1,000 hectares that are designed as national parks, natural monuments, nature reserves or wildlife sanctuaries, protected landscapes and seascapes, or scientific reserves with limited public access.

Public expenditure on education Public spending on public education plus subsidies to private education at the primary, secondary and tertiary levels.

Public expenditure on health Recurrent and capital spending from central and local government budgets, external borrowings and grants (including donations from international agencies and non-governmental organizations) and social health insurance funds.

Purchasing power parity (PPP) At the PPP rate, one dollar has the same purchasing power over domestic GDP that the US dollar has over US GDP. PPP could also be expressed in other national currencies or in special drawing rights (SDRs). PPP rates allow a standard comparison of real price levels between countries, just as conventional price indexes allow comparison of real values over time; otherwise, normal exchange rates may over- or undervalue purchasing power.

Real GDP per capita (PPP$) The GDP per capita of a country converted into US dollars on the basis of the purchasing power parity exchange rate.

Refugees People who have fled their countries because of a well-founded fear of persecution for reasons of their race, religion, nationality, political opinion or membership in a particular social group, and who cannot or do not want to return.

Research and development (R&D) Creative, systematic activity intended to increase the stock of knowledge and the use of this knowledge to devise new applications.

Scientists and technicians *Scientists* refers to scientists and engineers with scientific or technological training (usually completion of third-level education) in any field of science who are engaged in professional work in research and development activities, including administrators and other high-level personnel who direct the execution of research and development activities. *Technicians* refers to people engaged in scientific research and development activities who have received vocational or technical training for at least three years after the first stage of second-level education.

Secondary education Education at the second level (levels 2 and 3) based on at least four years of previous instruction at the first level and providing general or specialized instruction or both, such as middle school, secondary school, high school, teacher training school at this level and vocational or technical school.

Sovereign long-term debt rating As determined by Standard and Poor's, an assessment of a country's capacity and willingness to repay debt according to its terms. The ratings range from AAA to CC (investment grade AAA to BBB–, and speculative grade BB+ and lower).

Sulphur dioxide (SO_2) emissions Emissions of sulphur in the form of sulphur oxides and of nitrogen in the form of its various oxides, which together contribute to acid rain and adversely affect agriculture, forests, aquatic habitats and the weathering of building materials.

Tax revenue Compulsory, unrequited, non-repayable receipts collected by central governments for public purposes.

Tertiary education Education at the third level (levels 5, 6 and 7) such as universities, teachers colleges and higher-level professional schools—requiring as a minimum condition of admission the successful completion of education at the second level or evidence of the attainment of an equivalent level of knowledge.

Time allocation and time use Allocation of time between market (SNA) and non-market (non-SNA) activities according to the United Nations System of National Accounts (SNA).

Total armed forces Strategic, land, naval, air, administrative and support forces. Also included are paramilitary forces such as the gendarmerie, customs service and border guard if these are trained in military tactics.

Total debt service The sum of principal repayments and interest actually paid in foreign currency, goods, or services on long-term debt, interest paid on short-term debt, and repayments to the IMF. Total debt service is an important indicator to measure a country's relative burden to service external debt.

Total fertility rate The average number of children that would be born alive to a woman during her lifetime if she were to bear children at each age in accord with prevailing age-specific fertility rates.

Tourists Visitors who travel to a country other than that where they have their usual residence for a period not exceeding 12 months and whose main purpose in visiting is other than an activity remunerated from within the country visited.

Trade in conventional weapons (arms trade) Exports and imports of commodities designed for military use—military equipment such as weapons of war, parts thereof, ammunition and support equipment.

Traditional fuel use Estimated consumption of fuel wood, charcoal, bagasse and animal and vegetable wastes.

Under-five mortality rate The probability of dying between birth and exactly five years of age times 1,000.

Underweight (moderate and severe child malnutrition) *Moderate* refers to the percentage of children under age five who are below minus two standard deviations from the median weight for age of the reference population. *Severe* refers to the percentage of children under age five who are below minus three standard deviations from the median weight for age of the reference population.

Unemployment All people above a specified age who are not in paid employment or self-employed, but are available and have taken specific steps to seek paid employment or self-employment.

Unpaid family workers Household members involved in unremunerated subsistence and non-market activities, such as agricultural production for household consumption, and in household enterprises producing for the market for which more than one household member provides unpaid labor.

Waste recycling The reuse of material that diverts it from the waste stream, except for recycling within industrial plants and the reuse of material as fuel. The recycling rate is the ratio of the quantity recycled to the apparent consumption.

Classification of countries

Countries in the human development aggregates

High human development (HDI 0.800 and above)

Antigua and Barbuda
Argentina
Australia
Austria
Bahamas
Bahrain
Barbados
Belgium
Brunei Darussalam
Canada
Chile
Costa Rica
Cyprus
Czech Republic
Denmark
Finland
France
Germany
Greece
Hong Kong, China (SAR)
Iceland
Ireland
Israel
Italy
Japan
Korea, Rep. of
Kuwait
Luxembourg
Malta
Netherlands
New Zealand
Norway
Poland
Portugal
Qatar
Singapore
Slovakia
Slovenia
Spain
Sweden
Switzerland
United Arab Emirates
United Kingdom
United States
Uruguay

Medium human development (HDI 0.500 to 0.799)

Albania
Algeria
Armenia
Azerbaijan
Belarus
Belize
Bolivia
Botswana
Brazil
Bulgaria
Cambodia
Cameroon
Cape Verde
China
Colombia
Comoros
Congo
Croatia
Cuba
Dominica
Dominican Republic
Ecuador
Egypt
El Salvador
Equatorial Guinea
Estonia
Fiji
Gabon
Georgia
Ghana
Grenada
Guatemala
Guyana
Honduras
Hungary
India
Indonesia
Iran, Islamic Rep. of
Iraq
Jamaica
Jordan
Kazakhstan
Kenya
Kyrgyzstan
Latvia

Lebanon
Lesotho
Libyan Arab Jamahiriya
Lithuania
Macedonia, TFYR
Malaysia
Maldives
Mauritius
Mexico
Moldova, Rep. of
Mongolia
Morocco
Myanmar
Namibia
Nicaragua
Oman
Pakistan
Panama
Papua New Guinea
Paraguay
Peru
Philippines
Romania
Russian Federation
Saint Kitts and Nevis
Saint Lucia
Saint Vincent and the
    Grenadines
Samoa (Western)
São Tomé and Principe
Saudi Arabia
Seychelles
Solomon Islands
South Africa
Sri Lanka
Suriname
Swaziland
Syrian Arab Republic
Tajikistan
Thailand
Trinidad and Tobago
Tunisia
Turkey
Turkmenistan
Ukraine

Uzbekistan
Vanuatu
Venezuela
Viet Nam
Zimbabwe

Low human development (HDI below 0.500)

Angola
Bangladesh
Benin
Bhutan
Burkina Faso
Burundi
Central African Republic
Chad
Côte d'Ivoire
Congo, Dem. Rep. of the
Djibouti
Eritrea
Ethiopia
Gambia
Guinea
Guinea-Bissau
Haiti
Lao People's Dem. Rep.
Madagascar
Malawi
Mali
Mauritania
Mozambique
Nepal
Niger
Nigeria
Rwanda
Senegal
Sierra Leone
Sudan
Tanzania, U. Rep. of
Togo
Uganda
Yemen
Zambia

Countries in the major world aggregates

All developing countries

Algeria
Angola
Antigua and Barbuda
Argentina
Bahamas
Bahrain
Bangladesh
Barbados
Belize
Benin
Bhutan
Bolivia
Botswana
Brazil
Brunei Darussalam
Burundi
Cambodia
Cameroon
Cape Verde
Central African Republic
Chad
Chile
China
Colombia
Comoros
Congo
Congo, Dem. Rep. of the
Costa Rica
Côte d'Ivoire
Cuba
Cyprus
Djibouti
Dominica
Dominican Republic
Ecuador
Egypt
El Salvador
Equatorial Guinea
Eritrea
Ethiopia
Fiji
Gabon
Gambia
Ghana
Grenada
Guatemala
Guinea
Guinea-Bissau
Guyana
Haiti
Honduras
Hong Kong, China (SAR)
India
Indonesia

Iran, Islamic Rep. of
Iraq
Jamaica
Jordan
Kenya
Korea, Rep. of
Kuwait
Lao People's Dem. Rep.
Lebanon
Lesotho
Libyan Arab Jamahiriya
Madagascar
Malawi
Malaysia
Maldives
Mali
Mauritania
Mauritius
Mexico
Mongolia
Morocco
Mozambique
Myanmar
Namibia
Nepal
Nicaragua
Niger
Nigeria
Oman
Pakistan
Panama
Papua New Guinea
Paraguay
Peru
Philippines
Qatar
Rwanda
Saint Kitts and Nevis
Saint Lucia
Saint Vincent and the
    Grenadines
Samoa (Western)
São Tomé and Principe
Saudi Arabia
Senegal
Seychelles
Sierra Leone
Singapore
Solomon Islands
South Africa
Sri Lanka
Sudan
Suriname
Swaziland
Syrian Arab Republic

Tanzania, U. Rep. of
Thailand
Togo
Trinidad and Tobago
Tunisia
Turkey
Uganda
United Arab Emirates
Uruguay
Vanuatu
Venezuela
Viet Nam
Yemen
Zambia
Zimbabwe

Least developed countries

Angola
Bangladesh
Benin
Bhutan
Burkina Faso
Burundi
Cambodia
Cape Verde
Central African Republic
Chad
Comoros
Congo, Dem. Rep. of the
Djibouti
Equatorial Guinea
Eritrea
Ethiopia
Gambia
Guinea
Guinea-Bissau
Haiti
Lao People's Dem. Rep.
Lesotho
Madagascar
Malawi
Maldives
Mali
Mauritania
Mozambique
Myanmar
Nepal
Niger
Rwanda
Samoa (Western)
São Tomé and Principe
Sierra Leone
Solomon Islands

Sudan
Tanzania, U. Rep. of
Togo
Uganda
Vanuatu
Yemen
Zambia

Eastern Europe and the Commonwealth of Independent States (CIS)

Albania
Armenia
Azerbaijan
Belarus
Bulgaria
Croatia
Czech Republic
Estonia
Georgia
Hungary
Kazakhstan
Kyrgyzstan
Latvia
Lithuania
Macedonia, TFYR
Moldova, Rep. of
Poland
Romania
Russian Federation
Slovakia
Slovenia
Tajikistan
Turkmenistan
Ukraine
Uzbekistan

Industrialized countries

Australia
Austria
Belgium
Canada
Denmark
Finland
France
Germany
Greece
Iceland
Ireland
Israel
Italy
Japan
Luxembourg
Malta
Netherlands
New Zealand
Norway
Portugal
Spain
Sweden
Switzerland
United Kingdom
United States

Developing countries in the regional aggregates

Sub-Saharan Africa

Angola
Benin
Botswana
Burkina Faso
Burundi
Cameroon
Cape Verde
Central African Republic
Chad
Comoros
Congo
Congo, Dem. Rep. of the
Côte d'Ivoire
Equatorial Guinea
Eritrea
Ethiopia
Gabon
Gambia
Ghana
Guinea
Guinea-Bissau
Kenya
Lesotho
Madagascar
Malawi
Mali
Mauritania
Mauritius
Mozambique
Namibia
Niger
Nigeria
Rwanda
São Tomé and Principe
Senegal
Seychelles
Sierra Leone
South Africa
Swaziland
Tanzania, U. Rep. of
Togo
Uganda
Zambia
Zimbabwe

Arab States

Algeria
Bahrain
Djibouti
Egypt
Iraq
Jordan
Kuwait
Lebanon
Libyan Arab Jamahiriya
Morocco
Oman
Qatar
Saudi Arabia
Sudan
Syrian Arab Republic
Tunisia
United Arab Emirates
Yemen

Asia and the Pacific

East Asia
China
Hong Kong, China (SAR)
Korea, Rep. of
Mongolia

South-East Asia and the Pacific
Brunei Darussalam
Cambodia
Fiji
Indonesia
Lao People's Dem. Rep.
Malaysia
Myanmar
Papua New Guinea
Philippines
Samoa (Western)
Singapore
Solomon Islands
Thailand
Vanuatu
Viet Nam

South Asia
Bangladesh
Bhutan
India
Iran, Islamic Rep. of
Maldives
Nepal
Pakistan
Sri Lanka

Latin America and the Caribbean (including Mexico)

Antigua and Barbuda
Argentina
Bahamas
Barbados
Belize
Bolivia
Brazil
Chile
Colombia
Costa Rica
Cuba
Dominica
Dominican Republic
Ecuador
El Salvador
Grenada
Guatemala
Guyana
Haiti
Honduras
Jamaica
Mexico
Nicaragua
Panama
Paraguay
Peru
Saint Kitts and Nevis
Saint Lucia
Saint Vincent and the Grenadines
Suriname
Trinidad and Tobago
Uruguay
Venezuela

Southern Europe

Cyprus
Turkey

Key to countries

HDI rank

100	Albania	61	Fiji	169	Mozambique	158	Uganda
109	Algeria	13	Finland	128	Myanmar	91	Ukraine
160	Angola	11	France	115	Namibia	43	United Arab Emirates
38	Antigua and Barbuda	124	Gabon	144	Nepal	10	United Kingdom
39	Argentina	163	Gambia	8	Netherlands	3	United States
87	Armenia	85	Georgia	18	New Zealand	40	Uruguay
7	Australia	14	Germany	121	Nicaragua	92	Uzbekistan
16	Austria	133	Ghana	173	Niger	116	Vanuatu
103	Azerbaijan	27	Greece	146	Nigeria	48	Venezuela
31	Bahamas	52	Grenada	2	Norway	110	Viet Nam
37	Bahrain	117	Guatemala	89	Oman	148	Yemen
150	Bangladesh	161	Guinea	138	Pakistan	151	Zambia
29	Barbados	168	Guinea-Bissau	49	Panama	130	Zimbabwe
60	Belarus	99	Guyana	129	Papua New Guinea		
5	Belgium	152	Haiti	84	Paraguay		
83	Belize	114	Honduras	80	Peru		
155	Benin	24	Hong Kong, China (SAR)	77	Philippines		
145	Bhutan	47	Hungary	44	Poland		
112	Bolivia	9	Iceland	28	Portugal		
122	Botswana	132	India	41	Qatar		
79	Brazil	105	Indonesia	68	Romania		
25	Brunei Darussalam	95	Iran, Islamic Rep. of	71	Russian Federation		
63	Bulgaria	125	Iraq	164	Rwanda		
171	Burkina Faso	20	Ireland	51	Saint Kitts and Nevis		
170	Burundi	23	Israel	81	Saint Lucia		
137	Cambodia	19	Italy	75	Saint Vincent and the		
134	Cameroon	82	Jamaica		Grenadines		
1	Canada	4	Japan	70	Samoa (Western)		
106	Cape Verde	94	Jordan	123	São Tomé and Principe		
165	Central African Republic	76	Kazakhstan	78	Saudi Arabia		
162	Chad	136	Kenya	153	Senegal		
34	Chile	30	Korea, Rep. of	66	Seychelles		
98	China	35	Kuwait	174	Sierra Leone		
57	Colombia	97	Kyrgyzstan	22	Singapore		
139	Comoros	140	Lao People's Dem. Rep.	42	Slovakia		
135	Congo	74	Latvia	33	Slovenia		
141	Congo, Dem. Rep. of the	69	Lebanon	118	Solomon Islands		
45	Costa Rica	127	Lesotho	101	South Africa		
154	Côte d'Ivoire	65	Libyan Arab Jamahiriya	21	Spain		
55	Croatia	62	Lithuania	90	Sri Lanka		
58	Cuba	17	Luxembourg	142	Sudan		
26	Cyprus	73	Macedonia, TFYR	64	Suriname		
36	Czech Republic	147	Madagascar	113	Swaziland		
15	Denmark	159	Malawi	6	Sweden		
157	Djibouti	56	Malaysia	12	Switzerland		
53	Dominica	93	Maldives	111	Syrian Arab Republic		
88	Dominican Republic	166	Mali	108	Tajikistan		
72	Ecuador	32	Malta	156	Tanzania, U. Rep. of		
120	Egypt	149	Mauritania	67	Thailand		
107	El Salvador	59	Mauritius	143	Togo		
131	Equatorial Guinea	50	Mexico	46	Trinidad and Tobago		
167	Eritrea	104	Moldova, Rep. of	102	Tunisia		
54	Estonia	119	Mongolia	86	Turkey		
172	Ethiopia	126	Morocco	96	Turkmenistan		